Blackstone's Statutes on

Contract, Tort & Restitution

2015–2016

26th edition

edited by

F. D. Rose

PhD, LLD, DCL, of Gray's Inn, Barrister-at-Law
Professor of Maritime and Commercial Law, University of Southampton

OXFORD
UNIVERSITY PRESS

OXFORD
UNIVERSITY PRESS

Great Clarendon Street, Oxford, OX2 6DP,
United Kingdom

Oxford University Press is a department of the University of Oxford.
It furthers the University's objective of excellence in research, scholarship,
and education by publishing worldwide. Oxford is a registered trade mark of
Oxford University Press in the UK and in certain other countries

First published by Blackstone Press 1987

Twenty-third edition 2012
Twenty-fourth edition 2013
Twenty-fifth edition 2014
Twenty-sixth edition 2015

Impression: 1

Published in the United States of America by Oxford University Press
198 Madison Avenue, New York, NY 10016, United States of America

British Library Cataloguing in Publication Data
Data available

ISBN 978–0–19–873598–4

Printed in Italy by
L.E.G.O. S.p.A.

Blackstone's Statutes on

Contract, Tort & Restitution

Contents

Alphabetical contents

Editor's preface

The most useful piece of legislation for this year's compilation process was the Fixed-Term Parliaments Act 2011, which ensured that the primary legislative process was completed neatly in time not only for the 2015 General Election but also for submission of this year's collection. However, that did not prevent having to go up to the wire for this year's main enactment, namely the Consumer Rights Act 2015, which (along with the Small Business, Enterprise and Employment Act 2015) was passed at the very end of the 2014–2015 Parliamentary session and has necessitated extensive revision of existing major legislation. *Inter alia*, the Consumer Rights Act 2015 has necessitated amendment of the Misrepresentation Act 1967, the Consumer Credit Act 1974, the Unfair Contract Terms Act 1977 (substantially), the Sale of Goods Act 1979, the Supply of Goods and Services Act 1982 and the Consumer Protection Act 1987. Also, by absorbing the content of the Unfair Terms in Consumer Contracts Regulations 1999, it has caused the revocation of a core element of Contract and Contract-related courses. The Consumer Rights Act 2015 is typical of modern legislation rooted in Contract law in that, *inter alia*, it contains core matter of general interest together with an increasing amount of detailed application. In particular, it contains similar implied terms to those often considered by Contract students and also similar provisions in related areas, namely for services and, upgrading to the modern world, for digital content. As time passes and the amount of legal material increases, the process of compiling a manageable collection such as this continues to be more demanding.

The other major item of legislation for this book this year has been the Insurance Act 2015, which recasts the main area of study for the duty of disclosure in contract negotiations. In addition, the broader study of the law of torts has been affected by changes made by the Control of Horses Act 2015 to the Animals Act 1971. Also of interest are: the Civil Jurisdiction and Judgments (Amendment) Regulations 2014, which amend the Defamation Act 2013; the Collective Redundancies and Transfer of Undertakings (Protection of Employment) (Amendment) Regulations 2014, which amend the Transfer of Undertakings (Protection of Employment) Regulations 2014; the Modern Slavery Act 2015; the Serious Crimes Act 2015, which amends the Proceeds of Crime Act 2002; the Small Business, Enterprise and Employment Act 2015, which (topically) inserts provision into the Employment Rights Act 1996 on zero-hours contracts; and the Social Action, Responsibility and Heroism Act 2015, providing for allowance to be made for the socially beneficial conduct of a defendant accused of negligence or breach of statutory duty.

As usual, in most cases the material in this book is reproduced in its complete, most recent form, all amendments being incorporated within square brackets; occasional omissions are indicated by three dots. Supplementary notes and details of amending provisions, easily available elsewhere, are generally omitted for reasons of space.

As usual, in most cases the material in this book is reproduced in its complete, most recent form, all amendments being incorporated within square brackets; occasional omissions are indicated by three dots. Supplementary notes and details of amending provisions, easily available elsewhere, are generally omitted for reasons of space.

I continue to be grateful to my wife, Lynda, for her contribution to revision of these materials.

As always, I gladly acknowledge the holders' rights in copyright materials. And I continue to be grateful for suggestions as to possible revisions of this collection of materials, whether for additions or deletions.

Francis Rose
Easter Monday 2015

New to this edition

The twenty-sixth edition of *Blackstone's Statutes on Contract, Tort & Restitution* has been fully revised and updated with all relevant original and amending legislation and materials up to April 2015, including selections from:

- Consumer Rights Act 2015
- Control of Horses Act 2015
- Criminal Justice and Courts Act 2015
- Insurance Act 2015
- Modern Slavery Act 2015
- Social Action, Responsibility and Heroism Act 2015

Amendments have been made to the following materials:

- Misrepresentation Act 1967
- Animals Act 1971
- Consumer Credit Act 1974
- Unfair Contract Terms Act 1977
- Consumer Protection Act 1987
- Arbitration Act 1996

The following legislation has been re-enacted in the Consumer Rights Act 2015:

- Unfair Terms in Consumer Contracts Regulations 1999

For Christabel

Statutes

Statute of Frauds 1677

(29 Chas. II, c. 3)

4   No action against executors, etc. upon a special promise, or upon any agreement, or contract for sale of lands, etc. unless agreement, etc. be in writing and signed

[. . .] noe action shall be brought [. . .] whereby to charge the defendant upon any special promise to answere for the debt default or miscarriages of another person [. . .] unlesse the agreement upon which such action shall be brought or some memorandum or note thereof shall be in writeing and signed by the partie to be charged therewith or some other person thereunto by him lawfully authorised.

Libel Act 1843

(6 & 7 Vict., c. 96)

1   Offer of an apology admissible in evidence of mitigation of damages in action for defamation

[. . .] In any action for defamation it shall be lawful for the defendant (after notice in writing of his intention so to do, duly given to the plaintiff at the time of filing or delivering the plea in such action,) to give in evidence, in mitigation of damages, that he made or offered an apology to the plaintiff for such defamation before the commencement of the action, or as soon afterwards as he had an opportunity of doing so, in case the action shall have been commenced before there was an opportunity of making or offering such apology.

2   In an action against a newspaper for libel, the defendant may plead that it was inserted without malice and without neglect and may pay money into court as amends

[. . .] In an action for libel contained in any public newspaper or other periodical publication it shall be competent to the defendant to plead that such libel was inserted in such newspaper or other periodical publication without actual malice, and without gross negligence, and that before the commencement of the action, or at the earliest opportunity afterwards, he inserted in such newspaper or other periodical publication a full apology for the said libel, or, if the newspaper or periodical publication in which the said libel appeared should be ordinarily published at intervals exceeding one week, had offered to publish the said apology in any newspaper or periodical publication to be selected by the plaintiff in such action; [. . .] and to such plea to such action it shall be competent to the plaintiff to reply generally, denying the whole of such plea.

Libel Act 1845

(8 & 9 Vict., c. 75)

2   Defendant not to file such plea without paying money into court by way of amends

[. . .] It shall not be competent to any defendant in such action, whether in England or Ireland, to file any such plea, without at the same time making a payment of money into court by way of amends [. . .], but every such plea so filed without payment of money into court shall be deemed a nullity, and may be treated as such by the plaintiff in the action.

Mercantile Law Amendment Act 1856

(19 & 20 Vict., c. 97)

3   Consideration for guarantee need not appear in writing

No special promise to be made by any person [. . .] to answer for the debt, default, or miscarriage or another person, being in writing, and signed by the party to be charged therewith, or some other person by him thereunto lawfully authorised, shall be deemed invalid to support an action, suit, or other proceeding to charge the person by whom such promise shall have been made, by reason only that the consideration for such promise does not appear in writing, or by necessary inference from a written document.

5   A surety who discharges the liability to be entitled to assignment of all securities held by the creditor

Every person who, being surety for the debt or duty of another, or being liable with another for any debt or duty, shall pay such debt or perform such duty, shall be entitled to have assigned to him, or to a trustee for him, every judgment, specialty, or other security which shall be held by the creditor in respect of such debt or duty, whether such judgment, specialty, or other security shall or shall not be deemed at law to have been satisfied by the payment of the debt or performance of the duty, and such person shall be entitled to stand in the place of the creditor, and to use all the remedies, and, if need be, and upon a proper indemnity, to use the name of the creditor, in any action or other proceeding, at law or in equity, in order to obtain from the principal debtor, or any co-surety, co-contractor, or co-debtor, as the case may be, indemnification for the advances made and loss sustained by the person who shall have so paid such debt or performed such duty, and such payment or performance so made by such surety shall not be pleadable in bar of any such action or other proceeding by him: Provided always, that no co-surety, co-contractor, or co-debtor shall be entitled to recover from any other co-surety, co-contractor, or co-debtor, by the means aforesaid, more than the just proportion to which, as between those parties themselves, such last-mentioned person shall be justly liable.

Offences Against the Person Act 1861

(24 & 25 Vict., c. 100)

44   If the magistrates dismiss the complaint, they shall make out a certificate to that effect

If the Justices, upon the Hearing of any [. . .] Case of Assault or Battery upon the Merits, where the Complaint was preferred by or on the Behalf of the Party aggrieved, [. . .] shall deem the Offence not to be proved, or shall find the Assault or Battery to have been justified, or so trifling as not to merit any Punishment, and shall accordingly dismiss the Complaint, they shall forthwith make out a Certificate [. . .] stating the Fact of such Dismissal, and shall deliver such Certificate to the Party against whom the Complaint was preferred.

45 Certificate or conviction shall be a bar to any other proceedings

If any Person, against whom any such Complaint as [is mentioned in section 44 of this Act] shall have been preferred by or on the Behalf of the Party aggrieved, shall have obtained such Certificate, or, having been convicted, shall have paid the whole Amount adjudged to be paid, or shall have suffered the Imprisonment or Imprisonment with Hard Labour awarded, in every such Case he shall be released from all further or other Proceedings, Civil or Criminal, for the same Cause.

Apportionment Act 1870

(33 & 34 Vict., c. 35)

2 Rents, &c. to accrue from day to day and be apportionable in respect of time

[. . .] From and after the passing of this Act all rents, annuities, dividends, and other periodical payments in the nature of income (whether reserved or made payable under an instrument in writing or otherwise) shall, like interest on money lent, be considered as accruing from day to day, and shall be apportionable in respect of time accordingly.

3 Apportioned part of rent, &c. to be payable when the next entire portion shall have become due

The apportioned part of any such rent, annuity, dividend, or other payment shall be payable or recoverable in the case of a continuing rent, annuity, or other such payment when the entire portion of which such apportioned part shall form part shall become due and payable, and not before, and in the case of a rent, annuity, or other such payment determined by re-entry, death, or otherwise when the next entire portion of the same would have been payable if the same had not so determined, and not before.

5 Interpretation of terms

In the construction of this Act—

The word 'rents' includes rent service, rentcharge, and rent seck, and also tithes and all periodical payments or renderings in lieu of or in the nature of rent or tithe.

The word 'annuities' includes salaries and pensions.

The word 'dividends' includes (besides dividends strictly so called) all payments made by the name of dividend, bonus, or otherwise out of the revenue of trading or other public companies, divisible between all or any of the members of such respective companies, whether such payments shall be usually made or declared at any fixed times or otherwise; and all such divisible revenue shall, for the purposes of this Act, be deemed to have accrued by equal daily increment during and within the period for or in respect of which the payment of the same revenue shall be declared or expressed to be made, but the said word 'dividend' does not include payments in the nature of a return or reimbursement of capital.

6 Act not to apply to policies of assurance

Nothing in this Act contained shall render apportionable any annual sums made payable in policies of assurance of any description.

7 Nor where stipulation made to the contrary

The provisions of this Act shall not extend to any case in which it is or shall be expressly stipulated that no apportionment shall take place.

Law of Libel Amendment Act 1888

(51 & 52 Vict., c. 64)

5 Consolidation of actions

It shall be competent for a judge or the court, upon an application by or on behalf of two or more defendants in actions in respect to the same, or substantially the same, libel brought by one and the same person, to make an order for the consolidation of such actions, so that they shall be tried together; and after such order has been made, and before the trial of the said actions, the defendants in any new actions instituted in respect to the same, or substantially the same, libel shall also be entitled to be joined in a common action upon a joint application being made by such new defendants and the defendants in the actions already consolidated.

In a consolidated action under this section the jury shall assess the whole amount of the damages (if any) in one sum, but a separate verdict shall be taken for or against each defendant in the same way as if the actions consolidated had been tried separately; and if the jury shall have found a verdict against the defendant or defendants in more than one of the actions so consolidated, they shall proceed to apportion the amount of damages which they shall have so found between and against the said last-mentioned defendants; and the judge at the trial, if he awards to the plaintiff the costs of the action, shall thereupon make such order as he shall deem just for the apportionment of such costs between and against such defendants.

Factors Act 1889

(52 & 53 Vict., c. 45)

1 Definitions

For the purposes of this Act—

(1) The expression 'mercantile agent' shall mean a mercantile agent having in the customary course of his business as such agent authority either to sell goods or to consign goods for the purpose of sale, or to buy goods, or to raise money on the security of goods:

(2) A person shall be deemed to be in possession of goods or of the documents of title to goods, where the goods or documents are in the actual custody or are held by any other person subject to his control or for him or on his behalf:

(3) The expression 'goods' shall include wares and merchandise:

(4) The expression 'document of title' shall include any bill of lading, dock warrant, warehouse-keeper's certificate, and warrant or order for the delivery of goods, and any other document used in the ordinary course of business as proof of the possession or control of goods, or authorising or purporting to authorise, either by endorsement or by delivery, the possessor of the document to transfer or receive goods thereby represented:

(5) The expression 'pledge' shall include any contract pledging, or giving a lien or security on, goods, whether in consideration of an original advance or of any further or continuing advance or of any pecuniary liability:

(6) The expression 'person' shall include any body of persons corporate or unincorporate.

2 Powers of mercantile agent with respect to disposition of goods

(1) Where a mercantile agent is, with the consent of the owner, in possession of goods or of the documents of title to goods, any sale, pledge, or other disposition of the goods, made by him when acting in the ordinary course of business of a mercantile agent, shall, subject to the provisions of this Act, be as valid as if he were expressly authorised by the owner of the goods to make the same; provided that the person taking under the disposition acts in good faith, and has not at the time of the disposition notice that the person making the disposition has not authority to make the same.

(2) Where a mercantile agent has, with the consent of the owner, been in possession of goods or of the documents of title to goods, any sale, pledge, or other disposition, which would have been valid if the consent had continued, shall be valid notwithstanding the determination of the consent; provided that the person taking under the disposition has not at the time thereof notice that the consent has been determined.

(3) Where a mercantile agent has obtained possession of any documents of title to goods by reason of his being or having been, with the consent of the owner, in possession of the goods represented thereby, or of any other documents of title to the goods, his possession of the first-mentioned documents shall, for the purposes of this Act, be deemed to be with the consent of the owner.

(4) For the purposes of this Act the consent of the owner shall be presumed in the absence of evidence to the contrary.

Marine Insurance Act 1906

(6 Edw. VII, c. 41)

17 Insurance is uberrimae fidei

A contract of marine insurance is a contract based upon the utmost good faith, *and, if the utmost good faith be not observed by either party, the contract may be avoided by the other party.*
[Note: The words in italics in s 17 are repealed by the Insurance Act 2015, s 14(3)(a) from 12 August 2016.]

18 *Disclosure by assured*

(1) Subject to the provisions of this section, the assured must disclose to the insurer, before the contract is concluded, every material circumstance which is known to the assured, and the assured is deemed to know every circumstance which, in the ordinary course of business, ought to be known by him. If the assured fails to make such disclosure, the insurer may avoid the contract.

(2) Every circumstance is material which would influence the judgment of a prudent insurer in fixing the premium, or determining whether he will take the risk.

(3) In the absence of inquiry the following circumstances need not be disclosed, namely:

    (a) any circumstance which diminishes the risk;

    (b) any circumstance which is known or presumed to be known to the insurer. The insurer is presumed to know matters of common notoriety or knowledge, and matters which an insurer in the ordinary course of his business, as such, ought to know;

    (c) any circumstance as to which information is waived by the insurer;

    (d) any circumstance which it is superfluous to disclose by reason of any express or implied warranty.

(4) Whether any particular circumstance, which is not disclosed, be material or not is, in each case, a question of fact.

(5) The term 'circumstance' includes any communication made to, or information received by, the assured.

[(6) This section does not apply in relation to a contract of marine insurance if it is a consumer insurance contract within the meaning of the Consumer Insurance (Disclosure and Representations) Act 2012.]
[Note: Section 18 is repealed by the Insurance Act 2015, s 21(2) from 12 August 2016.]

20 *Representations pending negotiation of contract*

(1) Every material representation made by the assured or his agent to the insurer during the negotiations for the contract, and before the contract is concluded, must be true. If it be untrue the insurer may avoid the contract.

(2) A representation is material which would influence the judgment of a prudent insurer in fixing the premium, or determining whether he will take the risk.

(3) A representation may be either a representation as to a matter of fact, or as to a matter of expectation or belief.

(4) A representation as to a matter of fact is true, if it be substantially correct, that is to say, if the difference between what is represented and what is actually correct would not be considered material by a prudent insurer.

(5) A representation as to a matter of expectation or belief is true if it be made in good faith.

(6) A representation may be withdrawn or corrected before the contract is concluded.

(7) Whether a particular representation be material or not is, in each case, a question of fact.

[(8) This section does not apply in relation to a contract of marine insurance if it is a consumer insurance contract within the meaning of the Consumer Insurance (Disclosure and Representations) Act 2012.]

[Note: Section 20 is repealed by the Insurance Act 2015, s 21(2) from 12 August 2016.]

22   Contract must be embodied in policy

Subject to the provisions of any statute, a contract of marine insurance is inadmissible in evidence unless it is embodied in a marine policy in accordance with this Act. The policy may be executed and issued either at the time when the contract is concluded, or afterwards.

33   Nature of warranty

(1) A warranty, in the following sections relating to warranties, means a promissory warranty, that is to say, a warranty by which the assured undertakes that some particular thing shall or shall not be done, or that some condition shall be fulfilled, or whereby he affirms or negatives the existence of a particular state of facts.

(2) A warranty may be express or implied.

(3) A warranty, as above defined, is a condition which must be exactly complied with, whether it be material to the risk or not. *If it be not so complied with, then, subject to any express provision in the policy, the insurer is discharged from liability as from the date of the breach of warranty, but without prejudice to any liability incurred by him before that date.*

[Note: The words in italics in s 33(3) are repealed by the Insurance Act 2015, s 10(7) from 12 August 2016.]

34   *When breach of warranty excused*

(1) Non-compliance with a warranty is excused when, by reason of a change of circumstances, the warranty ceases to be applicable to the circumstances of the contract, or when compliance with the warranty is rendered unlawful by any subsequent law.

(2) Where a warranty is broken, the assured cannot avail himself of the defence that the breach has been remedied, and the warranty complied with, before loss.

(3) A breach of warranty may be waived by the insurer.

[Note: Section 34 is repealed by the Insurance Act 2015, s 10(7) from 12 August 2016.]

35   Express warranties

(1) An express warranty may be in any form of words from which the intention to warrant is to be inferred.

(2) An express warranty must be included in, or written upon, the policy, or must be contained in some document incorporated by reference into the policy.

(3) An express warranty does not exclude an implied warranty, unless it be inconsistent therewith.

49   Excuses for deviation or delay

(1) Deviation or delay in prosecuting the voyage contemplated by the policy is excused—

    (a) where authorised by any special term in the policy; or

    (b) where caused by circumstances beyond the control of the master and his employer; or

    (c) where reasonably necessary in order to comply with an express or implied warranty; or

    (d) where reasonably necessary for the safety of the ship or subject-matter insured; or

    (e) for the purpose of saving human life, or aiding a ship in distress where human life may be in danger; or

(f) where reasonably necessary for the purpose of obtaining medical or surgical aid for any person on board the ship; or

(g) where caused by the barratrous conduct of the master or crew, if barratry be one of the perils insured against.

(2) When the cause excusing the deviation or delay ceases to operate, the ship must resume her course, and prosecute her voyage, with reasonable dispatch.

82 Enforcement of return

Where the premium or a proportionate part thereof is, by this Act, declared to be returnable,—

(a) If already paid, it may be recovered by the assured from the insurer; and

(b) If unpaid, it may be retained by the assured or his agent.

83 Return by agreement

Where the policy contains a stipulation for the return of the premium, or a proportionate part thereof, on the happening of a certain event, and that event happens, the premium, or, as the case may be, the proportionate part thereof, is thereupon returnable to the assured.

84 Return for failure of consideration

(1) Where the consideration for the payment of the premium totally fails, and there has been no fraud or illegality on the part of the assured or his agents, the premium is thereupon returnable to the assured.

(2) Where the consideration for the payment of the premium is apportionable and there is a total failure of any apportionable part of the consideration, a proportionate part of the premium is, under the like conditions, thereupon returnable to the assured.

(3) In particular—

(a) Where the policy is void, or is avoided by the insurer as from the commencement of the risk, the premium is returnable, provided that there has been no fraud or illegality on the part of the assured; but if the risk is not apportionable, and has once attached, the premium is not returnable;

(b) Where the subject-matter insured, or part thereof, has never been imperilled, the premium, or, as the case may be, a proportionate part thereof, is returnable: Provided that where the subject-matter has been insured 'lost or not lost' and has arrived in safety at the time when the contract is concluded, the premium is not returnable unless, at such time, the insurer knew of the safe arrival;

(c) Where the assured has no insurable interest throughout the currency of the risk, the premium is returnable, provided that this rule does not apply to a policy effected by way of gaming or wagering;

(d) Where the assured has a defeasible interest which is terminated during the currency of the risk, the premium is not returnable;

(e) Where the assured has over-insured under an unvalued policy, a proportionate part of the premium is returnable;

(f) Subject to the foregoing provisions, where the assured has over-insured by double insurance, a proportionate part of the several premiums is returnable: Provided that, if the policies are effected at different times, and any earlier policy has at any time borne the entire risk, or if a claim has been paid on the policy in respect of the full sum insured thereby, no premium is returnable in respect of that policy, and when the double insurance is effected knowingly by the assured no premium is returnable.

87 Implied obligations varied by agreement or usage

(1) Where any right, duty, or liability would arise under a contract of marine insurance by implication of law, it may be negatived or varied by express agreement, or by usage, if the usage be such as to bind both parties to the contract.

Law of Property Act 1925

(15 & 16 Geo. V, c. 20)

41   Stipulations not of the essence of a contract
Stipulations in a contract, as to time or otherwise, which according to rules of equity are not deemed to be or to have become of the essence of the contract, are also construed and have effect at law in accordance with the same rules.

49   Applications to the court by vendor and purchaser
(2)   Where the court refuses to grant specific performance of a contract, or in any action for the return of a deposit, the court may, if it thinks fit, order the repayment of any deposit.

(3)   This section applies to a contract for the sale or exchange of any interest in land.

56   Persons taking who are not parties and as to indentures
(1)   A person may take an immediate or other interest in land or other property, or the benefit of any condition, right of entry, covenant or agreement over or respecting land or other property, although he may not be named as a party to the conveyance or other instrument.

136   Legal assignments of things in action
(1)   Any absolute assignment by writing under the hand of the assignor (not purporting to be by way of charge only) of any debt or other legal thing in action, of which express notice in writing has been given to the debtor, trustee or other person from whom the assignor would have been entitled to claim such debt or thing in action, is effectual in law (subject to equities having priority over the right of the assignee) to pass and transfer from the date of such notice—

   (a)   the legal right to such debt or thing in action;

   (b)   all legal and other remedies for the same; and

   (c)   the power to give a good discharge for the same without the concurrence of the assignor:

Provided that, if the debtor, trustee or other person liable in respect of such debt or thing in action has notice—

   (a)   that the assignment is disputed by the assignor or any person claiming under him; or

   (b)   of any other opposing or conflicting claims to such debt or thing in action; he may, if he thinks fit, either call upon the persons making claim thereto to interplead concerning the same, or pay the debt or other thing in action into court under the provisions of the Trustee Act 1925.

(2)   This section does not affect the provisions of the Policies of Assurance Act 1867.

146   Restrictions on and relief against forfeiture of leases and underleases
(1)   A right of re-entry or forfeiture under any proviso or stipulation in a lease for a breach of any covenant or condition in the lease shall not be enforceable, by action or otherwise, unless and until the lessor serves on the lessee a notice—

   (a)   specifying the particular breach complained of; and

   (b)   if the breach is capable of remedy, requiring the lessee to remedy the breach;

   (c)   in any case, requiring the lessee to make compensation in money for the breach;
and the lessee fails, within a reasonable time thereafter, to remedy the breach, if it is capable of remedy, and to make reasonable compensation in money, to the satisfaction of the lessor, for the breach.

(2)   Where a lessor is proceeding, by action or otherwise, to enforce such a right of re-entry or forfeiture, the lessee may, in the lessor s action, if any, or in any action brought by himself, apply to the court for relief; and the court may grant or refuse relief, as the court, having regard to the proceedings and conduct of the parties under the foregoing provisions of this section, and to all the other circumstances, thinks fit; and in case of relief may grant it on such terms, if any, as to costs, expenses, damages, compensation, penalty, or otherwise, including the granting of

an injunction to restrain any like breach in the future, as the court, in the circumstances of each case, thinks fit.

(11) This section does not, save as otherwise mentioned, affect the law relating to re-entry or forfeiture or relief in case of non-payment of rent.

(12) This section has effect notwithstanding any stipulation to the contrary.

205　General definitions

(1) In this Act unless the context otherwise requires, the following expressions have the meanings hereby assigned to them respectively, that is to say: . . .

(xvii) 'Notice' includes constructive notice;

(xx) 'Property' includes any thing in action, and any interest in real or personal property;

. . .

Law Reform (Miscellaneous Provisions) Act 1934

(24 & 25 Geo. V, c. 41)

1　Effect of death on certain causes of action

(1) Subject to the provisions of this section, on the death of any person after the commencement of this Act all causes of action subsisting against or vested in him shall survive against, or, as the case may be, for the benefit of, his estate. Provided that this subsection shall not apply to causes of action for defamation [. . .].

[(1A) The right of a person to claim under section 1A of the Fatal Accidents Act 1976 (bereavement) shall not survive for the benefit of his estate on his death.]

(2) Where a cause of action survives as aforesaid for the benefit of the estate of a deceased person, the damages recoverable for the benefit of the estate of that person:—

[(a) shall not include—

(i) any exemplary damages;

(ii) any damages for loss of income in respect of any period after that person's death;]

(b) [. . .]

(c) where the death of that person has been caused by the act or omission which gives rise to the cause of action, shall be calculated without reference to any loss or gain to his estate consequent on his death, except that a sum in respect of funeral expenses may be included.

(4) Where damage has been suffered by reason of any act or omission in respect of which a cause of action would have subsisted against any person if that person had not died before or at the same time as the damage was suffered, there shall be deemed, for the purposes of this Act, to have been subsisting against him before his death such cause of action in respect of that act or omission as would have subsisted if he had died after the damage was suffered.

(5) The rights conferred by this Act for the benefit of the estates of deceased persons shall be in addition to and not in derogation of any rights conferred on the dependants of deceased persons by [the Fatal Accidents Act 1976 . . .] and so much of this Act as relates to causes of action against the estates of deceased persons shall apply in relation to causes of action under the said Act as it applies in relation to other causes of action not expressly excepted from the operation of subsection (1) of this section.

(6) In the event of the insolvency of an estate against which proceedings are maintainable by virtue of this section, any liability in respect of the cause of action in respect of which the proceedings are maintainable shall be deemed to be a debt provable in the administration of the estate, notwithstanding that it is a demand in the nature of unliquidated damages arising otherwise than by a contract, promise or breach of trust.

Law Reform (Married Women and Tortfeasors) Act 1935

(25 & 26 Geo. V, c. 30)

3   Abolition of husband's liability for wife's torts and ante-nuptial contracts, debts and obligations

Subject to the provisions of this Part of this Act, the husband of a married woman shall not, by reason only of his being her husband, be liable—

    (a) in respect of any tort committed by her whether before or after the marriage, or in respect of any contract entered into, or debt or obligation incurred, by her before the marriage; or

    (b) to be sued, or made a party to any legal proceeding brought, in respect of any such tort, contract, debt, or obligation.

4   Savings

    (2) For the avoidance of doubt it is hereby declared that nothing in this Part of this Act—

    (a) renders the husband of a married woman liable in respect of any contract entered into, or debt or obligation incurred, by her after the marriage in respect of which he would not have been liable if this Act had not been passed;

    (b) exempts the husband of a married woman from liability in respect of any contract entered into, or debt or obligation (not being a debt or obligation arising out of a commission of a tort) incurred, by her after the marriage in respect of which he would have been liable if this Act had not been passed;

    (c) prevents a husband and wife from acquiring, holding, and disposing of, any property jointly or as tenants in common, or from rendering themselves, or being rendered, jointly liable in respect of any tort, contract, debt or obligation, and of suing and being sued either in tort or in contract or otherwise, in like manner as if they were not married;

    (d) prevents the exercise of any joint power given to a husband and wife.

Law Reform (Frustrated Contracts) Act 1943

(6 & 7 Geo. VI, c. 40)

1   Adjustment of rights and liabilities of parties to frustrated contracts

    (1) Where a contract governed by English law has become impossible of performance or been otherwise frustrated, and the parties thereto have for that reason been discharged from the further performance of the contract, the following provisions of this section shall, subject to the provisions of section two of this Act, have effect in relation thereto.

    (2) All sums paid or payable to any party in pursuance of the contract before the time when the parties were so discharged (in this Act referred to as 'the time of discharge') shall, in the case of sums so paid, be recoverable from him as money received by him for the use of the party by whom the sums were paid, and, in the case of sums so payable, cease to be so payable:

Provided that, if the party to whom the sums were so paid or payable incurred expenses before the time of discharge in, or for the purpose of, the performance of the contract, the court may, if it considers it just to do so having regard to all the circumstances of the case, allow him to retain or, as the case may be, recover the whole or any part of the sums so paid or payable, not being an amount in excess of the expenses so incurred.

    (3) Where any party to the contract has, by reason of anything done by any other party thereto in, or for the purpose of, the performance of the contract, obtained a valuable benefit (other than a payment of money to which the last foregoing subsection applies) before the time of discharge there shall be recoverable from him by the said other party such sum (if any), not exceeding the value of

the said benefit to the party obtaining it, as the court considers just, having regard to all the circumstances of the case and, in particular,—

(a) the amount of any expenses incurred before the time of discharge by the benefited party in, or for the purpose of, the performance of the contract, including any sums paid or payable by him to any other party in pursuance of the contract and retained or recoverable by that party under the last foregoing subsection, and

(b) the effect, in relation to the said benefit, of the circumstances giving rise to the frustration of the contract.

(4) In estimating, for the purposes of the foregoing provisions of this section, the amount of any expenses incurred by any party to the contract, the court may, without prejudice to the generality of the said provisions, include such sum as appears to be reasonable in respect of overhead expenses and in respect of any work or services performed personally by the said party.

(5) In considering whether any sum ought to be recovered or retained under the foregoing provisions of this section by any party to the contract, the court shall not take into account any sums which have, by reason of the circumstances giving rise to the frustration of the contract, become payable to that party under any contract of insurance unless there was an obligation to insure imposed by an express term of the frustrated contract or by or under any enactment.

(6) Where any person has assumed obligations under the contract in consideration of the conferring of a benefit by any other party to the contract upon any other person, whether a party to the contract or not, the court may, if in all the circumstances of the case it considers it just to do so, treat for the purposes of subsection (3) of this section any benefit so conferred as a benefit obtained by the person who has assumed the obligations as aforesaid.

2   Provision as to application of this Act

(1) This Act shall apply to contracts, whether made before or after the commencement of this Act, as respects which the time of discharge is on or after the first day of July, nineteen hundred and forty-three, but not to contracts as respects which the time of discharge is before the said date.

(2) This Act shall apply to contracts to which the Crown is a party in like manner as to contracts between subjects.

(3) Where any contract to which this Act applies contains any provision which, upon the true construction of the contract, is intended to have effect in the event of circumstances arising which operate, or would but for the said provision operate, to frustrate the contract, or is intended to have effect whether such circumstances arise or not, the court shall give effect to the said provision and shall only give effect to the foregoing section of this Act to such extent, if any, as appears to the court to be consistent with the said provision.

(4) Where it appears to the court that a part of any contract to which this Act applies can properly be severed from the remainder of the contract, being a part wholly performed before the time of discharge, or so performed except for the payment in respect of that part of the contract of sums which are or can be ascertained under the contract, the court shall treat that part of the contract as if it were a separate contract and had not been frustrated and shall treat the foregoing section of this Act as only applicable to the remainder of that contract.

(5) This Act shall not apply—

(a) to any charterparty, except a time charterparty or a charterparty by way of demise, or to any contract (other than a charterparty) for the carriage of goods by sea; or

(b) to any contract of insurance, save as is provided by subsection (5) of the foregoing section; or

(c) to any contract to which [section 7 of the Sale of Goods Act 1979] (which avoids contracts for the sale of specific goods which perish before the risk has passed to the buyer) applies, or to any other contract for the sale, or for the sale and delivery, of specific goods, where the contract is frustrated by reason of the fact that the goods have perished.

3   Short title and interpretation
(2) In this Act the expression 'court' means, in relation to any matter, the court or arbitrator by or before whom the matter falls to be determined.

Law Reform (Contributory Negligence) Act 1945

(8 & 9 Geo. VI, c. 28)

1   Apportionment of liability in case of contributory negligence
(1) Where any person suffers damage as the result partly of his own fault and partly of the fault of any other person or persons, a claim in respect of that damage shall not be defeated by reason of the fault of the person suffering the damage, but the damages recoverable in respect thereof shall be reduced to such extent as the court thinks just and equitable having regard to the claimant's share in the responsibility of the damage:

Provided that—
    (a) this subsection shall not operate to defeat any defence arising under a contract;
    (b) where any contract or enactment providing for the limitation of liability is applicable to the claim, the amount of damages recoverable by the claimant by virtue of this subsection shall not exceed the maximum limit so applicable.

(2) Where damages are recoverable by any person by virtue of the foregoing subsection subject to such reduction as is therein mentioned, the court shall find and record the total damages which would have been recoverable if the claimant had not been at fault.

(5) Where, in any case to which subsection (1) of this section applies, one of the persons at fault avoids liability to any other such person or his personal representative by pleading the Limitation Act, 1939, or any other enactment limiting the time within which proceedings may be taken, he shall not be entitled to recover any damages [. . .] from that other person or representative by virtue of the said subsection.

(6) Where any case to which subsection (1) of this section applies is tried with a jury, the jury shall determine the total damages which would have been recoverable if the claimant had not been at fault and the extent to which those damages are to be reduced.

4   Interpretation
The following expressions have the meanings hereby respectively assigned to them, that is to say—
   'court' means, in relation to any claim, the court or arbitrator by or before whom the claim falls to be determined;
   'damage' includes loss of life and personal injury; [. . .]
   'fault' means negligence, breach of statutory duty or other act or omission which gives rise to liability in tort or would, apart from this Act, give rise to the defence of contributory negligence.

Crown Proceedings Act 1947

(10 & 11 Geo. VI, c. 44)

2   Liability of the Crown in tort
(1) Subject to the provisions of this Act, the Crown shall be subject to all those liabilities in tort to which, if it were a private person of full age and capacity, it would be subject—
    (a) in respect of torts committed by its servants or agents;
    (b) in respect of any breach of those duties which a person owes to his servants or agents at common law by reason of being their employer; and
    (c) in respect of any breach of the duties attaching at common law to the ownership, occupation, possession or control of property:

provided that no proceedings shall lie against the Crown by virtue of paragraph (a) of this subsection in respect of any act or omission of a servant or agent of the Crown unless the act or omission would apart from the provisions of this Act have given rise to a cause of action in tort against that servant or agent or his estate.

(2) Where the Crown is bound by a statutory duty which is binding also upon persons other than the Crown and its officers, then, subject to the provisions of this Act, the Crown shall, in respect of a failure to comply with that duty, be subject to all those liabilities in tort (if any) to which it would be so subject if it were a private person of full age and capacity.

(3) Where any functions are conferred or imposed upon an officer of the Crown as such either by any rule of the common law or by statute, and that officer commits a tort while performing or purporting to perform those functions, the liabilities of the Crown in respect of the tort shall be such as they would have been if those functions had been conferred or imposed solely by virtue of instructions lawfully given by the Crown.

(4) Any enactment which negatives or limits the amount of the liability of any Government department[, part of the Scottish Administration,] or officer of the Crown in respect of any tort committed by that department[, part] or officer shall, in the case of proceedings against the Crown under this section in respect of a tort committed by that department[, part] or officer, apply in relation to the Crown as it would have applied in relation to that department[, part] or officer if the proceedings against the Crown had been proceedings against that department or officer.

(5) No proceedings shall lie against the Crown by virtue of this section in respect of anything done or omitted to be done by any person while discharging or purporting to discharge any responsibilities of a judicial nature vested in him, or any responsibilities which he has in connection with the execution of judicial process.

(6) No proceedings shall lie against the Crown by virtue of this section in respect of any act, neglect or default of any officer of the Crown, unless that officer has been directly or indirectly appointed by the Crown and was at the material time paid in respect of his duties as an officer of the Crown wholly out of the Consolidated Fund of the United Kingdom, moneys provided by Parliament, [the Scottish Consolidated Fund,] or any other Fund certified by the Treasury for the purposes of this subsection or was at the material time holding an office in respect of which the Treasury certify that the holder thereof would normally be so paid.

Law Reform (Personal Injuries) Act 1948

(11 & 12 Geo. VI, c. 41)

1   Common employment

(1) It shall not be a defence to an employer who is sued in respect of personal injuries caused by the negligence of a person employed by him, that that person was at the time the injuries were caused in common employment with the person injured.

(3) Any provision contained in a contract of service or apprenticeship, or in an agreement collateral thereto, (including a contract or agreement entered into before the commencement of this Act) shall be void in so far as it would have the effect of excluding or limiting any liability of the employer in respect of personal injuries caused to the person employed or apprenticed by the negligence of persons in common employment with him.

2   Measure of damages

(4) In an action for damages for personal injuries (including any such action arising out of a contract), there shall be disregarded, in determining the reasonableness of any expenses, the possibility of avoiding those expenses or part of them by taking advantage of facilities available under [the National Health Service Act 2006 or the National Health Service (Wales) Act 2006] or the [National Health Service (Scotland) Act 1978] or of any corresponding facilities in Northern Ireland.

3   Definition of 'personal injury'

In this Act the expression 'personal injury' includes any disease and any impairment of a person's physical or mental condition, and the expression 'injured' shall be construed accordingly.

Defamation Act 1952

(15 & 16 Geo. VI & 1 Eliz. II, c. 66)

2   Slander affecting official, professional or business reputation

In an action for slander in respect of words calculated to disparage the plaintiff in an office, profession, calling, trade or business held or carried on by him at the time of the publication, it shall not be necessary to allege or prove special damage, whether or not the words are spoken of the plaintiff in the way of his office, profession, calling, trade or business.

3   Slander of title, etc.

(1) In an action for slander of title, slander of goods or other malicious falsehood, it shall not be necessary to allege or prove special damage—

(a) if the words upon which the action is founded are calculated to cause pecuniary damage to the plaintiff and are published in writing or other permanent form; or

(b) if the said words are calculated to cause pecuniary damage to the plaintiff in respect of any office, profession, calling, trade or business held or carried on by him at the time of the publication.

(2) Section one of this Act shall apply for the purposes of this section as it applies for the purposes of the law of libel and slander.

9   Extension of certain defences to broadcasting

(1) Section three of the Parliamentary Papers Act, 1840 (which confers protection in respect of proceedings for printing extracts from or abstracts of parliamentary papers) shall have effect as if the reference to printing included a reference to broadcasting by means of wireless telegraphy.

10   Limitation on privilege at elections

A defamatory statement published by or on behalf of a candidate in any election to local government authority [to the Scottish Parliament] or to Parliament shall not be deemed to be published on a privileged occasion on the ground that it is material to a question in issue in the election, whether or not the person by whom it is published is qualified to vote at the election.

11   Agreements for indemnity

An agreement for indemnifying any person against civil liability for libel in respect of the publication of any matter shall not be unlawful unless at the time of the publication that person knows that the matter is defamatory, and does not reasonably believe that there is a good defence to any action brought upon it.

12   Evidence of other damages recovered by plaintiff

In any action for libel or slander the defendant may give evidence in mitigation of damages that the plaintiff has recovered damages, or has brought actions for damages, for libel or slander in respect of the publication of words to the same effect as the words on which the action is founded, or has received or agreed to receive compensation in respect of any such publication.

13   Consolidation of actions for slander etc.

Section five of the Law of Libel Amendment Act 1888 (which provides for the consolidation, on the application of the defendants, of two or more actions for libel by the same plaintiff) shall apply to actions for slander of title, slander of goods or other malicious falsehood as it applies to actions for libel; and references in that section to the same, or substantially the same, libel shall be construed accordingly.

16 Interpretation

(1) Any reference in this Act to words shall be construed as including a reference to pictures, visual images, gestures and other methods of signifying meaning.

Occupiers' Liability Act 1957

(5 & 6 Eliz. II, c. 31)

1 Preliminary

(1) The rules enacted by the two next following sections shall have effect, in place of the rules of the common law, to regulate the duty which an occupier of premises owes to his visitors in respect of dangers due to the state of the premises or to things done or omitted to be done on them.

(2) The rules so enacted shall regulate the nature of the duty imposed by law in consequence of a person's occupation or control of premises and of any invitation or permission he gives (or is to be treated as giving) to another to enter or use the premises, but they shall not alter the rules of the common law as to the persons on whom a duty is so imposed or to whom it is owed; and accordingly for the purpose of the rules so enacted the persons who are to be treated as an occupier and as his visitors are the same (subject to subsection (4) of this section) as the persons who would at common law be treated as an occupier and as his invitees or licensees.

(3) The rules so enacted in relation to an occupier of premises and his visitors shall also apply, in like manner and to the like extent as the principles applicable at common law to an occupier of premises and his invitees or licensees would apply, to regulate—

    (a) the obligations of a person occupying or having control over any fixed or moveable structure, including any vessel, vehicle or aircraft; and

    (b) the obligations of a person occupying or having control over any premises or structure in respect of damage to property, including the property of persons who are not themselves his visitors.

    [(4) A person entering any premises in exercise of rights conferred by virtue of—

    (a) section 2(1) of the Countryside and Rights of Way Act 2000, or

    (b) an access agreement or order under the National Parks and Access to the Countryside Act 1949,

is not, for the purposes of this Act, a visitor of the occupier of those premises.]

2 Extent of occupier's ordinary duty

(1) An occupier of premises owes the same duty, the 'common duty of care', to all his visitors, except in so far as he is free to and does extend, restrict, modify or exclude his duty to any visitor or visitors by agreement or otherwise.

(2) The common duty of care is a duty to take such care as in all the circumstances of the case is reasonable to see that the visitor will be reasonably safe in using the premises for the purposes for which he is invited or permitted by the occupier to be there.

(3) The circumstances relevant for the present purposes include the degree of care, and of want of care, which would ordinarily be looked for in such a visitor, so that (for example) in proper cases—

    (a) an occupier must be prepared for children to be less careful than adults; and

    (b) an occupier may expect that a person, in the exercise of his calling, will appreciate and guard against any special risks ordinarily incident to it, so far as the occupier leaves him free to do so.

(4) In determining whether the occupier of premises has discharged the common duty of care to a visitor, regard is to be had to all the circumstances, so that (for example)—

(a) where damage is caused to a visitor by a danger of which he had been warned by the occupier, the warning is not to be treated without more as absolving the occupier from liability, unless in all the circumstances it was enough to enable the visitor to be reasonably safe; and

(b) where damage is caused to a visitor by a danger due to the faulty execution of any work of construction, maintenance or repair by an independent contractor employed by the occupier, the occupier is not to be treated without more as answerable for the danger if in all the circumstances he had acted reasonably in entrusting the work to an independent contractor and had taken such steps (if any) as he reasonably ought in order to satisfy himself that the contractor was competent and that the work had been properly done.

(5) The common duty of care does not impose on an occupier any obligation to a visitor in respect of risks willingly accepted as his by the visitor (the question whether a risk was so accepted to be decided on the same principles as in other cases in which one person owes a duty of care to another).

(6) For the purposes of this section, persons who enter premises for any purpose in the exercise of a right conferred by law are to be treated as permitted by the occupier to be there for that purpose, whether they in fact have his permission or not.

3   Effect of contract on occupier's liability to third party

(1) Where an occupier of premises is bound by contract to permit persons who are strangers to the contract to enter or use the premises, the duty of care which he owes to them as his visitors cannot be restricted or excluded by that contract, but (subject to any provision of the contract to the contrary) shall include the duty to perform his obligations under the contract, whether undertaken for their protection or not, in so far as those obligations go beyond the obligations otherwise involved in that duty.

(2) A contract shall not by virtue of this section have the effect, unless it expressly so provides, of making an occupier who has taken all reasonable care answerable to strangers to the contract for dangers due to the faulty execution of any work of construction, maintenance or repair or other like operation by persons other than himself, his servants and persons acting under his direction and control.

(3) In this section, 'stranger to the contract' means a person not for the time being entitled to the benefit of the contract as a party to it or as the successor by assignment or otherwise of a party to it, and accordingly includes a party to the contract who has ceased to be so entitled.

(4) Where by the terms or conditions governing any tenancy (including a statutory tenancy which does not in law amount to a tenancy) either the landlord or the tenant is bound, though not by contract, to permit persons to enter or use premises of which he is the occupier, this section shall apply as if the tenancy were a contract between the landlord and the tenant.

(5) This section, in so far as it prevents the common duty of care from being restricted or excluded, applies to contracts entered into and tenancies created before the commencement of this Act, as well as to those entered into or created after its commencement; but, in so far as it enlarges the duty owed by an occupier beyond the common duty of care, it shall have effect only in relation to obligations which are undertaken after the commencement or which are renewed by agreement (whether express or implied) after that commencement.

5   Implied term in contracts

(1) Where persons enter or use, or bring or send goods to, any premises in exercise of a right conferred by contract with a person occupying or having control of the premises, the duty he owes them in respect of dangers due to the state of the premises or to things done or omitted to be done by them, in so far as the duty depends on a term to be implied in the contract by reason of its conferring that right, shall be the common duty of care.

(2) The foregoing subsection shall apply to fixed and moveable structures as it applies to premises.

(3) This section does not affect the obligations imposed on a person by or by virtue of any contract for the hire of, or for the carriage for reward of persons or goods in, any vehicle, vessel, aircraft or other means of transport, or by virtue of any contract of bailment.

(4) This section does not apply to contracts entered into before the commencement of this Act.

6 Application to the Crown

This Act shall bind the Crown, but as regards the Crown liability in tort shall not bind the Crown further than the Crown is made liable in tort by the Crown Proceedings Act, 1947, and that Act and in particular section two of it shall apply in relation to duties under sections two to four of this Act as statutory duties.

Law Reform (Husband and Wife) Act 1962

(10 & 11 Eliz. II, c. 48)

1 Actions in tort between husband and wife

(1) Subject to the provisions of this section, each of the parties to a marriage shall have the like right of action in tort against the other as if they were not married.

(2) Where an action in tort is brought by one of the parties to a marriage against the other during the subsistence of the marriage, the court may stay the action if it appears—

    (a) that no substantial benefit would accrue to either party from the continuation of the proceedings; or

    (b) that the question or questions in issue could more conveniently be disposed of on an application made under section seventeen of the Married Women's Property Act 1882 (determination of questions between husband and wife as to the title to or possession of property);

and without prejudice to paragraph (b) of this subsection the court may, in such an action, either exercise any power which could be exercised on an application under that said section seventeen, or give such directions as it thinks fit for the disposal under that section of any question arising in the proceedings.

Criminal Law Act 1967

(1967, c. 58)

3 Use of force in making arrest, etc.

(1) A person may use such force as is reasonable in the circumstances in the prevention of crime, or in effecting or assisting in the lawful arrest of offenders or suspected offenders or of persons unlawfully at large.

14 Civil rights in respect of maintenance and champerty

(1) No person shall, under the law of England and Wales, be liable in tort for any conduct on account of its being maintenance or champerty as known to the common law, except in the case of a cause of action accruing before this section has effect.

(2) The abolition of criminal and civil liability under the law of England and Wales for maintenance and champerty shall not affect any rule of that law as to the cases in which a contract is to be treated as contrary to public policy or otherwise illegal.

Misrepresentation Act 1967

(1967, c. 7)

1   Removal of certain bars to rescission for innocent misrepresentation

Where a person has entered into a contract after a misrepresentation has been made to him, and—

(a) the misrepresentation has become a term of the contract; or

(b) the contract has been performed;

or both, then, if otherwise he would be entitled to rescind the contract without alleging fraud, he shall be so entitled, subject to the provisions of this Act, notwithstanding the matters mentioned in paragraphs (a) and (b) of this section.

2   Damages for misrepresentation

(1) Where a person has entered into a contract after a misrepresentation has been made to him by another party thereto and as a result thereof he has suffered loss, then, if the person making the misrepresentation would be liable to damages in respect thereof had the misrepresentation been made fraudulently, that person shall be so liable notwithstanding that the misrepresentation was not made fraudulently, unless he proves that he had reasonable ground to believe and did believe up to the time the contract was made that the facts represented were true.

(2) Where a person has entered into a contract after a misrepresentation has been made to him otherwise than fraudulently, and he would be entitled, by reason of the misrepresentation, to rescind the contract, then, if it is claimed, in any proceedings arising out of the contract, that the contract ought to be or has been rescinded, the court or arbitrator may declare the contract subsisting and award damages in lieu of rescission, if of opinion that it would be equitable to do so, having regard to the nature of the misrepresentation and the loss that would be caused by it if the contract were upheld, as well as to the loss that rescission would cause to the other party.

(3) Damages may be awarded against a person under subsection (2) of this section whether or not he is liable to damages under subsection (1) thereof, but where he is so liable any award under the said subsection (2) shall be taken into account in assessing his liability under the said subsection (1).

[(4) This section does not entitle a person to be paid damages in respect of a misrepresentation if the person has a right to redress under Part 4A of the Consumer Protection from Unfair Trading Regulations 2008 (SI 2008/1277) in respect of the conduct constituting the misrepresentation.

(5) Subsection (4) does not prevent a debtor from bringing a claim under section 75(1) of the Consumer Credit Act 1974 against a creditor under a debtor-creditor-supplier agreement in a case where, but for subsection (4), the debtor would have a claim against the supplier in respect of a misrepresentation (and, where section 75 of that Act would otherwise apply, it accordingly applies as if the debtor had a claim against the supplier).]

3   Avoidance of provision excluding liability for misrepresentation

[(1) If a contract contains a term which would exclude or restrict—

(a) any liability to which a party to a contract may be subject by reason of any misrepresentation made by him before the contract was made; or

(b) any remedy available to another party to the contract by reason of such misrepresentation,

that term shall be of no effect except in so far as it satisfies the requirement of reasonableness as stated in section 11(1) of the Unfair Contract Terms Act 1977; and it is for those claiming that the term satisfies that requirement to show that it does.]

[(2) This section does not apply to a term in a consumer contract within the meaning of Part 2 of the Consumer Rights Act 2015 (but see the provision made about such contracts in section 62 of that Act).]

Civil Evidence Act 1968

(1968, c. 64)

11 Convictions as evidence in civil proceedings

(1) In any civil proceedings the fact that a person has been convicted of an offence by or before any court in the United Kingdom or by a court-martial there or elsewhere shall (subject to subsection (3) below) be admissible in evidence for the purpose of proving where to do so is relevant to any issue in those proceedings, that he committed that offence, whether he was so convicted upon a plea of guilty or otherwise and whether or not he is a party to the civil proceedings; but no conviction other than a subsisting one shall be admissible in evidence by virtue of this section.

(2) In any civil proceedings in which by virtue of this section a person is proved to have been convicted of an offence by or before any court in the United Kingdom or by a court-martial there or elsewhere—

    (a) he shall be taken to have committed that offence unless the contrary is proved; and

    (b) without prejudice to the reception of any other admissible evidence for the purpose of identifying the facts on which the conviction was based, the contents of any documents which is admissible as evidence of the conviction, and the contents of the information, complaint, indictment or charge-sheet on which the person in question was convicted, shall be admissible in evidence for that purpose.

(3) Nothing in this section shall prejudice the operation of section 13 of this Act or any other enactment whereby a conviction or a finding of fact in any criminal proceedings is for the purposes of any other proceedings made conclusive evidence of any fact.

(4) Where in any civil proceedings the contents of any document are admissible in evidence by virtue of subsection (2) above, a copy of that document, or of the material part thereof, purporting to be certified or otherwise authenticated by or on behalf of the court or authority having custody of that document shall be admissible in evidence and shall be taken to be a true copy of that document or part unless the contrary is shown.

13 Conclusiveness of convictions for purposes of defamation actions

(1) In an action for libel or slander in which the question whether [the plaintiff] did or did not commit a criminal offence is relevant to an issue arising in the action, proof that at the time when that issue falls to be determined, [he] stands convicted of that offence shall be conclusive evidence that he committed that offence; and his conviction thereof shall be admissible in evidence accordingly.

(2) In any such action as aforesaid in which by virtue of this section [the plaintiff] is proved to have been convicted of an offence, the contents of any document which is admissible as evidence of the conviction, and the contents of the information, complaint, indictment or charge-sheet on which [he] was convicted, shall, without prejudice to the reception of any other admissible evidence for the purpose of identifying the facts on which the conviction was based, be admissible in evidence for the purpose of identifying those facts.

[(2A) In the case of an action for libel or slander in which there is more than one plaintiff—

    (a) the references in subsections (1) and (2) above to the plaintiff shall be construed as references to any of the plaintiffs, and

    (b) proof that any of the plaintiffs stands convicted of an offence shall be conclusive evidence that he committed that offence so far as that fact is relevant to any issue arising in relation to his cause of action or that of any other plaintiff.]

(3) For the purposes of this section a person shall be taken to stand convicted of an offence if but only if there subsists against him a conviction of that offence by or before a court in the United Kingdom or by a court-martial there or elsewhere.

Theatres Act 1968

(1968, c. 54)

4   Amendment of law of defamation

(1) For the purposes of the law of libel and slander [. . .] the publication of words in the course of a performance of a play shall, subject to section 7 of this Act, be treated as publication in permanent form.

(2) The foregoing subsection shall apply for the purposes of section 3 (slander of title, etc.) of the Defamation Act 1952 as it applies for the purposes of the law of libel and slander.

(3) In this section 'words' includes pictures, visual images, gestures and other methods of signifying meaning.

Trade Descriptions Act 1968

(1968, c. 29)

35   Saving for civil rights

A contract for the supply of any goods shall not be void or unenforceable by reason only of a contravention of any provision of this Act.

Employers' Liability (Compulsory Insurance) Act 1969

(1969, c. 57)

1   Insurance against liability for employees

(1) Except as otherwise provided by this Act, every employer carrying on any business in Great Britain shall insure, and maintain insurance, under one or more approved policies with an authorised insurer or insurers against liability for bodily injury or disease sustained by his employees, and arising out of and in the course of their employment in Great Britain in that business, but except in so far as regulations otherwise provide not including injury or disease suffered or contracted outside Great Britain.

(2) Regulations may provide that the amount for which an employer is required by this Act to insure and maintain insurance shall, either generally or in such cases or classes of case as may be prescribed by the regulations, be limited in such manner as may be so prescribed.

2   Employees to be covered

(1) For the purposes of this Act the term 'employee' means an individual who has entered into or works under a contract of service or apprenticeship with an employer whether by way of manual labour, clerical work or otherwise, whether such contract is expressed or implied, oral or in writing.

(2) This Act shall not require an employer to insure—

    (a) in respect of an employee of whom the employer is the husband, wife, [civil partner,] father, mother, grandfather, grandmother, step-father, step-mother, son, daughter, grandson, granddaughter, stepson, stepdaughter, brother, sister, half-brother, half-sister; or

    (b) except as otherwise provided by regulations, in respect of employees not ordinarily resident in Great Britain.

Employer's Liability (Defective Equipment) Act 1969

(1969, c. 37)

1 Extension of employer's liability for defective equipment

(1) Where after the commencement of this Act—

(a) an employee suffers personal injury in the course of his employment in consequence of a defect in equipment provided by his employer for the purposes of the employer's business; and

(b) the defect is attributable wholly or partly to the fault of a third party (whether identified or not),

the injury shall be deemed to be also attributable to negligence on the part of the employer (whether or not he is liable in respect of the injury apart from this subsection), but without prejudice to the law relating to contributory negligence and to any remedy by way of contribution or in contract or otherwise which is available to the employer in respect of the injury.

(2) In so far as any agreement purports to exclude or limit any liability of an employer arising under subsection (1) of this section, the agreement shall be void.

(3) In this section—

'business' includes the activities carried on by any public body;

'employee' means a person who is employed by another person under a contract of service or apprenticeship and is so employed for the purposes of a business carried on by that other person, and 'employer' shall be construed accordingly;

'equipment' includes any plant and machinery, vehicle, aircraft and clothing;

'fault' means negligence, breach of statutory duty or other act or omission which gives rise to liability in tort in England and Wales or which is wrongful and gives rise to liability in damages in Scotland; and

'personal injury' includes loss of life, any impairment of a person's physical or mental condition and any disease.

(4) This section binds the Crown, and persons in the service of the Crown shall accordingly be treated for the purposes of this section as employees of the Crown if they would not be so treated apart from this subsection.

Administration of Justice Act 1970

(1970, c. 31)

40 Punishment for unlawful harassment of debtors

(1) A person commits an offence if, with the object of coercing another person to pay money claimed from the other as a debt due under a contract, he—

(a) harasses the other with demands for payment which, in respect of their frequency or the manner or occasion of making any such demand, or of any threat or publicity by which any demand is accompanied, are calculated to subject him or members of his family or household to alarm, distress or humiliation;

(b) falsely represents, in relation to the money claimed, that criminal proceedings lie for failure to pay it;

(c) falsely represents himself to be authorised in some official capacity to claim or enforce payment; or

(d) utters a document falsely represented by him to have some official character or purporting to have some official character which he knows it has not.

(2) A person may be guilty of an offence by virtue of subsection (1)(a) above if he concerts with others in the taking of such action as is described in that paragraph, notwithstanding that his own course of conduct does not by itself amount to harassment.

(3) Subsection (1)(a) above does not apply to anything done by a person which is reasonable (and otherwise permissible in law) for the purpose—

(a) of securing the discharge of an obligation due, or believed by him to be due, to himself or to persons for whom he acts, or protecting himself or them from future loss; or

(b) of the enforcement of any liability by legal process.

[(3A) Subsection (1) above does not apply to anything done by a person to another in circumstances where what is done is a commercial practice within the meaning of the Consumer Protection from Unfair Trading Regulations 2008 and the other is a consumer in relation to that practice.]

Taxes Management Act 1970

(1970, c. 9)

[30   Recovery of overpayment of tax, etc.

(1) Where an amount of [income tax or capital gains tax] has been repaid to any person which ought not to have been repaid to him, that amount of tax may be assessed and recovered as if it were unpaid tax.

(1A) Subsection (1) above shall not apply where the amount of tax which has been repaid is assessable under section 29 of this Act.

(1B) Subsections (2) to (8) of section 29 of this Act shall apply in relation to an assessment under subsection (1) above as they apply in relation to an assessment under subsection (1) of that section; and subsection (4) of that section as so applied shall have effect as if the reference to the loss of tax were a reference to the repayment of the amount of tax which ought not to have been repaid.

(2) In any case where—

(a) a repayment of tax has been increased in accordance with section 824 [. . .] of the principal Act or section 283 of the 1992 Act (supplements added to repayments of tax, etc.); and

(b) the whole or any part of that repayment has been paid to any person but ought not to have been paid to him; and

(c) that repayment ought not to have been increased either at all or to any extent;

then the amount of the repayment assessed under subsection (1) above may include an amount equal to the amount by which the repayment ought not to have been increased.

(3) In any case where—

(a) a payment, other than a repayment of tax to which subsection (2) above applies, is increased in accordance with section 824 or 825 of the principal Act or section 283 of the 1992 Act; and

(b) that payment ought not to have been increased either at all or to any extent;

then an amount equal to the amount by which the payment ought not to have been increased may be assessed and recovered as if it were unpaid income tax [. . .].

(5) An assessment under this section shall not be out of time under section 34 of this Act if it is made before the end of whichever of the following ends the later, namely—

(a) the [year of assessment] following that in which the amount assessed was repaid or paid as the case may be, or

(b) where a return delivered by the person concerned [. . .] is enquired into by an officer of the Board, the period ending with the day on which, by virtue of section 28A(5) of this Act, the officer's enquiries are treated as completed.

(6) Subsection (5) above is without prejudice to section 36 of this Act.

(7) In this section any reference to an amount repaid or paid includes a reference to an amount allowed by way of set-off.]

[33   Recovery of overpaid tax etc
Schedule 1AB contains provision for and in connection with claims for the recovery of overpaid income tax and capital gains tax.]

[Section 33   SCHEDULE 1AB
RECOVERY OF OVERPAID TAX ETC

1   Claim for relief for overpaid tax etc
(1) This paragraph applies where—
(a) a person has paid an amount by way of income tax or capital gains tax but the person believes that the tax was not due, or
(b) a person has been assessed as liable to pay an amount by way of income tax or capital gains tax, or there has been a determination or direction to that effect, but the person believes that the tax is not due.

(2) The person may make a claim to the Commissioners for repayment or discharge of the amount.

(6) The Commissioners are not liable to give relief in respect of a case described in sub-paragraph (1)(a) or (b) except as provided—
(a) by this Schedule and Schedule 1A (following a claim under this paragraph), or
(b) by or under another provision of the Income Tax Acts or an enactment relating to the taxation of capital gains.

(7) For the purposes of this Schedule an amount paid by one person on behalf of another is treated as paid by the other person.

2   Cases in which Commissioners not liable to give effect to claim
(1) The Commissioners are not liable to give effect to a claim under this Schedule if or to the extent that the claim falls within a case described in this paragraph (see also paragraph 4(5)).

(2) Case A is where the amount paid, or liable to be paid, is excessive by reason of—
(a) a mistake in a claim, election or notice,
(b) a mistake consisting of making or giving, or failing to make or give, a claim, election or notice,
(c) a mistake in allocating expenditure to a pool for the purposes of the Capital Allowances Act or a mistake consisting of making, or failing to make, such an allocation, or
(d) a mistake in bringing a disposal value into account for the purposes of that Act or a mistake consisting of bringing, or failing to bring, such a value into account.

(3) Case B is where the claimant is or will be able to seek relief by taking other steps under the Income Tax Acts or an enactment relating to the taxation of capital gains.

(4) Case C is where the claimant—
(a) could have sought relief by taking such steps within a period that has now expired, and
(b) knew, or ought reasonably to have known, before the end of that period that such relief was available.

(5) Case D is where the claim is made on grounds that—
(a) have been put to a court or tribunal in the course of an appeal by the claimant relating to the amount paid or liable to be paid, or
(b) have been put to Her Majesty's Revenue and Customs in the course of an appeal by the claimant relating to that amount that is treated as having been determined by a tribunal (by virtue of section 54 (settling of appeals by agreement)).

(6) Case E is where the claimant knew, or ought reasonably to have known, of the grounds for the claim before the latest of the following—

    (a) the date on which an appeal by the claimant relating to the amount paid, or liable to be paid, in the course of which the ground could have been put forward (a "relevant appeal") was determined by a court or tribunal (or is treated as having been so determined),

    (b) the date on which the claimant withdrew a relevant appeal to a court or tribunal, and

    (c) the end of the period in which the claimant was entitled to make a relevant appeal to a court or tribunal.

(7) Case F is where the amount in question was paid or is liable to be paid—

    (a) in consequence of proceedings enforcing the payment of that amount brought against the claimant by Her Majesty's Revenue and Customs, or

    (b) in accordance with an agreement between the claimant and Her Majesty's Revenue and Customs settling such proceedings.

(8) Case G is where—

    (a) the amount paid, or liable to be paid, is excessive by reason of a mistake in calculating the claimant's liability to income tax or capital gains tax (other than a mistake in a PAYE assessment or PAYE calculation), and

    (b) liability was calculated in accordance with the practice generally prevailing at the time.

(9) Case H is where—

    (a) the amount paid, or liable to be paid, is excessive by reason of a mistake in a PAYE assessment or PAYE calculation, and

    (b) the assessment or calculation was made in accordance with the practice generally prevailing at the end of the period of 12 months following the tax year for which the assessment or calculation was made.

(9A) Cases G and H do not apply where the amount paid, or liable to be paid, is tax which has been charged contrary to EU law.

(9B) For the purposes of sub-paragraph (9A), an amount of tax is charged contrary to EU law if, in the circumstances in question, the charge to tax is contrary to—

    (a) the provisions relating to the free movement of goods, persons, services and capital in Titles II and IV of Part 3 of the Treaty on the Functioning of the European Union, or

    (b) the provisions of any subsequent treaty replacing the provisions mentioned in paragraph (a).

(10) For the purposes of Cases G and H—

    (a) "PAYE assessment" means an assessment on the claimant made in accordance with section 709 of ITEPA 2003 (assessment in connection with PAYE deductions), and

    (b) "PAYE calculation" means a calculation of the amount of a deduction or repayment made or to be made under PAYE regulations in respect of tax estimated to be payable by the claimant.

3 Making a claim

(1) A claim under this Schedule may not be made more than 4 years after the end of the relevant tax year.

(2) In relation to a claim made in reliance on paragraph 1(1)(a), the relevant tax year is—

    (a) where the amount paid, or liable to be paid, is excessive by reason of a mistake in a return or returns under section 8, 8A or 12AA of this Act, the tax year to which the return (or, if more than one, the first return) relates, and

    (b) otherwise, the tax year in respect of which the payment was made.

(3) In relation to a claim made in reliance on paragraph 1(1)(b), the relevant tax year is the tax year to which the assessment, determination or direction relates.

(4) A claim under this Schedule may not be made by being included in a return under section 8, 8A or 12AA of this Act.

4 The claimant: one person accountable for amounts payable by another etc

(1) Sub-paragraph (2) applies where, under a relevant enactment, a person ("P") is accountable to the Commissioners for—

    (a) an amount representing income tax or capital gains tax that is or is estimated to be payable by another person ("T"), or

    (b) any other amount that, under a relevant enactment, has been or is to be set off against a liability of T.

(2) A claim under this Schedule in respect of the amount may be made only by T.

(3) Sub-paragraph (4) applies where—

    (a) a person ("P") has paid an amount described in sub-paragraph (1)(a) or (b) in the belief that P was accountable to the Commissioners for the amount under a relevant enactment, but

    (b) P was not so accountable.

(4) A claim under this Schedule in respect of the amount may be made only by P.

(5) The Commissioners are not liable to give effect to a claim under sub-paragraph (4) if or to the extent that the amount has been repaid to T or set against amounts payable to the Commissioners by T.

(6) "Relevant enactment" means—

    (a) PAYE regulations,

    (b) Chapter 3 of Part 3 of the Finance Act 2004 or regulations under that Chapter (construction industry scheme), or

    (c) any other provision of or made under the Taxes Acts.

5 The claimant: partnerships

(1) This paragraph applies where—

    (a) a trade, profession or business is carried on by two or more persons in partnership,

    (b) an amount is paid, or liable to be paid, by one or more of those persons in accordance with a self-assessment, and

    (c) the amount is excessive by reason of a mistake in a partnership return.

(2) A claim under this Schedule in respect of the amount—

    (a) may be made by the relevant partner nominated to make the claim by all of the relevant partners, and

    (b) may not be made by any other person.

(3) In relation to such a claim, references in this Schedule to the claimant are to any of the relevant partners.

(4) "Relevant partner" means—

    (a) a person who was a partner in the partnership at any time during the period in respect of which the partnership return was made, or

    (b) the personal representative of such a person.

6 Assessment of claimant in connection with claim

(1) This paragraph applies where—

    (a) a claim is made under this Schedule,

    (b) the grounds for giving effect to the claim also provide grounds for a discovery assessment or determination on the claimant in respect of any chargeable period, and

    (c) such an assessment or determination could be made but for a relevant restriction.

(2) "Discovery assessment or determination" means—

    (a) an assessment under section 29(1), or

    (b) a discovery assessment or discovery determination under Schedule 18 to the Finance Act 1998 (company tax return etc).

(3) The following are relevant restrictions—

    (a) the conditions in section 29(3) to (5),

    (b) the restrictions in paragraphs 42 to 45 of Schedule 18 to the Finance Act 1998, and

    (c) the expiry of a time limit for making a discovery assessment or determination.

(4) Where this paragraph applies—

    (a) the relevant restrictions are to be disregarded, and

    (b) the discovery assessment or determination is not out of time if it is made before the final determination of the claim.

7   Amendment of partnership return etc in connection with claim

(1) This paragraph applies where—

    (a) a claim is made under this Schedule,

    (b) the claimant is one of two or more persons carrying on a trade, profession or business in partnership,

    (c) the grounds for giving effect to the claim also provide grounds for amending, under section 30B(1) (discovery of loss of tax from partnership), a return made by the partnership or any of the partners in respect of any period, and

    (d) such an amendment could be made but for a relevant restriction.

(2) The following are relevant restrictions—

    (a) the conditions in section 30B(4) to (6), and

    (b) the expiry of a time limit for making an assessment under that section.

(3) Where this paragraph applies—

    (a) the relevant conditions are to be disregarded, and

    (b) the amendment is not out of time if it is made before the final determination of the claim.

8   Contract settlements

(1) In paragraph 1(1)(a) the reference to an amount paid by way of income tax or capital gains tax includes an amount paid under a contract settlement in connection with income tax or capital gains tax believed to be due from any person.

(2) Sub-paragraphs (3) to (6) apply if the person who paid the amount under the contract settlement ("the payer") and the person from whom the tax was due ("the taxpayer") are not the same person.

(3) In relation to a claim under this Schedule in respect of that amount—

    (a) the references to the claimant in paragraph 2(5) to (7) (Cases D, E and F) have effect as if they included the taxpayer,

    (b) the references to the claimant in paragraph 2(8) and (10) (Cases G and H) have effect as if they were references to the taxpayer,

    (c) the references to the claimant in paragraphs 6(1)(b) and 7(1)(b) have effect as if they were references to the taxpayer, and

    (d) references to tax in Schedule 1A (as it applies to a claim under this Schedule) include such an amount.

(4) Sub-paragraph (5) applies where the grounds for giving effect to a claim by the payer in respect of the amount also provide grounds for a discovery assessment or determination on the taxpayer in respect of any chargeable period.

(5) The Commissioners may set any amount repayable to the payer by virtue of the claim against any amount payable by the taxpayer by virtue of the assessment or determination.

(6) The obligations of the Commissioners and the taxpayer are discharged to the extent of any set-off under sub-paragraph (5).

(7) In this paragraph—

"contract settlement" means an agreement made in connection with any person's liability to make a payment to the Commissioners under or by virtue of an enactment;

"discovery assessment or determination" has the same meaning as in paragraph 6.

9 Interpretation

(1) In this Schedule "the Commissioners" means the Commissioners for Her Majesty's Revenue and Customs.

(2) For the purposes of this Schedule a claim is not finally determined until it, or the amount to which it relates, can no longer be varied (whether on appeal or otherwise).

Animals Act 1971

(1971, c. 22)

1 New provisions as to strict liability for damage done by animals

(1) The provisions of sections 2 to 5 of this Act replace—

  (a) the rules of the common law imposing a strict liability in tort for damage done by an animal on the ground that the animal is regarded as ferae naturae or that its vicious or mischievous propensities are known or presumed to be known;

  (b) subsections (1) and (2) of section 1 of the Dogs Act 1906 as amended by the Dogs (Amendment) Act 1928 (injury to cattle or poultry); and

  (c) the rules of the common law imposing a liability for cattle trespass.

(2) Expressions used in those sections shall be interpreted in accordance with the provisions of section 6 (as well as those of section 11) of this Act.

2 Liability for damage done by dangerous animals

(1) Where any damage is caused by an animal which belongs to a dangerous species, any person who is a keeper of the animal is liable for the damage, except as otherwise provided by this Act.

(2) Where damage is caused by an animal which does not belong to a dangerous species, a keeper of the animal is liable for the damage, except as otherwise provided by this Act, if—

  (a) the damage is of a kind which the animal, unless restrained, was likely to cause or which, if caused by the animal, was likely to be severe; and

  (b) the likelihood of the damage or of its being severe was due to characteristics of the animal which are not normally found in animals of the same species or are not normally so found except at particular times or in particular circumstances; and

  (c) those characteristics were known to that keeper or were at any time known to a person who at that time had charge of the animal as that keeper s servant or, where that keeper is the head of a household, were known to another keeper of the animal who is a member of that household and under the age of sixteen.

3 Liability for injury done by dogs to livestock

Where a dog causes damage by killing or injuring livestock, any person who is a keeper of the dog is liable for the damage, except as otherwise provided by this Act.

4 Liability for damage and expenses due to trespassing livestock

(1) Where livestock belonging to any person strays on to land in the ownership or occupation of another and—

  (a) damage is done by the livestock to the land or to any property on it which is in the ownership or possession of the other person; or

(b) any expenses are reasonably incurred by that other person in keeping the livestock while it cannot be restored to the person to whom it belongs or while it is detained in pursuance of section 7 of this Act, or in ascertaining to whom it belongs;

the person to whom the livestock belongs is liable for the damage or expenses, except as otherwise provided by this Act.

(2) For the purposes of this section any livestock belongs to the person in whose possession it is.

[(3) This section does not apply in relation to horses on land in England (as to which, see section 4A).]

[4A Liability for damage and expenses due to horses on land in England without lawful authority

(1) This section applies where a horse is on any land in England without lawful authority.

(2) The person to whom the horse belongs is liable for—

(a) any damage done by the horse to—

(i)   the land, or

(ii) any property on it which is in the ownership or possession of the freeholder or occupier of the land, and

(b) any expenses which are reasonably incurred by a person detaining the horse under section 7A or 7B of this Act—

(i)   in keeping the horse while it cannot be restored to the person to whom it belongs or while it is detained under section 7A or 7B of this Act, or

(ii) in ascertaining to whom it belongs.

This is subject to the other provisions of this Act.

(3) For the purposes of this section a horse belongs to the person in whose possession it is.]

5 Exceptions from liability under sections 2 to [4A]

(1) A person is not liable under sections 2 to [4A] of this Act for any damage which is due wholly to the fault of the person suffering it.

(2) A person is not liable under section 2 of this Act for any damage suffered by a person who has voluntarily accepted the risk thereof.

(3) A person is not liable under section 2 of this Act for any damage caused by an animal kept on any premises or structure to a person trespassing there, if it is proved either—

(a) that the animal was not kept there for the protection of persons or property; or

(b) (if the animal was kept there for the protection of persons or property) that keeping it there for that purpose was not unreasonable.

(4) A person is not liable under section 3 of this Act if the livestock was killed or injured on land on to which it had strayed and either the dog belonged to the occupier or its presence on the land was authorised by the occupier.

(5) A person is not liable under section 4 of this Act where the livestock strayed from a highway and its presence there was a lawful use of the highway.

[(5A) A person is not liable under section 4A of this Act in respect of a horse which strays from a highway when its presence there was a lawful use of the highway.]

(6) In determining whether any liability for damage under section 4 of this Act[, or under section 4A of this Act so far as relating to a straying horse in England,] is excluded by subsection (1) of this section the damage shall not be treated as due to the fault of the person suffering it by reason only that he could have prevented it by fencing; but a person is not liable under that section where it is proved that the straying of the livestock on to the land would not have occurred but for a breach by any other person, being a person having an interest in the land, of a duty to fence.

6 Interpretation of certain expressions used in sections 2 to 5

(1) The following provisions apply to the interpretation of sections 2 to 5 of this Act.

(2) A dangerous species is a species—

(a) which is not commonly domesticated in the British Islands; and

(b) whose fully grown animals normally have such characteristics that they are likely, unless restrained, to cause severe damage or that any damage they may cause is likely to be severe.

(3) Subject to subsection (4) of this section, a person is a keeper of an animal if—

(a) he owns the animal or has it in his possession; or

(b) he is the head of a household of which a member under the age of sixteen owns the animal or has it in his possession;

and if at any time an animal ceases to be owned by or to be in the possession of a person, any person who immediately before that time was a keeper thereof by virtue of the preceding provisions of this subsection continues to be a keeper of the animal until another person becomes a keeper thereof by virtue of those provisions.

(4) Where an animal is taken into and kept in possession for the purpose of preventing it from causing damage or of restoring it to its owner, a person is not a keeper of it by virtue only of that possession.

(5) Where a person employed as a servant by a keeper of an animal incurs a risk incidental to his employment he shall not be treated as accepting it voluntarily.

7 Detention and sale of trespassing livestock

(1) The right to seize and detain any animal by way of distress damage feasant is hereby abolished.

(2) Where any livestock strays on to any land and is not then under the control of any person the occupier of the land may detain it, subject to subsection (3) of this section, unless ordered to return it by a court.

(3) Where any livestock is detained in pursuance of this section the right to detain it ceases—

(a) at the end of a period of forty-eight hours, unless within that period notice of the detention has been given to the officer in charge of a police station and also, if the person detaining the livestock knows to whom it belongs, to that person; or

(b) when such amount is tendered to the person detaining the livestock as is sufficient to satisfy any claim he may have under section 4 of this Act in respect of the livestock; or,

(c) if he has no such claim, when the livestock is claimed by a person entitled to its possession.

(4) Where livestock has been detained in pursuance of this section for a period of not less than fourteen days the person detaining it may sell it at a market or by public auction, unless proceedings are then pending for the return of the livestock or for any claim under section 4 of this Act in respect of it.

(5) Where any livestock is sold in the exercise of the right conferred by this section and the proceeds of the sale, less the costs thereof and any costs incurred in connection with it, exceed the amount of any claim under section 4 of this Act which the vendor had in respect of the livestock, the excess shall be recoverable from him by the person who would be entitled to the possession of the livestock but for the sale.

(6) A person detaining any livestock in pursuance of this section is liable for any damage caused to it by a failure to treat it with reasonable care and supply it with adequate food and water while it is so detained.

(7) References in this section to a claim under section 4 of this Act in respect of any livestock do not include any claim under that section for damage done by or expenses incurred in respect of the livestock before the straying in connection with which it is detained under this section.

[(8) Subsections (2) to (7) do not apply to horses on land in England (as to which, see sections 7A to 7C).]

[7A Power of local authorities in England to detain horses

(1) A local authority in England may detain a horse which is in any public place in its area, if the conditions in subsection (2) are met.

(2) The conditions are—

    (a) the local authority has reasonable grounds for believing that the horse is there without lawful authority, and

    (b) if the land is lawfully occupied by a person—

        (i)   that person consents to the detention of the horse, or

        (ii) the local authority has reasonable grounds for believing that that person would consent to the detention of the horse (but this does not require the authority to seek consent).

(3) Section 7C contains further provision about detention under this section.

(4) In this section "local authority" means—

    (a) a county council,

    (b) a district council,

    (c) a London borough council,

    (d) the Common Council of the City of London, and

    (e) the Council of the Isles of Scilly.]

[7B   Powers of freeholders and occupiers in England to detain horses

(1) This section applies where a horse is on any land in England without lawful authority.

(2) The horse may be detained—

    (a) in any case, by the occupier of the land, and

    (b) if the freeholder is not the occupier, by the freeholder with the occupier's consent.

(3) Section 7C contains further provision about detention under this section.]

[7C   Detention of horses under sections 7A and 7B

(1) This section applies where a horse is detained under section 7A or 7B.

(2) The right to detain the horse ceases at the end of the period of 24 hours beginning with the time when it is first detained unless, within that period, the person detaining the horse gives notice of the detention to—

    (a) the officer in charge of a police station, and

    (b) if the person detaining the horse knows to whom the horse belongs, that person.

(3) Where notice is given under subsection (2), the right to detain the horse ceases if, within the period of 96 hours beginning with the time when it is first detained, the person entitled to possession of the horse—

    (a) claims it, and

    (b) complies with the condition in subsection (4).

(4) The condition is that the person tenders to each person with a claim under section 4A in respect of the horse such amount as is sufficient to satisfy the claim.

(5) If by the end of the 96 hour period referred to in subsection (3) the right to detain the horse has not ceased under this section—

    (a) ownership of the horse passes to the person detaining the horse, and

    (b) accordingly, the person detaining the horse may dispose of it by selling it, arranging for it to be destroyed or in any other way.

(6) Where a horse is sold under this section and the proceeds of sale, less the costs of the sale and any costs incurred in connection with it, exceed the amount of any claims under section 4A in respect of the horse, the excess is recoverable from the person detaining the horse by the person who would have been entitled to possession of the horse but for this section.

(7) A person detaining a horse under this section is liable for any damage caused to it by a failure to treat it with reasonable care and supply it with adequate food and water while it is so detained.

(8) References in this section to a claim under section 4A in respect of any horse do not include a claim under that section for damage done by or expenses incurred in respect of the horse before it was on the land without lawful authority.

(9) In calculating a period of 96 hours for the purposes of this section, disregard any time falling on—

    (a) a Saturday or Sunday,

    (b) Good Friday or Christmas Day, or

    (c) a day which is a bank holiday in England and Wales under the Banking and Financial Dealings Act 1971.]

8 Duty to take care to prevent damage from animals straying on to the highway

(1) So much of the rules of the common law relating to liability for negligence as excludes or restricts the duty which a person might owe to others to take such care as is reasonable to see that damage is not caused by animals straying on to a highway is hereby abolished.

(2) Where damage is caused by animals straying from unfenced land to a highway a person who placed them on the land shall not be regarded as having committed a breach of the duty to take care by reason only of placing them there if—

    (a) the land is common land, or is land situated in an area where fencing is not customary, or is a town or village green; and

    (b) he had a right to place the animals on that land.

9 Killing of or injury to dogs worrying livestock

(1) In any civil proceedings against a person (in this section referred to as the defendant) for killing or causing injury to a dog it shall be a defence to prove—

    (a) that the defendant acted for the protection of any livestock and was a person entitled to act for the protection of that livestock; and

    (b) that within forty-eight hours of the killing or injury notice thereof was given by the defendant to the officer in charge of a police station.

(2) For the purposes of this section a person is entitled to act for the protection of any livestock if, and only if—

    (a) the livestock or the land on which it is belongs to him or to any person under whose express or implied authority he is acting; and

    (b) the circumstances are not such that liability for killing or causing injury to the livestock would be excluded by section 5(4) of this Act.

(3) Subject to subsection (4) of this section, a person killing or causing injury to a dog shall be deemed for the purposes of this section to act for the protection of any livestock if, and only if, either—

    (a) the dog is worrying or is about to worry the livestock and there are no other reasonable means of ending or preventing the worrying; or

    (b) the dog has been worrying livestock, has not left the vicinity and is not under the control of any person and there are no practicable means of ascertaining to whom it belongs.

(4) For the purposes of this section the condition stated in either of the paragraphs of the preceding subsection shall be deemed to have been satisfied if the defendant believed that it was satisfied and had reasonable ground for that belief.

(5) For the purposes of this section—

    (a) an animal belongs to any person if he owns it or has it in his possession; and

    (b) land belongs to any person if he is the occupier thereof.

10 Application of certain enactments to liability under sections 2 to [4A]

For the purposes of [the Fatal Accidents Act 1976,] the Law Reform (Contributory Negligence) Act 1945 and [the Limitation Act 1980] any damage for which a person is liable under sections 2 to [4A] of this Act shall be treated as due to his fault.

11   General interpretation

In this Act—

'common land', and 'town or village green' have the same meanings as in the Commons Regulation Act 1965;

'damage' includes the death of, or injury to, any person (including any disease and any impairment of physical or mental condition);

'fault' has the same meaning as in the Law Reform (Contributory Negligence) Act 1945;

'fencing' includes the construction of any obstacle designed to prevent animals from straying;

["horse" includes an ass, mule or hinny;]

'livestock' means cattle, horses, [. . .] sheep, pigs, goats and poultry, and also deer not in the wild state and, in section 3 and 9 also, while in captivity, pheasants, partridges and grouse;

'poultry' means the domestic varieties of the following, that is to say, fowls, turkeys, geese, ducks, guinea-fowls, pigeons, peacocks and quails;

["public place" includes—

(a) any common land or town or village green;

(b) any highway (and the verges of any highway);]

and 'species' includes sub-species and variety.

12   Application to Crown

(1) This Act binds the Crown, but nothing in this section shall authorise proceedings to be brought against Her Majesty in her private capacity.

(2) Section 38(3) of the Crown Proceedings Act 1947 (interpretation of references to Her Majesty in her private capacity) shall apply as if this section were contained in that Act.

Carriage of Goods by Sea Act 1971

(1971, c. 19)

1   Application of Hague Rules as amended

(1) In this Act, 'the Rules' means the International Convention for the unification of certain rules of law relating to bills of lading signed at Brussels on 25 August 1924, as amended by the Protocol signed at Brussels on 23 February 1968 [and by the Protocol signed at Brussels on 21 December 1979.]

(2) The provisions of the Rules, as set out in the Schedule to this Act, shall have the force of law.

(3) Without prejudice to subsection (2) above, the said provisions shall have effect (and have the force of law) in relation to and in connection with the carriage of goods by sea in ships where the port of shipment is a port in the United Kingdom, whether or not the carriage is between ports in two different States within the meaning of Article X of the Rules.

(4) Subject to subsection (6) below, nothing in this section shall be taken as applying anything in the Rules to any contract for the carriage of goods by sea, unless the contract expressly or by implication provides for the issue of a bill of lading or any similar document of title.

(5) [. . .]

(6) Without prejudice to Article X(c) of the Rules, the Rules shall have the force of law in relation to—

(a) any bill of lading if the contract contained in or evidenced by it expressly provides that the Rules shall govern the contract, and

(b) any receipt which is a non-negotiable document marked as such if the contract contained in or evidenced by it is a contract for the carriage of goods by sea which expressly provides that the Rules are to govern the contract as if the receipt were a bill of lading,

but subject, where paragraph (b) applies, to any necessary modifications and in particular with the omission in Article III of the Rules of the second sentence of paragraph 4 and of paragraph 7.

(7) If and so far as the contract contained in or evidenced by a bill of lading or receipt within paragraph (a) or (b) of subsection (6) above applies to deck cargo or live animals, the Rules as given the force of law by that subsection shall have effect as if Article I(c) did not exclude deck cargo and live animals.

In this subsection 'deck cargo' means cargo which by the contract of carriage is stated as being carried on deck and is so carried.

[1A   Conversion of special drawing rights into sterling

(1) For the purposes of Article IV of the Rules the value on a particular day of one special drawing right shall be treated as equal to such a sum in sterling as the International Monetary Fund have fixed as being the equivalent of one special drawing right—

(a) for that day; or

(a) if no sum has been so fixed for that day, for the last day before that day for which a sum has been so fixed.

(2) A certificate given by or on behalf of the Treasury stating—

(a) that a particular sum in sterling has been fixed as aforesaid for a particular day; or

(b) that no sum has been so fixed for a particular day and that a particular sum in sterling has been so fixed for a day which is the last day for which a sum has been so fixed before the particular day,

shall be conclusive evidence of those matters for the purposes of subsection (1) above; and a document purporting to be such a certificate shall in any proceedings be received in evidence and, unless the contrary is proved, be deemed to be such a certificate.

(3) The Treasury may charge a reasonable fee for any certificate given in pursuance of subsection (2) above, and any fee received by the Treasury by virtue of this subsection shall be paid into the Consolidated Fund.]

2   Contracting States, etc.

(1) If Her Majesty by Order in council certifies to the following effect, that is to say, that for the purposes of the Rules—

(a) a State specified in the Order is a contracting State, or is a contracting State in respect of any place or territory so specified; or

(b) any place or territory specified in the Order forms part of a State so specified (whether a contracting State or not),

the Order shall, except so far as it has been superseded by a subsequent Order, be conclusive evidence of the matters so certified.

(2) An Order in Council under this section may be varied or revoked by a subsequent Order in Council.

3   Absolute warranty of seaworthiness not to be implied in contracts to which Rules apply

There shall not be implied in any contract for the carriage of goods by sea to which the Rules apply by virtue of this Act any absolute undertaking by the carrier of the goods to provide a seaworthy ship.

SCHEDULE
THE HAGUE RULES AS AMENDED
BY THE BRUSSELS PROTOCOL 1968

Article I

In these Rules the following words are employed, with the meanings set out below—

    (a) 'Carrier' includes the owner or the charter who enters into a contract of carriage with a shipper.

    (b) 'Contract of carriage' applies only to contracts of carriage covered by a bill of lading or any similar document of title, in so far as such document relates to the carriage of goods by sea, including any bill of lading or any similar document as aforesaid issued under or pursuant to a charter party from the moment at which such bill of lading or similar document of title regulates the relations between a carrier and a holder of the same.

    (c) 'Goods' includes goods, wares, merchandise, and articles of every kind whatsoever except live animals and cargo which by the contract of carriage is stated as being carried on deck and is so carried.

    (d) 'Ship' means any vessel used for the carriage of goods by sea.

    (e) 'Carriage of goods' covers the period from the time when the goods are loaded on to the time they are discharged from the ship.

Article II

Subject to the provisions of Article VI, under every contract of carriage of goods by sea the carrier, in relation to the loading, handling, stowage, carriage, custody, care and discharge of such goods, shall be subject to the responsibilities and liabilities, and entitled to the rights and immunities hereinafter set forth.

Article III

    (1) The carrier shall be bound before and at the beginning of the voyage to exercise due diligence to—

        (a) Make the ship seaworthy.

        (b) Properly man, equip and supply the ship.

        (c) Make the holds, refrigerating and cool chambers, and all other parts of the ship in which goods are carried, fit and safe for their reception, carriage and preservation.

    (2) Subject to the provisions of Article IV, the carrier shall properly and carefully load, handle, stow, carry, keep, care for, and discharge the goods carried.

    (3) After receiving the goods into his charge the carrier or the master or agent of the carrier shall, on demand of the shipper, issue to the shipper a bill of lading showing among other things—

        (a) The leading marks necessary for identification of the goods as the same are furnished in writing by the shipper before the loading of such goods starts, provided such marks are stamped or otherwise shown clearly upon the goods if uncovered, or on the cases or coverings in which such goods are contained, in such a manner as should ordinarily remain legible until the end of the voyage.

        (b) Either the number of packages or pieces, or the quantity, or weight, as the case may be, as furnished in writing by the shipper.

        (c) The apparent order and condition of the goods. Provided that no carrier, master or agent of the carrier shall be bound to state or show in the bill of lading any marks, number, quantity, or weight which he has reasonable ground for suspecting not accurately to represent the goods actually received, or which he has had no reasonable means of checking.

    (4) Such a bill of lading shall be prima facie evidence of the receipt by the carrier of the goods as therein described in accordance with paragraph 3(a), (b) and (c). However, proof to the contrary shall not be admissible when the bill of lading has been transferred to a third party acting in good faith.

(5) The shipper shall be deemed to have guaranteed to the carrier the accuracy at the time of shipment of the marks, number, quantity and weight, as furnished by him, and the shipper shall indemnify the carrier against all loss, damages and expenses arising or resulting from inaccuracies in such particulars. The right of the carrier to such indemnity shall in no way limit his responsibility and liability under the contract of carriage to any person other than the shipper.

(6) Unless notice of loss or damage and the general nature of such loss or damage be given in writing to the carrier or his agent at the port of discharge before or at the time of the removal of the goods into the custody of the person entitled to delivery thereof under the contract of carriage, or, if the loss or damage be not apparent, within three days, such removal shall be prima facie evidence of the delivery by the carrier of the goods as described in the bill of lading.

The notice in writing need not be given if the state of the goods has, at the time of their receipt, been the subject of joint survey or inspection.

Subject to paragraph 6bis the carrier and the ship shall in any event be discharged from all liability whatsoever in respect of the goods, unless suit is brought within one year of their delivery or of the date when they should have been delivered. This period may, however, be extended if the parties so agree after the cause of action has arisen.

In the case of any actual or apprehended loss or damage the carrier and the receiver shall give all reasonable facilities to each other for inspecting and tallying the goods.

(6bis) An action for indemnity against a third person may be brought even after the expiration of the year provided for in the preceding paragraph if brought within the time allowed by the law of the Court seized of the case. However, the time allowed shall be not less than three months, commencing from the day when the person bringing such action for indemnity has settled the claim or has been served with process in the action against himself.

(7) After the goods are loaded the bill of lading to be issued by the carrier, master, or agent of the carrier, to the shipper shall, if the shipper so demands, be a 'shipped' bill of lading, provided that if the shipper shall have previously taken up any document of title to such goods, he shall surrender the same as against the issue of the 'shipped' bill of lading, but at the option of the carrier such document of title may be noted at the port of shipment by the carrier, master, or agent with the name or names of the ship or ships upon which the goods have been shipped and the date or dates of shipment, and when so noted if it shows the particulars mentioned in paragraph 3 of Article III, shall for the purpose of this article be deemed to constitute a 'shipped' bill of lading.

(8) Any clause, covenant, or agreement in a contract of carriage relieving the carrier or the ship from liability for loss or damage to, or in connection with, goods arising from negligence, fault, or failure in the duties and obligations provided in this article or lessening such liability otherwise than as provided in these Rules, shall be null and void and of no effect. A benefit of insurance in favour of the carrier or similar clause shall be deemed to be a clause relieving the carrier from liability.

Article IV

(1) Neither the carrier nor the ship shall be liable for loss or damage arising or resulting from unseaworthiness unless caused by want of due diligence on the part of the carrier to make the ship seaworthy, and to secure that the ship is properly manned, equipped and supplied, and to make the holds, refrigerating and cool chambers and all other parts of the ship in which goods are carried fit and safe for their reception, carriage and preservation in accordance with the provisions of paragraph 1 of Article III. Whenever loss or damage has resulted from unseaworthiness the burden of proving the exercise of due diligence shall be on the carrier or other person claiming exemption under this article.

(2) Neither the carrier nor the ship shall be responsible for loss or damage arising or resulting from—

    (a) Act, neglect, or default of the master, mariner, pilot, or the servants of the carrier in the navigation or in the management of the ship.

    (b) Fire, unless caused by the actual fault or privity of the carrier.

    (c) Perils, dangers and accidents of the sea or other navigable waters.

(d) Act of God.

(e) Act of war.

(f) Act of public enemies.

(g) Arrest or restraint of princes, rulers or people, or seizure under legal process.

(h) Quarantine restrictions.

(i) Act or omission of the shipper or owner of the goods, his agent or representative.

(j) Strikes or lockouts or stoppage or restraint of labour from whatever cause, whether partial or general.

(k) Riots and civil commotions.

(l) Saving or attempting to save life or property at sea.

(m) Wastage in bulk or weight or any other loss or damage arising from inherent defect, quality or vice of the goods.

(n) Insufficiency of packing.

(o) Insufficiency or inadequacy of marks.

(p) Latent defects not discoverable by due diligence.

(q) Any other cause arising without the actual fault or privity of the carrier, or without the fault or neglect of the agents or servants of the carrier, but the burden of proof shall be on the person claiming the benefit of this exception to show that neither the actual fault or privity of the carrier nor the fault or neglect of the agents or servants of the carrier contributed to the loss or damage.

(3) The shipper shall not be responsible for the loss or damage sustained by the carrier or the ship arising or resulting from any cause without the act, fault or neglect of the shipper, his agents or his servants.

(4) Any deviation in saving or attempting to save life or property at sea or any reasonable deviation shall not be deemed to be an infringement or breach of these Rules or of the contract of carriage, and the carrier shall not be liable for any loss or damage resulting therefrom.

(5) (a) Unless the nature and value of such goods have been declared by the shipper before shipment and inserted in the bill of lading, neither the carrier nor the ship shall in any event be or become liable for any loss or damage to or in connection with the goods in an amount exceeding [666.67 units of account] per package or unit or [2 units of account per kilogramme] of gross weight of the goods lost or damaged, whichever is the higher.

(b) The total amount recoverable shall be calculated by reference to the value of such goods at the place and time at which the goods are discharged from the ship in accordance with the contract or should have been so discharged.

The value of the goods shall be fixed according to the commodity exchange price, or, if there be no such price, according to the current market price, or, if there be no commodity exchange price or current market price, by reference to the normal value of goods of the same kind and quality.

(c) Where a container, pallet or similar article of transport is used to consolidate goods, the number of packages or units enumerated in the bill of lading as packed in such article of transport shall be deemed the number of packages or units for the purpose of this paragraph as far as these packages or units are concerned. Except as aforesaid such article of transport shall be considered the package or unit.

[(d) The unit of account mentioned in this Article is the special drawing right as defined by the International Monetary Fund. The amounts mentioned in subparagraph (a) of this paragraph shall be converted into national currency on the basis of the value of that currency on a date to be determined by the law of the court seized of the case.]

(e) Neither the carrier nor the ship shall be entitled to the benefit of the limitation of liability provided for in this paragraph if it is proved that the damage resulted from an act or omission of the carrier done with intent to cause damage, or recklessly and with knowledge that damage would probably result.

(f) The declaration mentioned in sub-paragraph (a) of this paragraph, if embodied in the bill of lading, shall be prima facie evidence, but shall not be binding or conclusive on the carrier.

(g) By agreement between the carrier, master or agent of the carrier and the shipper other maximum amounts than those mentioned in sub-paragraph (a) of this paragraph may be fixed, provided that no maximum amount so fixed shall be less than the appropriate maximum mentioned in that sub-paragraph.

(h) Neither the carrier nor the ship shall be responsible in any event (nor loss or damage to, or in connection with, goods if the nature or value thereof has been knowingly mis-stated by the shipper in the bill of lading.

(6) Goods of an inflammable, explosive or dangerous nature to the shipment whereof the carrier, master or agent of the carrier has not consented with knowledge of their nature and character, may at any time before discharge be landed at any place, or destroyed or rendered innocuous by the carrier without compensation and the shipper of such goods shall be liable for all damages and expenses directly or indirectly arising out of or resulting from such shipment. If any such goods shipped with such knowledge and consent shall become a danger to the ship or cargo, they may in like manner be landed at any place, or destroyed or rendered innocuous by the carrier without liability on the part of the carrier except to general average, if any.

Article IV bis

(1) The defences and limits of liability provided for in these Rules shall apply in any action against the carrier in respect of loss or damage to goods covered by a contract of carriage whether the action be founded in contract or in tort.

(2) If such an action is brought against a servant or agent of the carrier (such servant or agent not being an independent contractor), such servant or agent shall be entitled to avail himself of the defences and limits of liability which the carrier is entitled to invoke under these Rules.

(3) The aggregate of the amounts recoverable from the carrier, and such servants and agents, shall in no case exceed the limit provided for in these Rules.

(4) Nevertheless, a servant or agent of the carrier shall not be entitled to avail himself of the provisions of this article, if it is proved that the damage resulted from an act or omission of the servant or agent done with intent to cause damage or recklessly and with knowledge that damage would probably result.

Article V

A carrier shall be at liberty to surrender in whole or in part all or any of his rights and immunities or to increase any of his responsibilities and obligations under these Rules, provided such surrender or increase shall be embodied in the bill of lading issued to the shipper. The provisions of the Rules shall not be applicable to charter parties, but if bills of lading are issued in the case of a ship under a charter party they shall comply with the terms of these Rules. Nothing in these Rules shall be held to prevent the insertion in a bill of lading of any lawful provisions regarding general average.

Article VI

Notwithstanding the provisions of the preceding articles, a carrier, master or agent of the carrier and a shipper shall in regard to any particular goods be at liberty to enter into any agreement in any terms as to the responsibility and liability of the carrier for such goods, and as to the rights and immunities of the carrier in respect of such goods, or his obligation as to seaworthiness, so far as this stipulation is not contrary to public policy, or the care or diligence of his servants or agents in regard to the loading, handling, stowage, carriage, custody, care and discharge of the goods carried by sea, provided that in this case no bill of lading has been or shall be issued and that the terms agreed shall be embodied in a receipt which shall be a non-negotiable document and shall be marked as such.

Any agreement so entered into shall have full legal effect. Provided that this article shall not apply to ordinary commercial shipments made in the ordinary course of trade, but only to other shipments where the character or condition of the property to be carried or the circumstances, terms and conditions under which the carriage is to be performed are such as reasonably to justify a special agreement.

Article VII
Nothing herein contained shall prevent a carrier or a shipper from entering into any agreement, stipulation, condition, reservation or exemption as to the responsibility and liability of the carrier or the ship for the loss or damage to, or in connection with, the custody and care and handling of goods prior to the loading on, and subsequent to the discharge from, the ship on which the goods are carried by sea.

Article VIII
The provisions of these Rules shall not affect the rights and obligations of the carrier under any statute for the time being in force relating to the limitation of the liability of owners of sea-going vessels.

Article IX
These rules shall not affect the provisions of any international Convention or national law governing liability for nuclear damage.

Article X
The provisions of these Rules shall apply to every bill of lading relating to the carriage of goods between ports in two different States if:

    (a) the bill of lading is issued in a contracting State,

or

    (b) the carriage is from a port in a contracting State,

or

    (c) the contract contained in or evidenced by the bill of lading provides that these Rules or legislation of any State giving effect to them are to govern the contract, whatever may be the nationality of the ship, the carrier, the shipper, the consignee, or any other interested person.

Unsolicited Goods and Services Act 1971

(1971, c. 30)

2 Demands and threats regarding payment

(1) A person who, not having reasonable cause to believe there is a right to payment, in the course of any trade or business makes a demand for payment, or asserts a present or prospective right to payment, for what he knows are unsolicited goods sent (after the commencement of this Act) to another person with a view to his acquiring them [for the purposes of his trade or business], shall be guilty of an offence and on summary conviction shall be liable to a fine not exceeding [level 4 on the standard scale].

(2) A person who, not having reasonable cause to believe there is a right to payment in the course of any trade or business and with a view to obtaining any payment for what he knows are unsolicited goods sent as aforesaid—

    (a) threatens to bring any legal proceedings; or

    (b) places or causes to be placed the name of any person on a list of defaulters or debtors or threatens to do so; or

    (c) invokes or causes to be invoked any other collection procedure or threatens to do so, shall be guilty of an offence and shall be liable on summary conviction to a fine not exceeding [level 5 on the standard scale].

3 Directory entries

[(1) A person ('the purchaser') shall not be liable to make any payment, and shall be entitled to recover any payment made by him, by way of charge for including or arranging for the inclusion in a directory of an entry relating to that person or his trade or business, unless—

    (a) there has been signed by the purchaser or on his behalf an order complying with this section,

    (b) there has been signed by the purchaser or on his behalf a note complying with this section of his agreement to the charge and before the note was signed, a copy of it was supplied, for retention by him, to him or a person acting on his behalf, . . .

    (c) there has been transmitted by the purchaser or a person acting on his behalf an electronic communication which includes a statement that the purchaser agrees to the charge and the relevant condition is satisfied in relation to that communication, or

    (d) the charge arises under a contract in relation to which the conditions in section 3B(1) (renewed and extended contracts) are met.]

(2) A person shall be guilty of an offence punishable on summary conviction with a fine not exceeding £400 if, in a case where a payment in respect of a charge would [. . .] be recoverable from him in accordance with the terms of subsection (1) above, he demands payment, or asserts a present or prospective right to payment, of the charge or any part of it, without knowing or having reasonable cause to believe [that—

    (a) the entry to which the charge relates was ordered in accordance with this section,

    (b) a proper note of the agreement has been duly signed, or

    (c) the requirements set out in subsection (1)(c) or (d) above have been met.]

(3) For the purposes of [this section—

    (a) an order for an entry in a directory must be made by means of an order form or other stationery belonging to the purchaser, which may be sent electronically but which must bear his name and address (or one or more of his addresses); and

    (b) the note of a person s agreement to a charge must—

        (i) specify the particulars set out in Part 1 of the Schedule to the Regulatory Reform (Unsolicited Goods and Services Act 1971) (Directory Entries and Demands for Payment) Order 2005, and

        (ii) give reasonable particulars of the entry in respect of which the charge would be payable.]

[(3A) In relation to an electronic communication which includes a statement that the purchaser agrees to a charge for including or arranging the inclusion in a directory of any entry, the relevant condition is that—

    (a) before the electronic communication was transmitted the information referred to in subsection (3B) below was communicated to the purchaser, and

    (b) the electronic communication can readily be produced and retained in a visible and legible form.

(3B) that information is—

    (a) the following particulars—

        (i) the amount of the charge;

        (ii) the name of the directory or proposed directory;

        (iii) the name of the person producing the directory;

        (iv) the geographic address at which that person is established;

        (v) if the directory is or is to be available in printed form, the proposed date of publication of the directory or of the issue in which the entry is to be included;

    (vi) if the directory or the issue in which the entry is to be included is to be put on sale, the price at which it is to be offered for sale and the minimum number of copies which are to be available for sale;

   (vii) if the directory or the issue in which the entry is to be included is to be distributed free of charge (whether or not it is also to be put on sale), the minimum number of copies which are to be so distributed;

  (viii) if the directory is or is to be available in a form other than in printed form, adequate details of how it may be accessed; and

  (b) reasonable particulars of the entry in respect of which the charge would be payable.

(3C) In this section 'electronic communication' has the same meaning as in the Electronic Communications Act 2000.]

[3B   Renewed and extended contracts

(1) The conditions referred to in section 3(1)(d) above are met in relation to a contract ('the new contract') if—

  (a) a person ('the purchaser') has entered into an earlier contract ('the earlier contract') for including or arranging for the inclusion in a particular issue or version of a directory ('the earlier directory') of an entry ('the earlier entry') relating to him or his trade or business;

  (b) the purchaser was liable to make a payment by way of a charge arising under the earlier contract for including or arranging for the inclusion of the earlier entry in the earlier directory;

  (c) the new contract is a contract for including or arranging for the inclusion in a later issue or version of a directory ('the later directory') of an entry ('the later entry') relating to the purchaser or his trade or business;

  (d) the form, content and distribution of the later directory is materially the same as the form, content and distribution of the earlier directory;

  (e) the form and content of the later entry is materially the same as the form and content of the earlier entry;

  (f) if the later directory is published other than in electronic form—

    (i) the earlier directory was the last, or the last but one, issue or version of the directory to be published before the later directory, and

   (ii) the date of publication of the later directory is not more than 13 months after the date of publication of the earlier directory;

  (g) if the later directory is published in electronic form, the first date on which the new contract requires the later entry to be published is not more than the relevant period after the last date on which the earlier contract required the earlier entry to be published;

  (h) if it was a term of the earlier contract that the purchaser renew or extend the contract—

    (i) before the start of the new contract the relevant publisher has given notice in writing to the purchaser containing the information set out in Part 3 of the Schedule to the Regulatory Reform (Unsolicited Goods and Services Act 1971) (Directory Entries and Demands for Payment) Order 2005; and

   (ii) the purchaser has not written to the relevant publisher withdrawing his agreement to the renewal or extension of the earlier contract within the period of 21 days starting when he receives the notice referred to in subparagraph (i); and

  (i) if the parties to the earlier contract and the new contract are different—

    (i) the parties to both contracts have entered into a novation agreement in respect of the earlier contract; or

   (ii) the relevant publisher has given the purchaser the information set out in Part 4 of the Schedule to the Regulatory Reform (Unsolicited Goods and Services Act 1971) (Directory Entries and Demands for Payment) Order 2005.

(2) For the purposes of subsection (1)(d) and (e), the form, content or distribution of the later directory, or the form or content of the later entry, shall be taken to be materially the same as that of the earlier directory or the earlier entry (as the case may be), if a reasonable person in the position of the purchaser would—
> (a) view the two as being materially the same; or
> (b) view that of the later directory or the later entry as being an improvement on that of the earlier directory or the earlier entry.

(3) For the purposes of subsection (1)(g) 'the relevant period' means the period of 13 months or (if shorter) the period of time between the first and last dates on which the earlier contract required the earlier entry to be published.

(4) For the purposes of subsection (1)(h) and (i) 'the relevant publisher' is the person with whom the purchaser has entered into the new contract.

(5) The information referred to in subsection (1) (i) (ii) must be given to the purchaser prior to the conclusion of the new contract.]

4   Unsolicited publications

(1) A person shall be guilty of an offence if he sends or causes to be sent to another person any book, magazine or leaflet (or advertising material for any such publication) which he knows or ought reasonably to know is unsolicited and which describes or illustrates human sexual techniques.

(2) A person found guilty of an offence under this section shall be liable on summary conviction to a fine not exceeding [level 5 on the standard scale] for a first offence and to a fine not exceeding [level 5 on the standard scale] for any subsequent offence.

(3) A prosecution for an offence under this section shall not in England and Wales be instituted except by, or with the consent of, the Director of Public Prosecutions.

5   Offences by corporations

(1) Where an offence under this Act which has been committed by a body corporate is proved to have been committed with the consent or connivance of, or to be attributable to any neglect on the part of, any director, manager, secretary, or other similar officer of the body corporate, or of any person who was purporting to act in any such capacity, he as well as the body corporate shall be guilty of that offence and shall be liable to be proceeded against and punished accordingly.

(2) Where the affairs of a body corporate are managed by its members, this section shall apply in relation to the acts or defaults of a member in connection with his functions of management as if he were a director of the body corporate.

6   Interpretation

(1) In this Act, unless the context or subject matter otherwise requires,—

'acquire' includes hire;

'send' includes deliver, and 'sender' shall be construed accordingly;

'unsolicited' means, in relation to goods sent to any person, that they are sent without any prior request made by him or on his behalf.

[(2) For the purposes of this Act, any invoice or similar document stating the amount of any payment shall be regarded as asserting a right to the payment unless it complies with the conditions set out in Part 2 of the Schedule to the Regulatory Reform (Unsolicited Goods and Services Act 1971) (Directory Entries and Demands for Payment) Order 2005.]

[(3) Nothing in section 3 or 3B affects the rights of any consumer under the Contracts (Information, Cancellation and Additional Charges) Regulations 2013.]

Defective Premises Act 1972

(1972, c. 35)

1 Duty to build dwellings properly

(1) A person taking on work for or in connection with the provision of a dwelling (whether the dwelling is provided by the erection or by the conversion or enlargement of a building) owes a duty—

    (a) if the dwelling is provided to the order of any person, to that person; and

    (b) without prejudice to paragraph (a) above, to every person who acquires an interest (whether legal or equitable) in the dwelling;

to see that the work which he takes on is done in a workmanlike or, as the case may be, professional manner, with proper materials and so that as regards that work the dwelling will be fit for habitation when completed.

(2) A person who takes on any such work for another on terms that he is to do it in accordance with instructions given by or on behalf of that other shall, to the extent to which he does it properly in accordance with those instructions, be treated for the purposes of this section as discharging the duty imposed on him by subsection (1) above except where he owes a duty to that other to warn him of any defects in the instructions and fails to discharge that duty.

(3) A person shall not be treated for the purposes of subsection (2) above as having given instructions for the doing of work merely because he has agreed to the work being done in a specified manner, with specified materials or to a specified design.

(4) A person who—

    (a) in the course of a business which consists of or includes providing or arranging for the provision of dwellings or installations in dwellings; or

    (b) in the exercise of a power of making such provision or arrangements conferred by or by virtue of any enactment;

arranges for another to take on work for or in connection with the provision of a dwelling shall be treated for the purposes of this section as included among the persons who have taken on the work.

(5) Any cause of action in respect of a breach of the duty imposed by this section shall be deemed, for the purposes of [the Limitation Act 1980], to have accrued at the time when the dwelling was completed, but if after that time a person who has done work for or in connection with the provision of the dwelling does further work to rectify the work he has already done, any such cause of action in respect of that further work shall be deemed for those purposes to have accrued at the time when the further work was finished.

2 Cases excluded from the remedy under section 1

(1) Where—

    (a) in connection with the provision of a dwelling or its first sale or letting for habitation any rights in respect of defects in the state of the dwelling are conferred by an approved scheme to which this section applies on a person having or acquiring an interest in the dwelling; and

    (b) it is stated in a document of a type approved for the purposes of this section that the requirements as to design or construction imposed by or under the scheme have, or appear to have, been substantially complied with in relation to the dwelling;

no action shall be brought by any person having or acquiring an interest in the dwelling for breach of the duty imposed by section 1 above in relation to the dwelling.

(2) A scheme to which this section applies—

    (a) may consist of any number of documents and any number of agreements or other transactions between any number of persons; but

(b) must confer, by virtue of agreements entered into with persons having or acquiring an interest in the dwellings to which the scheme applies, rights on such persons in respect of defects in the state of the dwellings.

(3) In this section 'approved' means approved by the Secretary of State, and the power of the Secretary of State to approve a scheme or document for the purposes of this section shall be exercisable by order, except that any requirements as to construction or design imposed under a scheme to which this section applies may be approved by him without making any order or, if he thinks fit, by order.

(4) The Secretary of State—

(a) may approve a scheme or document for the purposes of this section with or without limiting the duration of his approval; and

(b) may by order revoke or vary a previous order under this section or, without such an order, revoke or vary a previous approval under this section given otherwise than by order.

(5) The production of a document purporting to be a copy of an approval given by the Secretary of State otherwise than by order and certified by an officer of the Secretary of State to be a true copy of the approval shall be conclusive evidence of the approval, and without proof of the handwriting or official position of the person purporting to sign the certificate.

(6) The power to make an order under this section shall be exercisable by statutory instrument which shall be subject to annulment in pursuance of a resolution by either House of Parliament.

(7) Where an interest in a dwelling is compulsorily acquired—

(a) no action shall be brought by the acquiring authority for breach of the duty imposed by section 1 above in respect of the dwelling; and

(b) if any work for or in connection with the provision of the dwelling was done otherwise than in the course of a business by the person in occupation of the dwelling at the time of the compulsory acquisition, the acquiring authority and not that person shall be treated as the person who took on the work and accordingly as owing that duty.

3 Duty of care with respect to work done on premises not abated by disposal of premises

(1) Where work of construction, repair, maintenance or demolition or any other work is done on or in relation to premises, any duty of care owed, because of the doing of the work, to persons who might reasonably be expected to be affected by defects in the state of the premises created by the doing of the work shall not be abated by the subsequent disposal of the premises by the person who owed the duty.

(2) This section does not apply—

(a) in the case of premises which are let, where the relevant tenancy of the premises commenced, or the relevant tenancy agreement of the premises was entered into, before the commencement of this Act;

(b) in the case of premises disposed of in any other way, when the disposal of the premises was completed, or a contract for their disposal was entered into, before the commencement of this Act; or

(c) in either case, where the relevant transaction disposing of the premises is entered into in pursuance of an enforceable option by which the consideration for the disposal was fixed before the commencement of this Act.

4 Landlord's duty of care in virtue of obligation or right to repair premises demised

(1) Where premises are let under a tenancy which puts on the landlord an obligation to the tenant for the maintenance or repair of the premises the landlord owes to all persons who might reasonably be expected to be affected by defects in the state of the premises a duty to take such care as is reasonable in all the circumstances to see that they are reasonably safe from personal injury or from damage to their property caused by a relevant defect.

(2) The said duty is owed if the landlord knows (whether as the result of being notified by the tenant or otherwise) or if he ought in all the circumstances to have known of the relevant defect.

(3) In this section 'relevant defect' means a defect in the state of the premises existing at or after the material time and arising from, or continuing because of, an act or omission by the landlord which constituted or would if he had had notice of the defect, have constituted a failure by him to carry out his obligation to the tenant for the maintenance or repair of the premises; and for the purposes of the foregoing provision 'the material time' means—

(a) where the tenancy commenced before this Act, the commencement of this Act; and

(b) in all other cases, the earliest following times, that is to say—

(i)   the time when the tenancy commences;

(ii)   the time when the tenancy agreement is entered into;

(iii) the time when possession is taken of the premises in contemplation of the letting.

(4) Where premises are let under a tenancy which expressly or impliedly gives the landlord the right to enter the premises to carry out any description of maintenance or repair of the premises, then, as from the time when he first is, or by notice or otherwise can put himself, in a position to exercise the right and so long as he is or can put himself in that position, he shall be treated for the purposes of subsections (1) to (3) above (but for no other purpose) as if he were under an obligation to the tenant for that description of maintenance or repair of the premises; but the landlord shall not owe the tenant any duty by virtue of this subsection in respect of any defect in the state of the premises arising from, or continuing because of, a failure to carry out an obligation expressly imposed on the tenant by the tenancy.

(5) For the purposes of this section obligations imposed or rights given by any enactment in virtue of a tenancy shall be treated as imposed or given by the tenancy.

(6) This section applies to a right of occupation given by contract or any enactment and not amounting to a tenancy as if the right were a tenancy, and 'tenancy' and cognate expressions shall be construed accordingly.

5   Application to Crown

This Act shall bind the Crown, but as regards the Crown s liability in tort shall not bind the Crown further than the Crown is made liable in tort by the Crown Proceedings Act 1947.

6   Supplemental

(1) In this Act: 'disposal', in relation to premises, includes a letting, and an assignment or surrender of a tenancy, of the premises and the creation by contract of any other right to occupy the premises, and 'dispose' shall be construed accordingly; 'personal injury' includes any disease and any impairment of a person's physical or mental condition . . .

(2) Any duty imposed by or enforceable by virtue of any provision of this Act is in addition to any duty a person may owe apart from that provision.

(3) Any term of an agreement which purports to exclude or restrict, or has the effect of excluding or restricting, the operation of any of the provisions of this Act, or any liability arising by virtue of any such provision, shall be void.

Supply of Goods (Implied Terms) Act 1973

(1973, c. 13)

8   Implied terms as to title

[(1) In every relevant hire-purchase agreement, other than one to which subsection (2) below applies, there is—

(a) an implied term on the part of the creditor that he will have a right to sell the goods at the time when the property is to pass; and

     (b) an implied term that—
        (i) the goods are free, and will remain free until the time when the property is to pass, from any charge or encumbrance not disclosed or known to the person to whom the goods are bailed or (in Scotland) hired before the agreement is made, and
        (ii) that person will enjoy quiet possession of the goods except so far as it may be disturbed by any person entitled to the benefit of any charge or encumbrance so disclosed or known.

  (2) In a relevant hire-purchase agreement, in the case of which there appears from the agreement or is to be inferred from the circumstances of the agreement an intention that the creditor should transfer only such title as he or a third person may have, there is—
     (a) an implied term that all charges or encumbrances known to the creditor and not known to the person to whom the goods are bailed or hired have been disclosed to that person before the agreement is made; and
     (b) an implied term that neither—
        (i) the creditor; nor
        (ii) in a case where the parties to the agreement intend that any title which may be transferred shall be only such title as a third person may have, that person; nor
        (iii) anyone claiming through or under the creditor or that third person otherwise than under a charge or encumbrance disclosed or known to the person to whom the goods are bailed or hired, before the agreement is made;

will disturb the quiet possession of the person to whom the goods are bailed or hired.]

  [(3) As regards England and Wales and Northern Ireland, the term implied by subsection (1)(a) above is a condition and the terms implied by subsections (1)(b), (2)(a) and (2)(b) above are warranties.]

9 Bailing or hiring by description

  [(1) Where under a relevant hire-purchase agreement goods are bailed or (in Scotland) hired by description, there is an implied term that the goods will correspond with the description, and if under the agreement the goods are bailed or hired by reference to a sample as well as a description, it is not sufficient that the bulk of the goods corresponds with the sample if the goods do not also correspond with the description.]

  [(1A) As regards England and Wales and Northern Ireland, the term implied by subsection (1) above is a condition.]

  [(2) Goods shall not be prevented from being bailed or hired by description by reason only that, being exposed for sale, bailment or hire, they are selected by the person to whom they are bailed or hired.]

10 Implied undertakings as to quality or fitness

  [(1) Except as provided by this section and section 11 below and subject to the provisions of any other enactment, including any enactment of the Parliament of Northern Ireland or the Northern Ireland Assembly, there is no implied term as to the quality or fitness for any particular purpose of goods bailed or (in Scotland) hired under a relevant hire-purchase agreement.]

  [(2) Where the creditor bails or hires goods under a relevant hire-purchase agreement in the course of a business, there is an implied term that the goods supplied under the agreement are of satisfactory quality.

  (2A) For the purposes of this Act, goods are of satisfactory quality if they meet the standard that a reasonable person would regard as satisfactory, taking account of any description of the goods, the price (if relevant) and all the other relevant circumstances.

  (2B) For the purposes of this Act, the quality of goods includes their state and condition and the following (among others) are in appropriate cases aspects of the quality of goods—
     (a) fitness for all the purposes for which goods of the kind in question are commonly supplied,
     (b) appearance and finish,

    (c) freedom from minor defects,

    (d) safety, and

    (e) durability.

    (2C) The term implied by subsection (2) above does not extend to any matter making the quality of goods unsatisfactory—

        (a) which is specifically drawn to the attention of the person to whom the goods are bailed or hired before the agreement is made,

        (b) where that person examines the goods before the agreement is made, which that examination ought to reveal, or

        (c) where the goods are bailed or hired by reference to a sample, which would have been apparent on a reasonable examination of the sample.]

    [(3) Where the creditor bails or hires goods under a relevant hire-purchase agreement in the course of a business and the person to whom the goods are bailed or hired, expressly or by implication, makes known—

        (a) to the creditor in the course of negotiations conducted by the creditor in relation to the making of the relevant hire-purchase agreement, or

        (b) to a credit-broker in the course of negotiations conducted by that broker in relation to goods sold by him to the creditor before forming the subject matter of the relevant hire-purchase agreement,

any particular purpose for which the goods are being bailed or hired, there is an implied term that the goods supplied under the agreement are reasonably fit for that purpose, whether or not that is a purpose for which such goods are commonly supplied, except where the circumstances show that the person to whom the goods are bailed or hired does not rely, or that it is unreasonable for him to rely, on the skill or judgment of the creditor or credit-broker.

    (4) An implied term as to quality or fitness for a particular purpose may be annexed to a relevant hire-purchase agreement by usage.

    (5) The preceding provisions of this section apply to a relevant hire-purchase agreement made by a person who in the course of a business is acting as agent for the creditor as they apply to an agreement made by the creditor in the course of a business, except where the creditor is not bailing or hiring in the course of a business and either the person to whom the goods are bailed or hired knows that fact or reasonable steps are taken to bring it to the notice of that person before the agreement is made.

    (6) In subsection (3) above and this subsection—

        (a) 'credit-broker' means a person acting in the course of a business of credit brokerage;

        (b) 'credit brokerage' means the effecting of introductions of individuals desiring to obtain credit—

            (i) to persons carrying on any business so far as it relates to the provision of credit, or

            (ii) to other persons engaged in credit brokerage.]

    [(7) As regards England and Wales and Northern Ireland, the terms implied by subsections (2) and (3) above are conditions.]

11   Samples

    [(1) Where under a relevant hire-purchase agreement goods are bailed or (in Scotland) hired by reference to a sample, there is an implied term—

        (a) that the bulk will correspond with the sample in quality; and

        (b) that the person to whom the goods are bailed or hired will have a reasonable opportunity of comparing the bulk with the sample; and

        (c) that the goods will be free from any defect, making their quality unsatisfactory, which would not be apparent on reasonable examination of the sample.]

[(2) As regards England and Wales and Northern Ireland, the term implied by subsection (1) above is a condition.]

[11A   Modification of remedies for breach of statutory condition in non-consumer cases

(1) Where in the case of a relevant hire-purchase agreement—

(a) the person to whom goods are bailed would, apart from this subsection, have the right to reject them by reason of a breach on the part of the creditor of a term implied by section 9, 10 or 11(1)(a) or (c) above, but

(b) the breach is so slight that it would be unreasonable for him to reject them, the breach is not to be treated as a breach of condition but may be treated as a breach of warranty.

(2) This section applies unless a contrary intention appears in, or is to be implied from, the agreement.

(3) It is for the creditor to show—

(a) that a breach fell within subsection (1)(b) above, and

(b) that the agreement was a relevant hire-purchase agreement.]

[12   Exclusion of implied terms and conditions

(1) An express term does not negative a term implied by this Act unless inconsistent with it.]

15   Supplementary

[(1) In sections 8 to 14 above and this section—

'business' includes a profession and the activities of any government department (including a Northern Ireland department), [or local or public authority];

'buyer' and 'seller' includes a person to whom rights and duties under a conditional sale agreement have passed by assignment or operation of law;

'conditional sale agreement' means an agreement for the sale of goods under which the purchase price or part of it is payable by instalments, and the property in the goods is to remain in the seller (notwithstanding that the buyer is to be in possession of the goods) until such conditions as to the payment of instalments or otherwise as may be specified in the agreement are fulfilled;

['consumer sale' has the same meaning as in section 55 of the Sale of Goods Act 1979 (as set out in paragraph 11 of Schedule 1 to that Act)];

'creditor' means the person by whom the goods are bailed or (in Scotland) hired under a hire-purchase agreement or the person to whom his rights and duties under the agreement have passed by assignment or operation of law; and

'hire-purchase agreement' means an agreement, other than conditional sale agreement, under which—

(a) goods are bailed or (in Scotland) hired in return for periodical payments by the person to whom they are bailed or hired, and

(b) the property in the goods will pass to that person if the terms of the agreement are complied with and one or more of the following occurs—

(i)   the exercise of an option to purchase by that person,

(ii)   the doing of any other specified act by any party to the agreement,

(iii) the happening of any other specified event.

[and a hire-purchase agreement is relevant if it is not a contract to which Chapter 2 of Part 1 of the Consumer Rights Act 2015 applies.]

(4) Nothing in sections 8 to 13 above shall prejudice the operation of any other enactment including any enactment of the Parliament of Northern Ireland or the Northern Ireland Assembly or any rule of law whereby any term, other than one relating to quality or fitness, is to be implied in any hire-purchase agreement.]

Consumer Credit Act 1974

(1974, c. 39)

PART V

55 Disclosure of information

(1) Regulations may require specified information to be disclosed in the prescribed manner to the debtor or hirer before a regulated agreement is made.

[(2) If regulations under subsection (1) are not complied with, the agreement is enforceable against the debtor or hirer on an order of the court only (and for these purposes a retaking of goods or land to which the agreement relates is an enforcement of the agreement).]

56 Antecedent negotiations

(1) In this Act 'antecedent negotiations' means any negotiations with the debtor or hirer—

    (a) conducted by the creditor or owner in relation to the making of any regulated agreement, or

    (b) conducted by a credit-broker in relation to goods sold or proposed to be sold by the credit-broker to the creditor before forming the subject-matter of a debtor-creditor-supplier agreement within section 12(a), or

    (c) conducted by the supplier in relation to a transaction financed or proposed to be financed by a debtor-creditor-supplier agreement within section 12(b) or (c),

and 'negotiator' means the person by whom negotiations are so conducted with the debtor or hirer.

(2) Negotiations with the debtor in a case falling within subsection (1)(b) or (c) shall be deemed to be conducted by the negotiator in the capacity of agent of the creditor as well as in his actual capacity.

(3) An agreement is void if, and to the extent that, it purports in relation to an actual or prospective regulated agreement—

    (a) to provide that a person acting as, or on behalf of, a negotiator is to be treated as the agent of the debtor or hirer, or

    (b) to relieve a person from liability for acts or omissions of any person acting as, or on behalf of, a negotiator.

(4) For the purposes of this Act, antecedent negotiations shall be taken to begin when the negotiator and the debtor or hirer first enter into communication (including communication by advertisement), and to include any representations made by the negotiator to the debtor or hirer and any other dealings between them.

57 Withdrawal from prospective agreement

(1) The withdrawal of a party from a prospective regulated agreement shall operate to apply this Part to the agreement, any linked transaction and any other thing done in anticipation of the making of the agreement as it would apply if the agreement were made and then cancelled under section 69.

60 Form and content of agreements

(1) The [Treasury] shall make regulations as to the form and content of documents embodying regulated agreements, and the regulations shall contain such provisions as appear to [them] appropriate with a view to ensuring that the debtor or hirer is made aware of—

    (a) the rights and duties conferred or imposed on him by the agreement,

    (b) the amount and rate of the total charge for credit (in the case of a consumer credit agreement),

    (c) the protection and remedies available to him under this Act, and

    (d) any other matters which, in the opinion of the [Treasury], it is desirable for him to know about in connection with the agreement.

65 Consequences of improper execution

(1) An improperly-executed regulated agreement is enforceable against the debtor or hirer on an order of the court only.

67 Cancellable agreements

[(1) Subject to subsection (2)] A regulated agreement may be cancelled by the debtor or hirer in accordance with this Part if the antecedent negotiations included oral representations made when in the presence of the debtor or hirer by an individual acting as, or on behalf of, the negotiator, unless—

(a) the agreement is secured on land, or is a restricted-use credit agreement to finance the purchase of land or is an agreement for a bridging loan in connection with the purchase of land, or

(b) the unexecuted agreement is signed by the debtor or hirer at premises at which any of the following is carrying on any business (whether on a permanent or temporary basis)—

(i) the creditor or owner;

(ii) any party to a linked transaction (other than the debtor or hirer or a relative of his);

(iii) the negotiator in any antecedent negotiations.

[(2) This section does not apply where section 66A applies.]

68 Cooling-off period

The debtor or hirer may serve notice of cancellation of a cancellable agreement between his signing of the unexecuted agreement and—

(a) the end of the fifth day following the day on which he received a copy under section 63(2) or a notice under section 64(1)(b), or

(b) if (by virtue of regulations made under section 64(4)) section 64(1)(b) does not apply, the end of the fourteenth day following the day on which he signed the unexecuted agreement.

69 Notice of cancellation

(1) If within the period specified in section 68 the debtor or hirer under a cancellable agreement serves on—

(a) the creditor or owner, or

(b) the person specified in the notice under section 64(1), or

(c) a person who (whether by virtue of subsection (6) or otherwise) is the agent of the creditor or owner,

a notice (a 'notice of cancellation') which, however expressed and whether or not conforming to the notice given under section 64(1), indicates the intention of the debtor or hirer to withdraw from the agreement, the notice shall operate—

(i) to cancel the agreement, and any linked transaction, and

(ii) to withdraw any offer by the debtor or hirer, or his relative, to enter into a linked transaction.

(4) Except as otherwise provided by or under this Act, an agreement or transaction cancelled under subsection (1) shall be treated as if it had never been entered into.

70 Cancellation: recovery of money paid by debtor or hirer

(1) On the cancellation of a regulated agreement, and of any linked transaction,—

(a) any sum paid by the debtor or hirer, or his relative, under or in contemplation of the agreement or transaction, including any item in the total charge for credit, shall become repayable, and

(b) any sum, including any item in the total charge for credit, which but for the cancellation is, or would or might become, payable by the debtor or hirer, or his relative, under the agreement or transaction shall cease to be, or shall not become, so payable, and

(c) in the case of a debtor-creditor-supplier agreement falling within section 12(b), any sum paid on the debtor s behalf by the creditor to the supplier shall become repayable to the creditor.

(3) A sum repayable under subsection (1) is repayable by the person to whom it was originally paid, but in the case of a debtor-creditor-supplier agreement falling within section 12(b) the creditor and the supplier shall be under a joint and several liability to repay sums paid by the debtor, or his relative, under the agreement or under a linked transaction falling within section 19(1)(b) and

accordingly, in such a case, the creditor shall be entitled, in accordance with rules of court, to have the supplier made a party to any proceedings brought against the creditor to recover any such sums.

(4) Subject to any agreement between them, the creditor shall be entitled to be indemnified by the supplier for loss suffered by the creditor in satisfying his liability under subsection (3), including costs reasonably incurred by him in defending proceedings instituted by the debtor.

71   Cancellation: repayment of credit

(1) Notwithstanding the cancellation of a regulated consumer credit agreement, other than a debtor-creditor-supplier agreement for restricted-use credit, the agreement shall continue in force so far as it relates to repayment of credit and payment of interest.

PART VI

75   Liability of creditor for breaches by supplier

(1) If the debtor under a debtor-creditor-supplier agreement falling within section 12(b) or (c) has, in relation to a transaction financed by the agreement, any claim against the supplier in respect of a misrepresentation or breach of contract, he shall have a like claim against the creditor, who, with the supplier, shall accordingly be jointly and severally liable to the debtor.

(2) Subject to any agreement between them, the creditor shall be entitled to be indemnified by the supplier for loss suffered by the creditor in satisfying his liability under subsection (1), including costs reasonably incurred by him in defending proceedings instituted by the debtor.

(3) Subsection (1) does not apply to a claim—
    (a) under a non-commercial agreement, or [. . .]
    (b) so far as the claim relates to any single item to which the supplier has attached a cash price not exceeding [£100] or more than [£30,000] [. . .]

(4) This section applies notwithstanding that the debtor, in entering into the transaction, exceeded the credit limit or otherwise contravened any term of the agreement.

(5) In an action brought against the creditor under subsection (1) he shall be entitled, in accordance with rules of court, to have the supplier made a party to the proceedings.

76   Duty to give notice before taking certain action

(1) The creditor or owner is not entitled to enforce a term of a regulated agreement by—
    (a) demanding earlier payment of any sum, or
    (b) recovering possession of any goods or land, or
    (c) treating any right conferred on the debtor or hirer by the agreement as terminated, restricted or deferred,
except by or after giving the debtor or hirer not less than seven days' notice of his intention to do so.

(2) Subsection (1) applies only where—
    (a) a period for the duration of the agreement is specified in the agreement, and
    (b) that period has not ended when the creditor or owner does an act mentioned in subsection (1),
but so applies notwithstanding that, under the agreement, any party is entitled to terminate it before the end of the period so specified.

(6) Subsection (1) does not apply to a right of enforcement arising by reason of any breach by the debtor or hirer of the regulated agreement.

PART VII

87   Need for default notice

(1) Service of a notice on the debtor or hirer in accordance with section 88 (a 'default notice') is necessary before the creditor or owner can become entitled, by reason of any breach by the debtor or hirer of a regulated agreement,—

(a) to terminate the agreement, or

(b) to demand earlier payment of any sum, or

(c) to recover possession of any goods or land, or

(d) to treat any right conferred on the debtor or hirer by the agreement as terminated, restricted or deferred, or

(e) to enforce any security.

(2) Subsection (1) does not prevent the creditor from treating the right to draw upon any credit as restricted or deferred, and taking such steps as may be necessary to make the restriction or deferment effective.

(4) Regulations may provide that subsection (1) is not to apply to agreements described by the regulations.

88 Contents and effect of default notice

(1) The default notice must be in the prescribed form and specify—

(a) the nature of the alleged breach;

(b) if the breach is capable of remedy, what action is required to remedy it and the date before which that action is to be taken;

(c) if the breach is not capable of remedy, the sum (if any) required to be paid as compensation for the breach, and the date before which it is to be paid.

94 Right to complete payments ahead of time

(1) The debtor under a regulated consumer credit agreement is entitled at any time, by notice to the creditor and the payment to the creditor of all amounts payable by the debtor to him under the agreement [and any amount which the creditor claims under section 95A(2) or section 95B(2)] (less any rebate allowable under section 95), to discharge the debtor's indebtedness under the agreement.

96 Effect on linked transactions

(1) Where for any reason the indebtedness of the debtor under a regulated consumer credit agreement is discharged before the time fixed by the agreement, he, and any relative of his, shall at the same time be discharged from any liability under a linked transaction, other than a debt which has already become payable.

99 Right to terminate hire-purchase etc., agreements

(1) At any time before the final payment by the debtor under a regulated hire-purchase or regulated conditional sale agreement falls due, the debtor shall be entitled to terminate the agreement by giving notice to any person entitled or authorised to receive the sums payable under the agreement.

(2) Termination of an agreement under subsection (1) does not affect any liability under the agreement which has accrued before the termination.

(4) In the case of a conditional sale agreement relating to goods, where the property in the goods, having become vested in the debtor, is transferred to a person who does not become the debtor under the agreement, the debtor shall not thereafter be entitled to terminate the agreement under subsection (1).

100 Liability of debtor on termination of hire-purchase etc., agreement

(1) Where a regulated hire-purchase or regulated conditional sale agreement is terminated under section 99 the debtor shall be liable, unless the agreement provides for a smaller payment, or does not provide for any payment, to pay to the creditor the amount (if any) by which one-half of the total price exceeds the aggregate of the sums paid and the sums due in respect of the total price immediately before the termination.

(3) If in any action the court is satisfied that a sum less than the amount specified in subsection (1) would be equal to the loss sustained by the creditor in consequence of the termination of the agreement by the debtor, the court may make an order for the payment of that sum in lieu of the amount specified in subsection (1).

PART VIII

113   Act not to be evaded by use of security

(1) Where a security is provided in relation to an actual or prospective regulated agreement, the security shall not be enforced so as to benefit the creditor or owner, directly or indirectly, to an extent greater (whether as respects the amount of any payment or the time or manner of its being made) than would be the case if the security were not provided and any obligations of the debtor or hirer, or his relative, under or in relation to the agreement were carried out to the extent (if any) to which they would be enforced under this Act.

(2) In accordance with subsection (1), where a regulated agreement is enforceable on an order of the court or the [FCA] only, any security provided in relation to the agreement is enforceable (so far as provided in relation to the agreement) where such an order has been made in relation to the agreement, but not otherwise.

(7) Where an indemnity [or guarantee] is given in a case where the debtor or hirer is a minor, or [an indemnity is given in a case where he] is otherwise not of full capacity, the reference in subsection (1) to the extent to which his obligations would be enforced shall be read in relation to the indemnity [or guarantee] as a reference to the extent to which [those obligations] would be enforced if he were of full capacity.

PART IX

127   Enforcement orders in cases of infringement

(1) In the case of an application for an enforcement order under—

    [(za)   section 55(2) (disclosure of information), or]

    [(zb)   section 61B(3) (duty to supply copy of overdraft agreement), or]

    (a)   section 65(1) (improperly executed agreements), . . .

the court shall dismiss the application if, but (subject to subsections (3) and (4)) only if, it considers it just to do so having regard to—

        (i)   prejudice caused to any person by the contravention in question, and the degree of culpability for it; and

        (ii)   the powers conferred on the court by subsection (2) and sections 135 and 136.

(2) If it appears to the court just to do so, it may in an enforcement order reduce or discharge any sum payable by the debtor or hirer, or any surety, so as to compensate him for prejudice suffered as a result of the contravention in question.

129   Time orders

(1) [Subject to subsection (3) below,] If it appears to the court just to do so—

    (a)   on an application for an enforcement order;

    (b)   on an application made by a debtor or hirer under this paragraph after service on him of—

        (i)   a default notice, or

        (ii)   a notice under section 76(1) or 98(1);

    [(ba)   on an application made by a debtor or hirer under this paragraph after he has been given a notice under section 86B or 86C; or]

    (c)   in an action brought by a creditor or owner to enforce a regulated agreement or any security, or recover possession of any goods or land to which a regulated agreement relates,

the court may make an order under this section (a 'time order').

(2) A time order shall provide for one or both of the following, as the court considers just—

    (a)   the payment by the debtor or hirer or any surety of any sum owed under a regulated agreement or a security by such instalments, payable at such times, as the court, having regard to the means of the debtor or hirer and any surety, considers reasonable;

(b) the remedying by the debtor or hirer of any breach of a regulated agreement (other than non-payment of money) within such period as the court may specify.

132   Financial relief for hirer

(1) Where the owner under a regulated consumer hire agreement recovers possession of goods to which the agreement relates otherwise than by action, the hirer may apply to the court for an order that—

(a) the whole or part of any sum paid by the hirer to the owner in respect of the goods shall be repaid, and

(b) the obligation to pay the whole or part of any sum owed by the hirer to the owner in respect of the goods shall cease,

and if it appears to the court just to do so, having regard to the extent of the enjoyment of the goods by the hirer, the court shall grant the application in full or in part.

[140A   Unfair relationships between creditors and debtors

(1) The court may make an order under section 140B in connection with a credit agreement if it determines that the relationship between the creditor and the debtor arising out of the agreement (or the agreement taken with any related agreement) is unfair to the debtor because of one or more of the following—

(a) any of the terms of the agreement or of any related agreement;

(b) the way in which the creditor has exercised or enforced any of his rights under the agreement or any related agreement;

(c) any other thing done (or not done) by, or on behalf of, the creditor (either before or after the making of the agreement or any related agreement).

(2) In deciding whether to make a determination under this section the court shall have regard to all matters it thinks relevant (including matters relating to the creditor and matters relating to the debtor).

(3) For the purposes of this section the court shall (except to the extent that it is not appropriate to do so) treat anything done (or not done) by, or on behalf of, or in relation to, an associate or a former associate of the creditor as if done (or not done) by, or on behalf of, or in relation to, the creditor.

(4) A determination may be made under this section in relation to a relationship notwithstanding that the relationship may have ended.

(5) An order under section 140B shall not be made in connection with a credit agreement which is an exempt agreement for the purposes of Chapter 14A of Part 2 of the Regulated Activities Order by virtue of article 60C(2) of that Order (regulated mortgage contracts and regulated home purchase plans).]

[140B   Powers of court in relation to unfair relationships

(1) An order under this section in connection with a credit agreement may do one or more of the following—

(a) require the creditor, or any associate or former associate of his, to repay (in whole or in part) any sum paid by the debtor or by a surety by virtue of the agreement or any related agreement (whether paid to the creditor, the associate or the former associate or to any other person);

(b) require the creditor, or any associate or former associate of his, to do or not to do (or to cease doing) anything specified in the order in connection with the agreement or any related agreement;

(c) reduce or discharge any sum payable by the debtor or by a surety by virtue of the agreement or any related agreement;

(d) direct the return to a surety of any property provided by him for the purposes of a security;

(e) otherwise set aside (in whole or in part) any duty imposed on the debtor or on a surety by virtue of the agreement or any related agreement;

    (f) alter the terms of the agreement or of any related agreement;

    (g) direct accounts to be taken, or (in Scotland) an accounting to be made, between any persons.

(2) An order under this section may be made in connection with a credit agreement only—

    (a) on an application made by the debtor or by a surety;

    (b) at the instance of the debtor or a surety in any proceedings in any court to which the debtor and the creditor are parties, being proceedings to enforce the agreement or any related agreement; or

    (c) at the instance of the debtor or a surety in any other proceedings in any court where the amount paid or payable under the agreement or any related agreement is relevant.

(3) An order under this section may be made notwithstanding that its effect is to place on the creditor, or any associate or former associate of his, a burden in respect of an advantage enjoyed by another person.

(8) A party to any proceedings mentioned in subsection (2) shall be entitled, in accordance with rules of court, to have any person who might be the subject of an order under this section made a party to the proceedings.

(9) If, in any such proceedings, the debtor or a surety alleges that the relationship between the creditor and the debtor is unfair to the debtor, it is for the creditor to prove to the contrary.]

PART XI

162 Powers of entry and inspection

(1) A duly authorised officer of an enforcement authority, at all reasonable hours and on production, if required, of his credentials, may—

    (a) in order to ascertain whether a breach of any provision of or under this Act has been committed, inspect any goods and enter any premises (other than premises used only as a dwelling); . . .

    (c) if he has reasonable cause to believe that a breach of any provision of or under this Act has been committed, seize and detain any goods in order to ascertain (by testing or otherwise) whether such a breach has been committed;

    (d) seize and detain any goods, [. . .] or documents which he has reason to believe may be required as evidence in proceedings for an offence under this Act;

    (e) for the purpose of exercising his powers under this subsection to seize goods, [. . .] or documents, but only if and to the extent that it is reasonably necessary for securing that the provisions of this Act and of any regulations made under it are duly observed, require any person having authority to do so to break open any container and, if that person does not comply, break it open himself.

(2) An officer seizing goods, [. . .] or documents in exercise of his powers under this section shall not do so without informing the person he seizes them from.

(4) An officer entering premises by virtue of this section may take such other persons and equipment with him as he thinks necessary; and on leaving premises entered by virtue of a warrant under subsection (3) shall, if they are unoccupied or the occupier is temporarily absent, leave them as effectively secured against trespassers as he found them.

(6) A person who is not a duly authorised officer of an enforcement authority, but purports to act as such under this section, commits an offence.

163 Compensation for loss

(1) Where, in exercising his powers under section 162, an officer of an enforcement authority seizes and detains goods and their owner suffers loss by reason of—

    (a) that seizure, or

    (b) the loss, damage or deterioration of the goods during detention, then, unless the owner is convicted of an offence under this Act committed in relation to the goods, the authority shall compensate him for the loss so suffered.

165   Obstruction of authorised officers

(1) Any person who—

(a) wilfully obstructs an officer of an enforcement authority acting in pursuance of this Act; or

(b) wilfully fails to comply with any requirement properly made to him by such an officer under section 162; or

(c) without reasonable cause fails to give such an officer (so acting) other assistance or information he may reasonably require in performing his functions under this Act,

commits an offence.

170   No further sanctions for breach of Act

(1) A breach of any requirement made (otherwise than by any court) by or under this Act shall incur no civil or criminal sanction as being such a breach, except to the extent (if any) expressly provided by or under this Act [or by or under the Financial Services and Markets Act 2000 by virtue of an order made under section 107 of the Financial Services Act 2012].

173   Contracting-out forbidden

(1) A term contained in a regulated agreement or linked transaction, or in any other agreement relating to an actual or prospective regulated agreement or linked transaction, is void if, and to the extent that, it is inconsistent with a provision for the protection of the debtor or hirer or his relative or any surety contained in this Act or in any regulation made under this Act.

(2) Where a provision specifies the duty or liability of the debtor or hirer or his relative or any surety in certain circumstances, a term is inconsistent with that provision if it purports to impose, directly or indirectly, an additional duty or liability on him in those circumstances.

(3) Notwithstanding subsection (1), a provision of this Act under which a thing may be done in relation to any person on an order of the court or the [FCA] only shall not be taken to prevent its being done at any time with that person's consent given at that time, but the refusal of such consent shall not give rise to any liability.

175   Duty of persons deemed to be agents

Where under this Act a person is deemed to receive a notice or payment as agent of the creditor or owner under a regulated agreement, he shall be deemed to be under a contractual duty to the creditor or owner to transmit the notice, or remit the payment, to him forthwith.

181   Power to alter monetary limits etc.

(1) The [Treasury] may by order made by statutory instrument amend, or further amend, any of the following provisions of this Act so as to reduce or increase a sum mentioned in that provision, namely, sections . . . 75(3)(b) . . .

189   Definitions

(1) In this Act, unless the context otherwise requires—. . .

'representation' includes any condition or warranty, and any other statement or undertaking, whether oral or in writing; . . .

Health and Safety at Work Act 1974

(1974, c. 37)

2   General duties of employers to their employees

(1) It shall be the duty of every employer to ensure, so far as is reasonably practicable, the health, safety and welfare of work of all his employees.

3   General duties of employers and self-employed to persons other than their employees

(1) It shall be the duty of every employer to conduct his undertaking in such a way as to ensure, so far as is reasonably practicable, that persons not in his employment who may be affected thereby are not thereby exposed to risks to their health or safety.

(2) It shall be the duty of every self-employed person [who conducts an undertaking of a pre-scribed description] to conduct [the undertaking] in such a way as to ensure, so far as is reasonably practicable, that he and other persons (not being his employees) who may be affected thereby are not thereby exposed to risks to their health or safety.

(3) In such cases as may be prescribed, it shall be the duty of every employer and every self-employed person, in the prescribed circumstances and in the prescribed manner, to give to persons (not being his employees) who may be affected by the way in which he conducts his undertaking the prescribed information about such aspects of the way in which he conducts his undertaking as might affect their health or safety.

4   General duties of persons concerned with premises to persons other than their employees

(1) This section has effect for imposing on persons duties in relation to those who—
  (a) are not their employees; but
  (b) use non-domestic premises made available to them as a place of work or as a place where they may use plant or substances provided for their use there,
and applies to premises so made available and other non-domestic premises used in connection with them.

(2) It shall be the duty of each person who has, to any extent, control of premises to which this section applies or of the means of access thereto or egress therefrom or of any plant or substance in such premises to take such measures as it is reasonable for a person in his position to take to ensure, so far as is reasonably practicable, that the premises, all means of access thereto or egress therefrom available for use by persons using the premises, and any plant or substance in the premises or, as the case may be, provided for use there, is or are safe and without risks to health.

(3) Where a person has, by virtue of any contract or tenancy, an obligation of any extent in relation to—
  (a) the maintenance or repair of any premises to which this section applies or any means of access thereto or egress therefrom; or
  (b) the safety of or the absence of risks to health arising from plant or substances in any such premises;
that person shall be treated, for the purposes of subsection (2) above, as being a person who has control of the matters to which his obligation extends.

(4) Any reference in this section to a person having control of any premises or matter is a refer-ence to a person having control of the premises or matter in connection with the carrying on by him of a trade, business or other undertaking (whether for profit or not).

17   Use of approved codes of practice in criminal proceedings

(1) A failure on the part of any person to observe any provision of an approved code of practice shall not of itself render him liable to any civil or criminal proceedings; but where in any criminal proceedings a party is alleged to have committed an offence by reason of a contravention of any re-quirement or prohibition imposed by or under any such provision as is mentioned in section 16(1) being a provision for which there was an approved code of practice at the time of the alleged contra-vention, the following subsection shall have effect with respect to that code in relation to those proceedings.

47   Civil liability

(1) Nothing in this Part shall be construed—
  (a) as conferring a right of action in any civil proceedings in respect of any failure to comply with any duty imposed by sections 2 to 7 or any contravention of section 8; or

    (c) as affecting the operation of section 12 of the Nuclear Installations Act 1965 (right to compensation by virtue of certain provisions of that Act).

[(2) Breach of a duty imposed by a statutory instrument containing (whether alone or with other provision) health and safety regulations shall not be actionable except to the extent that regulations under this section so provide.

(2A) Breach of a duty imposed by an existing statutory provision shall not be actionable except to the extent that regulations under this section so provide (including by modifying any of the existing statutory provisions).

(2B) Regulations under this section may include provision for—

    (a) a defence to be available in any action for breach of the duty mentioned in subsection (2) or (2A);

    (b) any term of an agreement which purports to exclude or restrict any liability for such a breach to be void.]

(3) No provision made by virtue of section 15(6)(b) shall afford a defence in any civil proceedings [. . .].

(4) Subsections (1)(a)[, (2) and (2A)] above are without prejudice to any right of action which exists apart from the provisions of this Act, and subsection [(2B)(a)] above is without prejudice to any defence which may be available apart from the provisions of the regulations there mentioned.

[(7) The power to make regulations under this section shall be exercisable by the Secretary of State.]

Rehabilitation of Offenders Act 1974

(1974, c. 53)

4 Effect of rehabilitation

(1) Subject to sections 7 and 8 below, a person who has become a rehabilitated person for the purposes of this Act in respect of a conviction shall be treated for all purposes in law as a person who has not committed or been charged with or prosecuted for or convicted of or sentenced for the offence or offences which were the subject of that conviction; . . .

8 Defamation actions

(1) This section applies to any action for libel or slander begun after the commencement of this Act by a rehabilitated person and founded upon the publication of any matter imputing that the plaintiff has committed or been charged with or prosecuted for or convicted of or sentenced for an offence which was the subject of a spent conviction.

(2) Nothing in section 4(1) above shall affect an action to which this section applies where the publication complained of took place before the conviction in question became spent, and the following provisions of this section shall not apply in any such case.

(3) Subject to subsections (5) and (6) below, nothing in section 4(1) above shall prevent the defendant in an action to which this section applies from relying on any defence [under section 2 or 3 of the Defamation Act 2013 which is available to him or any defence] or of absolute or qualified privilege which is available to him, or restrict the matters he may establish in support of any such defence.

(4) Without prejudice to the generality of subsection (3) above, where in any such action malice is alleged against a defendant who is relying on a defence of qualified privilege, nothing in section 4(1) above shall restrict the matters he may establish in rebuttal of the allegation.

(5) A defendant in any such action shall not by virtue of subsection (3) above be entitled to rely upon [a defence under section 2 of the Defamation Act 2013] if the publication is proved to have been made with malice.

(6) Subject to subsection (7) below a defendant in any such action shall not, by virtue of subsection (3) above, be entitled to rely on any matter or adduce or require any evidence for the purpose

of establishing (whether under [section 14 of the Defamation Act 1996] or otherwise) the defence that the matter published constituted a fair and accurate report of judicial proceedings if it is proved that the publication contained a reference to evidence which was ruled to be inadmissible in the proceedings by virtue of section 4(1) above.

(7) Subsection (3) above shall apply without the qualifications imposed by subsection (6) above in relation to—

(a) any report of judicial proceedings contained in any bona fide series of law reports which does not form part of any other publication and consists solely of reports of proceedings in courts of law, and

(b) any report or account of judicial proceedings published for bona fide educational, scientific or professional purposes or given in the course of any lecture, class or discussion given or held for any of those purposes.

[(7A) Nothing in section 4(1) above shall restrict the evidence that may be adduced in mitigation of damages under section 13(2) of the Defamation Act 1996.]

Congenital Disabilities (Civil Liability) Act 1976

(1976, c. 28)

1   Civil liability to child born disabled

(1) If a child is born disabled as the result of such an occurrence before its birth as is mentioned in subsection (2) below, and a person (other than the child's own mother) is under this section answerable to the child in respect of the occurrence, the child's disabilities are to be regarded as damage resulting from the wrongful act of that person and actionable accordingly at the suit of the child.

(2) An occurrence to which this section applies is one which—

(a) affected either parent of the child in his or her ability to have a normal, healthy child; or

(b) affected the mother during her pregnancy, or affected her or the child in the course of its birth, so that the child is born with disabilities which would not otherwise have been present.

(3) Subject to the following subsections, a person (here referred to as 'the defendant') is answerable to the child if he was liable in tort to the parent or would, if sued in due time, have been so; and it is no answer that there could not have been such liability because the parent suffered no actionable injury, if there was a breach of legal duty which, accompanied by injury, would have given rise to the liability.

(4) In the case of an occurrence preceding the time of conception, the defendant is not answerable to the child if at that time either or both of the parents knew the risk of their child being born disabled (that is to say, the particular risk created by the occurrence); but should it be the child's father who is the defendant, this subsection does not apply if he knew of the risk and the mother did not.

(5) The defendant is not answerable to the child, for anything he did or omitted to do when responsible in a professional capacity for treating or advising the parent, if he took reasonable care having due regard to then received professional opinion applicable to the particular class of case; but this does not mean that he is answerable only because he departed from received opinion.

(6) Liability to the child under this section may be treated as having been excluded or limited by contract made with the parent affected, to the same extent and subject to the same restrictions as liability in the parent's own case; and a contract term which could have been set up by the defendant in an action by the parent, so as to exclude or limit his liability to him or her, operates in the defendant's favour to the same, but no greater, extent in an action under this section by the child.

(7) If in the child's action under this section it is shown that the parent affected shared the responsibility for the child being born disabled, the damages are to be reduced to such extent as the court thinks just and equitable having regard to the extent of the parent's responsibility.

[1A   Extension of section 1 to cover infertility treatments
(1) In any case where—
(a) a child carried by a woman as the result of the placing in her or an embryo or of sperm and eggs or her artificial insemination is born disabled,
(b) the disability results from an act or omission in the course of the selection, or the keeping or use outside the body, of the embryo carried by her or of the gametes used to bring about the creation of the embryo, and
(c) a person is under this section answerable to the child in respect of the act or omission,
the child's disabilities are to be regarded as damage resulting from the wrongful act of that person and actionable accordingly at the suit of the child.

(2) Subject to subsection (3) below and the applied provisions of section 1 of this Act, a person (here referred to as 'the defendant') is answerable to the child if he was liable in tort to one or both of the parents (here referred to as 'the parent or parents concerned') or would, if sued in due time, have been so; and it is no answer that there could not have been such liability because the parent or parents concerned suffered no actionable injury, if there was a breach of legal duty which, accompanied by injury, would have given rise to the liability.

(3) The defendant is not under this section answerable to the child if at the time the embryo, or the sperm and eggs, are placed in the woman or the time of her insemination (as the case may be) either or both of the parents knew the risk of their child being born disabled (that is to say, the particular risk created by the act or omission).

(4) Subsections (5) to (7) of section 1 of this Act apply for the purposes of this section as they apply for the purposes of that but as if references to the parent or the parent affected were references to the parent or parents concerned.

(4A) In the case of a child who has a parent by virtue of section 42 or 43 of the Human Fertilisation and Embryology Act 2008, the reference in subsection (4) to the child's father includes a reference to the woman who is a parent by virtue of that section.]

2   Liability of woman driving while pregnant
A woman driving a motor vehicle when she knows (or ought reasonably to know) herself to be pregnant is to be regarded as being under the same duty to take care for the safety of her unborn child as the law imposes on her with respect to the safety of other people; and if in consequence of her breach of that duty her child is born with disabilities which would not otherwise have been present, those disabilities are to be regarded as damage resulting from her wrongful act and actionable accordingly at the suit of the child.

3   Disabled birth due to radiation
(1) Section 1 of this Act does not affect the operation of the Nuclear Installations Act 1965 as to liability for, and compensation in respect of, injury or damage caused by occurrences involving nuclear matter or the emission of ionising radiations.

(2) For the avoidance of doubt anything which—
(a) affects a man in his ability to have a normal, healthy child; or
(b) affects a woman in that ability, or so affects her when she is pregnant that her child is born with disabilities which would not otherwise have been present,
is an injury for the purposes of that Act.

(3) If a child is born disabled as the result of an injury to either of its parents caused in breach of a duty imposed by any of sections 7 to 11 of that Act (nuclear site licensees and others to secure that nuclear incidents do not cause injury to persons, etc.), the child's disabilities are to be regarded under the subsequent provisions of that Act (compensation and other matters) as injuries caused on the same occasion, and by the same breach of duty, as was the injury to the parent.

(4) As respects compensation to the child, section 13(6) of that Act (contributory fault of person injured by radiation) is to be applied as if the reference there to fault were to the fault of the parent.

(5) Compensation is not payable in the child's case if the injury to the parent preceded the time of the child's conception and at that time either or both of the parents knew the risk of their child being born disabled (that is to say, the particular risk created by the injury).

4   Interpretation and other supplementary provisions

(1) References in this Act to a child being born disabled or with disabilities are to its being born with any deformity, disease or abnormality, including predisposition (whether or not susceptible or immediate prognosis) to physical or mental defect in the future.

(2) In this Act—

(a) 'born' means born alive (the moment of a child's birth being when it first has a life separate from its mother), and 'birth' has a corresponding meaning; and

(b) 'motor vehicle' means a mechanically propelled vehicle intended or adapted for use on roads.

[and references to embryos shall be construed in accordance with section 1(1) of the Human Fertilisation and Embryology Act 1990 and any regulations under section 1(6) of that Act.]

(3) Liability to a child under section 1 [1A] or 2 of this Act is to be regarded—

(a) as respects all its incidents and any matters arising or to arise out of it; and

(b) subject to any contrary context or intention, for the purpose of construing references in enactments and documents to personal or bodily injuries and cognate matters,

as liability for personal injuries sustained by the child immediately after its birth.

(4) No damages shall be recoverable under [any] of those sections in respect of any loss of expectation of life, nor shall any such loss be taken into account in the compensation payable in respect of a child under the Nuclear Installations Act 1965 as extended by section 3, unless (in either case) the child lives for at least 48 hours.

[(4A) In any case where a child carried by a woman as the result of the placing in her of an embryo or of sperm and eggs or her artificial insemination is born disabled, any reference in section 1 of this Act to a parent includes a reference to a person who would be a parent but for sections 27 to 29 of the Human Fertilisation and Embryology Act 1990 or sections 33 to 47 of the Human Fertilisation and Embryology Act 2008.]

(5) This Act applies in respect of births after (but not before) its passing, and in respect of any such birth it replaces any law in force before its passing, whereby a person could be liable to a child in respect of disabilities with which it might be born; but in section 1(3) of this Act the expression 'liable in tort' does not include any reference to liability by virtue of this Act or to liability by virtue of any such law.

5   Crown application

This Act binds the Crown.

Dangerous Wild Animals Act 1976

(1976, c. 38)

1   Licences

(1) Subject to section 5 of this Act, no person shall keep any dangerous wild animal except under the authority of a licence granted in accordance with the provisions of this Act by a local authority.

(3) A local authority shall not grant a licence under this Act unless it is satisfied that—

(a) it is not contrary to the public interest on the grounds of safety, nuisance or otherwise to grant the licence; . . .

(e) all reasonable precautions will be taken at all such times to prevent and control the spread of infectious diseases; . . .

4   Power to seize and to dispose of animals without compensation

(1) Where—

(a) an animal is being kept contrary to section 1(1) of the Act, or

(b) any condition of a licence under this Act is contravened or not complied with,

the local authority in whose area any animal concerned is for the time being may seize the animal, and either retain it in the authority's possession or destroy or otherwise dispose of it, and shall not be liable to pay compensation to any person in respect of the exercise of its powers under this subsection.

(2) A local authority which incurs any expenditure in exercising its powers under subsection (1)(a) of this section shall be entitled to recover the amount of the expenditure summarily as a civil debt from any person who was at the time of the seizure a keeper of the animal concerned.

(3) A local authority which incurs any expenditure in exercising its powers under subsection (1)(b) of this section shall be entitled to recover the amount of the expenditure summarily as a civil debt from the person to whom the licence concerned was granted.

Fatal Accidents Act 1976

(1976, c. 30)

1   Right of action for wrongful act causing death

[(1) If death is caused by any wrongful act, neglect or default which is such as would (if death had not ensued) have entitled the person injured to maintain an action and recover damages in respect thereof, the person who would have been liable if death had not ensued shall be liable to an action for damages, notwithstanding the death of the person injured.

(2) Subject to section 1A(2) below, every such action shall be for the benefit of the dependants of the person ('the deceased') whose death has been so caused.

(3) In this Act 'dependant' means—

  (a)   the wife or husband or former wife or husband of the deceased;

  [(aa) the civil partner or former civil partner of the deceased;]

  (b)   any person who—

      (i)   was living with the deceased in the same household immediately before the date of the death; and

      (ii) had been living with the deceased in the same household for at least two years before that date; and

      (iii) was living during the whole of that period as the husband or wife or civil partner of the deceased;

  (c)   any parent or other ascendant of the deceased;

  (d)   any person who was treated by the deceased as his parent;

  (e)   any child or other descendant of the deceased;

  (f)   any person (not being a child of the deceased) who, in the case of any marriage to which the deceased was at any time a party, was treated by the deceased as a child of the family in relation to that marriage;

  [(fa) any person (not being a child of the deceased) who, in the case of any civil partnership in which the deceased was at any time a civil partner, was treated by the deceased as a child of the family in relation to that civil partnership;]

  (g)   any person who is, or is the issue of, a brother, sister, uncle or aunt of the deceased.

(4) The reference to the former wife or husband of the deceased in subsection (3)(a) above includes a reference to a person whose marriage to the deceased has been annulled or declared void as well as a person whose marriage to the deceased has been dissolved.

[(4A) The reference to the former civil partner of the deceased in subsection (3)(aa) above includes a reference to a person whose civil partnership with the deceased has been annulled as well as a person whose civil partnership with the deceased has been dissolved.]

(5) In deducing any relationship for the purposes of subsection (3) above—

  (a)   any relationship by marriage or civil partnership shall be treated as a relationship of consanguinity, any relationship of the half blood as a relationship of the whole blood, and the stepchild of any person as his child, and

  (b)   an illegitimate person shall be treated as the legitimate child of his mother and reputed father.

(6) Any reference in this Act to injury includes any disease and any impairment of a person's physical or mental condition.]

[1A   Bereavement

(1) An action under this Act may consist of or include a claim for damages for bereavement.

(2) A claim for damages for bereavement shall only be for the benefit—

(a) of the wife or husband [or civil partner] of the deceased; and

(b) where the deceased was a minor who was never married [or a civil partner]—

(i)   his parents, if he was legitimate; and

(ii) of his mother, if he was illegitimate.

(3) Subject to subsection (5) below, the sum to be awarded as damages under this section shall be [£12,980].

(4) Where there is a claim for damages under this section for the benefit of both the parents of the deceased, the sum awarded shall be divided equally between them (subject to any deduction falling to be made in respect of costs not recovered from the defendant).

(5) The Lord Chancellor may by order made by statutory instrument, subject to annulment in pursuance of a resolution of either House of Parliament, amend this section by varying the sum for the time being specified in subsection (3) above.]

2   Persons entitled to bring the action

(1) The action shall be brought by and in the name of the executor or administrator of the deceased.

(2) If—

(a) there is no executor or administrator of the deceased, or

(b) no action is brought within six months after the death by and in the name of an executor or administrator of the deceased,

the action may be brought by and in the name of all or any of the persons for whose benefit an executor or administrator could have brought it.

(3) Not more than one action shall lie for and in respect of the same subject matter of complaint.

(4) The plaintiff in the action shall be required to deliver to the defendant or his solicitor full particulars of the persons for whom and on whose behalf the action is brought and of the nature of the claim in respect of which damages are sought to be recovered.

3   Assessment of damages

[(1) In the action such damages, other than damages for bereavement, may be awarded as are proportioned to the injury resulting from the death to the dependants respectively.

(2) After deducting the costs not recovered from the defendant any amount recovered otherwise than as damages for bereavement shall be divided among the dependants in such shares as may be directed.

(3) In an action under this Act where there fall to be assessed damages payable to a widow in respect of the death of her husband there shall not be taken into account the re-marriage of the widow or her prospects of re-marriage.

(4) In an action under this Act where there fall to be assessed damages payable to a person who is a dependant by virtue of section 1(3)(b) above in respect of the death of the person with whom the dependant was living as husband or wife [or civil partner] there shall be taken into account (together with any other matter that appears to the court to be relevant to the action) the fact that the dependant had no enforceable right to financial support by the deceased as a result of their living together.

(5) If the dependants have incurred funeral expenses in respect of the deceased, damages may be awarded in respect of those expenses.

(6) Money paid into court in satisfaction of a cause of action under this Act may be in one sum without specifying any person's share.]

4 Assessment of damages; disregard of benefits

[In assessing damages in respect of a person's death in an action under this Act, benefits which have accrued or will or may accrue to any person from his estate or otherwise as a result of his death shall be disregarded.]

5 Contributory negligence

Where any person dies as the result partly of his own fault and partly of the fault of any other person or persons, and accordingly if an action were brought for the benefit of the estate under the Law Reform (Miscellaneous Provisions) Act 1934 the damages recoverable would be reduced under section 1(1) of the Law Reform (Contributory Negligence) Act 1945, any damages recoverable in an action [. . .] under this Act shall be reduced to a proportionate extent.

Protection from Eviction Act 1977

(1977, c. 43)

1 Unlawful eviction and harassment of occupier

(1) In this section 'residential occupier', in relation to any premises, means a person occupying the premises as a residence, whether under a contract or by virtue of any enactment or rule of law giving him the right to remain in occupation or restricting the right of any other person to recover possession of the premises.

(2) If any person unlawfully deprives the residential occupier of any premises of his occupation of the premises or any part thereof, or attempts to do so, he shall be guilty of an offence unless he proves that he believed, and had reasonable cause to believe, that the residential occupier had ceased to reside in the premises.

(3) If any person with intent to cause the residential occupier of any premises—

(a) to give up the occupation of the premises or any part thereof; or

(b) to refrain from exercising any right or pursuing any remedy in respect of the premises or part thereof;

does acts [likely] to interfere with the peace or comfort of the residential occupier or members of his household, or persistently withdraws or withholds services reasonably required for the occupation of the premises as a residence, he shall be guilty of an offence.

[(3A) Subject to subsection (3B) below, the landlord of a residential occupier or an agent of the landlord shall be guilty of an offence if—

(a) he does acts likely to interfere with the peace or comfort of the residential occupier or members of his household, or

(b) he persistently withdraws or withholds services reasonably required for the occupation of the premises in question as a residence,

and (in either case) he knows, or has reasonable cause to believe, that that conduct is likely to cause the residential occupier to give up the occupation of the whole or part of the premises or to refrain from exercising any right or pursuing any remedy in respect of the whole or part of the premises.

(3B) A person shall not be guilty of an offence under subsection (3A) above if he proves that he had reasonable grounds for doing the acts or withdrawing or withholding the services in question.]

(5) Nothing in this section shall be taken to prejudice any liability or remedy to which a person guilty of an offence thereunder may be subject in civil proceedings.

2 Restriction on re-entry without due process of law

Where any premises are let as a dwelling on a lease which is subject to a right of re-entry or forfeiture it shall not be lawful to enforce that right otherwise than by proceedings in the court while any person is lawfully residing in the premises or part of them.

3 Prohibition of eviction without due process of law

(1) Where any premises have been let as a dwelling under a tenancy which is [neither a statutorily protected tenancy nor an excluded tenancy] and—

(a) the tenancy (in this section referred to as the former tenancy) has come to an end, but

(b) the occupier continues to reside in the premises or part of them,

it shall not be lawful for the owner to enforce against the occupier, otherwise than by proceedings in the court, his right to recover possession of the premises.

(2) In this section 'the occupier', in relation to any premises, means any person lawfully residing in the premises or part of them at the termination of the former tenancy.

Torts (Interference with Goods) Act 1977

(1977, c. 32)

1 Definition of 'wrongful interference with goods'

In this Act 'wrongful interference', or 'wrongful interference with goods', means—

(a) conversion of goods (also called trover),

(b) trespass to goods,

(c) negligence so far as it results in damage to goods or to an interest in goods,

(d) subject to section 2, any other tort so far as it results in damage to goods or to an interest in goods.

[and references in this Act (however worded) to proceedings for wrongful interference or to a claim or right to claim for wrongful interference shall include references to proceedings by virtue of Part I of the Consumer Protection Act 1987 or Part II of the Consumer Protection (Northern Ireland) Order 1987 (product liability) in respect of any damage to goods or to an interest in goods or, as the case may be, to a claim or right to claim by virtue of that Part in respect of any such damage.]

2 Abolition of detinue

(1) Detinue is abolished.

(2) An action lies in conversion for loss or destruction of goods which a bailee has allowed to happen in breach of his duty to his bailor (that is to say it lies in a case which is not otherwise conversion, but would have been detinue before detinue was abolished).

3 Forms of judgment where goods are detained

(1) In proceedings for wrongful interference against a person who is in possession or in control of the goods relief may be given in accordance with this section, so far as appropriate.

(2) The relief is—

(a) an order for delivery of the goods, and for payment of any consequential damages, or

(b) an order for delivery of the goods, but giving the defendant the alternative of paying damages by reference to the value of the goods, together in either alternative with payment of any consequential damages, or

(c) damages.

(3) Subject to rules of court—

(a) relief shall be given under only one of paragraphs (a), (b) and (c) of subsection (2),

(b) relief under paragraph (a) of subsection (2) is at the discretion of the court, and the claimant may choose between the others.

(4) If it is shown to the satisfaction of the court that an order under subsection (2)(a) had not been complied with, the court may—

(a) revoke the order, or the relevant part of it, and

(b) make an order for payment of damages by reference to the value of the goods.

(5) Where an order is made under subsection (2)(b) the defendant may satisfy the order by returning the goods at any time before execution of judgment, but without prejudice to liability to pay any consequential damages.

(6) An order for delivery of the goods under subsection (2)(a) or (b) may impose such conditions as may be determined by the court, or pursuant to rules of court, and in particular, where damages by reference to the value of the goods would not be the whole of the value of the goods, may require an allowance to be made by the claimant to reflect the difference.

For example, a bailor's action against the bailee may be one in which the measure of damages is not the full value of the goods, and then the court may order delivery of the goods, but require the bailor to pay the bailee a sum reflecting the difference.

(7) Where under subsection (1) or subsection (2) of section 6 an allowance is to be made in respect of an improvement of the goods, and an order is made under subsection (2)(a) or (b), the court may assess the allowance to be made in respect of the improvement, and by the order require, as a condition for delivery of the goods, that allowance to be made by the claimant.

(8) This section is without prejudice—

    (a) to the remedies afforded by section 133 of the Consumer Credit Act, or . . .

    (c) to any jurisdiction to afford ancillary or incidental relief.

4   Interlocutory relief where goods are detained

(1) In this section 'proceedings' means proceedings for wrongful interference.

(2) On the application of any person in accordance with rules of court, the High Court shall, in such circumstances as may be specified in the rules, have power to make an order providing for the delivery up of any goods which are or may become the subject matter of subsequent proceedings in the court, or as to which any question may arise in proceedings.

(3) Delivery shall be, as the order may provide, to the claimant or to a person appointed by the court for the purpose, and shall be on such terms and conditions as may be specified in the order.

5   Extinction of title on satisfaction of claim for damages

(1) Where damages for wrongful interference are, or would fall to be, assessed on the footing that the claimant is being compensated—

    (a) for the whole of his interest in the goods, or

    (b) for the whole of his interest in the goods subject to a reduction for contributory negligence,

payment of the assessed damages (under all heads), or as the case may be settlement of a claim for damages for the wrong (under all heads), extinguishes the claimant's title to that interest.

(2) In subsection (1) the reference to the settlement of the claim includes—

    (a) where the claim is made in court proceedings, and the defendant has paid a sum into court to meet the whole claim, the taking of that sum by the claimant, and

    (b) where the claim is made in court proceedings, and the proceedings are settled or compromised, the payment of what is due in accordance with the settlement or compromise, and

    (c) where the claim is made out of court and is settled or compromised, the payment of what is due in accordance with the settlement or compromise.

(3) It is hereby declared that subsection (1) does not apply where damages are assessed on the footing that the claimant is being compensated for the whole of his interest in the goods, but the damages paid are limited to some lesser amount by virtue of any enactment or rule of law.

(4) Where under section 7(3) the claimant accounts over to another person (the 'third party') so as to compensate (under all heads) the third party for the whole of his interest in the goods, the third party's title to that interest is extinguished.

(5) This section has effect subject to any agreement varying the respective rights of the parties to the agreement, and where the claim is made in court proceedings has effect subject to any order of the court.

6   Allowance for improvement of the goods

(1) If in proceedings for wrongful interference against a person (the 'improver') who has improved the goods, it is shown that the improver acted in the mistaken but honest belief that he had a good title to them, an allowance shall be made for the extent to which, at the time as at

which the goods fall to be valued in assessing damages, the value of the goods is attributable to the improvement.

(2) If, in proceedings for wrongful interference against a person ('the purchaser') who has purported to purchase the goods—

(a) from the improver, or

(b) where after such a purported sale the goods passed by a further purported sale on one or more occasions, on any such occasion,

it is shown that the purchaser acted in good faith, an allowance shall be made on the principle set out in subsection (1).

For example, where a person in good faith buys a stolen car from the improver and is sued in conversion by the true owner the damages may be reduced to reflect the improvement, but if the person who bought the stolen car from the improver sues the improver for failure of consideration, and the improver acted in good faith, subsection (3) below will ordinarily make a comparable reduction in the damages he recovers from the improver.

(3) If in a case within subsection (2) the person purporting to sell the goods acted in good faith, then in proceedings by the purchaser for recovery of the purchase price because of failure of consideration, or in any other proceedings founded on that failure of consideration, an allowance shall, where appropriate, be made on the principle set out in subsection (1).

(4) This section applies, with the necessary modifications, to a purported bailment or other disposition of goods as it applies to a purported sale of goods.

7 Double liability

(1) In this section 'double liability' means the double liability of the wrongdoer which can arise—

(a) where one of two or more rights of action for wrongful interference is founded on a possessory title, or

(b) where the measure of damages in an action for wrongful interference founded on a proprietary title is or includes the entire value of the goods, although the interest is one of two or more interests in the goods.

(2) In proceedings to which any two or more claimants are parties, the relief shall be such as to avoid double liability of the wrongdoer as between those claimants.

(3) On satisfaction, in whole or in part, of any claim for an amount exceeding that recoverable if subsection (2) applied, the claimant is liable to account over to the other person having a right to claim to such extent as will avoid double liability.

(4) Where, as the result of enforcement of a double liability, any claimant is unjustly enriched to an extent, he shall be liable to reimburse the wrongdoer to that extent.

For example, if a converter of goods pays damages first to a finder of the goods, and then to the true owner, the finder is unjustly enriched unless he accounts over to the true owner under subsection (3); and then the true owner is unjustly enriched and becomes liable to reimburse the converter of the goods.

8 Competing rights to the goods

(1) The defendant in an action for wrongful interference shall be entitled to show, in accordance with rules of court, that a third party has a better right than the plaintiff as respects all or any part of the interest claimed by the plaintiff, or in right of which he sues, and any rule of law (sometimes called jus tertii) to the contrary is abolished.

(2) Rules of court relating to proceedings for wrongful interference may—

(a) require the plaintiff to give particulars of his title,

(b) require the plaintiff to identify any person who, to his knowledge, has or claims any interest in the goods,

(c) authorise the defendant to apply for directions as to whether any person should be joined with a view to establishing whether he has a better right than the plaintiff, or has a claim as a result of which the defendant might be doubly liable,

(d) where a party fails to appear on an application within paragraph (c), or to comply with any direction given by the court on such an application, authorise the court to deprive him of any right of action against the defendant for the wrong either unconditionally, or subject to such terms or conditions as may be specified.

(3) Subsection (2) is without prejudice to any other power of making rules of court.

9   Concurrent actions

(1) This section applies where goods are the subject of two or more claims for wrongful interference (whether or not the claims are founded on the same wrongful act, and whether or not any of the claims relates also to other goods).

(2) Where the goods are the subject of two or more claims under section 6 this section shall apply as if any claim under section 6(3) were a claim for wrongful interference.

(3) If proceedings have been brought [in England and Wales in the county court or in Northern Ireland] in [the county court] on one of those claims, [rules of court or] county court rules may waive, or allow a court to waive, any limit (financial or territorial) on the jurisdiction of county courts in [the County Courts Act 1984] or the County Courts Act [(Northern Ireland) Order 1980] so as to allow another of those claims to be brought in the [same] court.

(4) If proceedings are brought [in England and Wales in the county court or in Northern Ireland] on one of the claims in the High Court, and proceedings on any other are brought in [the county court], whether prior to the High Court proceedings or not, the High Court may, on the application of the defendant, after notice has been given to the claimant in the county court proceedings—

(a) order that the county court proceedings be transferred to the High Court, and

(b) order security for costs or impose such other terms as the court thinks fit.

10   Co-owners

(1) Co-ownership is no defence to an action founded on conversion or trespass to goods where the defendant without the authority of the other co-owner—

(a) destroys the goods, or disposes of the goods in a way giving a good title to the entire property in the goods, or otherwise does anything equivalent to the destruction of the other's interest in the goods, or

(b) purports to dispose of the goods in a way which would give a good title to the entire property in the goods if he was acting with the authority of all co-owners of the goods.

(2) Subsection (1) shall not affect the law concerning execution or enforcement of judgments, or concerning any form of distress.

(3) Subsection (1)(a) is by way of restatement of existing law so far as it relates to conversion.

11   Minor amendments

(1) Contributory negligence is no defence in proceedings founded on conversion, or on intentional trespass to goods.

(2) Receipt of goods by way of pledge is conversion if the delivery of the goods is conversion.

(3) Denial of title is not of itself conversion.

12   Bailee's power of sale

(1) This section applies to goods in the possession or under the control of a bailee where—

(a) the bailor is in breach of an obligation to take delivery of the goods or, if the terms of the bailment so provide, to give directions as to their delivery, or

(b) the bailee could impose such an obligation by giving notice to the bailor, but is unable to trace or communicate with the bailor, or

(c) the bailee can reasonably expect to be relieved of any duty to safeguard the goods on giving notice to the bailor, but is unable to trace or communicate with the bailor.

(2) In the cases of Part I of Schedule 1 to this Act a bailee may, for the purposes of subsection (1), impose an obligation on the bailor to take delivery of the goods, or as the case may be to give directions as to their delivery, and in those cases the said Part I sets out the method of notification.

(3) If the bailee—

    (a) has in accordance with Part II of Schedule 1 to this Act given notice to the bailor of his intention to sell the goods under this subsection, or

    (b) has failed to trace or communicate with the bailor with a view to giving him such a notice, after having taken reasonable steps for the purpose,

and is reasonably satisfied that the bailor owns the goods, he shall be entitled, as against the bailor, to sell the goods.

(4) Where subsection (3) applies but the bailor did not in fact own the goods, a sale under this section, or under section 13, shall not give a good title as against the owner, or as against a person claiming under the owner.

(5) A bailee exercising his powers under subsection (3) shall be liable to account to the bailor for the proceeds of sale, less any cost of sale, and—

    (a) the account shall be taken on the footing that the bailee should have adopted the best method of sale reasonably available in the circumstances, and

    (b) where subsection (3)(a) applies, any sum payable in respect of the goods by the bailor to the bailee which accrued due before the bailee gave notice of intention to sell the goods shall be deductible from the proceeds of sale.

(6) A sale duly made under this section gives a good title to the purchaser as against the bailor.

(7) In this section, section 13, and Schedule 1 to this Act,

    (a) 'bailor' and 'bailee' include their respective successors in title, and

    (b) references to what is payable, paid or due to the bailee in respect of the goods include references to what would be payable by the bailor to the bailee as a condition of delivery of the goods at the relevant time.

(8) This section, and Schedule 1 to this Act, have effect subject to the terms of the bailment.

(9) This section shall not apply where the goods were bailed before the commencement of this Act.

13 Sale authorised by the court

(1) If a bailee of the goods to which section 12 applies satisfies the court that he is entitled to sell the goods under section 12, or that he would be so entitled if he had given any notice required in accordance with Schedule 1 to this Act, the court—

    (a) may authorise the sale of the goods subject to such terms and conditions, if any, as may be specified in the order, and

    (b) may authorise the bailee to deduct from the proceeds of sale any costs of sale and any amount due from the bailor to the bailee in respect of the goods, and

    (c) may direct the payment into court of the net proceeds of sale, less any amount deducted under paragraph (b), to be held to the credit of the bailor.

(2) A decision of the court authorising a sale under this section shall, subject to any right of appeal, be conclusive, as against the bailor, of the bailee's entitlement to sell the goods, and gives a good title to the purchaser as against the bailor.

(3) [In this section "the court", in relation to England and Wales, means the High Court or the county court and, in relation to Northern Ireland, means the High Court or a county court, save that a county court in Northern Ireland has jurisdiction in the proceedings only if the value of the goods does not exceed the county court limit mentioned in Article 10(1) of the County Courts (Northern Ireland) Order 1980.]

14 Interpretation

(1) In this Act, unless the context otherwise requires . . .

'goods' includes all chattels personal other than things in action and money . . .

16 Extent and application to the Crown

(3) This Act shall bind the Crown, but as regards the Crown's liability in tort shall not bind the Crown further than the Crown is made liable in tort by the Crown Proceedings Act 1947.

Section 12

SCHEDULE 1

UNCOLLECTED GOODS

PART I POWER TO IMPOSE OBLIGATION TO COLLECT GOODS

1. (1) For the purposes of section 12(1) a bailee may, in the circumstances specified in this Part of this Schedule, by notice given to the bailor impose on him an obligation to take delivery of the goods.

(2) The notice shall be in writing, and may be given either—

(a) by delivering it to the bailor, or

(b) by leaving it at his proper address, or

(c) by post.

(3) The notice shall—

(a) specify the name and address of the bailee, and give sufficient particulars of the goods and the address or place where they are held, and

(b) state that the goods are ready for delivery to the bailor, or where combined with a notice terminating the contract of bailment, will be ready for delivery when the contract is terminated, and

(c) specify the amount, if any, which is payable by the bailor to the bailee in respect of the goods and which became due before the giving of the notice.

(4) Where the notice is sent by post it may be combined with a notice under Part II of this Schedule if the notice is sent by post in a way complying with paragraph 6(4).

(5) References in this Part of this Schedule to taking delivery of the goods include, where the terms of the bailment admit, references to giving directions as to their delivery.

(6) This Part of this Schedule is without prejudice to the provisions of any contract requiring the bailor to take delivery of the goods.

Goods accepted for repair or other treatment

2. If a bailee has accepted goods for repair or other treatment on the terms (expressed or implied) that they will be re-delivered to the bailor when the repair or other treatment has been carried out, the notice may be given at any time after the repair or other treatment has been carried out.

Goods accepted for valuation or appraisal

3. If a bailee has accepted goods in order to value or appraise them, the notice may be given at any time after the bailee has carried out the valuation or appraisal.

Storage, warehousing, etc.

4. (1) If a bailee is in possession of goods which he has held as custodian, and his obligation as custodian has come to an end, the notice may be given at any time after the ending of the obligation, or may be combined with any notice terminating his obligation as custodian.

(2) This paragraph shall not apply to goods held by a person as mercantile agent, that is to say by a person having in the customary course of his business as a mercantile agent authority either to sell goods or to consign goods for the purpose of sale, or to buy goods, or to raise money on the security of goods.

Supplemental

5. Paragraphs 2, 3 and 4 apply whether or not the bailor has paid any amount due to the bailee in respect of the goods, and whether or not the bailment is for reward, or in the course of business, or gratuitous.

PART II NOTICE OF INTENTION TO SELL GOODS

6. (1) A notice under section 12(3) shall—

(a) specify the name and address of the bailee, and give sufficient particulars of the goods and the address or place where they are held, and

(b) specify the date on or after which the bailee proposes to sell the goods, and

(c) specify the amount, if any, which is payable by the bailor to the bailee in respect of the goods, and which became due before the giving of the notice.

(2) The period between giving of the notice and the date specified in the notice as that on or after which the bailee proposes to exercise the power of sale shall be such as will afford the bailor a reasonable opportunity of taking delivery of the goods.

(3) If any amount is payable in respect of the goods by the bailor to the bailee, and become due before giving of the notice, the said period shall be not less than three months.

(4) The notice shall be in writing and shall be sent by post in a registered letter, or by the recorded delivery service.

7. (1) The bailee shall not give a notice under section 12(3), or exercise his right to sell the goods pursuant to such a notice, at a time when he has notice that, because of a dispute concerning the goods, the bailor is questioning or refusing to pay all or any part of what the bailee claims to be due to him in respect of the goods.

(2) This paragraph shall be left out of account in determining under section 13(1) whether a bailee of goods is entitled to sell the goods under section 12, or would be so entitled if he had given any notice required in accordance with this Schedule.

Unfair Contract Terms Act 1977

(1977, c. 50)

PART I AMENDMENT OF THE LAW FOR ENGLAND AND WALES AND NORTHERN IRELAND

1 Scope of Part I

(1) For the purposes of this Part of this Act, 'negligence' means the breach—

(a) of any obligation, arising from the express or implied terms of a contract, to take reasonable care or exercise reasonable skill in the performance of the contract;

(b) of any common law duty to take reasonable care or exercise reasonable skill (but not any stricter duty);

(c) of the common duty of care imposed by the Occupiers' Liability Act 1957 or the Occupier's Liability Act (Northern Ireland) 1957.

(2) This Part of this Act is subject to Part III; and in relation to contracts, the operation of sections 2[, 3] and 7 is subject to the exceptions made by Schedule I.

(3) In the case of both contract and tort, sections 2 to 7 apply (except where the contrary is stated in section 6(4)) only to business liability, that is liability for breach of obligations or duties arising—

(a) from things done or to be done by a person in the course of a business (whether his own business or another's); or

(b) from the occupation of premises used for business purposes of the occupier; and references to liability are to be read accordingly [but liability of an occupier of premises for breach of an obligation or duty towards a person obtaining access to the premises for recreational or educational purposes, being liability for loss or damage suffered by reason of the dangerous state of the premises, is not a business liability of the occupier unless granting that person such access for the purposes concerned falls within the business purposes of the occupier.]

(4) In relation to any breach of duty or obligation, it is immaterial for any purpose of this Part of this Act whether the breach was inadvertent or intentional, or whether liability for it arises directly or vicariously.

2   Negligence liability

(1) A person cannot by reference to any contract term or to a notice given to persons generally or to particular persons exclude or restrict his liability for death or personal injury resulting from negligence.

(2) In the case of other loss or damage, a person cannot so exclude or restrict his liability for negligence except in so far as the term or notice satisfies the requirement of reasonableness.

(3) Where a contract term or notice purports to exclude or restrict liability for negligence a person's agreement to or awareness of it is not of itself to be taken as indicating his voluntary acceptance of any risk.

[(4) This section does not apply to—

    (a) a term in a consumer contract, or

    (b) a notice to the extent that it is a consumer notice,

(but see the provision made about such contracts and notices in sections 62 and 65 of the Consumer Rights Act 2015).]

3   Liability arising in contract

(1) This section applies as between contracting parties where one of them deals [...] on the other's written standard terms of business.

(2) As against that party, the other cannot by reference to any contract term—

    (a) when himself in breach of contract, exclude or restrict any liability of his in respect of the breach; or

    (b) claim to be entitled—

        (i) to render a contractual performance substantially different from that which was reasonably expected of him, or

        (ii) in respect of the whole or any part of his contractual obligation, to render no performance at all,

except in so far as (in any of the cases mentioned above in this subsection) the contract term satisfies the requirement of reasonableness.

[(3) This section does not apply to a term in a consumer contract (but see the provision made about such contracts in section 62 of the Consumer Rights Act 2015).]

6   Sale and hire-purchase

(1) Liability for breach of the obligations arising from—

    (a) [section 12 of the Sale of Goods Act 1979] (seller's implied undertakings as to title, etc.);

    (b) section 8 of the Supply of Goods (Implied Terms) Act 1973 (the corresponding thing in relation to hire-purchase),

cannot be excluded or restricted by reference to any contract term.

[(1A) Liability for breach of the obligations arising from—

    (a) section 13, 14 or 15 of the 1979 Act (seller's implied undertakings as to conformity of goods with description or sample, or as to their quality or fitness for a particular purpose);

    (b) section 9, 10 or 11 of the 1973 Act (the corresponding things in relation to hire purchase),

cannot be excluded or restricted by reference to a contract term except in so far as the term satisfies the requirement of reasonableness.]

(4) The liabilities referred to in this section are not only the business liabilities defined by section 1(3), but include those arising under any contract of sale of goods or hire-purchase agreement.

[(5) This section does not apply to a consumer contract (but see the provision made about such contracts in section 31 of the Consumer Rights Act 2015).]

7   Miscellaneous contracts under which goods pass

(1) Where the possession or ownership of goods passes under or in pursuance of a contract not governed by the law of sale of goods or hire-purchase, subsections (2) to (4) below apply as regards the effect (if any) to be given to contract terms excluding or restricting liability for breach of obligation arising by implication of law from the nature of the contract.

[(1A) Liability in respect of the goods' correspondence with description or sample, or their quality or fitness for any particular purpose, cannot be excluded or restricted by reference to such a term except in so far as the term satisfies the requirement of reasonableness.]

[(3A) Liability for breach of the obligations arising under section 2 of the Supply of Goods and Services Act 1982 (implied terms about title etc. in certain contracts for the transfer of the property in goods) cannot be excluded or restricted by reference to any such term.]

(4) Liability in respect of—

    (a) the right to transfer ownership of the goods, or give possession; or

    (b) the assurance of quiet possession to a person taking goods in pursuance of the contract,

cannot [(in a case to which subsection (3A) above does not apply)] be excluded or restricted by reference to any such term except in so far as the term satisfies the requirement of reasonableness.

[(4A) This section does not apply to a consumer contract (but see the provision made about such contracts in section 31 of the Consumer Rights Act 2015).]

10   Evasion by means of secondary contract

A person is not bound by any contract term prejudicing or taking away rights of his which arise under, or in connection with the performance of, another contract, so far as those rights extend to the enforcement of another's liability which this Part of this Act prevents that other from excluding or restricting.

11   The 'reasonableness' test

(1) In relation to a contract term, the requirement of reasonableness for the purposes of this Part of this Act, section 3 of the Misrepresentation Act 1967 and section 3 of the Misrepresentation Act (Northern Ireland) 1967 is that the term shall have been a fair and reasonable one to be included having regard to the circumstances which were, or ought reasonably to have been, known to or in the contemplation of the parties when the contract was made.

(2) In determining for the purposes of section 6 or 7 above whether a contract term satisfies the requirement of reasonableness, regard shall be had in particular to the matters specified in Schedule 2 to this Act; but this subsection does not prevent the court or arbitrator from holding, in accordance with any rule of law, that a term which purports to exclude or restrict any relevant liability is not a term of the contract.

(3) In relation to a notice (not being a notice having contractual effect), the requirement of reasonableness under this Act is that it should be fair and reasonable to allow reliance on it, having regard to all the circumstances obtaining when the liability arose or (but for the notice) would have arisen.

(4) Where by reference to a contract term or notice a person seeks to restrict liability to a specified sum of money, and the question arises (under this or any other Act) whether the term or notice satisfies the requirement of reasonableness, regard shall be had in particular (but without prejudice to subsection (2) above in the case of contract terms) to—

    (a) the resources which he could expect to be available to him for the purpose of meeting the liability should it arise; and

    (b) how far it was open to him to cover himself by insurance.

(5) It is for those claiming that a contract term or notice satisfies the requirement of reasonableness to show that it does.

13   Varieties of exemption clause

(1) To the extent that this Part of this Act prevents the exclusion or restriction of any liability it also prevents—

    (a) making the liability or its enforcement subject to restrictive or onerous conditions;

    (b) excluding or restricting any right or remedy in respect of the liability, or subjecting a person to any prejudice in consequence of his pursuing any such right or remedy;

    (c) excluding or restricting rules of evidence or procedure;

and (to that extent) sections 2[, 6 and] 7 also prevent excluding or restricting liability by reference to terms and notices which exclude or restrict the relevant obligation or duty.

(2) But an agreement in writing to submit present or future differences to arbitration is not to be treated under this Part of this Act as excluding or restricting any liability.

14 Interpretation of Part I

In this Part of the Act—

'business' includes a profession and the activities of any government department or local or public authority;

["consumer contract" has the same meaning as in the Consumer Rights Act 2015 (see section 61);]

["consumer notice" has the same meaning as in the Consumer Rights Act 2015 (see section 61);]

'goods' has the same meaning as in [the Sale of Goods Act 1979];

'hire-purchase agreement' has the same meaning as in the Consumer Credit Act 1974;

'negligence' has the meaning given by section 1(1);

'notice' includes an announcement, whether or not in writing, and any other communication or pretended communication; and

'personal injury' includes any disease and any impairment of physical or mental condition.

PART III PROVISIONS APPLYING TO WHOLE OF UNITED KINGDOM

26 International supply contracts

(1) The limits imposed by this Act on the extent to which a person may exclude or restrict liability by reference to a contract term do not apply to liability arising under such a contract as is described in subsection (3) below.

(2) The terms of such a contract are not subject to any requirement of reasonableness under section 3 [. . .]: and nothing in Part II of this Act shall require the incorporation of the terms of such a contract to be fair and reasonable for them to have effect.

(3) Subject to subsection (4), that description of contract is one whose characteristics are the following—

(a) either it is a contract of sale of goods or it is one under or in pursuance of which the possession or ownership of goods passes; and

(b) it is made by parties whose places of business (or, if they have none, habitual residences) are in the territories of different States (the Channel Islands and the Isle of Man being treated for this purpose as different States from the United Kingdom).

(4) A contract falls within subsection (3) above only if either—

(a) the goods in question are, at the time of the conclusion of the contract, in the course of carriage, or will be carried, from the territory of one State to the territory of another; or

(b) the acts constituting the offer and acceptance have been done in the territories of different States; or

(c) the contract provides for the goods to be delivered to the territory of a State other than that within whose territory those acts were done.

27 Choice of law clauses

(1) Where the [law applicable to] a contract is the law of any part of the United Kingdom only by choice of the parties (and apart from that choice would be the law of some country outside the United Kingdom) sections 2 to 7 and 16 to 21 of this Act do not operate as part [of the law applicable to the contract.]

(2) This Act has effect notwithstanding any contract term which applies or purports to apply the law of some country outside the United Kingdom, where [. . .]—

(a) the term appears to the court, or arbitrator or arbiter to have been imposed wholly or mainly for the purpose of enabling the party imposing it to evade the operation of this Act; [. . .]

29   Saving for other relevant legislation

(1) Nothing in this Act removes or restricts the effect of, or prevents reliance upon, any contractual provision which—

(a) is authorised or required by the express terms or necessary implication of an enactment; or

(b) being made with a view to compliance with an international agreement to which the United Kingdom is a party, does not operate more restrictively than is contemplated by the agreement.

(2) A contract term is to be taken—

(a) for the purposes of Part I of this Act, as satisfying the requirement of reasonableness . . .

if it is incorporated or approved by, or incorporated pursuant to a decision or ruling of, a competent authority acting in the exercise of any statutory jurisdiction or function and is not a term in a contract to which the competent authority is itself a party.

(3) In this section—

'competent authority' means any court, arbitrator or arbiter, government department or public authority;

'enactment' means any legislation (including subordinate legislation) of the United Kingdom or Northern Ireland and any instrument having effect by virtue of such legislation; and

'statutory' means conferred by an enactment.

Section 1(2)

SCHEDULE 1

SCOPE OF SECTIONS 2[, 3] AND 7

1. Sections 2 [and 3] of this Act do not extend to—

(a) any contract of insurance (including a contract to pay an annuity on human life);

(b) any contract so far as it relates to the creation or transfer of an interest in land, or to the termination of such an interest, whether by extinction, merger, surrender, forfeiture or otherwise;

(c) any contract so far as it relates to the creation or transfer of a right or interest in any patent, trade mark, copyright [or design right];

(d) any contract so far as it relates—

(i)   to the formation or dissolution of a company (which means any body corporate or unincorporated association and includes a partnership), or

(ii) to its constitution or the rights or obligations of its corporators or members;

(e) any contract so far as it relates to the creation or transfer of securities or of any right or interest in securities

[(f) anything that is governed by Article 6 of Regulation (EU) No 181/2011 of the European Parliament and of the Council of 16 February 2011 concerning the rights of passengers in bus and coach transport and amending Regulation (EC) No 2006/2004].

2. Section 2(1) extends to—

(a) any contract of marine salvage or towage;

(b) any charterparty of a ship or hovercraft; and

(c) any contract for the carriage of goods by ship or hovercraft;

but subject to this sections 2[, 3] and 7 do not extend to any such contract [. . .].

3. Where goods are carried by ship or hovercraft in pursuance of a contract which either—

(a) specifies that as the means of carriage over part of the journey to be covered, or

(b) makes no provision as to the means of carriage and does not exclude that means,

then sections 2(2)[and 3] do not [. . .] extend to the contract as it operates for and in relation to the carriage of the goods by that means.

4. Section 2(1) and (2) do not extend to a contract of employment, except in favour of the employee.

5. Section 2(1) does not affect the validity of any discharge and indemnity given by a person, on or in connection with an award to him of compensation for pneumoconiosis attributable to employment in the coal industry, in respect of any further claim arising from his contracting that disease.

Sections 11(2) and 24(2)   # SCHEDULE 2
'GUIDELINES' FOR APPLICATION
OF REASONABLENESS TEST

The matters to which regard is to be had in particular for the purposes of sections [6(1A), 7(1A) and (4),] 20 and 21 are any of the following which appear to be relevant—

(a) the strength of the bargaining positions of the parties relative to each other, taking into account (among other things) alternative means by which the customer's requirements could have been met;

(b) Whether the customer received an inducement to agree to the term, or in accepting it had an opportunity of entering into a similar contract with other persons, but without having to accept a similar term;

(c) whether the customer knew or ought reasonably to have known of the existence and extent of the term (having regard, among other things, to any custom of the trade and any previous course of dealing between the parties);

(d) where the term excludes or restricts any relevant liability if some condition is not complied with, whether it was reasonable at the time of the contract to expect that compliance with that condition would be practicable;

(e) whether the goods were manufactured, processed or adapted to the special order of the customer.

Civil Liability (Contribution) Act 1978

(1978, c. 47)

1 Entitlement to contribution

(1) Subject to the following provisions of this section, any person liable in respect of any damage suffered by another person may recover contribution from any other person liable in respect of the same damage (whether jointly with him or otherwise).

(2) A person shall be entitled to recover contribution by virtue of subsection (1) above notwithstanding that he has ceased to be liable in respect of the damage in question since the time when the damage occurred, provided that he was so liable immediately before he made or was ordered or agreed to make the payment in respect of which the contribution is sought.

(3) A person shall be liable to make contribution by virtue of subsection (1) above notwithstanding that he has ceased to be liable in respect of the damage in question since the time when the damage occurred, unless he ceased to be liable by virtue of the expiry of a period of limitation or prescription which extinguished the right on which the claim against him in respect of the damage was based.

(4) A person who has made or agreed to make any payment in bona fide settlement or compromise of any claim made against him in respect of any damage (including a payment into court which has been accepted) shall be entitled to recover contribution in accordance with this section without regard to whether or not he himself is or ever was liable in respect of the damage, provided, however, that he would have been liable assuming that the factual basis of the claim against him could be established.

(5) A judgment given in any action brought in any part of the United Kingdom by or on behalf of the person who suffered the damage in question against any person from whom contribution

is sought under this section shall be conclusive in the proceedings for contribution as to any issue determined by that judgment in favour of the person from whom the contribution is sought.

(6) References in this section to a person's liability in respect of any damage are references to any such liability which has been or could be established in an action brought against him in England and Wales by or on behalf of the person who suffered the damage; but it is immaterial whether any issue arising in any such action was or would be determined (in accordance with the rules of private international law) by reference to the law of a country outside England and Wales.

2 Assessment of contribution

(1) Subject to subsection (3) below, in any proceedings for contribution under section 1 above the amount of the contribution recoverable from any person shall be such as may be found by the court to be just and equitable having regard to the extent of that person's responsibility for the damage in question.

(2) Subject to subsection (3) below, the court shall have power in any such proceedings to exempt any person from liability to make contribution or to direct that the contribution to be recovered from any person shall amount to a complete indemnity.

(3) Where the amount of the damages which have or might have been awarded in respect of the damage in question in any action brought in England and Wales by or on behalf of the person who suffered it against the person from whom the contribution is sought was or would have been subject to—

(a) any limit imposed by or under any enactment or by any agreement made before the damage occurred;

(b) any reduction by virtue of section 1 of the Law Reform (Contributory Negligence) Act 1945 or section 5 of the Fatal Accidents Act 1976; or

(c) any corresponding limit or reduction under the law of a country outside England and Wales;

the person from whom the contribution is sought shall not by virtue of any contribution awarded under section 1 above be required to pay in respect of the damage a greater amount than the amount of those damages as so limited or reduced.

3 Proceedings against persons jointly liable for the same debt or damage

Judgment recovered against any person liable in respect of any debt or damage shall not be a bar to an action, or to the continuance of an action, against any other person who is (apart from any such bar) jointly liable with him in respect of the same debt or damage.

4 Successive actions against persons liable (jointly or otherwise) for the same damage

If more than one action is brought in respect of any damage by or on behalf of the person by whom it was suffered against persons liable in respect of the damage (whether jointly or otherwise) the plaintiff shall not be entitled to costs in any of those actions, other than that in which judgment is first given, unless the court is of the opinion that there was reasonable ground for bringing the action.

5 Application to the Crown

Without prejudice to section 4(1) of the Crown Proceedings Act 1947 (indemnity and contribution), this Act shall bind the Crown, but nothing in this Act shall be construed as in any way affecting Her Majesty in Her private capacity (including in right of Her Duchy of Lancaster) or the Duchy of Cornwall.

6 Interpretation

(1) A person is liable in respect of any damage for the purposes of this Act if the person who suffered it (or anyone representing his estate or dependants) is entitled to recover compensation

from him in respect of that damage (whatever the legal basis of his liability, whether tort, breach of contract, breach of trust or otherwise).

(2) References in this Act to an action brought by or on behalf of the person who suffered any damage include references to an action brought for the benefit of his estate or dependants.

(3) In this Act 'dependants' has the same meaning as in the Fatal Accidents Act 1976.

(4) In this Act, except in section 1(5) above, 'action' means an action brought in England and Wales.

7 Savings

(3) The right to recover contribution in accordance with section 1 above supersedes any right, other than an express contractual right, to recover contribution (as distinct from indemnity) otherwise than under this Act in corresponding circumstances; but nothing in this Act shall affect—

(a) any express or implied contractual or other right to indemnity; or

(b) any express contractual provision regulating or excluding contribution;

which would be enforceable apart from this Act (or render enforceable any agreement for indemnity or contribution which would not be enforceable apart from this Act).

Pneumoconiosis etc. (Workers' Compensation) Act 1979

(1979, c. 41)

1 Lump sum payments

(1) If, on a claim by a person who is disabled by a disease to which this Act applies, the Secretary of State is satisfied that the conditions of entitlement mentioned in section 2(1) below are fulfilled, he shall in accordance with this Act make to that person a payment of such amount as may be prescribed by regulations.

(2) If, on a claim by the dependant of a person who, immediately before he died, was disabled by a disease to which this Act applies, the Secretary of State is satisfied that the conditions of entitlement mentioned in section 2(2) below are fulfilled, he shall in accordance with this Act make to that dependant a payment of such amount as may be so prescribed.

(3) The diseases to which this Act applies are pneumoconiosis, byssinosis and diffuse mesothelioma [and any other disease which is specified by the Secretary of State for the purposes of this Act by order made by statutory instrument].

2 Conditions of entitlement

(1) In the case of a person who is disabled by a disease to which this Act applies, the conditions of entitlement are—

(a) that disablement benefit is payable to him in respect of the disease [or, subject to subsection (3A) below, would be payable to him in respect of it but for his disablement amounting to less than the appropriate percentage];

(b) that every relevant employer of his has ceased to carry on business;

[(ba) that no application has been made for a payment under the Diffuse Mesothelioma Payment Scheme in respect of the disease (for the scheme, see the Mesothelioma Act 2014);] and

(c) that he has not brought any action, or compromised any claim, for damages in respect of the disablement.

(2) In the case of the dependant of a person who, immediately before he died, was disabled by a disease to which this Act applies, the conditions of entitlement are—

(a) that no payment under this Act has been made to the deceased in respect of the disease;

(b)   [. . .] that disablement benefit was payable to the deceased in respect of the disease immediately before he died [or, subject to subsection (3A) below, would have been so payable to him—

     (i)   but for his disablement amounting to less than the appropriate percentage; or

     (ii)   but for his not having claimed the benefit; or

     (iii) but for his having died before he had suffered from the disease for the appropriate period];

(c)   that every relevant employer of the deceased has ceased to carry on business;

[(ca) that no application has been made by the deceased, or any dependant, for a payment under the Diffuse Mesothelioma Payment Scheme in respect of the disease (for the scheme, see the Mesothelioma Act 2014);] and

(d)   that neither the deceased nor his personal representatives nor any relative of his has brought any action, or compromised any claim, for damages in respect of the disablement or death.

   [(3A) No amount is payable under this Act in respect of disablement amounting to less than 1 per cent.]

   (4) For the purposes of this section any action which has been dismissed otherwise than on the merits (as for example for want of prosecution or under any enactment relating to the limitation of actions) shall be disregarded.

5   Reconsideration of determinations

   (1) Subject to subsection (2) below, the Secretary of State may reconsider a determination that a payment should not be made under this Act on the ground—

     (a) that there has been a material change of circumstances since the determination was made; or

     (b) that the determination was made in ignorance of, or was based on a mistake as to, some material fact;

and the Secretary of State may, on the ground set out in paragraph (b) above, reconsider a determination that such a payment should be made.

   (4) If, whether fraudulently or otherwise, any person misrepresents or fails to disclose any material fact and in consequence of the misrepresentation or failure a payment is made under this Act, the person to whom the payment was made shall be liable to repay the amount of that payment to the Secretary of State unless he can show that the misrepresentation or failure occurred without his connivance or consent.

9   Financial provisions

   (1) There shall be paid out of moneys provided by Parliament—

     (a) any expenditure incurred by the Secretary of State in making payments under this Act . . .

Sale of Goods Act 1979

(1979, c. 54)

PART I CONTRACTS TO WHICH ACT APPLIES

1   Contracts to which Act applies

   (1) This Act applies to contracts of sale of goods made on or after (but not to those made before) 1 January 1894.

   (2) In relation to contracts made on certain dates, this Act applies subject to the modification of certain of its sections as mentioned in Schedule 1 below.

   (3) Any such modification is indicated in the section concerned by a reference to Schedule 1 below.

   (4) Accordingly, where a section does not contain such a reference, this Act applies in relation to the contract concerned without such modification of the section.

   [(5) Certain sections or subsections of this Act do not apply to a contract to which Chapter 2 of Part 1 of the Consumer Rights Act 2015 applies.

   (6) Where that is the case it is indicated in the section concerned.]

PART II FORMATION OF THE CONTRACT

Contract of sale

2 Contract of sale

(1) A contract of sale of goods is a contract by which the seller transfers or agrees to transfer the property in goods to the buyer for a money consideration, called the price.

(2) There may be a contract of sale between one part owner and another.

(3) A contract of sale may be absolute or conditional.

(4) Where under a contract of sale the property in the goods is transferred from the seller to the buyer the contract is called a sale.

(5) Where under a contract of sale the transfer of the property in the goods is to take place at a future time or subject to some condition later to be fulfilled the contract is called an agreement to sell.

(6) An agreement to sell becomes a sale when the time elapses or the conditions are fulfilled subject to which the property in the goods is to be transferred.

3 Capacity to buy and sell

(1) Capacity to buy and sell is regulated by the general law concerning capacity to contract and to transfer and acquire property.

(2) Where necessaries are sold and delivered to a minor or to a person who by reason of [. . .] drunkenness is incompetent to contract, he must pay a reasonable price for them.

(3) In subsection (2) above 'necessaries' means goods suitable to the condition in life of the minor or other person concerned and to his actual requirements at the time of the sale and delivery.

4 How contract of sale is made

(1) Subject to this and any other Act, a contract of sale may be made in writing (either with or without seal), or by word of mouth, or partly in writing and partly by word of mouth, or may be implied from the conduct of the parties.

(2) Nothing in this section affects the law relating to corporations.

5 Existing or future goods

(1) The goods which form the subject of a contract of sale may be either existing goods, owned or possessed by the seller, or goods to be manufactured or acquired by him after the making of the contract of sale, in this Act called future goods.

(2) There may be a contract for the sale of goods the acquisition of which by the seller depends on a contingency which may or may not happen.

(3) Where by a contract of sale the seller purports to effect a present sale of future goods, the contract operates as an agreement to sell the goods.

6 Goods which have perished

Where there is a contract for the sale of specific goods, and the goods without the knowledge of the seller have perished at the time when the contract is made, the contract is void.

7 Goods perishing before sale but after agreement to sell

Where there is an agreement to sell specific goods and subsequently the goods, without any fault on the part of the seller or buyer, perish before the risk passes to the buyer, the agreement is avoided.

8 Ascertainment of price

(1) The price in a contract of sale may be fixed by the contract, or may be left to be fixed in a manner agreed by the contract, or may be determined by the course of dealing between the parties.

(2) Where the price is not determined as mentioned in subsection (1) above the buyer must pay a reasonable price.

(3) What is a reasonable price is a question of fact dependent on the circumstances of each particular case.

9   Agreement to sell at valuation

(1) Where there is an agreement to sell goods on the terms that the price is to be fixed by the valuation of a third party, and he cannot or does not make the valuation, the agreement is avoided; but if the goods or any part of them have been delivered to and appropriated by the buyer he must pay a reasonable price for them.

(2) Where the third party is prevented from making the valuation by the fault of the seller or buyer, the party not at fault may maintain an action for damages against the party at fault.

[Implied terms etc.]

10   Stipulations about time

(1) Unless a different intention appears from the terms of the contract, stipulations as to time of payment are not of the essence of a contract of sale.

(2) Whether any other stipulation as to time is or is not of the essence of the contract depends on the terms of the contract.

(3) In a contract of sale 'month' prima facie means calendar month.

11   When condition to be treated as warranty

[(1) This section does not apply to Scotland.]

(2) Where a contract of sale is subject to a condition to be fulfilled by the seller, the buyer may waive the condition, or may elect to treat the breach of the condition as a breach of warranty and not as a ground for treating the contract as repudiated.

(3) Whether a stipulation in a contract of sale is a condition, the breach of which may give rise to a right to treat the contract as repudiated, or a warranty, the breach of which may give rise to a claim for damages but not to a right to reject the goods and treat the contract as repudiated, depends in each case on the construction of the contract; and a stipulation may be a condition, though called a warranty in the contract.

(4) [Subject to section 35A below] Where a contract of sale is not severable and the buyer has accepted the goods or part of them, the breach of a condition to be fulfilled by the seller can only be treated as a breach of warranty, and not as a ground for rejecting the goods and treating the contract as repudiated, unless there is an express or implied term of the contract to that effect.

[(4A) Subsection (4) does not apply to a contract to which Chapter 2 of Part 1 of the Consumer Rights Act 2015 applies (but see the provision made about such contracts in sections 19 to 22 of that Act).]

(6) Nothing in this section affects a condition or warranty whose fulfilment is excused by law by reason of impossibility or otherwise.

(7) Paragraph 2 of Schedule 1 below applies in relation to a contract made before 22 April 1967 or (in the application of this Act to Northern Ireland) 28 July 1967.

12   Implied terms about title, etc.

(1) In a contract of sale, other than one to which subsection (3) below applies, there is an implied [term] on the part of the seller that in the case of a sale he has a right to sell the goods, and in the case of an agreement to sell he will have such a right at the time when the property is to pass.

(2) In a contract of sale, other than one to which subsection (3) below applies, there is also an implied [term] that—

  (a) the goods are free, and will remain free until the time when the property is to pass, from any charge or encumbrance not disclosed or known to the buyer before the contract is made, and

  (b) the buyer will enjoy quiet possession of the goods except so far as it may be disturbed by the owner or other person entitled to the benefit of any charge or encumbrance so disclosed or known.

(3) This subsection applies to a contract of sale in the case of which there appears from the contract or is to be inferred from its circumstances an intention that the seller should transfer only such title as he or a third person may have.

(4) In a contract to which subsection (3) above applies there is an implied [term] that all charges or encumbrances known to the seller and not known to the buyer have been disclosed to the buyer before the contract is made.

(5) In a contract to which subsection (3) above applies there is also an implied [term] that none of the following will disturb the buyer's quiet possession of the goods, namely—

    (a) the seller;

    (b) in a case where the parties to the contract intend that the seller should transfer only such title as a third person may have, that person;

    (c) anyone claiming through or under the seller or that third person otherwise than under a charge or encumbrance disclosed or known to the buyer before the contract is made.

[(5A) As regards England and Wales and Northern Ireland, the term implied by subsection (1) above is a condition and the terms implied by subsections (2), (4) and (5) above are warranties.]

(6) Paragraph 3 of Schedule 1 below applies in relation to a contract made before 18 May 1973.

13   Sale by description

(1) Where there is a contract for the sale of goods by description, there is an implied term that the goods will correspond with the description.

[(1A) As regards England and Wales and Northern Ireland, the term implied by subsection (1) above is a condition.]

(2) If the sale is by sample as well as by description it is not sufficient that the bulk of the goods corresponds with the sample if the goods do not also correspond with the description.

(3) A sale of goods is not prevented from being a sale by description by reason only that, being exposed for sale or hire, they are selected by the buyer.

(4) Paragraph 4 of Schedule 1 below applies in relation to a contract made before 18 May 1973.

[(5) This section does not apply to a contract to which Chapter 2 of Part 1 of the Consumer Rights Act 2015 applies (but see the provision made about such contracts in section 11 of that Act).]

14   Implied terms about quality or fitness

(1) Except as provided by this section and section 15 below and subject to any other enactment, there is no implied [term] about the quality or fitness for any particular purpose of goods supplied under a contract of sale.

[(2) Where the seller sells goods in the course of a business, there is an implied term that the goods supplied under the contract are of satisfactory quality.

(2A) For the purposes of this Act, goods are of satisfactory quality if they meet the standard that a reasonable person would regard as satisfactory, taking account of any description of the goods, the price (if relevant) and all the other relevant circumstances.

(2B) For the purposes of this Act, the quality of goods includes their state and condition and the following (among others) are in appropriate cases aspects of the quality of goods—

    (a) fitness for all the purposes for which goods of the kind in question are commonly supplied,

    (b) appearance and finish,

    (c) freedom from minor defects,

    (d) safety, and

    (e) durability.

(2C) The term implied by subsection (2) above does not extend to any matter making the quality of goods unsatisfactory—

    (a) which is specifically drawn to the buyer's attention before the contract is made,

    (b) where the buyer examines the goods before the contract is made, which that examination ought to reveal, or

    (c) in the case of a contract for sale by sample, which would have been apparent on a reasonable examination of the sample.]

(3) Where the seller sells goods in the course of a business and the buyer, expressly or by implication, makes known—

    (a) to the seller, or

(b) where the purchase price or part of it is payable by instalments and the goods were previously sold by a credit-broker to the seller, to that credit-broker,

any particular purpose for which the goods are being bought, there is an implied [term] that the
goods supplied under the contract are reasonably fit for that purpose, whether or not that is a purpose for which such goods are commonly supplied, except where the circumstances show that the
buyer does not rely, or that it is unreasonable for him to rely, on the skill or judgment of the seller or
credit-broker.

(4) An implied [term] about quality or fitness for a particular purpose may be annexed to a contract of sale by usage.

(5) The preceding provisions of this section apply to a sale by a person who in the course of
a business is acting as agent for another as they apply to a sale by a principal in the course of a
business, except where that other is not selling in the course of a business and either the buyer
knows that fact or reasonable steps are taken to bring it to the notice of the buyer before the contract is made.

[(6) As regards England and Wales and Northern Ireland, the terms implied by subsections
(2) and (3) above are conditions.]

(7) Paragraph 5 of Schedule 1 below applies in relation to a contract made on or after 18 May
1973 and before the appointed day, and paragraph 6 in relation to one made before 18 May 1973.

(8) In subsection (7) above and paragraph 5 of Schedule 1 below references to the appointed
day are to the day appointed for the purposes of those provisions by an order of the Secretary of State
made by statutory instrument.

[(9) This section does not apply to a contract to which Chapter 2 of Part 1 of the Consumer Rights
Act 2015 applies (but see the provision made about such contracts in sections 9, 10 and 18 of that
Act).]

Sale by sample

15   Sale by sample

(1) A contract of sale is a contract for sale by sample where there is an express or implied [term]
to that effect in the contract.

(2) In the case of a contract for sale by sample there is an implied [term]—

(a) that the bulk will correspond with the sample in quality;

[. . .]

(c) that the goods will be free from any defect, [making their quality unsatisfactory], which
would not be apparent on reasonable examination of the sample.

[(3) As regards England and Wales and Northern Ireland, the term implied by subsection
(2) above is a condition.]

(4) Paragraph 7 of Schedule 1 below applies in relation to a contract made before 18 May 1973.

[(5) This section does not apply to a contract to which Chapter 2 of Part 1 of the Consumer
Rights Act 2015 applies (but see the provision made about such contracts in sections 13 and 18 of
that Act).]

Miscellaneous

[15A   Modification of remedies for breach of condition in non-consumer cases

(1) Where in the case of a contract of sale—

(a) the buyer would, apart from this subsection, have the right to reject goods by reason of a
breach on the part of the seller of a term implied by section 13, 14 or 15 above, but

(b) the breach is so slight that it would be unreasonable for him to reject them, the breach is
not to be treated as a breach of condition but may be treated as a breach of warranty.

(2) This section applies unless a contrary intention appears in, or is to be implied from, the
contract.

(3) It is for the seller to show that a breach fell within subsection (1)(b) above.

PART III EFFECTS OF THE CONTRACT

Transfer of property as between seller and buyer

16 Goods must be ascertained

[Subject to section (20A) below] Where there is a contract for the sale of unascertained goods no property in the goods is transferred to the buyer unless and until the goods are ascertained.

17 Property passes when intended to pass

(1) Where there is a contract for the sale of specific or ascertained goods the property in them is transferred to the buyer at such time as the parties to the contract intend it to be transferred.

(2) For the purpose of ascertaining the intention of the parties regard shall be had to the terms of the contract, the conduct of the parties and the circumstances of the case.

18 Rules for ascertaining intention

Unless a different intention appears, the following are rules for ascertaining the intention of the parties as to the time at which the property in the goods is to pass to the buyer.

Rule 1.—Where there is an unconditional contract for the sale of specific goods in a deliverable state the property in the goods passes to the buyer when the contract is made, and it is immaterial whether the time of payment or the time of delivery, or both, be postponed.

Rule 2.—Where there is a contract for the sale of specific goods and the seller is bound to do something to the goods for the purpose of putting them into a deliverable state, the property does not pass until the thing is done and the buyer has notice that it has been done.

Rule 3.—Where there is a contract for the sale of specific goods in a deliverable state but the seller is bound to weigh, measure, test, or do some other act or thing with reference to the goods for the purpose of ascertaining the price, the property does not pass until the act or thing is done and the buyer has notice that it has been done.

Rule 4.—When goods are delivered to the buyer on approval or on sale or return or other similar terms the property in the goods passes to the buyer—

    (a) when he signifies his approval or acceptance to the seller or does any other act adopting the transaction;

    (b) if he does not signify his approval or acceptance to the seller but retains the goods without giving notice of rejection, then, if a time has been fixed for the return of the goods, on the expiration of that time, and, if no time has been fixed, on the expiration of a reasonable time.

Rule 5.—(1) Where there is a contract for the sale of unascertained or future goods by description, and goods of that description and in a deliverable state are unconditionally appropriated to the contract, either by the seller with the assent of the buyer or by the buyer with the assent of the seller, the property in the goods then passes to the buyer; and the assent may be express or implied, and may be given either before or after the appropriation is made.

(2) Where, in pursuance of the contract, the seller delivers the goods to the buyer or to a carrier or other bailee or custodier (whether named by the buyer or not) for the purpose of transmission to the buyer, and does not reserve the right of disposal, he is to be taken to have unconditionally appropriated the goods to the contract.

[(3) Where there is a contract for the sale of a specified quantity of unascertained goods in a deliverable state forming part of a bulk which is identified either in the contract or by subsequent agreement between the parties and the bulk is reduced to (or to less than) that quantity, then, if the buyer under that contract is the only buyer to whom goods are then due out of the bulk—

    (a) the remaining goods are to be taken as appropriated to that contract at the time when the bulk is so reduced; and

    (b) the property in those goods then passes to that buyer.

(4) Paragraph (3) above applies also (with the necessary modifications) where a bulk is reduced to (or to less than) the aggregate of the quantities due to a single buyer under separate contracts relating to that bulk and he is the only buyer to whom goods are then due out of that bulk.]

19   Reservation of right of disposal

(1) Where there is a contract for the sale of specific goods or where goods are subsequently appropriated to the contract, the seller may, by the terms of the contract or appropriation, reserve the right of disposal of the goods until certain conditions are fulfilled; and in such a case, notwithstanding the delivery of the goods to the buyer, or to a carrier or other bailee or custodier for the purpose of transmission to the buyer, the property in the goods does not pass to the buyer until the conditions imposed by the seller are fulfilled.

(2) Where goods are shipped, and by the bill of lading the goods are deliverable to the order of the seller or his agent, the seller is prima facie to be taken to reserve the right of disposal.

(3) Where the seller of goods draws on the buyer for the price, and transmits the bill of exchange and bill of lading to the buyer together to secure acceptance or payment of the bill of exchange, the buyer is bound to return the bill of lading if he does not honour the bill of exchange, and if he wrongfully retains the bill of lading the property in the goods does not pass to him.

20   [Passing of risk]

(1) Unless otherwise agreed, the goods remain at the seller's risk until the property in them is transferred to the buyer, but when the property in them is transferred to the buyer the goods are at the buyer's risk whether delivery has been made or not.

(2) But where delivery has been delayed through the fault of either buyer or seller the goods are at the risk of the party at fault as regards any loss which might not have occurred but for such fault.

(3) Nothing in this section affects the duties or liabilities of either seller or buyer as a bailee or custodier of the goods of the other party.

[(4) This section does not apply to a contract to which Chapter 2 of Part 1 of the Consumer Rights Act 2015 applies (but see the provision made about such contracts in section 29 of that Act).]

[20A   Undivided shares in goods forming part of a bulk

(1) This section applies to a contract for the sale of a specified quantity of unascertained goods if the following conditions are met—

    (a) the goods or some of them form part of a bulk which is identified either in the contract or by subsequent agreement between the parties; and

    (b) the buyer has paid the price for some or all of the goods which are the subject of the contract and which form part of the bulk.

(2) Where this section applies, then (unless the parties agree otherwise), as soon as the conditions specified in paragraphs (a) and (b) of subsection (1) above are met or at such later time as the parties may agree—

    (a) property in an undivided share in the bulk is transferred to the buyer; and

    (b) the buyer becomes an owner in common of the bulk.

(3) Subject to subsection (4) below, for the purposes of this section, the undivided share of a buyer in a bulk at any time shall be such share as the quantity of goods paid for and due to the buyer out of the bulk bears to the quantity of goods in the bulk at that time.

(4) Where the aggregate of the undivided shares of buyers in a bulk determined under subsection (3) above would at any time exceed the whole of the bulk at that time, the undivided share in the bulk of each buyer shall be reduced proportionately so that the aggregate of the undivided shares is equal to the whole bulk.

(5) Where a buyer has paid the price for only some of the goods due to him out of a bulk, any delivery to the buyer out of the bulk shall, for the purposes of this section, be ascribed in the first place to the goods in respect of which payment has been made.

(6) For the purpose of this section payment of part of the price for any goods shall be treated as payment for a corresponding part of the goods.]

[20B   Deemed consent by co-owner to dealings in bulk goods

(1) A person who has become an owner in common of a bulk by virtue of section 20A above shall be deemed to have consented to—

(a) any delivery of goods out of the bulk to any other owner in common of the bulk, being goods which are due to him under his contract;

(b) any removal, dealing with, delivery or disposal of goods in the bulk by any other person who is an owner in common of the bulk in so far as the goods fall within that co-owner's undivided share in the bulk at the time of the removal, dealing, delivery or disposal.

(2) No cause of action shall accrue to anyone against a person by reason of that person having acted in accordance with paragraph (a) or (b) of subsection (1) above in reliance on any consent deemed to have been given under that subsection.

(3) Nothing in this section or section 20A above shall—

(a) impose an obligation on a buyer of goods out of a bulk to compensate any other buyer of goods out of that bulk for any shortfall in the goods received by that other buyer;

(b) affect any contractual arrangement between buyers of goods out of a bulk for adjustments between themselves; or

(c) affect the rights of any buyer under his contract.]

Transfer of title

21   Sale by person not the owner

(1) Subject to this Act, where goods are sold by a person who is not their owner, and who does not sell them under the authority or with the consent of the owner, the buyer acquires no better title to the goods than the seller had, unless the owner of the goods is by his conduct precluded from denying the seller's authority to sell.

(2) Nothing in this Act affects—

(a) the provisions of the Factors Acts or any enactment enabling the apparent owner of goods to dispose of them as if he were their true owner;

(b) the validity of any contract of sale under any special common law or statutory power of sale or under the order of a court of competent jurisdiction.

22   Market overt

[. . .]

23   Sale under voidable title

When the seller of goods has a voidable title to them, but his title has not been avoided at the time of the sale, the buyer acquires a good title to the goods, provided he buys them in good faith and without notice of the seller's defect of title.

24   Seller in possession after sale

Where a person having sold goods continues or is in possession of the goods, or of the documents of title to the goods, the delivery or transfer by that person, or by a mercantile agent acting for him, of the goods or documents of title under any sale, pledge, or other disposition thereof, to any person receiving the same in good faith and without notice of the previous sale, has the same effect as if the person making the delivery or transfer were expressly authorised by the owner of the goods to make the same.

25   Buyer in possession after sale

(1) Where a person having bought or agreed to buy goods obtains, with the consent of the seller, possession of the goods or the documents of title to the goods, the delivery or transfer by that person, or by a mercantile agent acting for him, of the goods or documents of title, under any sale, pledge, or other disposition thereof, to any person receiving the same in good faith and without

notice of any lien or other right of the original seller in respect of the goods, has the same effect as if the person making the delivery or transfer were a mercantile agent in possession of the goods or documents of title with the consent of the owner.

(2) For the purposes of subsection (1) above—

(a) the buyer under a conditional sale agreement is to be taken not to be a person who has bought or agreed to buy goods, and

(b) 'conditional sale agreement' means an agreement for the sale of goods which is a consumer credit agreement within the meaning of the Consumer Credit Act 1974 under which the purchase price or part of it is payable by instalments, and the property in the goods is to remain in the seller (notwithstanding that the buyer is to be in possession of the goods) until such conditions as to the payment of instalments or otherwise as may be specified in the agreement are fulfilled.

(3) Paragraph 9 of Schedule 1 below applies in relation to a contract under which a person buys or agrees to buy goods and which is made before the appointed day.

(4) In subsection (3) above and paragraph 9 of Schedule 1 below references to the appointed day are to the day appointed for the purposes of those provisions by an order of the Secretary of State made by statutory instrument.

26   Supplementary to sections 24 and 25

In sections 24 and 25 above 'mercantile agent' means a mercantile agent having in the customary course of his business as such agent authority either—

(a) to sell goods, or

(b) to consign goods for the purpose of sale, or

(c) to buy goods, or

(d) to raise money on the security of goods.

PART IV PERFORMANCE OF THE CONTRACT

27   Duties of seller and buyer

It is the duty of the seller to deliver the goods, and of the buyer to accept and pay for them, in accordance with the terms of the contract of sale.

28   Payment and delivery are concurrent conditions

Unless otherwise agreed, delivery of the goods and payment of the price are concurrent conditions, that is to say, the seller must be ready and willing to give possession of the goods to the buyer in exchange for the price and the buyer must be ready and willing to pay the price in exchange for possession of the goods.

29   Rules about delivery

(1) Whether it is for the buyer to take possession of the goods or for the seller to send them to the buyer is a question depending in each case on the contract, express or implied, between the parties.

(2) Apart from any such contract, express or implied, the place of delivery is the seller's place of business if he has one, and if not, his residence; except that, if the contract is for the sale of specific goods, which to the knowledge of the parties when the contract is made are in some other place, then that place is the place of delivery.

(3) Where under the contract of sale the seller is bound to send the goods to the buyer, but no time for sending them is fixed, the seller is bound to send them within a reasonable time.

[(3A) Subsection (3) does not apply to a contract to which Chapter 2 of Part 1 of the Consumer Rights Act 2015 applies (but see the provision made about such contracts in section 28 of that Act).]

(4) Where the goods at the time of sale are in the possession of a third person, there is no delivery by seller to buyer unless and until the third person acknowledges to the buyer that he holds the goods on his behalf; but nothing in this section affects the operation of the issue or transfer of any document of title to goods.

(5) Demand or tender of delivery may be treated as ineffectual unless made at a reasonable hour; and what is a reasonable hour is a question of fact.

(6) Unless otherwise agreed, the expenses of and incidental to putting the goods into a deliverable state must be borne by the seller.

30   Delivery of wrong quantity

(1) Where the seller delivers to the buyer a quantity of goods less than he contracted to sell, the buyer may reject them, but if the buyer accepts the goods so delivered he must pay for them at the contract rate.

(2) Where the seller delivers to the buyer a quantity of goods larger than he contracted to sell, the buyer may accept the goods included in the contract and reject the rest, or he may reject the whole.

[(2A) A buyer may not—

(a) where the seller delivers a quantity of goods less than he contracted to sell, reject the goods under subsection (1) above, or

(b) where the seller delivers a quantity of goods larger than he contracted to sell, reject the whole under subsection (2) above,

if the shortfall or, as the case may be, excess is so slight that it would be unreasonable for him to do so.

(2B) It is for the seller to show that a shortfall or excess fell within subsection (2A) above.

(2C) Subsections (2A) and (2B) above do not apply to Scotland.]

[(2D) Where the seller delivers a quantity of goods—

(a) less than he contracted to sell, the buyer shall not be entitled to reject the goods under subsection (1) above,

(b) larger than he contracted to sell, the buyer shall not be entitled to reject the whole under subsection (2) above,

unless the shortfall or excess is material.

(2E) Subsection (2D) above applies to Scotland only.]

(3) Where the seller delivers to the buyer a quantity of goods larger than he contracted to sell and the buyer accepts the whole of the goods so delivered he must pay for them at the contract rate.

(5) This section is subject to any usage of trade, special agreement, or course of dealing between the parties.

[(6) This section does not apply to a contract to which Chapter 2 of Part 1 of the Consumer Rights Act 2015 applies (but see the provision made about such contracts in section 25 of that Act).]

31   Instalment deliveries

(1) Unless otherwise agreed, the buyer of goods is not bound to accept delivery of them by instalments.

(2) Where there is a contract for the sale of goods to be delivered by stated instalments, which are to be separately paid for, and the seller makes defective deliveries in respect of one or more instalments, or the buyer neglects or refuses to take delivery of or pay for one or more instalments, it is a question in each case depending on the terms of the contract and the circumstances of the case whether the breach of contract is a repudiation of the whole contract or whether it is a severable breach giving rise to a claim for compensation but not to a right to treat the whole contract as repudiated.

[(3) This section does not apply to a contract to which Chapter 2 of Part 1 of the Consumer Rights Act 2015 applies (but see the provision made about such contracts in section 26 of that Act).]

32   Delivery to carrier

(1) Where, in pursuance of a contract of sale, the seller is authorised or required to send the goods to the buyer, delivery of the goods to a carrier (whether named by the buyer or not) for the purpose of transmission to the buyer is prima facie deemed to be delivery of the goods to the buyer.

(2) Unless otherwise authorised by the buyer, the seller must make such contact with the carrier on behalf of the buyer as may be reasonable having regard to the nature of the goods and the

other circumstances of the case; and if the seller omits to do so, and the goods are lost or damaged in course of transit, the buyer may decline to treat the delivery to the carrier as a delivery to himself or may hold the seller responsible in damages.

(3) Unless otherwise agreed, where goods are sent by the seller to the buyer by a route involving sea transit, under circumstances in which it is usual to insure, the seller must give such notice to the buyer as may enable him to insure them during their sea transit, and if the seller fails to do so, the goods are at his risk during such sea transit.

[(4) This section does not apply to a contract to which Chapter 2 of Part 1 of the Consumer Rights Act 2015 applies (but see the provision made about such contracts in section 29 of that Act).]

33   Risk where goods are delivered at distant place

[(1)] Where the seller of goods agrees to deliver them at his own risk at a place other than that where they are when sold, the buyer must nevertheless (unless otherwise agreed) take any risk of deterioration in the goods necessarily incident to the course of transit.

[(2) This section does not apply to a contract to which Chapter 2 of Part 1 of the Consumer Rights Act 2015 applies (but see the provision made about such contracts in section 29 of that Act).]

34   Buyer's right of examining the goods

[(1)] Unless otherwise agreed, when the seller tenders delivery of goods to the buyer, he is bound on request to afford the buyer a reasonable opportunity of examining the goods for the purpose of ascertaining whether they are in conformity with the contract [and, in the case of a contract for sale by sample, of comparing the bulk with the sample].

[(2) Nothing in this section affects the operation of section 22 (time limit for short-term right to reject) of the Consumer Rights Act 2015.]

35   Acceptance

(1) The buyer is deemed to have accepted the goods [subject to subsection (2) below—
    (a) when he intimates to the seller that he has accepted them, or
    (b) when the goods have been delivered to him and he does any act in relation to them which is inconsistent with the ownership of the seller.

(2) Where goods are delivered to the buyer, and he has not previously examined them, he is not deemed to have accepted them under subsection (1) above until he has had a reasonable opportunity of examining them for the purpose—
    (a) of ascertaining whether they are in conformity with the contract, and
    (b) in the case of a contract for sale by sample, of comparing the bulk with the sample.

(4) The buyer is also deemed to have accepted the goods when after the lapse of a reasonable time he retains the goods without intimating to the seller that he has rejected them.

(5) The questions that are material in determining for the purposes of subsection (4) above whether a reasonable time has elapsed include whether the buyer has had a reasonable opportunity of examining the goods for the purpose mentioned in subsection (2) above.

(6) The buyer is not by virtue of this section deemed to have accepted the goods merely because—
    (a) he asks for, or agrees to, their repair by or under an arrangement with the seller, or
    (b) the goods are delivered to another under a sub-sale or other disposition.

(7) Where the contract is for the sale of goods making one or more commercial units, a buyer accepting any goods included in a unit is deemed to have accepted all the goods making the unit; and in this subsection 'commercial unit' means a unit division of which would materially impair the value of the goods or the character of the unit.]

[(9) This section does not apply to a contract to which Chapter 2 of Part 1 of the Consumer Rights Act 2015 applies (but see the provision made about such contracts in section 21 of that Act).]

[**35A   Right of partial rejection**

(1) If the buyer—

(a) has the right to reject the goods by reason of a breach on the part of the seller that affects some or all of them, but

(b) accepts some of the goods, including, where there are any goods unaffected by the breach, all such goods,

he does not by accepting them lose his right to reject the rest.

(2) In the case of a buyer having the right to reject an instalment of goods, subsection (1) above applies as if references to the goods were references to the goods comprised in the instalment.

(3) For the purposes of subsection (1) above, goods are affected by a breach if by reason of the breach they are not in conformity with the contract.

(4) This section applies unless a contrary intention appears in, or is to be implied from, the contract.]

36   Buyer not bound to return rejected goods

[(1)] Unless otherwise agreed, where goods are delivered to the buyer, and he refuses to accept them, having the right to do so, he is not bound to return them to the seller, but it is sufficient if he intimates to the seller that he refuses to accept them.

[(2) This section does not apply to a contract to which Chapter 2 of Part 1 of the Consumer Rights Act 2015 applies (but see the provision made about such contracts in section 20 of that Act).]

37   Buyer's liability for not taking delivery of goods

(1) When the seller is ready and willing to deliver the goods, and requests the buyer to take delivery, and the buyer does not within a reasonable time after such request take delivery of the goods, he is liable to the seller for any loss occasioned by his neglect or refusal to take delivery, and also for a reasonable charge for the care and custody of the goods.

(2) Nothing in this section affects the rights of the seller where the neglect or refusal of the buyer to take delivery amounts to a repudiation of the contract.

PART V RIGHTS OF UNPAID SELLER AGAINST THE GOODS

Preliminary

38   Unpaid seller defined

(1) The seller of goods is an unpaid seller within the meaning of this Act—

(a) when the whole of the price has not been paid or tendered;

(b) when a bill of exchange or other negotiable instrument has been received as conditional payment, and the condition on which it was received has not been fulfilled by reason of the dishonour of the instrument or otherwise.

(2) In this Part of this Act 'seller' includes any person who is in the position of a seller, as, for instance, an agent of the seller to whom the bill of lading has been indorsed, or a consignor or agent who has himself paid (or is directly responsible for) the price.

39   Unpaid seller's rights

(1) Subject to this and any other Act, notwithstanding that the property in the goods may have passed to the buyer, the unpaid seller of goods, as such, has by implication of law—

(a) a lien on the goods or right to retain them for the price while he is in possession of them;

(b) in the case of the insolvency of the buyer, a right of stopping the goods in transit after he has parted with the possession of them;

(c) a right of re-sale as limited by this Act.

(2) Where the property in goods has not passed to the buyer, the unpaid seller has (in addition to his other remedies) a right of withholding delivery similar to and coextensive with his rights of lien or retention and stoppage in transit where the property has passed to the buyer.

Unpaid seller's lien

41   Seller's lien

(1) Subject to this Act, the unpaid seller of goods who is in possession of them is entitled to retain possession of them until payment or tender of the price in the following cases:—
> (a) where the goods have been sold without any stipulation as to credit;
> (b) where the goods have been sold on credit but the term of credit has expired;
> (c) where the buyer becomes insolvent.

(2) The seller may exercise his lien or right of retention notwithstanding that he is in possession of the goods as agent or bailee or custodier for the buyer.

42   Part delivery

Where an unpaid seller has made part delivery of the goods, he may exercise his lien or right of retention on the remainder, unless such part delivery has been made under such circumstances as to show an agreement to waive the lien or right of retention.

43   Termination of lien

(1) The unpaid seller of goods loses his lien or right of retention in respect of them—
> (a) when he delivers the goods to a carrier or other bailee or custodier for the purpose of transmission to the buyer without reserving the right of disposal of the goods;
> (b) when the buyer or his agent lawfully obtains possession of the goods;
> (c) by waiver of the lien or right of retention.

(2) An unpaid seller of goods who has a lien or right of retention in respect of them does not lose his lien or right of retention by reason only that he has obtained judgment or decree for the price of the goods.

Stoppage in transit

44   Right of stoppage in transit

Subject to this Act, when the buyer of goods becomes insolvent the unpaid seller who has parted with the possession of the goods has the right of stopping them in transit, that is to say, he may resume possession of the goods as long as they are in course of transit, and may retain them until payment or tender of the price.

45   Duration of transit

(1) Goods are deemed to be in course of transit from the time when they are delivered to a carrier or other bailee or custodier for the purpose of transmission to the buyer, until the buyer or his agent in that behalf takes delivery of them from the carrier or other bailee or custodier.

(2) If the buyer or his agent in that behalf obtains delivery of the goods before their arrival at the appointed destination, the transit is at an end.

(3) If, after the arrival of the goods at the appointed destination, the carrier or other bailee or custodier acknowledges to the buyer or his agent that he holds the goods on his behalf and continues in possession of them as bailee or custodier for the buyer or his agent, the transit is at an end, and it is immaterial that a further destination for the goods may have been indicated by the buyer.

(4) If the goods are rejected by the buyer, and the carrier or other bailee or custodier continues in possession of them, the transit is not deemed to be at an end, even if the seller has refused to receive them back.

(5) When goods are delivered to a ship chartered by the buyer it is a question depending on the circumstances of the particular case whether they are in the possession of the master as a carrier or as agent to the buyer.

(6) Where the carrier or other bailee or custodier wrongfully refuses to deliver the goods to the buyer or his agent in that behalf, the transit is deemed to be at an end.

(7) Where part delivery of the goods has been made to the buyer or his agent in that behalf, the remainder of the goods may be stopped in transit, unless such part delivery has been made under such circumstances as to show an agreement to give up possession of the whole of the goods.

46 How stoppage in transit is effected

(1) The unpaid seller may exercise his right of stoppage in transit either by taking actual possession of the goods or by giving notice of his claim to the carrier or other bailee or custodier in whose possession the goods are.

(2) The notice may be given either to the person in actual possession of the goods or to his principal.

(3) If given to the principal, the notice is ineffective unless given at such time and under such circumstances that the principal, by the exercise of reasonable diligence, may communicate it to his servant or agent in time to prevent a delivery to the buyer.

(4) When notice of stoppage in transit is given by the seller to the carrier or other bailee or custodier in possession of the goods, he must re-deliver the goods to, or according to the directions of, the seller; and the expenses of the re-delivery must be borne by the seller.

Resale etc. by buyer

47 Effect of sub-sale etc. by buyer

(1) Subject to this Act, the unpaid seller's right of lien or retention or stoppage in transit is not affected by any sale or other disposition of the goods which the buyer may have made, unless the seller has assented to it.

(2) Where a document of title to goods has been lawfully transferred to any person as buyer or owner of the goods, and that person transfers the document to a person who takes it in good faith and for valuable consideration, then—

(a) if the last-mentioned transfer was by way of sale the unpaid seller's right of lien or retention or stoppage in transit is defeated; and

(b) if the last-mentioned transfer was made by way of pledge or other disposition for value, the unpaid seller's right of lien or retention of stoppage in transit can only be exercised subject to the rights of the transferee.

Rescission: and re-sale by seller

48 Rescission: and re-sale by seller

(1) Subject to this section, a contract of sale is not rescinded by the mere exercise by an unpaid seller of his right of lien or retention or stoppage in transit.

(2) Where an unpaid seller who has exercised his right of lien or retention or stoppage in transit re-sells the goods, the buyer acquires a good title to them as against the original buyer.

(3) Where the goods are of a perishable nature, or where the unpaid seller gives notice to the buyer of his intention to re-sell, and the buyer does not within a reasonable time pay or tender the price, the unpaid seller may re-sell the goods and recover from the original buyer damages for any loss occasioned by his breach of contract.

(4) Where the seller expressly reserves the right of re-sale in case the buyer should make default, and on the buyer making default re-sells the goods, the original contract of sale is rescinded but without prejudice to any claim the seller may have for damages.

PART VI ACTIONS FOR BREACH OF THE CONTRACT

Seller's remedies

49 Action for price

(1) Where, under a contract of sale, the property in the goods has passed to the buyer and he wrongfully neglects or refuses to pay for the goods according to the terms of the contract, the seller may maintain an action against him for the price of the goods.

50   Damages for non-acceptance

(1) Where the buyer wrongfully neglects or refuses to accept and pay for the goods, the seller may maintain an action against him for damages for non-acceptance.

(2) The measure of damages is the estimated loss directly and naturally resulting, in the ordinary course of events, from the buyer's breach of contract.

(3) Where there is an available market for the goods in question the measure of damages is prima facie to be ascertained by the difference between the contract price and the market or current price at the time or times when the goods ought to have been accepted or (if no time was fixed for acceptance) at the time of the refusal to accept.

Buyer's remedies

51   Damages for non-delivery

(1) Where the seller wrongfully neglects or refuses to deliver the goods to the buyer, the buyer may maintain an action against the seller for damages for non-delivery.

(2) The measure of damages is the estimated loss directly and naturally resulting, in the ordinary course of events, from the seller's breach of contract.

(3) Where there is an available market for the goods in question the measure of damages is prima facie to be ascertained by the difference between the contract price and the market or current price of the goods at the time or times when they ought to have been delivered or (if no time was fixed) at the time of the refusal to deliver.

[(4) This section does not apply to a contract to which Chapter 2 of Part 1 of the Consumer Rights Act 2015 applies (but see the provision made about such contracts in section 19 of that Act).]

52   Specific performance

(1) In any action for breach of contract to deliver specific or ascertained goods the court may, if it thinks fit, on the plaintiff's application, by its judgment or decree direct that the contract shall be performed specifically, without giving the defendant the option of retaining the goods on payment of damages.

(3) The judgment or decree may be unconditional, or on such terms and conditions as to damages, payment of the price and otherwise as seem just to the court.

[(5) This section does not apply to a contract to which Chapter 2 of Part 1 of the Consumer Rights Act 2015 applies (but see the provision made about such contracts in section 19 of that Act).]

53   Remedy for breach of warranty

(1) Where there is a breach of warranty by the seller, or where the buyer elects (or is compelled) to treat any breach of a condition on the part of the seller as a breach of warranty, the buyer is not by reason only of such breach of warranty entitled to reject the goods; but he may—

(a) set up against the seller the breach of warranty in diminution or extinction of the price, or

(b) maintain an action against the seller for damages for the breach of warranty.

(2) The measure of damages for breach of warranty is the estimated loss directly and naturally resulting, in the ordinary course of events, from the breach of warranty.

(3) In the case of breach of warranty of quality such loss is prima facie the difference between the value of the goods at the time of delivery to the buyer and the value they would have had if they had fulfilled the warranty.

(4) The fact that the buyer has set up the breach of warranty in diminution or extinction of the price does not prevent him from maintaining an action for the same breach of warranty if he has suffered further damage.

[(4A) This section does not apply to a contract to which Chapter 2 of Part 1 of the Consumer Rights Act 2015 applies (but see the provision made about such contracts in section 19 of that Act).]

[(5) This section does not apply to Scotland.]

Interest etc.

54   Interest, etc.

[(1)] Nothing in this Act affects the right of the buyer or the seller to recover interest or special damages in any case where by law interest or special damages may be recoverable, or to recover money paid where the consideration for the payment of it has failed.

[(2) This section does not apply to a contract to which Chapter 2 of Part 1 of the Consumer Rights Act 2015 applies (but see the provision made about such contracts in section 19 of that Act).]

PART VII SUPPLEMENTARY

55   Exclusion of implied terms

(1) Where a right, duty or liability would arise under a contract of sale of goods by implication of law, it may (subject to the Unfair Contract Terms Act 1977) be negatived or varied by express agreement, or by the course of dealing between the parties, or by such usage as binds both parties to the contract.

[(1A) Subsection (1) does not apply to a contract to which Chapter 2 of Part 1 of the Consumer Rights Act 2015 applies (but see the provision made about such contracts in section 31 of that Act).]

(2) An express [term] does not negative a [term] implied by this Act unless inconsistent with it.

(3) Paragraph 11 of Schedule 1 below applies in relation to a contract made on or after 18 May 1973 and before 1 February 1978, and paragraph 12 in relation to one made before 18 May 1973.

56   Conflict of laws

Paragraph 13 of Schedule 1 below applies in relation to a contract made on or after 18 May 1973 and before 1 February 1978, so as to make provision about conflict of laws in relation to such a contract.

57   Auction sales

(1) Where goods are put up for sale by auction in lots, each lot is prima facie deemed to be the subject of a separate contract of sale.

(2) A sale by auction is complete when the auctioneer announces its completion by the fall of the hammer, or in other customary manner; and until the announcement is made any bidder may retract his bid.

(3) A sale by auction may be notified to be subject to a reserve or upset price, and a right to bid may also be reserved expressly by or on behalf of the seller.

(4) Where a sale by auction is not notified to be subject to a right to bid by or on behalf of the seller, it is not lawful for the seller to bid himself or to employ any person to bid at the sale, or for the auctioneer knowingly to take any bid from the seller or any such person.

(5) A sale contravening subsection (4) above may be treated as fraudulent by the buyer.

(6) Where, in respect of a sale by auction, a right to bid is expressly reserved (but not otherwise) the seller or any one person on his behalf may bid at the auction.

59   Reasonable time a question of fact

Where a reference is made in this Act to a reasonable time the question what is a reasonable time is a question of fact.

60   Rights etc. enforceable by action

Where a right, duty or liability is declared by this Act, it may (unless otherwise provided by this Act) be enforced by action.

61   Interpretation

(1) In this Act, unless the context or subject matter otherwise requires,—

'action' includes counterclaim and set-off, and in Scotland condescendence and claim and compensation;

['bulk' means a mass or collection of goods of the same kind which—

    (a) is contained in a defined space or area; and

    (b) is such that any goods in the bulk are interchangeable with any other goods therein of the same number or quantity;]

'business' includes a profession and the activities of any government department (including a Northern Ireland department) or local or public authority;

'buyer' means a person who buys or agrees to buy goods;

'contract of sale' includes an agreement to sell as well as a sale;

'credit-broker' means a person acting in the course of a business of credit brokerage carried on by him, that is a business of effecting introductions of individuals desiring to obtain credit—

    (a) to persons carrying on any business so far as it relates to the provision of credit, or

    (b) to other persons engaged in credit brokerage;

'defendant' includes in Scotland defender, respondent, and claimant in a multiple poinding;

'delivery' means voluntary transfer of possession from one person to another; [except that in relation to sections 20A and 20B above it includes such appropriation of goods to the contract as results in property in the goods being transferred to the buyer;]

'document of title to goods' has the same meaning as it has in the Factors Acts;

'Factors Acts' means the Factors Act 1889, the Factors (Scotland) Act 1890, and any enactment amending or substituted for the same;

'fault' means wrongful act or default;

'future goods' means goods to be manufactured or acquired by the seller after the making of the contract of sale;

'goods' includes all personal chattels other than things in action and money, and in Scotland all corporeal moveables except money; and in particular 'goods' includes emblements, industrial growing crops, and things attached to or forming part of the land which are agreed to be severed before sale or under the contract of sale; [and includes an undivided share in goods;]

'plaintiff' includes pursuer, complainer, claimant in a multiplepoinding and defendant or defender counter-claiming;

'property' means the general property in goods, and not merely a special property;

'sale' includes a bargain and sale as well as a sale and delivery;

'seller' means a person who sells or agrees to sell goods;

'specific goods' means goods identified and agreed on at the time a contract of sale is made; [and includes an undivided share, specified as a fraction or percentage, of goods identified and agreed on as aforesaid]

'warranty' (as regards England and Wales and Northern Ireland) means an agreement with reference to goods which are the subject of a contract of sale, but collateral to the main purpose of such contract, the breach of which gives rise to a claim for damages, but not to a right to reject the goods and treat the contract as repudiated.

(3) A thing is deemed to be done in good faith within the meaning of this Act when it is in fact done honestly, whether it is done negligently or not.

(4) A person is deemed to be insolvent within the meaning of this Act if he has either ceased to pay his debts in the ordinary course of business or he cannot pay his debts as they become due, [. . .]

(5) Goods are in a deliverable state within the meaning of this Act when they are in such a state that the buyer would under the contract be bound to take delivery of them.

(6) As regards the definition of 'business' in subsection (1) above, paragraph 14 of Schedule 1 below applies in relation to a contract made on or after 18 May 1973 and before 1 February 1978, and paragraph 15 in relation to one made before 18 May 1973.

62 Savings: rule of law etc.

(1) The rules in bankruptcy relating to contracts of sale apply to those contracts, notwithstanding anything in this Act.

(2) The rules of the common law, including the law merchant, except in so far as they are inconsistent with the provisions of [legislation including this Act and the Consumer Rights Act 2015],

and in particular the rules relating to the law of principal and agent and the effect of fraud, misrepresentation, duress or coercion, mistake, or other invalidating cause, apply to contracts for the sale of goods.

(3) Nothing in this Act or the Sale of Goods Act 1893 affects the enactments relating to bills of sale, or any enactment relating to the sale of goods which is not expressly repealed or amended by this Act or that.

(4) The provisions of this Act about contracts of sale do not apply to a transaction in the form of a contract of sale which is intended to operate by way of mortgage, pledge, charge, or other security.

Limitation Act 1980

(1980, c. 58)

PART I

1 Time limits under Part I subject to exclusion under Part II

(1) This Part of this Act gives the ordinary time limits for bringing actions of the various classes mentioned in the following provisions of this Part.

(2) The ordinary time limits given in this Part of this Act are subject to extension or exclusion in accordance with the provisions of Part II of this Act.

2 Time limit for actions founded on tort

An action founded on tort shall not be brought after the expiration of six years from the date on which the cause of action accrued.

3 Time limit in case of successive conversions and extinction of title of owner of converted goods

(1) Where any cause of action in respect of the conversion of a chattel has accrued to any person and, before he recovers possession of the chattel, a further conversion takes place, no action shall be brought in respect of the further conversion after the expiration of six years from the accrual of the cause of action in respect of the original conversion.

(2) Where any such cause of action has accrued to any person and the period prescribed for bringing that action has expired and he has not during that period recovered possession of the chattel, the title of that person to the chattel shall be extinguished.

4 Special time limit in case of theft

(1) The right of any person from whom a chattel is stolen to bring an action in respect of the theft shall not be subject to the time limits under sections 2 and 3(1) of this Act, but if his title to the chattel is extinguished under section 3(2) of this Act he may not bring an action in respect of a theft preceding the loss of his title, unless the theft in question preceded the conversion from which time began to run for the purposes of section 3(2).

(2) Subsection (1) above shall apply to any conversion related to the theft of a chattel as it applies to the theft of a chattel; and, except as provided below, every conversion following the theft of a chattel before the person from whom it is stolen recovers possession of it shall be regarded for the purposes of this section as related to the theft.

If any one purchases the stolen chattel in good faith neither the purchase nor any conversion following it shall be regarded as related to the theft.

(3) Any cause of action accruing in respect of the theft or any conversion related to the theft of a chattel to any person from whom the chattel is stolen shall be disregarded for the purpose of applying section 3(1) or (2) of this Act to his case.

(4) Where in any action brought in respect of the conversion of a chattel it is proved that the chattel was stolen from the plaintiff or anyone through whom he claims it shall be presumed that any conversion following the theft is related to the theft unless the contrary is shown.

(5) In this section 'theft' includes—

    (a) any conduct outside England and Wales which would be theft if committed in England and Wales; and

    [(b) obtaining any chattel (in England and Wales or elsewhere) by—

        (i) blackmail (within the meaning of section 21 of the Theft Act 1968), or

        (ii) fraud (within the meaning of the Fraud Act 2006);]

and references in this section to a chattel being 'stolen' shall be construed accordingly.

[4A   Time limit for actions for defamation or malicious falsehood

The time limit under section 2 of this Act shall not apply to an action for—

    (a) libel or slander, or

    (b) slander of title, slander of goods or other malicious falsehood,

but no such action shall be brought after the expiration of one year from the date on which the cause of action accrued.]

5   Time limit for actions founded on simple contract

An action founded on simple contract shall not be brought after the expiration of six years from the date on which the cause of action accrued.

6   Special time limit for actions in respect of certain loans

(1) Subject to subsection (3) below, section 5 of this Act shall not bar the right of action on a contract of loan to which this section applies.

(2) This section applies to any contract of loan which—

    (a) does not provide for repayment of the debt on or before a fixed or determinable date; and

    (b) does not effectively (whether or not it purports to do so) make the obligation to repay the debt conditional on a demand for repayment made by or on behalf of the creditor or on any other matter;

except where in connection with taking the loan the debtor enters into any collateral obligation to pay the amount of the debt or any part of it (as, for example, by delivering a promissory note as security for the debt) on terms which would exclude the application of this section to the contract of loan if they applied directly to repayment of the debt.

(3) Where a demand in writing for repayment of the debt under a contract of loan to which this section applies is made by or on behalf of the creditor (or, where there are joint creditors, by or on behalf of any one of them) section 5 of this Act shall thereupon apply as if the cause of action to recover the debt had accrued on the date on which the demand was made.

(4) In this section 'promissory note' has the same meaning as in the Bills of Exchange Act 1882.

8   Time limit for actions on a specialty

(1) An action upon a specialty shall not be brought after the expiration of twelve years from the date on which the cause of action accrued.

(2) Subsection (1) above shall not affect any action for which a shorter period of limitation is prescribed by any other provision of this Act.

9   Time limit for actions for sums recoverable by statute

(1) An action to recover any sum recoverable by virtue of any enactment shall not be brought after the expiration of six years from the date on which the cause of action accrued.

(2) Subsection (1) above shall not affect any action to which section 10 of this Act applies.

10   Special time limit for claiming contribution

(1) Where under section 1 of the Civil Liability (Contribution) Act 1978 any person becomes entitled to a right to recover contribution in respect of any damage from any other person, no action to recover contribution by virtue of that right shall be brought after the expiration of two years from the date on which that right accrued.

(2) For the purposes of this section the date on which a right to recover contribution in respect of any damage accrues to any person (referred to below in this section as 'the relevant date') shall be ascertained as provided in subsections (3) and (4) below.

(3) If the person in question is held liable in respect of that damage—

(a) by a judgment given in any civil proceedings; or

(b) by an award made on any arbitration;

the relevant date shall be the date on which the judgment is given, or the date of the award (as the case may be).

For the purposes of this subsection no account shall be taken of any judgment or award given or made on appeal in so far as it varies the amount of damages awarded against the person in question.

(4) If, in any case not within subsection (3) above, the person in question makes or agrees to make any payment to one or more persons in compensation for that damage (whether he admits any liability in respect of the damage or not), the relevant date shall be the earliest date on which the amount to be paid by him is agreed between him (or his representative) and the person (or each of the persons, as the case may be) to whom the payment is to be made.

(5) An action to recover contribution shall be one to which sections 28, 32[, 33A] and 35 of this Act apply, but otherwise Parts II and III of this Act (except sections 34, 37 and 38) shall not apply for the purposes of this section.

11 Special time limit for actions in respect of personal injuries

(1) This section applies to any action for damages for negligence, nuisance or breach of duty (whether the duty exists by virtue of a contract or of provision made by or under a statute or independently of any contract or any such provision) where the damages claimed by the plaintiff for the negligence, nuisance or breach of duty consist of or include damages in respect of personal injuries to the plaintiff or any other person.

[(1A) This section does not apply to any action brought for damages under section 3 of the Protection from Harassment Act 1997.]

(3) An action to which this section applies shall not be brought after the expiration of the period applicable in accordance with subsection (4) or (5) below.

(4) Except where subsection (5) below applies, the period applicable is three years from—

(a) the date on which the cause of action accrued; or

(b) the date of knowledge (if later) of the person injured.

(5) If the injured person dies before the expiration of the period mentioned in subsection (4) above, the period applicable as respects the cause of action surviving for the benefit of his estate by virtue of section 1 of the Law Reform (Miscellaneous Provisions) Act 1934 shall be three years from—

(a) the date of death; or

(b) the date of the personal representative's knowledge; whichever is the later.

[11A Actions in respect of defective products

(1) This section shall apply to an action for damages by virtue of any provision of Part I of the Consumer Protection Act 1987.

[(1A) This section does not apply to any action brought for damages under section 3 of the Protection from Harassment Act 1977.]

(2) None of the time limits given in the preceding provisions of this Act shall apply to an action to which this section applies.

(3) An action to which this section applies shall not be brought after the expiration of the period of ten years from the relevant time, within the meaning of section 4 of the said Act of 1987; and this subsection shall operate to extinguish a right of action and shall do so whether or not that right of action had accrued, or time under the following provisions of this Act had begun to run, at the end of the said period of ten years.

(4) Subject to subsection (5) below, an action to which this section applies in which the damages claimed by the plaintiff consist of or include damages in respect of personal injuries to the plaintiff or any other person or loss of or damage to any property, shall not be brought after the expiration of the period of three years from whichever is the later of—

(a) the date on which the cause of action accrued; and

(b) the date of knowledge of the injured person or, in the case of loss of or damage to property, the date of knowledge of the plaintiff or (if earlier) of any person in whom his cause of action was previously vested.

(5) If in a case where the damages claimed by the plaintiff consist of or include damages in respect of personal injuries to the plaintiff or any other person the injured person died before the expiration of the period mentioned in subsection (4) above, the subsection shall have effect as respects the cause of action surviving for the benefit of his estate by virtue of section I of the Law Reform (Miscellaneous Provisions) Act 1934 as if for the reference to that period there were substituted a reference to the period of three years from whichever is the later of—

(a) the date of death; and

(b) the date of the personal representative's knowledge.

(6) For the purposes of this section 'personal representative' includes any person who is or has been a personal representative of the deceased, including an executor who has not proved the will (whether or not he has renounced probate) but not anyone appointed only as a special personal representative in relation to settled land; and regard shall be had to any knowledge acquired by any such person while a personal representative or previously.

(7) If there is more than one personal representative and their dates of knowledge are different, subsection (5)(b) above shall be read as referring to the earliest of those dates.

(8) Expressions used in this section or section 14 of this Act and in Part I of the Consumer Protection Act 1987 have the same meanings in this section or that section as in that Part; and section 1(1) of that Act (Part I to be construed as enacted for the purpose of complying with the product liability Directive) shall apply for the purpose of construing this section and the following provisions of this Act so far as they relate to an action by virtue of any provision of that Part as it applies for the purpose of construing that Part.]

12   Special time limit for actions under Fatal Accidents legislation

(1) An action under the Fatal Accidents Act 1976 shall not be brought if the death occurred when the person injured could no longer maintain an action and recover damages in respect of the injury (whether because of a time limit in this Act or in any other Act, or for any other reason).

Where any such action by the injured person would have been barred by the time limit in section 11 [or 11A] of this Act, no account shall be taken of the possibility of that time limit being overridden under section 33 of this Act.

(2) None of the time limits given in the preceding provisions of this Act shall apply to an action under the Fatal Accidents Act 1976, but no such action shall be brought after the expiration of three years from—

(a) the date of death; or

(b) the date of knowledge of the person for whose benefit the action is brought;
whichever is the later.

(3) An action under the Fatal Accidents Act 1976 shall be one to which sections 28, 33[, 33A] and 35 of this Act apply, and the application to any such action of the time limit under subsection (2) above shall be subject to section 39; but otherwise Parts II and III of this Act shall not apply to any such action.

13   Operation of time limit under section 12 in relation to different dependants

(1) Where there is more than one person for whose benefit an action under the Fatal Accidents Act 1976 is brought, section 12(2)(b) of this Act shall be applied separately to each of them.

(2) Subject to subsection (3) below, if by virtue of subsection (1) above the action would be outside the time limit given by section 12(2) as regards one or more, but not all, of the persons for whose benefit it is brought, the court shall direct that any person as regards whom the action would be outside that limit shall be excluded from those for whom the action is brought.

(3) The court shall not give such a direction if it is shown that if the action were brought exclusively for the benefit of the person in question it would not be defeated by a defence of limitation

(whether in consequence of section 28 of this Act or an agreement between the parties not to raise the defence, or otherwise).

14   Definition of date of knowledge for purposes of sections 11 and 12

(1) [Subject to subsection (1A) below,] In sections 11 and 12 of this Act references to a person's date of knowledge are references to the date on which he first had knowledge of the following facts—

    (a) that the injury in question was significant; and

    (b) that the injury was attributable in whole or in part to the act or omission which is alleged to constitute negligence, nuisance or breach of duty; and

    (c) the identity of the defendant; and

    (d) if it is alleged that the act or omission was that of a person other than the defendant, the identity of that person and the additional facts supporting the bringing of an action against the defendant;

and knowledge that any acts or omissions did or did not, as a matter of law, involve negligence, nuisance or breach of duty is irrelevant.

[(1A) In section 11A of this Act and in section 12 of this Act so far as that section applies to an action by virtue of section 6(1)(a) of the Consumer Protection Act 1987 (death caused by defective product) references to a person's date of knowledge are references to the date on which he first had knowledge of the following facts—

    (a) such facts about the damage caused by the defect as would lead a reasonable person who had suffered such damage to consider it sufficiently serious to justify his instituting proceedings for damages against a defendant who did not dispute liability and was able to satisfy a judgment; and

    (b) that the damage was wholly or partly attributable to the facts and circumstances alleged to constitute the defect; and

    (c) the identity of the defendant;

but, in determining the date on which a person first had such knowledge there shall be disregarded both the extent (if any) of that person's knowledge on any date of whether particular facts or circumstances would or would not, as a matter of law, constitute a defect and, in a case relating to loss of or damage to property, any knowledge which that person had on a date on which he had no right of action by virtue of Part of I of that Act in respect of the loss or damage.]

(2) For the purposes of this section an injury is significant if the person whose date of knowledge is in question would reasonably have considered it sufficiently serious to justify his instituting proceedings for damages against a defendant who did not dispute liability and was able to satisfy a judgment.

(3) For the purposes of this section a person's knowledge includes knowledge which he might reasonably have been expected to acquire—

    (a) from facts observable or ascertainable by him; or

    (b) from facts ascertainable by him with the help of medical or other appropriate expert advice which it is reasonable for him to seek;

but a person shall not be fixed under this subsection with knowledge of a fact ascertainable only with the help of expert advice so long as he has taken all reasonable steps to obtain (and, where appropriate, to act on) that advice.

[14A   Special time limit for negligence actions where facts relevant to cause of action are not known at date of accrual

(1) This section applies to any action for damages for negligence, other than one to which section 11 of this Act applies, where the starting date for reckoning the period of limitation under subsection (4)(b) below falls after the date on which the cause of action accrued.

(2) Section 2 of this Act shall not apply to an action to which this section applies.

(3) An action to which this section applies shall not be brought after the expiration of the period applicable in accordance with subsection (4) below.

(4) That period is either—

    (a) six years from the date on which the cause of action accrued; or

    (b) three years from the starting date as defined by subsection (5) below, if that period expires later than the period mentioned in paragraph (a) above.

    (5) For the purposes of this section, the starting date for reckoning the period of limitation under subsection (4)(b) above is the earliest date on which the plaintiff or any person in whom the cause of action was vested before him first had both the knowledge required for bringing an action for damages in respect of the relevant damage and a right to bring such an action.

    (6) In subsection (5) above 'the knowledge required for bringing an action for damages in respect of the relevant damage' means knowledge both—

        (a) of the material facts about the damage in respect of which damages are claimed; and

        (b) of the other facts relevant to the current action mentioned in subsection (8) below.

    (7) For the purposes of subsection (6)(a) above, the material facts about the damage are such facts about the damage as would lead a reasonable person who had suffered such damage to consider it sufficiently serious to justify his instituting proceedings for damages against a defendant who did not dispute liability and was able to satisfy a judgment.

    (8) The other facts referred to in subsection (6)(b) above are—

        (a) that the damage was attributable in whole or in part to the act or omission which is alleged to constitute negligence; and

        (b) the identity of the defendant; and

        (c) if it is alleged that the act or omission was that of a person other than the defendant, the identity of that person and the additional facts supporting the bringing of an action against the defendant.

    (9) Knowledge that any acts or omissions did or did not, as a matter of law, involve negligence is irrelevant for the purposes of subsection (5) above.

    (10) For the purposes of this section a person's knowledge includes knowledge which he might reasonably have been expected to acquire—

        (a) from facts observable or ascertainable by him; or

        (b) from facts ascertainable by him with the help of appropriate expert advice which it is reasonable for him to seek;

but a person shall not be taken by virtue of this subsection to have knowledge of a fact ascertainable only with the help of expert advice so long as he has taken all reasonable steps to obtain (and, where appropriate, to act on) that advice.]

[14B   Overriding time limit for negligence actions not involving personal injuries

    (1) An action for damages for negligence, other than one to which section 11 of this Act applies, shall not be brought after the expiration of fifteen years from the date (or, if more than one, from the last of the dates) on which there occurred any act or omission—

        (a) which is alleged to constitute negligence; and

        (b) to which the damage in respect of which damages are claimed is alleged to be attributable (in whole or in part).

    (2) This section bars the right of action in a case to which subsection (1) above applies notwithstanding that—

        (a) the cause of action has not yet accrued; or

        (b) where section 14A of this Act applies to the action, the date which is for the purposes of that section the starting date for reckoning the period mentioned in subsection (4)(b) of that section has not yet occurred;

before the end of the period of limitation prescribed by this section.]

15   Time limit for actions to recover land

    (1) No action shall be brought by any person to recover any land after the expiration of twelve years from the date on which the right of action accrued to him or, if it first accrued to some person through whom he claims, to that person.

(2) Subject to the following provisions of this section, where—

    (a) the estate or interest claimed was an estate or interest in reversion or remainder or any other future estate or interest and the right of action to recover the land accrued on the date on which the estate or interest fell into possession by the determination of the preceding estate or interest; and

    (b) the person entitled to the preceding estate or interest (not being a term of years absolute) was not in possession of the land on that date;

no action shall be brought by the person entitled to the succeeding estate or interest after the expiration of twelve years from the date on which the right of action accrued to the person entitled to the preceding estate or interest or six years from the date on which the right of action accrued to the person entitled to the succeeding estate or interest, whichever period last expires.

(3) Subsection (2) above shall not apply to any estate or interest which falls into possession on the determination of an entailed interest and which might have been barred by the person entitled to the entailed interest.

(4) No person shall bring an action to recover any estate or interest in land under an assurance taking effect after the right of action to recover the land had accrued to the person by whom the assurance was made or some person through whom he claimed or some person entitled to a preceding estate or interest, unless the action is brought within the period during which the person by whom the assurance was made could have brought such an action.

(5) Where any person is entitled to any estate or interest in land in possession and, while so entitled, is also entitled to any future estate or interest in that land, and his right to recover the estate or interest in possession is barred under this Act, no action shall be brought by that person, or by any person claiming through him, in respect of the future estate or interest, unless in the meantime possession of the land has been recovered by a person entitled to an intermediate estate or interest.

(6) Part I of Schedule 1 to this Act contains provisions for determining the date of accrual of rights of action to recover land in the cases there mentioned.

(7) Part II of that Schedule contains provisions modifying the provisions of this section in their application to actions brought by, or by a person claiming through, the Crown or any spiritual or eleemosynary corporation sole.

16 Time limit for redemption actions

When a mortgagee of land has been in possession of any of the mortgaged land for a period of twelve years, no action to redeem the land of which the mortgagee has been so in possession shall be brought after the end of that period by the mortgagor or any person claiming through him.

17 Extinction of title to land after expiration of time limit

Subject to—

    (a) section 18 of this Act; [. . .]

at the expiration of the period prescribed by this Act for any person to bring an action to recover land (including a redemption action) the title of that person to the land shall be extinguished.

18 Settled land and land held on trust

(1) Subject to section 21(1) and (2) of this Act, the provisions of this Act shall apply to equitable interests in land, [. . .] as they apply to legal estates. Accordingly a right of action to recover the land shall, for the purposes of this Act but not otherwise, be treated as accruing to a person entitled in possession to such an equitable interest in the like manner and circumstances, and on the same date, as it would accrue if his interest were a legal estate in the land (and any relevant provision of Part I of Schedule 1 to this Act shall apply in any such case accordingly).

(2) Where the period prescribed by this Act has expired for the bringing of an action to recover land by a tenant for life or a statutory owner of settled land—

    (a) his legal estate shall not be extinguished if and so long as the right of action to recover the land of any person entitled to a beneficial interest in the land either has not accrued or has not been barred by this Act; and

(b) the legal estate shall accordingly remain vested in the tenant for life or statutory owner and shall devolve in accordance with the Settled Land Act 1925;

but if and when every such right of action has been barred by this Act, his legal estate shall be extinguished.

(3) Where any land is held upon trust [. . .] and the period prescribed by this Act has expired for the bringing of an action to recover the land by the trustees, the estate of the trustees shall not be extinguished if and so long as the right of action to recover the land of any person entitled to a beneficial interest in the land [. . .] either has not accrued or has not been barred by this Act; but if and when every such right of action has been so barred the estate of the trustees shall be extinguished.

(4) Where—

(a) any settled land is vested in a statutory owner; or

(b) any land is held upon trust [. . .];

an action to recover the land may be brought by the statutory owner or trustees on behalf of any person entitled to a beneficial interest in possession in the land [. . .] whose right of action has not been barred by this Act, notwithstanding that the right of action of the statutory owner or trustees would apart from this provision have been barred by this Act.

19   Time limit for actions to recover rent

No action shall be brought, [and the power conferred by section 72(1) of the Tribunals, Courts and Enforcement Act 2007 shall not be exercisable], to recover arrears of rent, or damages in respect of arrears of rent, after the expiration of six years from the date on which the arrears became due.

[19A   Actions for breach of commonhold duty

An action in respect of a right or duty of a kind referred to in section 37(1) of the Commonhold and Leasehold Reform Act 2002 (enforcement) shall not be brought after the expiration of six years from the date on which the cause of action accrued.]

20   Time limit for actions to recover money secured by a mortgage or charge or to recover proceeds of the sale of land

(1) No action shall be brought to recover—

(a) any principal sum of money secured by a mortgage or other charge on property (whether real or personal); or

(b) proceeds of the sale of land;

after the expiration of twelve years from the date on which the right to receive the money accrued.

(2) No foreclosure action in respect of mortgaged personal property shall be brought after the expiration of twelve years from the date on which the right to foreclose accrued.

But if the mortgagee was in possession of the mortgaged property after that date, the right to foreclose on the property which was in his possession shall not be treated as having accrued for the purposes of this subsection until the date on which his possession discontinued.

(3) The right to receive any principal sum of money secured by a mortgage or other charge and the right to foreclose on the property subject to the mortgage or charge shall not be treated as accruing so long as that property comprises any future interest or any life insurance policy which has not matured or been determined.

(4) Nothing in this section shall apply to a foreclosure action in respect of mortgaged land, but the provisions of this Act relating to actions to recover land shall apply to such an action.

(5) Subject to subsections (6) and (7) below, no action to recover arrears of interest payable in respect of any sum of money secured by a mortgage or other charge or payable in respect of proceeds of the sale of land, or to recover damages in respect of such arrears shall be brought after the expiration of six years from the date on which the interest became due.

(6) Where—

(a) a prior mortgagee or other incumbrancer has been in possession of the property charged; and

(b) an action is brought within one year of the discontinuance of that possession by the subsequent incumbrancer;

the subsequent incumbrancer may recover by that action all the arrears of interest which fell due during the period of possession by the prior incumbrancer or damages in respect of those arrears, notwithstanding that the period exceeded six years.

(7) Where—

(a) the property subject to the mortgage or charge comprises any future interest or life insurance policy; and

(b) it is a term of the mortgage or charge that arrears of interest shall be treated as part of the principal sum of money secured by the mortgage or charge;

interest shall not be treated as becoming due before the right to recover the principal sum of money has accrued or is treated as having accrued.

21   Time limit for actions in respect of trust property

(1) No period of limitation prescribed by this Act shall apply to an action by a beneficiary under a trust, being an action—

(a) in respect of any fraud or fraudulent breach of trust to which the trustee was a party or privy; or

(b) to recover from the trustee trust property or the proceeds of trust property in the possession of the trustee, or previously received by the trustee and converted to his use.

(2) Where a trustee who is also a beneficiary under the trust receives or retains trust property or its proceeds as his share on a distribution of trust property under the trust, his liability in any action brought by virtue of subsection (1)(b) above to recover that property or its proceeds after the expiration of the period of limitation prescribed by this Act for bringing an action to recover trust property shall be limited to the excess over his proper share.

This subsection only applies if the trustee acted honestly and reasonably in making the distribution.

(3) Subject to the preceding provisions of this section, an action by a beneficiary to recover trust property or in respect of any breach of trust, not being an action for which a period of limitation is prescribed by any other provision of this Act, shall not be brought after the expiration of six years from the date on which the right of action accrued. For the purposes of this subsection, the right of action shall not be treated as having accrued to any beneficiary entitled to a future interest in the trust property until the interest fell into possession.

(4) No beneficiary as against whom there would be a good defence under this Act shall derive any greater or other benefit from a judgment or order obtained by any other beneficiary than he could have obtained if he had brought the action and this Act had been pleaded in defence.

22   Time limit for actions claiming personal estate of a deceased person

Subject to section 21(1) and (2) of this Act—

(a) no action in respect of any claim to the personal estate of a deceased person or to any share or interest in any such estate (whether under a will or on intestacy) shall be brought after the expiration of twelve years from the date on which the right to receive the share or interest accrued; and

(b) no action to recover arrears of interest in respect of any legacy, or damages in respect of such arrears, shall be brought after the expiration of six years from the date on which the interest became due.

23   Time limit in respect of actions for an account

An action for an account shall not be brought after the expiration of any time limit under this Act which is applicable to the claim which is the basis of the duty to account.

24   Time limit for actions to enforce judgments

(1) An action shall not be brought upon any judgment after the expiration of six years from the date on which the judgment became enforceable.

(2) No arrears of interest in respect of any judgment debt shall be recovered after the expiration of six years from the date on which the interest became due.

26   Administration to date back to death

For the purposes of the provisions of this Act relating to actions for the recovery of land and advowsons an administrator of the estate of a deceased person shall be treated as claiming as if there had been no interval of time between the death of the deceased person and the grant of the letters of administration.

[27A   Actions for recovery of property obtained through unlawful conduct etc.

(1) None of the time limits given in the preceding provisions of this Act applies to any proceedings under Chapter 2 of Part 5 of the Proceeds of Crime Act 2002 (civil recovery of proceeds of unlawful conduct).

(2) Proceedings under that Chapter for a recovery order in respect of any recoverable property shall not be brought after the expiration of the period of [20 years] from the date on which the [relevant person's] cause of action accrued.

(3) Proceedings under that Chapter are brought when—

    (a)   a claim form is issued, or

    [(aa) an application is made for a property freezing order, or]

    (b)   an application is made for an interim receiving order,

whichever is the [earliest].

(4) The [relevant person's] cause of action accrues in respect of any recoverable property—

    (a) in the case of proceedings for a recovery order in respect of property obtained through unlawful conduct, when the property is so obtained,

    (b) in the case of proceedings for a recovery order in respect of any other recoverable property, when the property obtained through unlawful conduct which it represents is so obtained.

(5) If—

    (a) a person would (but for the preceding provisions of this Act) have a cause of action in respect of the conversion of a chattel, and

    (b) proceedings are started under that Chapter for a recovery order in respect of the chattel,

section 3(2) of this Act does not prevent his asserting on an application under section 281 of that Act that the property belongs to him, or the court making a declaration in his favour under that section.

(6) If the court makes such a declaration, his title to the chattel is to be treated as not having been extinguished by section 3(2) of this Act.

(7) Expressions used in this section and Part 5 of that Act have the same meaning in this section as in that Part.]

    [(8) In this section 'relevant person' means—

    (a) the National Crime Agency,

    (b) the Director of Public Prosecutions,

    (c) the Director of Revenue and Customs Prosecutions, or

    (d) the Director of the Serious Fraud Office.]

[27AB   Actions to prohibit dealing with property subject to an external request

(1) None of the time limits given in the preceding provisions of this Act applies to any proceedings under Part 4A of the Proceeds of Crime Act 2002 (External Requests and Orders) Order 2005 (giving effect to external request by means of civil proceedings).

(2) Proceedings under that Part for a prohibition order in respect of relevant property shall not be brought after the expiration of the period of 20 years from the date on which the relevant person's cause of action accrued.

(3) Proceedings under that Part are brought when an application is made for a prohibition order.

(4) The relevant person's cause of action accrues in respect of relevant property when the property is obtained (or when it is believed to have been obtained) as a result of or in connection with criminal conduct.

(5) In this section—

(a) "criminal conduct" is to be construed in accordance with section 447(8) of the Act,

(b) expressions used in this section and Part 4A of the Proceeds of Crime Act 2002 (External Requests and Orders) Order 2005 have the same meaning in this section as in that Part.

(6) In this section "relevant person" means—

(a) the National Crime Agency,

(b) the Director of Public Prosecutions,

(c) the Director of Revenue and Customs Prosecutions, or

(d) the Director of the Serious Fraud Office.]

[27B   Actions for recovery of property for purposes of an external order

(1) None of the time limits given in the preceding provisions of this Act applies to any proceedings under Chapter 2 of Part 5 of the Proceeds of Crime Act 2002 (External Requests and Orders) Order 2005 (civil proceedings for the realisation of property to give effect to an external order).

(2) Proceedings under that Chapter for a recovery order in respect of any recoverable property shall not be brought after the expiration of the period of [20 years] from the date on which the [relevant person's] cause of action accrued.

(3) Proceedings under that Chapter are brought when—

(a) a claim form is issued, or

(b) an application is made for a property freezing order, or

(c) an application is made for an interim receiving order,

whichever is earliest.

[(3A) If, before an event mentioned in subsection (3) occurs, an application is made for a prohibition order under Part 4A of the Order, the proceedings under Chapter 2 of Part 5 of the Order are to be treated as having been brought when that application is made.]

(4) The [relevant person's] cause of action accrues in respect of any recoverable property—

(a) in the case of proceedings for a recovery order in respect of property obtained, or believed to have been obtained, as a result of or in connection with criminal conduct, when the property is so obtained,

(b) in the case of proceedings for a recovery order in respect of any other recoverable property, when the property obtained, or believed to have been obtained, as a result of or in connection with criminal conduct which it represents is so obtained.

(5) If—

(a) a person would (but for the preceding provisions of this Act) have a cause of action in respect of the conversion of a chattel, and

(b) proceedings are started under that Chapter for a recovery order in respect of the chattel,

section 3(2) of this Act does not prevent his asserting on an application under article 192 of that Order that the property belongs to him, or the court making a declaration in his favour under that article.

(6) If the court makes such a declaration, his title to the chattel is to be treated as not having been extinguished by section 3(2) of this Act.

(7) In this section—

(a) 'criminal conduct' is to be construed in accordance with section 447(8) of the Proceeds of Crime Act 2002, and

(b) expressions used in this section which are also used in Part 5 of the Proceeds of Crime Act 2002 (External Requests and Orders) Order 2005 have the same meaning in this section as in that Part.]

[(8) In this section 'relevant person' means—

(a) the National Crime Agency,

(b) the Director of Public Prosecutions,

(c) the Director of Revenue and Customs Prosecutions, or

(d) the Director of the Serious Fraud Office.]

[27C Actions for exploitation proceeds orders

(1) None of the time limits given in the preceding provisions of this Act applies to proceedings under Part 7 of the Coroners and Justice Act 2009 (criminal memoirs etc) for an exploitation proceeds order.

(2) Proceedings under that Part for such an order are not to be brought after the expiration of 6 years from the date on which the enforcement authority's cause of action accrued.

(3) Proceedings under that Part for such an order are brought when an application is made for the order.

(4) Where exploitation proceeds have been obtained by a person from a relevant offence, an enforcement authority's cause of action under that Part in respect of those proceeds accrues when the enforcement authority has actual knowledge that the proceeds have been obtained.

(5) Expressions used in this section and that Part have the same meaning in this section as in that Part.]

PART II

28 Extension of limitation period in case of disability

(1) Subject to the following provisions of this section, if on the date when any right of action accrued for which a period of limitation is prescribed by this Act, the person to whom it accrued was under a disability, the action may be brought at any time before the expiration of six years from the date when he ceased to be under a disability or died (whichever first occurred) notwithstanding that the period of limitation has expired.

(2) This section shall not affect any case where the right of action first accrued to some person (not under a disability) through whom the person under a disability claims.

(3) When a right of action which has accrued to a person under a disability accrues, on the death of that person while still under a disability, to another person under a disability, no further extension of time shall be allowed by reason of the disability of the second person.

[(4A) If the action is one to which section 4A of this Act applies, subsection (1) above shall have effect—

    (a) in the case of an action for libel or slander, as if for the words from 'at any time' to 'occurred)' there were substituted the words 'by him at any time before the expiration of one year from the date on which he ceased to be under a disability'; and

    (b) in the case of an action for slander of title, slander of goods or other malicious falsehood, as if for the words 'six years' there were substituted the words 'one year'.]

(5) If the action is one to which section 10 of this Act applies, subsection (1) above shall have effect as if for the words 'six years' there were substituted the words 'two years'.

(6) If the action is one to which section 11 or 12(2) of this Act applies, subsection (1) above shall have effect as if for the words 'six years' there were substituted the words 'three years'.

[(7) If the action is one to which section 11A of this Act applies or one by virtue of section 6(1)(a) of the Consumer Protection Act 1987 (death caused by defective product), subsection (1) above—

    (a) shall not apply to the time limit prescribed by subsection (3) of the said section 11A or to that time limit as applied by virtue of section 12(1) of this Act; and

    (b) in relation to any other time limit prescribed by this Act shall have effect as if for the words 'six years' there were substituted the words 'three years'.]

[28A Extension for cases where the limitation period is the period under section 14A(4)(b)

(1) Subject to subsection (2) below, if in the case of any action for which a period of limitation is prescribed by section 14A of this Act—

    (a) the period applicable in accordance with subsection (4) of that section is the period mentioned in paragraph (b) of that subsection;

(b) on the date which is for the purposes of that section the starting date for reckoning that period the person by reference to whose knowledge that date fell to be determined under subsection (5) of that section was under a disability; and

(c) section 28 of this Act does not apply to the action;

the action may be brought at any time before the expiration of three years from the date when he ceased to be under a disability or died (whichever first occurred) notwithstanding that the period mentioned above has expired.

(2) An action may not be brought by virtue of subsection (1) above after the end of the period of limitation prescribed by section 14B of this Act.]

29   Fresh accrual of action on acknowledgment or part payment

(5) Subject to subsection (6) below, where any right of action has accrued to recover—

(a) any debt or other liquidated pecuniary claim; or

(b) any claim to the personal estate of a deceased person or to any share or interest in any such estate;

and the person liable or accountable for the claim acknowledges the claim or makes any payment in respect of it the right shall be treated as having accrued on and not before the date of the acknowledgment or payment.

(6) A payment of a part of the rent or interest due at any time shall not extend the period for claiming the remainder then due, but any payment of interest shall be treated as a payment in respect of the principal debt.

(7) Subject to subsection (6) above, a current period of limitation may be repeatedly extended under this section by further acknowledgments or payments, but a right of action, once barred by this Act shall not be revived by any subsequent acknowledgment or payment.

30   Formal provisions as to acknowledgments and part payments

(1) To be effective for the purposes of section 29 of this Act, an acknowledgment must be in writing and signed by the person making it.

(2) For the purposes of section 29, any acknowledgment or payment—

(a) may be made by the agent of the person by whom it is required to be made under that section; and

(b) shall be made to the person, or to an agent of the person, whose title or claim is being acknowledged or, as the case may be, in respect of whose claim the payment is being made.

31   Effect of acknowledgment or part payment on persons other than the maker or recipient

(6) An acknowledgment of any debt or other liquidated pecuniary claim shall bind the acknowledgor and his successors but not any other person.

(7) A payment made in respect of any debt or other liquidated pecuniary claim shall bind all persons liable in respect of the debt or claim.

(8) An acknowledgment by one of several personal representatives of any claim to the personal estate of a deceased person or to any share or interest in any such estate, or a payment by one of several personal representatives in respect of any such claim, shall bind the estate of the deceased person.

(9) In this section 'successor', in relation to any mortgagee or person liable in respect of any debt or claim, means his personal representatives and any other person on whom the rights under the mortgage or, as the case may be, the liability in respect of the debt or claim devolve (whether on death or bankruptcy or the disposition of property or the determination of a limited estate or interest in settled property or otherwise).

32   Postponement of limitation period in case of fraud, concealment or mistake

(1) Subject to [subsections (3) and (4A)] below, where in the case of any action for which a period of limitation is prescribed by this Act, either—

(a) the action is based upon the fraud of the defendant; or

(b) any fact relevant to the plaintiff's right of action has been deliberately concealed from him by the defendant; or

(c) the action is for relief from the consequences of a mistake;

the period of limitation shall not begin to run until the plaintiff has discovered the fraud, conceal-ment or mistake (as the case may be) or could with reasonable diligence have discovered it.

References in this subsection to the defendant include references to the defendant's agent and to any person through whom the defendant claims and his agent.

(2) For the purposes of subsection (1) above, deliberate commission of a breach of duty in cir-cumstances in which it is unlikely to be discovered for some time amounts to deliberate conceal-ment of the facts involved in that breach of duty.

(3) Nothing in this section shall enable any action—

(a) to recover, or recover the value of, any property; or

(b) to enforce any charge against, or set aside any transaction affecting, any property;

to be brought against the purchaser of the property or any person claiming through him in any case where the property has been purchased for valuable consideration by an innocent third party since the fraud or concealment or (as the case may be) the transaction in which the mistake was made took place.

(4) A purchaser is an innocent third party for the purposes of this section—

(a) in the case of fraud or concealment of any fact relevant to the plaintiff's right of action, if he was not a party to the fraud or (as the case may be) to the concealment of that fact and did not at the time of the purchase know or have reason to believe that the fraud or concealment had taken place; and

(b) in the case of mistake, if he did not at the time of the purchase know or have reason to believe that the mistake had been made.

[(4A) Subsection (1) above shall not apply in relation to the time limit prescribed by section 11A(3) of this Act or in relation to that time limit as applied by virtue of section 12(1) of this Act.]

[(5) Sections 14A and 14B of this Act shall not apply to any action to which subsection (1)(b) above applies (and accordingly the period of limitation referred to in that subsection, in any case to which either of those sections would otherwise apply, is the period applicable under section 23 of this Act).]

[32A Discretionary exclusion of time limit for actions for defamation or malicious falsehood

(1) If it appears to the court that it would be equitable to allow an action to proceed having regard to the degree to which—

(a) the operation of section 4A of this Act prejudices the plaintiff or any person whom he represents, and

(b) any decision of the court under this subsection would prejudice the defendant or any person whom he represents,

the court may direct that that section shall not apply to the action or shall not apply to any specified cause of action to which the action relates.

(2) In acting under this section the court shall have regard to all the circumstances of the case and in particular to—

(a) the length of, and the reasons for, the delay on the part of the plaintiff;

(b) where the reason or one of the reasons for the delay was that all or any of the facts rele-vant to the cause of action did not become known to the plaintiff until after the end of the period mentioned in section 4A—

(i) the date on which any such facts did become known to him, and

(ii) the extent to which he acted promptly and reasonably once he knew whether or not the facts in question might be capable of giving rise to an action; and

(c) the extent to which, having regard to the delay, relevant evidence is likely—

(i) to be unavailable, or

(ii) to be less cogent than if the action had been brought within the period mentioned in section 4A.

(3) In the case of an action for slander of title, slander of goods or other malicious falsehood brought by a personal representative—

(a) the references in subsection (2) above to the plaintiff shall be construed as including the deceased person to whom the cause of action accrued and any previous personal representative of that person; and

(b) nothing in section 28(3) of this Act shall be construed as affecting the court's discretion under this section.

(4) In this section 'the court' means the court in which the action has been brought.]

33   Discretionary exclusion of time limit for actions in respect of personal injuries or death

(1) If it appears to the court that it would be equitable to allow an action to proceed having regard to the degree to which—

(a) the provisions of section 11 [or 11A] or 12 of this Act prejudice the plaintiff or any person whom he represents; and

(b) any decision of the court under this subsection would prejudice the defendant or any person whom he represents;

the court may direct that those provisions shall not apply to the action, or shall not apply to any specified cause of action to which the action relates.

[(1A) The court shall not under this section disapply—

(a) subsection (3) of section 11A; or

(b) where the damages claimed by the plaintiff are confined to damages for loss of or damage to any property, any other provision in its application to an action by virtue of Part I of the Consumer Protection Act 1987.]

(2) The court shall not under this section disapply section 12(1) except where the reason why the person injured could no longer maintain an action was because of the time limit in section 11 [or subsection (4) of section 11A].

If, for example, the person injured could at his death no longer maintain an action under the Fatal Accidents Act 1976 because of the time limit in Article 29 in Schedule 1 to the Carriage by Air Act 1961, the court has no power to direct that section 12(1) shall not apply.

(3) In acting under this section the court shall have regard to all the circumstances of the case and in particular to—

(a) the length of, and the reasons for, the delay on the part of the plaintiff;

(b) the extent to which, having regard to the delay, the evidence adduced or likely to be adduced by the plaintiff or the defendant is or is likely to be less cogent than if the action had been brought within the time allowed by section 11[, by section 11A] or (as the case may be) by section 12;

(c) the conduct of the defendant after the cause of action arose, including the extent (if any) to which he responded to requests reasonably made by the plaintiff for information or inspection for the purpose of ascertaining facts which were or might be relevant to the plaintiff's cause of action against the defendant;

(d) the duration of any disability of the plaintiff arising after the date of the accrual of the cause of action;

(e) the extent to which the plaintiff acted promptly and reasonably once he knew whether or not the act or omission of the defendant, to which the injury was attributable, might be capable at that time of giving rise to an action for damages;

(f) the steps, if any, taken by the plaintiff to obtain medical, legal or other expert advice and the nature of any such advice he may have received.

(4) In a case where the person injured died when, because of section 11 [or subsection (4) of section 11A], he could no longer maintain an action and recover damages in respect of the injury, the court shall have regard in particular to the length of, and the reasons for, the delay on the part of the deceased.

(5) In a case under subsection (4) above, or any other case where the time limit, or one of the time limits, depends on the date of knowledge of a person other than the plaintiff, subsection (3) above shall have effect with appropriate modifications, and shall have effect in particular as if

references to the plaintiff included references to any person whose date of knowledge is or was relevant in determining a time limit.

(6) A direction by the court disapplying the provisions of section 12(1) shall operate to disapply the provisions to the same effect in section 1(1) of the Fatal Accidents Act 1976.

(7) In this section 'the court' means the court in which the action has been brought.

(8) References in this section to section 11 or 11A include references to that section as extended by any of the [provisions of this Part of this Act other than this section] or by any provision of Part III of this Act.

[33A   Extension of time limits because of mediation in certain cross-border disputes

(1) In this section—

(a) "Mediation Directive" means Directive 2008/52/EC of the European Parliament and of the Council of 21 May 2008 on certain aspects of mediation in civil and commercial matters,

(b) "mediation" has the meaning given by article 3(a) of the Mediation Directive,

(c) "mediator" has the meaning given by article 3(b) of the Mediation Directive, and

(d) "relevant dispute" means a dispute to which article 8(1) of the Mediation Directive applies (certain cross-border disputes).

(2) Subsection (3) applies where—

(a) a time limit under this Act relates to the subject of the whole or part of a relevant dispute,

(b) a mediation in relation to the relevant dispute starts before the time limit expires, and

(c) if not extended by this section, the time limit would expire before the mediation ends or less than eight weeks after it ends.

(3) For the purposes of initiating judicial proceedings or arbitration, the time limit expires instead at the end of eight weeks after the mediation ends (subject to subsection (4)).

(4) If a time limit has been extended by this section, subsections (2) and (3) apply to the extended time limit as they apply to a time limit mentioned in subsection (2)(a).

(5) Where more than one time limit applies in relation to a relevant dispute, the extension by subsection (3) of one of those time limits does not affect the others.

(6) For the purposes of this section, a mediation starts on the date of the agreement to mediate that is entered into by the parties and the mediator.

(7) For the purposes of this section, a mediation ends on the date of the first of these to occur—

(a) the parties reach an agreement in resolution of the relevant dispute,

(b) a party completes the notification of the other parties that it has withdrawn from the mediation,

(c) a party to whom a qualifying request is made fails to give a response reaching the other parties within 14 days of the request,

(d) after the parties are notified that the mediator's appointment has ended (by death, resignation or otherwise), they fail to agree within 14 days to seek to appoint a replacement mediator,

(e) the mediation otherwise comes to an end pursuant to the terms of the agreement to mediate.

(8) For the purpose of subsection (7), a qualifying request is a request by a party that another (A) confirm to all parties that A is continuing with the mediation.

(9) In the case of any relevant dispute, references in this section to a mediation are references to the mediation so far as it relates to that dispute, and references to a party are to be read accordingly.]

35   New claims in pending actions; rules of court

(1) For the purposes of this Act, any new claim made in the course of any action shall be deemed to be a separate action and to have been commenced—

(a) in the case of a new claim made in or by way of third party proceedings, on the date on which those proceedings were commenced; and

(b) in the case of any other new claim, on the same date as the original action.

(2) In this section a new claim means any claim by way of set-off or counterclaim, and any claim involving either—

(a) the addition or substitution of a new cause of action; or

(b) the addition or substitution of a new party;

and 'third party proceedings' means any proceedings brought in the course of any action by any party to the action against a person not previously a party to the action, other than proceedings brought by joining any such person as defendant to any claim already made in the original action by the party bringing the proceedings.

(3) Except as provided by section 33 of this Act or by rules of court, neither the High Court nor [the county court] shall allow a new claim within subsection (1) (b) above, other than an original set-off or counterclaim, to be made in the course of any action after the expiry of any time limit under this Act which would affect a new action to enforce that claim.

For the purposes of this subsection, a claim is an original set-off or an original counterclaim if it is a claim made by way of set-off or (as the case may be) by way of counterclaim by a party who has not previously made any claim in the action.

(4) Rules of court may provide for allowing a new claim to which subsection (3) above applies to be made as there mentioned, but only if the conditions specified in subsection (5) below are satisfied, and subject to any further restrictions the rules may impose.

(5) The conditions referred to in subsection (4) above are the following—

(a) in the case of a claim involving a new cause of action, if the new cause of action arises out of the same facts or substantially the same facts as are already in issue on any claim previously made in the original action; and

(b) in the case of a claim involving a new party, if the addition or substitution of the new party is necessary for the determination of the original action.

(6) The addition or substitution of a new party shall not be regarded for the purposes of subsection (5)(b) above as necessary for the determination of the original action unless either—

(a) the new party is substituted for a party whose name was given in any claim made in the original action in mistake for the new party's name; or

(b) any claim already made in the original action cannot be maintained by or against an existing party unless the new party is joined or substituted as plaintiff or defendant in that action.

(7) Subject to subsection (4) above, rules of court may provide for allowing a party to any action to claim relief in a new capacity in respect of a new cause of action notwithstanding that he had no title to make that claim at the date of the commencement of the action.

This subsection shall not be taken as prejudicing the power of rules of court to provide for allowing a party to claim relief in a new capacity without adding or substituting a new cause of action.

(8) Subsections (3) to (7) above shall apply in relation to a new claim made in the course of third party proceedings as if those proceedings were the original action, and subject to such other modifications as may be prescribed by rules of court in any case or class of case.

PART III

36 Equitable jurisdiction and remedies

(1) The following time limits under this Act, that is to say—

(a)   the time limit under section 2 for actions founded on tort;

[(aa) the time limit under section 4A for actions for libel or slander;]

(b)   the time limit under section 5 for actions founded on simple contract;

(c)   the time limit under section 7 for actions to enforce awards where the submission is not by an instrument under seal;

(d)   the time limit under section 8 for actions on a specialty;

(e)   the time limit under section 9 for actions to recover a sum recoverable by virtue of any enactment; and

(f)   the time limit under section 24 for actions to enforce a judgment;

shall not apply to any claim for specific performance of a contract or for an injunction or for other equitable relief, except in so far as any such time limit may be applied by the court by analogy in like manner as the corresponding time limit under any enactment repealed by the Limitation Act 1939 was applied before 1st July 1940.

(2) Nothing in this Act shall affect any equitable jurisdiction to refuse relief on the ground of acquiescence or otherwise.

37   Application to the Crown and the Duke of Cornwall

(1) Except as otherwise expressly provided in this Act, and without prejudice to section 39, this Act shall apply to proceedings by or against the Crown in like manner as it applies to proceedings between subjects.

38   Interpretation

(1) In this Act, unless the context otherwise requires— . . .

'personal injuries' includes any disease and any impairment of a person's physical or mental condition, and 'injury' and cognate expressions shall be construed accordingly; . . .

(2) For the purposes of this Act a person shall be treated as under a disability while he is an infant, or [lacks capacity (within the meaning of the mental capacity Act 2005) to conduct legal proceedings].

(3) For the purposes of subsection (2) above a person is of unsound mind if he is a person who, by reason of mental disorder [is incapable of managing and administering his property and affairs; and in this section 'mental disorder' has the same meaning as in the Mental Health Act 1983].

[(11) References in this Act to an action do not include any method of recovery of a sum recoverable under—

(a) Part 3 of the Social Security Administration Act 1992,

(b) section 127(c) of the Social Security Contributions and Benefits Act 1992, or

(c) Part 1 of the Tax Credits Act 2002, other than a proceeding in a court of law.]

39   Saving for other limitation enactments

This Act shall not apply to any action or arbitration for which a period of limitation is prescribed by or under any other enactment (whether passed before or after the passing of this Act) or to any action or arbitration to which the Crown is a party and for which, if it were between subjects, a period of limitation would be prescribed by or under any such other enactment.

[Senior Courts Act 1981]

(1981, c. 54)

32   Orders for interim payment

(1) As regards proceedings pending in the High Court, provision may be made by rules of court for enabling the court, in such circumstances as may be prescribed, to make an order requiring a party to the proceedings to make an interim payment of such amount as may be specified in the order, with provision for the payment to be made to such other party to the proceedings as may be so specified or, if the order so provides, by paying it into court.

(2) Any rules of court which make provision in accordance with subsection (1) may include provision for enabling a party to any proceedings who, in pursuance of such an order, has made an interim payment to recover the whole or part of the amount of the payment in such circumstances, and from such other party to the proceedings, as may be determined in accordance with the rules.

(3) Any rules made by virtue of this section may include such incidental, supplementary and consequential provisions as the rule-making authority may consider necessary or expedient.

(4) Nothing in this section shall be construed as affecting the exercise of any power relating to costs, including any power to make rules of court relating to costs.

(5) In this section 'interim payment', in relation to a party to any proceedings, means a payment on account of any damages, debt or other sum (excluding any costs) which that party may be held liable to pay to or for the benefit of another party to the proceedings if a final judgment or order of the court in the proceedings is given or made in favour of that other party.

[32A   Orders for provisional damages for personal injuries

(1) This section applies to an action for damages for personal injuries in which there is proved or admitted to be a chance that at some definite or indefinite time in the future the injured person will, as a result of the act or omission which gave rise to the cause of action, develop some serious disease or suffer some serious deterioration in his physical or mental condition.

(2) Subject to subsection (4) below, as regards any action for damages to which this section applies in which a judgment is given in the High Court, provision may be made by rules of court for enabling the court, in such circumstances as may be prescribed, to award the injured person—

   (a) damages assessed on the assumption that the injured person will not develop the disease or suffer the deterioration in his condition; and

   (b) further damages at a future date if he develops the disease or suffers the deterioration.

(3) Any rules made by virtue of this section may include such incidental, supplementary and consequential provisions as the rule-making authority may consider necessary or expedient.

(4) Nothing in this section shall be construed—

   (a) as affecting the exercise of any power relating to costs, including any power to make rules of court relating to costs; or

   (b) as prejudicing any duty of the court under any enactment or rule of law to reduce or limit the total damages which would have been recoverable apart from any such duty.]

35   Provisions supplementary to ss. 33 and 34

(5) In sections [32A,] 33 and 34 and this section— . . .

'personal injuries' includes any disease and any impairment of a person's physical or mental condition.

[35A   Powers of High Court to award interest on debts and damages

(1) Subject to rules of court, in proceedings (whenever instituted) before the High Court for the recovery of a debt or damages there may be included in any sum for which judgment is given simple interest, at such rate as the court thinks fit or as rules of court may provide, on all or any part of the debt or damages in respect of which judgment is given, or payment is made before judgment, for all or any part of the period between the date when the cause of action arose and—

   (a) in the case of any sum paid before judgment, the date of the payment; and

   (b) in the case of the sum for which judgment is given, the date of the judgment.

(2) In relation to a judgment given for damages for personal injuries or death which exceed £200 subsection (1) shall have effect—

   (a) with the substitution of 'shall be included' for 'may be included'; and

   (b) with the addition of 'unless the court is satisfied that there are special reasons to the contrary' after 'given', where first occurring.

(3) Subject to rules of court, where—

   (a) there are proceedings (whenever instituted) before the High Court for the recovery of a debt; and

   (b) the defendant pays the whole debt to the plaintiff (otherwise than in pursuance of a judgment in the proceedings),

the defendant shall be liable to pay the plaintiff simple interest at such rate as the court thinks fit or as rules of court may provide on all or any part of the debt for all or any part of the period between the date when the cause of action arose and the date of the payment.

(4) Interest in respect of a debt shall not be awarded under this section for a period during which, for whatever reason, interest on the debt already runs.

(5) Without prejudice to the generality of section 84, rules of court may provide for a rate of interest by reference to the rate specified in section 17 of the Judgments Act 1838 as that section has effect from time to time or by reference to a rate for which any other enactment provides.

(6) Interest under this section may be calculated at different rates in respect of different periods.

(7) In this section 'plaintiff' means the person seeking the debt or damages and 'defendant' means the person from whom the plaintiff seeks the debt or damages and 'personal injuries' includes any disease and any impairment of a person's physical or mental condition.]

49   Concurrent administration of law and equity

(1) Subject to the provisions of this or any other Act, every court exercising jurisdiction in England and Wales in any civil cause or matter shall continue to administer law and equity on the basis that, wherever there is any conflict or variance between the rules of equity and the rules of the common law with reference to the same matter, the rules of equity shall prevail.

50   Power to award damages as well as, or in substitution for, injunction or specific performance

Where the Court of Appeal or the High Court has jurisdiction to entertain an application for an injunction or specific performance, it may award damages in addition to, or in substitution for, an injunction or specific performance.

69   Trial by jury

(1) Where, on the application of any party to an action to be tried in the Queen's Bench Division, the court is satisfied that there is in issue—

    (a) a charge of fraud against that party; or

    (b) a claim in respect of [. . .] malicious prosecution or false imprisonment; or

    (c) any question or issue of a kind prescribed for the purposes of this paragraph,

the action shall be tried with a jury, unless the court is of opinion that the trial requires any prolonged examination of documents or accounts or any scientific or local investigation which cannot conveniently be made with a jury [or unless the court is of opinion that the trial will involve section 6 proceedings].

Administration of Justice Act 1982

(1982, c. 53)

1   Abolition of right to damages for loss of expectation of life

(1) In an action under the law of England and Wales or the law of Northern Ireland for damages for personal injuries—

    (a) no damages shall be recoverable in respect of any loss of expectation of life caused to the injured person by the injuries; but

    (b) if the injured person's expectation of life has been reduced by the injuries, the court, in assessing damages in respect of pain and suffering caused by the injuries, shall take account of any suffering caused or likely to be caused to him by awareness that his expectation of life has been so reduced.

(2) The reference in subsection (1)(a) above to damages in respect of loss of expectation of life does not include damages in respect of loss of income.

2   Abolition of actions for loss of services, etc.

No person shall be liable in tort under the law of England and Wales or the law of Northern Ireland—

    (a) to a husband on the ground only of having deprived him of the services or society of his wife;

(b) to a parent (or person standing in the place of a parent) on the ground only of his having deprived him of the services of a child; or

(c) on the ground only—

    (i) of having deprived another of the services of his menial servant;

    (ii) of having deprived another of the services of his female servant by raping or seducing her; or

    (iii) of enticement of a servant or harbouring a servant.

5 Maintenance at public expense to be taken into account in assessment of damages

In an action under the law of England and Wales or the law of Northern Ireland for damages for personal injuries (including any such action arising out of a contract) any saving to the injured person which is attributable to his maintenance wholly or partly at public expense in a hospital, nursing home or other institution shall be set off against any income lost by him as a result of his injuries.

Civil Aviation Act 1982

(1982, c. 16)

[38A Noise control schemes

(1) An aerodrome operator may establish and maintain a scheme (referred to in this section and sections 38B and 38C below as a 'noise control scheme') for the purpose of avoiding, limiting or mitigating the effect of noise connected with the taking off or landing of aircraft at the aerodrome.]

[38C Breaches of noise control schemes

(6) An aerodrome operator which receives penalties under a noise control scheme shall make payments equal to the amount of those penalties for purposes which appear to it to be likely to be of benefit to persons who live in the area in which the aerodrome is situated.]

76 Liability of aircraft in respect of trespass, nuisance and surface damage

(1) No action shall lie in respect of trespass or in respect of nuisance, by reason only of the flight of an aircraft over any property at a height above the ground which, having regard to wind, weather and all the circumstances of the case is reasonable, or the ordinary incidents of such flight, so long as the provisions of any Air Navigation Order and of any orders under section 62 above have been duly complied with [. . .].

(2) Subject to subsection (3) below, where material loss or damage is caused to any person or property on land or water by, or by a person in, or an article, animal or person falling from, an aircraft while in flight, taking off or landing, then unless the loss or damage was caused or contributed to by the negligence of the person by whom it was suffered, damages in respect of the loss or damage shall be recoverable without proof of negligence or intention or other cause of action, as if the loss or damage had been caused by the wilful act, neglect, or default of the owner of the aircraft.

(3) Where material loss or damage is caused as aforesaid in circumstances in which—

(a) damages are recoverable in respect of the said loss or damage by virtue only of subsection (2) above, and

(b) a legal liability is created in some person other than the owner to pay damages in respect of the said loss or damage,

the owner shall be entitled to be indemnified by that other person against any claim in respect of the said loss or damage.

77 Nuisance caused by aircraft on aerodromes

(1) An Air Navigation Order may provide for regulating the conditions under which noise and vibration may be caused by aircraft on aerodromes and may provide that subsection (2) below shall apply to any aerodrome as respects which provision as to noise and vibration caused by aircraft is so made.

(2) No action shall lie in respect of nuisance by reason only of the noise and vibration caused by aircraft on an aerodrome to which this subsection applies by virtue of an Air Navigation Order, as long as the provisions of any such Order are duly complied with.

Forfeiture Act 1982

(1982, c. 34)

1 The 'forfeiture rule'

(1) In this Act, the 'forfeiture rule' means the rule of public policy which in certain circumstances precludes a person who has unlawfully killed another from acquiring a benefit in consequence of the killing . . .

2 Power to modify the rule

(1) Where a court determines that the forfeiture rule has precluded a person (in this section referred to as 'the offender') who has unlawfully killed another from acquiring any interest in property mentioned in subsection (4) below, the court may make an order under this section modifying the effect of that rule.

(2) The court shall not make an order under this section modifying the effect of the forfeiture rule in any case unless it is satisfied that, having regard to the conduct of the offender and of the deceased and to such other circumstances as appear to the court to be material, the justice of the case requires the effect of the rule to be so modified in that case.

(3) In any case where a person stands convicted of an offence of which unlawful killing is an element, the court shall not make an order under this section modifying the effect of the forfeiture rule in that case unless proceedings for the purpose are brought before the expiry of the period of three months beginning with his conviction.

(4) The interests in property referred to in subsection (1) above are—

(a) any beneficial interest in property which (apart from the forfeiture rule) the offender would have acquired—

  (i)   under the deceased's will (including, as respects Scotland, any writing having testamentary effect) or the law relating to intestacy or by way of ius relicti, ius relictae or legitim;

  (ii) on the nomination of the deceased in accordance with the provisions of any enactment;

  (iii) as a donatio mortis causa made by the deceased; or

  (iv) under a special destination (whether relating to heritable or moveable property); or

(b) any beneficial interest in property which (apart from the forfeiture rule) the offender would have acquired in consequence of the death of the deceased, being property which, before the death, was held on trust for any person.

(5) An order under this section may modify the effect of the forfeiture rule in respect of any interest in property to which the determination referred to in subsection (1) above relates and may do so in either or both of the following ways, that is—

(a) where there is more than one such interest, by excluding the application of the rule in respect of any (but not all) of those interests; and

(b) in the case of any such interest in property, by excluding the application of the rule in respect of part of the property.

(6) On the making of an order under this section, the forfeiture rule shall have effect for all purposes (including purposes relating to anything done before the order is made) subject to the modifications made by the order . . .

5 Exclusion of murderers

Nothing in this Act or in any order made under section 2 or referred to in section 3(1) of this Act [or in any decision made under section 4(1A) of this Act] shall affect the application of the forfeiture rule in the case of a person who stands convicted of murder.

Supply of Goods and Services Act 1982

(1982, c. 29)

PART I SUPPLY OF GOODS

Contracts for the transfer of property in goods

1 The contracts concerned

(1) In this Act [in its application to England and Wales and Northern Ireland 'relevant contract for the transfer of goods'] means a contract under which one person transfers or agrees to transfer to another the property in goods, other than an excepted contract[, and other than a contract to which Chapter 2 of Part 1 of the Consumer Rights Act 2015 applies.].

(2) For the purposes of this section an excepted contract means any of the following:—

(a) a contract of sale of goods;

(b) a hire-purchase agreement;

[. . .]

(d) a transfer or agreement to transfer which is made by deed and for which there is no consideration other than the presumed consideration imported by the deed;

(e) a contract intended to operate by way of mortgage, pledge, charge or other security.

(3) For the purposes of this Act [in its application to England and Wales and Northern Ireland] a contract is a [relevant contract for the transfer of goods] whether or not services are also provided or to be provided under the contract, and (subject to subsection (2) above) whatever is the nature of the consideration for the transfer or agreement to transfer.

2 Implied terms about title, etc.

(1) In a [relevant contract for the transfer of goods], other than one to which subsection (3) below applies, there is an implied condition on the part of the transferor that in the case of a transfer of the property in the goods he has a right to transfer the property and in the case of an agreement to transfer the property in the goods he will have such a right at the time when the property is to be transferred.

(2) In a [relevant contract for the transfer of goods], other than one to which subsection (3) below applies, there is also an implied warranty that—

(a) the goods are free, and will remain free until the time when the property is to be transferred, from any charge or encumbrance not disclosed or known to the transferee before the contract is made, and

(b) the transferee will enjoy quiet possession of the goods except so far as it may be disturbed by the owner or other person entitled to the benefit of any charge or encumbrance so disclosed or known.

(3) This subsection applies to a [relevant contract for the transfer of goods] in the case of which there appears from the contract or is to be inferred from its circumstances an intention that the transferor should transfer only such title as he or a third person may have.

(4) In a contract to which subsection (3) above applies there is an implied warranty that all charges or encumbrances known to the transferor and not known to the transferee have been disclosed to the transferee before the contract is made.

(5) In a contract to which subsection (3) above applies there is also an implied warranty that none of the following will disturb the transferee's quiet possession of the goods, namely—

(a) the transferor;

(b) in a case where the parties to the contract intend that the transferor should transfer only such title as a third person may have, that person;

(c) anyone claiming through or under the transferor or that third person otherwise than under a charge or encumbrance disclosed or known to the transferee before the contract is made.

3   Implied terms where transfer is by description

(1) This section applies where, under a [relevant contract for the transfer of goods], the transferor transfers or agrees to transfer the property in the goods by description.

(2) In such case there is an implied condition that the goods will correspond with the description.

(3) If the transferor transfers or agrees to transfer the property in the goods by sample as well as by description it is not sufficient that the bulk of the goods corresponds with the sample if the goods do not also correspond with the description.

(4) A contract is not prevented from falling within subsection (1) above by reason only that, being exposed for supply, the goods are selected by the transferee.

4   Implied terms about quality or fitness

(1) Except as provided by this section and section 5 below and subject to the provision of any other enactment, there is no implied condition or warranty about the quality or fitness for any particular purpose of goods supplied under a [relevant contract for the transfer of goods].

[(2) Where, under such a contract, the transferor transfers the property in goods in the course of a business, there is an implied condition that the goods supplied under the contract are of satisfactory quality.

(2A) For the purposes of this section and section 5 below, goods are of satisfactory quality if they meet the standard that a reasonable person would regard as satisfactory, taking account of any description of the goods, the price (if relevant) and all the other relevant circumstances.]

[(3) The condition implied by subsection (2) above does not extend to any matter making the quality of goods unsatisfactory—

(a) which is specifically drawn to the transferee's attention before the contract is made,

(b) where the transferee examines the goods before the contract is made, which that examination ought to reveal, or

(c) where the property in the goods is transferred by reference to a sample, which would have been apparent on a reasonable examination of the sample.]

(4) Subsection (5) below applies where, under a [relevant contract for the transfer of goods], the transferor transfers the property in goods in the course of a business and the transferee, expressly or by implication, makes known—

(a) to the transferor, or

(b) where the consideration or part of the consideration for the transfer is a sum payable by instalments and the goods were previously sold by a credit-broker to the transferor, to that credit-broker,

any particular purpose for which the goods are being acquired.

(5) In that case there is (subject to subsection (6) below) an implied condition that the goods supplied under the contract are reasonably fit for that purpose, whether or not that is a purpose for which such goods are commonly supplied.

(6) Subsection (5) above does not apply where the circumstances show that the transferee does not rely, or that it is unreasonable for him to rely, on the skill or judgment of the transferor or credit-broker.

(7) An implied condition or warranty about quality or fitness for a particular purpose may be annexed by usage to a [relevant contract for the transfer of goods].

(8) The preceding provisions of this section apply to a transfer by a person who in the course of a business is acting as agent for another as they apply to a transfer by a principal in the course of a business, except where that other is not transferring in the course of a business and either the transferee knows that fact or reasonable steps are taken to bring it to the transferee's notice before the contract concerned is made.

5 Implied terms where transfer is by sample

(1) This section applies where, under a [relevant contract for the transfer of goods], the transferor transfers or agrees to transfer the property in the goods by reference to a sample.

(2) In such a case there is an implied condition—

(a) that the bulk will correspond with the sample in quality; and

(b) that the transferee will have a reasonable opportunity of comparing the bulk with the sample; and

(c) that the goods will be free from any defect, making their quality unsatisfactory, which would not be apparent on reasonable examination of the sample.

(4) For the purposes of this section a transferor transfers or agrees to transfer the property in goods by reference to a sample where there is an express or implied term to that effect in the contract concerned.

[5A Modification of remedies for breach of statutory condition in non-consumer cases

(1) Where in the case of a [relevant contract for the transfer of goods]—

(a) the transferee would, apart from this subsection, have the right to treat the contract as repudiated by reason of a breach on the part of the transferor of a term implied by section 3, 4 or 5(2)(a) or (c) above, but

(b) the breach is so slight that it would be unreasonable for him to do so,

the breach is not to be treated as a breach of condition but may be treated as a breach of warranty.

(2) This section applies unless a contrary intention appears in, or is to be implied from, the contract.

(3) It is for the transferor to show that a breach fell within subsection (1)(b) above.]

Contracts for the hire of goods

6 The contracts concerned

(1) In this Act [in its application to England and Wales and Northern Ireland] a '[relevant contract for the hire of goods]' means a contract under which one person bails or agrees to bail goods to another by way of hire, other than [a hire-purchase agreement, and other than a contract to which Chapter 2 of Part 1 of the Consumer Rights Act 2015 applies].

(3) For the purposes of this Act [in its application to England and Wales and Northern Ireland] a contract is a [relevant contract for the hire of goods] whether or not services are also provided or to be provided under the contract, and [. . .] whatever is the nature of the consideration for the bailment or agreement to bail by way of hire.

7 Implied terms about right to transfer possession, etc.

(1) In a [relevant contract for the hire of goods] there is an implied condition on the part of the bailor that in the case of a bailment he has a right to transfer possession of the goods by way of hire for the period of the bailment and in the case of an agreement to bail he will have such a right at the time of the bailment.

(2) In a [relevant contract for the hire of goods] there is also an implied warranty that the bailee will enjoy quiet possession of the goods for the period of the bailment except so far as the possession may be disturbed by the owner or other person entitled to the benefit of any charge or encumbrance disclosed or known to the bailee before the contract is made.

(3) The preceding provisions of this section do not affect the right of the bailor to repossess the goods under an express or implied term of the contract.

8   Implied terms where hire is by description

(1) This section applies where, under a [relevant contract for the hire of goods], the bailor bails or agrees to bail the goods by description.

(2) In such a case there is an implied condition that the goods will correspond with the description.

(3) If under the contract the bailor bails or agrees to bail the goods by reference to a sample as well as a description it is not sufficient that the bulk of the goods corresponds with the sample if the goods do not also correspond with the description.

(4) A contract is not prevented from falling within subsection (1) above by reason only that, being exposed for supply, the goods are selected by the bailee.

9   Implied terms about quality or fitness

(1) Except as provided by this section and section 10 below and subject to the provisions of any other enactment, there is no implied condition or warranty about the quality or fitness for any particular purpose of goods bailed under a [relevant contract for the hire of goods].

[(2)   Where, under such a contract, the bailor bails goods in the course of a business, there is an implied condition that the goods supplied under the contract are of satisfactory quality.]

[(2A) For the purposes of this section and section 10 below, goods are of satisfactory quality if they meet the standard that a reasonable person would regard as satisfactory, taking account of any description of the goods, the consideration for the bailment (if relevant) and all the other relevant circumstances.]

[(3) The condition implied by subsection (2) above does not extend to any matter making the quality of goods unsatisfactory—
  (a) which is specifically drawn to the bailee's attention before the contract is made,
  (b) where the bailee examines the goods before the contract is made, which that examination ought to reveal, or
  (c) where the goods are bailed by reference to a sample, which would have been apparent on a reasonable examination of the sample.]

(4) Subsection (5) below applies where, under a [relevant contract for the hire of goods], the bailor bails goods in the course of a business and the bailee, expressly or by implication, makes known—
  (a) to the bailor in the course of negotiations conducted by him in relation to the making of the contract, or
  (b) to a credit-broker in the course of negotiations conducted by that broker in relation to goods sold by him to the bailor before forming the subject matter of the contract,
any particular purpose for which the goods are being bailed.

(5) In that case there is (subject to subsection (6) below) an implied condition that the goods supplied under the contract are reasonably fit for that purpose, whether or not that is a purpose for which such goods are commonly supplied.

(6) Subsection (5) above does not apply where the circumstances show that the bailee does not rely, or that it is unreasonable for him to rely, on the skill or judgment of the bailor or credit-broker.

(7) An implied condition or warranty about quality or fitness for a particular purpose may be annexed by usage to a [relevant contract for the hire of goods].

(8) The preceding provisions of this section apply to a bailment by a person who in the course of a business is acting as agent for another as they apply to a bailment by a principal in the course of a business, except where that other is not bailing in the course of a business and either the bailee knows that fact or reasonable steps are taken to bring it to the bailee's notice before the contract concerned is made.

10   Implied terms where hire is by sample

(1) This section applies where, under a [relevant contract for the hire of goods], the bailor bails or agrees to bail the goods by reference to a sample.

(2) In such a case there is an implied condition—

    (a) that the bulk will correspond with the sample in quality; and

    (b) that the bailee will have a reasonable opportunity of comparing the bulk with the sample; and

    (c) that the goods will be free from any defect, [making their quality unsatisfactory], which would not be apparent on reasonable examination of the sample.

(4) For the purposes of this section a bailor bails or agrees to bail goods by reference to a sample where there is an express or implied term to that effect in the contract concerned.

[10A Modification of remedies for breach of statutory condition in non-consumer cases

(1) Where in the case of a relevant contract for the hire of goods—

    (a) the bailee would, apart from this subsection, have the right to treat the contract as repudiated by reason of a breach on the part of the bailor of a term implied by section 8, 9 or 10(2)(a) or (c) above, but

    (b) the breach is so slight that it would be unreasonable for him to do so,

the breach is not to be treated as a breach of condition but may be treated as a breach of warranty.

(2) This section applies unless a contrary intention appears in, or is to be implied from, the contract.

(3) It is for the bailor to show that a breach fell within subsection (1)(b) above.]

Exclusion of implied terms, etc.

11 Exclusion of implied terms, etc.

(1) Where a right, duty or liability would arise under a [relevant contract for the transfer of goods] or a [relevant contract for the hire of goods] by implication of law, it may (subject to subsection (2) below and the 1977 Act) be negatived or varied by express agreement, or by the course of dealing between the parties, or by such usage as binds both parties to the contract.

(2) An express condition or warranty does not negative a condition or warranty implied by the preceding provisions of this Act unless inconsistent with it.

(3) Nothing in the preceding provisions of this Act prejudices the operation of any other enactment or any rule of law whereby any condition or warranty (other than one relating to quality or fitness) is to be implied in a [relevant contract for the transfer of goods] or a [relevant contract for the hire of goods].

PART II SUPPLY OF SERVICES

12 The contracts concerned

(1) In this Act a 'contract for the supply of a service' means, subject to subsection (2) below, a contract under which a person ('the supplier') agrees to carry out a service[, other than a contract to which Chapter 4 of Part 1 of the Consumer Rights Act 2015 applies.]

(2) For the purposes of this Act, a contract of service or apprenticeship is not a contract for the supply of a service.

(3) Subject to subsection (2) above, a contract is a contract for the supply of a service for the purposes of this Act whether or not goods are also—

    (a) transferred or to be transferred, or

    (b) bailed or to be bailed by way of hire,

under the contract, and whatever is the nature of the consideration for which the service is to be carried out.

(4) The Secretary of State may by order provide that one or more of sections 13 to 15 below shall not apply to services of a description specified in the order, and such an order may make different provision for different circumstances.

(5) The power to make an order under subsection (4) above shall be exercisable by statutory instrument subject to annulment in pursuance of a resolution of either House of Parliament.

13   Implied term about care and skill

In a contract for the supply of a service where the supplier is acting in the course of a business, there is an implied term that the supplier will carry out the service with reasonable care and skill.

14   Implied term about time of performance

(1) Where, under a contract for the supply of a service by a supplier acting in the course of a business, the time for the service to be carried out is not fixed by the contract, left to be fixed in a manner agreed by the contract or determined by the course of dealing between the parties, there is an implied term that the supplier will carry out the service within a reasonable time.

(2) What is a reasonable time is a question of fact.

15   Implied term about consideration

(1) Where, under a contract for the supply of a service, the consideration for the service is not determined by the contract, left to be determined in a manner agreed by the contract or determined by the course of dealing between the parties, there is an implied term that the party contracting with the supplier will pay a reasonable charge.

(2) What is a reasonable charge is a question of fact.

16   Exclusion of implied terms, etc.

(1) Where a right, duty or liability would arise under a contract for the supply of a service by virtue of this Part of this Act, it may (subject to subsection (2) below and the 1977 Act) be negatived or varied by express agreement, or by the course of dealing between the parties, or by such usage as binds both parties to the contract.

(2) An express term does not negative a term implied by this Part of this Act unless inconsistent with it.

(3) Nothing in this Part of this Act prejudices—
  (a) any rule of law which imposes on the supplier a duty stricter than that imposed by section 13 or 14 above; or
  (b) subject to paragraph (a) above, any rule of law whereby any term not inconsistent with this Part of this Act is to be implied in a contract for the supply of a service.

(4) This Part of this Act has effect subject to any other enactment which defines or restricts the rights, duties or liabilities arising in connection with a service of any description.

PART III SUPPLEMENTARY

18   Interpretation: general

(1) In the preceding provisions of this Act and this section—

'bailee', in relation to a [relevant contract for the hire of goods] means (depending on the context) a person to whom the goods are bailed under the contract, or a person to whom they are to be so bailed, or a person to whom the rights under the contract of either of those persons have passed;

'bailor', in relation to a [relevant contract for the hire of goods], means (depending on the context) a person who bails the goods under the contract, or a person who agrees to do so, or a person to whom the duties under the contract of either of those persons have passed;

'business' includes a profession and the activities of any government department or local or public authority;

'credit-broker' means a person acting in the course of a business of credit brokerage carried on by him;

'credit brokerage' means the effecting of introductions—
  (a) of individuals desiring to obtain credit to persons carrying on any business so far as it relates to the provision of credit; or

    (b) of individuals desiring to obtain goods on hire to persons carrying on a business which comprises or relates to the bailment [or as regards Scotland the hire] of goods under a [relevant contract for the hire of goods]; or

    (c) of individuals desiring to obtain credit, or to obtain goods on hire, to other credit-brokers;

'enactment' means any legislation (including subordinate legislation) of the United Kingdom or Northern Ireland;

'goods' [includes all personal chattels, other than things in action and money, and as regards Scotland all corporeal moveables; and in particular 'goods' includes] emblements, industrial growing crops, and things attached to or forming part of the land which are agreed to be severed before the transfer [bailment or hire] concerned or under the contract concerned [. . .];

'hire-purchase agreement' has the same meaning as in the 1974 Act;

'property', in relation to goods, means the general property in them and not merely a special property;

'transferee', in relation to a [relevant contract for the transfer of goods], means (depending on the context) a person to whom the property in the goods is transferred under the contract, or a person to whom the property is to be so transferred, or a person to whom the rights under the contract of either of those persons have passed;

'transferor', in relation to a [relevant contract for the transfer of goods], means (depending on the context) a person who transfers the property in the goods under the contract, or a person who agrees to do so, or a person to whom the duties under the contract of either of those persons have passed.

    (2) In subsection (1) above, in the definitions of bailee, bailor, transferee and transferor, a reference to rights or duties passing is to their passing by assignment, [assignation] operation of law or otherwise.

    [(3) For the purposes of this Act, the quality of goods includes their state and condition and the following (among others) are in appropriate cases aspects of the quality of goods—

    (a) fitness for all the purposes for which goods of the kind in question are commonly supplied,

    (b) appearance and finish,

    (c) freedom from minor defects,

    (d) safety, and

    (e) durability.]

19 Interpretation: references to Acts

In this Act—

'the 1973 Act' means the Supply of Goods (Implied Terms) Act 1973;

'the 1974 Act' means the Consumer Credit Act 1974;

'the 1977 Act' means the Unfair Contract Terms Act 1977; and

'the 1979 Act' means the Sale of Goods Act 1979.

Building Act 1984

(1984, c. 55)

38 Civil liability

    (1) Subject to this section—

    (a) breach of a duty imposed by building regulations, so far as it causes damage, is actionable, except in so far as the regulations provide otherwise, and

    (b) as regards such a duty, building regulations may provide for a prescribed defence to be available in an action for breach of that duty brought by virtue of this subsection.

    (4) In this section, 'damage' includes the death of, or injury to, any person (including any disease and any impairment of a person's physical or mental condition).

Occupiers' Liability Act 1984

(1984, c. 3)

1   Duty of occupier to persons other than his visitors

(1) The rules enacted by this section shall have effect, in place of the rules of the common law, to determine—

(a) whether any duty is owed by a person as occupier of premises to persons other than his visitors in respect of any risk of their suffering injury on the premises by reason of any danger due to the state of the premises or to things done or omitted to be done on them; and

(b) if so, what that duty is.

(2) For the purposes of this section, the persons who are to be treated respectively as an occupier of any premises (which, for those purposes, include any fixed or movable structure) and as his visitors are—

(a) any person who owes in relation to the premises the duty referred to in section 2 of the Occupiers' Liability Act 1957 (the common duty of care), and

(b) those who are his visitors for the purposes of that duty.

(3) An occupier of premises owes a duty to another (not being his visitor) in respect of any such risk as is referred to in subsection (1) above if—

(a) he is aware of the danger or has reasonable grounds to believe that it exists;

(b) he knows or has reasonable grounds to believe that the other is in the vicinity of the danger concerned or that he may come into the vicinity of the danger (in either case, whether the other has lawful authority for being in that vicinity or not); and

(c) the risk is one against which, in all the circumstances of the case, he may reasonably be expected to offer the other some protection.

(4) Where, by virtue of this section, an occupier of premises owes a duty to another in respect of such a risk, the duty is to take such care as is reasonable in all the circumstances of the case to see that he does not suffer injury on the premises by reason of the danger concerned.

(5) Any duty owed by virtue of this section in respect of a risk may, in an appropriate case, be discharged by taking such steps as are reasonable in all the circumstances of the case to give warning of the danger concerned or to discourage persons from incurring the risk.

(6) No duty is owed by virtue of this section to any person in respect of risks willingly accepted as his by that person (the question whether a risk was so accepted to be decided on the same principles as in other cases in which one person owes a duty of care to another).

[(6A) At any time when the right conferred by section 2(1) of the Countryside and Rights of Way Act 2000 is exercisable in relation to land which is access land for the purposes of Part I of that Act, an occupier of the land owes (subject to subsection (6C) below) no duty by virtue of this section to any person in respect of—

(a) a risk resulting from the existence of any natural feature of the landscape, or any river, stream, ditch or pond whether or not a natural feature, or

(b) a risk of that person suffering injury when passing over, under or through any wall, fence or gate, except by proper use of the gate or of a stile.

[(6AA) Where the land is coastal margin for the purposes of Part 1 of that Act (including any land treated as coastal margin by virtue of section 16 of that Act), subsection (6A) has effect as if for paragraphs (a) and (b) of that subsection there were substituted "a risk resulting from the existence of any physical feature (whether of the landscape or otherwise)".]

(6B) For the purposes of subsection (6A) above, any plant, shrub or tree, of whatever origin, is to be regarded as a natural feature of the landscape.

(6C) Subsection (6A) does not prevent an occupier from owing a duty by virtue of this section in respect of any risk where the danger concerned is due to anything done by the occupier—

(a) with the intention of creating that risk, or

(b) being reckless as to whether that risk is created.]

(7) No duty is owed by virtue of this section to persons using the highway, and this section does not affect any duty owed to such persons.

(8) Where a person owes a duty by virtue of this section, he does not, by reason of any breach of the duty, incur any liability in respect of any loss of or damage to property.

(9) In this section—

'highway' means any part of a highway other than a ferry or waterway;

'injury' means anything resulting in death or personal injury, including any disease and any impairment of physical or mental condition; and

'movable structure' includes any vessel, vehicle or aircraft.

[1A   Special considerations relating to access land

In determining whether any, and if so what, duty is owed by virtue of section 1 by an occupier of land at any time when the right conferred by section 2(1) of the Countryside and Rights of Way Act 2000 is exercisable in relation to the land, regard is to be had, in particular, to—

(a) the fact that the existence of that right ought not to place an undue burden (whether financial or otherwise) on the occupier,

(b) the importance of maintaining the character of the countryside, including features of historic, traditional or archaeological interest, and

(c) any relevant guidance given under section 20 of that Act.]

3   Application to Crown

Section 1 of this Act shall bind the Crown, but as regards the Crown's liability in tort shall not bind the Crown further than the Crown is made liable in tort by the Crown Proceedings Act 1947.

Police and Criminal Evidence Act 1984

(1984, c. 60)

17   Entry for purpose of arrest etc.

(1) Subject to the following provisions of this section, and without prejudice to any other enactment, a constable may enter and search any premises for the purpose—

(a) of executing—

(i)   a warrant of arrest issued in connection with or arising out of criminal proceedings; or

(ii)   a warrant of commitment issued under section 76 of the Magistrates' Courts Act 1980;

(b) of arresting a person for an [indictable] offence; . . .

(e) of saving life or limb or preventing serious damage to property.

(4) The power of search conferred by this section is only a power to search to the extent that is reasonably required for the purpose for which the power of entry is exercised.

(5) Subject to subsection (6) below, all the rules of common law under which a constable has power to enter premises without a warrant are hereby abolished.

(6) Nothing in subsection (5) above affects any power of entry to deal with or prevent a breach of the peace.

19   General power of seizure etc.

(1) The powers conferred by subsections (2), (3) and (4) below are exercisable by a constable who is lawfully on any premises.

(2) The constable may seize anything which is on the premises if he has reasonable grounds for believing—

    (a) that it has been obtained in consequence of the commission of an offence; and

    (b) that it is necessary to seize it in order to prevent it being concealed, lost, damaged, altered or destroyed.

22 Retention

(1) Subject to subsection (4) below, anything which has been seized by a constable or taken away by a constable following a requirement made by virtue of section 19 or 20 above may be retained so long as is necessary in all the circumstances.

(3) Nothing seized on the ground that it may be used—

    (a) to cause physical injury to any person;

    (b) to damage property;

    (c) to interfere with evidence; or

    (d) to assist in escape from police detention or lawful custody,

may be retained when the person from whom it was seized is no longer in police detention or the custody of a court or is in the custody of a court but has been released on bail.

[24   Arrest without warrant: constables

(1) A constable may arrest without a warrant—

    (a) anyone who is about to commit an offence;

    (b) anyone who is in the act of committing an offence;

    (c) anyone whom he has reasonable grounds for suspecting to be about to commit an offence;

    (d) anyone whom he has reasonable grounds for suspecting to be committing an offence.

(2) If a constable has reasonable grounds for suspecting that an offence has been committed, he may arrest without a warrant anyone whom he has reasonable grounds to suspect of being guilty of it.

(3) If an offence has been committed, a constable may arrest without a warrant—

    (a) anyone who is guilty of the offence;

    (b) anyone whom he has reasonable grounds for suspecting to be guilty of it.

(4) But the power of summary arrest conferred by subsection (1), (2) or (3) is exercisable only if the constable has reasonable grounds for believing that for any of the reasons mentioned in subsection (5) it is necessary to arrest the person in question.

(5) The reasons are—

    (a) to enable the name of the person in question to be ascertained (in the case where the constable does not know, and cannot readily ascertain, the person's name, or has reasonable grounds for doubting whether a name given by the person as his name is his real name);

    (b) correspondingly as regards the person's address;

    (c) to prevent the person in question—

        (i)   causing physical injury to himself or any other person;

        (ii) suffering physical injury;

        (iii) causing loss of or damage to property;

        (iv) committing an offence against public decency (subject to subsection (6)); or

        (v)   causing an unlawful obstruction of the highway;

    (d) to protect a child or other vulnerable person from the person in question;

    (e) to allow the prompt and effective investigation of the offence or of the conduct of the person in question;

    (f) to prevent any prosecution for the offence from being hindered by the disappearance of the person in question.

(6) Subsection (5)(c)(iv) applies only where members of the public going about their normal business cannot reasonably be expected to avoid the person in question.]

32   Search upon arrest

(1) A constable may search an arrested person, in any case where the person to be searched has been arrested at a place other than a police station, if the constable has reasonable grounds for believing that the arrested person may present a danger to himself or others.

34   Limitations on police detention

(1) A person arrested for an offence shall not be kept in police detention except in accordance with the provisions of this Part of this Act.

(2) Subject to subsection (3) below, if at any time a custody officer—

    (a) becomes aware, in relation to any person in police detention, that the grounds for the detention of that person have ceased to apply; and

    (b) is not aware of any other grounds on which the continued detention of that person could be justified under the provisions of this Part of this Act,

it shall be the duty of the custody officer, subject to subsection (4) below, to order his immediate release from custody.

55   Intimate searches

(2) An officer may not authorise an intimate search of a person for anything unless he has reasonable grounds for believing that it cannot be found without his being intimately searched.

62   Intimate samples

(1) [Subject to section 63B below] An intimate sample may be taken from a person in police detention only—

    (a) if a police officer of at least the rank of [inspector] authorises it to be taken; and

    (b) if the appropriate consent is given.

[(1A) An intimate sample may be taken from a person who is not in police detention but from whom, in the course of the investigation of an offence, two or more intimate samples suitable for the same means of analysis have been taken which have proved insufficient—

    (a) if a police officer of at least the rank of inspector authorises it to be taken; and

    (b) if the appropriate consent is given.]

65   Part V—supplementary

[(1)] In this Part of this Act— . . .

['intimate sample' means—

    (a) a sample of blood, semen or any other tissue fluid, urine or pubic hair;

    (b) a dental impression;

    (c) a swab taken from any part of a person's genitals (including pubic hair) or from a person's body orifice other than the mouth;]

Housing Act 1985

(1985, c. 68)

[118   The right to acquire

(1) A tenant of a registered social landlord who satisfies the conditions in section 16(1)(a) and (b) of the Housing Act 1996 has the right to acquire, that is to say, the right, in the circumstances and subject to the conditions and exceptions stated in the following provisions of this Part—

    (a) if the dwelling-house is a house and the landlord owns the freehold, to acquire the freehold of the dwelling-house;

    (b) if the landlord does not own the freehold or if the dwelling-house is a flat (whether or not the landlord owns the freehold), to be granted a lease of the dwelling-house.]

Landlord and Tenant Act 1985

(1985, c. 70)

8   Implied terms as to fitness for human habitation
   (1) In a contract to which this section applies for the letting of a house for human habitation there is implied, notwithstanding any stipulation to the contrary—
   (a) a condition that the house is fit for human habitation at the commencement of the tenancy, and
   (b) an undertaking that the house will be kept by the landlord fit for human habitation during the tenancy.

Insolvency Act 1986

(1986, c. 45)

238   Transactions at an undervalue (England and Wales)
   (1) This section applies in the case of a company where—
   [(a) the company enters administration,]
   (b) the company goes into liquidation;
and "the office-holder" means the administrator or the liquidator, as the case may be.
   (2) Where the company has at a relevant time (defined in section 240) entered into a transaction with any person at an undervalue, the office-holder may apply to the court for an order under this section.
   (3) Subject as follows, the court shall, on such an application, make such order as it thinks fit for restoring the position to what it would have been if the company had not entered into that transaction.
   (4) For the purposes of this section and section 241, a company enters into a transaction with a person at an undervalue if—
   (a) the company makes a gift to that person or otherwise enters into a transaction with that person on terms that provide for the company to receive no consideration, or
   (b) the company enters into a transaction with that person for a consideration the value of which, in money or money's worth, is significantly less than the value, in money or money's worth, of the consideration provided by the company.
   (5) The court shall not make an order under this section in respect of a transaction at an undervalue if it is satisfied—
   (a) that the company which entered into the transaction did so in good faith and for the purpose of carrying on its business, and
   (b) that at the time it did so there were reasonable grounds for believing that the transaction would benefit the company.

Latent Damage Act 1986

(1986, c. 37)

3   Accrual of cause of action to successive owners in respect of latent damage to property
   (1) Subject to the following provisions of this section, where—
   (a) a cause of action ('the original cause of action') has accrued to any person in respect of any negligence to which damage to any property in which he has an interest is attributable (in whole or in part); and

(b) another person acquires an interest in that property after the date on which the original cause of action accrued but before the material facts about the damage have become known to any person who, at the time when he first has knowledge of those facts, has any interest in the property;

a fresh cause of action in respect of that negligence shall accrue to that other person on the date on which he acquires his interest in the property.

(2) A cause of action accruing to any person by virtue of subsection (1) above—

(a) shall be treated as if based on breach of a duty of care at common law owed to the person to whom it accrues; and

(b) shall be treated for the purposes of section 14A of the 1980 Act (special time limit for negligence actions where facts relevant to cause of action are not known at date of accrual) as having accrued on the date on which the original cause of action accrued.

(3) Section 28 of the 1980 Act (extension of limitation period in case of disability) shall not apply in relation to any such cause of action.

(4) Subsection (1) above shall not apply in any case where the person acquiring an interest in the damaged property is either—

(a) a person in whom the original cause of action vests by operation of law; or

(b) a person in whom the interest in that property vests by virtue of any order made by a court under section 538 of the Companies Act 1985 (vesting of company property in liquidator).

[*The Companies Act 1985, s 538 has now been replaced by the Insolvency Act 1986, s 145.*]

(5) For the purposes of subsection (1)(b) above, the material facts about the damage are such facts about the damage as would lead a reasonable person who has an interest in the damaged property at the time when those facts become known to him to consider it sufficiently serious to justify his instituting proceedings for damages against a defendant who did not dispute liability and was able to satisfy a judgment.

(6) For the purposes of this section a person's knowledge includes knowledge which he might reasonably have been expected to acquire—

(a) from facts observable or ascertainable by him; or

(b) from facts ascertained by him with the help of appropriate expert advice which it is reasonable for him to seek;

but a person shall not be taken by virtue of this subsection to have knowledge of a fact ascertainable by him only with the help of expert advice so long as he has taken all reasonable steps to obtain (and, where appropriate, to act on) that advice.

(7) This section shall bind the Crown, but as regards the Crown's liability in tort shall not bind the Crown further than the Crown is made liable in tort by the Crown Proceedings Act 1947.

Consumer Protection Act 1987

(1987, c. 43)

PART I PRODUCT LIABILITY

1 Purpose and construction of Part I

(1) This Part shall have effect for the purpose of making such provision as is necessary in order to comply with the product liability Directive and shall be construed accordingly.

(2) In this Part, except in so far as the context otherwise requires—

'agricultural produce' means any produce of the soil, of stock-farming or of fisheries;

'dependant' and 'relative' have the same meaning as they have in, respectively, the Fatal Accidents Act 1976 and the [Damages (Scotland) Act 2011];

'producer', in relation to a product, means—

(a) the person who manufactured it;

(b) in the case of a substance which has not been manufactured but has been won or abstracted, the person who won or abstracted it;

(c) in the case of a product which has not been manufactured, won or abstracted but essential characteristics of which are attributable to an industrial or other process having been carried out (for example, in relation to agricultural produce), the person who carried out that process;

'product' means any goods or electricity and (subject to subsection (3) below) includes a product which is comprised in another product, whether by virtue of being a component part or raw material or otherwise; and

'the product liability Directive' means the Directive of the Council of the European Communities, dated 25th July 1985, (No. 85/374/EEC) on the approximation of the laws, regulations and administrative provisions of the member States concerning liability for defective products.

(3) For the purposes of this Part a person who supplies any product in which products are comprised, whether by virtue of being component parts or raw materials or otherwise, shall not be treated by reason only of his supply of that product as supplying any of the products so comprised.

2 Liability for defective products

(1) Subject to the following provisions of this Part, where any damage is caused wholly or partly by a defect in a product, every person to whom subsection (2) below applies shall be liable for the damage.

(2) This subsection applies to—

(a) the producer of the product;

(b) any person who, by putting his name on the product or using a trade mark or other distinguishing mark in relation to the product, has held himself out to be the producer of the product;

(c) any person who has imported the product into a member State from a place outside the member States in order, in the course of any business of his, to supply it to another.

(3) Subject as aforesaid, where any damage is caused wholly or partly by a defect in a product, any person who supplied the product (whether to the person who suffered the damage, to the producer of any product in which the product in question is comprised or to any other person) shall be liable for the damage if—

(a) the person who suffered the damage requests the supplier to identify one or more of the persons (whether still in existence or not) to whom subsection (2) above applies in relation to the product;

(b) that request is made within a reasonable period after the damage occurs and at a time when it is not reasonably practicable for the person making the request to identify all those persons; and

(c) the supplier fails, within a reasonable period after receiving the request, either to comply with the request or to identify the person who supplied the product to him.

(5) Where two or more persons are liable by virtue of this Part for the same damage, their liability shall be joint and several.

(6) This section shall be without prejudice to any liability arising otherwise than by virtue of this Part.

3 Meaning of 'defect'

(1) Subject to the following provisions of this section, there is a defect in a product for the purposes of this Part if the safety of the product is not such as persons generally are entitled to expect; and for those purposes 'safety', in relation to a product, shall include safety with respect to products comprised in that product and safety in the context of risks of damage to property, as well as in the context of risks of death or personal injury.

(2) In determining for the purposes of subsection (1) above what persons generally are entitled to expect in relation to a product all the circumstances shall be taken into account, including—

(a) the manner in which, and purposes for which, the product has been marketed, its get-up, the use of any mark in relation to the product and any instructions for, or warnings with respect to, doing or refraining from doing anything with or in relation to the product;

(b) what might reasonably be expected to be done with or in relation to the product; and

(c) the time when the product was supplied by its producer to another;

and nothing in this section shall require a defect to be inferred from the fact alone that the safety of a product which is supplied after that time is greater than the safety of the product in question.

4 Defences

(1) In any civil proceedings by virtue of this Part against any person ('the person proceeded against') in respect of a defect in a product it shall be a defence for him to show—

(a) that the defect is attributable to compliance with any requirement imposed by or under any enactment or with any [EU] obligation; or

(b) that the person proceeded against did not at any time supply the product to another; or

(c) that the following conditions are satisfied, that is to say—

  (i) that the only supply of the product to another by the person proceeded against was otherwise than in the course of a business of that person's; and

  (ii) that section 2(2) above does not apply to that person or applies to him by virtue only of things done otherwise than with a view to profit; or

(d) that the defect did not exist in the product at the relevant time; or

(e) that the state of scientific and technical knowledge at the relevant time was not such that a producer of products of the same description as the product in question might be expected to have discovered the defect if it had existed in his products while they were under his control; or

(f) that the defect—

  (i) constituted an defect in a product ('the subsequent product') in which the product in question had been comprised; and

  (ii) was wholly attributable to the design of the subsequent product or to compliance by the producer of the product in question with instructions given by the producer of the subsequent product.

(2) In this section 'the relevant time', in relation to electricity, means the time at which it was generated, being a time before it was transmitted or distributed, and in relation to any other product, means—

(a) if the person proceeded against is a person to whom subsection (2) of section 2 above applies in relation to the product, the time when he supplied the product to another;

(b) if that subsection does not apply to that person in relation to the product, the time when the product was last supplied by a person to whom that subsection does apply in relation to the product.

5 Damage giving rise to liability

(1) Subject to the following provisions of this section, in this Part 'damage' means death or personal injury or any loss of or damage to any property (including land).

(2) A person shall not be liable under section 2 above in respect of any defect in a product for the loss of or any damage to the product itself or for the loss of or any damage to the whole or any part of any product which has been supplied with the product in question comprised in it.

(3) A person shall not be liable under section 2 above for any loss of or damage to any property which, at the time it is lost or damaged, is not—

(a) of a description of property ordinarily intended for private use, occupation or consumption; and

(b) intended by the person suffering the loss or damage mainly for his own private use, occupation or consumption.

(4) No damages shall be awarded to any person by virtue of this Part in respect of any loss of or damage to any property if the amount which would fall to be so awarded to that person, apart from this subsection and any liability for interest, does not exceed £275.

(5) In determining for the purposes of this Part who has suffered any loss of or damage to property and when any such loss or damage occurred, the loss or damage shall be regarded as having occurred at the earliest time at which a person with an interest in the property had knowledge of the material facts about the loss or damage.

(6) For the purposes of subsection (5) above the material facts about any loss of or damage to any property are such facts about the loss or damage as would lead a reasonable person with an interest in the property to consider the loss or damage sufficiently serious to justify his instituting proceedings for damages against a defendant who did not dispute liability and was able to satisfy a judgment.

(7) For the purposes of subsection (5) above a person's knowledge includes knowledge which he might reasonably have been expected to acquire—

(a) from facts observable or ascertainable by him; or

(b) from facts ascertainable by him with the help of appropriate expert advice which it is reasonable for him to seek;

but a person shall not be taken by virtue of this subsection to have knowledge of a fact ascertainable by him only with the help of expert advice unless he has failed to take all reasonable steps to obtain (and, where appropriate, to act on) that advice.

6 Application of certain enactments etc.

(1) Any damage for which a person is liable under section 2 above shall be deemed to have been caused—

(a) for the purposes of the Fatal Accidents Act 1976, by that person's wrongful act, neglect or default; . . .

(2) Where—

(a) a person's death is caused wholly or partly by a defect in a product, or a person dies after suffering damage which has been so caused;

(b) a request such as mentioned in paragraph (a) of subsection (3) of section 2 above is made to a supplier of the product by that person's personal representatives or, in the case of a person whose death is caused wholly or partly by the defect, by any dependant or relative of that person; and

(c) the conditions specified in paragraphs (b) and (c) of that subsection are satisfied in relation to that request,

this Part shall have effect for the purposes of the Law Reform (Miscellaneous Provisions) Act 1934, the Fatal Accidents Act 1976 and the [Damages (Scotland) Act 2011] as if liability of the supplier to that person under that subsection did not depend on that person having requested the supplier to identify certain persons or on the said conditions having been satisfied in relation to a request made by that person.

(3) Section 1 of the Congenital Disabilities (Civil Liability) Act 1976 shall have effect for the purposes of this Part as if—

(a) a person were answerable to a child in respect of an occurrence caused wholly or partly by a defect in a product if he is or has been liable under section 2 above in respect of any effect of the occurrence on a parent of the child, or would be so liable if the occurrence caused a parent of the child to suffer damage;

(b) the provisions of this Part relating to liability under section 2 above applied in relation to liability by virtue of paragraph (a) above under the said section 1; and

(c) subsection (6) of the said section 1 (exclusion of liability) were omitted.

(4) Where any damage is caused partly by a defect in a product and partly by the fault of the person suffering the damage, the Law Reform (Contributory Negligence) Act 1945 and section 5 of the Fatal Accidents Act 1976 (contributory negligence) shall have effect as if the defect were the fault of every person liable by virtue of this Part for the damage caused by the defect.

(5) In subsection (4) above 'fault' has the same meaning as in the said Act of 1945.

(6) Schedule 1 to this Act shall have effect for the purpose of amending the Limitation Act 1980 and the Prescription and Limitation (Scotland) Act 1973 in their application in relation to the bringing of actions by virtue of this Part.

(7) It is hereby declared that liability by virtue of this Part is to be treated as liability in tort for the purposes of any enactment conferring jurisdiction on any court with respect to any matter.

(8) Nothing in this Part shall prejudice the operation of section 12 of the Nuclear Installations Act 1965 (rights to compensation for certain breaches of duties confined to rights under that Act).

7   Prohibition on exclusions from liability

The liability of a person by virtue of this Part to a person who has suffered damage caused wholly or partly by a defect in a product, or to a dependant or relative of such a person, shall not be limited or excluded by any contract term, by any notice or by any other provision.

8   Power to modify Part I

(1) Her Majesty may by Order in Council make such modifications of this Part and of any other enactment (including an enactment contained in the following Parts of this Act, or in an Act passed after this Act) as appear to Her Majesty in Council to be necessary or expedient in consequence of any modification of the product liability Directive which is made at any time after the passing of this Act.

9   Application of Part I to Crown

(1) Subject to subsection (2) below, this Part shall bind the Crown.

(2) The Crown shall not, as regards the Crown's liability by virtue of this Part, be bound by this Part further than the Crown is made liable in tort or in reparation under the Crown Proceedings Act 1947, as that Act has effect from time to time.

PART II CONSUMER SAFETY

11   Safety regulations

(1) The Secretary of State may by regulations under this section ('safety regulations') make such provision as he considers appropriate [. . .] for the purpose of securing—

(a) that goods to which this section applies are safe;

(b) that goods to which this section applies which are unsafe, or would be unsafe in the hands of persons of a particular description, are not made available to persons generally or, as the case may be, to persons of that description; and

(c) that appropriate information is, and inappropriate information is not, provided in relation to goods to which this section applies.

12   Offences against the safety regulations

(1) Where safety regulations prohibit a person from supplying or offering or agreeing to supply any goods or from exposing or possessing any goods for supply, that person shall be guilty of an offence if he contravenes the prohibition.

(2) Where safety regulations require a person who makes or processes any goods in the course of carrying on a business—

(a) to carry out a particular test or use a particular procedure in connection with the making or processing of the goods with a view to ascertaining whether the goods satisfy any requirements of such regulations; or

(b) to deal or not to deal in a particular way with a quantity of the goods of which the whole or part does not satisfy such a test or does not satisfy standards connected with such a procedure,

that person shall be guilty of an offence if he does not comply with the requirement.

(3) If a person contravenes a provision of safety regulations which prohibits or requires the provision, by means of a mark or otherwise, of information of a particular kind in relation to goods, he shall be guilty of an offence.

(4) Where safety regulations require any person to give information to another for the purpose of enabling that other to exercise any function, that person shall be guilty of an offence if—

    (a) he fails without reasonable cause to comply with the requirement; or

    (b) in giving the information which is required of him—

        (i) he makes any statement which he knows is false in a material particular; or

        (ii) he recklessly makes any statement which is false in a material particular.

PART IV ENFORCEMENT OF PARTS II AND III

29   Powers of search etc.

(1) Subject to the following provisions of this Part, a duly authorised officer of an enforcement authority may at any reasonable hour and on production, if required, of his credentials exercise [the power conferred by subsection (4)].

(4) If the officer has reasonable grounds for suspecting that any goods are manufactured or imported goods which have not been supplied in the United Kingdom since they were manufactured or imported he may—

    (a) for the purpose of ascertaining whether there has been any contravention of any safety provision in relation to the goods, require any person carrying on a business, or employed in connection with the business, to produce any records relating to the business;

    (b) for the purpose of ascertaining (by testing or otherwise) whether there has been any such contravention, seize and detain the goods;

    (c) take copies of, or of any entry in, any records produced by virtue of paragraph (a) above.

(7) If and to the extent that it is reasonably necessary to do so to prevent a contravention of any safety provision [. . .], the officer may, for the purpose of exercising his power under subsection (4) [. . .] above to seize any goods [. . .]—

    (a) require any person having authority to do so to open any container or to open any vending machine; and

    (b) himself open or break open any such container or machine where a requirement made under paragraph (a) above in relation to the container or machine has not been complied with.

30   Provisions supplemental to s. 29

(1) An officer seizing any goods [. . .] under section [29(4)] above shall inform the following persons that the goods [. . .] have been so seized, that is to say—

    (a) the person from whom they are seized; and

    (b) in the case of imported goods seized on any premises under the control of the Commissioners of Customs and Excise, the importer of those goods (within the meaning of the Customs and Excise Management Act 1979).

(2) If a justice of the peace—

    (a) is satisfied by any written information on oath that there are reasonable grounds for believing either—

        (i) that any [. . .] records which any officer has power to inspect under section [29(4)] above are on any premises and that their inspection is likely to disclose evidence that there has been a contravention of any safety provision [. . .]; or

        (ii) that such a contravention has taken place, is taking place or is about to take place on any premises; and

    (b) is also satisfied by any such information either—

        (i) that admission to the premises has been or is likely to be refused and that notice of intention to apply for a warrant under this subsection has been given to the occupier; or

(ii) that an application for admission, or the giving of such a notice, would defeat the object of the entry or that the premises are unoccupied or that the occupier is temporarily absent and it might defeat the object of the entry to await his return,

the justice may by warrant under his hand, which shall continue in force for a period of one month, authorise any officer of an enforcement authority to enter the premises, if need be by force.

(3) An officer entering any premises by virtue of [. . .] a warrant under subsection (2) above may take with him such other persons and such equipment as may appear to him necessary.

(4) On leaving any premises which a person is authorised to enter by a warrant under subsection (2) above, that person shall, if the premises are unoccupied or the occupier is temporarily absent, leave the premises as effectively secured against trespassers as he found them.

(6) Where any goods seized by an officer under section [29(4)] above are submitted to a test, the officer shall inform the persons mentioned in subsection (1) above of the result of the test and, if—

(a) proceedings are brought for an offence in respect of a contravention in relation to the goods of any safety provision [. . .] or for the forfeiture of the goods under section 16 or 17 above, or a suspension notice is served in respect of any goods; and

(b) the officer is requested to do so and it is practicable to comply with the request,

the officer shall allow any person who is a party to the proceedings or, as the case may be, has an interest in the g\oods to which the notice relates to have the goods tested.

(7) The Secretary of State may by regulations provide that any test of goods seized under section [29(4)] above by an officer of an enforcement authority shall—

(a) be carried out at the expense of the authority in a manner and by a person prescribed by or determined under the regulations; or

(b) be carried out either as mentioned in paragraph (a) above or by the authority in a manner prescribed by the regulations.

32   Obstruction of authorised officer

(1) Any person who—

(a) intentionally obstructs any officer of an enforcement authority who is acting in pursuance of [section 29(4)] or any customs officer who is [acting in pursuance of section 31]; or

(b) intentionally fails to comply with any requirement made of him by any officer of any enforcement authority under [section 29(4)]; or

(c) without reasonable cause fails to give any officer of an enforcement authority who is so acting any other assistance or information which the officer may reasonably require of him for the purposes of the exercise of the officer's functions under [section 29(4)],

shall be guilty of an \offence and liable on summary conviction to a fine not exceeding level 5 on the standard scale.

(2) A person shall be guilty of an offence if, in giving any information which is required of him by virtue of subsection (1)(c) above—

(a) he makes any statement which he knows is false in a material particular; or

(b) he recklessly makes a statement which is false in a material particular.

(3) A person guilty of an offence under subsection (2) above shall be liable—

(a) on conviction on indictment, to a fine;

(b) on summary conviction, to a fine not exceeding the statutory maximum.

33   Appeals against detention of goods

(1) Any person having an interest in any goods which are for the time being detained under [section 29(4)] by an enforcement authority or by an officer of such an authority may apply for an order requiring the goods to be released to him or to another person.

(2) An application under this section may be made—

(a) to any magistrates' court in which proceedings have been brought in England and Wales or Northern Ireland—

      (i) for an offence in respect of a contravention in relation to the goods of any safety provision [. . .]; or

      (ii) for the forfeiture of the goods under section 16 above;

    (b) where no such proceedings have been so brought, by way of complaint to a magistrates' court . . .

(3) On an application under this section to a magistrates' court . . . , an order requiring goods to be released shall be made only if the court . . . is satisfied—

    (a) that proceedings—

      (i) for an offence in respect of a contravention in relation to the goods of any safety provision [. . .]; or

      (ii) for the forfeiture of the goods under section 16 or 17 above, have not been brought or, having been brought, have been concluded without the goods being forfeited; and

    (b) where no such proceedings have been brought, that more than six months have elapsed since the goods were seized.

(4) Any person aggrieved by an order made under this section by a magistrates' court in England and Wales or Northern Ireland, or by a decision of such a court not to make such an order, may appeal against that order or decision—

    (a) in England and Wales, to the Crown Court;

    (b) in Northern Ireland, to the county court;

and an order so made may contain such provision as appears to the court to be appropriate for delaying the coming into force of the order pending the making and determination of any appeal (including any application under section 111 of the Magistrates' Courts Act 1980 or Article 146 of the Magistrates' Courts (Northern Ireland) Order 1981 (statement of case)).

34   Compensation for seizure and detention

(1) Where an officer of an enforcement authority exercises any power under section [29(4)] above to seize and detain goods, the enforcement authority shall be liable to pay compensation to any person having an interest in the goods in respect of any loss or damage caused by reason of the exercise of the power if—

    (a) there has been no contravention in relation to the goods of any safety provision [. . .]; and

    (b) the exercise of the power is not attributable to any neglect or default by that person.

(2) Any disputed question as to the right to or the amount of any compensation payable under this section shall be determined by arbitration . . .

PART V MISCELLANEOUS AND SUPPLEMENTAL

39   Defence of due diligence

(1) Subject to the following provisions of this section, in proceedings against any person for an offence to which this section applies it shall be a defence for that person to show that he took all reasonable steps and exercised all due diligence to avoid committing the offence.

41   Civil proceedings

(1) An obligation imposed by safety regulations shall be a duty owed to any person who may be affected by a contravention of the obligation and, subject to any provision to the contrary in the regulations and to the defences and other incidents applying to actions for breach of statutory duty, a contravention of any such obligation shall be actionable accordingly.

(2) This Act shall not be construed as conferring any other right of action in civil proceedings, apart from the right conferred by virtue of Part I of this Act, in respect of any loss or damage suffered in consequence of a contravention of a safety provision [. . .].

(3) Subject to any provision to the contrary in the agreement itself, an agreement shall not be void or unenforceable by reason only of a contravention of a safety provision [. . .].

(4) Liability by virtue of subsection (1) above shall not be limited or excluded by any contract term, by any notice or (subject to the power contained in subsection (1) above to limit or exclude it in safety regulations) by any other provision.

(5) Nothing in subsection (1) above shall prejudice the operation of section 12 of the Nuclear Installations Act 1965 (rights to compensation for certain breaches of duties confined to rights under that Act).

(6) In this section 'damage' includes personal injury and death.

45 Interpretation

(1) In this Act, except in so far as the context otherwise requires—

. . .

'business' includes a trade or profession and the activities of a professional or trade association or of a local authority or other public authority;

'conditional sale agreement', 'credit-sale agreement' and 'hire-purchase agreement' have the same meanings as in the Consumer Credit Act 1974 but as if in the definitions in that Act 'goods' had the same meaning as in this Act;

. . .

'goods' includes substances, growing crops and things comprised in land by virtue of being attached to it and any ship, aircraft or vehicle;

'information' includes accounts, estimates and returns;

. . .

'personal injury' includes any disease and any other impairment of a person's physical or mental condition;

'premises' includes any place and any ship, aircraft or vehicle;

'safety provision' means [. . .] any provision of safety regulations, a prohibition notice or a suspension notice;

'safety regulations' means regulations under section 11 above;

. . .

'substance' means any natural or artificial substance, whether in solid, liquid or gaseous form or in the form of a vapour, and includes substances that are comprised in or mixed with other goods;

'supply' and cognate expressions shall be construed in accordance with section 46 below;

Minors' Contracts Act 1987

(1987, c. 13)

2 Guarantees

Where—

    (a) a guarantee is given in respect of an obligation of a party to a contract made after the commencement of this Act, and

    (b) the obligation is unenforceable against him (or he repudiates the contract)

    (c) because he was a minor when the contract was made,

the guarantee shall not for that reason alone be unenforceable against the guarantor.

3 Restitution

(1) Where—

    (a) a person ('the plaintiff') has after the commencement of this Act entered into a contract with another ('the defendant'), and

    (b) the contract is unenforceable against the defendant (or he repudiates it) because he was a minor when the contract was made, the court may, if it is just and equitable to do so, require the defendant to transfer to the plaintiff any property acquired by the defendant under the contract, or any property representing it.

(2) Nothing in this section shall be taken to prejudice any other remedy available to the plaintiff.

Copyright, Designs and Patents Act 1988

(1988, c. 48)

96   Infringement actionable by copyright owner

(1) An infringement of copyright is actionable by the copyright owner.

(2) In an action for infringement of copyright all such relief by way of damages, injunctions, accounts or otherwise is available to the plaintiff as is available in respect of the infringement of any other property right.

97   Provisions as to damages in infringement action

(1) Where in an action for infringement of copyright it is shown that at the time of the infringement the defendant did not know, and had no reason to believe, that copyright subsisted in the work to which the action relates, the plaintiff is not entitled to damages against him, but without prejudice to any other remedy.

(2) The court may in an action for infringement of copyright having regard to all the circumstances, and in particular to—

(a) the flagrancy of the infringement, and

(b) any benefit accruing to the defendant by reason of the infringement,

award such additional damages as the justice of the case may require.

229   Rights and remedies of design right owner

(1) An infringement of design right is actionable by the design right owner.

(2) In an action for infringement of design right all such relief by way of damages, injunctions, accounts or otherwise is available to the plaintiff as is available in respect of the infringement of any other property right.

(3) The court may in an action for infringement of design right, having regard to all the circumstances and in particular to—

(a) the flagrancy of the infringement, and

(b) any benefit accruing to the defendant by reason of the infringement,

award such additional damages as the justice of the case may require.

253   Remedy for groundless threats of infringement proceedings.

(1) Where a person threatens another person with proceedings for infringement of design right, a person aggrieved by the threats may bring an action against him claiming—

(a) a declaration to the effect that the threats are unjustifiable;

(b) an injunction against the continuance of the threats;

(c) damages in respect of any loss which he has sustained by the threats.

(2) If the plaintiff proves that the threats were made and that he is a person aggrieved by them, he is entitled to the relief claimed unless the defendant shows that the acts in respect of which proceedings were threatened did constitute, or if done would have constituted, an infringement of the design right concerned.

(3) Proceedings may not be brought under this section in respect of a threat to bring proceedings for an infringement alleged to consist of making or importing anything.

(4) Mere notification that a design is protected by design right does not constitute a threat of proceedings for the purposes of this section.

Housing Act 1988

(1988, c. 50)

16   Access for repairs

It shall be an implied term of every assured tenancy that the tenant shall afford to the landlord access to the dwelling-house let on the tenancy and all reasonable facilities for executing therein any repairs which the landlord is entitled to execute.

27   Damages for unlawful eviction

(1) This section applies if, at any time after 9th June 1988, a landlord (in this section referred to as 'the landlord in default') or any person acting on behalf of the landlord in default unlawfully deprives the residential occupier of any premises of his occupation of the whole or part of the premises.

(2) This section also applies if, at any time after 9th June 1988, a landlord (in this section referred to as 'the landlord in default') or any person acting on behalf of the landlord in default—

    (a) attempts unlawfully to deprive the residential occupier of any premises of his occupation of the whole or part of the premises, or

    (b) knowing or having reasonable cause to believe that the conduct is likely to cause the residential occupier of any premises—

        (i)   to give up his occupation of the premises or any part thereof, or

        (ii)   to refrain from exercising any right or pursuing any remedy in respect of the premises or any part thereof,

does acts likely to interfere with the peace or comfort of the residential occupier or members of his household, or persistently withdraws or withholds services reasonably required for the occupation of the premises as a residence, and, as a result, the residential occupier gives up his occupation of the premises as a residence.

(3) Subject to the following provisions of this section, where this section applies, the landlord in default shall, by virtue of this section, be liable to pay to the former residential occupier, in respect of his loss of the right to occupy the premises in question as his residence, damages assessed on the basis set out in section 28 below.

(4) Any liability arising by virtue of subsection (3) above—

    (a) shall be in the nature of a liability in tort; and

    (b) subject to subsection (5) below, shall be in addition to any liability arising apart from this section (whether in tort, contract or otherwise).

(5) Nothing in this section affects the right of a residential occupier to enforce any liability which arises apart from this section in respect of his loss of the right to occupy premises as his residence; but damages shall not be awarded both in respect of such a liability and in respect of a liability arising by virtue of this section on account of the same loss.

(6) No liability shall arise by virtue of subsection (3) above if—

    (a) before the date on which proceedings to enforce the liability are finally disposed of, the former residential occupier is reinstated in the premises in question in such circumstances that he becomes again the residential occupier of them; or

    (b) at the request of the former residential occupier, a court makes an order (whether in the nature of an injunction or otherwise) as a result of which he is reinstated as mentioned in paragraph (a) above;

and, for the purposes of paragraph (a) above, proceedings to enforce a liability are finally disposed of on the earliest date by which the proceedings (including any proceedings on or in consequence of an appeal) have been determined and any time for appealing or further appealing has expired, except that if any appeal is abandoned, the proceedings shall be taken to be disposed of on the date of the abandonment.

(7) If, in proceedings to enforce a liability arising by virtue of subsection (3) above, it appears to the court—

(a) that, prior to the event which gave rise to the liability, the conduct of the former residential occupier or any person living with him in the premises concerned was such that it is reasonable to mitigate the damages for which the landlord in default would otherwise be liable, or

(b) that, before the proceedings were begun, the landlord in default offered to reinstate the former residential occupier in the premises in question and either it was unreasonable of the former residential occupier to refuse that offer or, if he had obtained alternative accommodation before the offer was made, it would have been unreasonable of him to refuse that offer if he had not obtained that accommodation,

the court may reduce the amount of damages which would otherwise be payable to such amount as it thinks appropriate.

(8) In proceedings to enforce a liability arising by virtue of subsection (3) above, it shall be a defence for the defendant to prove that he believed, and had reasonable cause to believe—

(b) that, where the liability would otherwise arise by virtue only of the doing of acts or the withdrawal or withholding of services, he had reasonable grounds for doing the acts or withdrawing or withholding the services in question.

28   The measure of damages

(1) The basis for the assessment of damages referred to in section 27(3) above is the difference in value, determined as at the time immediately before the residential occupier ceased to occupy the premises in question as his residence, between—

(a) the value of the interest of the landlord in default determined on the assumption that the residential occupier continues to have the same right to occupy the premises as before that time; and

(b) the value of that interest determined on the assumption that the residential occupier has ceased to have that right.

(3) For the purposes of the valuations referred to in subsection (1) above, it shall be assumed—

(a) that the landlord in default is selling his interest on the open market to a willing buyer;

(b) that neither the residential occupier nor any member of his family wishes to buy; and

(c) that it is unlawful to carry out any substantial development of any of the land in which the landlord's interest subsists or to demolish the whole or part of any building on that land.

Road Traffic Act 1988

(1988, c. 52)

38   The Highway Code

(7) A failure on the part of a person to observe a provision of the Highway Code shall not of itself render that person liable to criminal proceedings of any kind but any such failure may in any proceedings (whether civil or criminal, and including proceedings for an offence under the Traffic Acts, the Public Passenger Vehicles Act 1981 or sections 18 to 23 of the Transport Act 1985) be relied upon by any party to the proceedings as tending to establish or negative any liability which is in question in those proceedings.

143   Users of motor vehicles to be insured or secured against third-party risks

(1) Subject to the provisions of this Part of this Act—

(a) a person must not use a motor vehicle on a road [or other public place] unless there is in force in relation to the use of the vehicle by that person such a policy of insurance or such a security in respect of third party risks as complies with the requirements of this Part of this Act, and

(b) a person must not cause or permit any other person to use a motor vehicle on a road [or other public place] unless there is in force in relation to the use of the vehicle by that other person such a policy of insurance or such a security in respect of third party risks as complies with the requirements of this Part of this Act.

(2) If a person acts in contravention of subsection (1) above he is guilty of an offence.

(3) A person charged with using a motor vehicle in contravention of this section shall not be convicted if he proves—

(a) that the vehicle did not belong to him and was not in his possession under a contract of hiring or of loan,

(b) that he was using the vehicle in the course of his employment, and

(c) that he neither knew nor had reason to believe that there was not in force in relation to the vehicle such a policy of insurance or security as is mentioned in subsection (1) above.

(4) This Part of this Act does not apply to invalid carriages.

144   Exceptions from requirement of third-party insurance or security

(1) Section 143 of this Act does not apply to a vehicle owned by a person who has deposited and keeps deposited with the Accountant General of the [Senior Courts] the sum of [£500,000], at a time when the vehicle is being driven under the owner's control.

[(1A) The Secretary of State may by order made by statutory instrument substitute a greater sum for the sum for the time being specified in subsection (1) above.]

(2) Section 143 does not apply—

(a) to a vehicle owned—

(i) by the council of a county or county district in England and Wales [the Broads Authority], the Common Council of the City of London, the council of a London borough [a National Park Authority], the Inner London Education Authority [the London Fire and Emergency Planning Authority, an authority established for an area in England by an order under section 207 of the Local Government and Public Involvement in Health Act 2007 (joint waste authorities)], [, a joint authority . . . established by Part 4 of the Local Government Act 1985, an economic prosperity board established under section 88 of the Local Democracy, Economic Development and Construction Act 2009 or a combined authority established under section 103 of that Act,]

(ii) by a [council constituted under section 2 of the Local Government etc. (Scotland) Act 1994] in Scotland [or the Scottish Fire and Rescue Service], or

(iii) by a joint board or committee in England or Wales, or joint committee in Scotland, which is so constituted as to include among its members representatives of any such council,

at a time when the vehicle is being driven under the owner's control,

(b) to a vehicle owned by [a local policing body or] a police authority [or the Receiver for the Metropolitan Police district], at a time when it is being driven under the owner's control, or to a vehicle at a time when it is being driven for police purposes by or under the direction of a constable, [by a member of a police and crime commissioner's staff (within the meaning of Part 1 of the Police Reform and Social Responsibility Act 2011), by a member of the staff of the Mayor's Office for Policing and Crime (within the meaning of that Part of that Act), by a member of the civilian staff of a police force (within the meaning of that Part of that Act), by a member of the civilian staff of the metropolitan police force (within the meaning of that Part of that Act), by a person employed by the Common Council of the City of London in its capacity as a police authority,] or by a person employed by a police authority, or employed by the Receiver,

(c) to a vehicle at a time when it is being driven on a journey to or from any place undertaken for salvage purposes pursuant to the Merchant Shipping Act 1995,

[(da) to a vehicle owned by a health service body, as defined in section 60(7) of the National Health Service and Community Care Act 1990 . . . or by a Local Health Board established under section 11 of the National Health Service (Wales) Act 2006, at a time when the vehicle is being driven under the owner's control,

(db)   to an ambulance owned by a National Health Service trust established under . . . section 18 of the National Health Service (Wales) Act 2006 or the National Health Service (Scotland) Act 1978, at a time when a vehicle is being driven under the owner's control,

(dc)   to an ambulance owned by an NHS foundation trust, at a time when the vehicle is being driven under the owner's control,]

(e)   to a vehicle which is made available by the Secretary of State or the Welsh Ministers to any person, body or local authority in pursuance of [section 12 or 80 of the National Health Service (Wales) Act 2006, or section 10 or 38 of the National Health Service (Wales) Act 2006] at a time when it is being used in accordance with the terms on which it is so made available.

145   Requirements in respect of policies of insurance

(1) In order to comply with the requirements of this Part of this Act, a policy of insurance must satisfy the following conditions.

(2) The policy must be issued by an authorised insurer.

(3) Subject to subsection (4) below, the policy—

(a)   must insure such person, persons or classes of persons as may be specified in the policy in respect of any liability which may be incurred by him or them in respect of the death of or bodily injury to any person or damage to property caused by, or arising out of, the use of the vehicle on a road [or other public place] in Great Britain, and

[(aa) must, in the case of a vehicle normally based in the territory of another member State, insure him or them in respect of any civil liability which may be incurred by him or them as a result of an event related to the use of the vehicle in Great Britain if,—

(i)   according to the law of that territory, he or they would be required to be insured in respect of a civil liability which would arise under that law as a result of that event if the place where the vehicle was used when the event occurred were in that territory, and

(ii)   the cover required by that law would be higher than that required by paragraph (a) above, and]

(b)   must[, in the case of a vehicle normally based in Great Britain,] insure him or them in respect of any liability which may be incurred by him or them in respect of the use of the vehicle and of any trailer, whether or not coupled, in the territory other than Great Britain and Gibraltar of each of the member States of the Communities according to

[(i)   the law on compulsory insurance against civil liability in respect of the use of vehicles of the State in whose territory the event giving rise to the liability occurred; or

(ii)   if it would give higher cover, the law which would be applicable under this Part of this Act if the place where the vehicle was used when that event occurred were in Great Britain; and]

(c)   must also insure him or them in respect of any liability which may be incurred by him or them under the provisions of this Part of this Act relating to payment for emergency treatment.

(4) The policy shall not, by virtue of subsection (3)(a) above, be required—

(a)   to cover liability in respect of the death, arising out of and in the course of his employment, of a person in the employment of a person insured by the policy or of bodily injury sustained by such a person arising out of and in the course of his employment, or

(b)   to provide insurance of more than [£1,000,000] in respect of all such liabilities as may be incurred in respect of damage to property caused by, or arising out of, any one accident involving the vehicle, or

(c)   to cover liability in respect of damage to the vehicle, or

(d)   to cover liability in respect of damage to goods carried for hire or reward in or on the vehicle or in or on any trailer (whether or not coupled) drawn by the vehicle, or

(e)   to cover any liability of a person in respect of damage to property in his custody or under his control, or

(f)   to cover any contractual liability.

[(4A) In the case of a person—
>   (a) carried in or upon a vehicle, or
>   (b) entering or getting on to, or alighting from, a vehicle,

the provisions of paragraph (a) of subsection (4) above do not apply unless cover in respect of the liability referred to in that paragraph is in fact provided pursuant to a requirement of the Employers' Liability (Compulsory Insurance) Act 1969.]

148   Avoidance of certain exceptions to policies or securities

(1) Where a certificate of insurance or certificate of security has been delivered under section 147 of this Act to the person by whom a policy has been effected or to whom a security has been given, so much of the policy or security as purports to restrict—
>   (a) the insurance of the persons insured by the policy, or
>   (b) the operation of the security,

(as the case may be) by reference to any of the matters mentioned in subsection (2) below shall, as respects such liabilities as are required to be covered by a policy under section 145 of this Act, be of no effect.

(2) Those matters are—
>   (a) the age or physical or mental condition of persons driving the vehicle,
>   (b) the condition of the vehicle,
>   (c) the number of persons that the vehicle carries,
>   (d) the weight or physical characteristics of the goods that the vehicle carries,
>   (e) the time at which or the areas within which the vehicle is used,
>   (f) the horsepower or cylinder capacity or value of the vehicle,
>   (g) the carrying on the vehicle of any particular apparatus, or
>   (h) the carrying on the vehicle of any particular means of identification other than any means of identification required to be carried by or under [the Vehicles Excise and Registration Act 1994].

(3) Nothing in subsection (1) above requires an insurer or the giver of a security to pay any sum in respect of the liability of any person otherwise than in or towards the discharge of that liability.

(4) Any sum paid by an insurer or the giver of a security in or towards the discharge of any liability of any person which is covered by the policy or security by virtue only of subsection (1) above is recoverable by the insurer or giver of the security from that person.

(5) A condition in a policy or security issued or given for the purposes of this Part of this Act providing—
>   (a) that no liability shall arise under the policy or security, or
>   (b) that any liability so arising shall cease,

in the event of some specified thing being done or omitted to be done after the happening of the event giving rise to a claim under the policy or security, shall be of no effect in connection with such liabilities as are required to be covered by a policy under section 145 of this Act.

(6) Nothing in subsection (5) above shall be taken to render void any provision in a policy or security requiring the person insured or secured to pay to the insurer or the giver of the security any sums which the latter may have become liable to pay under the policy or security and which have been applied to the satisfaction of the claims of third parties.

(7) Notwithstanding anything in any enactment, a person issuing a policy of insurance under section 145 of this Act shall be liable to indemnify the persons or classes of persons specified in the policy in respect of any liability which the policy purports to cover in the case of those persons or classes of persons.

149   Avoidance of certain agreements as to liability towards passengers

(1) This section applies where a person uses a motor vehicle in circumstances such that under section 143 of this Act there is required to be in force in relation to his use of it such a policy of insurance or such a security in respect of third-party risks as complies with the requirements of this Part of this Act.

(2) If any other person is carried in or upon the vehicle when the user is so using it, any antecedent agreement or understanding between them (whether intended to be legally binding or not) shall be of no effect so far as it purports or might be held—

(a) to negative or restrict any such liability of the user in respect of persons carried in or upon the vehicle as is required by section 145 of this Act to be covered by a policy of insurance, or

(b) to impose any conditions with respect to the enforcement of any such liability of the user.

(3) The fact that a person so carried has willingly accepted as his the risk of negligence on the part of the user shall not be treated as negativing any such liability of the user.

(4) For the purposes of this section—

(a) references to a person being carried in or upon a vehicle include references to a person entering or getting on to, or alighting from, the vehicle, and

(b) the reference to an antecedent agreement is to one made at any time before the liability arose.

151 Duty of insurers of persons giving security to satisfy judgment against persons insured or secured against third-party risks

(1) This section applies where, after a certificate of insurance or certificate of security has been delivered under section 147 of this Act to the person by whom a policy has been effected or to whom a security has been given, a judgment to which this subsection applies is obtained.

(2) Subsection (1) above applies to judgments relating to a liability with respect to any matter where liability with respect to that matter is required to be covered by a policy of insurance under section 145 of this Act and either—

(a) it is a liability covered by the terms of the policy or security to which the certificate relates, and the judgment is obtained against any person who is insured by the policy or whose liability is covered by the security, as the case may be, or

(b) it is a liability, other than an excluded liability, which would be so covered if the policy insured all persons or, as the case may be, the security covered the liability of all persons, and the judgment is obtained against any person other than one who is insured by the policy or, as the case may be, whose liability is covered by the security.

(3) In deciding for the purposes of subsection (2) above whether a liability is or would be covered by the terms of a policy or security, so much of the policy or security as purports to restrict, as the case may be, the insurance of the persons insured by the policy or the operation of the security by reference to the holding by the driver of the vehicle of a licence authorising him to drive it shall be treated as of no effect.

(4) In subsection (2)(b) above 'excluded liability' means a liability in respect of the death of, or bodily injury to, or damage to the property of any person who, at the time of the use which gave rise to the liability, was allowing himself to be carried in or upon the vehicle and knew or had reason to believe that the vehicle had been stolen or unlawfully taken, not being a person who—

(a) did not know and had no reason to believe that the vehicle had been stolen or unlawfully taken until after the commencement of his journey, and

(b) could not reasonably have been expected to have alighted from the vehicle.

In this subsection the reference to a person being carried in or upon a vehicle includes a reference to a person entering or getting on to, or alighting from, the vehicle.

(5) Notwithstanding that the insurer may be entitled to avoid or cancel, or may have avoided or cancelled, the policy or security, he must, subject to the provisions of this section, pay to the persons entitled to the benefit of the judgment—

(a) as regards liability in respect of death or bodily injury, any sum payable under the judgment in respect of the liability, together with any sum which, by virtue of any enactment relating to interest on judgments, is payable in respect of interest on that sum,

(b) as regards liability in respect of damage to property, any sum required to be paid under subsection (6) below, and

(c) any amount payable in respect of costs.

(6) This subsection requires—

(a) where the total of any amounts paid, payable or likely to be payable under the policy or security in respect of damage to property caused by, or arising out of, the accident in question does not exceed [£1,000,000], the payment of any sum payable under the judgment in respect of the liability, together with any sum which, by virtue of any enactment relating to interest on judgments, is payable in respect of interest on that sum,

(b) where that total exceeds [£1,000,000], the payment of either—

    (i) such proportion of any sum payable under the judgment in respect of the liability as [£1,000,000] bears to that total, together with the same proportion of any sum which, by virtue of any enactment relating to interest on judgments, is payable in respect of interest on that sum, or

    (ii) the difference between the total of any amounts already paid under the policy or security in respect of such damage and [£1,000,000], together with such proportion of any sum which, by virtue of any enactment relating to interest on judgments, is payable in respect of interest on any sum payable under the judgment in respect of the liability as the difference bears to that sum,

whichever is the less, unless not less than [£1,000,000] has already been paid under the policy or security in respect of such damage (in which case nothing is payable).

(7) Where an insurer becomes liable under this section to pay an amount in respect of a liability of a person who is insured by a policy or whose liability is covered by a security, he is entitled to recover from that person—

(a) that amount, in a case where he became liable to pay it by virtue only of subsection (3) above, or

(b) in a case where that amount exceeds the amount for which he would, apart from the provisions of this section, be liable under the policy or security in respect of that liability, the excess.

(8) Where an insurer becomes liable under this section to pay an amount in respect of a liability of a person who is not insured by a policy or whose liability is not covered by a security, he is entitled to recover the amount from that person or from any person who—

(a) is insured by the policy, or whose liability is covered by the security, by the terms of which the liability would be covered if the policy insured all persons or, as the case may be, the security covered the liability of all persons, and

(b) caused or permitted the use of the vehicle which gave rise to the liability.

(9) In this section—

(a) 'insurer' includes a person giving a security,

(c) 'liability covered by the terms of the policy or security' means a liability which is covered by the policy or security or which would be so covered but for the fact that the insurer is entitled to avoid or cancel, or has avoided or cancelled, the policy or security.

153 Bankruptcy, etc., of insured or secured persons not to affect claims by third parties

(1) Where, after a certificate of insurance or certificate of security has been delivered under section 147 of this Act to the person by whom a policy has been effected or to whom a security has been given, any of the events mentioned in subsection (2) below happens, the happening of that event shall, notwithstanding anything in the Third Parties (Rights Against Insurers) Act 1930, not affect any such liability of that person as is required to be covered by a policy of insurance under section 145 of this Act.

(2) In the case of the person by whom the policy was effected or to whom the security was given, the events referred to in subsection (1) above are—

(a) that he becomes bankrupt or makes a composition or arrangement with his creditors or that his estate is sequestrated or he grants a trust deed for his creditors,

(b) that he dies and—

    (i) his estate falls to be administered in accordance with an order under section 421 of the Insolvency Act 1986,

    (ii) an award of sequestration of his estate is made, or

> (iii) a judicial factor is appointed to administer his estate under section 11A of the Judicial Factors (Scotland) Act 1889,
>
> (c) that if that person is a company—
>
> (i) a winding-up order [. . .] is made with respect of the company [or the company enters administration],
>
> (ii) a resolution for a voluntary winding-up is passed with respect to the company,
>
> (iii) a receiver or manager of the company's business or undertaking is duly appointed, or
>
> (iv) possession is taken, by or on behalf of the holders of any debentures secured by a floating charge, of any property comprised in or subject to the charge.

(3) Nothing in subsection (1) above affects any rights conferred by the Third Parties (Rights Against Insurers) Act 1930 on the person to whom the liability was incurred, being rights so conferred against the person by whom the policy was issued or the security was given.

157 Payment for hospital treatment of traffic casualties

(1) Subject to subsection (2) below, where—

> (a) a payment, other than a payment under section 158 of this Act, is made (whether or not with an admission of liability) in respect of the death of, or bodily injury to, any person arising out of the use of a motor vehicle on a road or in a place to which the public have a right of access, and
>
> (b) the payment is made—
>
> (i) by an authorised insurer, the payment being made under or in consequence of a policy issued under section 145 of this Act, or
>
> (ii) by the owner of a vehicle in relation to the use of which a security under this Part of this Act is in force, or
>
> (iii) by the owner of a vehicle who has made a deposit under this Part of this Act, and
>
> (c) the person who has so died or been bodily injured has to the knowledge of the insurer or owner, as the case may be, received treatment at a hospital, whether as an in-patient or as an out-patient, in respect of the injury so arising,

the insurer or owner must pay the expenses reasonably incurred by the hospital in affording the treatment, after deducting from the expenses any moneys actually received in payment of a specific charge for the treatment, not being moneys received under any contributory scheme.

(2) The amount to be paid shall not exceed [£2,949.00] for each person treated as an inpatient or [£295.00] for each person treated as an out-patient.

(3) For the purposes of this section 'expenses reasonably incurred' means—

> (a) in relation to a person who receives treatment at a hospital as an in-patient, an amount for each day he is maintained in the hospital representing the average daily cost, for each in-patient, of the maintenance of the hospital and the staff of the hospital and the maintenance and treatment of the in-patients in the hospital, and
>
> (b) in relation to a person who receives treatment at a hospital as an out-patient, reasonable expenses actually incurred.

158 Payment for emergency treatment of traffic casualties

(1) Subsection (2) below applies where—

> (a) medical or surgical treatment or examination is immediately required as a result of bodily injury (including fatal injury) to a person caused by, or arising out of, the use of a motor vehicle on a road and
>
> (b) the treatment or examination so required (in this Part of this Act referred to as 'emergency treatment') is effected by a legally qualified medical practitioner.

(2) The person who was using the vehicle at the time of the event out of which the bodily injury arose must, on a claim being made in accordance with the provisions of section 159 of this Act, pay to the practitioner (or, where emergency treatment is effected by more than one practitioner, to the practitioner by whom it is first effected)—

> (a) a fee of [£21.30] in respect of each person in whose case the emergency treatment is effected by him, and

(b) a sum, in respect of any distance in excess of two miles which he must cover in order—

    (i) to proceed from the place from which he is summoned to the place where the emergency treatment is carried out by him, and

    (ii) to return to the first mentioned place, equal to [41 pence] for every complete mile and additional part of a mile of that distance.

(3) Where emergency treatment is first effected in a hospital, the provisions of subsections (1) and (2) above with respect to payment of a fee shall, so far as applicable, but subject (as regards the recipient of a payment) to the provisions of section 159 of this Act, have effect with the substitution of references to the hospital for references to a legally qualified medical practitioner.

(4) Liability incurred under this section by the person using a vehicle shall, where the event out of which it arose was caused by the wrongful act of another person, be treated for the purposes of any claim to recover damage by reason of that wrongful act as damage sustained by the person using the vehicle.

159　Supplementary provisions as to payments for treatment

(2) A claim for a payment under section 158 of this Act may be made at the time when the emergency treatment is effected, by oral request to the person who was using the vehicle, and if not so made must be made by request in writing served on him within seven days from the day on which the emergency treatment was effected.

(4) A payment made under section 158 of this Act shall operate as a discharge, to the extent of the amount paid, of any liability of the person who was using the vehicle, or of any other person, to pay any sum in respect of the expenses of remuneration of the practitioner or hospital concerned of or for effecting the emergency treatment.

Road Traffic (Consequential Provisions) Act 1988

(1988, c. 54)

7　Saving for law of nuisance

Nothing in the Road Traffic Acts authorises a person to use on a road a vehicle so constructed or used as to cause a public or private nuisance . . . or affects the liability, whether under statute or common law, of the driver or owner so using a vehicle.

Employment Act 1989

(1989, c. 38)

11　Exemption of Sikhs from requirements as to wearing of safety helmets on construction sites

(1) Any requirement to wear a safety helmet which (apart from this section) would, by virtue of any statutory provision or rule of law, be imposed on a Sikh who is on a construction site shall not apply to him at any time when he is wearing a turban.

(2) Accordingly, where—

    (a) a Sikh who is on a construction site is for the time being wearing a turban, and

    (b) (apart from this section) any associated requirement would, by virtue of any statutory provision or rule of law, be imposed—

        (i) on the Sikh, or

        (ii) on the other person,

in connection with the wearing by the Sikh of a safety helmet, that requirement shall not apply to the Sikh or (as the case may be) to that other person.

(4) It is hereby declared that, where a person does not comply with any requirement, being a requirement which for the time being does not apply to him by virtue of subsection (1) or (2)—

    (a) he shall not be liable in tort to any person in respect of any injury, loss or damage caused by his failure to comply with that requirement . . .

(5) If a Sikh who is on a construction site—

(a) does not comply with any requirement to wear a safety helmet, being a requirement which for the time being does not apply to him by virtue of subsection (1), and

(b) in consequence of any act or omission of some other person sustains any injury, loss or damage which is to any extent attributable to the fact that he is not wearing a safety helmet in compliance with the requirement,

that other person shall, if liable to the Sikh in tort (or, in Scotland, in an action for reparation), be so liable only to the extent that injury, loss or damage would have been sustained by the Sikh even if he had been wearing a safety helmet in compliance with the requirement.

(6) Where—

(a) the act or omission referred to in subsection (5) causes the death of the Sikh, and

(b) the Sikh would have sustained some injury (other than loss of life) in consequence of the act or omission even if he had been wearing a safety helmet in compliance with the requirement in question,

the amount of any damages which, by virtue of that subsection, are recoverable in tort (or, in Scotland, in an action for reparation) in respect of that injury shall not exceed the amount of any damages which would (apart from that subsection) be so recoverable in respect of the Sikh's death.

(7) In this section—

'injury' includes loss of life, any impairment of a person's physical or mental condition and any disease; . . .

Law of Property (Miscellaneous Provisions) Act 1989

(1989, c. 34)

1 Deeds and their execution

(1) Any rule of law which—

(a) restricts the substances on which a deed may be written;

(b) requires a seal for the valid execution of an instrument as a deed by an individual; or

(c) requires authority by one person to another to deliver an instrument as a deed on his behalf to be given by deed,

is abolished.

(2) An instrument shall not be a deed unless—

(a) it makes it clear on its face that it is intended to be a deed by the person making it or, as the case may be, by the parties to it (whether by describing itself as a deed or expressing itself to be executed or signed as a deed or otherwise); and

(b) it is validly executed as a deed

[(i) by that person or a person authorised to execute it in the name or on behalf of that person, or

(ii) by one or more of those parties or a person authorised to execute it in the name or on behalf of one of more of those parties.]

[(2A) For the purposes of subsection (2)(a) above, an instrument shall not be taken to make it clear on its face that it is intended to be a deed merely because it is executed under seal.]

(3) An instrument is validly executed as a deed by an individual if, and only if—

(a) it is signed—

(i) by him in the presence of a witness who attests the signature; of

(ii) at his direction and in his presence and the presence of two witnesses who each attest the signature; and

(b) it is delivered as a deed [. . .].

(4) In subsections (2) and (3) above 'sign', in relation to an instrument, includes

[(a) an individual signing the name of the person or party on whose behalf he executes the instrument; and

(b) making one's mark on the instrument,

and 'signature' is to be construed accordingly.]

[(4A) Subsection (3) above applies in the case of an instrument executed by an individual in the name or on behalf of another person whether or not that person is also an individual.]

(5) Where [a relevant lawyer, or an agent or employee of a relevant lawyer], in the course of or in connection with a transaction [. . .], purports to deliver an instrument as a deed on behalf of a party to the instrument, it shall be conclusively presumed in favour of a purchaser that he is authorised so to deliver the instrument.

(6) In subsection (5) above—

['purchaser' has the same meaning] as in the Law of Property Act 1925;]

['relevant lawyer' means a person who, for the purposes of the Legal Services Act 2007, is an authorised person in relation to an activity which constitutes a reserved instrument activity (within the meaning of that Act);].

(7) Where an instrument under seal that constitutes a deed is required for the purposes of an Act passed before this section comes into force, this section shall have effect as to signing, sealing or delivery of an instrument by an individual in place of any provision of that Act as to signing, sealing or delivery.

(10) The references in this section to the execution of a deed by an individual do not include execution by a corporation sole and the reference in subsection (7) above to signing, sealing or delivery by an individual does not include signing, sealing or delivery by such a corporation.

(11) Nothing in this section applies in relation to instruments delivered as deeds before this section comes into force.

2 Contracts for sale etc. of land to be made by signed writing

(1) A contract for the sale or other disposition of an interest in land can only be made in writing and only by incorporating all the terms which the parties have expressly agreed in one document or, where contracts are exchanged, in each.

(2) The terms may be incorporated in a document either by being set out in it or by reference to some other document.

(3) The document incorporating the terms or, where contracts are exchanged, one of the documents incorporating them (but not necessarily the same one) must be signed by or on behalf of each party to the contract.

(4) Where a contract for the sale or other disposition of an interest in land satisfies the conditions of this section by reason only of the rectification of one or more documents in pursuance of an order of a court, the contract shall come into being, or be deemed to have come into being, at such time as may be specified in the order.

(5) This section does not apply in relation to—

    (a) a contract to grant such a lease as is mentioned in section 54(2) of the Law of Property Act 1925 (short leases);

    (b) a contract made in the course of a public auction; or

    [(c) a contract regulated under the Financial Services and Markets Act 2000, other than a regulated mortgage contract, a regulated home reversion plan or a regulated home purchase plan;]

and nothing in this section affects the creation or operation of resulting, implied or constructive trusts.

(6) In this section—

'disposition' has the same meaning as in the Law of Property Act 1925;

'interest in land' means any estate, interest or charge in or over land [. . .]

['regulated mortgage contract', 'regulated home reversion plan' and 'regulated home purchase plan' must be read with—

    (a) section 22 of the Financial Services and Markets Act 2000,

    (b) any relevant order under that section, and

    (c) Schedule 2 to that Act.]

(7) Nothing in this section shall apply in relation to contracts made before this section comes into force.

(8) Section 40 of the Law of Property Act 1925 (which is superseded by this section) shall cease to have effect.

3   Abolition of rule in *Brian v Fothergill*

The rule of law known as the rule in *Brian v Fothergill* is abolished in relation to contracts made after this section comes into force.

Broadcasting Act 1990

(1990, c. 42)

166   Defamatory material

(1) For the purposes of the law of libel and slander [. . .] the publication of words in the course of any programme included in a programme service shall be treated as publication in permanent form.

(2) Subsection (1) above shall apply for the purposes of section 3 of each of the Defamation Acts (slander of title etc.) as it applies for the purposes of the law of libel and slander.

(4) In this section 'the Defamation Acts' means the Defamation Act 1952 and the Defamation Act (Northern Ireland) 1955.

Section 203(1)   **SCHEDULE 20**

MINOR AND CONSEQUENTIAL AMENDMENTS

Parliamentary Papers Act 1840 (c. 9)

1. Section 3 (protection in respect of proceedings for printing extracts from or abstracts of parliamentary papers) shall have effect as if the reference to printing included a reference to including in a programme service.

Courts and Legal Services Act 1990

(1990, c. 41)

8   Powers of Court of Appeal to award damages

(1) In this section 'case' means any case where the Court of Appeal has power to order a new trial on the ground that damages awarded by a jury are excessive or inadequate.

(2) Rules of court may provide for the Court of Appeal, in such classes of case as may be specified in the rules, to have power, in place of ordering a new trial, to substitute for the sum awarded by the jury such sum as appears to the court to be proper.

[58B   Litigation funding agreements

(1) A litigation funding agreement which satisfies all of the conditions applicable to it by virtue of this section shall not be unenforceable by reason only of its being a litigation funding agreement.]

61   Right of barrister to enter into contract for the provision of his services

(1) Any rule of law which prevents a barrister from entering into a contract for the provision of his services as a barrister is hereby abolished.

(2) Nothing in subsection (1) prevents the General Council of the Bar from making rules (however described) which prohibit barristers from entering into contracts or restrict their right to do so.

Environmental Protection Act 1990

(1990, c. 43)

PART II WASTE ON LAND

33 Prohibition on unauthorised or harmful deposit, treatment or disposal etc. of waste

. . .

34 Duty of care etc. as respects waste

(1) Subject to subsection (2) below, it shall be the duty of any person who imports, produces, carries, keeps, treats or disposes of controlled waste or, [as a dealer or broker], has control of such waste, to take all such measures applicable to him in that capacity as are reasonable in the circumstances—

(a) to prevent any contravention by any other person of section 33 above;

[(aa) to prevent any contravention by any person of regulation 12 of the 2007 Regulations or of an environmental permit;]

(b) to prevent the escape of the waste from his control or that of any other person;

(c) on the transfer of the waste, to secure—

(i) that the transfer is only to an authorised person or to a person for authorised transport purposes; and

(ii) that there is transferred such a written description of the waste as will enable other persons to avoid a contravention of that section [or regulation 12 of the 2007 Regulations, or a contravention of a condition of an environmental permit] and to comply with the duty under this subsection as respects the escape of waste.

(2) The duty imposed by subsection (1) above does not apply to an occupier of domestic property as respects the household waste produced on the property.

(6) Any person who fails to comply with the duty imposed by subsection (1) above or with any requirement imposed under subsection (5) above shall be liable—

(a) on summary conviction, to a fine not exceeding the statutory maximum; and

(b) on conviction on indictment, to a fine.

(7) The Secretary of State shall, after consultation with such persons or bodies as appear to him representative of the interests concerned, prepare and issue a code of practice for the purpose of providing to persons practical guidance on how to discharge the duty imposed on them by subsection (1) above.

73 Appeals and other provisions relating to legal proceedings and civil liability

(6) Where any damage is caused by waste which has been deposited in or on land, any person who deposited it, or knowingly caused or knowingly permitted it to be deposited, in either case so as to commit an offence under section 33(1) or 63(2) above, is liable for the damage except where the damage—

(a) was due wholly to the fault of the person who suffered it; or

(b) was suffered by a person who voluntarily accepted the risk of the damage being caused;

but without prejudice to any liability arising otherwise than under this subsection.

(7) The matters which may be proved by way of defence under section 33(7) above may be proved also by way of defence to an action brought under subsection (6) above.

(8) In subsection (6) above—

'damage' includes the death of, or injury to, any person (including any disease and any impairment of physical or mental condition); and

'fault' has the same meaning as in the Law Reform (Contributory Negligence) Act 1945.

(9) For the purposes of the following enactments—

(a) the Fatal Accidents Act 1976;

(b) the Law Reform (Contributory Negligence) Act 1945; and

(c) the Limitation Act 1980; . . .

[PART IIA CONTAMINATED LAND]

[78A Preliminary

(2) 'Contaminated land' is any land which appears to the local authority in whose area it is situated to be in such a condition, by reason of substances in, on or under the land, that—

(a) significant harm is being caused or there is a significant possibility of such harm being caused; or

(b) [significant pollution of controlled waters is being caused or there is a significant possibility of such pollution being caused];

and, in determining whether any land appears to be such land, a local authority shall, subject to subsection (5) below, act in accordance with guidance issued by the Secretary of State in accordance with section 78YA below with respect to the manner in which that determination is to be made.

(7) 'Remediation' means—

(a) the doing of anything for the purpose of assessing the condition of—

(i)   the contaminated land in question;

(ii) any controlled waters affected by that land; or

(iii) any land adjoining or adjacent to that land;

(b) the doing of any works, the carrying out of any operations or the taking of any steps in relation to any such land or waters for the purpose—

(i)   of preventing or minimising, or remedying or mitigating the effects of, any significant harm, or any pollution of controlled waters, by reason of which the contaminated land is such land; or

(ii) of restoring the land or waters to their former state; or

(c) the making of subsequent inspections from time to time for the purpose of keeping under review the condition of the land or waters;

and cognate expressions shall be construed accordingly.]

[78E Duty of enforcing authority to require remediation of contaminated land etc.

(1) In any case where—

(a) any land has been designated as a special site by virtue of section 78C(7) or 78D(6) above, or

(b) a local authority has identified any contaminated land (other than a special site) in its area,

the enforcing authority shall, in accordance with such procedure as may be prescribed and subject to the following provisions of this Part, serve on each person who is an appropriate person a notice (in this Part referred to as a 'remediation notice') specifying what that person is to do by way of remediation and the periods within which he is required to do each of the things so specified.]

[78K   Liability in respect of contaminating substances which escape to other land

(1) A person who has caused or knowingly permitted any substances to be in, on or under any land shall also be taken for the purposes of this Part to have caused or, as the case may be, knowingly permitted those substances to be in, on or under any other land to which they appear to have escaped.

(2) Subsections (3) and (4) below apply in any case where it appears that any substances are or have been in, on or under any land (in this section referred to as 'land') as a result of their escape, whether directly or indirectly, from other land in, on or under which a person caused or knowingly permitted them to be.

(3) Where this subsection applies, no remediation notice shall require a person—

    (a) who is the owner or occupier of land A, and

    (b) who has not caused or knowingly permitted the substances in question to be in, on or under that land,

to do anything by way of remediation to any land or waters (other than land or waters of which he is the owner or occupier) in consequence of land A appearing to be in such a condition, by reason of the presence of those substances in, on or under it, that significant harm[, or significant pollution of controlled waters,] is being caused, or there is a significant possibility of such harm [or pollution] being caused, or that pollution of controlled waters is being, or is likely to be caused.

(4) Where this subsection applies, no remediation notice shall require a person—

    (a) who is the owner or occupier of land A, and

    (b) who has not caused or knowingly permitted the substances in question to be in, on or under that land,

to do anything by way of remediation in consequence of any further land in, on or under which those substances or any of them appear to be or to have been present as a result of their escape from land ('land B') appearing to be in such a condition, by reason of the presence of those substances in, on or under it, that significant harm[, or significant pollution of controlled waters,] is being caused, or there is a significant possibility of such harm [or pollution] being caused, or that pollution of controlled waters is being, or is likely to be caused, unless he is also the owner or occupier of land B.

(5) In any case where—

    (a) a person ('person A') has caused or knowingly permitted any substances to be in, on, or under any land,

    (b) another person ('person B') who has not caused or knowingly permitted those substances to be in, on or under that land becomes the owner or occupier of that land, and

    (c) the substances, or any of the substances, mentioned in paragraph (a) above appear to have escaped to other land,

no remediation notice shall require person B to do anything by way of remediation to that other land in consequence of the apparent acts or omissions of person A, except to the extent that person B caused or knowingly permitted the escape.

(6) Nothing in subsection (3), (4) or (5) above prevents the enforcing authority from doing anything by way of remediation under section 78N below which it could have done apart from that subsection, but the authority shall not be entitled under section 78P below to recover from any person any part of the cost incurred by the authority in doing by way of remediation anything which it is precluded by subsection (3), (4) or (5) above from requiring that person to do.

(7) in this section, 'appear' means appear to the enforcing authority, and cognate expressions shall be construed accordingly.]

[78M   Offences of not complying with a remediation notice

(1) If a person on whom an enforcing authority serves a remediation notice fails, without reasonable excuse, to comply with any of the requirements of the notice, he shall be guilty of an offence.]

[78N   Powers of the enforcing authority to carry out remediation

(1) Where this section applies, the enforcing authority shall itself have power, in a case falling within paragraph (a) or (b) of section 78E(1) above, to do what is appropriate by way of remediation to the relevant land or waters.]

[78P   Recovery of, and security for, the cost of remediation by the enforcing authority

(1) Where, by virtue of section 78N(3)(a), (c), (e) or (f) above, the enforcing authority does any particular thing by way of remediation, it shall be entitled, subject to sections 78J(7) and 78K(6) above, to recover the reasonable cost incurred in doing it from the appropriate person or, if there are two or more appropriate persons in relation to the thing in question, from those persons in proportions determined pursuant to section 78F(7) above.

(2) In deciding whether to recover the cost, and, if so, how much of the cost, which it is entitled to recover under subsection (1) above, the enforcing authority shall have regard—

    (a) to any hardship which the recovery may cause to the person from whom the cost is recoverable; and

    (b) to any guidance issued by the Secretary of State for the purposes of this subsection.

(3) Subsection (4) below shall apply in any case where—

    (a) any cost is recoverable under subsection (1) above from a person—

        (i)   who is the owner of any premises which consist of or include the contaminated land in question; and

        (ii) who caused or knowingly permitted the substances, or any of the substances, by reason of which the land is contaminated and to be in, on or under the land; and

    (b) the enforcing authority serves a notice under this subsection (in this Part referred to as a 'charging notice') on that person.

(4) Where this subsection applies—

    (a) the cost shall carry interest, at such reasonable rate as the enforcing authority may determine, from the date of service of the notice until the whole amount is paid; and

    (b) subject to the following provisions of this section, the cost and accrued interest shall be a charge on the premises mentioned in subsection (3)(a)(i) above.]

PART III   STATUTORY NUISANCES AND CLEAN AIR

79   Statutory nuisances and inspections therefor

(1) [Subject to subsections (1A) to (6A) below], the following matters constitute 'statutory nuisances' for the purposes of this Part, that is to say—

    (a)   any premises in such a state as to be prejudicial to health or a nuisance;

    (b)   smoke emitted from premises so as to be prejudicial to health or a nuisance;

    (c)   fumes or gases emitted from premises so as to be prejudicial to health or a nuisance;

    (d)   any dust, steam, smell or other effluvia arising on industrial, trade or business premises and being prejudicial to health or a nuisance;

    (e)   any accumulation or deposit which is prejudicial to health or a nuisance;

    (f)   any animal kept in such a place or manner as to be prejudicial to health or a nuisance;

    [(fa) any insects emanating from relevant industrial, trade or business premises and being prejudicial to health or a nuisance;]

    [(fb) artificial light emitted from premises so as to be prejudicial to health or a nuisance;]

    (g)   noise emitted from premises so as to be prejudicial to health or a nuisance;

    [(ga) noise that is prejudicial to health or a nuisance and is emitted from or caused by a vehicle, machinery or equipment in a street or, in Scotland, road;]

    (h)   any other matter declared by any enactment to be a statutory nuisance;

and it shall be the duty of every local authority to cause its area to be inspected from time to time to detect any statutory nuisances which ought to be dealt with under section 80 below or sections 80 and 80A below and, where a complaint of a statutory nuisance is made to it by a person living within its area, to take such steps as are reasonably practicable to investigate the complaint.

[(1A) No matter shall constitute a statutory nuisance to the extent that it consists of, or is caused by, any land being in a contaminated state.]

80 Summary proceedings for statutory nuisances

(1) [Subject to subsection (2A)] Where a local authority is satisfied that a statutory nuisance exists, or is likely to occur or recur, in the area of the authority, the local authority shall serve a notice ('an abatement notice') imposing all or any of the following requirements—

    (a) requiring the abatement of the nuisance or prohibiting or restricting its occurrence or recurrence;

    (b) requiring the execution of such works, and the taking of such other steps, as may be necessary for any of those purposes,

and the notice shall specify the time or times within which the requirements of the notice are to be complied with.

(2) [Subject to section 80A(1) below, the abatement notice] shall be served—

    (a) except in a case falling within paragraph (b) or (c) below, on the person responsible for the nuisance;

    (b) where the nuisance arises from any defect of a structural character, on the owner of the premises;

    (c) where the person responsible for the nuisance cannot be found or the nuisance has not yet occurred, on the owner or occupier of the premises.

[(2A) Where a local authority is satisfied that a statutory nuisance falling within paragraph (g) of section 79(1) above exists, or is likely to occur or recur, in the area of the authority, the authority shall—

    (a) serve an abatement notice in respect of the nuisance in accordance with subsections (1) and (2) above; or

    (b) take such other steps as it thinks appropriate for the purpose of persuading the appropriate person to abate the nuisance or prohibit or restrict its occurrence or recurrence.

(2B) If a local authority has taken steps under subsection (2A)(b) above and either of the conditions in subsection (2C) below is satisfied, the authority shall serve an abatement notice in respect of the nuisance.

(2C) The conditions are—

    (a) that the authority is satisfied at any time before the end of the relevant period that the steps taken will not be successful in persuading the appropriate person to abate the nuisance or prohibit or restrict its occurrence or recurrence;

    (b) that the authority is satisfied at the end of the relevant period that the nuisance continues to exist, or continues to be likely to occur or recur, in the area of the authority.

(2D) The relevant period is the period of seven days starting with the day on which the authority was first satisfied that the nuisance existed, or was likely to occur or recur.

(2E) The appropriate person is the person on whom the authority would otherwise be required under subsection (2A)(a) above to serve an abatement notice in respect of the nuisance.]

(3) [A person served with an abatement notice] may appeal against the notice to a magistrates' court [or, in Scotland, the sheriff] within the period of twenty-one days beginning with the date on which he was served with the notice.

(4) If a person on whom an abatement notice is served, without reasonable excuse, contravenes or fails to comply with any requirement or prohibition imposed by the notice, he shall be guilty of an offence.

(7) Subject to subsection (8) below, in any proceedings for an offence under subsection (4) above in respect of a statutory nuisance it shall be a defence to prove that the best practicable means were used to prevent, or to counteract the effects of, the nuisance.

(8) The defence under subsection (7) above is not available—

(a)   in the case of a nuisance falling within paragraph (a), (d), (e), (f)[, (fa)] or (g) of section 79(1) above except where the nuisance arises on industrial, trade or business premises;

[(aza) in the case of a nuisance falling within paragraph (fb) of section 79(1) above except where—

(i)   the artificial light is emitted from industrial, trade or business premises, or

(ii)   the artificial light (not being light to which sub-paragraph (i) applies) is emitted by lights used for the purpose only of illuminating an outdoor relevant sports facility;]

[(aa) in the case of a nuisance falling within paragraph (ga) o section 79(1) above except where the noise is emitted from or caused by a vehicle, machinery or equipment being used for industrial, trade or business purposes;]

(b)   in the case of a nuisance falling within paragraph (b) of section 79(1) above except where the smoke is emitted from a chimney; and

(c)   in the case of a nuisance falling within paragraph (c) or (h) of section 79(1) above.

[80A Abatement notice in respect of noise in street

. . .]

82 Summary proceedings by person aggrieved by statutory nuisances

(1) A magistrates' court may act under this section on a complaint [or, in Scotland, the sheriff may act under this section on a summary application,] made by any person on the ground that he is aggrieved by the existence of a statutory nuisance.

(2) If the magistrates' court [or, in Scotland, the sheriff] is satisfied that the alleged nuisance exists, or that although abated it is likely to recur on the same premises [or, in the case of a nuisance within section 79(1)(ga) above, in the same street or, in Scotland, road], the court [or the sheriff] shall make an order for either or both of the following purposes—

(a) requiring the defendant [or, in Scotland, the defender] to abate the nuisance, within a time specified in the order, and to execute any work necessary for that purpose;

(b) prohibiting a recurrence of the nuisance, and requiring the defendant [or defender], within a time specified in the order, to execute any works necessary to prevent the recurrence,

and[, in England and Wales,] may also impose on the defendant a fine not exceeding level 5 on the standard scale.

(3) If the magistrates' court [or the sheriff] is satisfied that the alleged nuisance exists and is such as, in the opinion of the court [or the sheriff], to render premises unfit for human habitation, an order under subsection (2) above may prohibit the use of the premises for human habitation until the premises are, to the satisfaction of the court, rendered fit for that purpose.

(4) Proceedings for an order under subsection (2) above shall be brought—

(a)   except in a case falling within [paragraph (b), (c) or (d) below], against the person responsible for the nuisance;

(b)   where the nuisance arises from any defect of a structural character, against the owner of the premises;

(c)   where the person responsible for the nuisance cannot be found, against the owner or occupier of the premises.

[(d)   in the case of a statutory nuisance within section 79(1)(ga) above caused by noise emitted from or caused by an unattended vehicle or unattended machinery or equipment, against the person responsible for the vehicle, machinery or equipment.]

(5) [Subject to subsection (5A) below, where] more than one person is responsible for a statutory nuisance, subsections (1) to (4) above shall apply to each of those persons whether or not what any one of them is responsible for would by itself amount to a nuisance.

[(5A) In relation to a statutory nuisance within section 79(1)(ga) above for which more than one person is responsible (whether or not what any one of those persons is responsible for would by itself amount to such a nuisance), subsection (4)(a) above shall apply with the substitution of 'each person responsible for the nuisance who can be found' for 'the person responsible for the nuisance'.

(5B) In relation to a statutory nuisance within section 79(1)(ga) above caused by noise emitted from or caused by an unattended vehicle or unattended machinery or equipment for which more than one person is responsible, subsection (4)(d) above shall apply with the substitution of 'any person' for 'the person'.]

(8) A person who, without reasonable excuse, contravenes any requirement or prohibition imposed by an order under subsection (2) above shall be guilty of an offence and liable on summary conviction to a fine not exceeding level 5 on the standard scale together with a further fine of an amount equal to one-tenth of that level for each day on which the offence continues after the conviction.

(9) Subject to subsection (1) below, in any proceedings for an offence under subsection (8) above in respect of a statutory nuisance it shall be a defence to prove that the best practicable means were used to prevent, or to counteract the effects of, the nuisance.

(10) The defence under subsection (9) above is not available—

    (a)   in the case of a nuisance falling within paragraph (a), (d), (e), (f)[, (fa)] or (g) of section 79(1) above except where the nuisance arises on industrial, trade or business premises;

   [(aza) in the case of a nuisance falling within paragraph (fb) of section 79(1) above except where—

        (i)   the artificial light is emitted from industrial, trade or business premises, or

       (ii)   the artificial light (not being light to which sub-paragraph (i) applies) is emitted by lights used for the purpose only of illuminating an outdoor relevant sports facility;]

   [(aa) in the case of a nuisance falling within paragraph (ga) of section 79(1) above except where the noise is emitted from or caused by a vehicle, machinery or equipment being used for industrial, trade or business purposes;]

    (b)   in the case of a nuisance falling within paragraph (b) of section 79(1) above except where the smoke is emitted from a chimney; and

    (c)   in the case of a nuisance falling within paragraph (c) or (h) or section 79(1) above; and

    (d)   in the case of a nuisance which is such as to render the premises unfit for human habitation.

(11) If a person is convicted of an offence under subsection (8) above, a magistrates' court [or the sheriff] may, after giving the local authority in whose area the nuisance has occurred an opportunity of being heard, direct the authority to do anything which the person convicted was required to do by the order to which the conviction relates.

(12) Where on the hearing of proceedings for an order under subsection (2) above it is proved that the alleged nuisance existed at the date of the making of the complaint [or summary application], then, whether or not at the date of the hearing it still exists or is likely to recur, the court [or the sheriff] shall order the [defendant or defender (or defendants or defenders] in such proportions as appears fair and reasonable) to pay to the person bringing the proceedings such amount as the court [or the sheriff] considers reasonably sufficient to compensate him for any expenses properly incurred by him in the proceedings.

(13) If it appears to the magistrates' court [or the sheriff]that neither the person responsible for the nuisance nor the owner or occupier of the premises [or (as the case may be) the person responsible for the vehicle, machinery or equipment] can be found the court [or the sheriff] may, after giving the local authority in whose area the nuisance has occurred an opportunity of being

heard, direct the authority to do anything which the court [or the sheriff] would have ordered that person to do.

Food Safety Act 1990

(1990, c. 16)

44   Protection of officers acting in good faith
(1) An officer of a food authority is not personally liable in respect of any act done by him—
  (a) in the execution or purported execution of this Act; and
  (b) within the scope of his employment,
if he did that act in the honest belief that his duty under this Act required or entitled him to do it.

(2) Nothing in subsection (1) above shall be construed as relieving any food authority from any liability in respect of the acts of their officers.

(3) Where an action has been brought against an officer of a food authority in respect of an act done by him—
  (a) in the execution or purported execution of this Act; but
  (b) outside the scope of his employment,
the authority may indemnify him against the whole or a part of any damages which he has been ordered to pay or any costs which he may have incurred if they are satisfied that he honestly believed that the act complained of was within the scope of his employment.

Water Industry Act 1991

(1991, c. 56)

209   Civil liability of undertakers for escapes of water etc.
(1) Where an escape of water, however caused, from a pipe vested in a water undertaker causes loss or damage, the undertaker shall be liable, except as otherwise provided in this section, for the loss or damage.

(2) A water undertaker shall not incur any liability under subsection (1) above if the escape was due wholly to the fault of the person who sustained the loss or damage or of any servant, agent or contractor of his.

(3) A water undertaker shall not incur any liability under subsection (1) above in respect of any loss or damage for which the undertaker would not be liable apart from that subsection and which is sustained—
  (a) by [the Environment Agency], [the NRBW,] a relevant undertaker or any statutory undertakers, within the meaning of section 336(1) of the Town and Country Planning Act 1990;
  (b) by any public gas supplier within the meaning of Part I of the Gas Act 1986 or the holder of a licence under section 6(1) of the Electricity Act 1989;
  (c) by any highway authority; or
  (d) by any person on whom a right to compensation is conferred by section 82 of the New Roads and Street Works Act 1991.

(4) The Law Reform (Contributory Negligence) Act 1945, the Fatal Accidents Act 1976 and the Limitation Act 1980 shall apply in relation to any loss or damage for which a water undertaker is liable under this section, but which is not due to the undertaker's fault, as if it were due to its fault.

(5) Nothing in subsection (1) above affects any entitlement which a water undertaker may have to recover contribution under the Civil Liability (Contribution) Act 1978; and for the purposes of that Act, any loss for which a water undertaker is liable under that subsection shall be treated as if it were damage.

(6) Where a water undertaker is liable under any enactment or agreement passed or made before April 1, 1982, to make any payment in respect of any loss or damage the undertaker shall not incur liability under subsection (1) above in respect of the same loss or damage.

(7) In this section 'fault' has the same meaning as in the Law Reform (Contributory Negligence) Act 1945.

Water Resources Act 1991

(1991, c. 57)

[Restoration and improvement works for controlled waters]

[161   Anti-pollution works and operations

(1) This section applies where it appears to the appropriate agency that any poisonous, noxious or polluting matter or any waste matter is or has been present in, or is likely to enter, any controlled waters.

(2) In a case where the matter appears to be or to have been present in the controlled waters, the appropriate agency shall be entitled to carry out works and operations for any of the following purposes—

   (a) removing or disposing of the matter;
   (b) remedying or mitigating any pollution caused by its presence in the waters; or
   (c) restoring (so far as it is reasonably practicable to do so) the waters, including any flora and fauna dependent on the aquatic environment of the waters, to their state immediately before the matter became present in the waters.

(3) In a case where the matter appears to be likely to enter the controlled waters, the appropriate agency shall be entitled to carry out works and operations for the purpose of preventing it from doing so.

(4) The appropriate agency shall be entitled to carry out investigations for the purpose of establishing any of the following—

   (a) the nature of the matter,
   (b) the source of the matter;
   (c) the nature and effects of any pollution caused or likely to be caused by the presence of the matter; and
   (d) the identity of any responsible persons.

(5) Without prejudice to the power of the appropriate agency to carry out those investigations, the powers conferred by subsection (2) or (3) shall only be exercisable in a case where—

   (a) the appropriate agency considers it necessary to carry out forthwith any works or operations falling within that subsection; or
   (b) it appears to the appropriate agency, after reasonable enquiry, that no responsible person can be found on whom to serve a works notice.

(6) In this section "responsible person" means a person who has caused or knowingly permitted the matter—

   (a) to be present in the controlled waters; or
   (b) to be at a place from which it was likely, in the opinion of the appropriate agency, to enter the controlled waters.]

[161ZA   Other works and operations in respect of harm to controlled waters

(1) This section applies where it appears to the appropriate agency that any controlled waters are being or have been harmed, or are likely to be harmed, by any event, process or other source of potential harm (and it is immaterial whether the source of potential harm has been identified).

(2) In this section "harm" means any adverse impact on the condition of any hydromorphological quality element affecting the controlled waters that would be likely to prevent the achievement of the environmental objectives applicable to the controlled waters (whether by itself or in combination with other factors), other than an adverse impact caused by the entry into or presence in those waters of any poisonous, noxious or polluting matter or waste matter.

(3) In subsection (2) "environmental objectives" and "hydromorphological quality element" have the same meaning as in the Water Framework Directive.

(4) The appropriate agency shall be entitled to carry out works and operations for any of the following purposes (so far as it is reasonably practicable to achieve them)—

    (a) removing the source of potential harm;

    (b) preventing any harm or further harm being caused to the controlled waters;

    (c) in a case where the controlled waters are being or have been harmed—

        (i)   remedying or mitigating the effects of the harm;

        (ii) restoring the waters, including any flora and fauna dependent on the aquatic environment of the waters, to their state immediately before any harm was caused.

(5) The appropriate agency shall be entitled to carry out investigations for the purpose of establishing any of the following—

    (a) the source of any harm or potential harm to the controlled waters;

    (b) the nature and effects of any harm caused or likely to be caused to those waters; and

    (c) the identity of any responsible persons.

(6) Without prejudice to the power of the appropriate agency to carry out those investigations, the powers conferred by subsection (4) shall only be exercisable in a case where—

    (a) the appropriate agency considers it necessary to carry out forthwith any works or operations falling within that subsection; or

    (b) it appears to the appropriate agency, after reasonable enquiry, that no responsible person can be found on whom to serve a works notice.

(7) In this section "responsible person" means a person who has caused or knowingly permitted—

    (a) any harm to be caused to the controlled waters; or

    (b) a source of potential harm to exist that is likely, in the opinion of the appropriate agency, to cause harm to the controlled waters.]

[161ZB   Works and operations for improving controlled waters

(1) This section applies where it appears to the appropriate agency that—

    (a) the condition of any hydromorphological quality element affecting any controlled waters is unsatisfactory; and

    (b) it is possible to improve the hydromorphological quality element by carrying out works or operations.

(2) For the purposes of this section the condition of a hydromorphological quality element affecting the controlled waters is unsatisfactory if (whether by itself or in combination with other factors) if it is likely to prevent the waters from achieving the applicable environmental objectives.

(3) In this section "environmental objectives" and "hydromorphological quality element" have the same meaning as in the Water Framework Directive.

(4) The appropriate agency shall be entitled to carry out works and operations for the purpose of improving the condition of the hydromorphological quality element in question with a view to achieving (or contributing to the achievement of) the applicable environmental objectives.

(5) The appropriate agency shall be entitled to carry out investigations for the purpose of establishing why the condition of the hydromorphological quality element in question is unsatisfactory.

(6) Without prejudice to the power of the appropriate agency to carry out those investigations, the powers conferred by subsection (4) shall only be exercisable if it appears to the appropriate agency that it is unable to secure that the necessary works or operations are carried out by exercising its powers under section 161 or 161ZA or by serving a works notice on any responsible person.]

[161ZC   Sections 161 to 161ZB: supplementary

(1) Nothing in sections 161 to 161ZB shall entitle the appropriate agency to impede or prevent the making of any discharge in pursuance of an environmental permit.

(2) Where the appropriate agency carries out any works, operations or investigations under any of the powers conferred by section 161 or 161ZA it shall, subject to subsection (3), be entitled to recover the expenses reasonably incurred in doing so from any responsible person (within the meaning of the section conferring the powers in question).

(6) Nothing in sections 161, 161ZA and 161ZB—

(a) derogates from any right of action or other remedy (whether civil or criminal) in proceedings instituted otherwise than under any of those sections; or

(b) affects any restriction imposed by or under any other enactment, whether public local or private.

(7) In this section—

"expenses" includes costs; . . .

"works notice" means a notice under section 161A.

(8) In sections 161, 161ZA and 161ZB and this section "controlled waters" has the same meaning as in Part 3 of this Act and in sections 161ZA and 161ZB, and "Water Framework Directive" has the same meaning as in section 93(7) of this Act.]

[161A   Notices requiring persons to carry out works and operations

(1) Where it appears to the appropriate agency that—

(a) any poisonous, noxious or polluting matter or any waste matter is or has been present in, or is likely to enter, any controlled waters (so that section 161 applies), or

(b) any controlled waters are being or have been harmed, or are likely to be harmed, by any event, process or other source of potential harm (so that section 161ZA applies),

the appropriate agency shall be entitled to serve a works notice on any responsible person.

(2) In this section "responsible person" has the same meaning as in section 161 or 161ZA) (as the case may be).

(3) For the purposes of this section a works notice is a notice requiring the person on whom it is served to carry out such works or operations as may be specified in the notice.

(4) The works or operations that may be so specified are works or operations which may be carried out under section 161(2) or (3) or section 161ZA(4) (as the case may be).

(5) Where the appropriate agency has carried out any such investigations as are mentioned in sections 161(4) or 161ZA(5) and serves a works notice on a responsible person in connection with the matters to which the investigations relate it shall (unless the notice is quashed or withdrawn) be entitled to recover from that person the costs or expenses reasonably incurred in carrying out those investigations.

(6) The appropriate national authority may, if it thinks fit in relation to any person, give directions to the appropriate agency as to whether or how it should exercise its powers under this section or section 161AA.]

[161B   Grant of, and compensation for, rights of entry etc.

. . .]

[161D   Consequences of not complying with a works notice

(1) If a person on whom the [appropriate agency] serves a works notice fails to comply with any of the requirements of the notice, he shall be guilty of an offence.]

208   Civil liability of the [Agency] for escapes of water etc.

(1) Where an escape of water, however caused, from a pipe vested in the [Agency] causes loss or damage, the [Agency] shall be liable, except as otherwise provided in this section, for the loss or damage.

(2) The [Agency] shall not incur any liability under subsection (1) above if the escape was due wholly to the fault of the person who sustained the loss or damage or of any servant, agent or contractor of his.

(3) The [Agency] shall not incur any liability under subsection (1) above in respect of any loss or damage for which the [Agency] would not be liable apart from that subsection and which is sustained—

(a) by any water undertaker or sewerage undertaker or by any statutory undertakers, within the meaning of section 336(1) of the Town and Country Planning Act 1990;

(b) by any public gas supplier within the meaning of Part I of the Gas Act 1986 or the holder of a licence under section 6(1) of the Electricity Act 1989;

(c) by any highway authority; or

(d) by any person on whom a right to compensation is conferred by section 82 of the New Roads and Street Works Act 1991.

(4) The Law Reform (Contributory Negligence) Act 1945, the Fatal Accidents Act 1976 and the Limitation Act 1980 shall apply in relation to any loss or damage for which the [Agency] is liable under this section, but which is not due to the [Agency's] fault, as if it were due to its fault.

(5) Nothing in subsection (1) above affects any entitlement which the [Agency] may have to recover contribution under the Civil Liability (Contribution) Act 1978; and for the purposes of that Act, any loss for which the Authority is liable under that subsection shall be treated as if it were damage.

(6) Where the [Agency] is liable under any enactment or agreement passed or made before April 1, 1982, to make any payment in respect of any loss or damage the [Agency] shall not incur liability under subsection (1) above in respect of the same loss or damage.

(7) In this section 'fault' has the same meaning as in the Law Reform (Contributory Negligence) Act 1945.

221   General interpretation

(1) In this Act, except in so far as the context otherwise requires—

. . .

['the Agency' means the Environment Agency;] . . .

Access to Neighbouring Land Act 1992

(1992, c. 23)

1   Access orders

(1) A person—

(a) who, for the purpose of carrying out works to any land (the 'dominant land'), desires to enter upon any adjoining or adjacent land (the 'servient land'), and

(b) who needs, but does not have, the consent of some other person to that entry, may make an application to the court for an order under this section ('an access order') against that other person.

(2) On an application under this section, the court shall make an access order if, and only if, it is satisfied—

(a) that the works are reasonably necessary for the preservation of the whole or any part of the dominant land; and

(b) that they cannot be carried out, or would be substantially more difficult to carry out, without entry upon the servient land;

but this subsection is subject to subsection (3) below.

(3) The court shall not make an access order in any case where it is satisfied that, were it to make such an order—

    (a) the respondent or any other person would suffer interference with, or disturbance of, his use or enjoyment of the servient land, or

    (b) the respondent, or any other person (whether of full age or capacity or not) in occupation of the whole or any part of the servient land, would suffer hardship,

to such a degree by reason of the entry (notwithstanding any requirement of this Act or any term or condition that may be imposed under it) that it would be unreasonable to make the order.

(4) Where the court is satisfied on an application under this section that it is reasonably necessary to carry out any basic preservation works to the dominant land, those works shall be taken for the purposes of this Act to be reasonably necessary for the preservation of the land; and in this subsection 'basic preservation works' means any of the following, that is to say—

    (a) the maintenance, repair or renewal of any part of a building or other structure comprised in, or situate on, the dominant land;

    (b) the clearance, repair or renewal of any drain, sewer, pipe or cable so comprised or situate;

    (c) the treatment, cutting back, felling, removal or replacement of any hedge, tree, shrub or other growing thing which is so comprised and which is, or is in danger of becoming, damaged, diseased, dangerous, insecurely rooted or dead;

    (d) the filling in, or clearance, of any ditch so comprised;

but this subsection is without prejudice to the generality of the works which may, apart from it, be regarded by the court as reasonably necessary for the preservation of any land.

(5) If the court considers it fair and reasonable in all the circumstances of the case, works may be regarded for the purposes of this Act as being reasonably necessary for the preservation of any land (or, for the purposes of subsection (4) above, as being basic preservation works which it is reasonably necessary to carry out to any land) notwithstanding that the works incidentally involve—

    (a) the making of some alteration, adjustment or improvement to the land, or

    (b) the demolition of the whole or any part of a building or structure comprised in or situate upon the land.

(6) Where any works are reasonably necessary for the preservation of the whole or any part of the dominant land, the doing to the dominant land of anything which is requisite for, incidental to, or consequential on, the carrying out of those works shall be treated for the purposes of this Act as the carrying out of works which are reasonably necessary for the preservation of that land; and references in this Act to works, or to the carrying out of works, shall be construed accordingly.

(7) Without prejudice to the generality of subsection (6) above, if it is reasonably necessary for a person to inspect the dominant land—

    (a) for the purpose of ascertaining whether any works may be reasonably necessary for the preservation of the whole or any part of that land,

    (b) for the purpose of making any map or plan, or ascertaining the course of any drain, sewer, pipe or cable, in preparation for, or otherwise in connection with, the carrying out of works which are so reasonably necessary, or

    (c) otherwise in connection with the carrying out of any such works,

the making of such an inspection shall be taken for the purposes of this Act to be the carrying out to the dominant land of works which are reasonably necessary for the preservation of that land; and references in this Act to works, or to the carrying out of works, shall be construed accordingly.

2   Terms and conditions of access orders

(1) An access order shall specify—

    (a) the works to the dominant land that may be carried out by entering upon the servient land in pursuance of the order;

    (b) the particular area of servient land that may be entered upon by virtue of the order for the purpose of carrying out those works to the dominant land; and

(c) the date on which, or the period during which, the land may be so entered upon;
and in the following provisions of this Act any reference to the servient land is a reference to the area specified in the order in pursuance of paragraph (b) above.

(2) An access order may impose upon the applicant or the respondent such terms and conditions as appear to the court to be reasonably necessary for the purpose of avoiding or restricting—

(a) any loss, damage, or injury which might otherwise be caused to the respondent or any other person by reason of the entry authorised by the order; or

(b) any inconvenience or loss of privacy that might otherwise be so caused to the respondent or any other person.

(3) Without prejudice to the generality of subsection (2) above, the terms and conditions which may be imposed under that subsection include provisions with respect to—

(a) the manner in which the specified works are to be carried out;

(b) the days on which, and the hours between which, the work involved may be executed;

(c) the persons who may undertake the carrying out of the specified works or enter upon the servient land under or by virtue of the order;

(d) the taking of any such precautions by the applicant as may be specified in the order.

(4) An access order may also impose terms and conditions—

(a) requiring the applicant to pay, or to secure that such person connected with him as may be specified in the order pays, compensation for—

(i) any loss, damage or injury, or

(ii) any substantial loss of privacy or other substantial inconvenience,

which will, or might, be caused to the respondent or any other person by reason of the entry authorised by the order;

(b) requiring the applicant to secure that he, or such person connected with him as may be specified in the order, is insured against any such risks as may be so specified;

(c) requiring such a record to be made of the condition of the servient land, or of such part of it as may be so specified, as the court may consider expedient with a view to facilitating the determination of any question that may arise concerning damage to that land.

(5) An access order may include provision requiring the applicant to pay the respondent such sum by way of consideration for the privilege of entering the servient land in pursuance of the order as appears to the court to be fair and reasonable having regard to all the circumstances of the case, including in particular—

(a) the likely financial advantage of the order to the applicant and any persons connected with him; and

(b) the degree of inconvenience likely to be caused to the respondent or any other person by the entry;

but no payment shall be ordered under this subsection if and to the extent that the works which the applicant desires to carry out by means of the entry are works to residential land.

(6) For the purposes of subsection (5)(a) above, the likely financial advantage of an access order to the applicant and any persons connected with him shall in all cases be taken to be a sum of money equal to the greater of the following amounts, that is to say—

(a) the amount (if any) by which so much of any likely increase in the value of any land—

(i) which consists of or includes the dominant land, and

(ii) which is owned or occupied by the same person as the dominant land,

as may reasonably be regarded as attributable to the carrying out of the specified works exceeds the likely cost of carrying out those works with the benefit of the access order; and

(b) the difference (if it would have been possible to carry out the specified works without entering upon the servient land) between—

(i) the likely cost of carrying out those works without entering upon the servient land; and

(ii) the likely cost of carrying them out with the benefit of the access order.

(7) For the purposes of subsection (5) above, 'residential land' means so much of any land as consists of—

(a) a dwelling or part of a dwelling;

(b) a garden, yard, private garage or outbuilding which is used and enjoyed wholly or mainly with a dwelling; or

(c) in the case of a building which includes one or more dwellings, any part of the building which is used and enjoyed wholly or mainly with those dwellings or any of them.

(8) The persons who are to be regarded for the purposes of this section as 'connected with' the applicant are—

(a) the owner of any estate or interest in, or right over, the whole or any part of the dominant land;

(b) the occupier of the whole or any part of the dominant land; and

(c) any person whom the applicant may authorise under section 3(7) below to exercise the power of entry conferred by the access order.

(9) The court may make provision—

(a) for the reimbursement by the applicant of any expenses reasonably incurred by the respondent in connection with the application which are not otherwise recoverable as costs;

(b) for the giving of security by the applicant for any sum that might become payable to the respondent or any other person by virtue of this section or section 3 below.

3   Effect of access order

(1) An access order requires the respondent, so far as he has power to do so, to permit the applicant or any of his associates to do anything which the applicant or associate is authorised or required to do under or by virtue of the order or this section.

(2) Except as otherwise provided by or under this Act, an access order authorises the applicant or any of his associates, without the consent of the respondent,—

(a) to enter upon the servient land for the purpose of carrying out the specified works;

(b) to bring on to that land, leave there during the period permitted by the order and, before the end of that period, remove, such materials, plant and equipment as are reasonably necessary for the carrying out of those works; and

(c) to bring on to that land any waste arising from the carrying out of those works, if it is reasonably necessary to do so in the course of removing it from the dominant land; but nothing in this Act or in any access order shall authorise the applicant or any of his associates to leave anything in, on or over the servient land (otherwise than in discharge of their duty to make good that land) after their entry for the purpose of carrying out works to the dominant land ceases to be authorised under or by virtue of the order.

(3) An access order requires the applicant—

(a) to secure that any waste arising from the carrying out of the specified works is removed from the servient land forthwith;

(b) to secure that, before the entry ceases to be authorised under or by virtue of the order, the servient land is, so far as reasonably practicable, made good; and

(c) to indemnify the respondent against any damage which may be caused to the servient land or any goods by the applicant or any of his associates which would not have been so caused had the order not been made;

but this subsection is subject to subsections (4) and (5) below.

(4) In making an access order, the court may vary or exclude, in whole or in part,—

(a) any authorisation that would otherwise be conferred by subsection 2(b) or (c) above; or

(b) any requirement that would otherwise be imposed by subsection (3) above.

(5) Without prejudice to the generality of subsection (4) above, if the court is satisfied that it is reasonably necessary for any such waste as may arise from the carrying out of the specified works to

be left on the servient land for some period before removal, the access order may, in place of subsection (3)(a) above, include provision—

    (a) authorising the waste to be left on that land for such period as may be permitted by the order; and

    (b) requiring the applicant to secure that the waste is removed before the end of that period.

(6) Where the applicant or any of his associates is authorised or required under or by virtue of an access order or this section to enter, or do any other thing, upon the servient land, he shall not (as respects that access order) be taken to be a trespasser from the beginning on account of his, or any other person's, subsequent conduct.

(7) For the purposes of this section, the applicant's 'associates' are such number of persons (whether or not servants or agents of his) whom he may reasonably authorise under this subsection to exercise the power of entry conferred by the access order as may be reasonably necessary for carrying out the specified works.

4   Persons bound by access order, unidentified persons and bar on contracting out

(1) In addition to the respondent, an access order shall, subject to the provisions of the Land Charges Act 1972 and the [Land Registration Act 2002], be binding on—

    (a) any of his successors in title to the servient land; and

    (b) any person who has an estate or interest in, or right over, the whole or any part of the servient land which was created after the making of the order and who derives his title to that estate, interest or right under the respondent;

and references to the respondent shall be construed accordingly.

(2) If and to the extent that the court considers it just and equitable to allow him to do so, a person on whom an access order becomes binding by virtue of subsection (1)(a) or (b) above shall be entitled, as respects anything falling to be done after the order becomes binding on him, to enforce the order or any of its terms or conditions as if he were the respondent, and references to the respondent shall be construed accordingly.

(3) Rules of court may—

    (a) provide a procedure which may be followed where the applicant does not know, and cannot reasonably ascertain, the name of any person whom he desires to make respondent to the application; and

    (b) make provision enabling such an applicant to make such a person respondent by description instead of by name;

and in this subsection 'applicant' includes a person who proposes to make an application for an access order.

(4) Any agreement, whenever made, shall be void if and to the extent that it would, apart from this subsection, prevent a person from applying for an access order or restrict his right to do so.

6   Variation of orders and damages for breach

(1) Where an access order or an order under this subsection has been made, the court may, on the application of any party to the proceedings in which the order was made or of any other person on whom the order is binding—

    (a) discharge or vary the order or any of its terms or conditions;

    (b) suspend any of its terms or conditions; or

    (c) revive any term or condition suspended under paragraph (b) above;

and in the application of subsections (1) and (2) of section 4 above in relation to an access order, any order under this subsection which relates to the access order shall be treated for the purposes of those subsections as included in the access order.

(2) If any person contravenes or fails to comply with any requirement, term or condition imposed upon him by or under this Act, the court may, without prejudice to any other remedy available, make an order for the payment of damages by him to any other person affected by the contravention or failure who makes an application for relief under this subsection.

Carriage of Goods by Sea Act 1992

(1992, c. 50)

1 Shipping documents etc. to which Act applies

(1) This Act applies to the following documents, that is to say—

    (a) any bill of lading;

    (b) any sea waybill; and

    (c) any ship's delivery order.

(2) References in this Act to a bill of lading—

    (a) do not include references to a document which is incapable of transfer either by indorsement or, as a bearer bill, by delivery without indorsement; but

    (b) subject to that, do include references to a received for shipment bill of lading.

(3) References in this Act to a sea waybill are references to any document which is not a bill of lading but—

    (a) is such a receipt for goods as contains or evidences a contract for the carriage of goods by sea; and

    (b) identifies the person to whom delivery of the goods is to be made by the carrier in accordance with that contract.

(4) References in this Act to a ship's delivery order are references to any document which is neither a bill of lading nor a sea waybill but contains an undertaking which—

    (a) is given under or for the purposes of a contract for the carriage by sea of the goods to which the document relates, or of goods which include those goods; and

    (b) is an undertaking by the carrier to a person identified in the document to deliver the goods to which the document relates to that person.

(5) The Secretary of State may by regulations make provision for the application of this Act to cases where[an electronic communications network] or any other information technology is used for effecting transactions corresponding to—

    (a) the issue of a document to which this Act applies;

    (b) the indorsement, delivery or other transfer of such a document; or

    (c) the doing of anything else in relation to such a document.

(6) Regulations under subsection (5) above may—

    (a) make such modifications of the following provisions of this Act as the Secretary of State considers appropriate in connection with the application of this Act to any case mentioned in that subsection; and

    (b) contain supplemental, incidental, consequential and transitional provision; and the power to make regulations under that subsection shall be exercisable by statutory instrument subject to annulment in pursuance of a resolution of either House of Parliament.

2 Rights under shipping documents

(1) Subject to the following provisions of this section, a person who becomes—

    (a) the lawful holder of a bill of lading;

    (b) the person who (without being an original party to the contract of carriage) is the person to whom delivery of the goods to which a sea waybill relates is to be made by the carrier in accordance with that contract; or

    (c) the person to whom delivery of the goods to which a ship's delivery order relates is to be made in accordance with the undertaking contained in the order,

shall (by virtue of becoming the holder of the bill or, as the case may be, the person to whom delivery is to be made) have transferred to and vested in him all rights of suit under the contract of carriage as if he had been a party to that contract.

(2) Where, when a person becomes the lawful holder of a bill of lading, possession of the bill no longer gives a right (as against the carrier) to possession of the goods to which the bill relates,

that person shall not have any rights transferred to him by virtue of subsection (1) above unless he becomes the holder of the bill—

    (a) by virtue of a transaction effected in pursuance of any contractual or other arrangements made before the time when such a right to possession ceased to attach to possession of the bill; or

    (b) as a result of the rejection to that person by another person of goods or documents delivered to the other person in pursuance of any such arrangements.

    (3) The rights vested in any person by virtue of the operation of subsection (1) above in relation to a ship's delivery order—

    (a) shall be so vested subject to the terms of the order; and

    (b) where the goods to which the order relates form a part only of the goods to which the contract of carriage relates, shall be confined to rights in respect of the goods to which the order relates.

    (4) Where, in the case of any document to which this Act applies—

    (a) a person with any interest or right in or in relation to goods to which the document relates sustains loss or damage in consequence of a breach of the contract of carriage; but

    (b) subsection (1) above operates in relation to that document so that rights of suit in respect of that breach are vested in another person,

the other person shall be entitled to exercise those rights for the benefit of the person who sustained the loss or damage to the same extent as they could have been exercised if they had been vested in the person for whose benefit they are exercised.

    (5) Where rights are transferred by virtue of the operation of subsection (1) above in relation to any document, the transfer for which that subsection provides shall extinguish any entitlement to those rights which derives—

    (a) where that document is a bill of lading, from a person's having been an original party to the contract of carriage; or

    (b) in the case of any document to which this Act applies, from the previous operation of that subsection in relation to that document;

but the operation of that subsection shall be without prejudice to any rights which derive from a person's having been an original party to the contract contained in, or evidenced by, a sea waybill and, in relation to a ship's delivery order, shall be without prejudice to any rights deriving otherwise than from the previous operation of that subsection in relation to that order.

3 Liabilities under shipping documents

    (1) Where subsection (1) of section 2 of this Act operates in relation to any document to which this Act applies and the person in whom rights are vested by virtue of that subsection—

    (a) takes or demands delivery from the carrier of any of the goods to which the document relates;

    (b) makes a claim under the contract of carriage against the carrier in respect of any of those goods; or

    (c) is a person who, at a time before those rights were vested in him, took or demanded delivery from the carrier of any of those goods,

that person shall (by virtue of taking or demanding delivery or making the claim or, in a case falling within paragraph (c) above, of having the rights vested in him) become subject to the same liabilities under that contract as if he had been a party to that contract.

    (2) Where the goods to which a ship's delivery order relates form a part only of the goods to which the contract of carriage relates, the liabilities to which any person is subject by virtue of the operation of this section in relation to that order shall exclude liabilities in respect of any goods to which the order does not relate.

    (3) This section, so far as it imposes liabilities under any contract on any person, shall be without prejudice to the liabilities under the contract of any person as an original party to the contract.

4   Representations in bills of lading

A bill of lading which—

(a) represents goods to have been shipped on board a vessel or to have been received for shipment on board a vessel; and

(b) has been signed by the master of the vessel or by a person who was not the master but had the express, implied or apparent authority of the carrier to sign bills of lading,

shall, in favour of a person who has become the lawful holder of the bill, be conclusive evidence against the carrier of the shipment of the goods or, as the case may be, of their receipt for shipment.

5   Interpretation etc.

(1) In this Act—

'bill of lading', 'sea way bill' and 'ship's delivery order' shall be construed in accordance with section 1 above;

'the contract of carriage'—

(a) in relation to a bill of lading or sea waybill, means the contract contained in or evidenced by that bill or waybill; and

(b) in relation to a ship's delivery order, means the contract under or for the purposes of which the undertaking contained in the order is given;

'holder', in relation to a bill of lading, shall be construed in accordance with subsection (2) below;

'information technology' includes any computer or other technology by means of which information or other matter may be recorded or communicated without being reduced to documentary form;

[. . .].

(2) References in this Act to the holder of a bill of lading are references to any of the following persons, that is to say—

(a) a person with possession of the bill who, by virtue of being the person identified in the bill, is the consignee of the goods to which the bill relates;

(b) a person with possession of the bill as a result of the completion, by delivery of the bill, of any indorsement of the bill or, in the case of a bearer bill, of any other transfer of the bill;

(c) a person with possession of the bill as a result of any transaction by virtue of which he would have become a holder falling within paragraph (a) or (b) above had not the transaction been effected at a time when possession of the bill no longer gave a right (as against the carrier) to possession of the goods to which the bill relates;

and a person shall be regarded for the purposes of this Act as having become the lawful holder of a bill of lading wherever he has become the holder of the bill in good faith.

(3) References in this Act to a person's being identified in a document include references to his being identified by a description which allows for the identity of the person in question to be varied, in accordance with the terms of the document, after its issue; and the reference in section 1(3)(b) of this Act to a document's identifying a person shall be construed accordingly.

(4) Without prejudice to sections 2(2) and 4 above, nothing in this Act shall preclude its operation in relation to a case where the goods to which a document relates—

(a) cease to exist after the issue of the document; or

(b) cannot be identified (whether because they are mixed with other goods or for any other reason);

and references in this Act to the goods to which a document relates shall be construed accordingly.

(5) The preceding provisions of this Act shall have effect without prejudice to the application, in relation to any case, of the rules (the Hague-Visby Rules) which for the time being have the force of law by virtue of section 1 of the Carriage of Goods by Sea Act 1971.

Social Security Contributions and Benefits Act 1992

(1992, c. 4)

94   Right to industrial injuries benefit

(1) Industrial injuries benefit shall be payable where an employed earner suffers personal injury caused [. . .] by accident arising out of and in the course of his employment, being employed earner's employment.

(3) For the purposes of industrial injuries benefit an accident arising in the course of an employed earner's employment shall be taken, in the absence of evidence to the contrary, also to have arisen out of that employment.

97   Accidents in course of illegal employments

(1) Subsection (2) below has effect in any case where—

(a) a claim is made for industrial injuries benefit in respect of an accident, or of a prescribed disease or injury; or

(b) an application is made under section 29 of the Social Security Act 1998 for a declaration that an accident was an industrial accident, or for a corresponding declaration as to a prescribed disease or injury.

(2) The Secretary of State may direct that the relevant employment shall, in relation to that accident, disease or injury, be treated as having been employed earner's employment notwithstanding that by reason of a contravention of, or non-compliance with, some provision contained in or having effect under an enactment passed for the protection of employed persons or any class of employed persons, either—

(a) the contract purporting to govern the employment was void; or

(b) the employed person was not lawfully employed in the relevant employment at the time when, or in the place where, the accident happened or the disease or injury was contracted or received.

(3) In subsection (2) above 'relevant employment' means—

(a) in relation to an accident, the employment out of and in the course of which the accident arises; and

(b) in relation to a prescribed disease or injury, the employment to the nature of which the disease or injury is due.

98   Earner acting in breach of regulations, etc.

An accident shall be taken to arise out of and in the course of an employed earner's employment, notwithstanding that he is at the time of the accident acting in contravention of any statutory or other regulations applicable to his employment, or of any orders given by or on behalf of his employer, or that he is acting without instructions from his employer, if—

(a) the accident would have been taken so to have arisen had the act not been done in contravention of any such regulations or orders, or without such instructions, as the case may be; and

(b) the act is done for the purposes of and in connection with the employer's trade or business.

100   Accidents happening while meeting emergency

An accident happening to an employed earner in or about any premises at which he is for the time being employed for the purposes of his employer's trade or business shall be taken to arise out of and in the course of his employment if it happens while he is taking steps, on an actual or supposed emergency at those premises, to rescue, succour or protect persons who are, or are thought to be or possibly to be, injured or imperilled, or to avert or minimise serious damage to property.

101 Accident caused by another's misconduct etc.

An accident happening after 19 December 1961 shall be treated for the purposes of industrial injuries benefit, where it would not apart from this section be so treated, as arising out of an employed earner's employment if—

    (a) the accident arises in the course of the employment; and

    (b) the accident either is caused—

        (i) by another person's misconduct, skylarking or negligence, or

        (ii) by steps taken in consequence of any such misconduct, skylarking or negligence, or

        (iii) by the behaviour or presence of an animal (including a bird, fish or insect), or is caused by or consists in the employed earner being struck by any object or by lightning; and

    (c) the employed earner did not directly or indirectly induce or contribute to the happening of the accident by his conduct outside the employment or by any act not incidental to the employment.

174 References to Acts

In this Act—

    'the Administration Act' means the Social Security Administration Act 1992;

Trade Union and Labour Relations (Consolidation) Act 1992

(1992, c. 52)

1 Meaning of 'trade union'

In this Act a 'trade union' means an organisation (whether temporary or permanent)—

    (a) which consists wholly or mainly of workers of one or more descriptions and whose principal purposes include the regulation of relations between workers of that description or those descriptions and employers or employers' associations; or . . .

10 Quasi-corporate status of trade unions

    (1) A trade union is not a body corporate but—

    (a) it is capable of making contracts;

    (b) it is capable of suing and being sued in its own name, whether in proceedings relating to property or founded on contract or tort or any other cause of action; and

    (c) proceedings for an offence alleged to have been committed by it or on its behalf may be brought against it in its own name.

11 Exclusion of common law rules as to restraint of trade

    (1) The purposes of a trade union are not, by reason only that they are in restraint of trade, unlawful so as—

    (a) to make any member of the trade union liable to criminal proceedings for conspiracy or otherwise, or

    (b) to make any agreement or trust void or voidable.

    (2) No rule of a trade union is unlawful or unenforceable by reason only that it is in restraint of trade.

20 Liability of trade union in certain proceedings in tort

    (1) Where proceedings in tort are brought against a trade union—

    (a) on the ground that an act—

        (i) induces another person to break a contract or interferes or induces another person to interfere with its performance, or

        (ii) consists in threatening that a contract (whether one to which the union is a party or not) will be broken or its performance interfered with, or that the union will induce another person to break a contract or interfere with its performance, or

    (b) in respect of an agreement or combination by two or more persons to do or to procure the doing of an act which, if it were done without any such agreement or combination, would be actionable in tort on such a ground,

then, for the purpose of determining in those proceedings whether the union is liable in respect of the act in question, that act shall be taken to have been done by the union if, but only if, it is to be taken to have been authorised or endorsed by the trade union in accordance with the following provisions.

    (5) Where for the purposes of any proceedings an act is by virtue of this section taken to have been done by a trade union, nothing in this section shall affect the liability of any other person, in those or any other proceedings, in respect of that act.

    (6) In proceedings arising out of an act which is by virtue of this section taken to have been done by a trade union, the power of the court to grant an injunction or interdict includes power to require the union to take such steps as the court considers appropriate for ensuring—

    (a) that there is no, or no further, inducement of persons to take part or to continue to take part in industrial action, and

    (b) that no person engages in any conduct after the granting of the injunction or interdict by virtue of having been induced before it was granted to take part or to continue to take part in industrial action.

The provisions of subsections (2) to (4) above apply in relation to proceedings for failure to comply with any such injunction or interdict as they apply in relation to the original proceedings.

22 Limit on damages awarded against trade unions in actions in tort

    (1) This section applies to any proceedings in tort brought against a trade union, except—

    (a) proceedings for personal injury as a result of negligence, nuisance or breach of duty;

    (b) proceedings for breach of duty in connection with the ownership, occupation, possession, control or use of property;

    (c) proceedings brought by virtue of Part I of the Consumer Protection Act 1987 (product liability).

In any proceedings in tort to which this section applies the amount which may be awarded against the union by way of damages shall not exceed the following limit—

Number of members of union	Maximum award of damages
Less than 5,000	£10,000
5,000 or more but less than 25,000	£50,000
25,000 or more but less than 100,000	£125,000
100,000 or more	£250,000

    (3) The Secretary of State may by order amend subsection (2) so as to vary any of the sums specified . . .

127 Corporate or quasi-corporate status of employers' associations

    (1) An employers' association may be either a body corporate or an unincorporated association.

    (2) Where an employers' association is unincorporated—

    (a) it is capable of making contracts;

    (b) it is capable of suing and being sued in its own name, whether in proceedings relating to property or founded on contract or tort or any other cause of action; and

    (c) proceedings for an offence alleged to have been committed by it or on its behalf may be brought against it in its own name.

128   Exclusion of common law rules as to restraint of trade

(1) The purposes of an unincorporated employers' association and, so far as they relate to the regulation of relations between employers and workers or trade unions, the purposes of an employers' association which is a body corporate are not, by reason only that they are in restraint of trade, unlawful so as—

(a) to make any member of the association liable to criminal proceedings for conspiracy or otherwise, or

(b) to make any agreement or trust void or voidable.

(2) No rule of an unincorporated employers' association or, so far as it relates to the regulation of relations between employers and workers or trade unions, of an employers' association which is a body corporate, is unlawful or unenforceable by reason only that it is in restraint of trade.

137   Refusal of employment on grounds related to union membership

(1) It is unlawful to refuse a person employment—

(a) because he is, or is not, a member of a trade union, or

(b) because he is unwilling to accept a requirement—

(i)   to take steps to become or cease to be, or to remain or not to become, a member of a trade union, or

(ii)   to make payments or suffer deductions in the event of his not being a member of a trade union.

(2) A person who is thus unlawfully refused employment has a right of complaint to an [employment tribunal].

138   Refusal of service of employment agency on grounds related to union membership

. . .

140   Remedies

(1) Where the [employment tribunal] finds that a complaint under section 137 or 138 is well-founded, it shall make a declaration to that effect and may make such of the following as it considers just and equitable—

(a) an order requiring the respondent to pay compensation to the complainant of such amount as the tribunal may determine;

(b) a recommendation that the respondent take within a specified period action appearing to the tribunal to be practicable for the purpose of obviating or reducing the adverse effect on the complainant of any conduct to which the complaint relates.

(2) Compensation shall be assessed on the same basis as damages for breach of statutory duty and may include compensation for injury to feelings.

(3) If the respondent fails without reasonable justification to comply with a recommendation to take action, the tribunal may increase its award of compensation or, if it has not made such an award, make one.

(4) The total amount of compensation shall not exceed the limit for the time being imposed by [section 124(1) of the Employment Rights Act 1996] (limit on compensation for unfair dismissal).

142   Awards against third parties

(1) If in proceedings on a complaint under section 137 or 138 either the complainant or the respondent claims that the respondent was induced to act in the manner complained of by pressure which a trade union or other person exercised on him by calling, organising, procuring or financing a strike or other industrial action, or by threatening to do so, the complainant or the respondent may request the [employment tribunal] to direct that the person who he claims exercised the pressure be joined or sisted as a party to the proceedings.

(3) Where a person has been so joined or sisted as a party to the proceedings and the tribunal—

(a) finds that the complaint is well-founded,

(b) makes an award of compensation, and

(c) also finds that the claim in subsection (1) above is well-founded,

it may order that the compensation shall be paid by the person joined instead of by the respondent, or partly by that person and partly by the respondent, as the tribunal may consider just and equitable in the circumstances.

143   Interpretation and other supplementary provisions

(4) The remedy of a person for conduct which is unlawful by virtue of section 137 or 138 is by way of a complaint to an [employment tribunal] in accordance with this Part, and not otherwise.

No other legal liability arises by reason that conduct is unlawful by virtue of either of those sections.

144   Union membership requirement in contract for goods or services void

A term or condition of a contract for the supply of goods or services is void in so far as it purports to require that the whole, or some part, of the work done for the purposes of the contract is done only by persons who are, or are not, members of trade unions or of a particular trade union.

145   Refusal to deal on union membership grounds prohibited

(1) A person shall not refuse to deal with a supplier or prospective supplier of goods or services on union membership grounds.

'Refuse to deal' and 'union membership grounds' shall be construed as follows.

(2) A person refuses to deal with a person if, where he maintains (in whatever form) a list of approved suppliers of goods or services, or of persons from whom tenders for the supply of goods or services may be invited, he fails to include the name of that person in that list.

He does so on union membership grounds if the grounds, or one of the grounds, for failing to include his name is that if that person were to enter into a contract with him for the supply of goods or services, work to be done for the purposes of the contract would, or would be likely to, be done by persons who were, or who were not, members of trade unions or of a particular trade union.

(3) A person refuses to deal with a person if, in relation to a proposed contract for the supply of goods or services—

(a) he excludes that person from the group of persons from whom tenders for the supply of the goods or services are invited, or

(b) he fails to permit that person to submit such a tender, or

(c) he otherwise determines not to enter into a contract with that person for the supply of the goods or services.

He does so on union membership grounds if the ground, or one of the grounds, on which he does so is that if the proposed contract were entered into with that person, work to be done for the purposes of the contract would, or would be likely to, be done by persons who were, or who were not, members of trade unions or of a particular trade union.

(4) A person refuses to deal with a person if he terminates a contract with him for the supply of goods or services.

He does so on union membership grounds if the ground, or one of the grounds, on which he does so is that work done, or to be done, for the purposes of the contract has been, or is likely to be, done by persons who are or are not members of trade unions or of a particular trade union.

(5) The obligation to comply with this section is a duty owed to the person with whom there is a refusal to deal and to any other person who may be adversely affected by its contravention; and a breach of the duty is actionable accordingly (subject to the defences and other incidents applying to actions for breach of statutory duty).

166   Consequences of failure to comply with order

(1) If on the application of an employee an [employment tribunal] is satisfied that the employer has not complied with the terms of an order for the reinstatement or re-engagement of the employee under section 163(4) or (5), the tribunal shall—

(a) make an order for the continuation of the employee's contract of employment, and

(b) order the employer to pay the employee such compensation as the tribunal considers just and equitable in all the circumstances having regard—

(i) to the infringement of the employee's right to be reinstated or re-engaged in pursuance of the order, and

(ii) to any loss suffered by the employee in consequence of the non-compliance.

(3) If on the application of an employee an [employment tribunal] is satisfied that the employer has not complied with the terms of an order for the continuation of a contract of employment, the following provisions apply.

(4) If the non-compliance consists of a failure to pay an amount by way of pay specified in the order, the tribunal shall determine the amount owed by the employer on the date of the determination.

If on that date the tribunal also determines the employee's complaint that he has been unfairly dismissed, it shall specify that amount separately from any other sum awarded to the employee.

(5) In any other case, the tribunal shall order the employer to pay the employee such compensation as the tribunal considers just and equitable in all the circumstances having regard to any loss suffered by the employee in consequence of the non-compliance.

178   Collective agreements and collective bargaining

(1) In this Act 'collective agreement' means any agreement or arrangement made by or on behalf of one or more trade unions and one or more employers or employers' associations and relating to one or more of the matters specified below; and 'collective bargaining' means negotiations relating to or connected with one or more of those matters.

(2) The matters referred to above are—

(a) terms and conditions of employment, or the physical conditions in which any workers are required to work;

(b) engagement or non-engagement, or termination or suspension of employment or the duties of employment, of one or more workers;

(c) allocation of work or the duties of employment between workers or groups of workers;

(d) matters of discipline;

(e) a worker's membership or non-membership of a trade union;

(f) facilities for officials of trade unions; and

(g) machinery for negotiation or consultation, and other procedures, relating to any of the above matters, including the recognition by employers or employers' associations of the right of a trade union to represent workers in such negotiation or consultation or in the carrying out of such procedures.

179   Whether agreement intended to be a legally enforceable contract

(1) A collective agreement shall be conclusively presumed not to have been intended by the parties to be a legally enforceable contract unless the agreement—

(a) is in writing, and

(b) contains a provision which (however expressed) states that the parties intend that the agreement shall be a legally enforceable contract.

(2) A collective agreement which does satisfy those conditions shall be conclusively presumed to have been intended by the parties to be a legally enforceable contract.

(3) If a collective agreement is in writing and contains a provision which (however expressed) states that the parties intend that one or more parts of the agreement specified in that provision, but not the whole of the agreement, shall be a legally enforceable contract, then—

(a) the specified part or parts shall be conclusively presumed to have been intended by the parties to be a legally enforceable contract, and

(b) the remainder of the agreement shall be conclusively presumed not to have been intended by the parties to be such a contract.

(4) A part of a collective agreement which by virtue of subsection (3)(b) is not a legally enforceable contract may be referred to for the purpose of interpreting a part of the agreement which is such a contract.

180   Effect of provisions restricting right to take industrial action

(1) Any terms of a collective agreement which prohibit or restrict the right of workers to engage in a strike or other industrial action, or have the effect of prohibiting or restricting that right, shall not form part of any contract between a worker and the person for whom he works unless the following conditions are met.

(2) The conditions are that the collective agreement—

    (a) is in writing,

    (b) contains a provision expressly stating that those terms shall or may be incorporated in such a contract,

    (c) is reasonably accessible at his place of work to the worker to whom it applies and is available for him to consult during working hours, and

    (d) is one where each trade union which is a party to the agreement is an independent trade union;

and that the contract with the worker expressly or impliedly incorporates those terms in the contract.

(3) The above provisions have effect notwithstanding anything in section 179 and notwithstanding any provision to the contrary in any agreement (including a collective agreement or a contract with any worker).

186   Recognition requirement in contract for goods or services void

A term or condition of a contract for the supply of goods or services is void in so far as it purports to require a party to the contract—

    (a) to recognise one or more trade unions (whether or not named in the contract) for the purpose of negotiating on behalf of workers, or any class of worker, employed by him, or

    (b) to negotiate or consult with, or with an official of, one or more trade unions (whether or not so named).

187   Refusal to deal on grounds of union exclusion prohibited

(1) A person shall not refuse to deal with a supplier or prospective supplier of goods or services if the ground or one of the grounds for his action is that the person against whom it is taken does not, or is not likely to—

    (a) recognise one or more trade unions for the purpose of negotiating on behalf of workers, or any class of worker, employed by him, or

    (b) negotiate or consult with, or with an official of, one or more trade unions.

(2) A person refuses to deal with a person if—

    (a) where he maintains (in whatever form) a list of approved suppliers of goods or services, or of persons from whom tenders for the supply of goods or services may be invited, he fails to include the name of that person in that list; or

    (b) in relation to a proposed contract for the supply of goods or services—

        (i)   he excludes that person from the group of persons from whom tenders for the supply of the goods or services are invited, or

        (ii)   he fails to permit that person to submit such a tender; or

        [(iii)] he otherwise determines not to enter into a contract with that person for the supply of the goods or services. [or

    (c) he terminates a contract with that person for the supply of goods or services.]

(3) The obligation to comply with this section is a duty owed to the person with whom there is a refusal to deal and to any other person who may be adversely affected by its contravention; and a breach of the duty is actionable accordingly (subject to the defences and other incidents applying to actions for breach of statutory duty).

219   Protection from certain tort liabilities

(1) An act done by a person in contemplation or furtherance of a trade dispute is not actionable in tort on the ground only—

    (a) that it induces another person to break a contract or interferes or induces another person to interfere with its performance, or

(b) that it consists in his threatening that a contract (whether one to which he is a party or not) will be broken or its performance interfered with, or that he will induce another person to break a contract or interfere with its performance.

(2) An agreement or combination by two or more persons to do or procure the doing of an act in contemplation or furtherance of a trade dispute is not actionable in tort if the act is one which if done without any such agreement or combination would not be actionable in tort.

(3) Nothing in subsections (1) and (2) prevents an act done in the course of picketing from being actionable in tort unless it is done in the course of attendance declared lawful by section 220 (peaceful picketing).

(4) Subsections (1) and (2) have effect subject to sections 222 to 225 (action excluded from protection) [and to sections 226 (requirement of ballot before action by trade union) and 234A (requirement of notice to employer of industrial action); and in those sections 'not protected' means excluded from the protection afforded by this section or, where the expression is used with reference to a particular person, excluded from that protection as respects that person.]

220   Peaceful picketing

(1) It is lawful for a person in contemplation or furtherance of a trade dispute to attend—
    (a) at or near his own place of work, or
    (b) if he is an official of a trade union, at or near the place of work of a member of the union whom he is accompanying and whom he represents,

for the purpose only of peacefully obtaining or communicating information, or peacefully persuading any person to work or abstain from working.

(2) If a person works or normally works—
    (a) otherwise than at any one place, or
    (b) at a place the location of which is such that attendance there for a purpose mentioned in subsection (1) is impracticable,

his place of work for the purposes of that subsection shall be any premises of his employer from which he works or from which his work is administered.

221   Restrictions on grant of injunctions and interdicts

(1) Where—
    (a) an application for an injunction or interdict is made to a court in the absence of the party against whom it is sought or any representative of his, and
    (b) he claims, or in the opinion of the court would be likely to claim, that he acted in contemplation or furtherance of a trade dispute,

the court shall not grant the injunction or interdict unless satisfied that all steps which in the circumstances were reasonable have been taken with a view to securing that notice of the application and an opportunity of being heard with respect to the application have been given to him.

(2) Where—
    (a) an application for an interlocutory injunction is made to a court pending the trial of an action, and
    (b) the party against whom it is sought claims that he acted in contemplation or furtherance of a trade dispute,

the court shall, in exercising its discretion whether or not to grant the injunction, have regard to the likelihood of that party's succeeding at the trial of the action in establishing any matter which would afford a defence to the action under section 219 (protection from certain tort liabilities) or section 220 (peaceful picketing).

This subsection does not extend to Scotland.

222   Action to enforce trade union membership

(1) An act is not protected if the reason, or one of the reasons, for which it is done is the fact or belief that a particular employer—
    (a) is employing, has employed or might employ a person who is not a member of a trade union, or

(b) is failing, has failed or might fail to discriminate against such a person.

(2) For the purposes of subsection (1)(b) an employer discriminates against a person if, but only if, he ensures that his conduct in relation to—

(a) persons, or persons of any description, employed by him, or who apply to be, or are, considered by him for employment, or

(b) that provision of employment for such persons, is different, in some or all cases, according to whether or not they are members of a trade union, and is more favourable to those who are.

(3) An act is not protected if it constitutes, or is one of a number of acts which together constitute, an inducement or attempted inducement of a person—

(a) to incorporate in a contract to which that person is a party, or a proposed contract to which he intends to be a party, a term or condition which is or would be void by virtue of section 144 (union membership requirement in contract for goods or services), or

(b) to contravene section 145 (refusal to deal with person on grounds relating to union membership).

224   Secondary action

(1) An Act is not protected if one of the facts relied on for the purpose of establishing liability is that there has been secondary action which is not lawful picketing.

(2) There is secondary action in relation to a trade dispute when, and only when, a person—

(a) induces another to break a contract of employment or interferes or induces another to interfere with its performance, or

(b) threatens that a contract of employment under which he or another is employed will be broken or its performance interfered with, or that he will induce another to break a contract of employment or to interfere with its performance,

and the employer under the contract of employment is not the employer party to the dispute.

(3) Lawful picketing means acts done in the course of such attendance as is declared lawful by section 220 (peaceful picketing)—

(a) by a worker employed (or, in the case of a worker not in employment, last employed) by the employer party to the dispute, or

(b) by a trade union official whose attendance is lawful by virtue of subsection (1)(b) of that section.

(4) For the purposes of this section an employer shall not be treated as party to a dispute between another employer and workers of that employer; and where more than one employer is in dispute with his workers, the dispute between each employer and his workers shall be treated as a separate dispute.

In this subsection 'worker' has the same meaning as in section 244 (meaning of 'trade dispute').

(5) An act in contemplation or furtherance of a trade dispute which is primary action in relation to that dispute may not be relied on as secondary action in relation to another trade dispute.

Primary action means such action as is mentioned in paragraph (a) or (b) of subsection (2) where the employer under the contract of employment is the employer party to the dispute.

(6) In this section 'contract of employment' includes any contract under which one person personally does work or performs services for another, and related expressions shall be construed accordingly.

225   Pressure to impose union recognition requirement

(1) An act is not protected if it constitutes, or is one of a number of acts which together constitute, an inducement or attempted inducement of a person—

(a) to incorporate in a contract to which that person is a party, or a proposed contract to which he intends to be a party, a term or condition which is or would be void by virtue of section 186 (recognition requirement in contract for goods or services), or

(b) to contravene section 187 (refusal to deal with person on grounds of union exclusion).

(2) An act is not protected if—
- (a) it interferes with the supply (whether or not under a contract) of goods or services, or can reasonably be expected to have that effect, and
- (b) one of the facts relied upon for the purpose of establishing liability is that a person has—
    - (i)   induced another to break a contract of employment or interfered or induced another to interfere with its performance, or
    - (ii) threatened that a contract of employment under which he or another is employed will be broken or its performance interfered with, or that he will induce another to break a contract of employment or to interfere with its performance, and
- (c) the reason, or one of the reasons, for doing the act is the fact or belief that the supplier (not being the employer under the contract of employment mentioned in paragraph (b)) does not, or might not—
    - (i)   recognise one or more trade unions for the purpose of negotiating on behalf of workers, or any class of worker, employed by him, or
    - (ii) negotiate or consult with, or with an official of, one or more trade unions.

226 Requirement of ballot before action by trade union

(1) An act done by a trade union to induce a person to take part, or continue to take part, in industrial action[—
- (a) is not protected unless the industrial action has the support of a ballot, and
- (b) where section 226A falls to be complied with in relation to the person's employer, is not protected as respects the employer unless the trade union has complied with section 226A in relation to him.]

236 No compulsion to work

No court shall, whether by way of—
- (a) an order for specific performance or specific implement of a contract of employment, or
- (b) an injunction or interdict restraining a breach or threatened breach of such a contract,

compel an employee to do any work or attend at any place for the doing of any work.

237 Dismissal of those taking part in unofficial industrial action

(1) An employee has no right to complain of unfair dismissal if at the time of dismissal he was taking part in an unofficial strike or other unofficial industrial action.

(2) A strike or other industrial action is unofficial in relation to an employee unless—
- (a) he is a member of a trade union and the action is authorised or endorsed by that union, or
- (b) he is not a member of a trade union but there are among those taking part in the industrial action members of a trade union by which the action has been authorised or endorsed.

Provided that, a strike or other industrial action shall not be regarded as unofficial if none of those taking part in it are members of a trade union.

240 Breach of contract involving injury to persons or property

(1) A person commits an offence who wilfully and maliciously breaks a contract of service or hiring, knowing or having reasonable cause to believe that the probable consequences of his so doing, either alone or in combination with others, will be—
- (a) to endanger human life or cause serious bodily injury, or
- (b) to expose valuable property, whether real or personal, to destruction or serious injury.

(2) Subsection (1) applies equally whether the offence is committed from malice conceived against the person endangered or injured or, as the case may be, the owner of the property destroyed or injured, or otherwise.

(4) This section does not apply to seamen.

241   Intimidation or annoyance by violence or otherwise

(1) A person commits an offence who, with a view to compelling another person to abstain from doing or to do any act which that person has a legal right to do or abstain from doing, wrongfully and without legal authority—

(a) uses violence to or intimidates that person or his [spouse or civil partner] or children, or injures his property,

(b) persistently follows that person about from place to place,

(c) hides any tools, clothes or other property owned or used by that person, or deprives him of or hinders him in the use thereof,

(d) watches or besets the house or other place where that person resides, works, carries on business or happens to be, or the approach to any such house or place, or

(e) follows that person with two or more other persons in a disorderly manner in or through any street or road.

244   Meaning of 'trade dispute' in Part V [ss 219–246]

(1) In this Part a 'trade dispute' means a dispute between workers and their employer which relates wholly or mainly to one or more of the following—

(a) terms and conditions of employment, or the physical conditions in which any workers are required to work;

(b) engagement or non-engagement, or termination or suspension of employment or the duties of employment, of one or more workers;

(c) allocation of work or the duties of employment between workers or groups of workers;

(d) matters of discipline;

(e) a worker's membership or non-membership of a trade union;

(f) facilities for officials of trade unions; and

(g) machinery for negotiation or consultation, and other procedures, relating to any of the above matters, including the recognition by employers or employers' associations of the right of a trade union to represent workers in such negotiation or consultation or in the carrying out of such procedures.

245   Crown employees and contracts

Where a person holds any office or employment under the Crown on terms which do not constitute a contract of employment between that person and the Crown, those terms shall nevertheless be deemed to constitute such a contract for the purposes of—

(a) the law relating to liability in tort of a person who commits an act which—

(i) induces another person to break a contract, interferes with the performance of a contract or induces another person to interfere with its performance, or

(ii) consists in a threat that a contract will be broken or its performance interfered with, or that any person will be induced to break a contract or interfere with its per-formance, and

(b) the provisions of this or any other Act which refer (whether in relation to contracts gen-erally or only in relation to contracts of employment) to such an act.

273   Crown employment

(1) The provisions of this Act have effect (except as mentioned below) in relation to Crown em-ployment and persons in Crown employment as in relation to other employment and other workers or employees.

(5) Sections 137 to 143 (rights in relation to trade union membership: access to employment) apply in relation to Crown employment otherwise than under a contract only where the terms of employment correspond to those of a contract of employment.

288   Restriction on contracting out

(1) Any provision in an agreement (whether a contract of employment or not) is void in so far as it purports—

(a) to exclude or limit the operation of any provision of this Act, or

(b) to preclude a person from bringing—

(i)   proceedings before an [employment tribunal] or the Central Arbitration Committee under any provision of this Act, [. . .]

[(2A) Subsection (1) does not apply to an agreement to refrain from instituting or continuing any proceedings, other than excepted proceedings, specified in subsection 1(b) of that section before an industrial tribunal if the conditions regulating compromise agreements under this Act are satisfied in relation to the agreement.

(2B) The conditions regulating compromise agreements under this Act are that—

(a) the agreement must be in writing;

(b) the agreement must relate to the particular proceedings;

(c) the complainant must have received advice from a relevant independent adviser as to the terms and effect of the proposed agreement and in particular its effect on his ability to pursue his rights before an industrial tribunal;

(d) there must be in force, when the adviser gives the advice, a contract of insurance, or an indemnity provided for members of a profession or professional body covering the risk of a claim by the complainant in respect of loss arising in consequence of the advice;

(e) the agreement must identify the adviser; and

(f) the agreement must state that the conditions regulating compromise agreements under this Act are satisfied.]

Railways Act 1993

(1993, c. 43)

122   Statutory authority as a defence to actions in nuisance etc.

(1) Subject to the following provisions of this section—

(a) any person shall have authority—

(i)   to use, or to cause or permit any agent or independent contractor of his to use, rolling stock on any track, or

(ii) to use, or to cause or permit any agent or independent contractor of his to use, any land comprised in a network, station or light maintenance depot for or in connection with the provision of network services, station services in light maintenance services, and

(b) any person who is the owner or occupier of any land shall have authority to authorise, consent to or acquiesce in—

(i)   the use by another of rolling stock on any track comprised in that land, or

(ii) the use by another of that land for or in connection with the provision of network services, station services or light maintenance services,

if and so long as the qualifying conditions are satisfied in the particular case.

(3) The authority conferred by this section is conferred only for the purpose of providing a defence of statutory authority—

(a) in England and Wales—

(i)   in any proceedings, whether civil or criminal, in nuisance; or

(ii) in any civil proceedings, other than proceedings for breach of statutory duty, in respect of the escape of things from land;

(4) Nothing in this section shall be construed as excluding a defence of statutory authority otherwise available under or by virtue of any enactment.

Criminal Justice and Public Order Act 1994

(1994, c. 33)

60   Powers to stop and search in anticipation of violence

[(1) If a police officer of or above the rank of inspector reasonably believes—

    (a) that incidents involving serious violence may take place in any locality in his police area, and that it is expedient to give an authorisation under this section to prevent their occurrence, or

    (b) that persons are carrying dangerous instruments or offensive weapons in any locality in his police area without good reason,

he may give an authorisation that the powers conferred by this section shall be exercisable at any place within that locality for a specified period not exceeding 24 hours.]

(5) A constable may, in the exercise of [the powers conferred by subsection (4) above], stop any person or vehicle and make any search he thinks fit whether or not he has any grounds for suspecting that the person or vehicle is carrying weapons or articles of that kind.

(6) If in the course of a search under this section a constable discovers a dangerous instrument or an article which he has reasonable grounds for suspecting to be an offensive weapon, he may seize it.

61   Power to remove trespassers on land

(1) If the senior police officer present at the scene reasonably believes that two or more persons are trespassing on land and are present there with the common purpose of residing there for any period, that reasonable steps have been taken by or on behalf of the occupier to ask them to leave and—

    (a) that any of those persons has caused damage to the land or to property on the land or used threatening, abusive or insulting words or behaviour towards the occupier, a member of his family or an employee or agent of his, or

    (b) that those persons have between them six or more vehicles on the land,

he may direct those persons, or any of them, to leave the land and to remove any vehicles or other property they have with them on the land.

(4) If a person knowing that a direction under subsection (1) above has been given which applies to him—

    (a) fails to leave the land as soon as reasonably practicable, or

    (b) having left again enters the land as a trespasser within the period of three months beginning with the day on which the direction was given, he commits an offence . . .

62   Supplementary powers of seizure

(1) If a direction has been given under section 61 and a constable reasonably suspects that any person to whom the direction applies has, without reasonable excuse—

    (a) failed to remove any vehicle on the land which appears to the constable to belong to him or to be in his possession or under his control; or

    (b) entered the land as a trespasser with a vehicle within the period of three months beginning with the day on which the direction was given,

the constable may seize and remove that vehicle.

63   Powers to remove persons attending or preparing for a rave

(1) This section applies to a gathering on land in the open air of [20] or more persons (whether or not trespassers) at which amplified music is played during the night (with or without intermissions) and is such as, by reason of its loudness and duration and the time at which it is played, is likely to cause serious distress to the inhabitants of the locality; and for this purpose—

(a) such a gathering continues during intermissions in the music and where the gathering extends over several days, throughout the period during which amplified music is played at night (with or without intermissions); and

(b) 'music' includes sounds wholly or predominantly characterised by the emission of a succession of repetitive beats.

[(1A) This section also applies to a gathering if—

(a) it is a gathering on land of 20 or more persons who are trespassing on the land; and

(b) it would be a gathering of a kind mentioned in subsection (1) above if it took place on land in the open air.]

(2) If, as respects any land [. . .], a police officer of at least the rank of superintendent reasonably believes that—

(a) two or more persons are making preparations for the holding there of a gathering to which this section applies,

(b) ten or more persons are waiting for such a gathering to begin there, or

(c) ten or more persons are attending such a gathering which is in progress,

he may give a direction that those persons and any other persons who come to prepare or wait for or to attend the gathering are to leave the land and remove any vehicles or other property which they have with them on the land.

(6) If a person knowing that a direction has been given which applies to him—

(a) fails to leave the land as soon as reasonably practicable, or

(b) having left again enters the land within the period of 7 days beginning with the day on which the direction was given,

he commits an offence . . .

64 Supplementary powers of entry and seizure

(4) If a direction has been given under section 63 and a constable reasonably suspects that any person to whom the direction applies has, without reasonable excuse—

(a) failed to remove any vehicle or sound equipment on the land which appears to the constable to belong to him or to be in his possession or under his control; or

(b) entered the land as a trespasser with a vehicle or sound equipment within the period of 7 days beginning with the day on which the direction was given,

the constable may seize and remove that vehicle or sound equipment.

65 Raves: power to stop persons from proceeding

(1) If a constable in uniform reasonably believes that a person is on his way to a gathering to which section 63 applies in relation to which a direction under section 63(2) is in force, he may, subject to subsections (2) and (3) below—

(a) stop that person, and

(b) direct him not to proceed in the direction of the gathering.

(2) The power conferred by subsection (1) above may only be exercised at a place within 5 miles of the boundary of the site of the gathering.

66 Power of court to forfeit sound equipment

(1) Where a person is convicted of an offence under section 63 in relation to a gathering to which that section applies and the court is satisfied that any sound equipment which has been seized from him under section 64(4), or which was in his possession or under his control at the relevant time, has been used at the gathering the court may make an order for forfeiture under this subsection in respect of that property.

(2) The court may make an order under subsection (1) above whether or not it also deals with the offender in respect of the offence in any other way and without regard to any restrictions on forfeiture in any enactment.

(3) In considering whether to make an order under subsection (1) above in respect of any property a court shall have regard—

(a) to the value of the property; and

(b) to the likely financial and other effects on the offender of the making of the order (taken together with any other order that the court contemplates making).

(4) An order under subsection (1) above shall operate to deprive the offender of his rights, if any, in the property to which it relates, and the property shall (if not already in their possession) be taken into the possession of the police.

(5) Except in a case to which subsection (6) below applies, where any property has been forfeited under subsection (1) above, a magistrates' court may, on application by a claimant of the property, other than the offender from whom it was forfeited under subsection (1) above, make an order for delivery of the property to the applicant if it appears to the court that he is the owner of the property.

(7) No application shall be made under subsection (5), or by virtue of subsection (6), above by any claimant of the property after the expiration of 6 months from the date on which an order under subsection (1) above was made in respect of the property.

(8) No such application shall succeed unless the claimant satisfies the court either that he had not consented to the offender having possession of the property or that he did not know, and had no reason to suspect, that the property was likely to be used at a gathering to which section 63 applies.

68   Offence of aggravated trespass

(1) A person commits the offence of aggravated trespass if he trespasses on land [. . .] and, in relation to any lawful activity which persons are engaging in or are about to engage in on that or adjoining land [. . .], does there anything which is intended by him to have the effect—

(a) of intimidating those persons or any of them so as to deter them or any of them from engaging in that activity,

(b) of obstructing that activity, or

(c) of disrupting that activity.

[(1A) The reference in subsection (1) above to trespass includes, in Scotland, the exercise of access rights (within the meaning of the Land Reform (Scotland) Act 2003 (asp 2) up to the point when they cease to be exercisable by virtue of the commission of the offence under that subsection.]

(2) Activity on any occasion on the part of a person or persons on land is 'lawful' for the purposes of this section if he or they may engage in the activity on the land on that occasion without committing an offence or trespassing on the land.

69   Powers to remove persons committing or participating in aggravated trespass

(1) If the senior police officer present at the scene reasonably believes—

(a) that a person is committing, has committed or intends to commit the offence of aggravated trespass on land [. . .]; or

(b) that two or more persons are trespassing on land [. . .] and are present there with the common purpose of intimidating persons so as to deter them from engaging in a lawful activity or of obstructing or disrupting a lawful activity,

he may direct that person or (as the case may be) those persons (or any of them) to leave the land.

(3) If a person knowing that a direction under subsection (1) above has been given which applies to him—

(a) fails to leave the land as soon as practicable, or

(b) having left again enters the land as a trespasser within the period of [51 weeks] beginning with the day on which the direction was given,

he commits an offence . . .

Value Added Tax Act 1994

(1994, c. 23)

80 **[Credit for, or repayment of, overstated or overpaid VAT]**
   [(1) Where a person—
      (a) has accounted to the Commissioners for VAT for a prescribed accounting period (when-
            ever ended), and
      (b) in doing so, has brought into account as output tax an amount that was not output tax due,
   the Commissioners shall be liable to credit the person with that amount.
   (1A) Where the Commissioners—
      (a) have assessed a person to VAT for a prescribed accounting period (whenever ended), and
      (b) in doing so, have brought into account as output tax an amount that was not output tax
            due,
   they shall be liable to credit the person with that amount.
   (1B) Where a person has for a prescribed accounting period (whenever ended) paid to the
Commissioners an amount by way of VAT that was not VAT due to them, otherwise than as a result of—
      (a) an amount that was not output tax due being brought into account as output tax, or
      (b) an amount of input tax allowable under section 26 not being brought into account,
   the Commissioners shall be liable to repay to that person the amount so paid.]
   (2) The Commissioners shall only be liable to [credit or] repay an amount under this section on
a claim being made for the purpose.
   [(2A) Where—
      (a) as a result of a claim under this section by virtue of subsection (1) or (1A) above an
            amount falls to be credited to a person, and
      (b) after setting any sums against it under or by virtue of this Act, some or all of that amount
            remains to his credit,
   the Commissioners shall be liable to pay (or repay) to him so much of that amount as so remains.]
   (3) It shall be a defence, in relation to a claim [under this section by virtue of subsection (1) or
(1A) above, that the crediting] of an amount would unjustly enrich the claimant.]
   [(3A) Subsection (3B) below applies for the purposes of subsection (3) above where—
      (a) an amount would (apart from subsection (3) above) fall to be credited under subsection
            (1) or (1A) above to any person ('the taxpayer'), and
      (b) the whole or a part of the amount brought into account as mentioned in paragraph
            (b) of that subsection has, for practical purposes, been borne by a person other than the
            taxpayer.
   (3B) Where, in a case to which this subsection applies, loss or damage has been or may be incurred by the taxpayer as a result of mistaken assumptions made in his case about the operation of
any VAT provisions, that loss or damage shall be disregarded, except to the extent of the quantified
amount, in the making of any determination—
      (a) of whether or to what extent the crediting of an amount to the taxpayer would enrich
            him; or
      (b) of whether or to what extent any enrichment of the taxpayer would be unjust.
   (3C) In subsection (3B) above—
   'the quantified amount' means the amount (if any) which is shown by the taxpayer to constitute
the amount that would appropriately compensate him for loss or damage shown by him to have
resulted, for any business carried on by him, from the making of the mistaken assumptions; and
   'VAT provisions' means the provisions of—
      (a) any enactment, subordinate legislation or [EU] legislation (whether or not still in force)
            which relates to VAT or to any matter connected with VAT; or

(b) any notice published by the Commissioners under or for the purposes of any such enactment or subordinate legislation.

(4) The Commissioners shall not be liable on a claim under this section—

(a) to credit an amount to a person under subsection (1) or (1A) above, or

(b) to repay an amount to a person under subsection (1B) above,

if the claim is made more than 4 years after the relevant date.

(4A) Where—

(a) an amount has been credited under subsection (1) or (1A) above to any person at any time on or after 26th May 2005, and

(b) the amount so credited exceeded the amount which the Commissioners were liable at that time to credit to that person,

the Commissioners may, to the best of their judgement, assess the excess credited to that person and notify it to him.

(4AA) An assessment under subsection (4A) shall not be made more than 2 years after the later of:

(a) the end of the prescribed accounting period in which the amount was credited to the person, and

(b) the time when evidence of facts sufficient in the opinion of the Commissioners to justify the making of the assessment comes to the knowledge of the Commissioners.

(4C) Subsections (3) to (8) of section 78A apply in the case of an assessment under subsection (4A) above as they apply in the case of an assessment under section 78A(1).

(6) A claim under this section shall be made in such form and manner and shall be supported by such documentary evidence as the Commissioners prescribe by regulations; and regulations under this subsection may make different provision for different cases.

(7) Except as provided by this section, the Commissioners shall not be liable to repay an amount accounted for or paid to them by way of VAT that was not VAT due to them.]

[80A Arrangements for reimbursing customers

(1) The Commissioners may by regulations make provision for reimbursement arrangements made by any person to be disregarded for the purposes of section 80(3) except where the arrangements—

(a) contain such provision as may be required by the regulations; and

(b) are supported by such undertakings to comply with the provisions of the arrangements as may be required by the regulations to be given to the Commissioners.

(2) In this section 'reimbursement arrangements' means any arrangements for the purposes of a claim under section 80 which—

(a) are made by any person for the purpose of securing that he is not unjustly enriched by the [crediting] of any amount in pursuance of the claim; and

(b) provide for the reimbursement of persons who have for practical purposes borne the whole or any part of [the amount bought into account as mentioned in paragraph (b) of subsection (1) or (1A) of that section].

(3) Without prejudice to the generality of subsection (1) above, the provision that may be required by regulations under this section to be contained in reimbursement arrangements includes—

(a) provision requiring a reimbursement for which the arrangements provide to be made within such period after the crediting of that amount to which it relates as may be specified in the regulations;

[(b) provision for cases where an amount is credited but an equal amount is not reimbursed in accordance with the arrangements;]

(c) provision requiring interest paid by the Commissioners on any amount [paid (or repaid)] by them to be treated in the same way as that amount for the purposes of any requirement under the arrangements to make reimbursement or to repay the Commissioners;

    (d) provision requiring such records relating to the carrying out of the arrangements as may be described in the regulations to be kept and produced to the Commissioners, or to an officer of theirs.

(4) Regulations under this section may impose obligations on such persons as may be specified in the regulations—

    (a) [to make the repayments, or give the notifications, to the Commissioners that they are required to make or give] in pursuance of any provisions contained in any reimbursement arrangements by virtue of subsection (3)(b) or (c) above;

    (e) to comply with any requirements contained in any such arrangements by virtue of subsection (3)(d) above.

(5) Regulations under this section may make provision for the form and manner in which, and the times at which, undertakings are to be given to the Commissioners in accordance with the regulations; and any such provision may allow for those matters to be determined by the Commissioners in accordance with the regulations.

(6) Regulations under this section may—

    (a) contain any such incidental, supplementary, consequential or transitional provision as appears to the Commissioners to be necessary or expedient; and

    (b) make different provision for different circumstances.

(7) Regulations under this section may have effect (irrespective of when the claim for [credit] was made) for the purposes of [the crediting of any amount] by the Commissioners after the time when the regulations are made; and, accordingly, such regulations may apply to arrangements made before that time.]

Criminal Injuries Compensation Act 1995

(1995, c. 53)

1   The Criminal Injuries Compensation Scheme

(1) The Secretary of State shall make arrangements for the payment of compensation to, or in respect of, persons who have sustained one or more criminal injuries.

(2) Any such arrangements shall include the making of a scheme providing, in particular, for—

    (a) the circumstances in which awards may be made; and

    (b) the categories of person to whom awards may be made.

(3) The scheme shall be known as the Criminal Injuries Compensation Scheme.

(4) In this Act—

'award' means an award of compensation made in accordance with the provisions of the Scheme;

'claim officer' means a person appointed by the Secretary of State under section 3(4)(b);

'compensation' means compensation payable under an award;

'criminal injury', 'loss of earnings' and 'special expenses' have such meaning as may be specified;

'the Scheme' means the Criminal Injuries Compensation Scheme;

'Scheme manager' means a person appointed by the Secretary of State to have overall responsibility for managing the provisions of the Scheme (other than those to which section 5(2) applies); and

'specified' means specified by the Scheme.

2   Basis on which compensation is to be calculated

(1) The amount of compensation payable under an award shall be determined in accordance with the provisions of the Scheme.

(2) Provision shall be made for—

    (a) a standard amount of compensation, determined by reference to the nature of the injury;

(b) in such cases as may be specified, an additional amount of compensation calculated with respect to loss of earnings;

(c) in such cases as may be specified, an additional amount of compensation calculated with respect to special expenses; and

(d) in cases of fatal injury, such additional amounts as may be specified or otherwise determined in accordance with the Scheme.

(3) Provision shall be made for the standard amount to be determined—

(a) in accordance with a table ('the Tariff') prepared by the Secretary of State as part of the Scheme and such other provisions of the Scheme as may be relevant; or

(b) where no provision is made in the Tariff with respect to the injury in question, in accordance with such provisions of the Scheme as may be relevant.

(4) The Tariff shall show, in respect of each description of injury mentioned in the Tariff, the standard amount of compensation payable in respect of that description of injury.

(5) An injury may be described in the Tariff in such a way, including by reference to the nature of the injury, its severity or the circumstances in which it was sustained, as the Secretary of State considers appropriate.

(6) The Secretary of State may at any time alter the Tariff—

(a) by adding to the descriptions of injury mentioned there;

(b) by removing a description of injury;

(c) by increasing or reducing the amount shown as the standard amount of compensation payable in respect of a particular description of injury; or

(d) in such other way as he considers appropriate.

(7) The Scheme may—

(a) provide for amounts of compensation not to exceed such maximum amounts as may be specified;

(b) include such transitional provision with respect to any alteration of its provisions relating to compensation as the Secretary of State considers appropriate.

3   Claims and awards

(1) The Scheme may, in particular, include provision—

(a) as to the circumstances in which an award may be withheld or the amount of compensation reduced;

(b) for an award to be made subject to conditions;

(c) for the whole or any part of any compensation to be repayable in specified circumstances;

(d) for compensation to be held subject to trusts, in such cases as may be determined in accordance with the Scheme;

(e) requiring claims under the Scheme to be made within such periods as may be specified by the Scheme; and

(f) imposing other time limits.

(2) Where, in accordance with any provision of the Scheme, it falls to one person to satisfy another as to any matter, the standard of proof required shall be that applicable in civil proceedings.

(3) Where, in accordance with any provision of the Scheme made by virtue of subsection (1)(c), any amount falls to be repaid it shall be recoverable as a debt due to the Crown.

(4) The Scheme shall include provision for claims for compensation to be determined and awards and payments of compensation to be made—

(a) if a Scheme manager has been appointed, by persons appointed for the purpose by the Scheme manager; but

(b) otherwise by persons ('claims officers') appointed for the purpose by the Secretary of State.

(5) A claims officer—

(a) shall be appointed on such terms and conditions as the Secretary of State considers appropriate; but

(b) shall not be regarded as having been appointed to exercise functions of the Secretary of State or to act on his behalf.

(6) No decision taken by a claims officer shall be regarded as having been taken by, or on behalf of, the Secretary of State.

(7) If a Scheme manager has been appointed—

(a) he shall not be regarded as exercising functions of the Secretary of State or as acting on his behalf; and

(b) no decision taken by him or by any person appointed by him shall be regarded as having been taken by, or on behalf of, the Secretary of State.

7   Inalienability of awards

(1) Every assignment (or, in Scotland, assignation) of, or charge on, an award and every agreement to assign or charge an award shall be void.

(2) On the bankruptcy of a person in whose favour an award is made (or, in Scotland, on the sequestration of such a person's estate), the award shall not pass to any trustee or other person acting on behalf of his creditors.

[7A   Recovery of compensation from offenders: general

(1) The Secretary of State may, by regulations made by statutory instrument, make provision for the recovery from an appropriate person of an amount equal to all or part of the compensation paid in respect of a criminal injury.

(2) An appropriate person is a person who has been convicted of an offence in respect of the criminal injury.

(3) The amount recoverable from a person under the regulations must be determined by reference only to the extent to which the criminal injury is directly attributable to an offence of which he has been convicted.

(4) The regulations may confer functions in respect of recovery on—

(a) claims officers;

(b) if a Scheme manager has been appointed, persons appointed by the Scheme manager under section 3(4)(a).

(5) The regulations may not authorise the recovery of an amount in respect of compensation from a person to the extent that the compensation has been repaid in accordance with the Scheme.]

[7B   Recovery notices

(1) If, under regulations made under section 7A(1), an amount has been determined as recoverable from a person, he must be given a notice (a 'recovery notice') in accordance with the regulations which—

(a) requires him to pay that amount, and

(b) contains the information mentioned in subsection (2).

(2) The information is—

(a) the reasons for the determination that an amount is recoverable from the person;

(b) the basis on which the amount has been determined;

(c) the way in which and the date before which the amount is required to be paid;

(d) the means by which the amount may be recovered if it is not paid in accordance with the notice;

(e) the grounds on which and the procedure by means of which he may seek a review if he objects to—

(i)   the determination that an amount is recoverable from him;

(ii)   the amount determined as recoverable from him.

(3) The Secretary of State may by order made by statutory instrument amend subsection (2) by—

(a) adding information;

(b) omitting information;

(c) changing the description of information.]

[7C   Review of recovery determinations

(1) Regulations under section 7A(1) shall include provision for the review, in such circumstances as may be prescribed by the regulations, of—

(a) a determination that an amount is recoverable from a person;

(b) the amount determined as recoverable from a person.

(2) A person from whom an amount has been determined as recoverable under the regulations may seek such a review only on the grounds—

(a) that he has not been convicted of an offence to which the injury is directly attributable;

(b) that the compensation paid was not determined in accordance with the Scheme;

(c) that the amount determined as recoverable from him was not determined in accordance with the regulations.

(3) Any such review must be conducted by a person other than the person who made the determination under review.

(4) The person conducting any such review may—

(a) set aside the determination that the amount is recoverable;

(b) reduce the amount determined as recoverable;

(c) increase the amount determined as recoverable;

(d) determine to take no action under paragraphs (a) to (c).

(5) But the person conducting any such review may increase the amount determined as recoverable if (but only if) it appears to that person that the interests of justice require the amount to be increased.]

[7D   Recovery proceedings

(1) An amount determined as recoverable from a person under regulations under section 7A(1) is recoverable from him as a debt due to the Crown if (but only if)—

(a) he has been given a recovery notice in accordance with the regulations which complies with the requirements of section 7B, and

(b) he has failed to pay the amount in accordance with the notice.

(2) In any proceedings for the recovery of the amount from a person, it is a defence for the person to show—

(a) that he has not been convicted of an offence to which the injury is directly attributable;

(b) that the compensation paid was not determined in accordance with the Scheme; or

(c) that the amount determined as recoverable from him was not determined in accordance with regulations under section 7A.

(3) In any such proceedings, except for the purposes of subsection (2)(b), no question may be raised or finding made as to the amount that was, or ought to have been, the subject of an award.

(4) For the purposes of section 9 of the Limitation Act 1980 (time limit for actions for sums recoverable by statute to run from date on which cause of action accrued) the cause of action to recover that amount shall be taken to have accrued—

(a) on the date on which the compensation was paid; or

(b) if later, on the date on which a person from whom an amount is sought to be recovered was convicted of an offence to which the injury is directly attributable.

(5) If that person is convicted of more than one such offence and the convictions are made on different dates, the reference in subsection (4)(b) to the date on which he was convicted of such an offence shall be taken to be a reference to the earlier or earliest (as the case may be) of the dates on which he was convicted of such an offence.]

9   Financial provisions

(1) The Secretary of State may pay such remuneration, allowances or gratuities to or in respect of claims officers and other persons appointed by him under this Act [. . .] as he considers appropriate.

(4) Sums required for the payment of compensation in accordance with the Scheme shall be provided by the Secretary of State out of money provided by Parliament.

(5) Where a Scheme manager has been appointed, the Secretary of State may make such payments to him, in respect of the discharge of his functions in relation to the Scheme, as the Secretary of State considers appropriate.

(6) Any expenses incurred by the Secretary of State under this Act shall be paid out of money provided by Parliament.

[(6A) Any expenses incurred by the Secretary of State under subsection (6) above as regards Scotland shall be reimbursed to the Secretary of State by the Scottish Minister.]

(7) Any sums received by the Secretary of State under any provision of the Scheme made by virtue of section 3(1)(c)[, or by virtue of regulations made under section 7A(1),] shall be paid by him into the Consolidated Fund.

Landlord and Tenant (Covenants) Act 1995

(1995, c. 30)

3 Transmission of benefit and burden of covenants

(1) The benefit and burden of all landlord and tenant covenants of a tenancy—

(a) shall be annexed and incident to the whole, and to each and every part, of the premises demised by the tenancy and of the reversion in them, and

(b) shall in accordance with this section pass on an assignment of the whole or any part of those premises or of the reversion in them.

(2) Where the assignment is by the tenant under the tenancy, then as from the assignment the assignee—

(a) becomes bound by the tenant covenants of the tenancy except to the extent that—

(i) immediately before the assignment they did not bind the assignor, or

(ii) they fall to be complied with in relation to any demised premises not comprised in the assignment; and

(b) becomes entitled to the benefit of the landlord covenants of the tenancy except to the extent that they fall to be complied with in relation to any such premises.

(3) Where the assignment is by the landlord under the tenancy, then as from the assignment the assignee—

(a) becomes bound by the landlord covenants of the tenancy except to the extent that—

(i) immediately before the assignment they did not bind the assignor, or

(ii) they fall to be complied with in relation to any demised premises not comprised in the assignment; and

(b) becomes entitled to the benefit of the tenant covenants of the tenancy except to the extent that they fall to be complied with in relation to any such premises.

(4) In determining for the purposes of subsection (2) or (3) whether any covenant bound the assignor immediately before the assignment, any waiver or release of the covenant (in whatever terms) is expressed to be personal to the assignor shall be disregarded.

(5) Any landlord or tenant covenant of a tenancy which is restrictive of the user of land shall, as well as being capable of enforcement against an assignee, be capable of being enforced against any other person who is the owner or occupier of any demised premises to which the covenant relates, even though there is no express provision in the tenancy to that effect.

(6) Nothing in this section shall operate—

(a) in the case of a covenant which (in whatever terms) is expressed to be personal to any person, to make the covenant enforceable by or (as the case may be) against any other person; or

(b) to make a covenant enforceable against any person if, apart from this section, it would not be enforceable against him by reason of its not having been registered under the [Land Registration Act 2002] or the Land Charges Act 1972.

(7) To the extent that there remains in force any rule of law by virtue of which the burden of a covenant whose subject matter is not in existence at the time when it is made does not run with the land affected unless the covenantor covenants on behalf of himself and his assigns, that rule of law is hereby abolished in relation to tenancies.

5   Tenant released from covenants on assignment of tenancy

(1) This section applies where a tenant assigns premises demised to him under a tenancy.

(2) If the tenant assigns the whole of the premises demised to him, he—

(a) is released from the tenant covenants of the tenancy, and

(b) ceases to be entitled to the benefit of the landlord covenants of the tenancy, as from the assignment.

(3) If the tenant assigns part only of the premises demised to him, then as from the assignment he—

(a) is released from the tenant covenants of the tenancy, and

(b) ceases to be entitled to the benefit of the landlord covenants of the tenancy, only to the extent that those covenants fall to be complied with in relation to that part of the demised premises.

(4) This section applies as mentioned in subsection (1) whether or not the tenant is tenant of the whole of the premises comprised in the tenancy.

13   Covenants binding two or more persons

(1) Where in consequence of this Act two or more persons are bound by the same covenant, they are so bound both jointly and severally.

(2) Subject to section 24(2), where by virtue of this Act—

(a) two or more persons are bound jointly and severally by the same covenant, and

(b) any of the persons so bound is released from the covenant, the release does not extend to any other of those persons.

(3) For the purpose of providing for contribution between persons who, by virtue of this Act, are bound jointly and severally by a covenant, the Civil Liability (Contribution) Act 1978 shall have effect as if—

(a) liability to a person under a covenant were liability in respect of damage suffered by that person;

(b) references to damage accordingly include a breach of a covenant of a tenancy; and

(c) section 7(2) of that Act were omitted.

23   Effects of becoming subject to liability under, or entitled to benefit of, covenant etc.

(1) Where as a result of an assignment a person becomes by virtue of this Act, bound by or entitled to the benefit of a covenant, he shall not by virtue of this Act have any liability or rights under the covenant in relation to any time falling before the assignment.

(2) Subsection (1) does not preclude any such rights being expressly assigned to the person in question.

(3) Where as a result of an assignment a person becomes, by virtue of this Act, entitled to a right of re-entry contained in a tenancy, that right shall be exercisable in relation to any breach of a covenant of the tenancy occurring before the assignment as in relation to one occurring thereafter, unless by reason of any waiver or release it was not so exercisable immediately before the assignment.

24 Effects of release from liability under, or loss of benefit of, covenant

(1) Any release of a person from a covenant by virtue of this Act does not affect any liability of his arising from a breach of the covenant occurring before the release.

(4) Where by virtue of this Act a person ceases to be entitled to the benefit of a covenant, this does not affect any rights of his arising from a breach of the covenant occurring before he ceases to be so entitled.

25 Agreement void if it restricts operation of the Act

(1) Any agreement relating to a tenancy is void to the extent that—

(a) it would apart from this section have effect to exclude, modify or otherwise frustrate the operation of any provision of this Act, or

(b) it provides for—

(i)   the termination or surrender of the tenancy, or

(ii) the imposition on the tenant of any penalty, disability or liability, in the event of the operation of any provision of this Act, or

(c) it provides for any of the matters referred to in paragraph (b)(i) or (ii) and does so (whether expressly or otherwise) in connection with, or in consequence of, the operation of any provision of this Act.

Merchant Shipping Act 1995

(1995, c. 21)

92 Duty of ship to assist the other in case of collision

(1) In every case of collision between two ships, it shall be the duty of the master of each ship, if and so far as he can do so without danger to his own ship, crew and passengers (if any)—

(a) to render to the other ship, its master, crew and passengers (if any) such assistance as may be practicable, and may be necessary to save them from any danger caused by the collision, and to stay by the other ship until he has ascertained that it has no need of further assistance; and

(b) to give to the master of the other ship the name of his own ship and also the names of the ports from which it comes and to which it is bound.

(2) The duties imposed on the master of a ship by subsection (1) above apply to the masters of United Kingdom ships and to the masters of foreign ships when in United Kingdom waters.

(3) The failure of the master of a ship to comply with the provisions of this section shall not raise any presumption of law that the collision was caused by his wrongful act, neglect, or default.

(4) If the master fails without reasonable excuse to comply with this section, he shall—

(a) in the case of a failure to comply with subsection (1)(a) above, be liable—

(i)   on summary conviction, to a fine not exceeding £50,000 or imprisonment for a term not exceeding six months or both;

(ii) on conviction on indictment, to a fine or imprisonment for a term not exceeding two years or both; and

(b) in the case of a failure to comply with subsection (1)(b) above, be liable—

(i)   on summary conviction, to a fine not exceeding the statutory maximum;

(ii) on conviction on indictment, to a fine;

and in either case if he is a certified officer, an inquiry into his conduct may be held, and his certificate cancelled or suspended.

93 Duty to assist ships, etc. in distress

(1) The master of a ship, on receiving at sea a signal of distress [from an aircraft] or information from any source that [an] aircraft is in distress, shall proceed with all speed to the assistance of the persons in distress (informing them if possible that he is doing so) unless he is unable, or in the special circumstances of the case considers it unreasonable or unnecessary, to do so, or unless he is released from this duty under subsection (4) or (5) below.

234   Power to pass over adjoining land

(1) In circumstances where this section applies by virtue of section 231 in relation to any vessel, all persons may, subject to subsections (3) and (4) below, for the purpose of—

(a) rendering assistance to the vessel,

(b) saving the lives of shipwrecked persons, or

(c) saving the cargo or equipment of the vessel,

pass and repass over any adjoining land without being subject to interruption by the owner or occupier and deposit on the land any cargo or other article recovered from the vessel.

(2) The right of passage conferred by subsection (1) above is a right of passage with or without vehicles.

(3) No right of passage is conferred by subsection (1) above where there is some public road equally convenient.

(4) The rights conferred by subsection (1) above shall be so exercised as to do as little damage as possible.

(5) Any damage sustained by an owner or occupier of land in consequence of the exercise of the right conferred by this section shall be a charge on the vessel, cargo or articles in respect of or by which the damage is caused.

(6) Any amount payable in respect of such damage shall, in case of dispute, be determined and shall, in default of payment, be recoverable in the same manner as the amount of salvage is determined and recoverable under this Part.

(7) If the owner or occupier of any land—

(a) impedes or hinders any person in the exercise of the rights conferred by this section;

(b) impedes or hinders the deposit on the land of any cargo or other article recovered from the vessel; or

(c) prevents or attempts to prevent any cargo or other article recovered from the vessel from remaining deposited on the land for a reasonable time until it can be removed to a safe place of public deposit;

he shall be liable, on summary conviction, to a fine not exceeding level 3 on the standard scale.

Arbitration Act 1996

(1996, c. 23)

8   Whether agreement discharged by death of a party

(1) Unless otherwise agreed by the parties, an arbitration agreement is not discharged by the death of a party and may be enforced by or against the personal representatives of that party.

(2) Subsection (1) does not affect the operation of any enactment or rule of law by virtue of which a substantive right or obligation is extinguished by death.

29   Immunity of arbitrator

(1) An arbitrator is not liable for anything done or omitted in the discharge or purported discharge of his functions as arbitrator unless the act or omission is shown to have been in bad faith.

40   General duty of parties

(1) The parties shall do all things necessary for the proper and expeditious conduct of the arbitral proceedings.

87   Effectiveness of agreement to exclude court's jurisdiction

(1) In the case of a domestic arbitration agreement any agreement to exclude the jurisdiction of the court under—

(a) section 45 (determination of preliminary point of law), or

(b) section 69 (challenging the award: appeal on point of law), is not effective unless entered into after the commencement of the arbitral proceedings in which the question arises or the award is made.

89 Application of unfair terms regulations to consumer arbitration agreements

(1) The following sections extend the application of [Part 2 (unfair terms) of the Consumer Rights Act 2015] in relation to a term which constitutes an arbitration agreement.

For this purpose 'arbitration agreement' means an agreement to submit to arbitration present or future disputes or differences (whether or not contractual).

[(2) In those sections "the Part" means Part 2 (unfair terms) of the Consumer Rights Act 2015.]

[90 Part applies where consumer is a legal person

The Part applies where the consumer is a legal person as it applies where the consumer is an individual.]

91 Arbitration agreement unfair where modest amount sought

(1) A term which constitutes an arbitration agreement is unfair for the purposes of the [Part] so far as it relates to a claim for a pecuniary remedy which does not exceed the amount specified by order for the purposes of this section.

Damages Act 1996

(1996, c. 48)

1 Assumed rate of return on investment of damages

(1) In determining the return to be expected from the investment of a sum awarded as general damages for future pecuniary loss in an action for personal injury the court shall, subject to and in accordance with rules of court made for the purposes of this section, take into account such rate of return as may from time to time be prescribed by an order made by the Lord Chancellor.

(2) Subsection (1) above shall not however prevent the court taking a different rate of return into account if any party to the proceedings shows that it is more appropriate in the case in question.

(3) An order under subsection (1) above may prescribe different rates of return for different classes of case.

(4) Before making an order under subsection (1) above the Lord Chancellor shall consult the Government Actuary and the Treasury; and any order under that subsection shall be made by statutory instrument subject to annulment in pursuance of a resolution of either House of Parliament.

[(5) In the application of this section to Scotland—
  (a) for the reference to the Lord Chancellor in subsections (1) and (4) there is substituted a reference to the Scottish Ministers; and
  (b) in subsection (4)—
  (c) 'and the Treasury' is omitted; and
  (d) for 'either House of Parliament' there is substituted 'the Scottish Parliament'.]

[2 Periodical payments

(1) A court awarding damages for future pecuniary loss in respect of personal injury—
  (a) may order that the damages are wholly or partly to take the form of periodical payments, and
  (b) shall consider whether to make that order.

(2) A court awarding other damages in respect of personal injury may, if the parties consent, order that the damages are wholly or partly to take the form of periodical payments.

(3) A court may not make an order for periodical payments unless satisfied that the continuity of payment under the order is reasonably secure.

(4) For the purpose of subsection (3) the continuity of payment under an order is reasonably secure if—

    (a) it is protected by a guarantee given under section 6 of or the Schedule to this Act,

    (b) it is protected by a scheme under section 213 of the Financial Services and Markets Act 2000 (compensation) (whether or not as modified by section 4 of this Act), or

    (c) the source of payment is a government or health service body.

  (5) An order for periodical payments may include provision—

    (a) requiring the party responsible for the payments to use a method (selected or to be selected by him) under which the continuity of payment is reasonably secure by virtue of subsection (4);

    (b) about how the payments are to be made, if not by a method under which the continuity of payment is reasonably secure by virtue of subsection (4);

    (c) requiring the party responsible for the payments to take specified action to secure continuity of payment, where continuity is not reasonably secure by virtue of subsection (4);

    (d) enabling a party to apply for a variation of provision included under paragraph (b), or (c).

  (6) Where a person has a right to receive payments under an order for periodical payments, or where an arrangement is entered into in satisfaction of an order which gives a person a right to receive periodical payments, that person's right under the order or arrangement may not be assigned or charged without the approval of the court which made the order; and—

    (a) a court shall not approve an assignment or charge unless satisfied that special circumstances make it necessary, and

    (b) a purported assignment or charge, or agreement to assign or charge, is void unless approved by the court.

  (7) Where an order is made for periodical payments, an alteration of the method by which the payments are made shall be treated as a breach of the order (whether or not the method was specified under subsection (5)(b)) unless—

    (a) the court which made the order declares its satisfaction that the continuity of payment under the new method is reasonably secure,

    (b) the new method is protected by a guarantee given under section 6 of or the Schedule to this Act,

    (c) the new method is protected by a scheme under section 213 of the Financial Services and Markets Act 2000 (compensation) (whether or not as modified by section 4 of this Act), or

    (d) the source of payment under the new method is a government or health service body.

  (8) An order for periodical payments shall be treated as providing for the amount of payments to vary by reference to the retail prices index (within the meaning of section 833(2) of the Income and Corporation Taxes Act 1988) at such times, and in such a manner, as may be determined by or in accordance with Civil Procedure Rules.

  (9) But an order for periodical payments may include provision—

    (a) disapplying subsection (8), or

    (b) modifying the effect of subsection (8).]

[2A Periodical payments: supplementary

  (1) Civil Procedure Rules may require a court to take specified matters into account in considering—

    (a) whether to order periodical payments;

    (b) the security of the continuity of payment;

    (c) whether to approve an assignment or charge.

  (2) For the purposes of section 2(4)(c) and (7)(d) 'government or health service body' means a body designated as a government body or a health service body by order made by the Lord Chancellor.

(3) An order under subsection (2)—

    (a) shall be made by statutory instrument, and

    (b) shall be subject to annulment in pursuance of a resolution of either House of Parliament.

(4) Section 2(6) is without prejudice to a person's power to assign a right to the scheme manager established under section 212 of the Financial Services and Markets Act 2000.

(5) In section 2 'damages' includes an interim payment which a court orders a defendant to make to a claimant.

(6) In the application of this section and section 2 to Northern Ireland—

    (a) a reference to Civil Procedure Rules shall be taken as a reference to rules of court, and

    (b) a reference to a claimant shall be taken as a reference to a plaintiff.

(7) Section 2 is without prejudice to any power exercisable apart from that section.]

[2B Variation of orders and settlements

(1) The Lord Chancellor may by order enable a court which has made an order for periodical payments to vary the order in specified circumstances (otherwise than in accordance with section 2(5)(d)).

(2) The Lord Chancellor may by order enable a court in specified circumstances to vary the terms on which a claim or action for damages for personal injury is settled by agreement between the parties if the agreement—

    (a) provides for periodical payments, and

    (b) expressly permits a party to apply to a court for variation in those circumstances.

(3) An order under this section may make provision—

    (a) which operates wholly or partly by reference to a condition or other term of the court's order or of the agreement;

    (b) about the nature of an order which may be made by a court on a variation;

    (c) about the matters to be taken into account on considering variation;

    (d) of a kind that could be made by Civil Procedure Rules or, in relation to Northern Ireland, rules of court (and which may be expressed to be with or without prejudice to the power to make those rules).

(4) An order under this section may apply (with or without modification) or amend an enactment about provisional or further damages.

(5) An order under this section shall be subject to any order under section 1 of the Courts and Legal Services Act 1990 (allocation between High Court and county courts).

(6) An order under this section—

    (a) shall be made by statutory instrument,

    (b) may not be made unless the Lord Chancellor has consulted such persons as he thinks appropriate,

    (c) may not be made unless a draft has been laid before and approved by resolution of each House of Parliament, and

    (d) may include transitional, consequential or incidental provision.

(7) In subsection (4)—

'provisional damages' means damages awarded by virtue of subsection (2)(a) of section 32A of the Supreme Court Act 1981 or section 51 of the County Courts Act 1984 (or, in relation to Northern Ireland, paragraph 10(2)(a) of Schedule 6 to the Administration of Justice Act 1982), and

'further damages' means damages awarded by virtue of subsection (2)(b) of either of those sections (or, in relation to Northern Ireland, paragraph 10(2)(b) of Schedule 6 to the Administration of Justice Act 1982).]

3 Provisional damages and fatal accident claims

(1) This section applies where a person—

    (a) is awarded provisional damages; and

(b) subsequently dies as a result of the act or omission which gave rise to the cause of action for which the damages were awarded.

(2) The award of the provisional damages shall not operate as a bar to an action in respect of that person's death under the Fatal Accidents Act 1976.

(3) Such part (if any) of—

(a) the provisional damages; and

(b) any further damages awarded to the person in question before his death,

as was intended to compensate him for pecuniary loss in a period which in the event falls after his death, shall be taken into account in assessing the amount of any loss of support suffered by the person or persons for whose benefit the action under the Fatal Accidents Act 1976 is brought.

(4) No award of further damages made in respect of that person after his death shall include any amount for loss of income in respect of any period after his death.

(5) In this section 'provisional damages' means damages awarded by virtue of subsection (2)(a) of section 32A of the [Senior Courts Act 1981] or section 51 of the County Courts Act 1984 and 'further damages' means damages awarded by virtue of subsection (2)(b) of either of those sections.

(6) Subsection (2) above applies whether the award of provisional damages was before or after the coming into force of that subsection; and subsections (3) and (4) apply to any award of damages under the 1976 Act or, as the case may be, further damages after the coming into force of those subsections.

(7) In the application of this section to Northern Ireland—

(a) for references to the Fatal Accidents Act 1976 there shall be substituted references to the Fatal Accidents (Northern Ireland) Order 1977;

(b) for the reference to subsection (2)(a) and (b) of section 32A of the [Senior Courts Act 1981] and section 51 of the County Courts Act 1984 there shall be substituted a reference to paragraph 10(2)(a) and (b) of Schedule 6 to the Administration of Justice Act 1982.

[4 Enhanced protection for periodical payments

(1) Subsection (2) applies where—

(a) a person has a right to receive periodical payments, and

(b) his right is protected by a scheme under section 213 of the Financial Services and Markets Act 2000 (compensation), but only as to part of the payments.

(2) The protection provided by the scheme shall extend by virtue of this section to the whole of the payments.

(3) Subsection (4) applies where—

(a) one person ('the claimant') has a right to receive periodical payments from another person ('the defendant'),

(b) a third person ('the insurer') is required by or in pursuance of an arrangement entered into with the defendant (whether or not together with other persons and whether before or after the creation of the claimant's right) to make payments in satisfaction of the claimant's right or for the purpose of enabling it to be satisfied, and

(c) the claimant's right to receive the payments would be wholly or partly protected by a scheme under section 213 of the Financial Services and Markets Act 2000 if it arose from an arrangement of the same kind as that mentioned in paragraph (b) but made between the claimant and the insurer.

(4) For the purposes of the scheme under section 213 of that Act—

(a) the claimant shall be treated as having a right to receive the payments from the insurer under an arrangement of the same kind as that mentioned in subsection (3)(b),

(b) the protection under the scheme in respect of those payments shall extend by virtue of this section to the whole of the payments, and

(c) no person other than the claimant shall be entitled to protection under the scheme in respect of the payments.

(5) In this section 'periodical payments' means periodical payments made pursuant to—

    (a) an order of a court in so far as it is made in reliance on section 2 above (including an order as varied), or

    (b) an agreement in so far as it settles a claim or action for damages in respect of personal injury (including an agreement as varied).

(6) In subsection (5)(b) the reference to an agreement in so far as it settles a claim or action for damages in respect of personal injury includes a reference to an undertaking given by the Motor Insurers' Bureau (being the company of that name incorporated on 14th June 1946 under the Companies Act 1929), or an Article 75 insurer under the Bureau's Articles of Association, in relation to a claim or action in respect of personal injury.]

6   Guarantees for public sector settlements

(1) This section applies where—

    (a) a claim or action for damages for personal injury is settled [on terms whereby the damages are to consist wholly or partly of periodical payments]; or

    (b) a court awarding damages for personal injury makes an order incorporating such terms.

(2) If it appears to a Minister of the Crown that the payments are to be made by a body in relation to which he has, by virtue of this section, power to do so, he may guarantee the payments to be made under the agreement or order.

(3) The bodies in relation to which a Minister may give such a guarantee shall, subject to subsection (4) below, be such bodies as are designated in relation to the relevant government department by guidelines agreed upon between that department and the Treasury.

(4) A guarantee purporting to be given by a Minister under this section shall not be invalidated by any failure on his part to act in accordance with such guidelines as are mentioned in subsection (3) above.

(5) A guarantee under this section shall be given on such terms as the Minister concerned may determine but those terms shall in every case require the body in question to reimburse the Minister, with interest, for any sums paid by him in fulfilment of the guarantee.

(6) Any sums required by a Minister for fulfilling a guarantee under this section shall be defrayed out of money provided by Parliament and any sums received by him by way of reimbursement or interest shall be paid into the Consolidated Fund.

(7) A Minister who has given one or more guarantees under this section shall, as soon as possible after the end of each financial year, lay before each House of Parliament a statement showing what liabilities are outstanding in respect of the guarantees in that year, what sums have been paid in that year in fulfilment of the guarantees and what sums (including interest) have been recovered in that year in respect of the guarantees or are still owing.

(8) In this section 'government department' means any department of Her Majesty's government in the United Kingdom and for the purposes of this section a government department is a relevant department in relation to a Minister if he has responsibilities in respect of that department.

[(8A) In the application of subsection (3) above to Scotland, for the words from 'guidelines' to the end there shall be substituted 'the Minister'.]

[(8B) In the application of this section to Scotland, 'relevant government department' shall be read as if it was a reference to any part of the Scottish Administration and subsection (8) shall cease to have effect.]

(9) The Schedule to this Act has effect for conferring corresponding powers on Northern Ireland departments.

7   Interpretation

(1) Subject to subsection (2) below, in this Act 'personal injury' includes any disease and any impairment of a person's physical or mental condition and references to a claim or action for personal injury include references to such a claim or action brought by virtue of the Law Reform (Miscellaneous Provisions) Act 1934 and to a claim or action brought by virtue of the Fatal Accidents Act 1976.

Defamation Act 1996

(1996, c. 31)

Responsibility for publication

1   Responsibility for publication

(1) In defamation proceedings a person has a defence if he shows that—

(a) he was not the author, editor or publisher of the statement complained of,

(b) he took reasonable care in relation to its publication, and

(c) he did not know, and had no reason to believe, that what he did caused or contributed to the publication of a defamatory statement.

(2) For this purpose 'author', 'editor' and 'publisher' have the following meanings, which are further explained in subsection (3)—

'author' means the originator of the statement, but does not include a person who did not intend that his statement be published at all;

'editor' means a person having editorial or equivalent responsibility for the content of the statement or the decision to publish it; and

'publisher' means a commercial publisher, that is, a person whose business is issuing material to the public, or a section of the public, who issues material containing the statement in the course of that business.

(3) A person shall not be considered the author, editor or publisher of a statement if he is only involved—

(a) in printing, producing, distributing or selling printed material containing the statement;

(b) in processing, making copies of, distributing, exhibiting or selling a film or sound recording (as defined in Part I of the Copyright, Designs and Patents Act 1988) containing the statement;

(c) in processing, making copies of, distributing or selling any electronic medium in or on which the statement is recorded, or in operating or providing any equipment, system or service by means of which the statement is retrieved, copied, distributed or made available in electronic form;

(d) as the broadcaster of a live programme containing the statement in circumstances in which he has no effective control over the maker of the statement;

(e) as the operator of or provider of access to a communications system by means of which the statement is transmitted, or made available, by a person over whom he has no effective control.

In a case not within paragraphs (a) to (e) the court may have regard to those provisions by way of analogy in deciding whether a person is to be considered the author, editor or publisher of a statement.

(4) Employees or agents of an author, editor or publisher are in the same position as their employer or principal to the extent that they are responsible for the content of the statement or the decision to publish it.

(5) In determining for the purposes of this section whether a person took reasonable care, or had reason to believe that what he did caused or contributed to the publication of a defamatory statement, regard shall be had to—

(a) the extent of his responsibility for the content of the statement or the decision to publish it,

(b) the nature or circumstances of the publication, and

(c) the previous conduct or character of the author, editor or publisher.

(6) This section does not apply to any cause of action which arose before the section came into force.

Offer to make amends

2   Offer to make amends

(1) A person who has published a statement alleged to be defamatory of another may offer to make amends under this section.

(2) The offer may be in relation to the statement generally or in relation to a specific defamatory meaning which the person making the offer accepts that the statement conveys ('a qualified offer').

(3) An offer to make amends—

(a) must be in writing,

(b) must be expressed to be an offer to make amends under section 2 of the Defamation Act 1996, and

(c) must state whether it is a qualified offer and, if so, set out the defamatory meaning in relation to which it is made.

(4) An offer to make amends under this section is an offer—

(a) to make a suitable correction of the statement complained of and a sufficient apology to the aggrieved party,

(b) to publish the correction and apology in a manner that is reasonable and practicable in the circumstances, and

(c) to pay the aggrieved party such compensation (if any), and such costs, as may be agreed or determined to be payable.

The fact that the offer is accompanied by an offer to take specific steps does not affect the fact that an offer to make amends under this section is an offer to do all the things mentioned in paragraphs (a) to (c).

(5) An offer to make amends under this section may not be made by a person after serving a defence in defamation proceedings brought against him by the aggrieved party in respect of the publication in question.

(6) An offer to make amends under this section may be withdrawn before it is accepted; and a renewal of an offer which has been withdrawn shall be treated as a new offer.

3   Accepting an offer to make amends

(1) If an offer to make amends under section 2 is accepted by the aggrieved party, the following provisions apply.

(2) The party accepting the offer may not bring or continue defamation proceedings in respect of the publication concerned against the person making the offer, but he is entitled to enforce the offer to make amends, as follows.

(3) If the parties agree on the steps to be taken in fulfilment of the offer, the aggrieved party may apply to the court for an order that the other party fulfil his offer by taking the steps agreed.

(4) If the parties do not agree on the steps to be taken by way of correction, apology and publication, the party who made the offer may take such steps as he thinks appropriate, and may in particular—

(a) make the correction and apology by a statement in open court in terms approved by the court, and

(b) give an undertaking to the court as to the manner of their publication.

(5) If the parties do not agree on the amount to be paid by way of compensation, it shall be determined by the court on the same principles as damages in defamation proceedings.

The court shall take account of any steps taken in fulfilment of the offer and (so far as not agreed between the parties) of the suitability of the correction, the sufficiency of the apology and whether the manner of their publication was reasonable in the circumstances, and may reduce or increase the amount of compensation accordingly.

(6) If the parties do not agree on the amount to be paid by way of costs, it shall be determined by the court on the same principles as costs awarded in court proceedings.

(7) The acceptance of an offer by one person to make amends does not affect any cause of action against another person in respect of the same publication, subject as follows.

(8) In England and Wales or Northern Ireland, for the purposes of the Civil Liability (Contribution) Act 1978—

    (a) the amount of compensation paid under the offer shall be treated as paid in bona fide settlement or compromise of the claim; and

    (b) where another person is liable in respect of the same damage (whether jointly or otherwise), the person whose offer to make amends was accepted is not required to pay by virtue of any contribution under section 1 of that Act a greater amount than the amount of the compensation payable in pursuance of the offer.

(9) In Scotland—

    (a) subsection (2) of section 3 of the Law Reform (Miscellaneous Provisions) (Scotland) Act 1940 (right of one joint wrongdoer as respects another to recover contribution towards damages) applies in relation to compensation paid under an offer to make amends as it applies in relation to damages in an action to which that section applies; and

    (b) where another person is liable in respect of the same damage (whether jointly or otherwise), the person whose offer to make amends was accepted is not required to pay by virtue of any contribution under section 3(2) of that Act a greater amount than the amount of compensation payable in pursuance of the offer.

(10) Proceedings under this section shall be heard and determined without a jury.

4   Failure to accept offer to make amends

(1) If an offer to make amends under section 2, duly made and not withdrawn, is not accepted by the aggrieved party, the following provisions apply.

(2) The fact that the offer was made is a defence (subject to subsection (3)) to defamation proceedings in respect of the publication in question by that party against the person making the offer.

A qualified offer is only a defence in respect of the meaning to which the offer related.

(3) There is no such defence if the person by whom the offer was made knew or had reason to believe that the statement complained of—

    (a) referred to the aggrieved party or was likely to be understood as referring to him, and

    (b) was both false and defamatory of that party;

but it shall be presumed until the contrary is shown that he did not know and had no reason to believe that was the case.

(4) The person who made the offer need not rely on it by way of defence, but if he does he may not rely on any other defence.

If the offer was a qualified offer, this applies only in respect of the meaning to which the offer related.

(5) The offer may be relied on in mitigation of damages whether or not it was relied on as a defence.

The meaning of a statement

7   Ruling on the meaning of a statement

In defamation proceedings the court shall not be asked to rule whether a statement is arguably capable, as opposed to capable, of bearing a particular meaning or meanings attributed to it.

Summary disposal of claim

8   Summary disposal of claim

(1) In defamation proceedings the court may dispose summarily of the plaintiffs claim in accordance with the following provisions.

(2) The court may dismiss the plaintiff's claim if it appears to the court that it has no realistic prospect of success and there is no reason why it should be tried.

(3) The court may give judgment for the plaintiff and grant him summary relief (see section 9) if it appears to the court that there is no defence to the claim which has a realistic prospect of success, and that there is no other reason why the claim should be tried.

Unless the plaintiff asks for summary relief, the court shall not act under this subsection unless it is satisfied that summary relief will adequately compensate him for the wrong he has suffered.

(4) In considering whether a claim should be tried the court shall have regard to—

(a) whether all the persons who are or might be defendants in respect of the publication complained of are before the court;

(b) whether summary disposal of the claim against another defendant would be inappropriate;

(c) the extent to which there is a conflict of evidence;

(d) the seriousness of the alleged wrong (as regards the content of the statement and the extent of publication); and

(e) whether it is justifiable in the circumstances to proceed to a full trial.

(5) Proceedings under this section shall be heard and determined without a jury.

9   Meaning of summary relief

(1) For the purposes of section 8 (summary disposal of claim) 'summary relief' means such of the following as may be appropriate—

(a) a declaration that the statement was false and defamatory of the plaintiff;

(b) an order that the defendant publish or cause to be published a suitable correction and apology;

(c) damages not exceeding £10,000 or such other amount as may be prescribed by order of the Lord Chancellor;

(d) an order restraining the defendant from publishing or further publishing the matter complained of.

(2) The content of any correction and apology, and the time, manner, form and place of publication, shall be for the parties to agree.

If they cannot agree on the content, the court may direct the defendant to publish or cause to be published a summary of the court's judgment agreed by the parties or settled by the court in accordance with rules of court.

If they cannot agree on the time, manner, form or place of publication, the court may direct the defendant to take such reasonable and practicable steps as the court considers appropriate.

[(2A) The Lord Chancellor must consult the Lord Chief Justice of England and Wales before making any order under subsection (1)(c) in relation to England and Wales.

(2B) The Lord Chancellor must consult the Lord Chief Justice of Northern Ireland before making any order under subsection (1)(c) in relation to Northern Ireland.

(2C) The Lord Chief Justice may nominate a judicial office holder (as defined in section 109(4) of the Constitutional Reform Act 2005) to exercise his functions under this section.

(2D) The Lord Chief Justice of Northern Ireland may nominate any of the following to exercise his functions under this section—

(a) the holder of one of the offices listed in Schedule 1 to the Justice (Northern Ireland) Act 2002;

(b) a Lord Justice of Appeal (as defined in section 88 of that Act).]

(3) Any order under subsection (1)(c) shall be made by statutory instrument which shall be subject to annulment in pursuance of a resolution of either House of Parliament.

10   Summary disposal: rules of court

(1) Provision may be made by rules of court as to the summary disposal of the plaintiff's claim in defamation proceedings.

(2) Without prejudice to the generality of that power, provision may be made—

(a) authorising a party to apply for summary disposal at any stage of the proceedings;

(b) authorising the court at any stage of the proceedings—

(i)   to treat any application, pleading or other step in the proceedings as an application for summary disposal, or

(ii) to make an order for summary disposal without any such application;

(c) as to the time for serving pleadings or taking any other step in the proceedings in a case where there are proceedings for summary disposal;

(d) requiring the parties to identify any question of law or construction which the court is to be asked to determine in the proceedings;

(e) as to the nature of any hearing on the question of summary disposal, and in particular—

(i)   authorising the court to order affidavits or witness statements to be prepared for use as evidence at the hearing, and

(ii) requiring the leave of the court for the calling of oral evidence, or the introduction of new evidence, at the hearing;

(f) authorising the court to require a defendant to elect, at or before the hearing, whether or not to make an offer to make amends under section 2.

Evidence concerning proceedings in Parliament

13   Evidence concerning proceedings in Parliament

(1) Where the conduct of a person in or in relation to proceedings in Parliament is in issue in defamation proceedings, he may waive for the purposes of those proceedings, so far as concerns him, the protection of any enactment or rule of law which prevents proceedings in Parliament being impeached or questioned in any court or place out of Parliament.

(2) Where a person waives that protection—

(a) any such enactment or rule of law shall not apply to prevent evidence being given, questions being asked or statements, submissions, comments or findings being made about his conduct, and

(b) none of those things shall be regarded as infringing the privilege of either House of Parliament.

(3) The waiver by one person of that protection does not affect its operation in relation to another person who has not waived it.

(4) Nothing in this section affects any enactment or rule of law so far as it protects a person (including a person who has waived the protection referred to above) from legal liability for words spoken or things done in the course of, or for the purposes of or incidental to, any proceedings in Parliament.

(5) Without prejudice to the generality of subsection (4), that subsection applies to—

(a) the giving of evidence before either House or a committee;

(b) the presentation or submission of a document to either House or a committee;

(c) the preparation of a document for the purposes of or incidental to the transacting of any such business;

(d) the formulation, making or publication of a document, including a report, by or pursuant to an order of either House or a committee; and

(e) any communication with the Parliamentary Commissioner for Standards or any person having functions in connection with the registration of Members' interests.

In this subsection 'a committee' means a committee of either House or a joint committee of both Houses of Parliament.

Statutory privilege

14   Reports of court proceedings absolutely privileged

(1) A fair and accurate report of proceedings in public before a court to which this section applies, if published contemporaneously with the proceedings, is absolutely privileged.

(2) A report of proceedings which by an order of the court, or as a consequence of any statutory provision, is required to be postponed shall be treated as published contemporaneously if it is published as soon as practicable after publication is permitted.

[(3) This section applies to—

(a) any court in the United Kingdom;

(b) any court established under the law of a country or territory outside the United Kingdom;

(c) any international court or tribunal established by the Security Council of the United Nations or by an international agreement;

and in paragraphs (a) and (b) "court" includes any tribunal or body exercising the judicial power of the State.]

15   Reports, etc. protected by qualified privilege

(1) The publication of any report or other statement mentioned in Schedule 1 to this Act is privileged unless the publication is shown to be made with malice, subject as follows.

(2) In defamation proceedings in respect of the publication of a report or other statement mentioned in Part II of that Schedule, there is no defence under this section if the plaintiff shows that the defendant—

(a) was requested by him to publish in a suitable manner a reasonable letter or statement by way of explanation or contradiction, and

(b) refused or neglected to do so.

For this purpose 'in a suitable manner' means in the same manner as the publication complained of or in a manner that is adequate and reasonable in the circumstances.

(3) This section does not apply to the publication to the public, or a section of the public, of matter which is not of [public interest] and the publication of which is not for the public benefit.

(4) Nothing in this section shall be construed—

(a) as protecting the publication of matter the publication of which is prohibited by law, or

(b) as limiting or abridging any privilege subsisting apart from this section.

Supplementary provisions

17   Interpretation

(1) In this Act—

'publication' and 'publish', in relation to a statement, have the meaning they have for the purposes of the law of defamation generally, but 'publisher' is specially defined for the purposes of section 1;

'statement' means words, pictures, visual images, gestures or any other method of signifying meaning; and

'statutory provision' means—

(a) a provision contained in an Act or in subordinate legislation within the meaning of the Interpretation Act 1978

[(aa) a provision contained in an Act of the Scottish Parliament or in an instrument made under such an Act], or

(b) a statutory provision within the meaning given by section 1(f) of the Interpretation Act (Northern Ireland) 1954.

Section 15

SCHEDULE 1

QUALIFIED PRIVILEGE

PART I STATEMENTS HAVING QUALIFIED PRIVILEGE WITHOUT EXPLANATION OR CONTRADICTION

1. A fair and accurate report of proceedings in public of a legislature anywhere in the world.

2. A fair and accurate report of proceedings in public before a court anywhere in the world.

3. A fair and accurate report of proceedings in public of a person appointed to hold a public inquiry by a government or legislature anywhere in the world.

4. A fair and accurate report of proceedings in public anywhere in the world of an international organisation or an international conference.

5. A fair and accurate copy of or extract from any register or other document required by law to be open to public inspection.

6. A notice or advertisement published by or on the authority of a court, or of a judge or officer of a court, anywhere in the world.

7. A fair and accurate copy of or extract from matter published by or on the authority of a government or legislature anywhere in the world.

8. A fair and accurate copy of or extract from matter published anywhere in the world by an international organisation or an international conference.

PART II STATEMENTS PRIVILEGED SUBJECT TO EXPLANATION OR CONTRADICTION

[**9.** (1) A fair and accurate copy of, extract from or summary of a notice or other matter issued for the information of the public by or on behalf of—

    (a) a legislature or government anywhere in the world;

    (b) an authority anywhere in the world performing governmental functions;

    (c) an international organisation or international conference.

(2) In this paragraph "governmental functions" includes police functions.

10. A fair and accurate copy of, extract from or summary of a document made available by a court anywhere in the world, or by a judge or officer of such a court.]

11. (1) A fair and accurate report of proceedings at any public meeting or sitting in the United Kingdom of—

    (a)   a local authority [or local authority committee];

    [(aa) in the case of a local authority which are operating executive arrangements, the executive of that authority or a committee of that executive;]

    (b)   a justice or justices of the peace acting otherwise than as a court exercising judicial authority;

    (c)   a commission, tribunal, committee or person appointed for the purposes of any inquiry by any statutory provision, by Her Majesty or by a Minister of the Crown [a member of the Scottish Executive] or a Northern Ireland Department;

    (d)   a person appointed by a local authority to hold a local inquiry in pursuance of any statutory provision;

    (e)   any other tribunal, board, committee or body constituted by or under, and exercising functions under, any statutory provision.

[(1A) In the case of a local authority which are operating executive arrangements, a fair and accurate record of any decision made by any member of the executive where that record is required to be made and available for public inspection by virtue of section 22 of the Local Government Act 2000 or of any provision in regulations made under that section.]

(2) [In sub-paragraphs (1)(a), (1)(aa) and (1A)—

'executive' and 'executive arrangements' have the same meaning as in Part II of the Local Government Act 2000;]

'local authority' means—

    (a) in relation to England and Wales, a principal council within the meaning of the Local Government Act 1972, any body falling within any paragraph of section 100J(1) of that Act or an authority or body to which the Public Bodies (Admission to Meetings) Act 1960 applies,

    (b) in relation to Scotland, a council constituted under section 2 of the Local Government etc. (Scotland) Act 1994 or an authority or body to which the Public Bodies (Admission to Meetings) Act 1960 applies,

(c) in relation to Northern Ireland, any authority or body to which sections 23 to 27 of the Local Government Act (Northern Ireland) 1972 apply; and

'local authority committee' means any committee of a local authority or of local authorities, and includes—

(a) any committee or sub-committee in relation to which sections 100A to 100D of the Local Government Act 1972 apply by virtue of section 100E of that Act (whether or not also by virtue of section 100J of that Act), and

(b) any committee or sub-committee in relation to which sections 50A to 50D of the Local Government (Scotland) Act 1973 apply by virtue of section 50E of that Act.

[(2A) In sub-paragraphs (1) and (1A)—

"executive" and "executive arrangements" have the same meaning as in Part II of the Local Government Act 2000.]

(3) A fair and accurate report of any corresponding proceedings in any of the Channel Islands or the Isle of Man or in another member State.

[**11A.** A fair and accurate report of proceedings at a press conference held anywhere in the world for the discussion of a matter of public interest.]

12. (1) A fair and accurate report of proceedings at any public meeting held [anywhere in the world].

(2) In this paragraph a 'public meeting' means a meeting bona fide and lawfully held for a lawful purpose and for the furtherance or discussion of a matter of [public interest], whether admission to the meeting is general or restricted.

13. (1) A fair and accurate report of proceedings at a general meeting of a [listed company].

[(2) A fair and accurate copy of, extract from or summary of any document circulated to members of a listed company—

(a) by or with the authority of the board of directors of the company,

(b) by the auditors of the company, or

(c) by any member of the company in pursuance of a right conferred by any statutory provision.

(3) A fair and accurate copy of, extract from or summary of any document circulated to members of a listed company which relates to the appointment, resignation, retirement or dismissal of directors of the company or its auditors.

(4) In this paragraph "listed company" has the same meaning as in Part 12 of the Corporation Tax Act 2009 (see section 1005 of that Act).]

14. A fair and accurate report of any finding or decision of any of the following descriptions of association, formed [anywhere in the world], or of any committee or governing body of such an association—

(a) an association formed for the purpose of promoting or encouraging the exercise of or interest in any art, science, religion or learning, and empowered by its constitution to exercise control over or adjudicate on matters of interest or concern to the association, or the actions or conduct of any person subject to such control or adjudication;

(b) an association formed for the purpose of promoting or safeguarding the interests of any trade, business, industry or profession, or of the persons carrying on or engaged in any trade, business, industry or profession, and empowered by its constitution to exercise control over or adjudicate upon matters connected with that trade, business, industry or profession, or the actions or conduct of those persons;

(c) an association formed for the purpose of promoting or safeguarding the interests of a game, sport or pastime to the playing or exercise of which members of the public are invited or admitted, and empowered by its constitution to exercise control over or adjudicate upon persons connected with or taking part in the game, sport or pastime;

(d) an association formed for the purpose of promoting charitable objects or other objects beneficial to the community and empowered by its constitution to exercise control over or to adjudicate on matters of interest or concern to the association, or the actions or conduct of any person subject to such control or adjudication.

[**14A.** A fair and accurate—

(a) report of proceedings of a scientific or academic conference held anywhere in the world, or

(b) copy of, extract from or summary of matter published by such a conference.]

[**15.** (1) A fair and accurate report of, or copy of or extract from, any adjudication, report, statement or notice issued by a body, officer or other person designated for the purposes of this paragraph—

(a) for England and Wales, by order of the Lord Chancellor;

(b) for Scotland, by order of the Secretary of State;

(c) for Northern Ireland, by order of the Department of Justice in Northern Ireland.

(2) Subject to sub-paragraph (3), an order under this paragraph shall be made by statutory instrument which shall be subject to annulment in pursuance of a resolution of either House of Parliament.]

PART III SUPPLEMENTARY PROVISIONS

[**16.** In this Schedule—

"court" includes—

(a) any tribunal or body established under the law of any country or territory exercising the judicial power of the State;

(b) any international tribunal established by the Security Council of the United Nations or by an international agreement;

(c) any international tribunal deciding matters in dispute between States;

"international conference" means a conference attended by representatives of two or more governments;

"international organisation" means an organisation of which two or more governments are members, and includes any committee or other subordinate body of such an organisation;

"legislature" includes a local legislature; and

"member State" includes any European dependent territory of a member State.]

Employment Rights Act 1996

(1996, c. 18)

[27A Exclusivity terms unenforceable in zero hours contracts

(1) In this section "zero hours contract" means a contract of employment or other worker's contract under which—

(a) the undertaking to do or perform work or services is an undertaking to do so conditionally on the employer making work or services available to the worker, and

(b) there is no certainty that any such work or services will be made available to the worker.

(2) For this purpose, an employer makes work or services available to a worker if the employer requests or requires the worker to do the work or perform the services.

(3) Any provision of a zero hours contract which—

(a) prohibits the worker from doing work or performing services under another contract or under any other arrangement, or

(b) prohibits the worker from doing so without the employer's consent,

is unenforceable against the worker.]

Police Act 1996

(1996, c. 16)

88　Liability for wrongful acts of constables

(1)　The chief officer of police for a police area shall be liable in respect of [any unlawful conduct of] constables under his direction and control in the performance or purported performance of their functions in like manner as a master is liable in respect of [any unlawful conduct of] his servants in the course of their employment, and accordingly shall[, in the case of a tort,] be treated for all purposes as a joint tortfeasor.

(2)　There shall be paid out of the police fund—

(a)　any damages or costs awarded against the chief officer of police in any proceedings brought against him by virtue of this section and any costs incurred by him in any such proceedings so far as not recovered by him in the proceedings; and

(b)　any sum required in connection with the settlement of any claim made against the chief officer of police by virtue of this section, if the settlement is approved by the [local policing body].

(4)　A [local policing body] may, in such cases and to such extent as appear to it to be appropriate, pay out of the police fund—

(a)　any damages or costs awarded against a person to whom this subsection applies in proceedings for [any unlawful conduct of] that person,

(b)　any costs incurred and not recovered by such a person in such proceedings, and

(c)　any sum required in connection with the settlement of a claim that has or might have given rise to such proceedings.

Local Government (Contracts) Act 1997

(1997, c. 65)

1　Functions to include power to enter into contracts

(1)　Every statutory provision conferring or imposing a function on a local authority confers power on the local authority to enter into a contract with another person for the provision or making available of assets or services, or both, (whether or not together with goods), for the purposes of, or in connection with, the discharge of the function by the local authority.

2　Certified contracts to be intra vires

(1)　Where a local authority has entered into a contract, the contract shall, if it is a certified contract, have effect (and be deemed always to have had effect) as if the local authority had had power to enter into it (and had exercised that power properly in entering into it).

(2)　For the purposes of this Act a contract entered into by a local authority is a certified contract if (and, subject to subsections (3) and (4), only if) the certification requirements have been satisfied by the local authority with respect to the contract and they were so satisfied before the end of the certification period.

Protection from Harassment Act 1997

(1997, c. 40)

1　Prohibition of harassment

(1)　A person must not pursue a course of conduct—

(a)　which amounts to harassment of another, and

(b)　which he knows or ought to know amounts to harassment of the other.

[(1A) A person must not pursue a course of conduct—

    (a) which involves harassment of two or more persons, and

    (b) which he knows or ought to know involves harassment of those persons, and

    (c) by which he intends to persuade any person (whether or not one of those mentioned above)—

        (i) not to do something that he is entitled or required to do, or

        (ii) to do something that he is not under any obligation to do.]

(2) For the purposes of this section [or section 2A(2)(c)], the person whose course of conduct is in question ought to know that it amounts to or involves harassment of another if a reasonable person in possession of the same information would think the course of conduct amounted to [or involved] harassment of the other.

(3) Subsection (1) [or (1A)] does not apply to a course of conduct if the person who pursued it shows—

    (a) that it was pursued for the purpose of presenting or detecting crime,

    (b) that it was pursued under any enactment or rule of law or to comply with any condition or requirement imposed by any person under any enactment, or

    (c) that in the particular circumstances the pursuit of the course of conduct was reasonable.

2   Offence of harassment

(1) A person who pursues a course of conduct in breach of [section 1 or (1A)] is guilty of an offence.

3   Civil remedy

(1) An actual or apprehended breach of [section 1(1)] may be the subject of a claim in civil proceedings by the person who is or may be the victim of the course of conduct in question.

(2) On such a claim, damages may be awarded for (among other things) any anxiety caused by the harassment and any financial loss resulting from the harassment.

(3) Where—

    (a) in such proceedings the High Court or [the county] court grants an injunction for the purpose of restraining the defendant from pursuing any conduct which amounts to harassment, and

    (b) the plaintiff considers that the defendant has done anything which he is prohibited from doing by the injunction,

the plaintiff may apply for the issue of a warrant for the arrest of the defendant.

(5) The judge [. . .] to whom an application under subsection (3) is made may only issue a warrant if—

    (a) the application is substantiated on oath, and

    (b) the judge [. . .] has reasonable grounds for believing that the defendant has done anything which he is prohibited from doing by the injunction.

(6) Where—

    (a) the High Court or [the county] court grants an injunction for the purpose mentioned in subsection (3)(a), and

    (b) without reasonable excuse the defendant does anything which he is prohibited from doing by the injunction,

he is guilty of an offence.

[3A   Injunctions to protect persons from harassment within section 1(1A)

(1) This section applies where there is an actual or apprehended breach of section 1(1A) by any person ('the relevant person').

(2) In such a case—

    (a) any person who is or may be a victim of the course of conduct in question, or

    (b) any person who is or may be a person falling within section 1(1A)(c),

may apply to the High Court or the county court for an injunction restraining the relevant person from pursuing any conduct which amounts to harassment in relation to any person or persons mentioned or described in the injunction.]

4   Putting people in fear of violence

(1) A person whose course of conduct causes another to fear, on at least two occasions, that violence will be used against him is guilty of an offence if he knows or ought to know that his course of conduct will cause the other so to fear on each of those occasions.

(2) For the purposes of this section, the person whose course of conduct is in question ought to know that it will cause another to fear that violence will be used against him on any occasion if a reasonable person in possession of the same information would think the course of conduct would cause the other so to fear on that occasion.

(3) It is a defence for a person charged with an offence under this section to show that—

    (a) his course of conduct was pursued for the purpose of preventing or detecting crime,

    (b) his course of conduct was pursued under any enactment or rule of law or to comply with any condition or requirement imposed by any person under any enactment, or

    (c) the pursuit of his course of conduct was reasonable for the protection of himself or another or for the protection of his or another's property.

5   Restraining orders [on conviction]

(1) A court sentencing or otherwise dealing with a person ('the defendant') convicted of an offence [. . .] may (as well as sentencing him or dealing with him in any other way) make an order under this section.

(2) The order may, for the purpose of protecting the victim [or victims] of the offence, or any other person mentioned in the order, from [. . .] conduct which—

    (a) amounts to harassment, or

    (b) will cause a fear of violence,

prohibit the defendant from doing anything described in the order.

(5) If without reasonable excuse the defendant does anything which he is prohibited from doing by an order under this section, he is guilty of an offence.

[5A   Restraining orders on acquittal

(1) A court before which a person ('the defendant') is acquitted of an offence may, if it considers it necessary to do so to protect a person from harassment by the defendant, make an order prohibiting the defendant from doing anything described in the order.]

7   Interpretation of this group of sections

(1) This section applies for the interpretation of [sections 1 to 5A].

(2) References to harassing a person include alarming the person or causing the person distress.

[(3) A 'course of conduct' must involve—

    (a) in the case of conduct in relation to a single person (see section 1(1)), conduct on at least two occasions in relation to that person, or

    (b) in the case of conduct in relation to two or more persons (see section 1(1A)), conduct on at least one occasion in relation to each of those persons.]

[(3A) A person's conduct on any occasion shall be taken, if aided, abetted, counselled or procured by another—

    (a) to be conduct on that occasion of the other (as well as conduct of the person whose conduct it is); and

    (b) to be conduct in relation to which the other's knowledge and purpose, and what he ought to have known, are the same as they were in relation to what was contemplated or reasonably foreseeable at the time of the aiding, abetting, counselling or procuring.]

(4) 'Conduct' includes speech.

[(5) References to a person, in the context of the harassment of a person, are references to a person who is an individual.]

12   National security, etc.

(1) If the Secretary of State certifies that in his opinion anything done by a specified person on a specified occasion related to—

    (a) national security,

(b) the economic well-being of the United Kingdom, or

(c) the prevention or detection of serious crime,

and was done on behalf of the Crown, the certificate is conclusive evidence that this Act does not apply to any conduct of that person on that occasion.

Data Protection Act 1998

(1998, c. 29)

10   Right to prevent processing likely to cause damage or distress

(1) Subject to subsection (2), an individual is entitled at any time by notice in writing to a data controller to require the data controller at the end of such period as is reasonable in the circumstances to cease, or not to begin, processing, or processing for a specified purpose or in a specified manner, any personal data in respect of which he is the data subject, on the ground that, for specified reasons—

(a) the processing of those data or their processing for that purpose or in that manner is causing or is likely to cause substantial damage or substantial distress to him or to another, and

(b) that damage or distress is or would be unwarranted.

(2) Subsection (1) does not apply—

(a) in a case where any of the conditions in paragraphs 1 to 4 of Schedule 2 is met, or

(b) on such other cases as may be prescribed by the [Secretary of State] by order.

(3) The data controller must within twenty-one days of receiving a notice under subsection (1) ('the data subject notice') give the individual who gave it a written notice—

(a) stating that he has complied or intends to comply with the data subject notice, or

(b) stating his reasons for regarding the data subject notice as to any extent unjustified and the extent (if any) to which he has complied or intends to comply with it.

(4) If a court is satisfied, on the application of any person who has given a notice under subsection (1) which appears to the court to be justified (or to be justified to any extent), that the data controller in question has failed to comply with the notice, the court may order him to take such steps for complying with the notice (or for complying with it to that extent) as the court thinks fit.

(5) The failure by a data subject to exercise the right conferred by subsection (1) or section 11(1) does not affect any other right conferred on him by this Part.

13   Compensation for failure to comply with certain requirements

(1) An individual who suffers damage by reason of any contravention by a data controller of any of the requirements of this Act is entitled to compensation from the data controller for that damage.

(2) An individual who suffers distress by reason of any contravention by a data controller of any of the requirements of this Act is entitled to compensation from the data controller for that distress if—

(a) the individual also suffers damage by reason of the contravention, or

(b) the contravention relates to the processing of personal data for the special purposes.

(3) On proceedings brought against a person by virtue of this section it is a defence to prove that he had taken such care as in all the circumstances was reasonably required to comply with the requirement concerned.

57   Avoidance of certain contractual terms relating to health records

(1) Any term or condition of a contract is void in so far as it purports to require an individual—

(a) to supply any other person with a record to which this section applies, or with a copy of such a record or a part of such a record, or

(b) to produce to any other person such a record, copy or part.

(2) This section applies to any record which—

(a) has been or is to be obtained by a data subject in the exercise of the right conferred by section 7, and

(b) consists of the information contained in any health record as defined by section 68(2).

Human Rights Act 1998

(1998, c. 42)

Introduction

1 The Convention Rights

(1) In this Act 'the Convention rights' means the rights and fundamental freedoms set out in—

    (a) Articles 2 to 12 and 14 of the Convention,

    (b) Articles 1 to 3 of the First Protocol, and

    (c) [Article 1 of the Thirteenth Protocol,]

as read with Articles 16 to 18 of the Convention.

(2) Those Articles are to have effect for the purposes of this Act subject to any designated derogation or reservation (as to which see sections 14 and 15).

(3) The Articles are set out in Schedule 1.

(4) The [Secretary of State] may by order make such amendments to this Act as he considers appropriate to reflect the effect, in relation to the United Kingdom, of a protocol.

(5) In subsection (4) 'protocol' means a protocol to the Convention—

    (a) which the United Kingdom has ratified; or

    (b) which the United Kingdom has signed with a view to ratification.

(6) No amendment may be made by an order under subsection (4) so as to come into force before the protocol concerned is in force in relation to the United Kingdom.

2 Interpretation of Convention rights

(1) A court or tribunal determining a question which has arisen in connection with a Convention right must take into account any—

    (a) judgment, decision, declaration or advisory opinion of the European Court of Human Rights,

    (b) opinion of the Commission given in a report adopted under Article 31 of the Convention,

    (c) decision of the Commission in connection with Article 26 or 27(2) of the Convention, or

    (d) decision of the Committee of Ministers taken under Article 46 of the Convention,

whenever made or given, so far as, in the opinion of the court or tribunal, it is relevant to the proceedings in which that question has arisen.

(2) Evidence of any judgment, decision, declaration or opinion of which account may have to be taken under this section is to be given in proceedings before any court or tribunal in such manner as may be provided by rules.

(3) In this section 'rules' means rules of court or, in the case of proceedings before a tribunal, rules made for the purposes of this section—

    (a) by [the Lord Chancellor or] the Secretary of State, in relation to any proceedings outside Scotland;

    (b) by the Secretary of State, in relation to proceedings in Scotland; or

    (c) by a Northern Ireland department, in relation to proceedings before a tribunal in Northern Ireland—

        (i) which deals with transferred matters; and

        (ii) for which no rules made under paragraph (a) are in force.

Legislation

3 Interpretation of legislation

(1) So far as it is possible to do so, primary legislation and subordinate legislation must be read and given effect in a way which is compatible with the Convention rights.

(2) This section—

    (a) applies to primary legislation and subordinate legislation whenever enacted;

(b) does not affect the validity, continuing operation or enforcement of any incompatible primary legislation; and

(c) does not affect the validity, continuing operation or enforcement of any incompatible subordinate legislation if (disregarding any possibility of revocation) primary legislation prevents removal of the incompatibility.

4   Declaration of incompatibility

(1) Subsection (2) applies in any proceedings in which a court determines whether a provision of primary legislation is compatible with a Convention right.

(2) If the court is satisfied that the provision is incompatible with a Convention right, it may make a declaration of that incompatibility.

(3) Subsection (4) applies in any proceedings in which a court determines whether a provision of subordinate legislation, made in the exercise of a power conferred by primary legislation, is compatible with a Convention right.

(4) If the court is satisfied—

(a) that the provision is incompatible with a Convention right, and

(b) that (disregarding any possibility of revocation) the primary legislation concerned prevents removal of the incompatibility,

it may make a declaration of that incompatibility.

(5) In this section 'court' means—

(a) the [Supreme Court];

(b) the Judicial Committee of the Privy Council;

(c) the [Courts Martial Appeal Court];

(d) in Scotland, the High Court of Justiciary sitting otherwise than as a trial court or the Court of Session;

(e) in England and Wales or Northern Ireland, the High Court or the Court of Appeal

[(f) the Court of Protection, in any matter being dealt with by the President of the Family Division, the Vice-Chancellor or a puisne judge of the High Court.]

(6) A declaration under this section ('a declaration of incompatibility')—

(a) does not affect the validity, continuing operation or enforcement of the provision in respect of which it is given; and

(b) is not binding on the parties to the proceedings in which it is made.

5   Right of Crown to intervene

(1) Where a court is considering whether to make a declaration of incompatibility, the Crown is entitled to notice in accordance with rules of court.

(2) In any case to which subsection (1) applies—

(a) a Minister of the Crown (or a person nominated by him),

(b) a member of the Scottish Executive,

(c) a Northern Ireland Minister,

(d) a Northern Ireland department,

is entitled, on giving notice in accordance with rules of court, to be joined as a party to the proceedings.

(3) Notice under subsection (2) may be given at any time during the proceedings.

(4) A person who has been made a party to criminal proceedings (other than in Scotland) as the result of a notice under subsection (2) may, with leave, appeal to the [Supreme Court] against any declaration of incompatibility made in the proceedings.

(5) In subsection (4)—

'criminal proceedings' includes all proceedings before the [Courts Martial Appeal Court]; and

'leave' means leave granted by the court making the declaration of incompatibility or by the [Supreme Court].

Public authorities

6   Acts of public authorities

(1) It is unlawful for a public authority to act in a way which is incompatible with a Convention right.

(2) Subsection (1) does not apply to an act if—

    (a) as the result of one or more provisions of primary legislation, the authority could not have acted differently; or

    (b) in the case of one or more provisions of, or made under, primary legislation which cannot be read or given effect in a way which is compatible with the Convention rights, the authority was acting so as to give effect to or enforce those provisions.

(3) In this section 'public authority' includes—

    (a) a court or tribunal, and

    (b) any person certain of whose functions are functions of a public nature,

but does not include either House of Parliament or a person exercising functions in connection with proceedings in Parliament.

(5) In relation to a particular act, a person is not a public authority by virtue only of subsection (3)(b) if the nature of the act is private.

(6) 'An act' includes a failure to act but does not include a failure to—

    (a) introduce in, or lay before, Parliament a proposal for legislation; or

    (b) make any primary legislation or remedial order.

7   Proceedings

(1) A person who claims that a public authority has acted (or proposes to act) in a way which is made unlawful by section 6(1) may—

    (a) bring proceedings against the authority under this Act in the appropriate court or tribunal, or

    (b) rely on the Convention right or rights concerned in any legal proceedings,

but only if he is (or would be) a victim of the unlawful act.

(2) In subsection (1)(a) 'appropriate court or tribunal' means such court or tribunal as may be determined in accordance with rules; and proceedings against an authority include a counterclaim or similar proceedings.

(3) If the proceedings are brought on an application for judicial review, the applicant is to be taken to have a sufficient interest in relation to the unlawful act only if he is, or would be, a victim of that act.

(4) If the proceedings are made by way of a petition for judicial review in Scotland, the applicant shall be taken to have title and interest to sue in relation to the unlawful act only if he is, or would be, a victim of that act.

(5) Proceedings under subsection (1)(a) must be brought before the end of—

    (a) the period of one year beginning with the date on which the act complained of took place; or

    (b) such longer period as the court or tribunal considers equitable having regard to all the circumstances,

but that is subject to any rule imposing a stricter time limit in relation to the procedure in question.

(6) In subsection (1)(b) 'legal proceedings' includes—

    (a) proceedings brought by or at the instigation of a public authority; and

    (b) an appeal against the decision of a court or tribunal.

(7) For the purposes of this section, a person is a victim of an unlawful act only if he would be a victim for the purposes of Article 34 of the Convention if proceedings were brought in the European Court of Human Rights in respect of that act.

(8) Nothing in this Act creates a criminal offence.

(9) In this section 'rules' means—

    (a) in relation to proceedings before a court or tribunal outside Scotland, rules made by [the Lord Chancellor or] the Secretary of State for the purposes of this section or rules of court,

    (b) in relation to proceedings before a court or tribunal in Scotland, rules made by the Secretary of State for those purposes,

    (c) in relation to proceedings before a tribunal in Northern Ireland—

        (i) which deals with transferred matters; and

        (ii) for which no rules made under paragraph (a) are in force,

rules made by a Northern Ireland department for those purposes,

and includes provision made by order under section 1 of the Courts and Legal Services Act 1990.

(10) In making rules, regard must be had to section 9.

(11) The Minister who has power to make rules in relation to a particular tribunal may, to the extent he considers it necessary to ensure that the tribunal can provide an appropriate remedy in relation to an act (or proposed act) of a public authority which is (or would be) unlawful as a result of section 6(1), by order add to—

    (a) the relief or remedies which the tribunal may grant; or

    (b) the grounds on which it may grant any of them.

(12) An order made under subsection (11) may contain such incidental, supplemental, consequential or transitional provision as the Minister making it considers appropriate.

(13) 'The Minister' includes the Northern Ireland department concerned.

8 Judicial remedies

(1) In relation to any act (or proposed act) of a public authority which the court finds is (or would be) unlawful, it may grant such relief or remedy, or make such order, within its powers as it considers just and appropriate.

(2) But damages may be awarded only by a court which has power to award damages, or to order the payment of compensation, in civil proceedings.

(3) No award of damages is to be made unless, taking account of all the circumstances of the case, including—

    (a) any other relief or remedy granted, or order made, in relation to the act in question (by that or any other court), and

    (b) the consequences of any decision (of that or any other court) in respect of that act,

the court is satisfied that the award is necessary to afford just satisfaction to the person in whose favour it is made.

(4) In determining—

    (a) whether to award damages, or

    (b) the amount of an award,

the court must take into account the principles applied by the European Court of Human Rights in relation to the award of compensation under Article 41 of the Convention.

(5) A public authority against which damages are awarded is to be treated—

    (a) in Scotland, for the purposes of section 3 of the Law Reform (Miscellaneous Provisions) (Scotland) Act 1940 as if the award were made in an action of damages in which the authority has been found liable in respect of loss or damage to the person to whom the award is made;

    (b) for the purposes of the Civil Liability (Contribution) Act 1978 as liable in respect of damage suffered by the person to whom the award is made.

(6) In this section—

'court' includes a tribunal;

'damages' means damages for an unlawful act of a public authority; and

'unlawful' means unlawful under section 6(1).

9   Judicial acts

(1) Proceedings under section 7(1)(a) in respect of a judicial act may be brought only—

   (a) by exercising a right of appeal;

   (b) on an application (in Scotland a petition) for judicial review; or

   (c) in such other forum as may be prescribed by rules.

(2) That does not affect any rule of law which prevents a court from being the subject of judicial review.

(3) In proceedings under this Act in respect of a judicial act done in good faith, damages may not be awarded otherwise than to compensate a person to the extent required by Article 5(5) of the Convention.

(4) An award of damages permitted by subsection (3) is to be made against the Crown; but no award may be made unless the appropriate person, if not a party to the proceedings, is joined.

(5) In this section—

'appropriate person' means the Minister responsible for the court concerned, or a person or government department nominated by him;

'court' includes a tribunal;

'judge' includes a member of a tribunal, a justice of the peace [or, in Northern Ireland, a lay magistrate] and a clerk or other officer entitled to exercise the jurisdiction of a court;

'judicial act' means a judicial act of a court and includes an act done on the instructions, or on behalf, of a judge; and

'rules' has the same meaning as in section 7(9).

Remedial action

10   Power to take remedial action

(1) This section applies if—

   (a) a provision of legislation has been declared under section 4 to be incompatible with a Convention right and, if an appeal lies—

      (i)   all persons who may appeal have stated in writing that they do not intend to do so;

      (ii) the time for bringing an appeal has expired and no appeal has been brought within that time; or

      (iii) an appeal brought within that time has been determined or abandoned; or

   (b) it appears to a Minister of the Crown or Her Majesty in Council that, having regard to a finding of the European Court of Human Rights made after the coming into force of this section in proceedings against the United Kingdom, a provision of legislation is incompatible with an obligation of the United Kingdom arising from the Convention.

(2) If a Minister of the Crown considers that there are compelling reasons for proceeding under this section, he may by order make such amendments to the legislation as he considers necessary to remove the incompatibility.

(3) If, in the case of subordinate legislation, a Minister of the Crown considers—

   (a) that it is necessary to amend the primary legislation under which the subordinate legislation in question was made, in order to enable the incompatibility to be removed, and

   (b) that there are compelling reasons for proceeding under this section,

he may by order make such amendments to the primary legislation as he considers necessary.

(4) This section also applies where the provision in question is in subordinate legislation and has been quashed, or declared invalid, by reason of incompatibility with a Convention right and the Minister proposes to proceed under paragraph 2(b) of Schedule 2.

(5) If the legislation is an Order in Council, the power conferred by subsection (2) or (3) is exercisable by Her Majesty in Council.

(6) In this section 'legislation' does not include a Measure of the Church Assembly or of the General Synod of the Church of England.

(7) Schedule 2 makes further provision about remedial orders.

Other rights and proceedings

11 Safeguard for existing human rights

A person's reliance on a Convention right does not restrict—

   (a) any other right or freedom conferred on him by or under any law having effect in any part of the United Kingdom; or

   (b) his right to make any claim or bring any proceedings which he could make or bring apart from sections 7 to 9.

12 Freedom of expression

   (1) This section applies if a court is considering whether to grant any relief which, if granted, might affect the exercise of the Convention right to freedom of expression.

   (2) If the person against whom the application for relief is made ('the respondent') is neither present nor represented, no such relief is to be granted unless the court is satisfied—

   (a) that the applicant has taken all practicable steps to notify the respondent; or

   (b) that there are compelling reasons why the respondent should not be notified.

   (3) No such relief is to be granted so as to restrain publication before trial unless the court is satisfied that the applicant is likely to establish that publication should not be allowed.

   (4) The court must have particular regard to the importance of the Convention right to freedom of expression and, where the proceedings relate to material which the respondent claims, or which appears to the court, to be journalistic, literary or artistic material (or to conduct connected with such material), to—

   (a) the extent to which—

      (i)   the material has, or is about to, become available to the public; or

      (ii) it is, or would be, in the public interest for the material to be published;

   (b) any relevant privacy code.

   (5) In this section—

'court' includes a tribunal; and

'relief' includes any remedy or order (other than in criminal proceedings).

13 Freedom of thought, conscience and religion

   (1) If a court's determination of any question arising under this Act might affect the exercise by a religious organisation (itself or its members collectively) of the Convention right to freedom of thought, conscience and religion, it must have particular regard to the importance of that right.

   (2) In this section 'court' includes a tribunal.

Parliamentary procedure

19 Statements of compatibility

   (1) A Minister of the Crown in charge of a Bill in either House of Parliament must, before Second Reading of the Bill—

   (a) make a statement to the effect that in his view the provisions of the Bill are compatible with the Convention rights ('a statement of compatibility'); or

   (b) make a statement to the effect that although he is unable to make a statement of compatibility the government nevertheless wishes the House to proceed with the Bill.

   (2) The statement must be in writing and be published in such manner as the Minister making it considers appropriate.

Supplemental

21 Interpretation, etc.

   (1) In this Act—

'amend' includes repeal and apply (with or without modifications);

'the appropriate Minister' means the Minister of the Crown having charge of the appropriate authorised government department (within the meaning of the Crown Proceedings Act 1947);

'the Commission' means the European Commission of Human Rights;

'the Convention' means the Convention for the Protection of Human Rights and Fundamental Freedoms, agreed by the Council of Europe at Rome on 4th November 1950 as it has effect for the time being in relation to the United Kingdom;

'declaration of incompatibility' means a declaration under section 4;

'Minister of the Crown' has the same meaning as in the Ministers of the Crown Act 1975;

'Northern Ireland Minister' includes the First Minister and the deputy First Minister in Northern Ireland;

'primary legislation' means any—

(a) public general Act;

(b) local and personal Act;

(c) private Act;

(d) Measure of the Church Assembly;

(e) Measure of the General Synod of the Church of England;

(f) Order in Council—

   (i) made in exercise of Her Majesty's Royal Prerogative;

   (ii) made under section 38(1)(a) of the Northern Ireland Constitution Act 1973 or the corresponding provision of the Northern Ireland Act 1998; or

   (iii) amending an Act of a kind mentioned in paragraph (a), (b) or (c);

and includes an order or other instrument made under primary legislation (otherwise than by the [Welsh Ministers, the First Minister for Wales, the Counsel General to the Welsh Assembly Government,] a member of the Scottish Executive, a Northern Ireland Minister or a Northern Ireland department) to the extent to which it operates to bring one or more provisions of that legislation into force or amends any primary legislation;

'the First Protocol' means the protocol to the Convention agreed at Paris on 20th March 1952;

'the Eleventh Protocol' means the protocol to the Convention (restructuring the control machinery established by the Convention) agreed at Strasbourg on 11th May 1994;

['the Thirteenth Protocol' means the protocol to the Convention (concerning the abolition of the death penalty in all circumstances) agreed at Vilnius on 3rd May 2002;]

'remedial order' means an order under section 10;

'subordinate legislation' means any—

(a) Order in Council other than one—

   (i) made in exercise of Her Majesty's Royal Prerogative;

   (ii) made under section 38(1)(a) of the Northern Ireland Constitution Act 1973 or the corresponding provision of the Northern Ireland Act 1998; or

   (iii) amending an Act of a kind mentioned in the definition of primary legislation;

(b) Act of the Scottish Parliament;

[(ba) Measure of the National Assembly for Wales;

(bb) Act of the National Assembly for Wales;]

(c) Act of the Parliament of Northern Ireland;

(d) Measure of the Assembly established under section 1 of the Northern Ireland Assembly Act 1973;

(e) Act of the Northern Ireland Assembly;

(f) order, rules, regulations, scheme, warrant, byelaw or other instrument made under primary legislation (except to the extent to which it operates to bring one or more provisions of that legislation into force or amends any primary legislation);

(g) order, rules, regulations, scheme, warrant, byelaw or other instrument made under legislation mentioned in paragraph (b), (c), (d) or (e) or made under an Order in Council applying only to Northern Ireland;

(h)   order, rules, regulations, scheme, warrant, byelaw or other instrument made by a member of the Scottish Executive, [Welsh Ministers, the First Minister for Wales, the Counsel General to the Welsh Assembly Government,] a Northern Ireland Minister or a Northern Ireland department in exercise of prerogative or other executive functions of Her Majesty which are exercisable by such a person on behalf of Her Majesty;

'transferred matters' has the same meaning as in the Northern Ireland Act 1998; and

'tribunal' means any tribunal in which legal proceedings may be brought.

(2) The references in paragraphs (b) and (c) of section 2(1) to Articles are to Articles of the Convention as they had effect immediately before the coming into force of the Eleventh Protocol.

(3) The reference in paragraph (d) of section 2(1) to Article 46 includes a reference to Articles 32 and 54 of the Convention as they had effect immediately before the coming into force of the Eleventh Protocol.

(4) The references in section 2(1) to a report or decision of the Commission or a decision of the Committee of Ministers include references to a report or decision made as provided by paragraphs 3, 4 and 6 of Article 5 of the Eleventh Protocol (transitional provisions).

(5) Any liability under the Army Act 1955, the Air Force Act 1955 or the Naval Discipline Act 1957 to suffer death for an offence is replaced by a liability to imprisonment for life or any less punishment authorised by those Acts; and those Acts shall accordingly have effect with the necessary modifications.

22   Short title, commencement, application and extent

(5) This Act binds the Crown.

(6) This Act extends to Northern Ireland.

Section 1(3)

SCHEDULE 1
THE ARTICLES

PART I THE CONVENTION

Rights and freedoms

Article 2   Right to life

1. Everyone's right to life shall be protected by law. No one shall be deprived of his life intentionally save in the execution of a sentence of a court following his conviction of a crime for which this penalty is provided by law.

2. Deprivation of life shall not be regarded as inflicted in contravention of this Article when it results from the use of force which is no more than absolutely necessary:

(a) in defence of any person from unlawful violence;

(b) in order to effect a lawful arrest or to prevent the escape of a person lawfully detained;

(c) in action lawfully taken for the purpose of quelling a riot or insurrection.

Article 3   Prohibition of torture

No one shall be subjected to torture or to inhuman or degrading treatment or punishment.

Article 4   Prohibition of slavery and forced labour

1. No one shall be held in slavery or servitude.

2. No one shall be required to perform forced or compulsory labour.

3. For the purpose of this Article the term 'forced or compulsory labour' shall not include:

(a) any work required to be done in the ordinary course of detention imposed according to the provisions of Article 5 of this Convention or during conditional release from such detention;

(b) any service of a military character or, in case of conscientious objectors in countries where they are recognised, service exacted instead of compulsory military service;

(c) any service exacted in case of an emergency or calamity threatening the life or well-being of the community;

(d) any work or service which forms part of normal civic obligations.

Article 5   Right to liberty and security

1. Everyone has the right to liberty and security of person. No one shall be deprived of his liberty save in the following cases and in accordance with a procedure prescribed by law:

(a) the lawful detention of a person after conviction by a competent court;

(b) the lawful arrest or detention of a person for non-compliance with the lawful order of a court or in order to secure the fulfilment of any obligation prescribed by law;

(c) the lawful arrest or detention of a person effected for the purpose of bringing him before the competent legal authority on reasonable suspicion of having committed an offence or when it is reasonably considered necessary to prevent his committing an offence or fleeing after having done so;

(d) the detention of a minor by lawful order for the purpose of educational supervision or his lawful detention for the purpose of bringing him before the competent legal authority.

(e) the lawful detention of persons for the prevention of the spreading of infectious diseases, of persons of unsound mind, alcoholics or drug addicts or vagrants;

(f) the lawful arrest or detention of a person to prevent his effecting an unauthorised entry into the country or of a person against whom action is being taken with a view to deportation or extradition.

2. Everyone who is arrested shall be informed promptly, in a language which he understands, of the reasons for his arrest and of any charge against him.

3. Everyone arrested or detained in accordance with the provisions of paragraph 1(c) of this Article shall be brought promptly before a judge or other officer authorised by law to exercise judicial power and shall be entitled to trial within a reasonable time or to release pending trial. Release may be conditioned by guarantees to appear for trial.

4. Everyone who is deprived of his liberty by arrest or detention shall be entitled to take proceedings by which the lawfulness of his detention shall be decided speedily by a court and his release ordered if the detention is not lawful.

5. Everyone who has been the victim of arrest or detention in contravention of the provisions of this Article shall have an enforceable right to compensation.

Article 6   Right to a fair trial

1. In the determination of his civil rights and obligations or of any criminal charge against him, everyone is entitled to a fair and public hearing within a reasonable time by an independent and impartial tribunal established by law. Judgment shall be pronounced publicly but the press and public may be excluded from all or part of the trial in the interest of morals, public order or national security in a democratic society, where the interests of juveniles or the protection of the private life of the parties so require, or to the extent strictly necessary in the opinion of the court in special circumstances where publicity would prejudice the interests of justice.

2. Everyone charged with a criminal offence shall be presumed innocent until proved guilty according to law.

3. Everyone charged with a criminal offence has the following minimum rights:

(a) to be informed promptly, in a language which he understands and in detail, of the nature and cause of the accusation against him;

(b) to have adequate time and facilities for the preparation of his defence;

(c) to defend himself in person or through legal assistance of his own choosing or, if he has not sufficient means to pay for legal assistance, to be given it free when the interests of justice so require;

(d) to examine or have examined witnesses against him and to obtain the attendance and examination of witnesses on his behalf under the same conditions as witnesses against him;

(e) to have the free assistance of an interpreter if he cannot understand or speak the language used in court.

Article 7   No punishment without law

1. No one shall be held guilty of any criminal offence on account of any act or omission which did not constitute a criminal offence under national or international law at the time when it was committed. Nor shall a heavier penalty be imposed than the one that was applicable at the time the criminal offence was committed.

2. This Article shall not prejudice the trial and punishment of any person for any act or omission which, at the time when it was committed, was criminal according to the general principles of law recognised by civilised nations.

Article 8   Right to respect for private and family life

1. Everyone has the right to respect for his private and family life, his home and his correspondence.

2. There shall be no interference by a public authority with the exercise of this right except such as is in accordance with the law and is necessary in a democratic society in the interests of national security, public safety or the economic well-being of the country, for the prevention of disorder or crime, for the protection of health or morals, or for the protection of the rights and freedoms of others.

Article 9   Freedom of thought, conscience and religion

1. Everyone has the right to freedom of thought, conscience and religion; this right includes freedom to change his religion or belief and freedom, either alone or in community with others and in public or private, to manifest his religion or belief, in worship, teaching, practice and observance.

2. Freedom to manifest one's religion or beliefs shall be subject only to such limitations as are prescribed by law and are necessary in a democratic society in the interests of public safety, for the protection of public order, health or morals, or for the protection of the rights and freedoms of others.

Article 10   Freedom of expression

1. Everyone has the right to freedom of expression. This right shall include freedom to hold opinions and to receive and impart information and ideas without interference by public authority and regardless of frontiers. This Article shall not prevent States from requiring the licensing of broadcasting, television or cinema enterprises.

2. The exercise of these freedoms, since it carries with it duties and responsibilities, may be subject to such formalities, conditions, restrictions or penalties as are prescribed by law and are necessary in a democratic society, in the interests of national security, territorial integrity or public safety, for the prevention of disorder or crime, for the protection of health or morals, for the protection of the reputation or rights of others, for preventing the disclosure of information received in confidence, or for maintaining the authority and impartiality of the judiciary.

Article 11   Freedom of assembly and association

1. Everyone has the right to freedom of peaceful assembly and to freedom of association with others, including the right to form and to join trade unions for the protection of his interests.

2. No restrictions shall be placed on the exercise of these rights other than such as are prescribed by law and are necessary in a democratic society in the interests of national security or public safety, for the prevention of disorder or crime, for the protection of health or morals or for

the protection of the rights and freedoms of others. This Article shall not prevent the imposition of lawful restrictions on the exercise of these rights by members of the armed forces, of the police or of the administration of the State.

Article 12   Right to marry

Men and women of marriageable age have the right to marry and to found a family, according to the national laws governing the exercise of this right.

Article 14   Prohibition of discrimination

The enjoyment of the rights and freedoms set forth in this Convention shall be secured without discrimination on any ground such as sex, race, colour, language, religion, political or other opinion, national or social origin, association with a national minority, property, birth or other status.

Article 16   Restrictions on political activity of aliens

Nothing in Articles 10, 11 and 14 shall be regarded as preventing the High Contracting Parties from imposing restrictions on the political activity of aliens.

Article 17   Prohibition of abuse of rights

Nothing in this Convention may be interpreted as implying for any State, group or person any right to engage in any activity or perform any act aimed at the destruction of any of the rights and freedoms set forth herein or at their limitation to a greater extent than is provided for in the Convention.

Article 18   Limitation on use of restrictions on rights

The restrictions permitted under this Convention to the said rights and freedoms shall not be applied for any purpose other than those for which they have been prescribed.

PART II THE FIRST PROTOCOL

Article 1   Protection of property

Every natural or legal person is entitled to the peaceful enjoyment of his possessions. No one shall be deprived of his possessions except in the public interest and subject to the conditions provided for by law and by the general principles of international law.

The preceding provisions shall not, however, in any way impair the right of a State to enforce such laws as it deems necessary to control the use of property in accordance with the general interest or to secure the payment of taxes or other contributions or penalties.

Article 2   Right to education

No person shall be denied the right to education. In the exercise of any functions which it assumes in relation to education and to teaching, the State shall respect the right of parents to ensure such education and teaching in conformity with their own religious and philosophical convictions.

Article 3   Right to free elections

The High Contracting Parties undertake to hold free elections at reasonable intervals by secret ballot, under conditions which will ensure the free expression of the opinion of the people in the choice of the legislature.

[PART 3 ARTICLE 1 OF THE THIRTEENTH PROTOCOL

Abolition of the death penalty

The death penalty shall be abolished. No one shall be condemned to such penalty or executed.]

Late Payment of Commercial Debts (Interest) Act 1998

(1998, c. 20)

PART I STATUTORY INTEREST ON QUALIFYING DEBTS

1 Statutory interest

(1) It is an implied term in a contract to which this Act applies that any qualifying debt created by the contract carries simple interest subject to and in accordance with this Part.

(2) Interest carried under that implied term (in this Act referred to as 'statutory interest') shall be treated, for the purposes of any rule of law or enactment (other than this Act) relating to interest on debts, in the same way as interest carried under an express contract term.

(3) This Part has effect subject to Part II (which in certain circumstances permits contract terms to oust or vary the right to statutory interest that would otherwise be conferred by virtue of the term implied by subsection (1)).

2   Contracts to which Act applies

(1) This Act applies to a contract for the supply of goods or services where the purchaser and the supplier are each acting in the course of a business, other than an excepted contract.

(2) In this Act 'contract for the supply of goods or services' means—

   (a) a contract of sale of goods; or
   (b) a contract (other than a contract of sale of goods) by which a person does any, or any combination, of the things mentioned in subsection (3) for a consideration that is (or includes) a money consideration.

(3) Those things are—

   (a) transferring or agreeing to transfer to another the property in goods;
   (b) bailing or agreeing to bail goods to another by way of hire or, in Scotland, hiring or agreeing to hire goods to another; and
   (c) agreeing to carry out a service.

(4) For the avoidance of doubt a contract of service or apprenticeship is not a contract for the supply of goods or services.

(5) The following are excepted contracts—

   (a) a consumer credit agreement;
   (b) a contract intended to operate by way of mortgage, pledge, charge or other security; and
   [. . .]

(7) In this section—

   'business' includes a profession and the activities of any government department or local or public authority;

   'consumer credit agreement' has the same meaning as in the Consumer Credit Act 1974;

   'contract of sale of goods' and 'goods' have the same meaning as in the Sale of Goods Act 1979;

   ['government department' includes any part of the Scottish Administration;]

   'property in goods' means the general property in them and not merely a special property.

3 Qualifying debts

(1) A debt created by virtue of an obligation under a contract to which this Act applies to pay the whole or any part of the contract price is a 'qualifying debt' for the purposes of this Act, unless (when created) the whole of the debt is prevented from carrying statutory interest by this section.

(2) A debt does not carry statutory interest if or to the extent that it consists of a sum to which a right to interest or to charge interest applies by virtue of any enactment (other than section 1 of this Act).

This subsection does not prevent a sum from carrying statutory interest by reason of the fact that a court, arbitrator or arbiter would, apart from this Act, have power to award interest on it.

(3) A debt does not carry (and shall be treated as never having carried) statutory interest if or to the extent that a right to demand interest on it, which exists by virtue of any rule of law, is exercised.

4   Period for which statutory interest runs

(1) Statutory interest runs in relation to a qualifying debt in accordance with this section (unless section 5 applies).

(2) Statutory interest starts to run on the day after the relevant day for the debt, at the rate prevailing under section 6 at the end of the relevant day.

(3) Where the supplier and the purchaser agree a date for payment of the debt (that is, the day on which the debt is to be created by the contract), that is the relevant day unless the debt relates to an obligation to make an advance payment.

A date so agreed may be a fixed one or may depend on the happening of an event or the failure of an event to happen.

[(3A) If, in a case where the purchaser is a public authority, the relevant day under subsection (3) would (but for this subsection) be later than the day which would be the relevant day if subsection (5) applied, it is to be treated for the purposes of subsection (3) as being the day which would be the relevant day if subsection (5) applied.

(3B) If, in a case where the purchaser is not a public authority, the relevant day under subsection (3) would (but for this subsection) be more than 30 days after the day which would be the relevant day if subsection (5) applied, it is to be treated for the purposes of subsection (3) as being the day which is 30 days after the day which would be the relevant day if subsection (5) applied.

(3C) Subsection (3B) does not apply if—

(a) the supplier and the purchaser expressly agree in the contract a date for payment of the debt that is later than the day which would otherwise be the relevant day by virtue of that subsection, and

(b) that later date is not grossly unfair to the supplier (see subsection (7A)).]

(4) Where the debt relates to an obligation to make an advance payment, the relevant day is the day on which the debt is treated by section 11 as having been created.

(5) In any other case, the relevant day is the last day of the period of 30 days beginning with—

(a) the day on which the obligation of the supplier to which the debt relates is performed; [. . .]

(b) the day on which the purchaser has notice of the amount of the debt or (where the amount is unascertained) the sum which the supplier claims is the amount of the debt, whichever is the later[; or

(c) where subsection (5A) applies, the day determined under subsection (5B)], whichever is the later.

[(5A) This subsection applies where—

(a) there is a procedure of acceptance or verification (whether provided for by an enactment or by the contract), under which the conforming of goods or services with the contract is to be ascertained, and

(b) the purchaser has notice of the amount of the debt on or before the day on which the procedure is completed.

(5B) For the purposes of subsection (5)(c), the day in question is the day . . . after the day on which the procedure is completed.

(5C) Where, in a case where subsection (5A) applies, the procedure in question is completed after the end of the period of 30 days beginning with the day on which the obligation of the supplier to which the debt relates is performed, the procedure is to be treated for the purposes of subsection (5B) as being completed immediately after the end of that period.

(5D) Subsection (5C) does not apply if—

    (a) the supplier and the purchaser expressly agree in the contract a period for completing the procedure in question that is longer than the period mentioned in that subsection, and

    (b) that longer period is not grossly unfair to the supplier (see subsection (7A)).]

(6) Where the debt is created by virtue of an obligation to pay a sum due in respect of a period of hire of goods, subsection (5)(a) has effect as if it referred to the last day of that period.

(7) Statutory interest ceases to run when the interest would cease to run if it were carried under an express contract term.

[(7A) In determining for the purposes of subsection (3C) or (5D) whether something is grossly unfair, all circumstances of the case shall be considered; and for that purpose, the circumstances of the case include in particular—

    (a) anything that is a gross deviation from good commercial practice and contrary to good faith and fair dealing,

    (b) the nature of the goods or services in question, and

    (c) whether the purchaser has any objective reason to deviate from the result which is provided for by subsection (3B) or (5C).]

[(8) In this section—

"advance payment" has the same meaning as in section 11;

"enactment" includes an enactment contained in subordinate legislation (within the meaning of the Interpretation Act 1978);

"public authority" means a contracting authority (within the meaning of regulation 3 of the Public Contracts Regulations 2006).]

5   Remission of statutory interest

(1) This section applies where, by reason of any conduct of the supplier, the interests of justice require that statutory interest should be remitted in whole or part in respect of a period for which it would otherwise run in relation to a qualifying debt.

(2) If the interests of justice require that the supplier should receive no statutory interest for a period, statutory interest shall not run for that period.

(3) If the interests of justice require that the supplier should receive statutory interest at a reduced rate for a period, statutory interest shall run at such rate as meets the justice of the case for that period.

(4) Remission of statutory interest under this section may be required—

    (a) by reason of conduct at any time (whether before or after the time at which the debt is created); and

    (b) for the whole period for which statutory interest would otherwise run or for one or more parts of that period.

(5) In this section 'conduct' includes any act or omission.

[5A   Compensation arising out of late payment

(1) Once statutory interest begins to run in relation to a qualifying debt, the supplier shall be entitled to a fixed sum (in addition to the statutory interest on the debt).

(2) That sum shall be—

    (a) for a debt less than £1,000, the sum of £40;

    (b) for a debt of £1,000 or more, but less than £10,000, the sum of £70;

    (c) for a debt of £10,000 or more, the sum of £100.

(2A) If the reasonable costs of the supplier in recovering the debt are not met by the fixed sum, the supplier shall also be entitled to a sum equivalent to the difference between the fixed sum and those costs.

(3) The obligation to pay a sum under this section in respect of a qualifying debt shall be treated as part of the term implied by section 1(1) in the contract creating the debt.

(4) Section 3(2)(b) of the Unfair Contract Terms Act 1977 (no reliance to be placed on certain contract terms) shall apply in cases where a contract term is not contained in written standard terms of the purchaser as well as in cases where the term is contained in such standard terms.

(5) In this section "contract term" means a term of the contract relating to a sum due to the supplier under this section.]

6 Rate of statutory interest

(1) The Secretary of State shall by order made with the consent of the Treasury set the rate of statutory interest by prescribing—

    (a) a formula for calculating the rate of statutory interest; or

    (b) the rate of statutory interest.

(2) Before making such an order the Secretary of State shall, among other things, consider the extent to which it may be desirable to set the rate so as to—

    (a) protect suppliers whose financial position makes them particularly vulnerable if their qualifying debts are paid late; and

    (b) deter generally the late payment of qualifying debts.

PART II CONTRACT TERMS RELATING TO LATE PAYMENT OF QUALIFYING DEBTS

7 Purpose of Part II

(1) This Part deals with the extent to which the parties to a contract to which this Act applies may by reference to contract terms oust or vary the right to statutory interest that would otherwise apply when a qualifying debt created by the contract (in this Part referred to as 'the debt') is not paid.

(2) This Part applies to contract terms agreed before the debt is created; after that time the parties are free to agree terms dealing with the debt.

(3) This Part has effect without prejudice to any other ground which may affect the validity of a contract term.

8 Circumstances where statutory interest may be ousted or varied

(1) Any contract terms are void to the extent that they purport to exclude the right to statutory interest in relation to the debt, unless there is a substantial contractual remedy for late payment of the debt.

(2) Where the parties agree a contractual remedy for late payment of the debt that is a substantial remedy, statutory interest is not carried by the debt (unless they agree otherwise).

(3) The parties may not agree to vary the right to statutory interest in relation to the debt unless either the right to statutory interest as varied or the overall remedy for late payment of the debt is a substantial remedy.

(4) Any contract terms are void to the extent that they purport to—

    (a) confer a contractual right to interest that is not a substantial remedy for late payment of the debt, or

    (b) vary the right to statutory interest so as to provide for a right to statutory interest that is not a substantial remedy for late payment of the debt,

unless the overall remedy for late payment of the debt is a substantial remedy.

(5) Subject to this section, the parties are free to agree contract terms which deal with the consequences of late payment of the debt.

9 Meaning of 'substantial remedy'

(1) A remedy for the late payment of the debt shall be regarded as a substantial remedy unless—

    (a) the remedy is insufficient either for the purpose of compensating the supplier for late payment or for deterring late payment; and

(b) it would not be fair or reasonable to allow the remedy to be relied on to oust or (as the case may be) to vary the right to statutory interest that would otherwise apply in relation to the debt.

(2) In determining whether a remedy is not a substantial remedy, regard shall be had to all the relevant circumstances at the time the terms in question are agreed.

(3) In determining whether subsection (1)(b) applies, regard shall be had (without prejudice to the generality of subsection (2)) to the following matters—

(a) the benefits of commercial certainty;

(b) the strength of the bargaining positions of the parties relative to each other;

(c) whether the term was imposed by one party to the detriment of the other (whether by the use of standard terms or otherwise); and

(d) whether the supplier received an inducement to agree to the term.

10   Interpretation of Part II

(1) In this Part—

'contract term' means a term of the contract creating the debt or any other contract term binding the parties (or either of them);

'contractual remedy' means a contractual right to interest or any contractual remedy other than interest;

'contractual right to interest' includes a reference to a contractual right to charge interest;

'overall remedy', in relation to the late payment of the debt, means any combination of a contractual right to interest, a varied right to statutory interest or a contractual remedy other than interest;'substantial remedy' shall be construed in accordance with section 9.

(2) In this Part a reference (however worded) to contract terms which vary the right to statutory interest is a reference to terms altering in any way the effect of Part I in relation to the debt (for example by postponing the time at which interest starts to run or by imposing conditions on the right to interest).

(3) In this Part a reference to late payment of the debt is a reference to late payment of the sum due when the debt is created (excluding any part of that sum which is prevented from carrying statutory interest by section 3).

PART III GENERAL AND SUPPLEMENTARY

11   Treatment of advance payments of the contract price

(1) A qualifying debt created by virtue of an obligation to make an advance payment shall be treated for the purposes of this Act as if it was created on the day mentioned in subsection (3), (4) or (5) (as the case may be).

(2) In this section 'advance payment' means a payment falling due before the obligation of the supplier to which the whole contract price relates ('the supplier's obligation') is performed, other than a payment of a part of the contract price that is due in respect of any part performance of that obligation and payable on or after the day on which that part performance is completed.

(3) Where the advance payment is the whole contract price, the debt shall be treated as created on the day on which the supplier's obligation is performed.

(4) Where the advance payment is a part of the contract price, but the sum is not due in respect of any part performance of the supplier's obligation, the debt shall be treated as created on the day on which the supplier's obligation is performed.

(5) Where the advance payment is a part of the contract price due in respect of any part performance of the supplier's obligation, but is payable before that part performance is completed, the debt shall be treated as created on the day on which the relevant part performance is completed.

(6) Where the debt is created by virtue of an obligation to pay a sum due in respect of a period of hire of goods, this section has effect as if—

(a) references to the day on which the supplier's obligation is performed were references to the last day of that period; and

(b) references to part performance of that obligation were references to part of that period.

(7) For the purposes of this section an obligation to pay the whole outstanding balance of the contract price shall be regarded as an obligation to pay the whole contract price and not as an obligation to pay a part of the contract price.

13 Assignments, etc.

(1) The operation of this Act in relation to a qualifying debt is not affected by—

(a) any change in the identity of the parties to the contract creating the debt; or

(b) the passing of the right to be paid the debt, or the duty to pay it (in whole or in part) to a person other than the person who is the original creditor or the original debtor when the debt is created.

(2) Any reference in this Act to the supplier or the purchaser is a reference to the person who is for the time being the supplier or the purchaser or, in relation to a time after the debt in question has been created, the person who is for the time being the creditor or the debtor, as the case may be.

(3) Where the right to be paid part of a debt passes to a person other than the person who is the original creditor when the debt is created, any reference in this Act to a debt shall be construed as (or, if the context so requires, as including) a reference to part of a debt.

(4) A reference in this section to the identity of the parties to a contract changing, or to a right or duty passing, is a reference to it changing or passing by assignment or assignation, by operation of law or otherwise.

14 Contract terms relating to the date for payment of the contract price

(1) This section applies to any contract term which purports to have the effect of postponing the time at which a qualifying debt would otherwise be created by a contract to which this Act applies.

(2) Sections 3(2)(b) and 17(1)(b) of the Unfair Contract Terms Act 1977 (no reliance to be placed on certain contract terms) shall apply in cases where such a contract term is not contained in written standard terms of the purchaser as well as in cases where the term is contained in such standard terms.

(3) In this section 'contract term' has the same meaning as in section 10(1).

15 Orders and regulations

(1) Any power to make an order or regulations under this Act is exercisable by statutory instrument.

(2) Any statutory instrument containing an order or regulations under this Act, other than an order under section 17(2), shall be subject to annulment in pursuance of a resolution of either House of Parliament.

16 Interpretation

(1) In this Act—

'contract for the supply of goods or services' has the meaning given in section 2(2);

'contract price' means the price in a contract of sale of goods or the money consideration referred to in section 2(2)(b) in any other contract for the supply of goods or services;

'purchaser' means (subject to section 13(2)) the buyer in a contract of sale or the person who contracts with the supplier in any other contract for the supply of goods or services;

'qualifying debt' means a debt falling within section 3(1);

'statutory interest' means interest carried by virtue of the term implied by section 1(1); and 'supplier' means (subject to section 13(2)) the seller in a contract of sale of goods or the person who does one or more of the things mentioned in section 2(3) in any other contract for the supply of goods or services.

(2) In this Act any reference (however worded) to an agreement or to contract terms includes a reference to both express and implied terms (including terms established by a course of dealing or by such usage as binds the parties).

17   Short title, commencement and extent

(5) This Act extends to Northern Ireland.

National Minimum Wage Act 1998

(1998, c. 39)

1   Workers to be paid at least the national minimum wage

(1) A person who qualifies for the national minimum wage shall be remunerated by his employer in respect of his work in any pay reference period at a rate which is not less than the national minimum wage.

Contracts (Rights of Third Parties) Act 1999

(1999, c. 31)

1   Right of third party to enforce contractual term

(1) Subject to the provisions of this Act, a person who is not a party to a contract (a 'third party') may in his own right enforce a term of the contract if—

    (a) the contract expressly provides that he may, or

    (b) subject to subsection (2), the term purports to confer a benefit on him.

(2) Subsection (1)(b) does not apply if on a proper construction of the contract it appears that the parties did not intend the term to be enforceable by the third party.

(3) The third party must be expressly identified in the contract by name, as a member of a class or as answering a particular description but need not be in existence when the contract is entered into.

(4) This section does not confer a right on a third party to enforce a term of a contract otherwise than subject to and in accordance with any other relevant terms of the contract.

(5) For the purpose of exercising his right to enforce a term of the contract, there shall be available to the third party any remedy that would have been available to him in an action for breach of contract if he had been a party to the contract (and the rules relating to damages, injunctions, specific performance and other relief shall apply accordingly).

(6) Where a term of a contract excludes or limits liability in relation to any matter references in this Act to the third party enforcing the term shall be construed as references to his availing himself of the exclusion or limitation.

(7) In this Act, in relation to a term of a contract which is enforceable by a third party—

'the promisor' means the party to the contract against whom the term is enforceable by the third party, and

'the promisee' means the party to the contract by whom the term is enforceable against the promisor.

2   Variation and rescission of contract

(1) Subject to the provisions of this section, where a third party has a right under section 1 to enforce a term of the contract, the parties to the contract may not, by agreement, rescind the contract, or vary it in such a way as to extinguish or alter his entitlement under that right, without his consent if—

    (a) the third party has communicated his assent to the term to the promisor,

    (b) the promisor is aware that the third party has relied on the term, or

    (c) the promisor can reasonably be expected to have foreseen that the third party would rely on the term and the third party has in fact relied on it.

(2) The assent referred to in subsection (1)(a)—

    (a) may be by words or conduct, and

    (b) if sent to the promisor by post or other means, shall not be regarded as communicated to the promisor until received by him.

(3) Subsection (1) is subject to any express term of the contract under which—

    (a) the parties to the contract may by agreement rescind or vary the contract without the consent of the third party, or

    (b) the consent of the third party is required in circumstances specified in the contract instead of those set out in subsection (1)(a) to (c).

(4) Where the consent of a third party is required under subsection (1) or (3), the court or arbitral tribunal may, on the application of the parties to the contract, dispense with his consent if satisfied—

    (a) that his consent cannot be obtained because his whereabouts cannot reasonably be ascertained, or

    (b) that he is mentally incapable of giving his consent.

(5) The court or arbitral tribunal may, on the application of the parties to a contract, dispense with any consent that may be required under subsection (1)(c) if satisfied that it cannot reasonably be ascertained whether or not the third party has in fact relied on the term.

(6) If the court or arbitral tribunal dispenses with a third party's consent, it may impose such conditions as it thinks fit, including a condition requiring the payment of compensation to the third party.

(7) The jurisdiction conferred on the court by subsections (4) to (6) is exercisable [in England and Wales by both the High Court and the county court and in Northern Ireland] by both the High Court and a county court.

3 Defences etc. available to promisor

(1) Subsections (2) to (5) apply where, in reliance on section 1, proceedings for the enforcement of a term of a contract are brought by a third party.

(2) The promisor shall have available to him by way of defence or set-off any matter that—

    (a) arises from or in connection with the contract and is relevant to the term, and

    (b) would have been available to him by way of defence or set-off if the proceedings had been brought by the promisee.

(3) The promisor shall also have available to him by way of defence or set-off any matter if—

    (a) an express term of the contract provides for it to be available to him in proceedings brought by the third party, and

    (b) it would have been available to him by way of defence or set-off if the proceedings had been brought by the promisee.

(4) The promisor shall also have available to him—

    (a) by way of defence or set-off any matter, and

    (b) by way of counterclaim any matter not arising from the contract, that would have been available to him by way of defence or set-off or, as the case maybe, by way of counterclaim against the third party if the third party had been a party to the contract.

(5) Subsections (2) and (4) are subject to any express term of the contract as to the matters that are not to be available to the promisor by way of defence, set-off or counterclaim.

(6) Where in any proceedings brought against him a third party seeks in reliance on section 1 to enforce a term of a contract (including, in particular, a term purporting to exclude or limit liability), he may not do so if he could not have done so (whether by reason of any particular circumstances relating to him or otherwise) had he been a party to the contract.

4   Enforcement of contract by promisee

Section 1 does not affect any right of the promisee to enforce any term of the contract.

5   Protection of promisor from double liability

Where under section 1 a term of a contract is enforceable by a third party, and the promisee has recovered from the promisor a sum in respect of—

(a) the third party's loss in respect of the term, or

(b) the expense to the promisee of making good to the third party the default of the promisor,

then, in any proceedings brought in reliance on that section by the third party, the court or arbitral tribunal shall reduce any award to the third party to such extent as it thinks appropriate to take account of the sum recovered by the promisee.

6   Exceptions

(1) Section 1 confers no rights on a third party in the case of a contract on a bill of exchange, promissory note or other negotiable instrument.

(2) Section 1 confers no rights on a third party in the case of any contract binding on a company and its members under [section 33 of the Companies Act 2006 (effect of company's constitution)].

[(2A) Section 1 confers no rights on a third party in the case of any incorporation document of a limited liability partnership or any agreement (express or implied) between the members of a limited liability partnership, or between a limited liability partnership and its members, that determines the mutual rights and duties of the members and their rights and duties in relation to the limited liability partnership.]

(3) Section 1 confers no right on a third party to enforce—

(a) any term of a contract of employment against an employee,

(b) any term of a worker's contract against a worker (including a home worker), or

(c) any term of a relevant contract against an agency worker.

(4) In subsection (3)—

(a) 'contract of employment', 'employee', 'worker's contract', and 'worker' have the meaning given by section 54 of the National Minimum Wage Act 1998,

(b) 'home worker' has the meaning given by section 35(2) of that Act,

(c) 'agency worker' has the same meaning as in section 34(1) of that Act, and

(d) 'relevant contract' means a contract entered into, in a case where section 34 of that Act applies, by the agency worker as respects work falling within subsection (1)(a) of that section.

(5) Section 1 confers no rights on a third party in the case of—

(a) a contract for the carriage of goods by sea, or

(b) a contract for the carriage of goods by rail or road, or for the carriage of cargo by air, which is subject to the rules of the appropriate international transport convention,

except that a third party may in reliance on that section avail himself of an exclusion or limitation of liability in such a contract.

(6) In subsection (5) 'contract for the carriage of goods by sea' means a contract of carriage—

(a) contained in or evidenced by a bill of lading, sea waybill or a corresponding electronic transaction, or

(b) under or for the purposes of which there is given an undertaking which is contained in a ship's delivery order or a corresponding electronic transaction.

(7) For the purposes of subsection (6)—

(a) 'bill of lading', 'sea waybill' and 'ship's delivery order' have the same meaning as in the Carriage of Goods by Sea Act 1992, and

(b) a corresponding electronic transaction is a transaction within section 1(5) of that Act which corresponds to the issue, indorsement, delivery or transfer of a bill of lading, sea waybill or ship's delivery order.

(8) In subsection (5) 'the appropriate international transport convention' means—

(a) in relation to a contract for the carriage of goods by rail, the Convention which has the force of law in the United Kingdom under [regulation 3 of the Railways (Convention on International Carriage by Rail) Regulations 2005],

(b) in relation to a contract for the carriage of goods by road, the Convention which has the force of law in the United Kingdom under section 1 of the Carriage of Goods by Road Act 1965, and

(c) in relation to a contract for the carriage of cargo by air—

(i) the Convention which has the force of law in the United Kingdom under section 1 of the Carriage by Air Act 1961, or

(ii) the Convention which has the force of law under section 1 of the Carriage by Air (Supplementary Provisions) Act 1962, or

(iii) either of the amended Conventions set out in Part B of Schedule 2 or 3 to the Carriage by Air Acts (Application of Provisions) Order 1967.

7 Supplementary provisions relating to third party

(1) Section 1 does not affect any right or remedy of a third party that exists or is available apart from this Act.

(2) Section 2(2) of the Unfair Contract Terms Act 1977 (restriction on exclusion etc. of liability for negligence) shall not apply where the negligence consists of the breach of an obligation arising from a term of a contract and the person seeking to enforce it is a third party acting in reliance on section 1.

(3) In sections 5 and 8 of the Limitation Act 1980 the references to an action founded on a simple contract and an action upon a specialty shall respectively include references to an action brought in reliance on section 1 relating to a simple contract and an action brought in reliance on that section relating to a specialty.

(4) A third party shall not, by virtue of section 1(5) or 3(4) or (6), be treated as a party to the contract for the purposes of any other Act (or any instrument made under any other Act).

8 Arbitration provisions

(1) Where—

(a) a right under section 1 to enforce a term ('the substantive term') is subject to a term providing for the submission of disputes to arbitration ('the arbitration agreement'), and

(b) the arbitration agreement is an agreement in writing for the purposes of Part I of the Arbitration Act 1996,

the third party shall be treated for the purposes of that Act as a party to the arbitration agreement as regards disputes between himself and the promisor relating to the enforcement of the substantive term by the third party.

(2) Where—

(a) a third party has a right under section 1 to enforce a term providing for one or more descriptions of dispute between the third party and the promisor to be submitted to arbitration ('the arbitration agreement'),

(b) the arbitration agreement is an agreement in writing for the purposes of Part I of the Arbitration Act 1996, and

(c) the third party does not fall to be treated under subsection (1) as a party to the arbitration agreement,

the third party shall, if he exercises the right, be treated for the purposes of that Act as a party to the arbitration agreement in relation to the matter with respect to which the right is exercised, and be treated as having been so immediately before the exercise of the right.

EXPLANATORY NOTES

1. These explanatory notes . . . have been prepared by the Lord Chancellor's Department in order to assist the reader in understanding the Act. They do not form part of the Act and have not been endorsed by Parliament.

Section 3: Defences etc. available to promisor

15. *Section 3* enables the promisor, in a claim by the third party, to rely on any defence or set-off arising out of the contract and relevant to the term being enforced, which would have been available to him had the claim been by the promisee. He may also rely on any defence or set-off, or make any counterclaim, where this would have been possible had the third party been a party to the contract.

16. *Subsection (2)* can be illustrated as follows—

    (I) a third party can no more enforce a void, discharged or unenforceable contract than a promisee could;

    (II) P1 (the promisor) and P2 (the promisee) contract that P2 will sell goods to P1, who will pay the contract price to P3 (the third party). In breach of contract, P2 delivers goods that are not of the standard contracted for. In an action for the price by P3 (just as in an action for the price by P2) P1 is entitled to reduce or extinguish the price by reason of the damages for breach of contract.

17. *Subsection (3)* can be illustrated as follows—

P1 and P2 contract that P1 will pay P3 if P2 transfers his car to P1. P2 owes P1 money under a wholly unrelated contract. P1 and P2 agree to an express term in the contract which provides that P1 can raise against a claim by P3 any matter which would have given P1 a defence or set-off to a claim by P2.

18. *Subsection (4)* makes it clear that the promisor also has available any defence or setoff, and any counterclaim not arising from the contract, which is specific to the third party. It can be illustrated as follows.

    (I) P1 contracts with P2 to pay P3 £1000. P3 already owes P1 £600. P1 has a set-off to P3's claim so that P1 is only bound to pay P3 £400.

    (II) P3 induced P1 to enter into the contract with P2 by misrepresentation, but P2 has no actual or constructive notice of that misrepresentation. P1 may have a defence (or a counterclaim for damages) against P3 which would not have been available had the action been brought by P2.

19. *Subsection (5)* makes subsections (2) and (4) subject to any express term of the contract which narrows the defences or set-offs available under section 3(2) or narrows the defences, set-offs or counterclaims available under section 3(4). For example—

    (I) in relation to subsection (2), P2 agrees with P1 to purchase a painting, the painting to be delivered to P3, who is expressly given a right to enforce the delivery obligation. P2 owes P1 considerable sums for other art works purchased. P2 wishes to ensure that P3's right is not affected. P1 and P2 expressly agree that P1 may not raise against P3 defences and set-offs that would have been available to P1 in an action by P2.

    (II) in relation to subsection (4), P1 agrees with P2 to pay £5000 to P3 if P2 will transfer a number of cases of wine to P1. P3 is in dispute with P1 over a prior contract and P1 alleges that P3 owes P1 money. P2 is concerned that P1 may seek to withhold part of the £5000 payable to P3 by raising a set-off or counterclaim against P3 in relation to the prior contract. Consequently P1 and P2 include an express term that P1 may raise no defences, set-offs or counterclaims of any nature whatever against a claim by P3 to enforce P1's obligation to pay the £5000.

20. *Subsection (6)* ensures that an analogous approach to that set out in subsections (2) to (5) applies where the proceedings are brought against the third party and he seeks to avail himself of, for example, an exclusion section.

Countryside and Rights of Way Act 2000

(2000, c. 37)

1 Principal definitions for Part I

(1) In this Part 'access land' means any land which—

(a) is shown as open country on a map in conclusive form issued by the appropriate countryside body for the purposes of this Part,

(b) is shown on such a map as registered common land,

(c) is registered common land in any area outside Inner London for which no such map relating to registered common land has been issued,

(d) is situated more than 600 metres above sea level in any area for which no such map relating to open country has been issued,

[(da) is coastal margin, or]

(e) is dedicated for the purposes of this Part under section 16,

but does not (in any of those cases) include excepted land or land which is treated by section 15(1) as being accessible to the public apart from this Act.

2 Rights of public in relation to access land

(1) Any person is entitled by virtue of this subsection to enter and remain on any access land for the purposes of open-air recreation, if and so long as—

(a) he does so without breaking or damaging any wall, fence, hedge, stile or gate, and

(b) he observes the general restrictions in Schedule 2 and any other restrictions imposed in relation to the land under Chapter II.

(2) Subsection (1) has effect subject to subsections (3) and (4) and to the provisions of Chapter II.

(3) Subsection (1) does not entitle a person to enter or be on any land, or do anything on any land, in contravention of any [relevant statutory prohibition].

[(3A) In subsection (3) "relevant statutory prohibition" means—

(a) in the case of land which is coastal margin, a prohibition contained in or having effect under any enactment, and

(b) in any other case, a prohibition contained in or having effect under any enactment other than an enactment contained in a local or private Act.]

(4) If a person becomes a trespasser on any access land by failing to comply with—

(a) subsection (1)(a),

(b) the general restrictions in Schedule 2, or

(c) any other restrictions imposed in relation to the land under Chapter II, he may not, within 72 hours after leaving that land, exercise his right under subsection (1) to enter that land again or to enter other land in the same ownership.

12 Effect of right of access on rights and liabilities of owners

(1) The operation of section 2(1) in relation to any access land does not increase the liability, under any enactment not contained in this Act or under any rule of law, of a person interested in the access land or any adjoining land in respect of the state of the land or of things done or omitted to be done on the land.

(2) Any restriction arising under a covenant or otherwise as to the use of any access land shall have effect subject to the provisions of this Part, and any liability of a person interested in any access land in respect of such a restriction is limited accordingly.

(3) For the purposes of any enactment or rule of law as to the circumstances in which the dedication of a highway or the grant of an easement may be presumed, or may be established by prescription, the use by the public or by any person of a way across land in the exercise of the right conferred by section 2(1) is to be disregarded.

(4) The use of any land by the inhabitants of any locality for the purposes of open-air recreation in the exercise of the right conferred by section 2(1) is to be disregarded in determining whether the land has become a town or village green.

Finance Act 2000

(2000, c. 17)

Section 30   **SCHEDULE 6**

CLIMATE CHANGE LEVY

142   Adjustment of contracts

(1) Sub-paragraph (2) applies in the case of a contract for the supply of a taxable commodity if—

    (a) the contract is entered into before 1 April 2001 (whether before or after the passing of this Act) or at a time when supplies such as are provided for by the contract are not taxable supplies, but

    (b) supplies falling to be made under the contract will be, or become or will become, taxable supplies.

(2) The supplier of the commodity may unilaterally vary the contract by adjusting the price chargeable for any supply made under the contract if he does so for the purpose of passing on, to the person liable to pay for the supply, the burden (or any part of the burden) of the levy for which the supplier is liable to account on the supply.

(3) Sub-paragraph (4) applies in the case of a contract for the supply of a taxable commodity if it provides (whether as a result of a variation under sub-paragraph (2) or otherwise) for the passing on, to the person liable to pay for the supply, of the burden (or any part of the burden) of any levy for which the supplier is liable to account on the supply.

    (a) any change in the rate at which levy is charged on the supply;

    (b) levy ceasing to be chargeable on the supply.

(5) The powers conferred by this paragraph are in addition to any contractual powers.

Financial Services and Markets Act 2000

(2000, c. 8)

19   [Regulated activities]

(1) No person may carry on a regulated activity in the United Kingdom, or purport to do so, unless he is—

    (a) an authorised person; or

    (b) an exempt person.

[(1A) An activity is also a regulated activity for the purposes of this Act if it is an activity of a specified kind which is carried on by way of business and relates to—

    (a) information about a person's financial standing, or

    (b) the setting of a specified benchmark.]

(2) The prohibition is referred to in this Act as the general prohibition.

26   Agreements made by unauthorised persons

(1) An agreement made by a person in the course of carrying on a regulated activity in contravention of the general prohibition is unenforceable against the other party.

(2) The other party is entitled to recover—

    (a) any money or other property paid or transferred by him under the agreement; and

    (b) compensation for any loss sustained by him as a result of having parted with it.

(3) 'Agreement' means an agreement—

    (a) made after this section comes into force; and

    (b) the making or performance of which constitutes, or is part of, the regulated activity in question.

[26A   Agreements relating to credit

(1) An agreement that is made by an authorised person in contravention of section 20 is unenforceable against the other party if the agreement is entered into in the course of carrying on a credit-related regulated activity involving matters falling within section 23(1C)(a).

(2) The other party is entitled to recover—

(a) any money or other property paid or transferred by that party under the agreement, and

(b) compensation for any loss sustained by that party as a result of having parted with it.]

27   Agreements made through unauthorised persons

[(1) This section applies to an agreement that—

(a) is made by an authorised person ("the provider") in the course of carrying on a regulated activity,

(b) is not made in contravention of the general prohibition,

(c) if it relates to a credit-related regulated activity, is not made in contravention of section 20, and

(d) is made in consequence of something said or done by another person ("the third party") in the course of—

(i) a regulated activity carried on by the third party in contravention of the general prohibition, or

(ii) a credit-related regulated activity carried on by the third party in contravention of section 20.

(1A) The agreement is unenforceable against the other party.]

(2) The other party is entitled to recover—

(a) any money or other property paid or transferred by him under the agreement; and

(b) compensation for any loss sustained by him as a result of having parted with it.

(3) 'Agreement' means an agreement—

(a) made after this section comes into force; and

(b) the making or performance of which constitutes, or is part of, the regulated activity in question carried on by the provider.

71   Actions for damages

(1) A contravention of section 56(6) or 59(1) or (2) is actionable at the suit of a private person who suffers loss as a result of the contravention, subject to the defences and other incidents applying to actions for breach of statutory duty.

(2) In prescribed cases, a contravention of that kind which would be actionable at the suit of a private person is actionable at the suit of a person who is not a private person, subject to the defences and other incidents applying to actions for breach of statutory duty.

80   General duty of disclosure in listing particulars

(1) Listing particulars submitted to the [FCA] under section 79 must contain all such information as investors and their professional advisers would reasonably require, and reasonably expect to find there, for the purpose of making an informed assessment of—

(a) the assets and liabilities, financial position, profits and losses, and prospects of the issuer of the securities; and

(b) the rights attaching to the securities.

90   [Compensation for statements in listing particulars or prospectus]

(1) Any person responsible for listing particulars is liable to pay compensation to a person who has—

(a) acquired securities to which the particulars apply; and

(b) suffered loss in respect of them as a result of—

(i) any untrue or misleading statement in the particulars; or

(ii) the omission from the particulars of any matter required to be included by section 80 or 81.

(2) Subsection (1) is subject to exemptions provided by Schedule 10.

(3) If listing particulars are required to include information about the absence of a particular matter, the omission from the particulars of that information is to be treated as a statement in the listing particulars that there is no such matter.

(4) Any person who fails to comply with section 81 is liable to pay compensation to any person who has—

(a) acquired securities of the kind in question; and

(b) suffered loss in respect of them as a result of the failure.

(5) Subsection (4) is subject to exemptions provided by Schedule 10.

(6) This section does not affect any liability which may be incurred apart from this section.

(7) References in this section to the acquisition by a person of securities include references to his contracting to acquire them or any interest in them.

(8) No person shall, by reason of being a promoter of a company or otherwise, incur any liability for failing to disclose information which he would not be required to disclose in listing particulars in respect of a company's securities—

(a) if he were responsible for those particulars; or

(b) if he is responsible for them, which he is entitled to omit by virtue of section 82.

(9) The reference in subsection (8) to a person incurring liability includes a reference to any other person being entitled as against that person to be granted any civil remedy or to rescind or repudiate an agreement.

[(12) A person is not to be subject to civil liability solely on the basis of a summary in a prospectus unless the summary, when read with the rest of the prospectus—

(a) is misleading, inaccurate or inconsistent; or

(b) does not provide key information (as defined in section 87A(9) and (10)),

and in this subsection a summary includes any translation of it.]

131   Effect on transactions

The imposition of a penalty under this Part does not make any transaction void or unenforceable.

[138D   Actions for damages

(1) A rule made by the PRA may provide that contravention of the rule is actionable at the suit of a private person who suffers loss as a result of the contravention, subject to the defences and other incidents applying to actions for breach of statutory duty.

(2) A contravention by an authorised person of a rule made by the FCA is actionable at the suit of a private person who suffers loss as a result of the contravention, subject to the defences and other incidents applying to actions for breach of statutory duty.]

213   The compensation scheme

(1) The [regulators] must by rules [made in accordance with an order under subsection (1A)] establish a scheme for compensating persons in [cases where —

(a) relevant persons are unable, or likely to be unable, to satisfy claims against them, or

(b) persons who have assumed responsibility for liabilities arising from acts or omissions of relevant persons ("successors") are unable, or likely to be unable, to satisfy claims against the successors that are based on those acts or omissions.]

[(1A) The Treasury must by order specify—

(a) the cases in which the FCA may, or may not, make rules under subsection (1), and

(b) the cases in which the PRA may, or may not, make rules under that subsection.]

(2) The rules [(taken together)] are to be known as the Financial Services Compensation Scheme (but are referred to in this Act as 'the compensation scheme').

(3) The compensation scheme must, in particular, provide for the scheme manager—

(a) to assess and pay compensation, in accordance with the scheme, to claimants in respect of claims made in connection with regulated activities carried on (whether or not with permission) by relevant persons; and

(b) to have power to impose levies on authorised persons, or any class of authorised person, for the purpose of meeting its expenses (including in particular expenses incurred, or expected to be incurred, in paying compensation, borrowing or insuring risks).

(4) The compensation scheme may provide for the scheme manager to have power to impose levies on authorised persons, or any class of authorised person, for the purpose of recovering the cost (whenever incurred) of establishing the scheme.

(5) In making any provision of the scheme by virtue of subsection (3)(b), the [regulators] must take account of the desirability of ensuring that the amount of the levies imposed on a particular class of authorised person reflects, so far as practicable, the amount of the claims made, or likely to be made, in respect of that class of person.

(6) An amount payable to the scheme manager as a result of any provision of the scheme made by virtue of subsection (3)(b) or (4) may be recovered as a debt due to the scheme manager.

222   Statutory immunity

(1) Neither the scheme manager nor any person who is, or is acting as, its [. . .] officer[, scheme agent] or member of staff is to be liable in damages for anything done or omitted in the discharge, or purported discharge, of the scheme manager's functions.

(2) Subsection (1) does not apply—

(a) if the act or omission is shown to have been in bad faith; or

(b) so as to prevent an award of damages made in respect of an act or omission on the ground that the act or omission was unlawful as a result of section 6(1) of the Human Rights Act 1998.

291   Liability in relation to recognised body's regulatory functions

(1) A recognised body and its officers and staff [and an Operator and its officers and staff] are not to be liable in damages for anything done or omitted in the discharge of the recognised body's [or the Operator's] regulatory functions unless it is shown that the act or omission was in bad faith.

(2) But subsection (1) does not prevent an award of damages made in respect of an act or omission on the ground that the act or omission was unlawful as a result of section 6(1) of the Human Rights Act 1998.

380   Injunctions

(3) If, on the application of the [appropriate regulator] or the Secretary of State, the court is satisfied that any person may have—

(a) contravened a relevant requirement, or

(b) been knowingly concerned in the contravention of such a requirement,

it may make an order restraining (or in Scotland an interdict prohibiting) him from disposing of, or otherwise dealing with, any assets of his which it is satisfied he is reasonably likely to dispose of or otherwise deal with.

381   Injunctions in cases of market abuse

(3) Subsection (4) applies if, on the application of the [FCA], the court is satisfied that any person—

(a) may be engaged in market abuse; or

(b) may have been engaged in market abuse.

(4) The court [may] make an order restraining (or in Scotland an interdict prohibiting) the person concerned from disposing of, or otherwise dealing with, any assets of his which it is satisfied that he is reasonably likely to dispose of, or otherwise deal with.

382   Restitution orders

(1) The court may, on the application of the [appropriate regulator] or the Secretary of State, make an order under subsection (2) if it is satisfied that a person has contravened a relevant requirement, or been knowingly concerned in the contravention of such a requirement, and—

(a) that profits have accrued to him as a result of the contravention; or

(b) that one or more persons have suffered loss or been otherwise adversely affected as a result of the contravention.

(2) The court may order the person concerned to pay to the [regulator concerned] such sum as appears to the court to be just having regard—

(a) in a case within paragraph (a) of subsection (1), to the profits appearing to the court to have accrued;

(b) in a case within paragraph (b) of that subsection, to the extent of the loss or other adverse effect;

(c) in a case within both of those paragraphs, to the profits appearing to the court to have accrued and to the extent of the loss or other adverse effect.

(3) Any amount paid to the [regulator concerned] in pursuance of an order under subsection (2) must be paid by it to such qualifying person or distributed by it among such qualifying persons as the court may direct.

(4) On an application under subsection (1) the court may require the person concerned to supply it with such accounts or other information as it may require for any one or more of the following purposes—

(a) establishing whether any and, if so, what profits have accrued to him as mentioned in paragraph (a) of that subsection;

(b) establishing whether any person or persons have suffered any loss or adverse effect as mentioned in paragraph (b) of that subsection and, if so, the extent of that loss or adverse effect; and

(c) determining how any amounts are to be paid or distributed under subsection (3).

(5) The court may require any accounts or other information supplied under subsection (4) to be verified in such manner as it may direct.

(6) The jurisdiction conferred by this section is exercisable by the High Court and the Court of Session.

(7) Nothing in this section affects the right of any person other than the [appropriate regulator] or the Secretary of State to bring proceedings in respect of the matters to which this section applies.

(8) 'Qualifying person' means a person appearing to the court to be someone—

(a) to whom the profits mentioned in subsection (1)(a) are attributable; or

(b) who has suffered the loss or adverse effect mentioned in subsection (1)(b).

(9) 'Relevant requirement'—

(a) in relation to an application by the [appropriate regulator], means a requirement—

[(i)   which is imposed by or under this Act or by a qualifying EU provision specified, or of a description specified, for the purposes of this subsection by the Treasury by order;

(ii)   which is imposed by or under any other Act and whose contravention constitutes an offence mentioned in section 402(1); or

(iii) which is imposed by the Alternative Investment Fund Managers Regulations 2013];

(b) in relation to an application by the Secretary of State, means a requirement which is imposed by or under this Act and whose contravention constitutes an offence which the Secretary of State has power to prosecute under this Act.

[*Subsections (11)–(15) define in detail "appropriate regulator".*]

383   Restitution orders in cases of market abuse

(1) The court may, on the application of the [FCA], make an order under subsection (4) if it is satisfied that a person ('the person concerned')—

(a) has engaged in market abuse, or

(b) by taking or refraining from taking any action has required or encouraged another person or persons to engage in behaviour which, if engaged in by the person concerned, would amount to market abuse,

and the condition mentioned in subsection (2) is fulfilled.

(2) The condition is—

(a) that profits have accrued to the person concerned as a result; or

(b) that one or more persons have suffered loss or been otherwise adversely affected as a result.

(3) But the court may not make an order under subsection (4) if it is satisfied that—

(a) the person concerned believed, on reasonable grounds, that his behaviour did not fall within paragraph (a) or (b) of subsection (1); or

(b) he took all reasonable precautions and exercised all due diligence to avoid behaving in a way which fell within paragraph (a) or (b) of subsection (1).

(4) The court may order the person concerned to pay to the [FCA] such sum as appears to the court to be just having regard—

(a) in a case within paragraph (a) of subsection (2), to the profits appearing to the court to have accrued;

(b) in a case within paragraph (b) of that subsection, to the extent of the loss or other adverse effect;

(c) in a case within both of those paragraphs, to the profits appearing to the court to have accrued and to the extent of the loss or other adverse effect.

(5) Any amount paid to the [FCA] in pursuance of an order under subsection (4) must be paid by it to such qualifying person or distributed by it among such qualifying persons as the court may direct.

(6) On an application under subsection (1) the court may require the person concerned to supply it with such accounts or other information as it may require for any one or more of the following purposes—

(a) establishing whether any and, if so, what profits have accrued to him as mentioned in subsection (2)(a);

(b) establishing whether any person or persons have suffered any loss or adverse effect as mentioned in subsection (2)(b) and, if so, the extent of that loss or adverse effect; and

(c) determining how any amounts are to be paid or distributed under subsection (5).

(7) The court may require any accounts or other information supplied under subsection (6) to be verified in such manner as it may direct.

(8) The jurisdiction conferred by this section is exercisable by the High Court and the Court of Session.

(9) Nothing in this section affects the right of any person other than the [FCA] to bring proceedings in respect of the matters to which this section applies.

(10) 'Qualifying person' means a person appearing to the court to be someone—

(a) to whom the profits mentioned in paragraph (a) of subsection (2) are attributable; or

(b) who has suffered the loss or adverse effect mentioned in paragraph (b) of that subsection.

384   Power of [FCA or PRA] to require restitution

(1) [The appropriate regulator] may exercise the power in subsection (5) if it is satisfied that an authorised person [or recognised investment exchange] ('the person concerned') has contravened a relevant requirement, or been knowingly concerned in the contravention of such a requirement, and—

(a) that profits have accrued to him as a result of the contravention; or

(b) that one or more persons have suffered loss or been otherwise adversely affected as a result of the contravention.

(2) The [FCA] may exercise the power in subsection (5) if it is satisfied that a person ('the person concerned')—

    (a) has engaged in market abuse, or

    (b) by taking or refraining from taking any action has required or encouraged another person or persons to engage in behaviour which, if engaged in by the person concerned, would amount to market abuse,

and the condition mentioned in subsection (3) is fulfilled.

(3) The condition is—

    (a) that profits have accrued to the person concerned as a result of the market abuse; or

    (b) that one or more persons have suffered loss or been otherwise adversely affected as a result of the market abuse.

(4) But the [FCA] may not exercise that power as a result of subsection (2) if, having considered any representations made to it in response to a warning notice, there are reasonable grounds for it to be satisfied that—

    (a) the person concerned believed, on reasonable grounds, that his behaviour did not fall within paragraph (a) or (b) of that subsection; or

    (b) he took all reasonable precautions and exercised all due diligence to avoid behaving in a way which fell within paragraph (a) or (b) of that subsection.

(5) The power referred to in subsections (1) and (2) is a power to require the person concerned, in accordance with such arrangements as the [regulator exercising the power ("the regulator concerned")] considers appropriate, to pay to the appropriate person or distribute among the appropriate persons such amount as appears to the [regulator concerned] to be just having regard—

    (a) in a case within paragraph (a) of subsection (1) or (3), to the profits appearing to the [regulator concerned] to have accrued;

    (b) in a case within paragraph (b) of subsection (1) or (3), to the extent of the loss or other adverse effect;

    (c) in a case within paragraphs (a) and (b) of subsection (1) or (3), to the profits appearing to the [regulator concerned] to have accrued and to the extent of the loss or other adverse effect.

(6) 'Appropriate person' means a person appearing to the [regulator concerned] to be someone—

    (a) to whom the profits mentioned in paragraph (a) of subsection (1) or (3) are attributable; or

    (b) who has suffered the loss or adverse effect mentioned in paragraph (b) of subsection (1) or (3).

(7) 'Relevant requirement' means—

    (a) a requirement imposed by or under this Act [or by a qualifying EU provision specified, or of a description specified, for the purposes of this subsection by the Treasury by order]; [. . .]

    (b) a requirement which is imposed by or under any other Act and whose contravention constitutes an offence [mentioned in section 402(1); and

    (c) a requirement imposed by the Alternative Investment Fund Managers Regulations 2013].

[Subsections (9)–(13) define in detail "appropriate regulator".]

385   Warning notices

(1) If [a regulator] proposes to exercise the power under section 384(5) in relation to a person, it must give him a warning notice.

(2) A warning notice under this section must specify the amount which the [the regulator] proposes to require the person concerned to pay or distribute as mentioned in section 384(5).

386 Decision notices

(1) If the [the regulator] decides to exercise the power under section 384(5), it must give a decision notice to the person in relation to whom the power is exercised.

(2) The decision notice must—

(a) state the amount that he is to pay or distribute as mentioned in section 384(5);

(b) identify the person or persons to whom that amount is to be paid or among whom that amount is to be distributed; and

(c) state the arrangements in accordance with which the payment or distribution is to be made.

(3) If the [regulator] decides to exercise the power under section 384(5), the person in relation to whom it is exercised may refer the matter to the Tribunal.

Freedom of Information Act 2000

(2000, c. 36)

56 No action against public authority

(1) This Act does not confer any right of action in civil proceedings in respect of any failure to comply with any duty imposed by or under this Act.

79 Defamation

Where any information communicated by a public authority to a person ('the applicant') under section 1 was supplied to the public authority by a third person, the publication to the applicant of any defamatory matter contained in the information shall be privileged unless the publication is shown to have been made with malice.

Postal Services Act 2000

(2000, c. 26)

89 Schemes as to terms and conditions for provision of [postal services]

. . .

90 Exclusion of liability

(1) No proceedings in tort shall lie or, in Scotland, be competent against [the operator] provider in respect of loss or damage suffered by any person in connection with the provision of [the service] because of—

(a) anything done or omitted to be done in relation to any postal packet in the course of transmission by post, or

(b) any omission to carry out arrangements for the collection of anything to be conveyed by post.

(2) No officer, servant, employee, agent or sub-contractor of [the operator] shall be subject, except at the suit or instance of [the operator], to any civil liability for—

(a) any loss or damage in the case of which liability of [the operator] is excluded by subsection (1), or

(b) any loss of, or damage to, [a postal packet] to which section 91 applies.

(3) No person engaged in or about the conveyance of postal packets and no officer, servant, employee, agent or sub-contractor of any such person shall be subject, except at the suit or instance of [the operator] concerned, to any civil liability for—

(a) any loss or damage in the case of which liability of [the operator] is excluded by subsection (1), or

(b) any loss of, or damage to, [a postal packet] to which section 91 applies.

(5) This section is subject to section 91.

91 Limited liability for [postal packets]

(1) Proceedings shall lie or, in Scotland, be competent against [a postal operator] under this section, but not otherwise, in respect of relevant loss of, or relevant damage to, [a postal packet] in respect of which [the operator] accepts liability under this section in pursuance of a scheme made under section 89.

(2) The references in subsection (1) to relevant loss or damage are to loss or damage so far as it is due to any wrongful act of, or any neglect or default by, an officer, servant, employee, agent or sub-contractor of [the postal operator] while performing or purporting to perform in that capacity his functions in relation to the receipt, conveyance, delivery or other dealing with the packet.

(3) No proceedings shall lie or, in Scotland, be competent under this section in relation to a packet unless they are begun within the period of twelve months starting with the day on which the packet was posted.

Powers of Criminal Courts (Sentencing) Act 2000

(2000, c. 6)

73 Reparation orders

(1) Where a child or young person (that is to say, any person aged under 18) is convicted of an offence other than one for which the sentence is fixed by law, the court by or before which he is convicted may make an order requiring him to make reparation specified in the order—

    (a) to a person or persons so specified; or

    (b) to the community at large;

and any person so specified must be a person identified by the court as a victim of the offence or a person otherwise affected by it.

(3) In this section and section 74 below 'make reparation', in relation to an offender, means make reparation for the offence otherwise than by the payment of compensation; and the requirements that may be specified in a reparation order are subject to section 74(1) to (3).

130 Compensation orders against convicted persons

(1) A court by or before which a person is convicted of an offence, instead of or in addition to dealing with him in any other way, may, on application or otherwise, make an order (in this Act referred to as a 'compensation order') requiring him—

    (a) to pay compensation for any personal injury, loss or damage resulting from that offence or any other offence which is taken into consideration by the court in determining sentence; or

    (b) to make payments for funeral expenses or bereavement in respect of a death resulting from any such offence, other than a death due to an accident arising out of the presence of a motor vehicle on a road;

but this is subject to the following provisions of this section and to section 131 below.

[(2A) A court must consider making a compensation order in any case where this section empowers it to do so.]

(3) A court shall give reasons, on passing sentence, if it does not make a compensation order in a case where this section empowers it to do so.

(4) Compensation under subsection (1) above shall be of such amount as the court considers appropriate, having regard to any evidence and to any representations that are made by or on behalf of the accused or the prosecutor.

(5) In the case of an offence under the Theft Act 1968 [or Fraud Act 2006], where the property in question is recovered, any damage to the property occurring while it was out of the owner's possession shall be treated for the purposes of subsection (1) above as having resulted from the offence, however and by whomever the damage was caused.

(6)   A compensation order may only be made in respect of injury, loss or damage (other than loss suffered by a person's dependants in consequence of his death) which was due to an accident arising out of the presence of a motor vehicle on a road, if

(a) it is in respect of damage which is treated by subsection (5) above as resulting from an offence under the Theft Act 1968 [or Fraud Act 2006]; or

(b) it is in respect of injury, loss or damage as respects which—

(i)   the offender is uninsured in relation to the use of the vehicle; and

(ii)   compensation is not payable under any arrangements to which the Secretary of State is a party.

(7)   Where a compensation order is made in respect of injury, loss or damage due to an accident arising out of the presence of a motor vehicle on a road, the amount to be paid may include an amount representing the whole or part of any loss of or reduction in preferential rates of insurance attributable to the accident.

(8)   A vehicle the use of which is exempted from insurance by section 144 of the Road Traffic Act 1988 is not uninsured for the purposes of subsection (6) above.

(9)   A compensation order in respect of funeral expenses may be made for the benefit of anyone who incurred the expenses.

(10)   A compensation order in respect of bereavement may be made only for the benefit of a person for whose benefit a claim for damages for bereavement could be made under section 1A of the Fatal Accidents Act 1976; and the amount of compensation in respect of bereavement shall not exceed the amount for the time being specified in section 1A(3) of that Act.

(11)   In determining whether to make a compensation order against any person, and in determining the amount to be paid by any person under such an order, the court shall have regard to his means so far as they appear or are known to the court.

(12)   Where the court considers—

(a) that it would be appropriate both to impose a fine and to make a compensation order, but

(b) that the offender has insufficient means to pay both an appropriate fine and appropriate compensation,

the court shall give preference to compensation (though it may impose a fine as well).

134   Effect of compensation order on subsequent award of damages in civil proceedings

(1)   This section shall have effect where a compensation order, or a service compensation order [...], has been made in favour of any person in respect of any injury, loss or damage and a claim by him in civil proceedings for damages in respect of the injury, loss or damage subsequently falls to be determined.

(2)   The damages in the civil proceedings shall be assessed without regard to the order [...], but the plaintiff may only recover an amount equal to the aggregate of the following—

(a) any amount by which they exceed the compensation; and

(b) a sum equal to any portion of the compensation which he fails to recover,

and may not enforce the judgment, so far as it relates to a sum such as is mentioned in paragraph (b) above, without the leave of the court.

[(3)   In this section 'service compensation order' means a service compensation order under the Armed Forces Act 2006.]

137   Power to order parent or guardian to pay fine, costs or [compensation or surcharge]

(1)   Where—

(a) a child or young person (that is to say, any person aged under 18) is convicted of any offence for the commission of which a fine or costs may be imposed or a compensation order may be made, and

(b) the court is of the opinion that the case would best be met by the imposition of a fine or costs or the making of such an order, whether with or without any other punishment, the court shall order that the fine, compensation or costs awarded be paid by the parent or guardian of the child or young person instead of by the child or young person himself, unless the court is satisfied—

      (i)   that the parent or guardian cannot be found; or

      (ii) that it would be unreasonable to make an order for payment, having regard to the circumstances of the case.

(3) In the case of a young person aged 16 or over, subsections (1) to (2) above shall have effect as if, instead of imposing a duty, they conferred a power to make such an order as is mentioned in those subsections.

143   Powers to deprive offender of property used etc. for purposes of crime

  . . .

145   Application of proceeds of forfeited property

(1) Where a court makes an order under section 143 above in a case where—

    (a) the offender has been convicted of an offence which has resulted in a person suffering personal injury, loss or damage, or

    (b) any such offence is taken into consideration by the court in determining sentence,

the court may also make an order that any proceeds which arise from the disposal of the property and which do not exceed a sum specified by the court shall be paid to that person.

(2) The court may make an order under this section only if it is satisfied that but for the inadequacy of the offender's means it would have made a compensation order under which the offender would have been required to pay compensation of an amount not less than the specified amount.

148   Restitution orders

(1) This section applies where goods have been stolen, and either—

    (a) a person is convicted of any offence with reference to the theft (whether or not the stealing is the gist of his offence); or

    (b) a person is convicted of any other offence, but such an offence as is mentioned in paragraph (a) above is taken into consideration in determining his sentence.

(2) Where this section applies, the court by or before which the offender is convicted may on the conviction (whether or not the passing of sentence is in other respects deferred) exercise any of the following powers—

    (a) the court may order anyone having possession or control of the stolen goods to restore them to any person entitled to recover them from him; or

    (b) on the application of a person entitled to recover from the person convicted any other goods directly or indirectly representing the stolen goods (as being the proceeds of any disposal or realisation of the whole or part of them or of goods so representing them), the court may order those other goods to be delivered or transferred to the applicant; or

    (c) the court may order that a sum not exceeding the value of the stolen goods shall be paid, out of any money of the person convicted which was taken out of his possession on his apprehension, to any person who, if those goods were in the possession of the person convicted, would be entitled to recover them from him;

and in this subsection 'the stolen goods' means the goods referred to in subsection (1) above.

(3) Where the court has power on a person's conviction to make an order against him both under paragraph (b) and under paragraph (c) of subsection (2) above with reference to the stealing of the same goods, the court may make orders under both paragraphs provided that the person in whose favour the orders are made does not thereby recover more than the value of those goods.

(4) Where the court on a person's conviction makes an order under subsection (2)(a) above for the restoration of any goods, and it appears to the court that the person convicted—

    (a) has sold the goods to a person acting in good faith, or

    (b) has borrowed money on the security of them from a person so acting, the court may order that there shall be paid to the purchaser or lender, out of any money of the person convicted which was taken out of his possession on his apprehension, a sum not exceeding the amount paid for the purchase by the purchaser or, as the case may be, the amount owed to the lender in respect of the loan.

(10) In this section and section 149 below, 'goods', except in so far as the context otherwise requires, includes money and every other description of property (within the meaning of the Theft Act 1968) except land, and includes things severed from the land by stealing.

(11) An order may be made under this section in respect of money owed by the Crown.

149   Restitution orders: supplementary
(1) The following provisions of this section shall have effect with respect to section 148 above.

(2) The powers conferred by subsections (2)(c) and (4) of that section shall be exercisable without any application being made in that behalf or on the application of any person appearing to the court to be interested in the property concerned.

Enterprise Act 2002

(2002, c. 40)

108   Defamation
For the purposes of the law relating to defamation, absolute privilege attaches to any advice, guidance, notice or direction given, or decision or report made, by the [CMA, OFCOM,] the Commission or the Secretary of State in the exercise of any of their functions under this Part [ss 22–130].

173   Defamation: Part 4 [ss 131–184]
For the purposes of the law relating to defamation, absolute privilege attaches to any advice, guidance, notice or direction given, or decision or report made, by the [CMA, by the Secretary of State or] by the appropriate Minister (other than the Secretary of State acting alone) [. . .] in the exercise of any of their functions under this Part.

273   Interpretation
In this Act—
    ["the CMA" means the Competition and Markets Authority;]

Proceeds of Crime Act 2002

(2002, c. 29)

7   Recoverable amount
(1) The recoverable amount for the purposes of section 6 is an amount equal to the defendant's benefit from the conduct concerned.

304   Property obtained through unlawful conduct
(1) Property obtained through unlawful conduct is recoverable property.

(2) But if property obtained through unlawful conduct has been disposed of (since it was so obtained), it is recoverable property only if it is held by a person into whose hands it may be followed.

(3) Recoverable property obtained through unlawful conduct may be followed into the hands of a person obtaining it on a disposal by—
    (a) the person who through the conduct obtained the property, or
    (b) a person into whose hands it may (by virtue of this subsection) be followed.

305   Tracing property, etc.
(1) Where property obtained through unlawful conduct ('the original property') is or has been recoverable, property which represents the original property is also recoverable property.

(2) If a person enters into a transaction by which—

 (a) he disposes of recoverable property, whether the original property or property which (by virtue of this Chapter) represents the original property, and

 (b) he obtains other property in place of it,

the other property represents the original property.

(3) If a person disposes of recoverable property which represents the original property, the property may be followed into the hands of the person who obtains it (and it continues to represent the original property).

306 Mixing property

(1) Subsection (2) applies if a person's recoverable property is mixed with other property (whether his property or another's).

(2) The portion of the mixed property which is attributable to the recoverable property represents the property obtained through unlawful conduct.

(3) Recoverable property is mixed with other property if (for example) it is used—

 (a) to increase funds held in a bank account,

 (b) in part payment for the acquisition of an asset,

 (c) for the restoration or improvement of land,

 (d) by a person holding a leasehold interest in the property to acquire the freehold.

307 Recoverable property: accruing profits

(1) This section applies where a person who has recoverable property obtains further property consisting of profits accruing in respect of the recoverable property.

(2) The further property is to be treated as representing the property obtained through unlawful conduct.

338 Authorised disclosures

[(4A) Where an authorised disclosure is made in good faith, no civil liability arises in respect of the disclosure on the part of the person by or on whose behalf it is made.]

Criminal Justice Act 2003

(2003, c. 44)

329 Civil proceedings for trespass to the person brought by offender

(1) This section applies where—

 (a) a person ('the claimant') claims that another person ('the defendant') did an act amounting to trespass to the claimant's person, and

 (b) the claimant has been convicted in the United Kingdom of an imprisonable offence committed on the same occasion as that on which the act is alleged to have been done.

(2) Civil proceedings relating to the claim may be brought only with the permission of the court.

(3) The court may give permission for the proceedings to be brought only if there is evidence that either—

 (a) the condition in subsection (5) is not met, or

 (b) in all the circumstances, the defendant's act was grossly disproportionate.

(4) If the court gives permission and the proceedings are brought, it is a defence for the defendant to prove both—

 (a) that the condition in subsection (5) is met, and

 (b) that, in all the circumstances, his act was not grossly disproportionate.

(5) The condition referred to in subsection (3)(a) and (4)(a) is that the defendant did the act only because—

 (a) he believed that the claimant—

        (i)   was about to commit an offence,

        (ii) was in the course of committing an offence, or

        (iii) had committed an offence immediately beforehand; and

   (b) he believed that the act was necessary to—

        (i)   defend himself or another person,

        (ii) protect or recover property,

        (iii) prevent the commission or continuation of an offence, or

        (iv) apprehend, or secure the conviction, of the claimant after he had committed an offence;

or was necessary to assist in achieving any of those things.

   (6) Subsection (4) is without prejudice to any other defence.

   (8) In this section—

   (a) the reference to trespass to the person is a reference to—

        (i)   assault,

        (ii) battery, or

        (iii) false imprisonment;

   (b) references to a defendant's belief are to his honest belief, whether or not the belief was also reasonable;

   (c) 'court' means the High Court or [the county court]; and

   (d) 'imprisonable offence' means an offence which, in the case of a person aged 18 or over, is punishable by imprisonment.

Health and Social Care (Community Health and Standards) Act 2003

(2003, c. 43)

PART 3 RECOVERY OF NHS CHARGES

NHS charges

150 Liability to pay NHS charges

   (1) This section applies if—

   (a) a person makes a compensation payment to or in respect of any other person (the 'injured person') in consequence of any injury, whether physical or psychological, suffered by the injured person, and

   (b) the injured person has—

        (i)   received NHS treatment at a health service hospital as a result of the injury,

        (ii) been provided with NHS ambulance services as a result of the injury for the purpose of taking him to a health service hospital for NHS treatment (unless he was dead on arrival at that hospital), or

        (iii) received treatment as mentioned in sub-paragraph (i) and been provided with ambulance services as mentioned in sub-paragraph (ii).

   (2) The person making the compensation payment is liable to pay the relevant NHS charges—

   (a) in respect of—

        (i)   the treatment, in so far as received at a hospital in England or Wales,

        (ii) the ambulance services, in so far as provided to take the injured person to such a hospital,

     to the Secretary of State,

   (b) in respect of—

        (i)   the treatment, in so far as received at a hospital in Scotland,

    (ii) the ambulance services, in so far as provided to take the injured person to such a hospital,

to the Scottish Ministers.

(3) 'Compensation payment' means a payment, including a payment in money's worth, made—

  (a) by or on behalf of a person who is, or is alleged to be, liable to any extent in respect of the injury, or

  (b) in pursuance of a compensation scheme for motor accidents,

but does not include a payment mentioned in Schedule 10.

(4) Subsection (1)(a) applies—

  (a) to a payment made—

    (i) voluntarily, or in pursuance of a court order or an agreement, or otherwise, and

    (ii) in the United Kingdom or elsewhere, and

  (b) if more than one payment is made, to each payment.

(5) 'Injury' does not include any disease.

(6) Nothing in subsection (5) prevents this Part from applying to—

  (a) treatment received as a result of any disease suffered by the injured person, or

  (b) ambulance services provided as a result of any disease suffered by him,

if the disease in question is attributable to the injury suffered by the injured person (and accordingly that treatment is received or those services are provided as a result of the injury).

(11) 'Compensation scheme for motor accidents' means any scheme or arrangement under which funds are available for the payment of compensation in respect of motor accidents caused, or alleged to have been caused, by uninsured or unidentified persons.

(14) For the purpose of this Part, it is irrelevant whether a compensation payment is made with or without an admission of liability.

Certificates of NHS charges

151   Applications for certificates of NHS charges

(1) Before a person makes a compensation payment in consequence of any injury suffered by an injured person, he may apply for a certificate to the Secretary of State, the Scottish Ministers or both, according to whether he believes the relevant NHS charges payable by him (if any) would be due to the Secretary of State, the Scottish Ministers or both.

153   Information contained in certificates

(1) A certificate must specify the amount (or amounts) for which the person to whom it is issued is liable under section 150 (2).

(2) The amount (or amounts) to be specified is (or are) to be that (or those) set out in, or determined in accordance with, regulations, reduced if applicable in accordance with subsection (3) or regulations under subsection (10).

(3) If a certificate relates to a claim made by or on behalf of an injured person—

  (a) in respect of which a court in England and Wales or Scotland has ordered a reduction of damages in accordance with section 1 of the Law Reform (Contributory Negligence) Act 1945,

  ...

  (d) in respect of which an officer of a court in England and Wales or Northern Ireland has entered or sealed an agreed judgement or order which specifies—

    (i) that the damages are to be reduced to reflect the injured person's share in the responsibility for the injury in question, and

    (ii) the amount or proportion by which they are to be so reduced,

  ...

  (f) in respect of which a document has been made under any provision of the law of a country other than England and Wales, Scotland or Northern Ireland—

      (i)   which appears to the Secretary of State to correspond to an agreed judgement or order entered or sealed by an officer of a court in England and Wales, and

      (ii) which specifies the matters mentioned in paragraph (d)(i) and (ii), or

   ...

the amount (or amounts) specified in the certificate is (or are) to be that (or those) which would be so specified apart from this subsection, reduced by the same proportion as the reduction of damages.

  (4) If a certificate relates to an injured person who has not received NHS treatment at a health service hospital or been provided with NHS ambulance services as a result of the injury, it must indicate that no amount is payable to the Secretary of State or the Scottish Ministers (as the case may be) by reference to that certificate.

155 Recovery of NHS charges

  (1) This section applies if a person has made a compensation payment and either—

     (a) subsection (7) of section 151 applies but he has not applied for a certificate as required by that subsection, or

     (b) he has not made payment, in full, of any amount due under section 150(2) by the end of the period allowed under section 154.

  (2) The Secretary of State, the Scottish Ministers or both, according to the circumstances of the case, may—

     (a) in a case within subsection (1)(a), issue the person who made the compensation payment with a certificate, and

     (b) in a case within subsection (1)(b), issue him with a copy of the certificate or (if more than one has been issued) the most recent one,

and, in either case, issue him with a demand that payment of any amount due under section 150(2) be made immediately.

  (6) The Secretary of State or the Scottish Ministers may recover the amount for which a demand for payment is made under subsection (2) from the person who made the compensation payment.

Payments to hospitals or ambulance trusts

162 Payment of NHS charges to hospitals or ambulance trusts

  (1) If the Secretary of State receives or the Scottish Ministers receive a payment of relevant NHS charges under section 150(2)—

     (a) if the payment relates only to NHS treatment received at a health service hospital, he or they must pay the amount received to the responsible body of the health service hospital,

     (b) if the payment relates only to the provision of NHS ambulance services, he or they must pay the amount received to the relevant ambulance trust,

     (c) if the payment relates to NHS treatment received at more than one health service hospital, he or they must divide the amount received among the responsible bodies of the hospitals concerned in such manner as he considers or they consider appropriate,

     (d) if the payment relates to NHS treatment received at one or more health service hospitals and the provision of NHS ambulance services, he or they must divide the amount received among the responsible body or bodies of the hospital or hospitals and any relevant ambulance trusts concerned in such manner as he considers or they consider appropriate.

  (2) Subsection (1) does not apply to any amount received by the Secretary of State or the Scottish Ministers under section 150(2) which he is or they are required to repay in accordance with regulations under section 153(2).

  (4) Any amounts received under this section by the responsible bodies of the health service hospitals concerned must be used for the purposes of providing goods and services for the benefit of patients receiving NHS treatment at those hospitals.

  (5) Any amounts received under this section by the relevant ambulance trusts concerned must be used for the purposes of NHS ambulance services.

Miscellaneous and general

163　Regulations governing lump sums, periodical payments etc.

(1) Regulations may make provision (including provision modifying this Part)—

    (a) for cases to which section 150(2) applies in which two or more compensation payments in the form of lump sums are made by the same person in respect of the same injury,

    (b) for cases to which section 150(2) applies in which an agreement is entered into for the making of—

        (i) periodical compensation payments (whether of an income or capital nature), or

        (ii) periodical compensation payments and lump sum compensation payments,

    (c) for cases in which the compensation payment to which section 150(2) applies is an interim payment of damages which a court orders to be repaid.

(2) Regulations made by virtue of subsection (1)(a) may (among other things) provide—

    (a) for giving credit for amounts already paid, and

    (b) for the payment by any person of any balance or the recovery from any person of any excess.

(3) Regulations may make provision modifying the application of this Part in relation to cases in which a payment into court is made and, in particular, may provide—

    (a) for the making of a payment into court to be treated in prescribed circumstances as the making of a compensation payment,

    (b) for application for, and issue of, certificates.

164　Liability of insurers

(1) If a compensation payment is made in a case where—

    (a) a person is liable to any extent in respect of the injury, and

    (b) the liability is covered to any extent by a policy of insurance,

the policy is also to be treated as covering any liability of that person under section 150(2).

(2) Liability imposed on the insurer by subsection (1) cannot be excluded or restricted.

(3) For that purpose excluding or restricting liability includes—

    (a) making the liability or its enforcement subject to restrictive or onerous conditions,

    (b) excluding or restricting any right or remedy in respect of the liability, or subjecting a person to any prejudice in consequence of his pursuing any such right or remedy, or

    (c) excluding or restricting rules of evidence or procedure.

(4) Regulations may in prescribed cases limit the amount of the liability imposed on the insurer by subsection (1).

(5) This section applies in relation to policies of insurance issued before (as well as those issued after) the date on which it comes into force.

(6) References in this section to policies of insurance and their issue include references to contracts of insurance and their making.

165　Power to apply Part 3 to treatment at non-health service hospitals

. . .

166　The Crown

This Part binds the Crown.

Civil Partnership Act 2004

(2004, c. 33)

1　Civil partnership

(1) A civil partnership is a relationship between two people of the same sex ('civil partners')—

    (a) which is formed when they register as civil partners of each other— . . . or

(b) which they are treated under Chapter 2 of Part 5 as having formed (at the time determined under that Chapter) by virtue of having registered an overseas relationship.

69 Actions in tort between civil partners

(1) This section applies if an action in tort is brought by one civil partner against the other during the subsistence of the civil partnership.

(2) The court may stay the proceedings if it appears—

(a) that no substantial benefit would accrue to either civil partner from the continuation of the proceedings, or

(b) that the question or questions in issue could more conveniently be disposed of on an application under section 66.

73 Civil partnership agreements unenforceable

(1) A civil partnership agreement does not under the law of England and Wales have effect as a contract giving rise to legal rights.

(2) No action lies in England and Wales for breach of a civil partnership agreement, whatever the law applicable to the agreement.

(3) In this section and section 74 'civil partnership agreement' means an agreement between two people—

(a) to register as civil partners of each other—...

Gambling Act 2005

(2005, c. 19)

335 Enforceability of gambling contracts

(1) The fact that a contract relates to gambling shall not prevent its enforcement.

(2) Subsection (1) is without prejudice to any rule of law preventing the enforcement of a contract on the grounds of unlawfulness (other than a rule relating specifically to gambling).

336 Power of Gambling Commission to void bet

(1) The Commission may make an order under this subsection in relation to a bet accepted by or through the holder of—

(a) a general betting operating licence,

(b) a pool betting operating licence, or

(c) a betting intermediary operating licence.

(2) Where the Commission makes an order under subsection (1) in relation to a bet—

(a) any contract or other arrangement in relation to the bet is void, and

(b) any money paid in relation to the bet (whether by way of stake, winnings, commission or otherwise) shall be repaid to the person who paid it, and repayment may be enforced as a debt due to that person.

(3) The Commission may make an order under subsection (1) in relation to a bet only if satisfied that the bet was substantially unfair.

(4) In considering whether a bet was unfair the Commission shall, in particular, take account of any of the following that applies—

(a) the fact that either party to the bet supplied insufficient, false or misleading information in connection with it,

(b) the fact that either party to the bet believed or ought to have believed that a race, competition or other event or process to which the bet related was or would be conducted in contravention of industry rules,

(c) the fact that either party to the bet believed or ought to have believed that an offence under section 42 had been or was likely to be committed in respect of anything to which the bet related, and

(d) the fact that either party to the bet was convicted of an offence under section 42 in relation to the bet.

(5) An order under subsection (1) may be made in relation to a bet only during the period of six months beginning with the day on which the result of the bet is determined.

(6) But subsection (5) shall not apply to an order made taking account of the fact that a party to the bet was convicted of an offence under section 42 in relation to it.

337 Section 336: supplementary

(1) Where the Commission makes an order under section 336(1) in relation to a bet a party to the bet or to any contract or other arrangement in relation to the bet may appeal to the [First-tier Tribunal]; . . .

(2) The Commission may make an order under section 336(1) in relation to the whole, or any part or aspect of, a betting transaction.

(3) An order under section 336(1) may make incidental provision; in particular, an order may make provision about—

(a) the consequences of the order for bets connected with the bet which becomes void under the order;

(b) the consequences of the order for other parts or aspects of a betting transaction one part or aspect of which becomes void under the order.

(7) In section 336(4)(b) 'industry rules' means rules established by an organisation having, by virtue of an agreement, instrument or enactment, responsibility for the conduct of races, competitions or other events or processes.

338 Interim moratorium

(1) Where the Commission has reason to suspect that it may wish to make an order under section 336(1) in relation to a bet, the Commission may make an order under this subsection in relation to the bet.

(2) While an order under subsection (1) has effect in relation to a bet, an obligation to pay money in relation to the bet (whether by way of stake, winnings, commission or otherwise) shall have no effect.

(3) An order under subsection (1) shall have effect for the period of 14 days beginning with the day on which the order is made (subject to extension under subsection (4) and without prejudice to the making of a new order).

Mental Capacity Act 2005

(2005, c. 9)

PART 1 PERSONS WHO LACK CAPACITY

The principles

1 The principles

(1) The following principles apply for the purposes of this Act.

(2) A person must be assumed to have capacity unless it is established that he lacks capacity.

(3) A person is not to be treated as unable to make a decision unless all practicable steps to help him to do so have been taken without success.

(4) A person is not to be treated as unable to make a decision merely because he makes an unwise decision.

(5) An act done, or decision made, under this Act for or on behalf of a person who lacks capacity must be done, or made, in his best interests.

(6) Before the act is done, or the decision is made, regard must be had to whether the purpose for which it is needed can be as effectively achieved in a way that is less restrictive of the person's rights and freedom of action.

Preliminary

2   People who lack capacity

(1) For the purposes of this Act, a person lacks capacity in relation to a matter if at the material time he is unable to make a decision for himself in relation to the matter because of an impairment of, or a disturbance in the functioning of, the mind or brain.

(2) It does not matter whether the impairment or disturbance is permanent or temporary.

(3) A lack of capacity cannot be established merely by reference to—

(a) a person's age or appearance, or

(b) a condition of his, or an aspect of his behaviour, which might lead others to make unjustified assumptions about his capacity.

(4) In proceedings under this Act or any other enactment, any question whether a person lacks capacity within the meaning of this Act must be decided on the balance of probabilities.

(5) No power which a person ('D') may exercise under this Act—

(a) in relation to a person who lacks capacity, or

(b) where D reasonably thinks that a person lacks capacity,

is exercisable in relation to a person under 16.

(6) Subsection (5) is subject to section 18(3).

3   Inability to make decisions

(1) For the purposes of section 2, a person is unable to make a decision for himself if he is unable—

(a) to understand the information relevant to the decision,

(b) to retain that information,

(c) to use or weigh that information as part of the process of making the decision, or

(d) to communicate his decision (whether by talking, using sign language or any other means).

(2) A person is not to be regarded as unable to understand the information relevant to a decision if he is able to understand an explanation of it given to him in a way that is appropriate to his circumstances (using simple language, visual aids or any other means).

(3) The fact that a person is able to retain the information relevant to a decision for a short period only does not prevent him from being regarded as able to make the decision.

(4) The information relevant to a decision includes information about the reasonably foreseeable consequences of—

(a) deciding one way or another, or

(b) failing to make the decision.

4   Best interests

(1) In determining for the purposes of this Act what is in a person's best interests, the person making the determination must not make it merely on the basis of—

(a) the person's age or appearance, or

(b) a condition of his, or an aspect of his behaviour, which might lead others to make unjustified assumptions about what might be in his best interests.

(2) The person making the determination must consider all the relevant circumstances and, in particular, take the following steps.

(3) He must consider—

(a) whether it is likely that the person will at some time have capacity in relation to the matter in question, and

(b) if it appears likely that he will, when that is likely to be.

(4) He must, so far as reasonably practicable, permit and encourage the person to participate, or to improve his ability to participate, as fully as possible in any act done for him and any decision affecting him.

(5) Where the determination relates to life-sustaining treatment he must not, in considering whether the treatment is in the best interests of the person concerned, be motivated by a desire to bring about his death.

(6) He must consider, so far as is reasonably ascertainable—

(a) the person's past and present wishes and feelings (and, in particular, any relevant written statement made by him when he had capacity),

(b) the beliefs and values that would be likely to influence his decision if he had capacity, and

(c) the other factors that he would be likely to consider if he were able to do so.

(7) He must take into account, if it is practicable and appropriate to consult them, the views of—

(a) anyone named by the person as someone to be consulted on the matter in question or on matters of that kind,

(b) anyone engaged in caring for the person or interested in his welfare,

(c) any donee of a lasting power of attorney granted by the person, and

(d) any deputy appointed for the person by the court,

as to what would be in the person's best interests and, in particular, as to the matters mentioned in subsection (6).

(8) The duties imposed by subsections (1) to (7) also apply in relation to the exercise of any powers which—

(a) are exercisable under a lasting power of attorney, or

(b) are exercisable by a person under this Act where he reasonably believes that another person lacks capacity.

(9) In the case of an act done, or a decision made, by a person other than the court, there is sufficient compliance with this section if (having complied with the requirements of subsections (1) to (7)) he reasonably believes that what he does or decides is in the best interests of the person concerned.

(10) 'Life-sustaining treatment' means treatment which in the view of a person providing health care for the person concerned is necessary to sustain life.

(11) 'Relevant circumstances' are those—

(a) of which the person making the determination is aware, and

(b) which it would be reasonable to regard as relevant.

[4A   Restriction on deprivation of liberty

(1) This Act does not authorise any person ('D') to deprive any other person ('P') of his liberty.

(2) But that is subject to—

(a) the following provisions of this section, and

(b) section 4B.

(3) D may deprive P of his liberty if, by doing so, D is giving effect to a relevant decision of the court.

(4) A relevant decision of the court is a decision made by an order under section 16(2)(a) in relation to a matter concerning P's personal welfare.

(5) D may deprive P of his liberty if the deprivation is authorised by Schedule A1 (hospital and care home residents: deprivation of liberty).]

[4B   Deprivation of liberty necessary for life-sustaining treatment etc

(1) If the following conditions are met, D is authorised to deprive P of his liberty while a decision as respects any relevant issue is sought from the court.

(2) The first condition is that there is a question about whether D is authorised to deprive P of his liberty under section 4A.

(3) The second condition is that the deprivation of liberty—

(a) is wholly or partly for the purpose of—

(i)   giving P life-sustaining treatment, or

(ii) doing any vital act, or

(b) consists wholly or partly of—

    (i)   giving P life-sustaining treatment, or

    (ii) doing any vital act.

(4) The third condition is that the deprivation of liberty is necessary in order to—

    (a) give the life-sustaining treatment, or

    (b) do the vital act.

(5) A vital act is any act which the person doing it reasonably believes to be necessary to prevent a serious deterioration in P's condition.]

5 Acts in connection with care or treatment

(1) If a person ('D') does an act in connection with the care or treatment of another person ('P'), the act is one to which this section applies if—

    (a) before doing the act, D takes reasonable steps to establish whether P lacks capacity in relation to the matter in question, and

    (b) when doing the act, D reasonably believes—

        (i)   that P lacks capacity in relation to the matter, and

        (ii) that it will be in P's best interests for the act to be done.

(2) D does not incur any liability in relation to the act that he would not have incurred if P—

    (a) had had capacity to consent in relation to the matter, and

    (b) had consented to D's doing the act.

(3) Nothing in this section excludes a person's civil liability for loss or damage, or his criminal liability, resulting from his negligence in doing the act.

(4) Nothing in this section affects the operation of sections 24 to 26 (advance decisions to refuse treatment).

6 Section 5 acts: limitations

(1) If D does an act that is intended to restrain P, it is not an act to which section 5 applies unless two further conditions are satisfied.

(2) The first condition is that D reasonably believes that it is necessary to do the act in order to prevent harm to P.

(3) The second is that the act is a proportionate response to—

    (a) the likelihood of P's suffering harm, and

    (b) the seriousness of that harm.

(4) For the purposes of this section D restrains P if he—

    (a) uses, or threatens to use, force to secure the doing of an act which P resists, or

    (b) restricts P's liberty of movement, whether or not P resists.

(6) Section 5 does not authorise a person to do an act which conflicts with a decision made, within the scope of his authority and in accordance with this Part, by—

    (a) a donee of a lasting power of attorney granted by P, or

    (b) a deputy appointed for P by the court.

(7) But nothing in subsection (6) stops a person—

    (a) providing life-sustaining treatment, or

    (b) doing any act which he reasonably believes to be necessary to prevent a serious deterioration in P's condition,

while a decision as respects any relevant issue is sought from the court.

7 Payment for necessary goods and services

(1) If necessary goods or services are supplied to a person who lacks capacity to contract for the supply, he must pay a reasonable price for them.

(2) 'Necessary' means suitable to a person's condition in life and to his actual requirements at the time when the goods or services are supplied.

8 Expenditure

(1) If an act to which section 5 applies involves expenditure, it is lawful for D—

    (a) to pledge P's credit for the purpose of the expenditure, and

(b) to apply money in P's possession for meeting the expenditure.

(2) If the expenditure is borne for P by D, it is lawful for D—

    (a) to reimburse himself out of money in P's possession, or

    (b) to be otherwise indemnified by P.

(3) Subsections (1) and (2) do not affect any power under which (apart from those subsections) a person—

    (a) has lawful control of P's money or other property, and

    (b) has power to spend money for P's benefit.

Advance decisions to refuse treatment

24   Advance decisions to refuse treatment: general

(1) 'Advance decision' means a decision made by a person ('P'), after he has reached 18 and when he has capacity to do so, that if—

    (a) at a later time and in such circumstances as he may specify, a specified treatment is proposed to be carried out or continued by a person providing health care for him, and

    (b) at that time he lacks capacity to consent to the carrying out or continuation of the treatment,

the specified treatment is not to be carried out or continued.

(2) For the purposes of subsection (1)(a), a decision may be regarded as specifying a treatment or circumstances even though expressed in layman's terms.

(3) P may withdraw or alter an advance decision at any time when he has capacity to do so.

(4) A withdrawal (including a partial withdrawal) need not be in writing.

(5) An alteration of an advance decision need not be in writing (unless section 25(5) applies in relation to the decision resulting from the alteration).

25   Validity and applicability of advance decisions

(1) An advance decision does not affect the liability which a person may incur for carrying out or continuing a treatment in relation to P unless the decision is at the material time—

    (a) valid, and

    (b) applicable to the treatment.

(2) An advance decision is not valid if P—

    (a) has withdrawn the decision at a time when he had capacity to do so,

    (b) has, under a lasting power of attorney created after the advance decision was made, conferred authority on the donee (or, if more than one, any of them) to give or refuse consent to the treatment to which the advance decision relates, or

    (c) has done anything else clearly inconsistent with the advance decision remaining his fixed decision.

(3) An advance decision is not applicable to the treatment in question if at the material time P has capacity to give or refuse consent to it.

(4) An advance decision is not applicable to the treatment in question if—

    (a) that treatment is not the treatment specified in the advance decision,

    (b) any circumstances specified in the advance decision are absent, or

    (c) there are reasonable grounds for believing that circumstances exist which P did not anticipate at the time of the advance decision and which would have affected his decision had he anticipated them.

(5) An advance decision is not applicable to life-sustaining treatment unless—

    (a) the decision is verified by a statement by P to the effect that it is to apply to that treatment even if life is at risk, and

    (b) the decision and statement comply with subsection (6).

(6) A decision or statement complies with this subsection only if—

    (a) it is in writing,

    (b) it is signed by P or by another person in P's presence and by P's direction,

    (c) the signature is made or acknowledged by P in the presence of a witness, and

(d) the witness signs it, or acknowledges his signature, in P's presence.

(7) The existence of any lasting power of attorney other than one of a description mentioned in subsection (2)(b) does not prevent the advance decision from being regarded as valid and applicable.

26 Effect of advance decisions

(1) If P has made an advance decision which is—

(a) valid, and

(b) applicable to a treatment,

the decision has effect as if he had made it, and had had capacity to make it, at the time when the question arises whether the treatment should be carried out or continued.

(2) A person does not incur liability for carrying out or continuing the treatment unless, at the time, he is satisfied that an advance decision exists which is valid and applicable to the treatment.

(3) A person does not incur liability for the consequences of withholding or withdrawing a treatment from P if, at the time, he reasonably believes that an advance decision exists which is valid and applicable to the treatment.

(4) The court may make a declaration as to whether an advance decision—

(a) exists;

(b) is valid;

(c) is applicable to a treatment.

(5) Nothing in an apparent advance decision stops a person—

(a) providing life-sustaining treatment, or

(b) doing any act he reasonably believes to be necessary to prevent a serious deterioration in P's condition,

while a decision as respects any relevant issue is sought from the court.

Excluded decisions

27 Family relationships etc.

(1) Nothing in this Act permits a decision on any of the following matters to be made on behalf of a person—

(a) . . .

(b) consenting to have sexual relations, . . .

28 Mental Health Act matters

(1) Nothing in this Act authorises anyone—

(a) to give a patient medical treatment for mental disorder, or

(b) to consent to a patient's being given medical treatment for mental disorder,

if, at the time when it is proposed to treat the patient, his treatment is regulated by Part 4 of the Mental Health Act.

Research

30 Research

(1) Intrusive research carried out on, or in relation to, a person who lacks capacity to consent to it is unlawful unless it is carried out—

(a) as part of a research project which is for the time being approved by the appropriate body for the purposes of this Act in accordance with section 31, and

(b) in accordance with sections 32 and 33.

(2) Research is intrusive if it is of a kind that would be unlawful if it was carried out—

(a) on or in relation to a person who had capacity to consent to it, but

(b) without his consent.

(3) A clinical trial which is subject to the provisions of clinical trials regulations is not to be treated as research for the purposes of this section.

(4) 'Appropriate body', in relation to a research project, means the person, committee or other body specified in regulations made by the appropriate authority as the appropriate body in relation to a project of the kind in question.

(5) 'Clinical trials regulations' means—

    (a) the Medicines for Human Use (Clinical Trials) Regulations 2004 (S.I. 2004/1031) and any other regulations replacing those regulations or amending them, and

    (b) any other regulations relating to clinical trials and designated by the Secretary of State as clinical trials regulations for the purposes of this section.

(6) In this section, section 32 and section 34, 'appropriate authority' means—

    (a) in relation to the carrying out of research in England, the Secretary of State, and

    (b) in relation to the carrying out of research in Wales, the National Assembly for Wales.

31   Requirements for approval

(1) The appropriate body may not approve a research project for the purposes of this Act unless satisfied that the following requirements will be met in relation to research carried out as part of the project on, or in relation to, a person who lacks capacity to consent to taking part in the project ('P').

(2) The research must be connected with—

    (a) an impairing condition affecting P, or

    (b) its treatment.

(3) 'Impairing condition' means a condition which is (or may be) attributable to, or which causes or contributes to (or may cause or contribute to), the impairment of, or disturbance in the functioning of, the mind or brain.

(4) There must be reasonable grounds for believing that research of comparable effectiveness cannot be carried out if the project has to be confined to, or relate only to, persons who have capacity to consent to taking part in it.

(5) The research must—

    (a) have the potential to benefit P without imposing on P a burden that is disproportionate to the potential benefit to P, or

    (b) be intended to provide knowledge of the causes or treatment of, or of the care of persons affected by, the same or a similar condition.

(6) If the research falls within paragraph (b) of subsection (5) but not within paragraph (a), there must be reasonable grounds for believing—

    (a) that the risk to P from taking part in the project is likely to be negligible, and

    (b) that anything done to, or in relation to, P will not—

        (i)   interfere with P's freedom of action or privacy in a significant way, or

        (ii)   be unduly invasive or restrictive.

(7) There must be reasonable arrangements in place for ensuring that the requirements of sections 32 and 33 will be met.

32   Consulting carers etc.

(1) This section applies if a person ('R')—

    (a) is conducting an approved research project, and

    (b) wishes to carry out research, as part of the project, on or in relation to a person ('P') who lacks capacity to consent to taking part in the project.

(2) R must take reasonable steps to identify a person who—

    (a) otherwise than in a professional capacity or for remuneration, is engaged in caring for P or is interested in P's welfare, and

    (b) is prepared to be consulted by R under this section.

(3) If R is unable to identify such a person he must, in accordance with guidance issued by the appropriate authority, nominate a person who—

    (a) is prepared to be consulted by R under this section, but

    (b) has no connection with the project.

(4) R must provide the person identified under subsection (2), or nominated under subsection (3), with information about the project and ask him—

    (a) for advice as to whether P should take part in the project, and

    (b) what, in his opinion, P's wishes and feelings about taking part in the project would be likely to be if P had capacity in relation to the matter.

(5) If, at any time, the person consulted advises R that in his opinion P's wishes and feelings would be likely to lead him to decline to take part in the project (or to wish to withdraw from it) if he had capacity in relation to the matter, R must ensure—

    (a) if P is not already taking part in the project, that he does not take part in it;

    (b) if P is taking part in the project, that he is withdrawn from it.

(6) But subsection (5)(b) does not require treatment that P has been receiving as part of the project to be discontinued if R has reasonable grounds for believing that there would be a significant risk to P's health if it were discontinued.

(7) The fact that a person is the donee of a lasting power of attorney given by P, or is P's deputy, does not prevent him from being the person consulted under this section.

(8) Subsection (9) applies if treatment is being, or is about to be, provided for P as a matter of urgency and R considers that, having regard to the nature of the research and of the particular circumstances of the case—

    (a) it is also necessary to take action for the purposes of the research as a matter of urgency, but

    (b) it is not reasonably practicable to consult under the previous provisions of this section.

(9) R may take the action if—

    (a) he has the agreement of a registered medical practitioner who is not involved in the organisation or conduct of the research project, or

    (b) where it is not reasonably practicable in the time available to obtain that agreement, he acts in accordance with a procedure approved by the appropriate body at the time when the research project was approved under section 31.

(10) But R may not continue to act in reliance on subsection (9) if he has reasonable grounds for believing that it is no longer necessary to take the action as a matter of urgency.

33 Additional safeguards

(1) This section applies in relation to a person who is taking part in an approved research project even though he lacks capacity to consent to taking part.

(2) Nothing may be done to, or in relation to, him in the course of the research—

    (a) to which he appears to object (whether by showing signs of resistance or otherwise) except where what is being done is intended to protect him from harm or to reduce or prevent pain or discomfort, or

    (b) which would be contrary to—

        (i) an advance decision of his which has effect, or

        (ii) any other form of statement made by him and not subsequently withdrawn, of which R is aware.

(3) The interests of the person must be assumed to outweigh those of science and society.

(4) If he indicates (in any way) that he wishes to be withdrawn from the project he must be withdrawn without delay.

(5) P must be withdrawn from the project, without delay, if at any time the person conducting the research has reasonable grounds for believing that one or more of the requirements set out in section 31(2) to (7) is no longer met in relation to research being carried out on, or in relation to, P.

(6) But neither subsection (4) nor subsection (5) requires treatment that P has been receiving as part of the project to be discontinued if R has reasonable grounds for believing that there would be a significant risk to P's health if it were discontinued.

34   Loss of capacity during research project

(1) This section applies where a person ('P')—

   (a) has consented to take part in a research project begun before the commencement of section 30, but

   (b) before the conclusion of the project, loses capacity to consent to continue to take part in it.

(2) The appropriate authority may by regulations provide that, despite P's loss of capacity, research of a prescribed kind may be carried out on, or in relation to, P if—

   (a) the project satisfies prescribed requirements,

   (b) any information or material relating to P which is used in the research is of a prescribed description and was obtained before P's loss of capacity, and

   (c) the person conducting the project takes in relation to P such steps as may be prescribed for the purpose of protecting him.

(3) The regulations may, in particular,—

   (a) make provision about when, for the purposes of the regulations, a project is to be treated as having begun;

   (b) include provision similar to any made by section 31, 32 or 33.

Independent mental capacity advocate service

35   Appointment of independent mental capacity advocates

(1) The [responsible authority] must make such arrangements as it considers reasonable to enable persons ('independent mental capacity advocates') to be available to represent and support persons to whom acts or decisions proposed under sections 37, 38 and 39 relate [or persons who fall within section 39A, 39C or 39D].

36   Functions of independent mental capacity advocates

(1) The appropriate authority may make regulations as to the functions of independent mental capacity advocates.

37   Provision of serious medical treatment by NHS body

(1) This section applies if an NHS body—

   (a) is proposing to provide, or secure the provision of, serious medical treatment for a person ('P') who lacks capacity to consent to the treatment, and

   (b) is satisfied that there is no person, other than one engaged in providing care or treatment for P in a professional capacity or for remuneration, whom it would be appropriate to consult in determining what would be in P's best interests.

(2) But this section does not apply if P's treatment is regulated by Part 4 of the Mental Health Act.

(3) Before the treatment is provided, the NHS body must instruct an independent mental capacity advocate to represent P.

(4) If the treatment needs to be provided as a matter of urgency, it may be provided even though the NHS body has not been able to comply with subsection (3).

(5) The NHS body must, in providing or securing the provision of treatment for P, take into account any information given, or submissions made, by the independent mental capacity advocate.

(6) 'Serious medical treatment' means treatment which involves providing, withholding or withdrawing treatment of a kind prescribed by regulations made by the appropriate authority.

Miscellaneous and supplementary

42 Codes of practice

   (1) The Lord Chancellor must prepare and issue one or more codes of practice—

     (a) for the guidance of persons assessing whether a person has capacity in relation to any matter,

     (b) for the guidance of persons acting in connection with the care or treatment of another person (see section 5),

     (c) for the guidance of donees of lasting powers of attorney,

     (d) for the guidance of deputies appointed by the court,

     (e) for the guidance of persons carrying out research in reliance on any provision made by or under this Act (and otherwise with respect to sections 30 to 34),

     (f) for the guidance of independent mental capacity advocates,

    [(fa) for the guidance of persons exercising functions under Schedule A1,

    (fb) for the guidance of representatives appointed under Part 10 of Schedule A1,]

     (g) with respect to the provisions of sections 24 to 26 (advance decisions and apparent advance decisions), and

     (h) with respect to such other matters concerned with this Act as he thinks fit.

   (4) It is the duty of a person to have regard to any relevant code if he is acting in relation to a person who lacks capacity and is doing so in one or more of the following ways—

     (a) as the donee of a lasting power of attorney,

     (b) as a deputy appointed by the court,

     (c) as a person carrying out research in reliance on any provision made by or under this Act (see sections 30 to 34),

     (d) as an independent mental capacity advocate,

    [(da) in the exercise of functions under Schedule A1,

    (db) as a representative appointed under Part 10 of Schedule A1,]

     (e) in a professional capacity,

     (f) for remuneration.

   (5) If it appears to a court or tribunal conducting any criminal or civil proceedings that—

     (a) a provision of a code, or

     (b) a failure to comply with a code,

is relevant to a question arising in the proceedings, the provision or failure must be taken into account in deciding the question.

Companies Act 2006

(2006, c. 46)

17 A company's constitution

Unless the context otherwise requires, references in the Companies Acts to a company's constitution include—

     (a) the company's articles, and

     (b) any resolutions and agreements to which Chapter 3 applies (see section 29).

33 Effect of company's constitution

   (1) The provisions of a company's constitution bind the company and its members to the same extent as if there were covenants on the part of the company and of each member to observe those provisions.

   (2) Money payable by a member to the company under its constitution is a debt due from him to the company.

   In England and Wales and Northern Ireland it is of the nature of an ordinary contract debt.

39 A company's capacity

(1) The validity of an act done by a company shall not be called into question on the ground of lack of capacity by reason of anything in the company's constitution.

40 Power of directors to bind the company

(1) In favour of a person dealing with a company in good faith, the power of the directors to bind the company, or authorise others to do so, is deemed to be free of any limitation under the company's constitution.

(2) For this purpose—

(a) a person 'deals with' a company if he is a party to any transaction or other act to which the company is a party,

(b) a person dealing with a company—

(i) is not bound to enquire as to any limitation on the powers of the directors to bind the company or authorise others to do so,

(ii) is presumed to have acted in good faith unless the contrary is proved, and

(iii) is not to be regarded as acting in bad faith by reason only of his knowing that an act is beyond the powers of the directors under the company's constitution.

41 Constitutional limitations: transactions involving directors or their associates

(1) This section applies to a transaction if or to the extent that its validity depends on section 40 (power of directors deemed to be free of limitations under company's constitution in favour of person dealing with company in good faith).

Nothing in this section shall be read as excluding the operation of any other enactment or rule of law by virtue of which the transaction may be called in question or any liability to the company may arise.

(2) Where—

(a) a company enters into such a transaction, and

(b) the parties to the transaction include—

(i) a director of the company or of its holding company, or

(ii) a person connected with any such director,

the transaction is voidable at the instance of the company.

(3) Whether or not it is avoided, any such party to the transaction as is mentioned in subsection (2)(b)(i) or (ii), and any director of the company who authorised the transaction, is liable—

(a) to account to the company for any gain he has made directly or indirectly by the transaction, and

(b) to indemnify the company for any loss or damage resulting from the transaction.

(4) The transaction ceases to be voidable if—

(a) restitution of any money or other asset which was the subject matter of the transaction is no longer possible, or

(b) the company is indemnified for any loss or damage resulting from the transaction, or

(c) rights acquired bona fide for value and without actual notice of the directors' exceeding their powers by a person who is not party to the transaction would be affected by the avoidance, or

(d) the transaction is affirmed by the company.

(5) A person other than a director of the company is not liable under subsection (3) if he shows that at the time the transaction was entered into he did not know that the directors were exceeding their powers.

(6) Nothing in the preceding provisions of this section affects the rights of any party to the transaction not within subsection (2)(b)(i) or (ii).

But the court may, on the application of the company or any such party, make an order affirming, severing or setting aside the transaction on such terms as appear to the court to be just.

(7) In this section—

    (a) 'transaction' includes any act; and

    (b) the reference to a person connected with a director has the same meaning as in Part 10 (company directors).

43 Company contracts

(1) Under the law of England and Wales or Northern Ireland a contract may be made—

    (a) by a company, by writing under its common seal, or

    (b) on behalf of a company, by a person acting under its authority, express or implied.

(2) Any formalities required by law in the case of a contract made by an individual also apply, unless a contrary intention appears, to a contract made by or on behalf of a company.

51 Pre-incorporation contracts, deeds and obligations

(1) A contract that purports to be made by or on behalf of a company at a time when the company has not been formed has effect, subject to any agreement to the contrary, as one made with the person purporting to act for the company or as agent for it, and he is personally liable on the contract accordingly.

(2) Subsection (1) applies—

    (a) to the making of a deed under the law of England and Wales or Northern Ireland, and

    (b) to the undertaking of an obligation under the law of Scotland,

as it applies to the making of a contract.

83 Civil consequences of failure to make required disclosure

(1) This section applies to any legal proceedings brought by a company to which section 82 applies (requirement to disclose company name etc) to enforce a right arising out of a contract made in the course of a business in respect of which the company was, at the time the contract was made, in breach of regulations under that section.

(2) The proceedings shall be dismissed if the defendant (in Scotland, the defender) to the proceedings shows—

    (a) that he has a claim against the claimant (pursuer) arising out of the contract that he has been unable to pursue by reason of the latter's breach of the regulations, or

    (b) that he has suffered some financial loss in connection with the contract by reason of the claimant's (pursuer's) breach of the regulations,

unless the court before which the proceedings are brought is satisfied that it is just and equitable to permit the proceedings to continue.

(3) This section does not affect the right of any person to enforce such rights as he may have against another person in any proceedings brought by that person.

170 Scope and nature of general duties

(1) The general duties specified in sections 171 to 177 are owed by a director of a company to the company.

(3) The general duties are based on certain common law rules and equitable principles as they apply in relation to directors and have effect in place of those rules and principles as regards the duties owed to a company by a director.

(4) The general duties shall be interpreted and applied in the same way as common law rules or equitable principles, and regard shall be had to the corresponding common law rules and equitable principles in interpreting and applying the general duties.

174 Duty to exercise reasonable care, skill and diligence

(1) A director of a company must exercise reasonable care, skill and diligence.

(2) This means the care, skill and diligence that would be exercised by a reasonably diligent person with—

(a) the general knowledge, skill and experience that may reasonably be expected of a person carrying out the functions carried out by the director in relation to the company, and

(b) the general knowledge, skill and experience that the director has.

176 Duty not to accept benefits from third parties

(1) A director of a company must not accept a benefit from a third party conferred by reason of—

(a) his being a director, or

(b) his doing (or not doing) anything as director.

178 Civil consequences of breach of general duties

(1) The consequences of breach (or threatened breach) of sections 171 to 177 are the same as would apply if the corresponding common law rule or equitable principle applied.

(2) The duties in those sections (with the exception of section 174 (duty to exercise reasonable care, skill and diligence)) are, accordingly, enforceable in the same way as any other fiduciary duty owed to a company by its directors.

189 Directors' long-term service contracts: civil consequences of contravention

If a company agrees to provision in contravention of section 188 (directors' long-term service contracts: requirement of members' approval)—

(a) the provision is void, to the extent of the contravention, and

(b) the contract is deemed to contain a term entitling the company to terminate it at any time by the giving of reasonable notice.

195 Property transactions: civil consequences of contravention

(1) This section applies where a company enters into an arrangement in contravention of section 190 (requirement of members' approval for substantial property transactions).

(2) The arrangement, and any transaction entered into in pursuance of the arrangement (whether by the company or any other person), is voidable at the instance of the company, unless—

(a) restitution of any money or other asset that was the subject matter of the arrangement or transaction is no longer possible,

(b) the company has been indemnified in pursuance of this section by any other persons for the loss or damage suffered by it, or

(c) rights acquired in good faith, for value and without actual notice of the contravention by a person who is not a party to the arrangement or transaction would be affected by the avoidance.

(3) Whether or not the arrangement or any such transaction has been avoided, each of the persons specified in subsection (4) is liable—

(a) to account to the company for any gain that he has made directly or indirectly by the arrangement or transaction, and

(b) (jointly and severally with any other person so liable under this section) to indemnify the company for any loss or damage resulting from the arrangement or transaction.

(4) The persons so liable are—

(a) any director of the company or of its holding company with whom the company entered into the arrangement in contravention of section 190,

(b) any person with whom the company entered into the arrangement in contravention of that section who is connected with a director of the company or of its holding company,

(c) the director of the company or of its holding company with whom any such person is connected, and

(d) any other director of the company who authorised the arrangement or any transaction entered into in pursuance of such an arrangement.

(5) Subsections (3) and (4) are subject to the following two subsections.

(6) In the case of an arrangement entered into by a company in contravention of section 190 with a person connected with a director of the company or of its holding company, that director is not liable by virtue of subsection (4)(c) if he shows that he took all reasonable steps to secure the company's compliance with that section.

(7) In any case—

(a) a person so connected is not liable by virtue of subsection (4)(b), and

(b) a director is not liable by virtue of subsection (4)(d),

if he shows that, at the time the arrangement was entered into, he did not know the relevant circumstances constituting the contravention.

(8) Nothing in this section shall be read as excluding the operation of any other enactment or rule of law by virtue of which the arrangement or transaction may be called in question or any liability to the company may arise.

196 Property transactions: effect of subsequent affirmation

Where a transaction or arrangement is entered into by a company in contravention of section 190 (requirement of members' approval) but, within a reasonable period, it is affirmed—

(a) in the case of a contravention of subsection (1) of that section, by resolution of the members of the company, and

(b) in the case of a contravention of subsection (2) of that section, by resolution of the members of the holding company,

the transaction or arrangement may no longer be avoided under section 195.

222 Payments made without approval: civil consequences

(1) If a payment is made in contravention of section 217 (payment by company)—

(a) it is held by the recipient on trust for the company making the payment, and

(b) any director who authorised the payment is jointly and severally liable to indemnify the company that made the payment for any loss resulting from it.

(2) If a payment is made in contravention of section 218 (payment in connection with transfer of undertaking etc), it is held by the recipient on trust for the company whose undertaking or property is or is proposed to be transferred.

(3) If a payment is made in contravention of section 219 (payment in connection with share transfer)—

(a) it is held by the recipient on trust for persons who have sold their shares as a result of the offer made, and

(b) the expenses incurred by the recipient in distributing that sum amongst those persons shall be borne by him and not retained out of that sum.

(4) If a payment is in contravention of section 217 and section 218, subsection (2) of this section applies rather than subsection (1).

(5) If a payment is in contravention of section 217 and section 219, subsection (3) of this section applies rather than subsection (1), unless the court directs otherwise.

[*Sections 226A–226F (restrictions on payments to directors).*]

[226E Payments made without approval: civil consequences

(1) An obligation (however arising) to make a payment which would be in contravention of section 226B or 226C has no effect.

(2) If a payment is made in contravention of section 226B or 226C—

(a) it is held by the recipient on trust for the company or other person making the payment, and

(b) in the case of a payment by a company, any director who authorised the payment is jointly and severally liable to indemnify the company that made the payment for any loss resulting from it.

(3) If a payment for loss of office is made in contravention of section 226C to a director of a quoted company in connection with the transfer of the whole or any part of the undertaking or property of the company or a subsidiary of the company—

(a) subsection (2) does not apply, and

(b) the payment is held by the recipient on trust for the company whose undertaking or property is or is proposed to be transferred.

(4) If a payment for loss of office is made in contravention of section 226C to a director of a quoted company in connection with a transfer of shares in the company, or in a subsidiary of the company, resulting from a takeover bid—

(a) subsection (2) does not apply,

(b) the payment is held by the recipient on trust for persons who have sold their shares as a result of the offer made, and

(c) the expenses incurred by the recipient in distributing that sum amongst those persons shall be borne by the recipient and not retained out of that sum.

(5) If in proceedings against a director for the enforcement of a liability under subsection (2)(b)—

(a) the director shows that he or she has acted honestly and reasonably, and

(b) the court considers that, having regard to all the circumstances of the case, the director ought to be relieved of liability,

the court may relieve the director, either wholly or in part, from liability on such terms as the court thinks fit.]

232   Provisions protecting directors from liability

(1) Any provision that purports to exempt a director of a company (to any extent) from any liability that would otherwise attach to him in connection with any negligence, default, breach of duty or breach of trust in relation to the company is void.

(2) Any provision by which a company directly or indirectly provides an indemnity (to any extent) for a director of the company, or of an associated company, against any liability attaching to him in connection with any negligence, default, breach of duty or breach of trust in relation to the company of which he is a director is void, except as permitted by—

(a) section 233 (provision of insurance),

(b) section 234 (qualifying third party indemnity provision), or

(c) section 235 (qualifying pension scheme indemnity provision).

463   Liability for false or misleading statements in reports

(1) The reports to which this section applies are—

[(za) the strategic report,]

(a) the directors' report,

(b) the directors' remuneration report, [. . .].

(2) A director of a company is liable to compensate the company for any loss suffered by it as a result of—

(a) any untrue or misleading statement in a report to which this section applies, or

(b) the omission from a report to which this section applies of anything required to be included in it.

(3) He is so liable only if—

(a) he knew the statement to be untrue or misleading or was reckless as to whether it was untrue or misleading, or

(b) he knew the omission to be dishonest concealment of a material fact.

(4) No person shall be subject to any liability to a person other than the company resulting from reliance, by that person or another, on information in a report to which this section applies.

(5) The reference in subsection (4) to a person being subject to a liability includes a reference to another person being entitled as against him to be granted any civil remedy or to rescind or re-pudiate an agreement.

(6) This section does not affect—

(a) liability for a civil penalty, or

(b) liability for a criminal offence.

532　Voidness of provisions protecting auditors from liability

(1) This section applies to any provision—

 (a) for exempting an auditor of a company (to any extent) from any liability that would otherwise attach to him in connection with any negligence, default, breach of duty or breach of trust in relation to the company occurring in the course of the audit of accounts, or

 (b) by which a company directly or indirectly provides an indemnity (to any extent) for an auditor of the company, or of an associated company, against any liability attaching to him in connection with any negligence, default, breach of duty or breach of trust in relation to the company of which he is auditor occurring in the course of the audit of accounts.

(2) Any such provision is void, except as permitted by—

 (a) section 533 (indemnity for costs of successfully defending proceedings), or

 (b) sections 534 to 536 (liability limitation agreements).

534　Liability limitation agreements

(1) A 'liability limitation agreement' is an agreement that purports to limit the amount of a liability owed to a company by its auditor in respect of any negligence, default, breach of duty or breach of trust, occurring in the course of the audit of accounts, of which the auditor may be guilty in relation to the company.

537　Effect of liability limitation agreement

(1) A liability limitation agreement is not effective to limit the auditor's liability to less than such amount as is fair and reasonable in all the circumstances of the case having regard (in particular) to—

 (a) the auditor's responsibilities under this Part,

 (b) the nature and purpose of the auditor's contractual obligations to the company, and

 (c) the professional standards expected of him.

(2) A liability limitation agreement that purports to limit the auditor's liability to less than the amount mentioned in subsection (1) shall have effect as if it limited his liability to that amount.

(3) In determining what is fair and reasonable in all the circumstances of the case no account is to be taken of—

 (a) matters arising after the loss or damage in question has been incurred, or

 (b) matters (whenever arising) affecting the possibility of recovering compensation from other persons liable in respect of the same loss or damage.

655　Shares no bar to damages against company

A person is not debarred from obtaining damages or other compensation from a company by reason only of his holding or having held shares in the company or any right to apply or subscribe for shares or to be included in the company's register of members in respect of shares.

847　Consequences of unlawful distribution

(1) This section applies where a distribution, or part of one, made by a company to one of its members is made in contravention of this Part.

(2) If at the time of the distribution the member knows or has reasonable grounds for believing that it is so made, he is liable—

 (a) to repay it (or that part of it, as the case may be) to the company, or

 (b) in the case of a distribution made otherwise than in cash, to pay the company a sum equal to the value of the distribution (or part) at that time.

(3) This is without prejudice to any obligation imposed apart from this section on a member of a company to repay a distribution unlawfully made to him.

942   The Panel

(1) The body known as the Panel on Takeovers and Mergers ('the Panel') is to have the functions conferred on it by or under this Chapter.

954   Compensation

(1) Rules may confer power on the Panel to order a person to pay such compensation as it thinks just and reasonable if he is in breach of a rule the effect of which is to require the payment of money.

(2) Rules made by virtue of this section may include provision for the payment of interest (including compound interest).

956   No action for breach of statutory duty etc.

(1) Contravention of a rule-based requirement or a disclosure requirement does not give rise to any right of action for breach of statutory duty.

(2) Contravention of a rule-based requirement does not make any transaction void or unenforceable or (subject to any provision made by rules) affect the validity of any other thing.

1218   Exemption from liability for damages

(1) No person within subsection (2) is to be liable in damages for anything done or omitted in the discharge or purported discharge of functions to which this subsection applies.

(2) The persons within this subsection are—

    (a) any recognised supervisory body,

    (b) any officer or employee of a recognised supervisory body, and

    (c) any member of the governing body of a recognised supervisory body.

Compensation Act 2006

(2006, c. 29)

PART 1 STANDARD OF CARE

1   Deterrent effect of potential liability

A court considering a claim in negligence or breach of statutory duty may, in determining whether the defendant should have taken particular steps to meet a standard of care (whether by taking precautions against a risk or otherwise), have regard to whether a requirement to take those steps might—

    (a) prevent a desirable activity from being undertaken at all, to a particular extent or in a particular way, or

    (b) discourage persons from undertaking functions in connection with a desirable activity.

2   Apologies, offers of treatment or other redress

An apology, an offer of treatment or other redress, shall not of itself amount to an admission of negligence or breach of statutory duty.

3   Mesothelioma: damages

(1) This section applies where—

    (a) a person ('the responsible person') has negligently or in breach of statutory duty caused or permitted another person ('the victim') to be exposed to asbestos,

    (b) the victim has contracted mesothelioma as a result of exposure to asbestos,

(c) because of the nature of mesothelioma and the state of medical science, it is not possible to determine with certainty whether it was the exposure mentioned in paragraph (a) or another exposure which caused the victim to become ill, and

(d) the responsible person is liable in tort, by virtue of the exposure mentioned in paragraph (a), in connection with damage caused to the victim by the disease (whether by reason of having materially increased a risk or for any other reason).

(2) The responsible person shall be liable—

(a) in respect of the whole of the damage caused to the victim by the disease (irrespective of whether the victim was also exposed to asbestos—

(i) other than by the responsible person, whether or not in circumstances in which another person has liability in tort, or

(ii) by the responsible person in circumstances in which he has no liability in tort), and

(b) jointly and severally with any other responsible person.

(3) Subsection (2) does not prevent—

(a) one responsible person from claiming a contribution from another, or

(b) a finding of contributory negligence.

(4) In determining the extent of contributions of different responsible persons in accordance with subsection (3)(a), a court shall have regard to the relative lengths of the periods of exposure for which each was responsible; but this subsection shall not apply—

(a) if or to the extent that responsible persons agree to apportion responsibility amongst themselves on some other basis, or

(b) if or to the extent that the court thinks that another basis for determining contributions is more appropriate in the circumstances of a particular case.

(5) In subsection (1) the reference to causing or permitting a person to be exposed to asbestos includes a reference to failing to protect a person from exposure to asbestos.

(6) In the application of this section to Scotland—

(a) a reference to tort shall be taken as a reference to delict, and

(b) a reference to a court shall be taken to include a reference to a jury.

(7) The Treasury may make regulations about the provision of compensation to a responsible person where—

(a) he claims, or would claim, a contribution from another responsible person in accordance with subsection (3)(a), but

(b) he is unable or likely to be unable to obtain the contribution, because an insurer of the other responsible person is unable or likely to be unable to satisfy the claim for a contribution.

(8) The regulations may, in particular—

(b) replicate or apply (with or without modification) a transitional compensation provision;

(c) provide for a specified person to assess and pay compensation;

(d) provide for expenses incurred (including the payment of compensation) to be met out of levies collected in accordance with section 213(3)(b) of the Financial Services and Markets Act 2000 (c. 8) (the Financial Services Compensation Scheme);

(e) modify the effect of a transitional compensation provision;

(f) enable the [Financial Conduct Authority or the Prudential Regulation Authority] to amend the Financial Services Compensation Scheme;

(g) modify the Financial Services and Markets Act 2000 in its application to an amendment pursuant to paragraph (f);

(h) make, or require the making of, provision for the making of a claim by a responsible person for compensation whether or not he has already satisfied claims in tort against him;

(i) make, or require the making of, provision which has effect in relation to claims for contributions made on or after the date on which this Act is passed.

(10) In subsections (7) and (8)—

    (a) a reference to a responsible person includes a reference to an insurer of a responsible person, and

    (b) 'transitional compensation provision' means a provision of an enactment which is made under the Financial Services and Markets Act 2000 and—

        (i)   preserves the effect of the Policyholders Protection Act 1975 (c. 75), or

        (ii) applies the Financial Services Compensation Scheme in relation to matters arising before its establishment.

(11) Regulations under subsection (7)—

    (a) may include consequential or incidental provision,

    (b) may make provision which has effect generally or only in relation to specified cases or circumstances,

    (c) may make different provision for different cases or circumstances,

    (d) shall be made by statutory instrument, and

    (e) may not be made unless a draft has been laid before and approved by resolution of each House of Parliament.

PART 2 CLAIMS MANAGEMENT SERVICES

4   Provision of regulated claims management services

(1) A person may not provide regulated claims management services unless—

    (a) he is an authorised person,

    (b) he is an exempt person,

    (c) the requirement for authorisation has been waived in relation to him in accordance with regulations under section 9, or

    (d) he is an individual acting otherwise than in the course of a business.

Government of Wales Act 2006

(2006, c. 32)

1   The Assembly

(1) There is to be an Assembly for Wales to be known as the National Assembly for Wales or Cynulliad Cenedlaethol Cymru (referred to in this Act as 'the Assembly').

42   Defamation

(1) For the purposes of the law of defamation—

    (a) any statement made in Assembly proceedings, and

    (b) the publication under the authority of the Assembly of any statement, is absolutely privileged.

(2) The Welsh Ministers may by regulations make provision for and in connection with establishing in any legal proceedings that any statement or publication is absolutely privileged by virtue of subsection (1).

(3) No regulations are to be made under subsection (2) unless a draft of the statutory instrument containing them has been laid before, and approved by a resolution of, the Assembly.

(4) In this section 'statement' has the same meaning as in the Defamation Act 1996 (c. 31).

130   Payments in by mistake

Where a sum is paid into the Welsh Consolidated Fund which should not or need not have been paid into the Fund, the Auditor General may grant an approval to draw a payment equal to the amount of that sum out of the Fund.

National Health Service Act 2006

(2006, c. 41)

9 NHS contracts

(1) In this Act, an NHS contract is an arrangement under which one health service body ('the commissioner') arranges for the provision to it by another health service body ('the provider') of goods or services which it reasonably requires for the purposes of its functions.

(5) Whether or not an arrangement which constitutes an NHS contract would apart from this subsection be a contract in law, it must not be regarded for any purpose as giving rise to contractual rights or liabilities.

(6) But if any dispute arises with respect to such an arrangement, either party may refer the matter to the Secretary of State for determination under this section

(7) If, in the course of negotiations intending to lead to an arrangement which will be an NHS contract, it appears to a health service body—

    (a) that the terms proposed by another health service body are unfair by reason that the other is seeking to take advantage of its position as the only, or the only practicable, provider of the goods or services concerned or by reason of any other unequal bargaining position as between the prospective parties to the proposed arrangement, or

    (b) that for any other reason arising out of the relative bargaining position of the prospective parties any of the terms of the proposed arrangement cannot be agreed,

that health service body may refer the terms of the proposed arrangement to the Secretary of State for determination under this section.

(8) Where a reference is made to the Secretary of State under subsection (6) or (7), he may determine the matter himself or appoint a person to consider and determine it in accordance with regulations.

NHS Redress Act 2006

(2006, c. 44)

England

1 Power to establish redress scheme

(1) The Secretary of State may by regulations establish a scheme for the purpose of enabling redress to be provided without recourse to civil proceedings in circumstances in which this section applies.

(2) This section applies where under the law of England and Wales qualifying liability in tort on the part of a body or other person mentioned in subsection (3) arises in connection with the provision, as part of the health service in England, of qualifying services.

(3) The bodies and other persons referred to are—

    (a) the Secretary of State,

  [(aa) the National Health Service Commissioning Board,

    (ab) a clinical commissioning group,] and

    (d) a body or other person providing, or arranging for the provision of, services whose provision is the subject of arrangements with a body or other person mentioned in paragraph (a), [(aa) or (ab)].

(4) The reference in subsection (2) to qualifying liability in tort is to liability in tort owed—

    (a) in respect of or consequent upon personal injury or loss arising out of or in connection with breach of a duty of care owed to any person in connection with the diagnosis of illness, or the care or treatment of any patient, and

(b) in consequence of any act or omission by a health care professional.

(5) For the purposes of subsection (2), services are qualifying services if—

    (a) they are provided in a hospital (in England or elsewhere), or

    (b) they are of such other description (including a description involving provision outside England) as the Secretary of State may specify by regulations.

(6) Regulations under subsection (5)(b) may not specify services of any of the following descriptions—

    (a) primary dental services,

    (b) primary medical services,

    (c) services provided under section 38 of the National Health Service Act 1977 (c. 49) (general ophthalmic services),

    (d) services provided under [section 126 of the National Health Service Act 2006] (arrangements for pharmaceutical services) or by virtue of [section 127] of that Act (arrangements for additional pharmaceutical services), and

    (e) services of a kind which may be provided under [section 126 of that Act, or by virtue of section 127 of that Act, which are provided under Schedule 12 to that Act (local pharmaceutical services schemes) or under section 134 of that Act (local pharmaceutical services pilot schemes).]

(7) The references in subsection (6) to primary dental services and primary medical services are to primary dental services and primary medical services under [the National Health Service Act 2006], except that the Secretary of State may by regulations provide that services of a description specified in the regulations are not to be regarded as primary dental services or primary medical services for the purposes of that subsection.

(8) Regulations under subsection (5)(b) or (7) may, in particular, describe services by reference to the manner or circumstances in which they are provided.

(9) In subsection (3)(d), the reference to a person providing services does not include a person providing services under a contract of employment.

(10) In subsection (4), the reference to a health care professional is to a member of a profession (whether or not regulated by, or by virtue of, any enactment) which is concerned (wholly or partly) with the physical or mental health of individuals.

(11) In this section, 'hospital' has the same meaning as in [the National Health Service Act 2006].

2 Application of scheme

(1) Subject to subsection (2), a scheme may make such provision defining its application as the Secretary of State thinks fit.

(2) A scheme must provide that it does not apply in relation to a liability that is or has been the subject of civil proceedings.

3 Redress under scheme

(1) Subject to subsections (2) and (5), a scheme may make such provision as the Secretary of State thinks fit about redress under the scheme.

(2) A scheme must provide for redress ordinarily to comprise—

    (a) the making of an offer of compensation in satisfaction of any right to bring civil proceedings in respect of the liability concerned,

    (b) the giving of an explanation,

    (c) the giving of an apology, and

    (d) the giving of a report on the action which has been, or will be, taken to prevent similar cases arising,

but may specify circumstances in which one or more of those forms of redress is not required.

(3) A scheme may, in particular—

    (a) make provision for the compensation that may be offered to take the form of entry into a contract to provide care or treatment or of financial compensation, or both;

    (b) make provision about the circumstances in which different forms of compensation may be offered.

(4) A scheme that provides for financial compensation to be offered may, in particular—

    (a) make provision about the matters in respect of which financial compensation may be offered;

    (b) make provision with respect to the assessment of the amount of any financial compensation.

(5) A scheme that provides for financial compensation to be offered—

    (a) may specify an upper limit on the amount of financial compensation that may be included in an offer under the scheme;

    (b) if it does not specify a limit under paragraph (a), must specify an upper limit on the amount of financial compensation that may be included in such an offer in respect of pain and suffering;

    (c) may not specify any other limit on what may be included in such an offer by way of financial compensation.

6 Proceedings under scheme

(1) Subject to subsections (3) to (6), a scheme may make such provision as the Secretary of State thinks fit about proceedings under the scheme.

(2) A scheme may, in particular, make provision—

    (a) about the investigation of cases under the scheme (including provision for the overseeing of the investigation by an individual of a specified description);

    (b) about the making of decisions about the application of the scheme;

    (c) for time limits in relation to acceptance of an offer of compensation under the scheme;

    (d) about the form and content of settlement agreements under the scheme;

    (e) for settlement agreements under the scheme to be subject in cases of a specified description to approval by a court;

    (f) about the termination of proceedings under the scheme.

(3) A scheme must—

    (a) make provision for the findings of an investigation of a case under the scheme to be recorded in a report, and

    (b) subject to subsection (4), make provision for a copy of the report to be provided on request to the individual seeking redress.

(4) A scheme may provide that no copy of an investigation report need be provided—

    (a) before an offer is made under the scheme or proceedings under the scheme are terminated, or

    (b) in such other circumstances as may be specified.

(5) A scheme must provide for a settlement agreement under the scheme to include a waiver of the right to bring civil proceedings in respect of the liability to which the settlement relates.

(6) A scheme must provide for the termination of proceedings under the scheme if the liability to which the proceedings relate becomes the subject of civil proceedings.

7 Suspension of limitation period

(1) A scheme must make provision for the period during which a liability is the subject of proceedings under the scheme to be disregarded for the purposes of calculating whether any relevant limitation period has expired.

(2) In subsection (1), the reference to any relevant limitation period is to any period of time for the bringing of civil proceedings in respect of the liability which is prescribed by or under the Limitation Act 1980 (c. 58) or any other enactment.

(3) A scheme may define for the purposes of provision in pursuance of subsection (1) when liability is the subject of proceedings under the scheme.

8   Legal advice etc.

(1) Subject to subsections (2) and (4), a scheme may make such provision as the Secretary of State thinks fit—

    (a) for the provision of legal advice without charge to individuals seeking redress under the scheme;

    (b) for the provision in connection with proceedings under the scheme of other services, including the services of medical experts.

(2) A scheme must make such provision as the Secretary of State considers appropriate in order to secure that individuals to whom an offer under the scheme is made have access to legal advice without charge in relation to—

    (a) the offer, and

    (b) any settlement agreement.

(3) Provision under subsection (1)(a) or (2) about who may provide the legal advice may operate by reference to whether a potential provider is included in a list prepared by a specified person.

(4) A scheme that makes provision for the provision of the services of medical experts must provide for such experts to be instructed jointly by the scheme authority and the individual seeking redress under the scheme.

9   Assistance for individuals seeking redress under scheme

(1) It is the duty of the Secretary of State to arrange, to such extent as he considers necessary to meet all reasonable requirements, for the provision of assistance (by way of representation or otherwise) to individuals seeking, or intending to seek, redress under a scheme.

(2) The Secretary of State may make such other arrangements as he thinks fit for the provision of assistance to individuals in connection with cases which are the subject of proceedings under a scheme.

(3) The Secretary of State may make payments to any person in pursuance of arrangements under this section.

(4) In making arrangements under this section, the Secretary of State must have regard to the principle that the provision of services under the arrangements in connection with a particular case should, so far as practicable, be independent of any person to whose conduct the case relates or who is involved in dealing with the case.

10   Scheme members

(1) Subject to subsection (3), a scheme may make such provision as the Secretary of State thinks fit—

    (a) about membership of the scheme on the part of any body or other person to whose liability the scheme applies, and

    (b) about the functions of members in connection with the scheme.

11   Scheme authority

(1) A scheme must make provision for a specified Special Health Authority (in this Act referred to as 'the scheme authority') to have such functions in connection with the scheme as the Secretary of State thinks fit.

12   General duty to promote resolution under scheme

A scheme must include provision requiring the scheme authority and the members of the scheme, in carrying out their functions under the scheme, to have regard in particular to the desirability of redress being provided without recourse to civil proceedings.

13   Duties of co-operation

(1) The scheme authority under a scheme and [the Care Quality Commission] must co-operate with each other where it appears to them that it is appropriate to do so for the efficient and effective discharge of their respective functions.

(2) The scheme authority under a scheme and the National Patient Safety Agency must co-operate with each other where it appears to them that it is appropriate to do so for the efficient and effective discharge of their respective functions.

14 Complaints

(1) The Secretary of State may by regulations make provision about the handling and consideration of complaints made under the regulations about maladministration by any body or other person—

    (a) in the exercise of functions under a scheme,

    (b) in the exercise of other functions relating to proceedings under a scheme, or

    (c) in connection with a settlement agreement entered into under a scheme.

Income Tax Act 2007

(2007, c. 3)

762 [and 781] Tracing value

(1) This section applies if it is necessary to determine the extent to which the value of any property or right is derived from any other property or right for the purposes of this Chapter.

(2) Value may be traced through any number of companies, partnerships and trusts.

(3) The property held by a company, partnership or trust must be attributed to the shareholders, partners or beneficiaries at each stage in such manner as is appropriate in the circumstances.

Legal Services Act 2007

(2007, c. 29)

131 Acts and omissions by employees etc

(1) For the purposes of this Part and the ombudsman scheme, any act or omission by a person in the course of the person's employment is to be treated as also an act or omission by the person's employer, whether or not it was done with the employer's knowledge or approval.

154 Protection from defamation claims

For the purposes of the law of defamation—

    (a) proceedings in relation to a complaint under the ombudsman scheme are to be treated as if they were proceedings before a court, and

    (b) the publication of any matter by the OLC ['the Office for Legal Complaints'] under this Part is absolutely privileged.

176 Duties of regulated persons

(1) A person who is a regulated person in relation to an approved regulator has a duty to comply with the regulatory arrangements of the approved regulator as they apply to that person.

Tribunals, Courts and Enforcement Act 2007

(2007, c. 15)

62 Enforcement by taking control of goods

(1) Schedule 12 applies where an enactment, writ or warrant confers power to use the procedure in that Schedule (taking control of goods and selling them to recover a sum of money).

(2) The power conferred by a writ or warrant of control to recover a sum of money, and any power conferred by a writ or warrant of possession or delivery to take control of goods and sell them to recover a sum of money, is exercisable only by using that procedure.

63 Enforcement agents

(1) This section and section 64 apply for the purposes of Schedule 12.

(2) An individual may act as an enforcement agent only if one of these applies—

    (a) he acts under a certificate under section 64;

    (b) he is exempt;

    (c) he acts in the presence and under the direction of a person to whom paragraph (a) or (b) applies.

(3) An individual is exempt if he acts in the course of his duty as one of these—

    (a) a constable;

    (b) an officer of Revenue and Customs;

    (c) a person appointed under section 2(1) of the Courts Act 2003 (c. 39) (court officers and staff).

65 Common law rules replaced

(1) This Chapter replaces the common law rules about the exercise of the powers which under it become powers to use the procedure in Schedule 12.

(2) The rules replaced include—

    (a) rules distinguishing between an illegal, an irregular and an excessive exercise of a power;

    (b) rules that would entitle a person to bring proceedings of a kind for which paragraph 66 of Schedule 12 provides (remedies available to the debtor);

    (c) rules of replevin;

    (d) rules about rescuing goods.

85 Contracts for similar rights to be void

(1) A provision of a contract is void to the extent that it would do any of these—

    (a) confer a right to seize or otherwise take control of goods to recover amounts within subsection (2);

    (b) confer a right to sell goods to recover amounts within subsection (2);

    (c) modify the effect of section 72(1), except in accordance with subsection (3).

(2) The amounts are any amounts payable—

    (a) as rent;

    (b) under a lease (other than as rent);

    (c) under an agreement collateral to a lease;

    (d) under an instrument creating a rentcharge;

    (e) in respect of breach of a covenant or condition in a lease, in an agreement collateral to a lease or in an instrument creating a rentcharge;

    (f) under an indemnity in respect of a payment within paragraphs (a) to (e).

(3) A provision of a contract is not void under subsection (1)(c) to the extent that it prevents or restricts the exercise of CRAR [*commercial rent arrears recovery*].

89 Application to the Crown

(1) This Part binds the Crown.

(2) But the procedure in Schedule 12 may not be used—

    (a) to recover debts due from the Crown,

    (b) to take control of or sell goods of the Crown (including goods owned by the Crown jointly or in common with another person), or

    (c) to enter premises occupied by the Crown.

Banking Act 2009

(2009, c. 1)

[191 Directions

(1) The Bank of England may give directions in writing to the operator of a recognised inter-bank payment system.

(2) A direction may—

    (a) require or prohibit the taking of specified action in the operation of the system;

    (b) set standards to be met in the operation of the system.

(3) If a direction is given for the purpose of resolving or reducing a threat to the stability of the UK financial system, the operator (including its officers and staff) has immunity from liability in damages in respect of action or inaction in accordance with the direction.

(4) A direction given for the purpose mentioned in subsection (3) must—

    (a) include a statement that it is given for that purpose, and

    (b) inform the operator of the effect of that subsection.

(5) The Treasury may by order confer immunity on any person from liability in damages in respect of action or inaction in accordance with a direction (including a direction given for the purpose mentioned in subsection (3)).

(6) An order—

    (a) is to be made by statutory instrument, and

    (b) is subject to annulment in pursuance of a resolution of either House of Parliament.

(7) An immunity conferred by or under this section does not extend to action or inaction—

    (a) in bad faith, or

    (b) in contravention of section 6(1) of the Human Rights Act 1998.]

244 Immunity

(1) The Bank of England has immunity in its capacity as a monetary authority.

(2) In this section—

    (a) a reference to the Bank of England is a reference to the Bank and anyone who acts or purports to act as a director, officer, [employee] or agent of the Bank,

    (b) "immunity" means immunity from liability in damages in respect of action or inaction, and

(3) The immunity does not extend to action or inaction—

    (a) in bad faith, or

    (b) in contravention of section 6(1) of the Human Rights Act 1998.

Equality Act 2010

(2010, c. 15)

PART 2 EQUALITY: KEY CONCEPTS

4 The protected characteristics

The following characteristics are protected characteristics—

age;

disability;

gender reassignment;

marriage and civil partnership;

pregnancy and maternity;

race;

religion or belief;

sex;

sexual orientation.

13 Direct discrimination

(1) A person (A) discriminates against another (B) if, because of a protected characteristic, A treats B less favourably than A treats or would treat others.

26   Harassment

(1) A person (A) harasses another (B) if—

(a) A engages in unwanted conduct related to a relevant protected characteristic, and

(b) the conduct has the purpose or effect of—

(i)   violating B's dignity, or

(ii) creating an intimidating, hostile, degrading, humiliating or offensive environment for B.

27   Victimisation

(1) A person (A) victimises another person (B) if A subjects B to a detriment because—

(a) B does a protected act, or

(b) A believes that B has done, or may do, a protected act.

(2) Each of the following is a protected act—

(a) bringing proceedings under this Act;

(b) giving evidence or information in connection with proceedings under this Act;

(c) doing any other thing for the purposes of or in connection with this Act;

(d) making an allegation (whether or not express) that A or another person has contravened this Act.

(3) Giving false evidence or information, or making a false allegation, is not a protected act if the evidence or information is given, or the allegation is made, in bad faith.

(4) This section applies only where the person subjected to a detriment is an individual.

(5) The reference to contravening this Act includes a reference to committing a breach of an equality clause or rule.

PART 3 SERVICES AND PUBLIC FUNCTIONS

28   Application of this Part

(1) This Part does not apply to the protected characteristic of—

(a) age, so far as relating to persons who have not attained the age of 18;

(b) marriage and civil partnership.

(2) This Part does not apply to discrimination, harassment or victimisation—

(a) that is prohibited by Part 4 (premises), 5 (work) or 6 (education), or

(b) that would be so prohibited but for an express exception.

(3) This Part does not apply to—

(a) a breach of an equality clause or rule;

(b) anything that would be a breach of an equality clause or rule but for section 69 or Part 2 of Schedule 7;

(c) a breach of a non-discrimination rule.

29   Provision of services, etc.

(1) A person (a "service-provider") concerned with the provision of a service to the public or a section of the public (for payment or not) must not discriminate against a person requiring the service by not providing the person with the service.

(2) A service-provider (A) must not, in providing the service, discriminate against a person (B)—

(a) as to the terms on which A provides the service to B;

(b) by terminating the provision of the service to B;

(c) by subjecting B to any other detriment.

(3) A service-provider must not, in relation to the provision of the service, harass—

(a) a person requiring the service, or

(b) a person to whom the service-provider provides the service.

(4) A service-provider must not victimise a person requiring the service by not providing the person with the service.

(5) A service-provider (A) must not, in providing the service, victimise a person (B)—

  (a) as to the terms on which A provides the service to B;

  (b) by terminating the provision of the service to B;

  (c) by subjecting B to any other detriment.

(6) A person must not, in the exercise of a public function that is not the provision of a service to the public or a section of the public, do anything that constitutes discrimination, harassment or victimisation.

(8) In the application of section 26 for the purposes of subsection (3), and subsection (6) as it relates to harassment, neither of the following is a relevant protected characteristic—

  (a) religion or belief;

  (b) sexual orientation.

31 Interpretation and exceptions

(1) This section applies for the purposes of this Part.

(2) A reference to the provision of a service includes a reference to the provision of goods or facilities.

PART 4 PREMISES

32 Application of this Part

(1) This Part does not apply to the following protected characteristics—

  (a) age;

  (b) marriage and civil partnership.

33 Disposals, etc.

(1) A person (A) who has the right to dispose of premises must not discriminate against another (B)—

  (a) as to the terms on which A offers to dispose of the premises to B;

  (b) by not disposing of the premises to B;

  (c) in A's treatment of B with respect to things done in relation to persons seeking premises.

PART 5 WORK

39 Employees and applicants

(1) An employer (A) must not discriminate against a person (B)—

  (a) in the arrangements A makes for deciding to whom to offer employment;

  (b) as to the terms on which A offers B employment;

  (c) by not offering B employment.

(2) An employer (A) must not discriminate against an employee of A's (B)—

  (a) as to B's terms of employment;

  (b) in the way A affords B access, or by not affording B access, to opportunities for promotion, transfer or training or for receiving any other benefit, facility or service;

  (c) by dismissing B;

  (d) by subjecting B to any other detriment.

66 Sex equality clause

(1) If the terms of A's work do not (by whatever means) include a sex equality clause, they are to be treated as including one.

(2) A sex equality clause is a provision that has the following effect—

  (a) if a term of A's is less favourable to A than a corresponding term of B's is to B, A's term is modified so as not to be less favourable;

(b) if A does not have a term which corresponds to a term of B's that benefits B, A's terms are modified so as to include such a term.

PART 9 ENFORCEMENT

119   Remedies

(1) This section applies if [the county court] or the sheriff finds that there has been a contravention of a provision referred to in section 114(1).

(2) The county court has power to grant any remedy which could be granted by the High Court—

(a) in proceedings in tort;

(b) on a claim for judicial review.

(4) An award of damages may include compensation for injured feelings (whether or not it includes compensation on any other basis).

(7) The county court or sheriff must not grant a remedy other than an award of damages or the making of a declaration unless satisfied that no criminal matter would be prejudiced by doing so.

PART 10 CONTRACTS ETC.

142   Unenforceable terms

(1) A term of a contract is unenforceable against a person in so far as it constitutes, promotes or provides for treatment of that or another person that is of a description prohibited by this Act.

(2) A relevant non-contractual term is unenforceable against a person in so far as it constitutes, promotes or provides for treatment of that or another person that is of a description prohibited by this Act, in so far as this Act relates to disability.

(3) A relevant non-contractual term is a term which—

(a) is a term of an agreement that is not a contract, and

(b) relates to the provision of an employment service within section 56(2)(a) to (e) or to the provision under a group insurance arrangement of facilities by way of insurance.

143   Removal or modification of unenforceable terms

(1) [The county court] or the sheriff may, on an application by a person who has an interest in a contract or other agreement which includes a term that is unenforceable as a result of section 142, make an order for the term to be removed or modified.

(2) An order under this section must not be made unless every person who would be affected by it—

(a) has been given notice of the application (except where notice is dispensed with in accordance with rules of court), and

(b) has been afforded an opportunity to make representations to the county court or sheriff.

(3) An order under this section may include provision in respect of a period before the making of the order.

144   Contracting out

(1) A term of a contract is unenforceable by a person in whose favour it would operate in so far as it purports to exclude or limit a provision of or made under this Act.

(2) A relevant non-contractual term (as defined by section 142) is unenforceable by a person in whose favour it would operate in so far as it purports to exclude or limit a provision of or made under this Act, in so far as the provision relates to disability.

(3) This section does not apply to a contract which settles a claim within section 114 [*Civil courts: Jurisdiction*].

(4) This section does not apply to a contract which settles a complaint within section 120 [*Employment Tribunals: Jurisdiction*] if the contract—

    (a) is made with the assistance of a conciliation officer, or

    (b) is a qualifying [settlement agreement].

(5) A contract within subsection (4) includes a contract which settles a complaint relating to a breach of an equality clause or rule or of a non-discrimination rule.

(6) A contract within subsection (4) includes an agreement by the parties to a dispute to submit the dispute to arbitration if—

    (a) the dispute is covered by a scheme having effect by virtue of an order under section 212A of the Trade Union and Labour Relations (Consolidation) Act 1992, and

    (b) the agreement is to submit the dispute to arbitration in accordance with the scheme.

145   Void and unenforceable terms

(1) A term of a collective agreement is void in so far as it constitutes, promotes or provides for treatment of a description prohibited by this Act.

(2) A rule of an undertaking is unenforceable against a person in so far as it constitutes, promotes or provides for treatment of the person that is of a description prohibited by this Act.

146   Declaration in respect of void term, etc.

(1) A qualifying person (P) may make a complaint to an employment tribunal that a term is void, or that a rule is unenforceable, as a result of section 145.

(2) But subsection (1) applies only if—

    (a) the term or rule may in the future have effect in relation to P, and

    (b) where the complaint alleges that the term or rule provides for treatment of a description prohibited by this Act, P may in the future be subjected to treatment that would (if P were subjected to it in present circumstances) be of that description.

PART 16   GENERAL AND MISCELLANEOUS

212   General interpretation

(2) A reference (however expressed) to an act includes a reference to an omission.

(3) A reference (however expressed) to an omission includes (unless there is express provision to the contrary) a reference to—

    (a) a deliberate omission to do something;

    (b) a refusal to do it;

    (c) a failure to do it.

Section 31

SCHEDULE 3

SERVICES AND PUBLIC FUNCTIONS: EXCEPTIONS

[Age

20A.—(1) A person (A) does not contravene section 29, so far as relating to age discrimination, by doing anything in connection with the provision of a financial service.

(2) Where A conducts an assessment of risk for the purposes of providing the financial service to another person (B), A may rely on sub-paragraph (1) only if the assessment of risk, so far as it involves a consideration of B's age, is carried out by reference to information which is relevant to the assessment of risk and from a source on which it is reasonable to rely.

(3) In this paragraph, "financial service" includes a service of a banking, credit, insurance, personal pension, investment or payment nature.]

Third Parties (Rights against Insurers) Act 2010

(2010, c. 10)

1 Rights against insurer of insolvent person etc

(1) This section applies if—

    (a) a relevant person incurs a liability against which that person is insured under a contract of insurance, or

    (b) a person who is subject to such a liability becomes a relevant person.

(2) The rights of the relevant person under the contract against the insurer in respect of the liability are transferred to and vest in the person to whom the liability is or was incurred (the "third party").

(3) The third party may bring proceedings to enforce the rights against the insurer without having established the relevant person's liability; but the third party may not enforce those rights without having established that liability.

(4) For the purposes of this Act, a liability is established only if its existence and amount are established; and, for that purpose, "establish" means establish—

    (a) by virtue of a declaration under section 2 . . .,

    (b) by a judgment or decree,

    (c) by an award in arbitral proceedings or by an arbitration, or

    (d) by an enforceable agreement.

(5) In this Act—

    (a) references to an "insured" are to a person who incurs or who is subject to a liability to a third party against which that person is insured under a contract of insurance;

    (b) references to a "relevant person" are to a person within sections 4 to 7 7 [(and see also paragraph 1A of Schedule 3)];

    (c) references to a "third party" are to be construed in accordance with subsection (2);

    (d) references to "transferred rights" are to rights under a contract of insurance which are transferred under this section.

2 Establishing liability in England and Wales and Northern Ireland

(1) This section applies where a person (P)—

    (a) claims to have rights under a contract of insurance by virtue of a transfer under section 1, but

    (b) has not yet established the insured's liability which is insured under that contract.

(2) P may bring proceedings against the insurer for either or both of the following—

    (a) a declaration as to the insured's liability to P;

    (b) a declaration as to the insurer's potential liability to P.

(3) In such proceedings P is entitled, subject to any defence on which the insurer may rely, to a declaration under subsection (2)(a) or (b) on proof of the insured's liability to P or (as the case may be) the insurer's potential liability to P.

(4) Where proceedings are brought under subsection (2)(a) the insurer may rely on any defence on which the insured could rely if those proceedings were proceedings brought against the insured in respect of the insured's liability to P.

(5) Subsection (4) is subject to section 12(1).

(6) Where the court makes a declaration under this section, the effect of which is that the insurer is liable to P, the court may give the appropriate judgment against the insurer.

(9) When bringing proceedings under subsection (2)(a), P may also make the insured a defendant to those proceedings.

(10) If (but only if) the insured is a defendant to proceedings under this section (whether by virtue of subsection (9) or otherwise), a declaration under subsection (2) binds the insured as well as the insurer.

(11) In this section, references to the insurer's potential liability to P are references to the insurer's liability in respect of the insured's liability to P, if established.

4 Individuals

(1) An individual is a relevant person if any of the following is in force in respect of that individual in England and Wales—

    (a) a deed of arrangement registered in accordance with the Deeds of Arrangement Act 1914,

    (b) an administration order made under Part 6 of the County Courts Act 1984,

    (c) an enforcement restriction order made under Part 6A of that Act,

    (d) subject to subsection (4), a debt relief order made under Part 7A of the Insolvency Act 1986,

    (e) a voluntary arrangement approved in accordance with Part 8 of that Act, or

    (f) a bankruptcy order made under Part 9 of that Act.

(4) If an individual is a relevant person by virtue of subsection (1)(d) [or (3)(ba)], that person is a relevant person for the purposes of section 1(1)(b) only.

6 Corporate bodies etc

(1) A body corporate or an unincorporated body is a relevant person if—

    (a) a compromise or arrangement between the body and its creditors (or a class of them) is in force, having been sanctioned in accordance with section 899 of the Companies Act 2006, or

    (b) the body has been dissolved under section 1000, 1001 or 1003 of that Act, and the body has not been—

        (i) restored to the register by virtue of section 1025 of that Act, or

        (ii) ordered to be restored to the register by virtue of section 1031 of that Act.

(2) A body corporate or an unincorporated body is a relevant person if, in England and Wales . . .—

    (a) a voluntary arrangement approved in accordance with Part 1 of the Insolvency Act 1986 is in force in respect of it,

    [(b) the body is in administration under Schedule B1 to that Act,]

    (c) there is a person appointed in accordance with Part 3 of that Act who is acting as receiver or manager of the body's property (or there would be such a person so acting but for a temporary vacancy),

    (d) the body is, or is being, wound up voluntarily in accordance with Chapter 2 of Part 4 of that Act,

    (e) there is a person appointed under section 135 of that Act who is acting as provisional liquidator in respect of the body (or there would be such a person so acting but for a temporary vacancy), or

    (f) the body is, or is being, wound up by the court following the making of a winding-up order under Chapter 6 of Part 4 of that Act or Part 5 of that Act.

(5) A body within subsection (1)(a) is not a relevant person in relation to a liability that is transferred to another body by the order sanctioning the compromise or arrangement.

(6) Where a body is a relevant person by virtue of subsection (1)(a), section 1 has effect to transfer rights only to a person on whom the compromise or arrangement is binding.

(9) In this section—

    (a) a reference to a person appointed in accordance with Part 3 of the Insolvency Act 1986 includes a reference to a person appointed under section 101 of the Law of Property Act 1925;

    (b) a reference to a receiver or manager of a body's property includes a reference to a receiver or manager of part only of the property and to a receiver only of the income arising from the property or from part of it;

(c) for the purposes of subsection (3) "body corporate or unincorporated body" includes any entity, other than a trust, the estate of which may be sequestrated under section 6 of the Bankruptcy (Scotland) Act 1985; . . .

8   Limit on rights transferred

Where the liability of an insured to a third party is less than the liability of the insurer to the insured (ignoring the effect of section 1), no rights are transferred under that section in respect of the difference.

10   Insurer's right of set off

(1) This section applies if—

  (a) rights of an insured under a contract of insurance have been transferred to a third party under section 1,

  (b) the insured is under a liability to the insurer under the contract ("the insured's liability"), and

  (c) if there had been no transfer, the insurer would have been entitled to set off the amount of the insured's liability against the amount of the insurer's own liability to the insured.

(2) The insurer is entitled to set off the amount of the insured's liability against the amount of the insurer's own liability to the third party in relation to the transferred rights.

14   Effect of transfer on insured's liability

(1) Where rights in respect of an insured's liability to a third party are transferred under section 1, the third party may enforce that liability against the insured only to the extent (if any) that it exceeds the amount recoverable from the insurer by virtue of the transfer.

(2) Subsection (3) applies if a transfer of rights under section 1 occurs because the insured person is a relevant person by virtue of—

  (a) section 4(1)(a) or (e), (2)(b) or (3)(b) or (c),

  (b) section 6(1)(a), (2)(a), (3)(c) or (4)(a), or

  (c) section 7(1)(b).

(3) If the liability is subject to the arrangement, trust deed or compromise by virtue of which the insured is a relevant person, the liability is to be treated as subject to that arrangement, trust deed or compromise only to the extent that the liability exceeds the amount recoverable from the insurer by virtue of the transfer.

(6) For the purposes of this section the amount recoverable from the insurer does not include any amount that the third party is unable to recover as a result of—

  (a) a shortage of assets on the insurer's part, in a case where the insurer is a relevant person, or

  (b) a limit set by the contract of insurance on the fund available to meet claims in respect of a particular description of liability of the insured.

16   Voluntarily-incurred liabilities

It is irrelevant for the purposes of section 1 whether or not the liability of the insured is or was incurred voluntarily.

17   Avoidance

(1) A contract of insurance to which this section applies is of no effect in so far as it purports, whether directly or indirectly, to avoid or terminate the contract or alter the rights of the parties under it in the event of the insured—

  (a) becoming a relevant person, or

  (b) dying insolvent (within the meaning given by section 5(2)).

(2) A contract of insurance is one to which this section applies if the insured's rights under it are capable of being transferred under section 1.

[19   Power to change the meaning of "relevant person"
. . .]

Civil Aviation Act 2012

(2012, c. 19)

38 Civil proceedings

(1) A person who is given an enforcement order must comply with it (unless it is revoked).

(2) The obligation to comply with an enforcement order is a duty owed to every person who may be affected by a contravention of a requirement of the order.

(3) A person who is given an urgent enforcement order must comply with it, whether or not it has been confirmed (unless it is revoked).

(4) The obligation to comply with an urgent enforcement order that has been confirmed is a duty owed to every person who may be affected by a contravention of a requirement of the order.

(5) Where a duty is owed to a person under subsection (2) or (4), the following are actionable by the person—

    (a) a breach of the duty that causes the person to sustain loss or damage, and

    (b) an act that—

        (i)   by inducing a breach of the duty or interfering with its performance, causes that person to sustain loss or damage, and

        (ii) is done entirely or partly for achieving that result.

(6) In proceedings brought against a person ("P") by virtue of subsection (5)(a), it is a defence for P to show that P took all reasonable steps and exercised all due diligence to avoid contravening the requirements of the order.

(7) The CAA may enforce the duties under subsections (1) and (3) in—

    (a) civil proceedings for an injunction,

    (b) civil proceedings in Scotland for an interdict or for specific performance of a statutory duty under section 45 of the Court of Session Act 1988, or

    (c) civil proceedings for any other appropriate remedy or relief.

(8) Enforcement of a duty under subsection (1) or (3) by the CAA does not prejudice any rights that a person may have by virtue of subsection (5).

Consumer Insurance (Disclosure and Representations) Act 2012

(2012, c. 6)

1 Main definitions

In this Act—

  "consumer insurance contract" means a contract of insurance between—

    (a) an individual who enters into the contract wholly or mainly for purposes unrelated to the individual's trade, business or profession, and

    (b) a person who carries on the business of insurance and who becomes a party to the contract by way of that business (whether or not in accordance with permission for the purposes of the Financial Services and Markets Act 2000);

  "consumer" means the individual who enters into a consumer insurance contract, or proposes to do so;

  "insurer" means the person who is, or would become, the other party to a consumer insurance contract.

Pre-contract and pre-variation information

2 Disclosure and representations before contract or variation

(1) This section makes provision about disclosure and representations by a consumer to an insurer before a consumer insurance contract is entered into or varied.

(2) It is the duty of the consumer to take reasonable care not to make a misrepresentation to the insurer.

(3) A failure by the consumer to comply with the insurer's request to confirm or amend particulars previously given is capable of being a misrepresentation for the purposes of this Act (whether or not it could be apart from this subsection).

(4) The duty set out in subsection (2) replaces any duty relating to disclosure or representations by a consumer to an insurer which existed in the same circumstances before this Act applied.

(5) *Accordingly—*

  (a) *any rule of law to the effect that a consumer insurance contract is one of the utmost good faith is modified to the extent required by the provisions of this Act, and*

  (b) *the application of section 17 of the Marine Insurance Act 1906 (contracts of marine insurance are of utmost good faith), in relation to a contract of marine insurance which is a consumer insurance contract, is subject to the provisions of this Act.*

[*Note: Section 2(5) is repealed by the Insurance Act 2015, s 14(4) from 12 August 2016.*]

3   Reasonable care

(1) Whether or not a consumer has taken reasonable care not to make a misrepresentation is to be determined in the light of all the relevant circumstances.

(2) The following are examples of things which may need to be taken into account in making a determination under subsection (1)—

  (a) the type of consumer insurance contract in question, and its target market,

  (b) any relevant explanatory material or publicity produced or authorised by the insurer,

  (c) how clear, and how specific, the insurer's questions were,

  (d) in the case of a failure to respond to the insurer's questions in connection with the renewal or variation of a consumer insurance contract, how clearly the insurer communicated the importance of answering those questions (or the possible consequences of failing to do so),

  (e) whether or not an agent was acting for the consumer.

(3) The standard of care required is that of a reasonable consumer: but this is subject to subsections (4) and (5).

(4) If the insurer was, or ought to have been, aware of any particular characteristics or circumstances of the actual consumer, those are to be taken into account.

(5) A misrepresentation made dishonestly is always to be taken as showing lack of reasonable care.

4   Qualifying misrepresentations: definition and remedies

(1) An insurer has a remedy against a consumer for a misrepresentation made by the consumer before a consumer insurance contract was entered into or varied only if—

  (a) the consumer made the misrepresentation in breach of the duty set out in section 2(2), and

  (b) the insurer shows that without the misrepresentation, that insurer would not have entered into the contract (or agreed to the variation) at all, or would have done so only on different terms.

(2) A misrepresentation for which the insurer has a remedy against the consumer is referred to in this Act as a "qualifying misrepresentation".

(3) The only such remedies available are set out in Schedule 1.

5   Qualifying misrepresentations: classification and presumptions

(1) For the purposes of this Act, a qualifying misrepresentation (see section 4(2)) is either—

  (a) deliberate or reckless, or

  (b) careless.

(2) A qualifying misrepresentation is deliberate or reckless if the consumer—

  (a) knew that it was untrue or misleading, or did not care whether or not it was untrue or misleading, and

(b) knew that the matter to which the misrepresentation related was relevant to the insurer, or did not care whether or not it was relevant to the insurer.

(3) A qualifying misrepresentation is careless if it is not deliberate or reckless.

(4) It is for the insurer to show that a qualifying misrepresentation was deliberate or reckless.

(5) But it is to be presumed, unless the contrary is shown—

(a) that the consumer had the knowledge of a reasonable consumer, and

(b) that the consumer knew that a matter about which the insurer asked a clear and specific question was relevant to the insurer.

6   Warranties and representations

(1) This section applies to representations made by a consumer—

(a) in connection with a proposed consumer insurance contract, or

(b) in connection with a proposed variation to a consumer insurance contract.

(2) Such a representation is not capable of being converted into a warranty by means of any provision of the consumer insurance contract (or of the terms of the variation), or of any other contract (and whether by declaring the representation to form the basis of the contract or otherwise).

10   Contracting out

(1) A term of a consumer insurance contract, or of any other contract, which would put the consumer in a worse position as respects the matters mentioned in subsection (2) than the consumer would be in by virtue of the provisions of this Act is to that extent of no effect.

(2) The matters are—

(a) disclosure and representations by the consumer to the insurer before the contract is entered into or varied, and

(b) any remedies for qualifying misrepresentations (see section 4(2)).

(3) This section does not apply in relation to a contract for the settlement of a claim arising under a consumer insurance contract.

SCHEDULES

Section 4(3)   # SCHEDULE 1

INSURERS' REMEDIES FOR QUALIFYING MISREPRESENTATIONS

PART 1 CONTRACTS

1   General

This Part of this Schedule applies in relation to qualifying misrepresentations made in connection with consumer insurance contracts (for variations to them, see Part 2).

2   Deliberate or reckless misrepresentations

If a qualifying misrepresentation was deliberate or reckless, the insurer—

(a) may avoid the contract and refuse all claims, and

(b) need not return any of the premiums paid, except to the extent (if any) that it would be unfair to the consumer to retain them.

Careless misrepresentations—claims

3 If the qualifying misrepresentation was careless, paragraphs 4 to 8 apply in relation to any claim.

4 The insurer's remedies are based on what it would have done if the consumer had complied with the duty set out in section 2(2), and paragraphs 5 to 8 are to be read accordingly.

5 If the insurer would not have entered into the consumer insurance contract on any terms, the insurer may avoid the contract and refuse all claims, but must return the premiums paid.

6 If the insurer would have entered into the consumer insurance contract, but on different terms (excluding terms relating to the premium), the contract is to be treated as if it had been entered into on those different terms if the insurer so requires.

7 In addition, if the insurer would have entered into the consumer insurance contract (whether the terms relating to matters other than the premium would have been the same or different), but would have charged a higher premium, the insurer may reduce proportionately the amount to be paid on a claim.

8 "Reduce proportionately" means that the insurer need pay on the claim only X% of what it would otherwise have been under an obligation to pay under the terms of the contract (or, if applicable, under the different terms provided for by virtue of paragraph 6), where—

$$X = \frac{Pr\,emium\ actually\ charged \times 100}{Higher\ premium}$$

9 Careless misrepresentations—treatment of contract for the future

(1) This paragraph—

    (a) applies if the qualifying misrepresentation was careless, but

    (b) does not relate to any outstanding claim.

(2) Paragraphs 5 and 6 (as read with paragraph 4) apply as they apply where a claim has been made.

(3) Paragraph 7 (as read with paragraph 4) applies in relation to a claim yet to be made as it applies in relation to a claim which has been made.

(4) If by virtue of sub-paragraph (2) or (3), the insurer would have either (or both) of the rights conferred by paragraph 6 or 7, the insurer may—

    (a) give notice to that effect to the consumer, or

    (b) terminate the contract by giving reasonable notice to the consumer.

(5) But the insurer may not terminate a contract under sub-paragraph (4)(b) if it is wholly or mainly one of life insurance.

(6) If the insurer gives notice to the consumer under sub-paragraph (4)(a), the consumer may terminate the contract by giving reasonable notice to the insurer.

(7) If either party terminates the contract under this paragraph, the insurer must refund any premiums paid for the terminated cover in respect of the balance of the contract term.

(8) Termination of the contract under this paragraph does not affect the treatment of any claim arising under the contract in the period before termination.

(9) Nothing in this paragraph affects any contractual right to terminate the contract.

PART 4 SUPPLEMENTARY

17 Section 84 of the Marine Insurance Act 1906 (return of premium for failure of consideration) is to be read subject to the provisions of this Schedule in relation to contracts of marine insurance which are consumer insurance contracts.

Financial Services Act 2012

(2012, c. 21)

88 Exemption from liability in damages

(1) Neither the investigator appointed under section 84 nor a person appointed to conduct an investigation on the investigator's behalf under section 87(8) is to be liable in damages for anything

done or omitted in the discharge, or purported discharge, of functions in relation to the investigation of a complaint.

(2) Subsection (1) does not apply—

(a) if the act or omission is shown to have been in bad faith, or

(b) so as to prevent an award of damages made in respect of an act or omission on the ground that the act or omission was unlawful as a result of section 6(1) of the Human Rights Act 1998.

Crime and Courts Act 2013

(2013, c. 22)

Publishers of news-related material: damages and costs

34 Awards of exemplary damages

(1) This section applies where—

(a) a relevant claim is made against a person ("the defendant"),

(b) the defendant was a relevant publisher at the material time,

(c) the claim is related to the publication of news-related material, and

(d) the defendant is found liable in respect of the claim.

(2) Exemplary damages may not be awarded against the defendant in respect of the claim if the defendant was a member of an approved regulator at the material time.

(3) But the court may disregard subsection (2) if—

(a) the approved regulator imposed a penalty on the defendant in respect of the defendant's conduct or decided not to do so,

(b) the court considers, in light of the information available to the approved regulator when imposing the penalty or deciding not to impose one, that the regulator was manifestly irrational in imposing the penalty or deciding not to impose one, and

(c) the court is satisfied that, but for subsection (2), it would have made an award of exemplary damages under this section against the defendant.

(4) Where the court is not prevented from making an award of exemplary damages by subsection (2) (whether because that subsection does not apply or the court is permitted to disregard that subsection as a result of subsection (3)), the court—

(a) may make an award of exemplary damages if it considers it appropriate to do so in all the circumstances of the case, but

(b) may do so only under this section.

(5) Exemplary damages may be awarded under this section only if they are claimed.

(6) Exemplary damages may be awarded under this section only if the court is satisfied that—

(a) the defendant's conduct has shown a deliberate or reckless disregard of an outrageous nature for the claimant's rights,

(b) the conduct is such that the court should punish the defendant for it, and

(c) other remedies would not be adequate to punish that conduct.

(7) Exemplary damages may be awarded under this section whether or not another remedy is granted.

(8) The decision on the question of—

(a) whether exemplary damages are to be awarded under this section, or

(b) the amount of such damages,

must not be left to a jury.

35 Relevant considerations

(1) This section applies where the court is deciding whether the circumstances of the case make it appropriate for exemplary damages to be awarded under section 34.

(2) The court must have regard to the principle that exemplary damages must not usually be awarded if, at any time before the decision comes to be made, the defendant has been convicted of an offence involving the conduct complained of.

(3) The court must take account of the following—

   (a) whether membership of an approved regulator was available to the defendant at the material time;

   (b) if such membership was available, the reasons for the defendant not being a member;

   (c) so far as relevant in the case of the conduct complained of, whether internal compliance procedures of a satisfactory nature were in place and, if so, the extent to which they were adhered to in that case.

(4) The reference in subsection (3)(c) to "internal compliance procedures" being in place is a reference to any procedures put in place by the defendant for the purpose of ensuring that—

   (a) material is not obtained by or on behalf of the defendant in an inappropriate way, and

   (b) material is not published by the defendant in inappropriate circumstances.

(5) The court may regard deterring the defendant and others from similar conduct as an object of punishment.

(6) This section is not to be read as limiting the power of the court to take account of any other matters it considers relevant to its decision.

36 Amount of exemplary damages

(1) This section applies where the court decides to award exemplary damages under section 34.

(2) The court must have regard to these principles in determining the amount of exemplary damages—

   (a) the amount must not be more than the minimum needed to punish the defendant for the conduct complained of;

   (b) the amount must be proportionate to the seriousness of the conduct.

(3) The court must take account of these matters in determining the amount of exemplary damages—

   (a) the nature and extent of any loss or harm caused, or intended to be caused, by the defendant's conduct;

   (b) the nature and extent of any benefit the defendant derived or intended to derive from such conduct.

(4) The court may regard deterring the defendant and others from similar conduct as an object of punishment.

(5) This section is not to be read as limiting the power of the court to take account of any other matters it considers relevant to its decision.

37 Multiple claimants

(1) This section applies where a relevant publisher—

   (a) is a defendant to a relevant claim, and

   (b) is found liable to two or more persons in respect of the claim ("the persons affected").

(2) In deciding whether to award exemplary damages under section 34 or the amount of such damages to award (whether to one or more of the persons affected), the court must take account of any settlement or compromise by any persons of a claim in respect of the conduct.

(3) But the court may take account of any such settlement or compromise only if the defendant agrees.

(4) If the court awards exemplary damages under section 34 to two or more of the persons affected, the total amount awarded must be such that it does not punish the defendant excessively.

(5) If the court awards exemplary damages under section 34 to one or more of the persons affected, no later claim may be made for exemplary damages as regards the conduct.

38 Multiple defendants

(1) Any liability of two or more persons for exemplary damages awarded under section 34 is several (and not joint or joint and several).

(2) Subsection (1) has effect subject to the law relating to the liability of a partner for the conduct of another partner.

(3) Where the liability of two or more persons for exemplary damages is several, no contribution in respect of the damages may be recovered by any of them under section 1 of the Civil Liability (Contribution) Act 1978.

39   Awards of aggravated damages

(1) This section applies where—

    (a) a relevant claim is made against a person ("the defendant"),

    (b) the defendant was a relevant publisher at the material time,

    (c) the claim is related to the publication of news-related material, and

    (d) the defendant is found liable in respect of the claim.

(2) Aggravated damages may be awarded against the defendant only to compensate for mental distress and not for purposes of punishment.

(3) In this section, "aggravated damages" means damages that were commonly called aggravated before the passing of this Act and which—

    (a) are awarded against a person in respect of the person's motive or exceptional conduct, but

    (b) are not exemplary damages or restitutionary damages.

(4) Nothing in this section is to be read as implying that, in cases where this section does not apply, aggravated damages may be awarded for purposes of punishment.

40   Awards of costs

(1) This section applies where—

    (a) a relevant claim is made against a person ("the defendant"),

    (b) the defendant was a relevant publisher at the material time, and

    (c) the claim is related to the publication of news-related material.

(2) If the defendant was a member of an approved regulator at the time when the claim was commenced (or was unable to be a member at that time for reasons beyond the defendant's control or it would have been unreasonable in the circumstances for the defendant to have been a member at that time), the court must not award costs against the defendant unless satisfied that—

    (a) the issues raised by the claim could not have been resolved by using an arbitration scheme of the approved regulator, or

    (b) it is just and equitable in all the circumstances of the case to award costs against the defendant.

(3) If the defendant was not a member of an approved regulator at the time when the claim was commenced (but would have been able to be a member at that time and it would have been reasonable in the circumstances for the defendant to have been a member at that time), the court must award costs against the defendant unless satisfied that—

    (a) the issues raised by the claim could not have been resolved by using an arbitration scheme of the approved regulator (had the defendant been a member), or

    (b) it is just and equitable in all the circumstances of the case to make a different award of costs or make no award of costs.

(4) The Secretary of State must take steps to put in place arrangements for protecting the position in costs of parties to relevant claims who have entered into agreements under section 58 of the Courts and Legal Services Act 1990.

(5) This section is not to be read as limiting any power to make rules of court.

(6) This section does not apply until such time as a body is first recognised as an approved regulator.

41   Meaning of "relevant publisher"

(1) In sections 34 to 40, "relevant publisher" means a person who, in the course of a business (whether or not carried on with a view to profit), publishes news-related material—

    (a) which is written by different authors, and

    (b) which is to any extent subject to editorial control.

This is subject to subsections (5) and (6).

(2) News-related material is "subject to editorial control" if there is a person (whether or not the publisher of the material) who has editorial or equivalent responsibility for—

(a) the content of the material,

(b) how the material is to be presented, and

(c) the decision to publish it.

(3) A person who is the operator of a website is not to be taken as having editorial or equivalent responsibility for the decision to publish any material on the site, or for content of the material, if the person did not post the material on the site.

(4) The fact that the operator of the website may moderate statements posted on it by others does not matter for the purposes of subsection (3).

(5) A person is not a "relevant publisher" if the person is specified by name in Schedule 15.

(6) A person is not a "relevant publisher" in so far as the person's publication of news-related material is in a capacity or case of a description specified in Schedule 15.

(7) But a person who is not a "relevant publisher" as a result of paragraph 8 of that Schedule (micro-businesses) is nevertheless to be regarded as such if the person was a member of an approved regulator at the material time.

42   Other interpretative provisions

(1) This section applies for the purposes of sections 34 to 41.

(2) "Approved regulator" means a body recognised as a regulator of relevant publishers.

(3) For the purposes of subsection (2), a body is "recognised" as a regulator of relevant publishers if it is so recognised by any body established by Royal Charter (whether established before or after the coming into force of this section) with the purpose of carrying on activities relating to the recognition of independent regulators of relevant publishers.

(4) "Relevant claim" means a civil claim made in respect of any of the following—

(a) libel;

(b) slander;

(c) breach of confidence;

(d) misuse of private information;

(e) malicious falsehood;

(f) harassment.

(5) For the purposes of subsection (4)—

(a) the reference to a claim made in respect of the misuse of private information does not include a reference to a claim made by virtue of section 13 of the Data Protection Act 1998 (damage or distress suffered as a result of a contravention of a requirement of that Act);

(b) the reference to a claim made in respect of harassment is a reference to a claim made under the Protection from Harassment Act 1997.

(6) The "material time", in relation to a relevant claim, is the time of the events giving rise to the claim.

(7) "News-related material" means—

(a) news or information about current affairs,

(b) opinion about matters relating to the news or current affairs, or

(c) gossip about celebrities, other public figures or other persons in the news.

(8) A relevant claim is related to the publication of news-related material if the claim results from—

(a) the publication of news-related material, or

(b) activities carried on in connection with the publication of such material (whether or not the material is in fact published).

(9) A reference to the "publication" of material is a reference to publication—

(a) on a website,

(b) in hard copy, or

(c) by any other means;

and references to a person who "publishes" material are to be read accordingly.

(10) A reference to "conduct" includes a reference to omissions; and a reference to a person's conduct includes a reference to a person's conduct after the events giving rise to the claim concerned.

Defamation Act 2013

(2013, c. 26)

Requirement of serious harm

1 Serious harm

(1) A statement is not defamatory unless its publication has caused or is likely to cause serious harm to the reputation of the claimant.

(2) For the purposes of this section, harm to the reputation of a body that trades for profit is not "serious harm" unless it has caused or is likely to cause the body serious financial loss.

Defences

2 Truth

(1) It is a defence to an action for defamation for the defendant to show that the imputation conveyed by the statement complained of is substantially true.

(2) Subsection (3) applies in an action for defamation if the statement complained of conveys two or more distinct imputations.

(3) If one or more of the imputations is not shown to be substantially true, the defence under this section does not fail if, having regard to the imputations which are shown to be substantially true, the imputations which are not shown to be substantially true do not seriously harm the claimant's reputation.

(4) The common law defence of justification is abolished and, accordingly, section 5 of the Defamation Act 1952 (justification) is repealed.

3 Honest opinion

(1) It is a defence to an action for defamation for the defendant to show that the following conditions are met.

(2) The first condition is that the statement complained of was a statement of opinion.

(3) The second condition is that the statement complained of indicated, whether in general or specific terms, the basis of the opinion.

(4) The third condition is that an honest person could have held the opinion on the basis of—

(a) any fact which existed at the time the statement complained of was published;

(b) anything asserted to be a fact in a privileged statement published before the statement complained of.

(5) The defence is defeated if the claimant shows that the defendant did not hold the opinion.

(6) Subsection (5) does not apply in a case where the statement complained of was published by the defendant but made by another person ("the author"); and in such a case the defence is defeated if the claimant shows that the defendant knew or ought to have known that the author did not hold the opinion.

(7) For the purposes of subsection (4)(b) a statement is a "privileged statement" if the person responsible for its publication would have one or more of the following defences if an action for defamation were brought in respect of it—

(a) a defence under section 4 (publication on matter of public interest);

(b) a defence under section 6 (peer-reviewed statement in scientific or academic journal);

(c) a defence under section 14 of the Defamation Act 1996 (reports of court proceedings protected by absolute privilege);

(d) a defence under section 15 of that Act (other reports protected by qualified privilege).

(8) The common law defence of fair comment is abolished and, accordingly, section 6 of the Defamation Act 1952 (fair comment) is repealed.

4 Publication on matter of public interest

(1) It is a defence to an action for defamation for the defendant to show that—

(a) the statement complained of was, or formed part of, a statement on a matter of public interest; and

(b) the defendant reasonably believed that publishing the statement complained of was in the public interest.

(2) Subject to subsections (3) and (4), in determining whether the defendant has shown the matters mentioned in subsection (1), the court must have regard to all the circumstances of the case.

(3) If the statement complained of was, or formed part of, an accurate and impartial account of a dispute to which the claimant was a party, the court must in determining whether it was reasonable for the defendant to believe that publishing the statement was in the public interest disregard any omission of the defendant to take steps to verify the truth of the imputation conveyed by it.

(4) In determining whether it was reasonable for the defendant to believe that publishing the statement complained of was in the public interest, the court must make such allowance for editorial judgement as it considers appropriate.

(5) For the avoidance of doubt, the defence under this section may be relied upon irrespective of whether the statement complained of is a statement of fact or a statement of opinion.

(6) The common law defence known as the Reynolds defence is abolished.

5 Operators of websites

(1) This section applies where an action for defamation is brought against the operator of a website in respect of a statement posted on the website.

(2) It is a defence for the operator to show that it was not the operator who posted the statement on the website.

(3) The defence is defeated if the claimant shows that—

(a) it was not possible for the claimant to identify the person who posted the statement,

(b) the claimant gave the operator a notice of complaint in relation to the statement, and

(c) the operator failed to respond to the notice of complaint in accordance with any provision contained in regulations.

(4) For the purposes of subsection (3)(a), it is possible for a claimant to "identify" a person only if the claimant has sufficient information to bring proceedings against the person.

(5) Regulations may—

(a) make provision as to the action required to be taken by an operator of a website in response to a notice of complaint (which may in particular include action relating to the identity or contact details of the person who posted the statement and action relating to its removal);

(b) make provision specifying a time limit for the taking of any such action;

(c) make provision conferring on the court a discretion to treat action taken after the expiry of a time limit as having been taken before the expiry;

(d) make any other provision for the purposes of this section.

(6) Subject to any provision made by virtue of subsection (7), a notice of complaint is a notice which—

(a) specifies the complainant's name,

(b) sets out the statement concerned and explains why it is defamatory of the complainant,

(c) specifies where on the website the statement was posted, and

(d) contains such other information as may be specified in regulations.

(7) Regulations may make provision about the circumstances in which a notice which is not a notice of complaint is to be treated as a notice of complaint for the purposes of this section or any provision made under it.

(8) Regulations under this section—

(a) may make different provision for different circumstances;

(b) are to be made by statutory instrument.

(9) A statutory instrument containing regulations under this section may not be made unless a draft of the instrument has been laid before, and approved by a resolution of, each House of Parliament.

(10) In this section "regulations" means regulations made by the Secretary of State.

(11) The defence under this section is defeated if the claimant shows that the operator of the website has acted with malice in relation to the posting of the statement concerned.

(12) The defence under this section is not defeated by reason only of the fact that the operator of the website moderates the statements posted on it by others.

6   Peer-reviewed statement in scientific or academic journal etc

(1) The publication of a statement in a scientific or academic journal (whether published in electronic form or otherwise) is privileged if the following conditions are met.

(2) The first condition is that the statement relates to a scientific or academic matter.

(3) The second condition is that before the statement was published in the journal an independent review of the statement's scientific or academic merit was carried out by—

(a) the editor of the journal, and

(b) one or more persons with expertise in the scientific or academic matter concerned.

(4) Where the publication of a statement in a scientific or academic journal is privileged by virtue of subsection (1), the publication in the same journal of any assessment of the statement's scientific or academic merit is also privileged if—

(a) the assessment was written by one or more of the persons who carried out the independent review of the statement; and

(b) the assessment was written in the course of that review.

(5) Where the publication of a statement or assessment is privileged by virtue of this section, the publication of a fair and accurate copy of, extract from or summary of the statement or assessment is also privileged.

(6) A publication is not privileged by virtue of this section if it is shown to be made with malice.

(7) Nothing in this section is to be construed—

(a) as protecting the publication of matter the publication of which is prohibited by law;

(b) as limiting any privilege subsisting apart from this section.

(8) The reference in subsection (3)(a) to "the editor of the journal" is to be read, in the case of a journal with more than one editor, as a reference to the editor or editors who were responsible for deciding to publish the statement concerned.

Single publication rule

8   Single publication rule

(1) This section applies if a person—

(a) publishes a statement to the public ("the first publication"), and

(b) subsequently publishes (whether or not to the public) that statement or a statement which is substantially the same.

(2) In subsection (1) "publication to the public" includes publication to a section of the public.

(3) For the purposes of section 4A of the Limitation Act 1980 (time limit for actions for defamation etc) any cause of action against the person for defamation in respect of the subsequent publication is to be treated as having accrued on the date of the first publication.

(4) This section does not apply in relation to the subsequent publication if the manner of that publication is materially different from the manner of the first publication.

(5) In determining whether the manner of a subsequent publication is materially different from the manner of the first publication, the matters to which the court may have regard include (amongst other matters)—

    (a) the level of prominence that a statement is given;

    (b) the extent of the subsequent publication.

(6) Where this section applies—

    (a) it does not affect the court's discretion under section 32A of the Limitation Act 1980 (discretionary exclusion of time limit for actions for defamation etc), and

    (b) the reference in subsection (1)(a) of that section to the operation of section 4A of that Act is a reference to the operation of section 4A together with this section.

Jurisdiction

9   Action against a person not domiciled in the UK or a Member State etc

(1) This section applies to an action for defamation against a person who is not domiciled—

    (a) in the United Kingdom;

    (b) in another Member State; or

    (c) in a state which is for the time being a contracting party to the Lugano Convention.

(2) A court does not have jurisdiction to hear and determine an action to which this section applies unless the court is satisfied that, of all the places in which the statement complained of has been published, England and Wales is clearly the most appropriate place in which to bring an action in respect of the statement.

(3) The references in subsection (2) to the statement complained of include references to any statement which conveys the same, or substantially the same, imputation as the statement complained of.

(4) For the purposes of this section—

    (a) a person is domiciled in the United Kingdom or in another Member State if the person is domiciled there for the purposes of the Brussels Regulation;

    (b) a person is domiciled in a state which is a contracting party to the Lugano Convention if the person is domiciled in the state for the purposes of that Convention.

(5) In this section—

"the Brussels Regulation" means [Regulation (EU) No. 1215/2012 of the European Parliament and of the Council of 12 December 2012 on jurisdiction and the recognition and enforcement of judgments in civil and commercial matters (recast), as amended from time to time and as applied by virtue of the Agreement made on 19 October 2005 between the European Community and the Kingdom of Denmark on jurisdiction and the recognition and enforcement of judgments in civil and commercial matters (OJ No L 299, 16.11.2005, p62; OJ No L79, 21.3.2013, p4)];

"the Lugano Convention" means the Convention on jurisdiction and the recognition and enforcement of judgments in civil and commercial matters, between the European Community and the Republic of Iceland, the Kingdom of Norway, the Swiss Confederation and the Kingdom of Denmark signed on behalf of the European Community on 30th October 2007.

10   Action against a person who was not the author, editor etc

(1) A court does not have jurisdiction to hear and determine an action for defamation brought against a person who was not the author, editor or publisher of the statement complained of unless the court is satisfied that it is not reasonably practicable for an action to be brought against the author, editor or publisher.

(2) In this section "author", "editor" and "publisher" have the same meaning as in section 1 of the Defamation Act 1996.

Summary of court judgment

12   Power of court to order a summary of its judgment to be published

(1) Where a court gives judgment for the claimant in an action for defamation the court may order the defendant to publish a summary of the judgment.

(2) The wording of any summary and the time, manner, form and place of its publication are to be for the parties to agree.

(3) If the parties cannot agree on the wording, the wording is to be settled by the court.

(4) If the parties cannot agree on the time, manner, form or place of publication, the court may give such directions as to those matters as it considers reasonable and practicable in the circumstances.

(5) This section does not apply where the court gives judgment for the claimant under section 8(3) of the Defamation Act 1996 (summary disposal of claims).

Removal, etc of statements

13   Order to remove statement or cease distribution etc

(1) Where a court gives judgment for the claimant in an action for defamation the court may order—

   (a) the operator of a website on which the defamatory statement is posted to remove the statement, or

   (b) any person who was not the author, editor or publisher of the defamatory statement to stop distributing, selling or exhibiting material containing the statement.

(2) In this section "author", "editor" and "publisher" have the same meaning as in section 1 of the Defamation Act 1996.

(3) Subsection (1) does not affect the power of the court apart from that subsection.

Slander

14   Special damage

(2) The publication of a statement that conveys the imputation that a person has a contagious or infectious disease does not give rise to a cause of action for slander unless the publication causes the person special damage.

General provisions

15   Meaning of "publish" and "statement"

In this Act—

   "publish" and "publication", in relation to a statement, have the meaning they have for the purposes of the law of defamation generally;

   "statement" means words, pictures, visual images, gestures or any other method of signifying meaning.

Marriage (Same Sex Couples) Act 2013

(2013, c. 30)

2   Marriage according to religious rites: no compulsion to solemnize etc

(1) A person may not be compelled by any means (including by the enforcement of a contract or a statutory or other legal requirement) to—

   (a) undertake an opt-in activity, or

   (b) refrain from undertaking an opt-out activity.

(2) A person may not be compelled by any means (including by the enforcement of a contract or a statutory or other legal requirement)—

    (a) to conduct a relevant marriage,

    (b) to be present at, carry out, or otherwise participate in, a relevant marriage, or

    (c) to consent to a relevant marriage being conducted,

where the reason for the person not doing that thing is that the relevant marriage concerns a same sex couple.

Prevention of Social Housing Fraud Act 2013

(2013, c. 3)

5 Unlawful profit orders: civil proceedings

(1) The court may, on the application of the landlord of a dwelling-house let under a secure or an assured tenancy, make an unlawful profit order if—

    (a) in the case of a secure tenancy, the conditions in subsection (3) are met, and

    (b) in the case of an assured tenancy, the conditions in subsection (4) are met.

(2) An "unlawful profit order" is an order requiring the tenant against whom it is made to pay the landlord an amount representing the profit made by the tenant from the conduct described in subsection (3)(a) or (4)(c).

(3) The conditions in the case of a secure tenancy are that a tenant under the tenancy—

    (a) in breach of an express or implied term of the tenancy, has sub-let or parted with possession of—

        (i) the whole of the dwelling-house, or

        (ii) part of the dwelling-house without the landlord's written consent,

    (b) has ceased to occupy the dwelling-house as the tenant's only or principal home, and

    (c) has received money as a result of the conduct described in paragraph (a).

(4) The conditions in the case of an assured tenancy are that—

    (a) the landlord is a private registered provider of social housing or a registered social landlord,

    (b) the tenancy is not a shared ownership lease,

    (c) in breach of an express or implied term of the tenancy, a tenant under the tenancy has sub-let or parted with possession of the whole or part of the dwelling-house,

    (d) the tenant has ceased to occupy the dwelling-house as the tenant's only or principal home, and

    (e) the tenant has received money as a result of the conduct described in paragraph (c).

(5) The amount payable under an unlawful profit order must be such amount as the court considers appropriate, having regard to any evidence and to any representations that are made by or on behalf of the landlord or the tenant, but subject to subsections (6) and (7).

(6) The maximum amount payable under an unlawful profit order is calculated as follows—

Step 1 Determine the total amount the tenant received as a result of the conduct described in subsection (3)(a) or (4)(c) (or the best estimate of that amount).

Step 2 Deduct from the amount determined under step 1 the total amount, if any, paid by the tenant as rent to the landlord (including service charges) over the period during which the conduct described in subsection (3)(a) or (4)(c) took place.

(7) Where an unlawful profit order has been made against the tenant under section 4, an order under this section may only provide for the landlord to recover an amount equal to the aggregate of the following—

    (a) any amount by which the amount of the tenant's profit found under this section exceeds the amount payable under the order made under section 4, and

(b) a sum equal to any portion of the amount payable under the order made under section 4 that the landlord fails to recover,

and the landlord may not enforce the order under this section, so far as it relates to a sum mentioned in paragraph (b), without the leave of the court.

Anti-social Behaviour, Crime and Policing Act 2014

(2014, c. 12)

1 Power to grant injunctions

(1) A court may grant an injunction under this section against a person aged 10 or over ("the respondent") if two conditions are met.

(2) The first condition is that the court is satisfied, on the balance of probabilities, that the respondent has engaged or threatens to engage in anti-social behaviour.

(3) The second condition is that the court considers it just and convenient to grant the injunction for the purpose of preventing the respondent from engaging in anti-social behaviour.

(4) An injunction under this section may for the purpose of preventing the respondent from engaging in anti-social behaviour—

(a) prohibit the respondent from doing anything described in the injunction;

(b) require the respondent to do anything described in the injunction.

2 Meaning of "anti-social behaviour"

(1) In this Part "anti-social behaviour" means—

(a) conduct that has caused, or is likely to cause, harassment, alarm or distress to any person,

(b) conduct capable of causing nuisance or annoyance to a person in relation to that person's occupation of residential premises, or

(c) conduct capable of causing housing-related nuisance or annoyance to any person.

4 Power of arrest

(1) A court granting an injunction under section 1 may attach a power of arrest to a prohibition or requirement of the injunction if the court thinks that—

(a) the anti-social behaviour in which the respondent has engaged or threatens to engage consists of or includes the use or threatened use of violence against other persons, or

(b) there is a significant risk of harm to other persons from the respondent.

9 Arrest without warrant

(1) Where a power of arrest is attached to a provision of an injunction under section 1, a constable may arrest the respondent without warrant if he or she has reasonable cause to suspect that the respondent is in breach of the provision.

10 Issue of arrest warrant

(1) If the person who applied for an injunction under section 1 thinks that the respondent is in breach of any of its provisions, the person may apply for the issue of a warrant for the respondent's arrest.

22 Power to make orders

(1) This section applies where a person ("the offender") is convicted of an offence.

(2) The court may make a criminal behaviour order against the offender if two conditions are met.

(3) The first condition is that the court is satisfied, beyond reasonable doubt, that the offender has engaged in behaviour that caused or was likely to cause harassment, alarm or distress to any person.

(4) The second condition is that the court considers that making the order will help in preventing the offender from engaging in such behaviour.

(5) A criminal behaviour order is an order which, for the purpose of preventing the offender from engaging in such behaviour—

(a) prohibits the offender from doing anything described in the order;

(b) requires the offender to do anything described in the order.

30   Breach of order

(1) A person who without reasonable excuse—

(a) does anything he or she is prohibited from doing by a criminal behaviour order, or

(b) fails to do anything he or she is required to do by a criminal behaviour order,

commits an offence.

35   Directions excluding a person from an area

(1) If the conditions in subsections (2) and (3) are met and an authorisation is in force under section 34, a constable in uniform may direct a person who is in a public place in the locality specified in the authorisation—

(a) to leave the locality (or part of the locality), and

(b) not to return to the locality (or part of the locality) for the period specified in the direction ("the exclusion period").

(2) The first condition is that the constable has reasonable grounds to suspect that the behaviour of the person in the locality has contributed or is likely to contribute to—

(a) members of the public in the locality being harassed, alarmed or distressed, or

(b) the occurrence in the locality of crime or disorder.

(3) The second condition is that the constable considers that giving a direction to the person is necessary for the purpose of removing or reducing the likelihood of the events mentioned in subsection (2)(a) or (b).

37   Surrender of property

(1) A constable who gives a person a direction under section 35 may also direct the person to surrender to the constable any item in the person's possession or control that the constable reasonably believes has been used or is likely to be used in behaviour that harasses, alarms or distresses members of the public.

50   Forfeiture of item used in commission of offence

(1) A court before which a person is convicted of an offence under section 48 may order the forfeiture of any item that was used in the commission of the offence.

54   Exemption from liability

(1) A local authority exercising or purporting to exercise a power under section 47(2) is not liable to an occupier or owner of land for damages or otherwise (whether at common law or otherwise) arising out of anything done or omitted to be done in the exercise or purported exercise of that power.

(2) A person carrying out work under section 47(2), or a person by or on whose behalf work is carried out under section 49(2)(b), is not liable to an occupier or owner of land for damages or otherwise (whether at common law or otherwise) arising out of anything done or omitted to be done in carrying out that work.

(3) Subsections (1) and (2) do not apply—

(a) to an act or omission shown to have been in bad faith, or

(b) to liability arising out of a failure to exercise due care and attention.

(4) Subsections (1) and (2) do not apply so as to prevent an award of damages made in respect of an act or omission on the ground that the act or omission was unlawful by virtue of section 6(1) of the Human Rights Act 1998.

(5) This section does not affect any other exemption from liability (whether at common law or otherwise).

64   Orders restricting public right of way over highway

(1) A local authority may not make a public spaces protection order that restricts the public right of way over a highway without considering—

(a) the likely effect of making the order on the occupiers of premises adjoining or adjacent to the highway;

(b) the likely effect of making the order on other persons in the locality;

(c) in a case where the highway constitutes a through route, the availability of a reasonably convenient alternative route.

76   Power to issue closure notices

(1) A police officer of at least the rank of inspector, or the local authority, may issue a closure notice if satisfied on reasonable grounds—

(a) that the use of particular premises has resulted, or (if the notice is not issued) is likely soon to result, in nuisance to members of the public, or

(b) that there has been, or (if the notice is not issued) is likely soon to be, disorder near those premises associated with the use of those premises,

and that the notice is necessary to prevent the nuisance or disorder from continuing, recurring or occurring.

80   Power of court to make closure orders

(1) Whenever a closure notice is issued an application must be made to a magistrates' court for a closure order (unless the notice has been cancelled under section 78).

(2) An application for a closure order must be made—

(a) by a constable, if the closure notice was issued by a police officer;

(b) by the authority that issued the closure notice, if the notice was issued by a local authority.

(5) The court may make a closure order if it is satisfied—

(a) that a person has engaged, or (if the order is not made) is likely to engage, in disorderly, offensive or criminal behaviour on the premises, or

(b) that the use of the premises has resulted, or (if the order is not made) is likely to result, in serious nuisance to members of the public, or

(c) that there has been, or (if the order is not made) is likely to be, disorder near those premises associated with the use of those premises,

and that the order is necessary to prevent the behaviour, nuisance or disorder from continuing, recurring or occurring.

(6) A closure order is an order prohibiting access to the premises for a period specified in the order.

The period may not exceed 3 months.

(7) A closure order may prohibit access—

(a) by all persons, or by all persons except those specified, or by all persons except those of a specified description;

(b) at all times, or at all times except those specified;

(c) in all circumstances, or in all circumstances except those specified.

(8) A closure order—

(a) may be made in respect of the whole or any part of the premises;

(b) may include provision about access to a part of the building or structure of which the premises form part.

88   Reimbursement of costs

(1) A local policing body or a local authority that incurs expenditure for the purpose of clearing, securing or maintaining premises in respect of which a closure order is in force may apply to the court that made the order for an order under this section.

(2) On an application under this section the court may make whatever order it thinks appropriate for the reimbursement (in full or in part) by the owner or occupier of the premises of the expenditure mentioned in subsection (1).

89   Exemption from liability

(1) A police officer, or the chief officer of police under whose direction or control he or she acts, is not liable for damages in proceedings for—

(a) judicial review, or

(b) the tort of negligence or misfeasance in public office,

arising out of anything done or omitted to be done by the police officer in the exercise or purported exercise of a power under this Chapter.

(2) A local authority is not liable for damages in proceedings for—

(a) judicial review, or

(b) the tort of negligence or misfeasance in public office,

arising out of anything done or omitted to be done by the authority in the exercise or purported exercise of a power under this Chapter.

(3) Subsections (1) and (2) do not apply to an act or omission shown to have been in bad faith.

(4) Subsections (1) and (2) do not apply so as to prevent an award of damages made in respect of an act or omission on the ground that the act or omission was unlawful by virtue of section 6(1) of the Human Rights Act 1998.

(5) This section does not affect any other exemption from liability (whether at common law or otherwise).

90   Compensation

(1) A person who claims to have incurred financial loss in consequence of a closure notice or a closure order may apply to the appropriate court for compensation.

(5) On an application under this section the court may order the payment of compensation out of central funds if it is satisfied—

(a) that the applicant is not associated with the use of the premises, or the behaviour on the premises, on the basis of which the closure notice was issued or the closure order made,

(b) if the applicant is the owner or occupier of the premises, that the applicant took reasonable steps to prevent that use or behaviour,

(c) that the applicant has incurred financial loss in consequence of the notice or order, and

(d) that having regard to all the circumstances it is appropriate to order payment of compensation in respect of that loss.

Immigration Act 2014

(2014, c. 22)

22   Persons disqualified by immigration status not to be leased premises

(1) A landlord must not authorise an adult to occupy premises under a residential tenancy agreement if the adult is disqualified as a result of their immigration status.

(9) A contravention of this section does not affect the validity or enforceability of any provision of a residential tenancy agreement by virtue of any rule of law relating to the validity or enforceability of contracts in circumstances involving illegality.

Local Audit and Accountability Act 2014

(2014, c. 2)

14   Limitation of local auditor's liability

(1) This section applies in relation to an agreement (a "liability limitation agreement") that purports to limit the amount of a liability owed to a relevant authority by its local auditor in respect of any negligence, default, breach of duty or breach of trust occurring in the course of the audit of accounts, of which the auditor may be guilty in relation to the authority.

(2) A liability limitation agreement must comply with regulations made by the Secretary of State.

(7) A liability limitation agreement that complies with regulations under subsection (2) is not subject to section 2(2) or 3(2)(a) of the Unfair Contract Terms Act 1977.

Consumer Rights Act 2015

(2015, c. 15)

Chapter 1   Introduction

1   Where Part 1 applies

(1) This Part applies where there is an agreement between a trader and a consumer for the trader to supply goods, digital content or services, if the agreement is a contract.

(2) It applies whether the contract is written or oral or implied from the parties' conduct, or more than one of these combined.

(3) Any of Chapters 2, 3 and 4 may apply to a contract—
  (a) if it is a contract for the trader to supply goods, see Chapter 2;
  (b) if it is a contract for the trader to supply digital content, see Chapter 3 (also, subsection (6));
  (c) if it is a contract for the trader to supply a service, see Chapter 4 (also, subsection (6)).

(4) In each case the Chapter applies even if the contract also covers something covered by another Chapter (a mixed contract).

(5) Two or all three of those Chapters may apply to a mixed contract.

2   Key definitions

(1) These definitions apply in this Part (as well as the definitions in section 59).

(2) "Trader" means a person acting for purposes relating to that person's trade, business, craft or profession, whether acting personally or through another person acting in the trader's name or on the trader's behalf.

(3) "Consumer" means an individual acting for purposes that are wholly or mainly outside that individual's trade, business, craft or profession.

(4) A trader claiming that an individual was not acting for purposes wholly or mainly outside the individual's trade, business, craft or profession must prove it.

(5) For the purposes of Chapter 2, except to the extent mentioned in subsection (6), a person is not a consumer in relation to a sales contract if—
  (a) the goods are second hand goods sold at public auction, and
  (b) individuals have the opportunity of attending the sale in person.

(6) A person is a consumer in relation to such a contract for the purposes of—
  (a) sections 11(4) and (5), 12, 28 and 29, and
  (b) the other provisions of Chapter 2 as they apply in relation to those sections.

(8) "Goods" means any tangible moveable items, but that includes water, gas and electricity if and only if they are put up for supply in a limited volume or set quantity.

(9) "Digital content" means data which are produced and supplied in digital form.

Chapter 2 Goods

What goods contracts are covered?

3   Contracts covered by this Chapter

(1) This Chapter applies to a contract for a trader to supply goods to a consumer.

(2) It applies only if the contract is one of these (defined for the purposes of this Part in sections 5 to 8)—

    (a) a sales contract;

    (b) a contract for the hire of goods;

    (c) a hire-purchase agreement;

    (d) a contract for transfer of goods.

(4) A contract to which this Chapter applies is referred to in this Part as a "contract to supply goods".

(5) Contracts to supply goods include—

    (a) contracts entered into between one part owner and another;

    (b) contracts for the transfer of an undivided share in goods;

    (c) contracts that are absolute and contracts that are conditional.

4   Ownership of goods

(1) In this Chapter ownership of goods means the general property in goods, not merely a special property.

5   Sales contracts

(1) A contract is a sales contract if under it—

    (a) the trader transfers or agrees to transfer ownership of goods to the consumer, and

    (b) the consumer pays or agrees to pay the price.

(2) A contract is a sales contract (whether or not it would be one under subsection (1)) if under the contract—

    (a) goods are to be manufactured or produced and the trader agrees to supply them to the consumer,

    (b) on being supplied, the goods will be owned by the consumer, and

    (c) the consumer pays or agrees to pay the price.

(3) A sales contract may be conditional (see section 3(5)), but in this Part "conditional sales contract" means a sales contract under which—

    (a) the price for the goods or part of it is payable by instalments, and

    (b) the trader retains ownership of the goods until the conditions specified in the contract (for the payment of instalments or otherwise) are met;

and it makes no difference whether or not the consumer possesses the goods.

6   Contracts for the hire of goods

(1) A contract is for the hire of goods if under it the trader gives or agrees to give the consumer possession of the goods with the right to use them, subject to the terms of the contract, for a period determined in accordance with the contract.

(2) But a contract is not for the hire of goods if it is a hire-purchase agreement.

7   Hire-purchase agreements

(1) A contract is a hire-purchase agreement if it meets the two conditions set out below.

(2) The first condition is that under the contract goods are hired by the trader in return for periodical payments by the consumer (and "hired" is to be read in accordance with section 6(1)).

(3) The second condition is that under the contract ownership of the goods will transfer to the consumer if the terms of the contract are complied with and—

(a) the consumer exercises an option to buy the goods,

(b) any party to the contract does an act specified in it, or

(c) an event specified in the contract occurs.

(4) But a contract is not a hire-purchase agreement if it is a conditional sales contract.

8 Contracts for transfer of goods

A contract to supply goods is a contract for transfer of goods if under it the trader transfers or agrees to transfer ownership of the goods to the consumer and—

(a) the consumer provides or agrees to provide consideration otherwise than by paying a price, or

(b) the contract is, for any other reason, not a sales contract or a hire-purchase agreement.

What statutory rights are there under a goods contract?

9 Goods to be of satisfactory quality

(1) Every contract to supply goods is to be treated as including a term that the quality of the goods is satisfactory.

(2) The quality of goods is satisfactory if they meet the standard that a reasonable person would consider satisfactory, taking account of—

(a) any description of the goods,

(b) the price or other consideration for the goods (if relevant), and

(c) all the other relevant circumstances (see subsection (5)).

(3) The quality of goods includes their state and condition; and the following aspects (among others) are in appropriate cases aspects of the quality of goods—

(a) fitness for all the purposes for which goods of that kind are usually supplied;

(b) appearance and finish;

(c) freedom from minor defects;

(d) safety;

(e) durability.

(4) The term mentioned in subsection (1) does not cover anything which makes the quality of the goods unsatisfactory—

(a) which is specifically drawn to the consumer's attention before the contract is made,

(b) where the consumer examines the goods before the contract is made, which that examination ought to reveal, or

(c) in the case of a contract to supply goods by sample, which would have been apparent on a reasonable examination of the sample.

(5) The relevant circumstances mentioned in subsection (2)(c) include any public statement about the specific characteristics of the goods made by the trader, the producer or any representative of the trader or the producer.

(6) That includes, in particular, any public statement made in advertising or labelling.

(7) But a public statement is not a relevant circumstance for the purposes of subsection (2)(c) if the trader shows that—

(a) when the contract was made, the trader was not, and could not reasonably have been, aware of the statement,

(b) before the contract was made, the statement had been publicly withdrawn or, to the extent that it contained anything which was incorrect or misleading, it had been publicly corrected, or

(c) the consumer's decision to contract for the goods could not have been influenced by the statement.

(8) In a contract to supply goods a term about the quality of the goods may be treated as included as a matter of custom.

(9) See section 19 for a consumer's rights if the trader is in breach of a term that this section requires to be treated as included in a contract.

10   Goods to be fit for particular purpose

(1) Subsection (3) applies to a contract to supply goods if before the contract is made the consumer makes known to the trader (expressly or by implication) any particular purpose for which the consumer is contracting for the goods.

(2) Subsection (3) also applies to a contract to supply goods if—

    (a) the goods were previously sold by a credit-broker to the trader,

    (b) in the case of a sales contract or contract for transfer of goods, the consideration or part of it is a sum payable by instalments, and

    (c) before the contract is made, the consumer makes known to the credit-broker (expressly or by implication) any particular purpose for which the consumer is contracting for the goods.

(3) The contract is to be treated as including a term that the goods are reasonably fit for that purpose, whether or not that is a purpose for which goods of that kind are usually supplied.

(4) Subsection (3) does not apply if the circumstances show that the consumer does not rely, or it is unreasonable for the consumer to rely, on the skill or judgment of the trader or credit-broker.

(5) In a contract to supply goods a term about the fitness of the goods for a particular purpose may be treated as included as a matter of custom.

11   Goods to be as described

(1) Every contract to supply goods by description is to be treated as including a term that the goods will match the description.

(2) If the supply is by sample as well as by description, it is not sufficient that the bulk of the goods matches the sample if the goods do not also match the description.

(3) A supply of goods is not prevented from being a supply by description just because—

    (a) the goods are exposed for supply, and

    (b) they are selected by the consumer.

(4) Any information that is provided by the trader about the goods and is information mentioned in paragraph (a) of Schedule 1 or 2 to the Consumer Contracts (Information, Cancellation and Additional Charges) Regulations 2013 (SI 2013/3134) (main characteristics of goods) is to be treated as included as a term of the contract.

(5) A change to any of that information, made before entering into the contract or later, is not effective unless expressly agreed between the consumer and the trader.

12   Other pre-contract information included in contract

(1) This section applies to any contract to supply goods.

(2) Where regulation 9, 10 or 13 of the Consumer Contracts (Information, Cancellation and Additional Charges) Regulations 2013 (SI 2013/3134) required the trader to provide information to the consumer before the contract became binding, any of that information that was provided by the trader other than information about the goods and mentioned in paragraph (a) of Schedule 1 or 2 to the Regulations (main characteristics of goods) is to be treated as included as a term of the contract.

(3) A change to any of that information, made before entering into the contract or later, is not effective unless expressly agreed between the consumer and the trader.

13   Goods to match a sample

(1) This section applies to a contract to supply goods by reference to a sample of the goods that is seen or examined by the consumer before the contract is made.

(2) Every contract to which this section applies is to be treated as including a term that—

    (a) the goods will match the sample except to the extent that any differences between the sample and the goods are brought to the consumer's attention before the contract is made, and

(b) the goods will be free from any defect that makes their quality unsatisfactory and that would not be apparent on a reasonable examination of the sample.

14 Goods to match a model seen or examined

(1) This section applies to a contract to supply goods by reference to a model of the goods that is seen or examined by the consumer before entering into the contract.

(2) Every contract to which this section applies is to be treated as including a term that the goods will match the model except to the extent that any differences between the model and the goods are brought to the consumer's attention before the consumer enters into the contract.

15 Installation as part of conformity of the goods with the contract

(1) Goods do not conform to a contract to supply goods if—

(a) installation of the goods forms part of the contract,

(b) the goods are installed by the trader or under the trader's responsibility, and

(c) the goods are installed incorrectly.

16 Goods not conforming to contract if digital content does not conform

(1) Goods (whether or not they conform otherwise to a contract to supply goods) do not conform to it if—

(a) the goods are an item that includes digital content, and

(b) the digital content does not conform to the contract to supply that content (for which see section 42(1)).

17 Trader to have right to supply the goods etc

(1) Every contract to supply goods, except one within subsection (4), is to be treated as including a term—

(a) in the case of a contract for the hire of goods, that at the beginning of the period of hire the trader must have the right to transfer possession of the goods by way of hire for that period,

(b) in any other case, that the trader must have the right to sell or transfer the goods at the time when ownership of the goods is to be transferred.

(2) Every contract to supply goods, except a contract for the hire of goods or a contract within subsection (4), is to be treated as including a term that—

(a) the goods are free from any charge or encumbrance not disclosed or known to the consumer before entering into the contract,

(b) the goods will remain free from any such charge or encumbrance until ownership of them is to be transferred, and

(c) the consumer will enjoy quiet possession of the goods except so far as it may be disturbed by the owner or other person entitled to the benefit of any charge or encumbrance so disclosed or known.

(3) Every contract for the hire of goods is to be treated as including a term that the consumer will enjoy quiet possession of the goods for the period of the hire except so far as the possession may be disturbed by the owner or other person entitled to the benefit of any charge or encumbrance disclosed or known to the consumer before entering into the contract.

(4) This subsection applies to a contract if the contract shows, or the circumstances when they enter into the contract imply, that the trader and the consumer intend the trader to transfer only—

(a) whatever title the trader has, even if it is limited, or

(b) whatever title a third person has, even if it is limited.

(5) Every contract within subsection (4) is to be treated as including a term that all charges or encumbrances known to the trader and not known to the consumer were disclosed to the consumer before entering into the contract.

(6) Every contract within subsection (4) is to be treated as including a term that the consumer's quiet possession of the goods—

(a) will not be disturbed by the trader, and

(b) will not be disturbed by a person claiming through or under the trader, unless that person is claiming under a charge or encumbrance that was disclosed or known to the consumer before entering into the contract.

(7) If subsection (4)(b) applies (transfer of title that a third person has), the contract is also to be treated as including a term that the consumer's quiet possession of the goods—

(a) will not be disturbed by the third person, and

(b) will not be disturbed by a person claiming through or under the third person, unless the claim is under a charge or encumbrance that was disclosed or known to the consumer before entering into the contract.

(8) In the case of a contract for the hire of goods, this section does not affect the right of the trader to repossess the goods where the contract provides or is to be treated as providing for this.

18   No other requirement to treat term about quality or fitness as included

(1) Except as provided by sections 9, 10, 13 and 16, a contract to supply goods is not to be treated as including any term about the quality of the goods or their fitness for any particular purpose, unless the term is expressly included in the contract.

(2) Subsection (1) is subject to provision made by any other enactment (whenever passed or made).

What remedies are there if statutory rights under a goods contract are not met?

19   Consumer's rights to enforce terms about goods

(1) In this section and sections 22 to 24 references to goods conforming to a contract are references to—

(a) the goods conforming to the terms described in sections 9, 10, 11, 13 and 14,

(b) the goods not failing to conform to the contract under section 15 or 16, and

(c) the goods conforming to requirements that are stated in the contract.

(2) But, for the purposes of this section and sections 22 to 24, a failure to conform as mentioned in subsection (1)(a) to (c) is not a failure to conform to the contract if it has its origin in materials supplied by the consumer.

(3) If the goods do not conform to the contract because of a breach of any of the terms described in sections 9, 10, 11, 13 and 14, or if they do not conform to the contract under section 16, the consumer's rights (and the provisions about them and when they are available) are—

(a) the short-term right to reject (sections 20 and 22);

(b) the right to repair or replacement (section 23); and

(c) the right to a price reduction or the final right to reject (sections 20 and 24).

(4) If the goods do not conform to the contract under section 15 or because of a breach of requirements that are stated in the contract, the consumer's rights (and the provisions about them and when they are available) are—

(a) the right to repair or replacement (section 23); and

(b) the right to a price reduction or the final right to reject (sections 20 and 24).

(5) If the trader is in breach of a term that section 12 requires to be treated as included in the contract, the consumer has the right to recover from the trader the amount of any costs incurred by the consumer as a result of the breach, up to the amount of the price paid or the value of other consideration given for the goods.

(6) If the trader is in breach of the term that section 17(1) (right to supply etc) requires to be treated as included in the contract, the consumer has a right to reject (see section 20 for provisions about that right and when it is available).

(7) Subsections (3) to (6) are subject to section 25 and subsections (3)(a) and (6) are subject to section 26.

(9) This Chapter does not prevent the consumer seeking other remedies—

(a) for a breach of a term that this Chapter requires to be treated as included in the contract,

     (b) on the grounds that, under section 15 or 16, goods do not conform to the contract, or

     (c) for a breach of a requirement stated in the contract.

(10) Those other remedies may be ones—

     (a) in addition to a remedy referred to in subsections (3) to (6) (but not so as to recover twice for the same loss), or

     (b) instead of such a remedy, or

     (c) where no such remedy is provided for.

(11) Those other remedies include any of the following that is open to the consumer in the circumstances—

     (a) claiming damages;

     (b) seeking specific performance;

     (c) seeking an order for specific implement;

     (d) relying on the breach against a claim by the trader for the price;

     (e) for breach of an express term, exercising a right to treat the contract as at an end.

(12) It is not open to the consumer to treat the contract as at an end for breach of a term that this Chapter requires to be treated as included in the contract, or on the grounds that, under section 15 or 16, goods do not conform to the contract, except as provided by subsections (3), (4) and (6).

(13) In this Part, treating a contract as at an end means treating it as repudiated.

(14) For the purposes of subsections (3)(b) and (c) and (4), goods which do not conform to the contract at any time within the period of six months beginning with the day on which the goods were delivered to the consumer must be taken not to have conformed to it on that day.

(15) Subsection (14) does not apply if—

     (a) it is established that the goods did conform to the contract on that day, or

     (b) its application is incompatible with the nature of the goods or with how they fail to conform to the contract.

20 Right to reject

(1) The short-term right to reject is subject to section 22.

(2) The final right to reject is subject to section 24.

(3) The right to reject under section 19(6) is not limited by those sections.

(4) Each of these rights entitles the consumer to reject the goods and treat the contract as at an end, subject to subsections (20) and (21).

(5) The right is exercised if the consumer indicates to the trader that the consumer is rejecting the goods and treating the contract as at an end.

(6) The indication may be something the consumer says or does, but it must be clear enough to be understood by the trader.

(7) From the time when the right is exercised—

     (a) the trader has a duty to give the consumer a refund, subject to subsection (18), and

     (b) the consumer has a duty to make the goods available for collection by the trader or (if there is an agreement for the consumer to return rejected goods) to return them as agreed.

(8) Whether or not the consumer has a duty to return the rejected goods, the trader must bear any reasonable costs of returning them, other than any costs incurred by the consumer in returning the goods in person to the place where the consumer took physical possession of them.

(9) The consumer's entitlement to receive a refund works as follows.

(10) To the extent that the consumer paid money under the contract, the consumer is entitled to receive back the same amount of money.

(11) To the extent that the consumer transferred anything else under the contract, the consumer is entitled to receive back the same amount of what the consumer transferred, unless subsection (12) applies.

(12) To the extent that the consumer transferred under the contract something for which the same amount of the same thing cannot be substituted, the consumer is entitled to receive back in its original state whatever the consumer transferred.

(13) If the contract is for the hire of goods, the entitlement to a refund extends only to anything paid or otherwise transferred for a period of hire that the consumer does not get because the contract is treated as at an end.

(14) If the contract is a hire-purchase agreement or a conditional sales contract and the contract is treated as at an end before the whole of the price has been paid, the entitlement to a refund extends only to the part of the price paid.

(15) A refund under this section must be given without undue delay, and in any event within 14 days beginning with the day on which the trader agrees that the consumer is entitled to a refund.

(16) If the consumer paid money under the contract, the trader must give the refund using the same means of payment as the consumer used, unless the consumer expressly agrees otherwise.

(17) The trader must not impose any fee on the consumer in respect of the refund.

(18) There is no entitlement to receive a refund—

    (a) if none of subsections (10) to (12) applies,

    (b) to the extent that anything to which subsection (12) applies cannot be given back in its original state, or

    (c) where subsection (13) applies, to the extent that anything the consumer transferred under the contract cannot be divided so as to give back only the amount, or part of the amount, to which the consumer is entitled.

(19) It may be open to a consumer to claim damages where there is no entitlement to receive a refund, or because of the limits of the entitlement, or instead of a refund.

(20) Subsection (21) qualifies the application in relation to England and Wales and Northern Ireland of the rights mentioned in subsections (1) to (3) where—

    (a) the contract is a severable contract,

    (b) in relation to the final right to reject, the contract is a contract for the hire of goods, a hire-purchase agreement or a contract for transfer of goods, and

    (c) section 26(3) does not apply.

(21) The consumer is entitled, depending on the terms of the contract and the circumstances of the case—

    (a) to reject the goods to which a severable obligation relates and treat that obligation as at an end (so that the entitlement to a refund relates only to what the consumer paid or transferred in relation to that obligation), or

    (b) to exercise any of the rights mentioned in subsections (1) to (3) in respect of the whole contract.

21 Partial rejection of goods

(1) If the consumer has any of the rights mentioned in section 20(1) to (3), but does not reject all of the goods and treat the contract as at an end, the consumer—

    (a) may reject some or all of the goods that do not conform to the contract, but

    (b) may not reject any goods that do conform to the contract.

(2) If the consumer is entitled to reject the goods in an instalment, but does not reject all of those goods, the consumer—

    (a) may reject some or all of the goods in the instalment that do not conform to the contract, but

    (b) may not reject any goods in the instalment that do conform to the contract.

(3) If any of the goods form a commercial unit, the consumer cannot reject some of those goods without also rejecting the rest of them.

(4) A unit is a "commercial unit" if division of the unit would materially impair the value of the goods or the character of the unit.

(5) The consumer rejects goods under this section by indicating to the trader that the consumer is rejecting the goods.

(6) The indication may be something the consumer says or does, but it must be clear enough to be understood by the trader.

(7) From the time when a consumer rejects goods under this section—

    (a) the trader has a duty to give the consumer a refund in respect of those goods (subject to subsection (10)), and

    (b) the consumer has a duty to make those goods available for collection by the trader or (if there is an agreement for the consumer to return rejected goods) to return them as agreed.

(8) Whether or not the consumer has a duty to return the rejected goods, the trader must bear any reasonable costs of returning them, other than any costs incurred by the consumer in returning those goods in person to the place where the consumer took physical possession of them.

(9) Section 20(10) to (17) apply to a consumer's right to receive a refund under this section (and in section 20(13) and (14) references to the contract being treated as at an end are to be read as references to goods being rejected).

(10) That right does not apply—

    (a) if none of section 20(10) to (12) applies,

    (b) to the extent that anything to which section 20(12) applies cannot be given back in its original state, or

    (c) to the extent that anything the consumer transferred under the contract cannot be divided so as to give back only the amount, or part of the amount, to which the consumer is entitled.

(11) It may be open to a consumer to claim damages where there is no right to receive a refund, or because of the limits of the right, or instead of a refund.

(12) References in this section to goods conforming to a contract are to be read in accordance with section 19(1) and (2), but they also include the goods conforming to the terms described in section 17.

(13) Where section 20(21)(a) applies the reference in subsection (1) to the consumer treating the contract as at an end is to be read as a reference to the consumer treating the severable obligation as at an end.

22 Time limit for short-term right to reject

(1) A consumer who has the short-term right to reject loses it if the time limit for exercising it passes without the consumer exercising it, unless the trader and the consumer agree that it may be exercised later.

(2) An agreement under which the short-term right to reject would be lost before the time limit passes is not binding on the consumer.

(3) The time limit for exercising the short-term right to reject (unless subsection (4) applies) is the end of 30 days beginning with the first day after these have all happened—

    (a) ownership or (in the case of a contract for the hire of goods, a hire-purchase agreement or a conditional sales contract) possession of the goods has been transferred to the consumer,

    (b) the goods have been delivered, and

    (c) where the contract requires the trader to install the goods or take other action to enable the consumer to use them, the trader has notified the consumer that the action has been taken.

(4) If any of the goods are of a kind that can reasonably be expected to perish after a shorter period, the time limit for exercising the short-term right to reject in relation to those goods is the end of that shorter period (but without affecting the time limit in relation to goods that are not of that kind).

(5) Subsections (3) and (4) do not prevent the consumer exercising the short-term right to reject before something mentioned in subsection (3)(a), (b) or (c) has happened.

(6) If the consumer requests or agrees to the repair or replacement of goods, the period mentioned in subsection (3) or (4) stops running for the length of the waiting period.

(7) If goods supplied by the trader in response to that request or agreement do not conform to the contract, the time limit for exercising the short-term right to reject is then either—

    (a) 7 days after the waiting period ends, or

    (b) if later, the original time limit for exercising that right, extended by the waiting period.

(8) The waiting period—

    (a) begins with the day the consumer requests or agrees to the repair or replacement of the goods, and

    (b) ends with the day on which the consumer receives goods supplied by the trader in response to the request or agreement.

23   Right to repair or replacement

(1) This section applies if the consumer has the right to repair or replacement (see section 19(3) and (4)).

(2) If the consumer requires the trader to repair or replace the goods, the trader must—

    (a) do so within a reasonable time and without significant inconvenience to the consumer, and

    (b) bear any necessary costs incurred in doing so (including in particular the cost of any labour, materials or postage).

(3) The consumer cannot require the trader to repair or replace the goods if that remedy (the repair or the replacement)—

    (a) is impossible, or

    (b) is disproportionate compared to the other of those remedies.

(4) Either of those remedies is disproportionate compared to the other if it imposes costs on the trader which, compared to those imposed by the other, are unreasonable, taking into account—

    (a) the value which the goods would have if they conformed to the contract,

    (b) the significance of the lack of conformity, and

    (c) whether the other remedy could be effected without significant inconvenience to the consumer.

(5) Any question as to what is a reasonable time or significant inconvenience is to be determined taking account of—

    (a) the nature of the goods, and

    (b) the purpose for which the goods were acquired.

(6) A consumer who requires or agrees to the repair of goods cannot require the trader to replace them, or exercise the short-term right to reject, without giving the trader a reasonable time to repair them (unless giving the trader that time would cause significant inconvenience to the consumer).

(7) A consumer who requires or agrees to the replacement of goods cannot require the trader to repair them, or exercise the short-term right to reject, without giving the trader a reasonable time to replace them (unless giving the trader that time would cause significant inconvenience to the consumer).

(8) In this Chapter, "repair" in relation to goods that do not conform to a contract, means making them conform.

24   Right to price reduction or final right to reject

(1) The right to a price reduction is the right—

    (a) to require the trader to reduce by an appropriate amount the price the consumer is required to pay under the contract, or anything else the consumer is required to transfer under the contract, and

(b) to receive a refund from the trader for anything already paid or otherwise transferred by the consumer above the reduced amount.

(2) The amount of the reduction may, where appropriate, be the full amount of the price or whatever the consumer is required to transfer.

(3) Section 20(10) to (17) applies to a consumer's right to receive a refund under subsection (1)(b).

(4) The right to a price reduction does not apply—

    (a) if what the consumer is (before the reduction) required to transfer under the contract, whether or not already transferred, cannot be divided up so as to enable the trader to receive or retain only the reduced amount, or

    (b) if anything to which section 20(12) applies cannot be given back in its original state.

(5) A consumer who has the right to a price reduction and the final right to reject may only exercise one (not both), and may only do so in one of these situations—

    (a) after one repair or one replacement, the goods do not conform to the contract;

    (b) because of section 23(3) the consumer can require neither repair nor replacement of the goods; or

    (c) the consumer has required the trader to repair or replace the goods, but the trader is in breach of the requirement of section 23(2)(a) to do so within a reasonable time and without significant inconvenience to the consumer.

(6) There has been a repair or replacement for the purposes of subsection (5)(a) if—

    (a) the consumer has requested or agreed to repair or replacement of the goods (whether in relation to one fault or more than one), and

    (b) the trader has delivered goods to the consumer, or made goods available to the consumer, in response to the request or agreement.

(7) For the purposes of subsection (6) goods that the trader arranges to repair at the consumer's premises are made available when the trader indicates that the repairs are finished.

(8) If the consumer exercises the final right to reject, any refund to the consumer may be reduced by a deduction for use, to take account of the use the consumer has had of the goods in the period since they were delivered, but this is subject to subsections (9) and (10).

(9) No deduction may be made to take account of use in any period when the consumer had the goods only because the trader failed to collect them at an agreed time.

(10) No deduction may be made if the final right to reject is exercised in the first 6 months (see subsection (11)), unless—

    (a) the goods consist of a motor vehicle, or

    (b) the goods are of a description specified by order made by the Secretary of State by statutory instrument.

(11) In subsection (10) the first 6 months means 6 months beginning with the first day after these have all happened—

    (a) ownership or (in the case of a contract for the hire of goods, a hire-purchase agreement or a conditional sales contract) possession of the goods has been transferred to the consumer,

    (b) the goods have been delivered, and

    (c) where the contract requires the trader to install the goods or take other action to enable the consumer to use them, the trader has notified the consumer that the action has been taken.

(12) In subsection (10)(a) "motor vehicle"—

    (a) in relation to Great Britain, has the same meaning as in the Road Traffic Act 1988 (see sections 185 to 194 of that Act); . . .

(13) But a vehicle is not a motor vehicle for the purposes of subsection (10)(a) if it is constructed or adapted—

    (a) for the use of a person suffering from some physical defect or disability, and

    (b) so that it may only be used by one such person at any one time.

(14) An order under subsection (10)(b)—

    (a) may be made only if the Secretary of State is satisfied that it is appropriate to do so because of significant detriment caused to traders as a result of the application of subsection (10) in relation to goods of the description specified by the order;

    (b) may contain transitional or transitory provision or savings.

(15) No order may be made under subsection (10)(b) unless a draft of the statutory instrument containing it has been laid before, and approved by a resolution of, each House of Parliament.

Other rules about remedies under goods contracts

25 Delivery of wrong quantity

(1) Where the trader delivers to the consumer a quantity of goods less than the trader contracted to supply, the consumer may reject them, but if the consumer accepts them the consumer must pay for them at the contract rate.

(2) Where the trader delivers to the consumer a quantity of goods larger than the trader contracted to supply, the consumer may accept the goods included in the contract and reject the rest, or may reject all of the goods.

(3) Where the trader delivers to the consumer a quantity of goods larger than the trader contracted to supply and the consumer accepts all of the goods delivered, the consumer must pay for them at the contract rate.

(4) Where the consumer is entitled to reject goods under this section, any entitlement for the consumer to treat the contract as at an end depends on the terms of the contract and the circumstances of the case.

(5) The consumer rejects goods under this section by indicating to the trader that the consumer is rejecting the goods.

(6) The indication may be something the consumer says or does, but it must be clear enough to be understood by the trader.

(7) Subsections (1) to (3) do not prevent the consumer claiming damages, where it is open to the consumer to do so.

(8) This section is subject to any usage of trade, special agreement, or course of dealing between the parties.

26 Instalment deliveries

(1) Under a contract to supply goods, the consumer is not bound to accept delivery of the goods by instalments, unless that has been agreed between the consumer and the trader.

(2) The following provisions apply if the contract provides for the goods to be delivered by stated instalments, which are to be separately paid for.

(3) If the trader makes defective deliveries in respect of one or more instalments, the consumer, apart from any entitlement to claim damages, may be (but is not necessarily) entitled—

    (a) to exercise the short-term right to reject or the right to reject under section 19(6) (as applicable) in respect of the whole contract, or

    (b) to reject the goods in an instalment.

(4) Whether paragraph (a) or (b) of subsection (3) (or neither) applies to a consumer depends on the terms of the contract and the circumstances of the case.

(5) In subsection (3), making defective deliveries does not include failing to make a delivery in accordance with section 28.

(6) If the consumer neglects or refuses to take delivery of or pay for one or more instalments, the trader may—

    (a) be entitled to treat the whole contract as at an end, or

    (b) if it is a severable breach, have a claim for damages but not a right to treat the whole contract as at an end.

(7) Whether paragraph (a) or (b) of subsection (6) (or neither) applies to a trader depends on the terms of the contract and the circumstances of the case.

Other rules about goods contracts

28 Delivery of goods

(1) This section applies to any sales contract.

(2) Unless the trader and the consumer have agreed otherwise, the contract is to be treated as including a term that the trader must deliver the goods to the consumer.

(3) Unless there is an agreed time or period, the contract is to be treated as including a term that the trader must deliver the goods—
- (a) without undue delay, and
- (b) in any event, not more than 30 days after the day on which the contract is entered into.

(4) In this section—
- (a) an "agreed" time or period means a time or period agreed by the trader and the consumer for delivery of the goods;
- (b) if there is an obligation to deliver the goods at the time the contract is entered into, that time counts as the "agreed" time.

(5) Subsections (6) and (7) apply if the trader does not deliver the goods in accordance with subsection (3) or at the agreed time or within the agreed period.

(6) If the circumstances are that—
- (a) the trader has refused to deliver the goods,
- (b) delivery of the goods at the agreed time or within the agreed period is essential taking into account all the relevant circumstances at the time the contract was entered into, or
- (c) the consumer told the trader before the contract was entered into that delivery in accordance with subsection (3), or at the agreed time or within the agreed period, was essential,

then the consumer may treat the contract as at an end.

(7) In any other circumstances, the consumer may specify a period that is appropriate in the circumstances and require the trader to deliver the goods before the end of that period.

(8) If the consumer specifies a period under subsection (7) but the goods are not delivered within that period, then the consumer may treat the contract as at an end.

(9) If the consumer treats the contract as at an end under subsection (6) or (8), the trader must without undue delay reimburse all payments made under the contract.

(10) If subsection (6) or (8) applies but the consumer does not treat the contract as at an end—
- (a) that does not prevent the consumer from cancelling the order for any of the goods or rejecting goods that have been delivered, and
- (b) the trader must without undue delay reimburse all payments made under the contract in respect of any goods for which the consumer cancels the order or which the consumer rejects.

(11) If any of the goods form a commercial unit, the consumer cannot reject or cancel the order for some of those goods without also rejecting or cancelling the order for the rest of them.

(12) A unit is a "commercial unit" if division of the unit would materially impair the value of the goods or the character of the unit.

(13) This section does not prevent the consumer seeking other remedies where it is open to the consumer to do so.

(14) See section 2(5) and (6) for the application of this section where goods are sold at public auction.

29 Passing of risk

(1) A sales contract is to be treated as including the following provisions as terms.

(2) The goods remain at the trader's risk until they come into the physical possession of—
- (a) the consumer, or
- (b) a person identified by the consumer to take possession of the goods.

(3) Subsection (2) does not apply if the goods are delivered to a carrier who—

    (a) is commissioned by the consumer to deliver the goods, and

    (b) is not a carrier the trader named as an option for the consumer.

(4) In that case the goods are at the consumer's risk on and after delivery to the carrier.

(5) Subsection (4) does not affect any liability of the carrier to the consumer in respect of the goods.

(6) See section 2(5) and (6) for the application of this section where goods are sold at public auction.

30 Goods under guarantee

(1) This section applies where—

    (a) there is a contract to supply goods, and

    (b) there is a guarantee in relation to the goods.

(2) "Guarantee" here means an undertaking to the consumer given without extra charge by a person acting in the course of the person's business (the "guarantor") that, if the goods do not meet the specifications set out in the guarantee statement or in any associated advertising—

    (a) the consumer will be reimbursed for the price paid for the goods, or

    (b) the goods will be repaired, replaced or handled in any way.

(3) The guarantee takes effect, at the time the goods are delivered, as a contractual obligation owed by the guarantor under the conditions set out in the guarantee statement and in any associated advertising.

(4) The guarantor must ensure that—

    (a) the guarantee sets out in plain and intelligible language the contents of the guarantee and the essential particulars for making claims under the guarantee,

    (b) the guarantee states that the consumer has statutory rights in relation to the goods and that those rights are not affected by the guarantee, and

    (c) where the goods are offered within the territory of the United Kingdom, the guarantee is written in English.

(5) The contents of the guarantee to be set out in it include, in particular—

    (a) the name and address of the guarantor, and

    (b) the duration and territorial scope of the guarantee.

(6) The guarantor and any other person who offers to supply to consumers the goods which are the subject of the guarantee must, on request by the consumer, make the guarantee available to the consumer within a reasonable time, in writing and in a form accessible to the consumer.

(7) What is a reasonable time is a question of fact.

(8) If a person fails to comply with a requirement of this section, the enforcement authority may apply to the court for an injunction ... against that person requiring that person to comply.

(9) On an application the court may grant an injunction ... an order of specific implement on such terms as it thinks appropriate.

(10) In this section—

"court" means—

    (a) in relation to England and Wales, the High Court or the county court, ...

"enforcement authority" means—

    (a) the Competition and Markets Authority,

    (b) a local weights and measures authority in Great Britain, ...

Can a trader contract out of statutory rights and remedies under a goods contract?

31 Liability that cannot be excluded or restricted

(1) A term of a contract to supply goods is not binding on the consumer to the extent that it would exclude or restrict the trader's liability arising under any of these provisions—

    (a) section 9 (goods to be of satisfactory quality);

(b) section 10 (goods to be fit for particular purpose);

(c) section 11 (goods to be as described);

(d) section 12 (other pre-contract information included in contract);

(e) section 13 (goods to match a sample);

(f) section 14 (goods to match a model seen or examined);

(g) section 15 (installation as part of conformity of the goods with the contract);

(h) section 16 (goods not conforming to contract if digital content does not conform);

(i) section 17 (trader to have right to supply the goods etc);

(j) section 28 (delivery of goods);

(k) section 29 (passing of risk).

(2) That also means that a term of a contract to supply goods is not binding on the consumer to the extent that it would—

(a) exclude or restrict a right or remedy in respect of a liability under a provision listed in subsection (1),

(b) make such a right or remedy or its enforcement subject to a restrictive or onerous condition,

(c) allow a trader to put a person at a disadvantage as a result of pursuing such a right or remedy, or

(d) exclude or restrict rules of evidence or procedure.

(3) The reference in subsection (1) to excluding or restricting a liability also includes preventing an obligation or duty arising or limiting its extent.

(4) An agreement in writing to submit present or future differences to arbitration is not to be regarded as excluding or restricting any liability for the purposes of this section.

(5) Subsection (1)(i), and subsection (2) so far as it relates to liability under section 17, do not apply to a term of a contract for the hire of goods.

(6) But an express term of a contract for the hire of goods is not binding on the consumer to the extent that it would exclude or restrict a term that section 17 requires to be treated as included in the contract, unless it is inconsistent with that term (and see also section 62 (requirement for terms to be fair)).

(7) See Schedule 3 for provision about the enforcement of this section.

Chapter 5 General and supplementary provisions

58 Powers of the court

(1) In any proceedings in which a remedy is sought by virtue of section 19(3) or (4), 42(2) or 54(3), the court, in addition to any other power it has, may act under this section.

(2) On the application of the consumer the court may make an order requiring specific performance . . . by the trader of any obligation imposed on the trader by virtue of section 23, 43 or 55.

(3) Subsection (4) applies if—

(a) the consumer claims to exercise a right under the relevant remedies provisions, but

(b) the court decides that those provisions have the effect that exercise of another right is appropriate.

(4) The court may proceed as if the consumer had exercised that other right.

(5) If the consumer has claimed to exercise the final right to reject, the court may order that any reimbursement to the consumer is reduced by a deduction for use, to take account of the use the consumer has had of the goods in the period since they were delivered.

(6) Any deduction for use is limited as set out in section 24(9) and (10).

(7) The court may make an order under this section unconditionally or on such terms and conditions as to damages, payment of the price and otherwise as it thinks just.

(8) The "relevant remedies provisions" are—

(a) where Chapter 2 applies, sections 23 and 24;

59 Interpretation

(1) These definitions apply in this Part (as well as the key definitions in section 2)—

"conditional sales contract" has the meaning given in section 5(3);

"Consumer Rights Directive" means Directive 2011/83/EU of the European Parliament and of the Council of 25 October 2011 on consumer rights, amending Council Directive 93/13/EEC and Directive 1999/44/EC of the European Parliament and of the Council and repealing Council Directive 85/577/EEC and Directive 97/7/EC of the European Parliament and of the Council;

"credit-broker" means a person acting in the course of a business of credit brokerage carried on by that person;

"credit brokerage" means—

(a) introducing individuals who want to obtain credit to persons carrying on any business so far as it relates to the provision of credit,

(b) introducing individuals who want to obtain goods on hire to persons carrying on a business which comprises or relates to supplying goods under a contract for the hire of goods, or

(c) introducing individuals who want to obtain credit, or to obtain goods on hire, to other persons engaged in credit brokerage;

"delivery" means voluntary transfer of possession from one person to another;

"enactment" includes—

(a) an enactment contained in subordinate legislation within the meaning of the Interpretation Act 1978...;

"producer", in relation to goods or digital content, means—

(a) the manufacturer,

(b) the importer into the European Economic Area, or

(c) any person who purports to be a producer by placing the person's name, trade mark or other distinctive sign on the goods or using it in connection with the digital content.

(2) References in this Part to treating a contract as at an end are to be read in accordance with section 19(13).

PART 2 UNFAIR TERMS

What contracts and notices are covered by this Part?

61 Contracts and notices covered by this Part

(1) This Part applies to a contract between a trader and a consumer.

(2) This does not include a contract of employment or apprenticeship.

(3) A contract to which this Part applies is referred to in this Part as a "consumer contract".

(4) This Part applies to a notice to the extent that it—

(a) relates to rights or obligations as between a trader and a consumer, or

(b) purports to exclude or restrict a trader's liability to a consumer.

(5) This does not include a notice relating to rights, obligations or liabilities as between an employer and an employee.

(6) It does not matter for the purposes of subsection (4) whether the notice is expressed to apply to a consumer, as long as it is reasonable to assume it is intended to be seen or heard by a consumer.

(7) A notice to which this Part applies is referred to in this Part as a "consumer notice".

(8) In this section "notice" includes an announcement, whether or not in writing, and any other communication or purported communication.

What are the general rules about fairness of contract terms and notices?

62   Requirement for contract terms and notices to be fair

(1) An unfair term of a consumer contract is not binding on the consumer.

(2) An unfair consumer notice is not binding on the consumer.

(3) This does not prevent the consumer from relying on the term or notice if the consumer chooses to do so.

(4) A term is unfair if, contrary to the requirement of good faith, it causes a significant imbalance in the parties' rights and obligations under the contract to the detriment of the consumer.

(5) Whether a term is fair is to be determined—

　　(a) taking into account the nature of the subject matter of the contract, and

　　(b) by reference to all the circumstances existing when the term was agreed and to all of the other terms of the contract or of any other contract on which it depends.

(6) A notice is unfair if, contrary to the requirement of good faith, it causes a significant imbalance in the parties' rights and obligations to the detriment of the consumer.

(7) Whether a notice is fair is to be determined—

　　(a) taking into account the nature of the subject matter of the notice, and

　　(b) by reference to all the circumstances existing when the rights or obligations to which it relates arose and to the terms of any contract on which it depends.

(8) This section does not affect the operation of—

　　(a) section 31 (exclusion of liability: goods contracts),

　　(b) section 47 (exclusion of liability: digital content contracts),

　　(c) section 57 (exclusion of liability: services contracts), or

　　(d) section 65 (exclusion of negligence liability).

63   Contract terms which may or must be regarded as unfair

(1) Part 1 of Schedule 2 contains an indicative and non-exhaustive list of terms of consumer contracts that may be regarded as unfair for the purposes of this Part.

(2) Part 1 of Schedule 2 is subject to Part 2 of that Schedule; but a term listed in Part 2 of that Schedule may nevertheless be assessed for fairness under section 62 unless section 64 or 73 applies to it.

(3) The Secretary of State may by order made by statutory instrument amend Schedule 2 so as to add, modify or remove an entry in Part 1 or Part 2 of that Schedule.

(4) An order under subsection (3) may contain transitional or transitory provision or savings.

(5) No order may be made under subsection (3) unless a draft of the statutory instrument containing it has been laid before, and approved by a resolution of, each House of Parliament.

(6) A term of a consumer contract must be regarded as unfair if it has the effect that the consumer bears the burden of proof with respect to compliance by a distance supplier or an intermediary with an obligation under any enactment or rule implementing the Distance Marketing Directive.

(7) In subsection (6)—

"the Distance Marketing Directive" means Directive 2002/65/EC of the European Parliament and of the Council of 23 September 2002 concerning the distance marketing of consumer financial services and amending Council Directive 90/619/EEC and Directives 97/7/EC and 98/27/EC;

"distance supplier" means—

　　(a) a supplier under a distance contract within the meaning of the Financial Services (Distance Marketing) Regulations 2004 (SI 2004/2095), or

　　(b) a supplier of unsolicited financial services within the meaning of regulation 15 of those regulations;

"enactment" includes an enactment contained in subordinate legislation within the meaning of the Interpretation Act 1978;

"intermediary" has the same meaning as in the Financial Services (Distance Marketing) Regulations 2004;

"rule" means a rule made by the Financial Conduct Authority or the Prudential Regulation Authority under the Financial Services and Markets Act 2000 or by a designated professional body within the meaning of section 326(2) of that Act.

64   Exclusion from assessment of fairness

(1) A term of a consumer contract may not be assessed for fairness under section 62 to the extent that—

    (a) it specifies the main subject matter of the contract, or

    (b) the assessment is of the appropriateness of the price payable under the contract by comparison with the goods, digital content or services supplied under it.

(2) Subsection (1) excludes a term from an assessment under section 62 only if it is transparent and prominent.

(3) A term is transparent for the purposes of this Part if it is expressed in plain and intelligible language and (in the case of a written term) is legible.

(4) A term is prominent for the purposes of this section if it is brought to the consumer's attention in such a way that an average consumer would be aware of the term.

(5) In subsection (4) "average consumer" means a consumer who is reasonably well-informed, observant and circumspect.

(6) This section does not apply to a term of a contract listed in Part 1 of Schedule 2.

65   Bar on exclusion or restriction of negligence liability

(1) A trader cannot by a term of a consumer contract or by a consumer notice exclude or restrict liability for death or personal injury resulting from negligence.

(2) Where a term of a consumer contract, or a consumer notice, purports to exclude or restrict a trader's liability for negligence, a person is not to be taken to have voluntarily accepted any risk merely because the person agreed to or knew about the term or notice.

(3) In this section "personal injury" includes any disease and any impairment of physical or mental condition.

(4) In this section "negligence" means the breach of—

    (a) any obligation to take reasonable care or exercise reasonable skill in the performance of a contract where the obligation arises from an express or implied term of the contract,

    (b) a common law duty to take reasonable care or exercise reasonable skill,

    (c) the common duty of care imposed by the Occupiers' Liability Act 1957 or the Occupiers' Liability Act (Northern Ireland) 1957, or

    (d) the duty of reasonable care imposed by section 2(1) of the Occupiers' Liability (Scotland) Act 1960.

(5) It is immaterial for the purposes of subsection (4)—

    (a) whether a breach of duty or obligation was inadvertent or intentional, or

    (b) whether liability for it arises directly or vicariously.

(6) This section is subject to section 66 (which makes provision about the scope of this section).

66   Scope of section 65

(1) Section 65 does not apply to—

    (a) any contract so far as it is a contract of insurance, including a contract to pay an annuity on human life, or

    (b) any contract so far as it relates to the creation or transfer of an interest in land.

(2) Section 65 does not affect the validity of any discharge or indemnity given by a person in consideration of the receipt by that person of compensation in settlement of any claim the person has.

(4) Section 65 does not apply to the liability of an occupier of premises to a person who obtains access to the premises for recreational purposes if—

    (a) the person suffers loss or damage because of the dangerous state of the premises, and

    (b) allowing the person access for those purposes is not within the purposes of the occupier's trade, business, craft or profession.

67   Effect of an unfair term on the rest of a contract

Where a term of a consumer contract is not binding on the consumer as a result of this Part, the contract continues, so far as practicable, to have effect in every other respect.

68   Requirement for transparency

(1) A trader must ensure that a written term of a consumer contract, or a consumer notice in writing, is transparent.

(2) A consumer notice is transparent for the purposes of subsection (1) if it is expressed in plain and intelligible language and it is legible.

69   Contract terms that may have different meanings

(1) If a term in a consumer contract, or a consumer notice, could have different meanings, the meaning that is most favourable to the consumer is to prevail.

(2) Subsection (1) does not apply to the construction of a term or a notice in proceedings on an application for an injunction or interdict under paragraph 3 of Schedule 3.

How are the general rules enforced?

70   Enforcement of the law on unfair contract terms

(1) Schedule 3 confers functions on the Competition and Markets Authority and other regulators in relation to the enforcement of this Part.

(2) For provision about the investigatory powers that are available to those regulators for the purposes of that Schedule, see Schedule 5.

Supplementary provisions

71   Duty of court to consider fairness of term

(1) Subsection (2) applies to proceedings before a court which relate to a term of a consumer contract.

(2) The court must consider whether the term is fair even if none of the parties to the proceedings has raised that issue or indicated that it intends to raise it.

(3) But subsection (2) does not apply unless the court considers that it has before it sufficient legal and factual material to enable it to consider the fairness of the term.

72   Application of rules to secondary contracts

(1) This section applies if a term of a contract ("the secondary contract") reduces the rights or remedies or increases the obligations of a person under another contract ("the main contract").

(2) The term is subject to the provisions of this Part that would apply to the term if it were in the main contract.

(3) It does not matter for the purposes of this section—
  (a) whether the parties to the secondary contract are the same as the parties to the main contract, or
  (b) whether the secondary contract is a consumer contract.

(4) This section does not apply if the secondary contract is a settlement of a claim arising under the main contract.

73   Disapplication of rules to mandatory terms and notices

(1) This Part does not apply to a term of a contract, or to a notice, to the extent that it reflects—
  (a) mandatory statutory or regulatory provisions, or
  (b) the provisions or principles of an international convention to which the United Kingdom or the EU is a party.

(2) In subsection (1) "mandatory statutory or regulatory provisions" includes rules which, according to law, apply between the parties on the basis that no other arrangements have been established.

74   Contracts applying law of non-EEA State

(1) If—

(a) the law of a country or territory other than an EEA State is chosen by the parties to be applicable to a consumer contract, but

(b) the consumer contract has a close connection with the United Kingdom,

this Part applies despite that choice.

(2) For cases where the law applicable has not been chosen or the law of an EEA State is chosen, see Regulation (EC) No. 593/2008 of the European Parliament and of the Council of 17 June 2008 on the law applicable to contractual obligations.

76   Interpretation of Part 2

(1) In this Part—

"consumer contract" has the meaning given by section 61(3);

"consumer notice" has the meaning given by section 61(7);

"transparent" is to be construed in accordance with sections 64(3) and 68(2).

(2) The following have the same meanings in this Part as they have in Part 1—

"trader" (see section 2(2));

"consumer" (see section 2(3));

"goods" (see section 2(8));

"digital content" (see section 2(9)).

(3) Section 2(4) (trader who claims an individual is not a consumer must prove it) applies in relation to this Part as it applies in relation to Part 1.

Section 63   SCHEDULE 2

CONSUMER CONTRACT TERMS WHICH MAY BE REGARDED AS UNFAIR

PART 1 LIST OF TERMS

1. A term which has the object or effect of excluding or limiting the trader's liability in the event of the death of or personal injury to the consumer resulting from an act or omission of the trader.

2. A term which has the object or effect of inappropriately excluding or limiting the legal rights of the consumer in relation to the trader or another party in the event of total or partial non-performance or inadequate performance by the trader of any of the contractual obligations, including the option of offsetting a debt owed to the trader against any claim which the consumer may have against the trader.

3. A term which has the object or effect of making an agreement binding on the consumer in a case where the provision of services by the trader is subject to a condition whose realisation depends on the trader's will alone.

4. A term which has the object or effect of permitting the trader to retain sums paid by the consumer where the consumer decides not to conclude or perform the contract, without providing for the consumer to receive compensation of an equivalent amount from the trader where the trader is the party cancelling the contract.

5. A term which has the object or effect of requiring that, where the consumer decides not to conclude or perform the contract, the consumer must pay the trader a disproportionately high sum in compensation or for services which have not been supplied.

6. A term which has the object or effect of requiring a consumer who fails to fulfil his obligations under the contract to pay a disproportionately high sum in compensation.

7. A term which has the object or effect of authorising the trader to dissolve the contract on a discretionary basis where the same facility is not granted to the consumer, or permitting the trader to retain the sums paid for services not yet supplied by the trader where it is the trader who dissolves the contract.

8. A term which has the object or effect of enabling the trader to terminate a contract of indeterminate duration without reasonable notice except where there are serious grounds for doing so.

9. A term which has the object or effect of automatically extending a contract of fixed duration where the consumer does not indicate otherwise, when the deadline fixed for the consumer to express a desire not to extend the contract is unreasonably early.

10. A term which has the object or effect of irrevocably binding the consumer to terms with which the consumer has had no real opportunity of becoming acquainted before the conclusion of the contract.

11. A term which has the object or effect of enabling the trader to alter the terms of the contract unilaterally without a valid reason which is specified in the contract.

12. A term which has the object or effect of permitting the trader to determine the characteristics of the subject matter of the contract after the consumer has become bound by it.

13. A term which has the object or effect of enabling the trader to alter unilaterally without a valid reason any characteristics of the goods, digital content or services to be provided.

14. A term which has the object or effect of giving the trader the discretion to decide the price payable under the contract after the consumer has become bound by it, where no price or method of determining the price is agreed when the consumer becomes bound.

15. A term which has the object or effect of permitting a trader to increase the price of goods, digital content or services without giving the consumer the right to cancel the contract if the final price is too high in relation to the price agreed when the contract was concluded.

16. A term which has the object or effect of giving the trader the right to determine whether the goods, digital content or services supplied are in conformity with the contract, or giving the trader the exclusive right to interpret any term of the contract.

17. A term which has the object or effect of limiting the trader's obligation to respect commitments undertaken by the trader's agents or making the trader's commitments subject to compliance with a particular formality.

18. A term which has the object or effect of obliging the consumer to fulfil all of the consumer's obligations where the trader does not perform the trader's obligations.

19. A term which has the object or effect of allowing the trader to transfer the trader's rights and obligations under the contract, where this may reduce the guarantees for the consumer, without the consumer's agreement.

20. A term which has the object or effect of excluding or hindering the consumer's right to take legal action or exercise any other legal remedy, in particular by—

    (a) requiring the consumer to take disputes exclusively to arbitration not covered by legal provisions,

    (b) unduly restricting the evidence available to the consumer, or

    (c) imposing on the consumer a burden of proof which, according to the applicable law, should lie with another party to the contract.

PART 2 SCOPE OF PART 1

Financial services

21. Paragraph 8 (cancellation without reasonable notice) does not include a term by which a supplier of financial services reserves the right to terminate unilaterally a contract of indeterminate duration without notice where there is a valid reason, if the supplier is required to inform the consumer of the cancellation immediately.

22. Paragraph 11 (variation of contract without valid reason) does not include a term by which a supplier of financial services reserves the right to alter the rate of interest payable by or due to the consumer, or the amount of other charges for financial services without notice where there is a valid reason, if—

  (a) the supplier is required to inform the consumer of the alteration at the earliest opportunity, and

  (b) the consumer is free to dissolve the contract immediately.

23. Contracts which last indefinitely

Paragraphs 11 (variation of contract without valid reason), 12 (determination of characteristics of goods etc after consumer bound) and 14 (determination of price after consumer bound) do not include a term under which a trader reserves the right to alter unilaterally the conditions of a contract of indeterminate duration if—

  (a) the trader is required to inform the consumer with reasonable notice, and

  (b) the consumer is free to dissolve the contract.

24. Sale of securities, foreign currency etc

Paragraphs 8 (cancellation without reasonable notice), 11 (variation of contract without valid reason), 14 (determination of price after consumer bound) and 15 (increase in price) do not apply to—

  (a) transactions in transferable securities, financial instruments and other products or services where the price is linked to fluctuations in a stock exchange quotation or index or a financial market rate that the trader does not control, and

  (b) contracts for the purchase or sale of foreign currency, traveller's cheques or international money orders denominated in foreign currency.

25. Price index clauses

Paragraphs 14 (determination of price after consumer bound) and 15 (increase in price) do not include a term which is a price-indexation clause (where otherwise lawful), if the method by which prices vary is explicitly described.

Section 70   **SCHEDULE 3**

ENFORCEMENT OF THE LAW ON UNFAIR CONTRACT TERMS AND NOTICES

1. Application of Schedule

This Schedule applies to—

  (a) a term of a consumer contract,

  (b) a term proposed for use in a consumer contract,

  (c) a term which a third party recommends for use in a consumer contract, or

  (d) a consumer notice.

2. Consideration of complaints

  (1) A regulator may consider a complaint about a term or notice to which this Schedule applies (a "relevant complaint").

  (2) If a regulator other than the CMA intends to consider a relevant complaint, it must notify the CMA that it intends to do so, and must then consider the complaint.

  (3) If a regulator considers a relevant complaint, but decides not to make an application under paragraph 3 in relation to the complaint, it must give reasons for its decision to the person who made the complaint.

3. Application for injunction or interdict

  (1) A regulator may apply for an injunction . . . against a person if the regulator thinks that—

  (a) the person is using, or proposing or recommending the use of, a term or notice to which this Schedule applies, and

  (b) the term or notice falls within any one or more of sub-paragraphs (2), (3) or (5).

(2) A term or notice falls within this sub-paragraph if it purports to exclude or restrict liability of the kind mentioned in—

    (a) section 31 (exclusion of liability: goods contracts),

    (b) section 47 (exclusion of liability: digital content contracts),

    (c) section 57 (exclusion of liability: services contracts), or

    (d) section 65(1) (business liability for death or personal injury resulting from negligence).

(3) A term or notice falls within this sub-paragraph if it is unfair to any extent.

(4) A term within paragraph 1(1)(b) or (c) (but not within paragraph 1(1)(a)) is to be treated for the purposes of section 62(4) and (5) (assessment of fairness) as if it were a term of a contract.

(5) A term or notice falls within this sub-paragraph if it breaches section 68 (requirement for transparency).

(6) A regulator may apply for an injunction or interdict under this paragraph in relation to a term or notice whether or not it has received a relevant complaint about the term or notice.

4. Notification of application

(1) Before making an application under paragraph 3, a regulator other than the CMA must notify the CMA that it intends to do so.

(2) The regulator may make the application only if—

    (a) the period of 14 days beginning with the day on which the regulator notified the CMA has ended, or

    (b) before the end of that period, the CMA agrees to the regulator making the application.

5. Determination of application

(1) On an application for an injunction under paragraph 3, the court may grant an injunction on such conditions, and against such of the respondents, as it thinks appropriate.

(2) On an application for an interdict under paragraph 3, the court may grant an interdict on such conditions, and against such of the defenders, as it thinks appropriate.

(3) The injunction or interdict may include provision about—

    (a) a term or notice to which the application relates, or

    (b) any term of a consumer contract, or any consumer notice, of a similar kind or with a similar effect.

(4) It is not a defence to an application under paragraph 3 to show that, because of a rule of law, a term to which the application relates is not, or could not be, an enforceable contract term.

(5) If a regulator other than the CMA makes the application, it must notify the CMA of—

    (a) the outcome of the application, and

    (b) if an injunction or interdict is granted, the conditions on which, and the persons against whom, it is granted.

6. Undertakings

(1) A regulator may accept an undertaking from a person against whom it has applied, or thinks it is entitled to apply, for an injunction or interdict under paragraph 3.

(2) The undertaking may provide that the person will comply with the conditions that are agreed between the person and the regulator about the use of terms or notices, or terms or notices of a kind, specified in the undertaking.

(3) If a regulator other than the CMA accepts an undertaking, it must notify the CMA of—

    (a) the conditions on which the undertaking is accepted, and

    (b) the person who gave it.

7. Publication, information and advice

(1) The CMA must arrange the publication of details of—

    (a) any application it makes for an injunction or interdict under paragraph 3,

    (b) any injunction or interdict under this Schedule, and

    (c) any undertaking under this Schedule.

(2) The CMA must respond to a request whether a term or notice, or one of a similar kind or with a similar effect, is or has been the subject of an injunction, interdict or undertaking under this Schedule.

(3) Where the term or notice, or one of a similar kind or with a similar effect, is or has been the subject of an injunction or interdict under this Schedule, the CMA must give the person making the request a copy of the injunction or interdict.

(4) Where the term or notice, or one of a similar kind or with a similar effect, is or has been the subject of an undertaking under this Schedule, the CMA must give the person making the request—

    (a) details of the undertaking, and

    (b) if the person giving the undertaking has agreed to amend the term or notice, a copy of the amendments.

(5) The CMA may arrange the publication of advice and information about the provisions of this Part.

(6) In this paragraph—

    (a) references to an injunction or interdict under this Schedule are to an injunction or interdict granted on an application by the CMA under paragraph 3 or notified to it under paragraph 5, and

    (b) references to an undertaking are to an undertaking given to the CMA under paragraph 6 or notified to it under that paragraph.

8. Meaning of "regulator"

(1) In this Schedule "regulator" means—

    (a) the CMA,

    (b) the Department of Enterprise, Trade and Investment in Northern Ireland,

    (c) a local weights and measures authority in Great Britain,

    (d) the Financial Conduct Authority,

    (e) the Office of Communications,

    (f) the Information Commissioner,

    (g) the Gas and Electricity Markets Authority,

    (h) the Water Services Regulation Authority,

    (i) the Office of Rail Regulation,

    (j) the Northern Ireland Authority for Utility Regulation, or

    (k) the Consumers' Association.

(2) The Secretary of State may by order made by statutory instrument amend sub-paragraph (1) so as to add, modify or remove an entry.

(3) An order under sub-paragraph (2) may amend sub-paragraph (1) so as to add a body that is not a public authority only if the Secretary of State thinks that the body represents the interests of consumers (or consumers of a particular description).

(4) The Secretary of State must publish (and may from time to time vary) other criteria to be applied by the Secretary of State in deciding whether to add an entry to, or remove an entry from, sub-paragraph (1).

(5) An order under sub-paragraph (2) may make consequential amendments to this Schedule (including with the effect that any of its provisions apply differently, or do not apply, to a body added to sub-paragraph (1)).

(6) An order under sub-paragraph (2) may contain transitional or transitory provision or savings.

(7) No order may be made under sub-paragraph (2) unless a draft of the statutory instrument containing it has been laid before, and approved by a resolution of, each House of Parliament.

(8) In this paragraph "public authority" has the same meaning as in section 6 of the Human Rights Act 1998.

9. Other definitions

In this Schedule—

"the CMA" means the Competition and Markets Authority;

"injunction" includes an interim injunction; . . .

Criminal Justice and Courts Act 2015

(2015, c. 2)

Civil proceedings relating to personal injury

57 Personal injury claims: cases of fundamental dishonesty

(1) This section applies where, in proceedings on a claim for damages in respect of personal injury ("the primary claim")—

(a) the court finds that the claimant is entitled to damages in respect of the claim, but

(b) on an application by the defendant for the dismissal of the claim under this section, the court is satisfied on the balance of probabilities that the claimant has been fundamentally dishonest in relation to the primary claim or a related claim.

(2) The court must dismiss the primary claim, unless it is satisfied that the claimant would suffer substantial injustice if the claim were dismissed.

(3) The duty under subsection (2) includes the dismissal of any element of the primary claim in respect of which the claimant has not been dishonest.

(4) The court's order dismissing the claim must record the amount of damages that the court would have awarded to the claimant in respect of the primary claim but for the dismissal of the claim.

(5) When assessing costs in the proceedings, a court which dismisses a claim under this section must deduct the amount recorded in accordance with subsection (4) from the amount which it would otherwise order the claimant to pay in respect of costs incurred by the defendant.

(6) If a claim is dismissed under this section, subsection (7) applies to—

(a) any subsequent criminal proceedings against the claimant in respect of the fundamental dishonesty mentioned in subsection (1)(b), and

(b) any subsequent proceedings for contempt of court against the claimant in respect of that dishonesty.

(7) If the court in those proceedings finds the claimant guilty of an offence or of contempt of court, it must have regard to the dismissal of the primary claim under this section when sentencing the claimant or otherwise disposing of the proceedings.

(8) In this section—

"claim" includes a counter-claim and, accordingly, "claimant" includes a counter-claimant and "defendant" includes a defendant to a counter-claim;

"personal injury" includes any disease and any other impairment of a person's physical or mental condition;

"related claim" means a claim for damages in respect of personal injury which is made—

(a) in connection with the same incident or series of incidents in connection with which the primary claim is made, and

(b) by a person other than the person who made the primary claim.

58 Rules against inducements to make personal injury claims

(1) A regulated person is in breach of this section if—

(a) the regulated person offers another person a benefit or is treated as doing so under subsection (4),

(b) the offer of the benefit is an inducement to make a claim in civil proceedings for—

    (i) damages for personal injury or death, or

    (ii) damages arising out of circumstances involving personal injury or death, and

(c) the benefit is not related to the provision of legal services in connection with the claim.

(2) An offer of a benefit to another person is an inducement to make a claim if the offer of the benefit—

(a) is intended to encourage the person to make a claim or to seek advice from a regulated person with a view to making a claim, or

(b) is likely to have the effect of encouraging the person to do so.

(3) An offer of a benefit may be an inducement to make a claim regardless of—

(a) when or by what means the offer is made,

(b) whether the receipt of the benefit pursuant to the offer is subject to conditions,

(c) when the benefit may be received pursuant to the offer, or

(d) whether the benefit may be received by the person to whom the offer is made or by a third party.

(4) If a person other than a regulated person offers a benefit in accordance with arrangements made by or on behalf of a regulated person—

(a) the regulated person is to be treated as offering the benefit, and

(b) the offer of the benefit is to be treated as satisfying subsection (2)(a) if the arrangements were intended to encourage people to make claims or seek advice from a regulated person with a view to making a claim.

(5) The Lord Chancellor may by regulations make provision as to the circumstances in which a benefit is related to the provision of legal services in connection with a claim, including provision about benefits relating to—

(a) fees to be charged in respect of the legal services,

(b) expenses which are or would be necessarily incurred in connection with the claim, or

(c) insurance to cover legal costs and expenses in connection with the claim.

59   Effect of rules against inducements

(1) The relevant regulator must ensure that it has appropriate arrangements for monitoring and enforcing the restriction imposed on regulated persons by section 58.

Insurance Act 2015

(2015, c. 4)

PART 1 INSURANCE CONTRACTS: MAIN DEFINITIONS

1   Insurance contracts: main definitions

In this Act (apart from Part 6)—

"consumer insurance contract" has the same meaning as in the Consumer Insurance (Disclosure and Representations) Act 2012;

"non-consumer insurance contract" means a contract of insurance that is not a consumer insurance contract;

"insured" means the party to a contract of insurance who is the insured under the contract, or would be if the contract were entered into;

"insurer" means the party to a contract of insurance who is the insurer under the contract, or would be if the contract were entered into;

"the duty of fair presentation" means the duty imposed by section 3(1).

PART 2 THE DUTY OF FAIR PRESENTATION

2   Application and interpretation
(1) This Part applies to non-consumer insurance contracts only.

(2) This Part applies in relation to variations of non-consumer insurance contracts as it applies to contracts, but—
  (a) references to the risk are to be read as references to changes in the risk relevant to the proposed variation, and
  (b) references to the contract of insurance are to the variation.

3   The duty of fair presentation
(1) Before a contract of insurance is entered into, the insured must make to the insurer a fair presentation of the risk.

(2) The duty imposed by subsection (1) is referred to in this Act as "the duty of fair presentation".

(3) A fair presentation of the risk is one—
  (a) which makes the disclosure required by subsection (4),
  (b) which makes that disclosure in a manner which would be reasonably clear and accessible to a prudent insurer, and
  (c) in which every material representation as to a matter of fact is substantially correct, and every material representation as to a matter of expectation or belief is made in good faith.

(4) The disclosure required is as follows, except as provided in subsection (5)—
  (a) disclosure of every material circumstance which the insured knows or ought to know, or
  (b) failing that, disclosure which gives the insurer sufficient information to put a prudent insurer on notice that it needs to make further enquiries for the purpose of revealing those material circumstances.

(5) In the absence of enquiry, subsection (4) does not require the insured to disclose a circumstance if—
  (a) it diminishes the risk,
  (b) the insurer knows it,
  (c) the insurer ought to know it,
  (d) the insurer is presumed to know it, or
  (e) it is something as to which the insurer waives information.

4   Knowledge of insured
(1) This section provides for what an insured knows or ought to know for the purposes of section 3(4)(a).

(2) An insured who is an individual knows only—
  (a) what is known to the individual, and
  (b) what is known to one or more of the individuals who are responsible for the insured's insurance.

(3) An insured who is not an individual knows only what is known to one or more of the individuals who are—
  (a) part of the insured's senior management, or
  (b) responsible for the insured's insurance.

(4) An insured is not by virtue of subsection (2)(b) or (3)(b) taken to know confidential information known to an individual if—
  (a) the individual is, or is an employee of, the insured's agent; and
  (b) the information was acquired by the insured's agent (or by an employee of that agent) through a business relationship with a person who is not connected with the contract of insurance.

(5) For the purposes of subsection (4) the persons connected with a contract of insurance are—
  (a) the insured and any other persons for whom cover is provided by the contract, and

(b) if the contract re-insures risks covered by another contract, the persons who are (by virtue of this subsection) connected with that other contract.

(6) Whether an individual or not, an insured ought to know what should reasonably have been revealed by a reasonable search of information available to the insured (whether the search is conducted by making enquiries or by any other means).

(7) In subsection (6) "information" includes information held within the insured's organisation or by any other person (such as the insured's agent or a person for whom cover is provided by the contract of insurance).

(8) For the purposes of this section—

(a) "employee", in relation to the insured's agent, includes any individual working for the agent, whatever the capacity in which the individual acts,

(b) an individual is responsible for the insured's insurance if the individual participates on behalf of the insured in the process of procuring the insured's insurance (whether the individual does so as the insured's employee or agent, as an employee of the insured's agent or in any other capacity), and

(c) "senior management" means those individuals who play significant roles in the making of decisions about how the insured's activities are to be managed or organised.

5   Knowledge of insurer

(1) For the purposes of section 3(5)(b), an insurer knows something only if it is known to one or more of the individuals who participate on behalf of the insurer in the decision whether to take the risk, and if so on what terms (whether the individual does so as the insurer's employee or agent, as an employee of the insurer's agent or in any other capacity).

(2) For the purposes of section 3(5)(c), an insurer ought to know something only if—

(a) an employee or agent of the insurer knows it, and ought reasonably to have passed on the relevant information to an individual mentioned in subsection (1), or

(b) the relevant information is held by the insurer and is readily available to an individual mentioned in subsection (1).

(3) For the purposes of section 3(5)(d), an insurer is presumed to know—

(a) things which are common knowledge, and

(b) things which an insurer offering insurance of the class in question to insureds in the field of activity in question would reasonably be expected to know in the ordinary course of business.

6   Knowledge: general

(1) For the purposes of sections 3 to 5, references to an individual's knowledge include not only actual knowledge, but also matters which the individual suspected, and of which the individual would have had knowledge but for deliberately refraining from confirming them or enquiring about them.

(2) Nothing in this Part affects the operation of any rule of law according to which knowledge of a fraud perpetrated by an individual ("F") either on the insured or on the insurer is not to be attributed to the insured or to the insurer (respectively), where—

(a) if the fraud is on the insured, F is any of the individuals mentioned in section 4(2)(b) or (3), or

(b) if the fraud is on the insurer, F is any of the individuals mentioned in section 5(1).

7   Supplementary

(1) A fair presentation need not be contained in only one document or oral presentation.

(2) The term "circumstance" includes any communication made to, or information received by, the insured.

(3) A circumstance or representation is material if it would influence the judgement of a prudent insurer in determining whether to take the risk and, if so, on what terms.

(4) Examples of things which may be material circumstances are—

    (a) special or unusual facts relating to the risk,

    (b) any particular concerns which led the insured to seek insurance cover for the risk,

    (c) anything which those concerned with the class of insurance and field of activity in question would generally understand as being something that should be dealt with in a fair presentation of risks of the type in question.

(5) A material representation is substantially correct if a prudent insurer would not consider the difference between what is represented and what is actually correct to be material.

(6) A representation may be withdrawn or corrected before the contract of insurance is entered into.

8   Remedies for breach

(1) The insurer has a remedy against the insured for a breach of the duty of fair presentation only if the insurer shows that, but for the breach, the insurer—

    (a) would not have entered into the contract of insurance at all, or

    (b) would have done so only on different terms.

(2) The remedies are set out in Schedule 1.

(3) A breach for which the insurer has a remedy against the insured is referred to in this Act as a "qualifying breach".

(4) A qualifying breach is either—

    (a) deliberate or reckless, or

    (b) neither deliberate nor reckless.

(5) A qualifying breach is deliberate or reckless if the insured —

    (a) knew that it was in breach of the duty of fair presentation, or

    (b) did not care whether or not it was in breach of that duty.

(6) It is for the insurer to show that a qualifying breach was deliberate or reckless.

PART 3 WARRANTIES AND OTHER TERMS

9   Warranties and representations

(1) This section applies to representations made by the insured in connection with—

    (a) a proposed non-consumer insurance contract, or

    (b) a proposed variation to a non-consumer insurance contract.

(2) Such a representation is not capable of being converted into a warranty by means of any provision of the non-consumer insurance contract (or of the terms of the variation), or of any other contract (and whether by declaring the representation to form the basis of the contract or otherwise).

10   Breach of warranty

(1) Any rule of law that breach of a warranty (express or implied) in a contract of insurance results in the discharge of the insurer's liability under the contract is abolished.

(2) An insurer has no liability under a contract of insurance in respect of any loss occurring, or attributable to something happening, after a warranty (express or implied) in the contract has been breached but before the breach has been remedied.

(3) But subsection (2) does not apply if—

    (a) because of a change of circumstances, the warranty ceases to be applicable to the circumstances of the contract,

    (b) compliance with the warranty is rendered unlawful by any subsequent law, or

    (c) the insurer waives the breach of warranty.

(4) Subsection (2) does not affect the liability of the insurer in respect of losses occurring, or attributable to something happening—

    (a) before the breach of warranty, or

(b) if the breach can be remedied, after it has been remedied.

(5) For the purposes of this section, a breach of warranty is to be taken as remedied—

(a) in a case falling within subsection (6), if the risk to which the warranty relates later becomes essentially the same as that originally contemplated by the parties,

(b) in any other case, if the insured ceases to be in breach of the warranty.

(6) A case falls within this subsection if—

(a) the warranty in question requires that by an ascertainable time something is to be done (or not done), or a condition is to be fulfilled, or something is (or is not) to be the case, and

(b) that requirement is not complied with.

11   Terms not relevant to the actual loss

(1) This section applies to a term (express or implied) of a contract of insurance, other than a term defining the risk as a whole, if compliance with it would tend to reduce the risk of one or more of the following—

(a) loss of a particular kind,

(b) loss at a particular location,

(c) loss at a particular time.

(2) If a loss occurs, and the term has not been complied with, the insurer may not rely on the non-compliance to exclude, limit or discharge its liability under the contract for the loss if the insured satisfies subsection (3).

(3) The insured satisfies this subsection if it shows that the non-compliance with the term could not have increased the risk of the loss which actually occurred in the circumstances in which it occurred.

(4) This section may apply in addition to section 10.

PART 4 FRAUDULENT CLAIMS

12   Remedies for fraudulent claims

(1) If the insured makes a fraudulent claim under a contract of insurance—

(a) the insurer is not liable to pay the claim,

(b) the insurer may recover from the insured any sums paid by the insurer to the insured in respect of the claim, and

(c) in addition, the insurer may by notice to the insured treat the contract as having been terminated with effect from the time of the fraudulent act.

(2) If the insurer does treat the contract as having been terminated—

(a) it may refuse all liability to the insured under the contract in respect of a relevant event occurring after the time of the fraudulent act, and

(b) it need not return any of the premiums paid under the contract.

(3) Treating a contract as having been terminated under this section does not affect the rights and obligations of the parties to the contract with respect to a relevant event occurring before the time of the fraudulent act.

(4) In subsections (2)(a) and (3), "relevant event" refers to whatever gives rise to the insurer's liability under the contract (and includes, for example, the occurrence of a loss, the making of a claim, or the notification of a potential claim, depending on how the contract is written).

13   Remedies for fraudulent claims: group insurance

(1) This section applies where—

(a) a contract of insurance is entered into with an insurer by a person ("A"),

(b) the contract provides cover for one or more other persons who are not parties to the contract ("the Cs"), whether or not it also provides cover of any kind for A or another insured party, and

(c) a fraudulent claim is made under the contract by or on behalf of one of the Cs ("CF").

(2) Section 12 applies in relation to the claim as if the cover provided for CF were provided under an individual insurance contract between the insurer and CF as the insured; and, accordingly—

(a) the insurer's rights under section 12 are exercisable only in relation to the cover provided for CF, and

(b) the exercise of any of those rights does not affect the cover provided under the contract for anyone else.

(3) In its application by virtue of subsection (2), section 12 is subject to the following particular modifications—

(a) the first reference to "the insured" in subsection (1)(b) of that section, in respect of any particular sum paid by the insurer, is to whichever of A and CF the insurer paid the sum to; but if a sum was paid to A and passed on by A to CF, the reference is to CF,

(b) the second reference to "the insured" in subsection (1)(b) is to A or CF,

(c) the reference to "the insured" in subsection (1)(c) is to both CF and A,

(d) the reference in subsection (2)(b) to the premiums paid under the contract is to premiums paid in respect of the cover for CF.

PART 5 GOOD FAITH AND CONTRACTING OUT

Good faith

14 Good faith

(1) Any rule of law permitting a party to a contract of insurance to avoid the contract on the ground that the utmost good faith has not been observed by the other party is abolished.

(2) Any rule of law to the effect that a contract of insurance is a contract based on the utmost good faith is modified to the extent required by the provisions of this Act and the Consumer Insurance (Disclosure and Representations) Act 2012.

Contracting out

15 Contracting out: consumer insurance contracts

(1) A term of a consumer insurance contract, or of any other contract, which would put the consumer in a worse position as respects any of the matters provided for in Part 3 or 4 of this Act than the consumer would be in by virtue of the provisions of those Parts (so far as relating to consumer insurance contracts) is to that extent of no effect.

(2) In subsection (1) references to a contract include a variation.

(3) This section does not apply in relation to a contract for the settlement of a claim arising under a consumer insurance contract.

16 Contracting out: non-consumer insurance contracts

(1) A term of a non-consumer insurance contract, or of any other contract, which would put the insured in a worse position as respects representations to which section 9 applies than the insured would be in by virtue of that section is to that extent of no effect.

(2) A term of a non-consumer insurance contract, or of any other contract, which would put the insured in a worse position as respects any of the other matters provided for in Part 2, 3 or 4 of this Act than the insured would be in by virtue of the provisions of those Parts (so far as relating to non-consumer insurance contracts) is to that extent of no effect, unless the requirements of section 17 have been satisfied in relation to the term.

(3) In this section references to a contract include a variation.

(4) This section does not apply in relation to a contract for the settlement of a claim arising under a non-consumer insurance contract.

17   The transparency requirements

(1) In this section, "the disadvantageous term" means such a term as is mentioned in section 16(2).

(2) The insurer must take sufficient steps to draw the disadvantageous term to the insured's attention before the contract is entered into or the variation agreed.

(3) The disadvantageous term must be clear and unambiguous as to its effect.

(4) In determining whether the requirements of subsections (2) and (3) have been met, the characteristics of insured persons of the kind in question, and the circumstances of the transaction, are to be taken into account.

(5) The insured may not rely on any failure on the part of the insurer to meet the requirements of subsection (2) if the insured (or its agent) had actual knowledge of the disadvantageous term when the contract was entered into or the variation agreed.

18   Contracting out: group insurance contracts

(1) This section applies to a contract of insurance referred to in section 13(1)(a); and in this section—

"A" and "the Cs" have the same meaning as in section 13,

"consumer C" means an individual who is one of the Cs, where the cover provided by the contract for that individual would have been a consumer insurance contract if entered into by that person rather than by A, and

"non-consumer C" means any of the Cs who is not a consumer C.

(2) A term of the contract of insurance, or any other contract, which puts a consumer C in a worse position as respects any matter dealt with in section 13 than that individual would be in by virtue of that section is to that extent of no effect.

(3) A term of the contract of insurance, or any other contract, which puts a non-consumer C in a worse position as respects any matter dealt with in section 13 than that person would be in by virtue of that section is to that extent of no effect, unless the requirements of section 17 have been met in relation to the term.

(4) Section 17 applies in relation to such a term as it applies to a term mentioned in section 16(2), with references to the insured being read as references to A rather than the non-consumer C.

(5) In this section references to a contract include a variation.

(6) This section does not apply in relation to a contract for the settlement of a claim arising under a contract of insurance to which this section applies.

PART 7   GENERAL

21   Provision consequential on Part 2

(2) In the Marine Insurance Act 1906, sections 18 (disclosure by assured), 19 (disclosure by agent effecting insurance) and 20 (representations pending negotiation of contract) are omitted.

(3) Any rule of law to the same effect as any of those provisions is abolished.

Section 8(2)

SCHEDULE 1

INSURERS' REMEDIES FOR QUALIFYING BREACHES

PART 1   CONTRACTS

1.   General

This Part of this Schedule applies to qualifying breaches of the duty of fair presentation in relation to non-consumer insurance contracts (for variations to them, see Part 2).

2. Deliberate or reckless breaches

If a qualifying breach was deliberate or reckless, the insurer—

    (a) may avoid the contract and refuse all claims, and

    (b) need not return any of the premiums paid.

Other breaches

  3. Paragraphs 4 to 6 apply if a qualifying breach was neither deliberate nor reckless.

  4. If, in the absence of the qualifying breach, the insurer would not have entered into the contract on any terms, the insurer may avoid the contract and refuse all claims, but must in that event return the premiums paid.

  5. If the insurer would have entered into the contract, but on different terms (other than terms relating to the premium), the contract is to be treated as if it had been entered into on those different terms if the insurer so requires.

  6. (1) In addition, if the insurer would have entered into the contract (whether the terms relating to matters other than the premium would have been the same or different), but would have charged a higher premium, the insurer may reduce proportionately the amount to be paid on a claim.

    (2) In sub-paragraph (1), "reduce proportionately" means that the insurer need pay on the claim only X% of what it would otherwise have been under an obligation to pay under the terms of the contract (or, if applicable, under the different terms provided for by virtue of paragraph 5), where—

$$X = \frac{\text{Premium actually charged}}{\text{Higher premium}} \times 100$$

PART 2 VARIATIONS

7. General

This Part of this Schedule applies to qualifying breaches of the duty of fair presentation in relation to variations to non-consumer insurance contracts.

8. Deliberate or reckless breaches

If a qualifying breach was deliberate or reckless, the insurer—

    (a) may by notice to the insured treat the contract as having been terminated with effect from the time when the variation was made, and

    (b) need not return any of the premiums paid.

Other breaches

  9. (1) This paragraph applies if—

    (a) a qualifying breach was neither deliberate nor reckless, and

    (b) the total premium was increased or not changed as a result of the variation.

    (2) If, in the absence of the qualifying breach, the insurer would not have agreed to the variation on any terms, the insurer may treat the contract as if the variation was never made, but must in that event return any extra premium paid.

    (3) If sub-paragraph (2) does not apply—

      (a) if the insurer would have agreed to the variation on different terms (other than terms relating to the premium), the variation is to be treated as if it had been entered into on those different terms if the insurer so requires, and

      (b) paragraph 11 also applies if (in the case of an increased premium) the insurer would have increased the premium by more than it did, or (in the case of an unchanged premium) the insurer would have increased the premium.

  10. (1) This paragraph applies if—

    (a) a qualifying breach was neither deliberate nor reckless, and

    (b) the total premium was reduced as a result of the variation.

(2) If, in the absence of the qualifying breach, the insurer would not have agreed to the variation on any terms, the insurer may treat the contract as if the variation was never made, and paragraph 11 also applies.

(3) If sub-paragraph (2) does not apply—

(a) if the insurer would have agreed to the variation on different terms (other than terms relating to the premium), the variation is to be treated as if it had been entered into on those different terms if the insurer so requires, and

(b) paragraph 11 also applies if the insurer would have increased the premium, would not have reduced the premium, or would have reduced it by less than it did.

11. Proportionate reduction

(1) If this paragraph applies, the insurer may reduce proportionately the amount to be paid on a claim arising out of events after the variation.

(2) In sub-paragraph (1), "reduce proportionately" means that the insurer need pay on the claim only Y% of what it would otherwise have been under an obligation to pay under the terms of the contract (whether on the original terms, or as varied, or under the different terms provided for by virtue of paragraph 9(3)(a) or 10(3)(a), as the case may be), where—

$$Y = \frac{\text{Total Premium actually charged}}{P} \times 100$$

(3) In the formula in sub-paragraph (2), "P"—

(a) in a paragraph 9(3)(b) case, is the total premium the insurer would have charged,

(b) in a paragraph 10(2) case, is the original premium,

(c) in a paragraph 10(3)(b) case, is the original premium if the insurer would not have changed it, and otherwise the increased or (as the case may be) reduced total premium the insurer would have charged.

PART 3 SUPPLEMENTARY

12. Relationship with section 84 of the Marine Insurance Act 1906

Section 84 of the Marine Insurance Act 1906 (return of premium for failure of consideration) is to be read subject to the provisions of this Schedule in relation to contracts of marine insurance which are non-consumer insurance contracts.

Modern Slavery Act 2015

(2015, c. 30)

1 Slavery, servitude and forced or compulsory labour

(1) A person commits an offence if—

(a) the person holds another person in slavery or servitude and the circumstances are such that the person knows or ought to know that the other person is held in slavery or servitude, or

(b) the person requires another person to perform forced or compulsory labour and the circumstances are such that the person knows or ought to know that the other person is being required to perform forced or compulsory labour.

(5) The consent of a person (whether an adult or a child) to any of the acts alleged to constitute holding the person in slavery or servitude, or requiring the person to perform forced or compulsory labour, does not preclude a determination that the person is being held in slavery or servitude, or required to perform forced or compulsory labour.

2 Human trafficking

(1) A person commits an offence if the person arranges or facilitates the travel of another person ("V") with a view to V being exploited.

(2) It is irrelevant whether V consents to the travel (whether V is an adult or a child).

8 Power to make slavery and trafficking reparation orders

(1) The court may make a slavery and trafficking reparation order against a person if—

(a) the person has been convicted of an offence under section 1, 2 or 4, and

(b) a confiscation order is made against the person in respect of the offence.

(2) The court may make a slavery and trafficking reparation order against the person in addition to dealing with the person in any other way (subject to section 10(1)).

(5) In determining whether to make a slavery and trafficking reparation order against the person the court must have regard to the person's means.

(6) If the court considers that—

(a) it would be appropriate both to impose a fine and to make a slavery and trafficking reparation order, but

(b) the person has insufficient means to pay both an appropriate fine and appropriate compensation under such an order,

the court must give preference to compensation (although it may impose a fine as well).

9 Effect of slavery and trafficking reparation orders

(1) A slavery and trafficking reparation order is an order requiring the person against whom it is made to pay compensation to the victim of a relevant offence for any harm resulting from that offence.

(2) The amount of the compensation is to be such amount as the court considers appropriate having regard to any evidence and to any representations made by or on behalf of the person or the prosecutor, but subject to subsection (4).

(3) The amount of the compensation payable under the slavery and trafficking reparation order (or if more than one order is made in the same proceedings, the total amount of the compensation payable under those orders) must not exceed the amount the person is required to pay under the confiscation order.

(4) In determining the amount to be paid by the person under a slavery and trafficking reparation order the court must have regard to the person's means.

10 Slavery and trafficking reparation orders: supplementary provision

(1) A slavery and trafficking reparation order and a compensation order under section 130 of the Powers of Criminal Courts (Sentencing) Act 2000 may not both be made in respect of the same offence.

11 Forfeiture of land vehicle, ship or aircraft

(1) This section applies if a person is convicted on indictment of an offence under section 2.

(2) The court may order the forfeiture of a land vehicle used or intended to be used in connection with the offence if the convicted person—

(a) owned the vehicle at the time the offence was committed,

(b) was at that time a director, secretary or manager of a company which owned the vehicle,

(c) was at that time in possession of the vehicle under a hire-purchase agreement,

(d) was at that time a director, secretary or manager of a company which was in possession of the vehicle under a hire-purchase agreement, or

(e) was driving the vehicle in the course of the commission of the offence.

12 Detention of land vehicle, ship or aircraft

(1) If a person ("P") has been arrested for an offence under section 2, a constable or senior immigration officer may detain a relevant land vehicle, ship or aircraft.

15   Slavery and trafficking prevention orders on application

(1) A magistrates' court may make a slavery and trafficking prevention order against a person ("the defendant") on an application by—

    (a) a chief officer of police,

    (b) an immigration officer, or

    (c) the Director General of the National Crime Agency ("the Director General").

17   Effect of slavery and trafficking prevention orders

(1) A slavery and trafficking prevention order is an order prohibiting the defendant from doing anything described in the order.

23   Slavery and trafficking risk orders

(1) A magistrates' court may make a slavery and trafficking risk order against a person ("the defendant") on an application by—

    (a) a chief officer of police,

    (b) an immigration officer, or

    (c) the Director General of the National Crime Agency ("the Director General").

24   Effect of slavery and trafficking risk orders

(1) A slavery and trafficking risk order is an order which prohibits the defendant from doing anything described in the order.

30   Offences

(1) A person who, without reasonable excuse, does anything that the person is prohibited from doing by—

    (a) a slavery and trafficking prevention order,

    (b) an interim slavery and trafficking prevention order,

    (c) a slavery and trafficking risk order,

    …

commits an offence.

Small Business, Enterprise and Employment Act 2015

(2015, c. 26)

1   Power to invalidate certain restrictive terms of business contracts

(1) The appropriate authority may by regulations make provision for the purpose of securing that any non-assignment of receivables term of a relevant contract—

    (a) has no effect;

    (b) has no effect in relation to persons of a prescribed description;

    (c) has effect in relation to persons of a prescribed description only for such purposes as may be prescribed.

(2) A "non-assignment of receivables term" of a contract is a term which prohibits or imposes a condition, or other restriction, on the assignment … by a party to the contract of the right to be paid any amount under the contract or any other contract between the parties.

(3) A contract is a relevant contract if—

    (a) it is a contract for goods, services or intangible assets (including intellectual property) which is not an excluded financial services contract, and

    (b) at least one of the parties has entered into it in connection with the carrying on of a business.

Social Action, Responsibility and Heroism Act 2015

(2015, c. 3)

1 When this Act applies

This Act applies when a court, in considering a claim that a person was negligent or in breach of statutory duty, is determining the steps that the person was required to take to meet a standard of care.

2 Social action

The court must have regard to whether the alleged negligence or breach of statutory duty occurred when the person was acting for the benefit of society or any of its members.

3 Responsibility

The court must have regard to whether the person, in carrying out the activity in the course of which the alleged negligence or breach of statutory duty occurred, demonstrated a predominantly responsible approach towards protecting the safety or other interests of others.

4 Heroism

The court must have regard to whether the alleged negligence or breach of statutory duty occurred when the person was acting heroically by intervening in an emergency to assist an individual in danger.

Part II

Proposed Statutes

(Draft) Negligence (Psychiatric Illness) Bill

(Law Com. No. 249)

An Act to amend and clarify the law relating to liability in negligence for psychiatric illness.   [1998]

New duties of care

1 Close tie: duty of care

(1) Subsection (2) imposes a duty of care for the purposes of the tort of negligence, and that subsection has effect subject to (and only to) subsections (3) to (6).

(2) A person (the defendant) owes a duty to take reasonable care to avoid causing another person (the plaintiff) to suffer a recognisable psychiatric illness as a result of the death, injury or imperilment of a third person (the immediate victim) if it is reasonably foreseeable that the defendant's act or omission might cause the plaintiff to suffer such an illness.

(3) The defendant must be taken not to have owed the duty unless—

   (a) his act or omission caused the death, injury or imperilment of the immediate victim, and

   (b) the plaintiff and the immediate victim had a close tie of love and affection immediately before the act or omission occurred or immediately before the onset of the plaintiff's illness (or both).

(4) The duty is not imposed if the court is satisfied that its imposition would not be just and reasonable—

   (a) because of any factor by virtue of which the defendant owed no duty of care to the immediate victim,

   (b) because the immediate victim voluntarily accepted the risk that the defendant's act or omission might cause his death, injury or imperilment, or

   (c) because the plaintiff was involved in conduct which is illegal or contrary to public policy.

(5) The duty is not imposed if the plaintiff—

   (a) voluntarily accepted the risk of suffering the illness, or

   (b) excluded the duty.

(6) The duty is not imposed if a provision which is contained in or made under another enactment, or which has the force of law by virtue of another enactment, regulates the defendant's duty to the plaintiff as regards the act or omission in place of the common law rules of the tort of negligence.

2 Close tie: duty of care if defendant is victim

(1) Subsection (2) imposes a duty of care for the purposes of the tort of negligence, and that subsection has effect subject to (and only to) subsections (3) to (6).

(2) A person (the defendant) owes a duty to take reasonable care to avoid causing another person (the plaintiff) to suffer a recognisable psychiatric illness as a result of the death, injury or imperilment of the defendant if it is reasonably foreseeable that the defendant's act or omission might cause the plaintiff to suffer such an illness.

(3) The defendant must be taken not to have owed the duty unless—

(a) his act or omission caused his death, injury or imperilment, and

(b) the plaintiff and the defendant had a close tie of love and affection immediately before the act or omission occurred or immediately before the onset of the plaintiff's illness (or both).

(4) The duty is not imposed if the court is satisfied that its imposition would not be just and reasonable—

(a) because the defendant chose to cause his death, injury or imperilment, or

(b) because the plaintiff was involved in conduct which is illegal or contrary to public policy.

(5) The duty is not imposed if the plaintiff—

(a) voluntarily accepted the risk of suffering the illness, or

(b) excluded the duty.

(6) The duty is not imposed if a provision which is contained in or made under another enactment, or which has the force of law by virtue of another enactment, regulates the defendant's duty to the plaintiff as regards the act or omission in place of the common law rules of the tort of negligence.

3 Meaning of close tie

(1) Subsections (2) to (5) have effect to determine whether for the purposes of section 1 the plaintiff and the immediate victim had a close tie of love and affection at a particular time.

(2) If at the time concerned the plaintiff fell within any of the categories listed in subsection (4) he and the immediate victim must be conclusively taken to have had a close tie of love and affection at that time.

(3) Otherwise it is for the plaintiff to show that he and the immediate victim had a close tie of love and affection at the time concerned.

(4) The categories are—

(a) the immediate victim's spouse;

(b) either parent of the immediate victim;

(c) any child of the immediate victim;

(d) any brother or sister of the immediate victim;

(e) the immediate victim's cohabitant.

(5) The plaintiff was the immediate victim's cohabitant at the time concerned if and only if—

(a) though not married to each other, they lived together as man and wife for a period of at least two years immediately before the time concerned, or

(b) though of the same gender, they had a relationship equivalent to that described in paragraph (a) for such a period.

(6) Subsections (2) to (5) also have effect to determine whether for the purposes of section 2 the plaintiff and the defendant had a close tie of love and affection at a particular time, reading references in those subsections to the immediate victim as references to the defendant.

Common law duty of care

4 Close tie: abolition of common law duty

The common law duty of care under the tort of negligence is abolished to the extent that (apart from this section)—

(a) it would arise in respect of a recognisable psychiatric illness suffered by a person (A) as a result of the death, injury or imperilment of another (B),

(b) it would depend on the existence of a close tie of love and affection between A and B, and

(c) it would be imposed on the person (whether B or a third person) causing the death, injury or imperilment.

5   Removal of certain restrictions

(1) This section amends and clarifies the law relating to a claim which—

(a) Is founded on the common law duty of care under the tort of negligence, and

(b) is made in respect of a recognisable psychiatric illness.

(2) It is not a condition of the claim's success that the illness was induced by a shock.

(3) The court may allow the claim even if the illness results from the defendant causing his own death, injury or imperilment.

Part III

Statutory Instruments

Package Travel, Package Holidays and Package Tours Regulations 1992

(SI 1992, No. 3288)

2. Interpretation

(1) In these Regulations—

'brochure' means any brochure in which packages are offered for sale;

'contract' means the agreement linking the consumer to the organiser or to the retailer, or to both, as the case may be;

'the Directive' means Council Directive 90/314/EEC on package travel, package holidays and package tours;

["member State" means a member State of the European Union or another State in the European Economic Area;]

'offer' includes an invitation to treat whether by means of advertising or otherwise, and cognate expressions shall be construed accordingly;

'organiser' means the person who, otherwise than occasionally, organises packages and sells or offers them for sale, whether directly or through a retailer;

'the other party to the contract' means the party, other than the consumer, to the contract, that is, the organiser or the retailer, or both, as the case may be;

'package' means the pre-arranged combination of at least two of the following components when sold or offered for sale at an inclusive price and when the service covers a period of more than twenty-four hours or includes overnight accommodation—

(a) transport;

(b) accommodation;

(c) other tourist services not ancillary to transport or accommodation and accounting for a significant proportion of the package,

and

(i) the submission of separate accounts for different components shall not cause the arrangements to be other than a package;

(ii) the fact that a combination is arranged at the request of the consumer and in accordance with his specific instructions (whether modified or not) shall not of itself cause it to be treated as other than pre-arranged;

and

'retailer' means the person who sells or offers for sale the package put together by the organiser.

(2) In the definition of 'contract' in paragraph (1) above, 'consumer' means the person who takes or agrees to take the package ('the principal contractor') and elsewhere in these Regulations 'consumer' means, as the context requires, the principal contractor, any person on whose behalf the principal contractor agrees to purchase the package ('the other beneficiaries') or any person to whom the principal contractor or any of the other beneficiaries transfers the package ('the transferee').

3.   Application of Regulations

(1) These Regulations apply to packages sold or offered for sale in the territory of the United Kingdom.

4.   Descriptive matter relating to packages must not be misleading

(1) No organiser or retailer shall supply to a consumer any descriptive matter concerning a package, the price of a package or any other conditions applying to the contract which contains any misleading information.

(2) If an organiser or retailer is in breach of paragraph (1) he shall be liable to compensate the consumer for any loss which the consumer suffers in consequence.

5.   Requirements as to brochures

(1) Subject to paragraph (4) below, no organiser shall make available a brochure to a possible consumer unless it indicates in a legible, comprehensive and accurate manner the price and adequate information about the matters specified in Schedule 1 to these Regulations in respect of the packages offered for sale in the brochure to the extent that those matters are relevant to the packages so offered.

(2) Subject to paragraph (4) below, no retailer shall make available to a possible consumer a brochure which he knows or has reasonable cause to believe does not comply with the requirements of paragraph (1).

(3) An organiser who contravenes paragraph (1) of this regulation and a retailer who contravenes paragraph (2) thereof shall be guilty of an offence and liable—

    (a) on summary conviction, to a fine not exceeding level 5 on the standard scale;

    (b) on conviction on indictment, to a fine.

(4) Where a brochure was first made available to consumers generally before 31 December 1992 no liability shall arise under this regulation in respect of an identical brochure being made available to a consumer at any time.

6.   Circumstances in which particulars in brochure are to be binding

(1) Subject to paragraphs (2) and (3) of this regulation, the particulars in the brochure (whether or not they are required by regulation 5(1) above to be included in the brochure) shall constitute implied warranties (or, as regards Scotland, implied terms) for the purposes of any contract to which the particulars relate.

(2) Paragraph (1) of this regulation does not apply—

    (a) in relation to information required to be included by virtue of paragraph 9 of Schedule 1 to these Regulations; or

    (b) where the brochure contains an express statement that changes may be made in the particulars contained in it before a contract is concluded and changes in the particulars so contained are clearly communicated to the consumer before a contract is concluded.

(3) Paragraph (1) of this regulation does not apply when the consumer and the other party to the contract agree after the contract has been made that the particulars in the brochure, or some of those particulars, should not form part of the contract.

7.   Information to be provided before contract is concluded

(1) Before a contract is concluded, the other party to the contract shall provide the intending consumer with the information specified in paragraph (2) below in writing or in some other appropriate form.

(2) The information referred to in paragraph (1) is—

    (a) general information about passport and visa requirements which apply to [nationals of the member State or States concerned] who purchase the package in question, including information about the length of time it is likely to take to obtain the appropriate passports and visas;

    (b) information about health formalities required for the journey and the stay; and

(c) the arrangements for security for the money paid over and (where applicable) for the repatriation of the consumer in the event of insolvency.

(3) If the intending consumer is not provided with the information required by paragraph (1) in accordance with that paragraph the other party to the contract shall be guilty of an offence and liable—

(a) on summary conviction, to a fine not exceeding level 5 on the standard scale; and

(b) on conviction on indictment, to a fine.

8. Information to be provided in good time

(1) The other party to the contract shall in good time before the start of the journey provide the consumer with the information specified in paragraph (2) below in writing or in some other appropriate form.

(2) The information referred to in paragraph (1) is the following—

(a) the times and places of intermediate stops and transport connections and particulars of the place to be occupied by the traveller (for example, cabin or berth on ship, sleeper compartment on train);

(b) the name, address and telephone number—

(i) of the representative of the other party to the contract in the locality where the consumer is to stay,

or, if there is no such representative,

(ii) of an agency in that locality on whose assistance a consumer in difficulty would be able to call,

or, if there is no such representative or agency, a telephone number or other information which will enable the consumer to contact the other party to the contract during the stay; and

(c) in the case of a journey or stay abroad by a child under the age of 16 on the day when the journey or stay is due to start, information enabling direct contact to be made with the child or the person responsible at the place where he is to stay; and

(d) except where the consumer is required as a term of the contract to take out an insurance policy in order to cover the cost of cancellation by the consumer or the cost of assistance, including repatriation, in the event of accident or illness, information about an insurance policy which the consumer may, if he wishes, take out in respect of the risk of those costs being incurred.

(3) If the consumer is not provided with the information required by paragraph (1) in accordance with that paragraph the other party to the contract shall be guilty of an offence and liable—

(a) on summary conviction, to a fine not exceeding level 5 on the standard scale;

(b) on conviction on indictment, to a fine.

9. Contents and form of contract

(1) The other party to the contract shall ensure that—

(a) depending on the nature of the package being purchased, the contract contains at least the elements specified in Schedule 2 to these Regulations;

(b) subject to paragraph (2) below, all the terms of the contract are set out in writing or such other form as is comprehensible and accessible to the consumer and are communicated to the consumer before the contract is made; and

(c) a written copy of these terms is supplied to the consumer.

(2) Paragraph (1)(b) above does not apply when the interval between the time when the consumer approaches the other party to the contract with a view to entering it is impracticable to comply with the sub-paragraph.

(3) It is an implied condition (or, as regards Scotland, an implied term) of the contract that the other party to the contract complies with the provisions of paragraph (1).

10.   Transfer of bookings

(1) In every contract there is an implied term that where the consumer is prevented from proceeding with the package the consumer may transfer his booking to a person who satisfies all the conditions applicable to the package, provided that the consumer gives reasonable notice to the other party to the contract of his intention to transfer before the date when departure is due to take place.

(2) Where a transfer is made in accordance with the implied term set out in paragraph (1) above, the transferor and the transferee shall be jointly and severally liable to the other party to the contract for payment of the price of the package (or, if part of the price has been paid, for payment of the balance) and for any additional costs arising from such transfer.

11.   Price revision

(1) Any term in a contract to the effect that the prices laid down in the contract may be revised shall be void and of no effect unless the contract provides for the possibility of upward or downward revision and satisfies the conditions laid down in paragraph (2) below.

(2) The conditions mentioned in paragraph (1) are that—

    (a) the contract states precisely how the revised price is to be calculated;

    (b) the contract provides that price revisions are to be made solely to allow for variations in—

        (i)   transportation costs, including the cost of fuel,

        (ii) dues, taxes or fees chargeable for services such as landing taxes or embarkation or disembarkation fees at ports and airports, or

        (iii) the exchange rates applied to the particular package; and

(3) Notwithstanding any terms of a contract,

    (i)   no price increase may be made in a specified period which may not be less than 30 days before the departure date stipulated; and

    (ii) as against an individual consumer liable under the contract, no price increase may be made in respect of variations which would produce an increase of less than 2 per cent, or such greater percentage as the contract may specify ('non-eligible variations') and that the non-eligible variations shall be left out of account in the calculation.

12.   Significant alterations to essential terms

In every contract there are implied terms to the effect that—

    (a) where the organiser is constrained before the departure to alter significantly an essential term of the contract, such as the price (so far as regulation 11 permits him to do so), he will notify the consumer as quickly as possible in order to enable him to take appropriate decisions and in particular to withdraw from the contract without penalty or to accept a rider to the contract specifying the alterations made and their impact on the price; and

    (b) the consumer will inform the organiser or the retailer of his decision as soon as possible.

13.   Withdrawal by consumer pursuant to regulation 12 and cancellation by organiser

(1) The terms set out in paragraphs (2) and (3) below are implied in every contract and apply where the consumer withdraws from the contract pursuant to the term in it implied by virtue of regulation 12(a), or where the organiser, for any reason other than the fault of the consumer, cancels the package before the agreed date of departure.

(2) The consumer is entitled—

    (a) to take a substitute package of equivalent or superior quality if the other party to the contract is able to offer him such a substitute; or

    (b) to take a substitute package of lower quality if the other party to the contract is able to offer him one and to recover from the organiser the difference in price between the price of the package purchased and that of the substitute package; or

    (c) to have repaid to him as soon as possible all the monies paid by him under the contract.

(3) The consumer is entitled, if appropriate, to be compensated by the organiser for non-performance of the contract except where—

    (a) the package is cancelled because the number of persons who agree to take it is less than the minimum number required and the consumer is informed of the cancellation, in writing, within the period indicated in the description of the package; or

    (b) the package is cancelled by reason of unusual and unforeseeable circumstances beyond the control of the party by whom this exception is pleaded, the consequences of which could not have been avoided even if all due care had been exercised.

(4) Overbooking shall not be regarded as a circumstance falling within the provisions of sub-paragraph (b) of paragraph (3) above.

14. Significant proportion of services not provided

(1) The terms set out in paragraphs (2) and (3) below are implied in every contract and apply where, after departure, a significant proportion of the services contracted for is not provided or the organiser becomes aware that he will be unable to procure a significant proportion of the services to be provided.

(2) The organiser will make suitable alternative arrangements, at no extra cost to the consumer, for the continuation of the package and will, where appropriate, compensate the consumer for the difference between the services to be supplied under the contract and those supplied.

(3) If it is impossible to make arrangements as described in paragraph (2), or these are not accepted by the consumer for good reasons, the organiser will, where appropriate, provide the consumer with equivalent transport back to the place of departure or to another place to which the consumer has agreed and will, where appropriate, compensate the consumer.

15. Liability of other party to the contract for proper performance of obligations under contract

(1) The other party to the contract is liable to the consumer for the proper performance of the obligations under the contract, irrespective of whether such obligations are to be performed by that other party or by other suppliers of services but this shall not affect any remedy or right of action which that other party may have against those other suppliers of services.

(2) The other party to the contract is liable to the consumer for any damage caused to him by the failure to perform the contract or the improper performance of the contract unless the failure or the improper performance is due neither to any fault of that other party nor to that of another supplier of services, because—

    (a) the failures which occur in the performance of the contract are attributable to the consumer;

    (b) such failures are attributable to a third party unconnected with the provision of the services contracted for, and are unforeseeable or unavoidable; or

    (c) such failures are due to—

        (i) unusual and unforeseeable circumstances beyond the control of the party by whom this exception is pleaded, the consequences of which could not have been avoided even if all due care had been exercised; or

        (ii) an event which the other party to the contract or the supplier of services, even with all due care, could not foresee or forestall.

(3) In the case of damage arising from the non-performance or improper performance of the services involved in the package, the contract may provide for compensation to be limited in accordance with the international conventions which govern such services.

(4) In the case of damage other than personal injury resulting from the non-performance or improper performance of the services involved in the package, the contract may include a term limiting the of compensation which will be paid to the consumer, provided that the limitation is not unreasonable.

(5) Without prejudice to paragraph (3) and paragraph (4) above, liability under paragraphs (1) and (2) above cannot be excluded by any contractual term.

(6) The terms set out in paragraphs (7) and (8) below are implied in every contract.

(7) In the circumstances described in paragraph (2)(b) and (c) of this regulation, the other party to the contract will give prompt assistance to a consumer in difficulty.

(8) If the consumer complains about a defect in the performance of the contract, the other party to the contract, or his local representative, if there is one, will make prompt efforts to find appropriate solutions.

(9) The contract must clearly and explicitly oblige the consumer to communicate at the earliest opportunity, in writing or any other appropriate form, to the supplier of the services concerned and to the other party to the contract any failure which he perceives at the place where the services concerned are supplied.

27. Saving for civil consequences

No contract shall be void or unenforceable, and no right of action in civil proceedings in respect of any loss shall arise, by reason only of the commission of an offence under regulations 5, 7, 8, 16 or 22 of these Regulations.

28. Terms implied in contract

Where it is provided in these Regulations that a term (whether so described or whether described as a condition or warranty) is implied in the contract it is so implied irrespective of the law which governs the contract.

Regulation 5

SCHEDULE 1

INFORMATION TO BE INCLUDED (IN ADDITION TO THE PRICE) IN BROCHURES WHERE RELEVANT TO PACKAGES OFFERED

1. The destination and the means, characteristics and categories of transport used.

2. The type of accommodation, its location, category or degree of comfort and its main features and, where the accommodation is to be provided in a member State, its approval or tourist classification under the rules of that member State.

3. The meals which are included in the package.

4. The itinerary.

5. General information about passport and visa requirements which apply for [nationals of the member State or States in which the brochure is made available] and health formalities required for the journey and the stay.

6. Either the monetary amount or the percentage of the price which is to be paid on account and the timetable for payment of the balance.

7. Whether a minimum number of persons is required for the package to take place and, if so, the deadline for informing the consumer in the event of cancellation.

8. The arrangements (if any) which apply if consumers are delayed at the outward or homeward points of departure.

9. The arrangements for security for money paid over and for the repatriation of the consumer in the event of insolvency.

Regulation 9

SCHEDULE 2

ELEMENTS TO BE INCLUDED IN THE CONTRACT IF RELEVANT TO THE PARTICULAR PACKAGE

1. The travel destination(s) and, where periods of stay are involved, the relevant periods, with dates.

2. The means, characteristics and categories of transport to be used and the dates, times and points of departure and return.

3. Where the package includes accommodation, its location, its tourist category of degree of comfort, its main features and, where the accommodation is to be provided in a member State, its compliance with the rules of that member State.

4. The meals which are included in the package.

5. Whether a minimum number of persons is required for the package to take place and, if so, the deadline for informing the consumer in the event of cancellation.

6. The itinerary.

7. Visits, excursions or other services which are included in the total price agreed for the package.

8. The name and address of the organiser, the retailer and, where appropriate, the insurer.

9. The price of the package, if the price may be revised in accordance with the term which may be included in the contract under regulation 11, an indication of the possibility of such price revisions, and an indication of any dues, taxes or fees chargeable for certain services (landing, embarkation or disembarkation fees at ports and airports and tourist taxes) where such costs are not included in the package.

10. The payment schedule and method of payment.

11. Special requirements which the consumer has communicated to the organiser or retailer when making the booking and which both have accepted.

12. The periods within which the consumer must make any complaint about the failure to perform or the inadequate performance of the contract.

Regulation 23

SCHEDULE 3
ENFORCEMENT

1. Enforcement authority

(1) Every local weights and measures authority in Great Britain shall be an enforcement authority for the purposes of regulations 5, 7, 8, 16 and 22 of these Regulations ('the relevant regulations'), and it shall be the duty of each such authority to enforce those provisions within their area.

Employers' Liability (Compulsory Insurance) Regulations 1998

(SI 1998, No. 2573)

1. Citation, commencement and interpretation

(2) In these Regulations—

'the 1969 Act' means the Employers' Liability (Compulsory Insurance) Act 1969;

. . .

2. Prohibition of certain conditions in policies of insurance

(1) For the purposes of the 1969 Act, there is prohibited in any contract of insurance any condition which provides (in whatever terms) that no liability (either generally or in respect of a particular claim) shall arise under the policy, or that any such liability so arising shall cease, if—

    (a) some specified thing is done or omitted to be done after the happening of the event giving rise to a claim under the policy,

    (b) the policy holder does not take reasonable care to protect his employees against the risk of bodily injury or disease in the course of their employment;

    (c) the policy holder fails to comply with the requirements of any enactment for the protection of employees against the risk of bodily injury or disease in the course of their employment; or

(d) the policy holder does not keep specified records or fails to provide the insurer with or make available to him information from such records.

(2) For the purposes of the 1969 Act there is also prohibited in a policy of insurance any condition which requires—

(a) a relevant employee to pay; or

(b) an insured employer to pay the relevant employee, the first amount of any claim or any aggregation of claims.

(3) Paragraphs (1) and (2) above do not prohibit for the purposes of the 1969 Act a condition in a policy of insurance which requires the employer to pay or contribute any sum to the insurer in respect of the satisfaction of any claim made under the contract of insurance by a relevant employee or any costs and expenses incurred in relation to any such claim.

3.   Limit of amount of compulsory insurance

(1) Subject to paragraph (2) below, the amount for which an employer is required by the 1969 Act to insure and maintain insurance in respect of relevant employees under one or more policies of insurance shall be, or shall in aggregate be not less than £5 million in respect of—

(a) a claim relating to any one or more of those employees arising out of any one occurrence; and

(b) any costs and expenses incurred in relation to any such claim.

Provision and Use of Work Equipment Regulations 1998

(SI 1998, No. 2306)

2.   Interpretation

(1) In these Regulations, unless the context otherwise requires—

'the 1974 Act' means the Health and Safety at Work etc. Act 1974;

'employer' except in regulation 3(2) and (3) includes a person to whom the requirements imposed by the Regulations apply by virtue of regulation 3(3)(a) and (b);

'essential requirements' means requirements described in regulation 10(1);

'the Executive' means the Health and Safety Executive;

'inspection' in relation to an inspection under paragraph (1) or (2) of regulation 6—

(a) means such visual or more rigorous inspection by a competent person as is appropriate for the purpose described in the paragraph;

(b) where it is appropriate to carry out testing for the purpose, includes testing the nature and extent of which are appropriate for the purpose;

'power press' means a press or press brake for the working of metal by means of tools, or for die proving, which is power driven and which embodies a flywheel and clutch;

'thorough examination' in relation to a thorough examination under paragraph (1), (2), (3) or (4) of regulation 32—

(a) means a thorough examination by a competent person;

(b) includes testing the nature and extent of which are appropriate for the purpose described in the paragraph;

'use' in relation to work equipment means any activity involving work equipment and includes starting, stopping, programming, setting, transporting, repairing, modifying, maintaining, servicing and cleaning;

'work equipment' means any machinery, appliance, apparatus, tool or installation for use at work (whether exclusively or not);

and related expressions shall be construed accordingly.

4. Suitability of work equipment

(1) Every employer shall ensure that work equipment is so constructed or adapted as to be suitable for the purpose for which it is used or provided.

(2) In selecting work equipment, every employer shall have regard to the working conditions and to the risks to the health and safety of persons which exist in the premises or undertaking in which that work equipment is to be used and any additional risk posed by the use of that work equipment.

(3) Every employer shall ensure that work equipment is used only for operations for which, and under conditions for which, it is suitable.

(4) In this regulation 'suitable' [—

> (a) subject to paragraph (b), means suitable in any respect which it is reasonably foreseeable will affect the health and safety of any person; . . .]

5. Maintenance

(1) Every employer shall ensure that work equipment is maintained in an efficient state, in efficient working order and in good repair.

(2) Every employer shall ensure that where any machinery has a maintenance log, the log is kept up to date.

6. Inspection

(1) Every employer shall ensure that, where the safety of work equipment depends on the installation conditions, it is inspected—

> (a) after installation and before being put into service for the first time; or
> (b) after assembly at a new site or in a new location, to ensure that it has been installed correctly and is safe to operate.

(2) Every employer shall ensure that work equipment exposed to conditions causing deterioration which is liable to result in dangerous situations is inspected—

> (a) at suitable intervals; and
> (b) each time that exceptional circumstances which are liable to jeopardise the safety of the work equipment have occurred,

to ensure that health and safety conditions are maintained and that any deterioration can be detected and remedied in good time.

(3) Every employer shall ensure that the result of an inspection made under this regulation is recorded and kept until the next inspection under this regulation is recorded.

(4) Every employer shall ensure that no work equipment—

> (a) leaves his undertaking; or
> (b) if obtained from the undertaking of another person, is used in his undertaking, unless it is accompanied by physical evidence that the last inspection required to be carried out under this regulation has been carried out.

7. Specific risks

(1) Where the use of work equipment is likely to involve a specific risk to health or safety, every employer shall ensure that—

> (a) the use of that work equipment is restricted to those persons given the task of using it; and
> (b) repairs, modifications, maintenance or servicing of that work equipment is restricted to those persons who have been specifically designated to perform operations of that description (whether or not also authorised to perform other operations).

(2) The employer shall ensure that the persons designated for the purposes of subparagraph (b) of paragraph (1) have received adequate training related to any operations in respect of which they have been so designated.

8. Information and instructions

(1) Every employer shall ensure that all persons who use work equipment have available to them adequate health and safety information and, where appropriate, written instructions pertaining to the use of the work equipment.

(2) Every employer shall ensure that any of his employees who supervises or manages the use of work equipment has available to him adequate health and safety information and, where appropriate, written instructions pertaining to the use of the work equipment.

(3) Without prejudice to the generality of paragraphs (1) or (2), the information and instructions required by either of those paragraphs shall include information and, where appropriate, written instructions on—

(a) the conditions in which and the methods by which the work equipment may be used;

(b) foreseeable abnormal situations and the action to be taken if such a situation were to occur; and

(c) any conclusions to be drawn from experience in using the work equipment.

(4) Information and instructions required by this regulation shall be readily comprehensive to those concerned.

9. Training

(1) Every employer shall ensure that all persons who use work equipment have received adequate training for purposes of health and safety, including training in the methods which may be adopted when using the work equipment, any risks which such use may entail and precautions to be taken.

(2) Every employer shall ensure that any of his employees who supervises or manages the use of work equipment has received adequate training for purposes of health and safety, including training in the methods which may be adopted when using the work equipment, any risks which such use may entail and precautions to be taken.

10. Conformity with Community requirements

[(1) Every employer shall ensure that an item of work equipment conforms at all times with any essential requirements, other than requirements which, at the time of its being first supplied or put into service in any place in which these Regulations apply, did not apply to work equipment of its type.

(2) In this regulation "essential requirements", in relation to an item of work equipment, means requirements relating to the design and construction of work equipment of its type in any of the instruments listed in Schedule 1 (being instruments which give effect to Community directives concerning the safety of products);]

(3) This regulation applies to items of work equipment provided for use in the premises or undertaking of the employer for the first time after 31 December 1992.

11. Dangerous parts of machinery

(1) Every employer shall ensure that measures are taken in accordance with paragraph (2) which are effective—

(a) to prevent access to any dangerous part of machinery or to any rotating stock-bar; or

(b) to stop the movement of any dangerous part of machinery or rotating stock-bar before any part of a person enters a danger zone.

[(2) The measures required by paragraph (1) shall consist of—

(a) the provision of fixed guards enclosing every dangerous part or rotating stock-bar where and to the extent that it is practicable to do so, but where or to the extent that it is not, then

(b) the provision of other guards or protection devices where and to the extent that it is practicable to do so, but where or to the extent that it is not, then

(c) the provision of jigs, holders, push-sticks or similar protection appliances used in conjunction with the machinery where and to the extent that it is practicable to do so,

and the provision of such information, instruction, training and supervision as is necessary.]

(3) All guards and protection devices provided under sub-paragraphs (a) or (b) of paragraph (2) shall—

(a) be suitable for the purpose for which they are provided;

(b) be of good construction, sound material and adequate strength;

(c) be maintained in an efficient state, in efficient working order and in good repair;

(d) not give rise to any increased risk to health or safety;

(e) not be easily bypassed or disabled;

(f) be situated at sufficient distance from the danger zone;

(g) not unduly restrict the view of the operating cycle of the machinery, where such a view is necessary;

(h) be so constructed or adapted that they allow operations necessary to fit or replace parts and for maintenance work, restricting access so that it is allowed only to the area where the work is to be carried out and, if possible, without having to dismantle the guard or protection device.

(4) All protection appliances provided under sub-paragraph (c) of paragraph (2) shall comply with sub-paragraphs (a) to (d) and (g) of paragraph (3).

(5) In this regulation—

'danger zone' means any zone in or around machinery in which a person is exposed to a risk to health or safety from contact with a dangerous part of machinery or a rotating stock-bar;

'stock-bar' means any part of a stock-bar which projects beyond the head-stock of a lathe.

12.   Protection against specified hazards

(1) Every employer shall take measures to ensure that the exposure of a person using work equipment to any risk to his health or safety from any hazard specified in paragraph (3) is either prevented, or, where that is not reasonably practicable, adequately controlled.

(2) The measures required by paragraph (1) shall—

(a) be measures other than the provision of personal protective equipment or of information, instruction, training and supervision, so far as is reasonably practicable; and

(b) include, where appropriate, measures to minimise the effects of the hazard as well as to reduce the likelihood of the hazard occurring.

(3) The hazards referred to in paragraph (1) are—

(a) any article or substance falling or being ejected from work equipment;

(b) rupture or disintegration of parts of work equipment;

(c) work equipment catching fire or overheating;

(d) the unintended or premature discharge of any article or of any gas, dust, liquid, vapour or other substance which, in each case, is produced, used or stored in the work equipment;

(e) the unintended or premature explosion of the work equipment or any article or substance produced, used or stored in it.

(4) For the purposes of this regulation 'adequately' means adequately having regard only to the nature of the hazard and the nature and degree of exposure to the risk.

(5) This regulation shall not apply where any of the following Regulations apply in respect of any risk to a person's health or safety for which such Regulations require measures to be taken to prevent or control such risk, namely—

(a)   the Ionising Radiations Regulations 1985;

(b)   the [Control of Asbestos Regulations 2012];

(c)   the Control of Substances Hazardous to Health Regulations 1994;

(d)   the [Control of Noise at Work Regulations 2005];

(f)   the Control of Lead at Work Regulations 1998

[(g) the Control of Vibration at Work Regulations 2005].

13.   High or very low temperature

Every employer shall ensure that work equipment, parts of work equipment and any article or substance produced, used or stored in work equipment which, in each case, is at a high or very low temperature shall have protection where appropriate so as to prevent injury to any person by burn, scald or sear.

14. Controls for starting or making a significant change in operating conditions

(1) Every employer shall ensure that, where appropriate, work equipment is provided with one or more controls for the purposes of—

(a) starting the work equipment (including re-starting after a stoppage for any reason); or

(b) controlling any change in the speed, pressure or other operating conditions of the work equipment where such conditions after the change result in risk to health and safety which is greater than or of a different nature from such risks before the change.

(2) Subject to paragraph (3), every employer shall ensure that, where a control is required by paragraph (1), it shall not be possible to perform any operation mentioned in sub-paragraph (a) or (b) of that paragraph except by a deliberate action on such control.

(3) Paragraph (1) shall not apply to re-starting or changing operating conditions as a result of the normal operating cycle of an automatic device.

15. Stop controls

(1) Every employer shall ensure that, where appropriate, work equipment is provided with one or more readily accessible controls the operation of which will bring the work equipment to a safe condition in a safe manner.

(2) Any control required by paragraph (1) shall bring the work equipment to a complete stop where necessary for reasons of health and safety.

(3) Any control required by paragraph (1) shall, if necessary for reasons of health and safety, switch off all sources of energy after stopping the functioning of the work equipment.

(4) Any control required by paragraph (1) shall operate in priority to any control which starts or changes the operating conditions of the work equipment.

16. Emergency stop controls

(1) Every employer shall ensure that, where appropriate, work equipment is provided with one or more readily accessible emergency stop controls unless it is not necessary by reason of the nature of the hazards and the time taken for the work equipment to come to a complete stop as a result of the action of any control provided by virtue of regulation 15(1).

(2) Any control required by paragraph (1) shall operate in priority to any control required by regulation 15(1).

17. Controls

(1) Every employer shall ensure that all controls for work equipment are clearly visible and identifiable, including by appropriate marking where necessary.

(2) Except where necessary, the employer shall ensure that no control for work equipment is in a position where any person operating the control is exposed to a risk to his health or safety.

(3) Every employer shall ensure where appropriate—

(a) that, so far as is reasonably practicable, the operator of any control is able to ensure from the position of that control that no person is in a place where he would be exposed to any risk to his health or safety as a result of the operation of that control, but where or to the extent that it is not reasonably practicable;

(b) that, so far as is reasonably practicable, systems of work are effective to ensure that, when work equipment is about to start, no person is in a place where he would be exposed to a risk to his health or safety as a result of the work equipment starting, but where neither of these is reasonably practicable;

(c) that an audible, visible or other suitable warning is given by virtue of regulation 24 whenever work equipment is about to start.

(4) Every employer shall take appropriate measures to ensure that any person who is in a place where he would be exposed to a risk to his health or safety as a result of the starting or stopping of work equipment has sufficient time and suitable means to avoid that risk.

18.   Control systems

[(1) Every employer shall ensure, so far as is reasonably practicable, that all control systems of work equipment—

   (a) are safe; and
   (b) are chosen making due allowance for the failures, faults and constraints to be expected in the planned circumstances of use.]

(2) Without prejudice to the generality of paragraph (1), a control system shall not be safe unless—

   (a) its operation does not create any increased risk to health or safety;
   (b) it ensures, so far as is reasonably practicable, that any fault in or damage to any part of the control system or the loss of supply of any source of energy used by the work equipment cannot result in additional or increased risk to health or safety;
   (c) it does not impede the operation of any control required by regulation 15 or 16.

19.   Isolation from sources of energy

(1) Every employer shall ensure that where appropriate work equipment is provided with suitable means to isolate it from all its sources of energy.

(2) Without prejudice to the generality of paragraph (1), the means mentioned in that paragraph shall not be suitable unless they are clearly identifiable and readily accessible.

(3) Every employer shall take appropriate measures to ensure that re-connection of any energy source to work equipment does not expose any person using the work equipment to any risk to his health or safety.

20.   Stability

Every employer shall ensure that work equipment or any part of work equipment is stabilised by clamping or otherwise where necessary for purposes of health or safety.

21.   Lighting

Every employer shall ensure that suitable and sufficient lighting, which takes account of the operations to be carried out, is provided at any place where a person uses work equipment.

22.   Maintenance operations

Every employer shall take appropriate measures to ensure that work equipment is so constructed or adapted that, so far as is reasonably practicable, maintenance operations which involve a risk to health or safety can be carried out while the work equipment is shut down, or in other cases—

   (a) maintenance operations can be carried out without exposing the person carrying them out to a risk to his health or safety; or
   (b) appropriate measures can be taken for the protection of any person carrying out maintenance operations which involve a risk to his health or safety.

23.   Markings

Every employer shall ensure that work equipment is marked in a clearly visible manner with any marking appropriate for reasons of health and safety.

24.   Warnings

(1) Every employer shall ensure that work equipment incorporates any warnings or warning devices which are appropriate for reasons of health and safety.

(2) Without prejudice to the generality of paragraph (1), warnings given by warning devices on work equipment shall not be appropriate unless they are unambiguous, easily perceived and easily understood.

Electronic Commerce (EC Directive) Regulations 2002

(SI 2002, No. 2013)

2. Interpretation

(1) In these Regulations and in the Schedule . . .

'consumer' means any natural person who is acting for purposes other than those of his trade, business or profession; . . .

'the Directive' means Directive 2000/31/EC of the European Parliament and of the Council of 8 June 2000 on certain legal aspects of information society services, in particular electronic commerce, in the Internal Market (Directive on electronic commerce); . . .

'information society services' (which is summarised in recital 17 of the Directive as covering 'any service normally provided for remuneration, at a distance, by means of electronic equipment for the processing (including digital compression) and storage of data, and at the individual request of a recipient of a service') has the meaning set out in Article 2(a) of the Directive, (which refers to Article 1(2) of Directive 98/34/EC of the European Parliament and of the Council of 22 June 1998 laying down a procedure for the provision of information in the field of technical standards and regulations, as amended by Directive 98/48/EC of 20 July 1998); . . .

'recipient of the service' means any person who, for professional ends or otherwise, uses an information society service, in particular for the purposes of seeking information or making it accessible; . . .

'service provider' means any person providing an information society service;

'the Treaty' means [the Treaty on the Functioning of the European Union].

(3) Terms used in the Directive other than those in paragraph (1) above shall have the same meaning as in the Directive.

9. Information to be provided where contracts are concluded by electronic means

(1) Unless parties who are not consumers have agreed otherwise, where a contract is to be concluded by electronic means a service provider shall, prior to an order being placed by the recipient of a service, provide to that recipient in a clear, comprehensible and unambiguous manner the information set out in (a) to (d) below—

    (a) the different technical steps to follow to conclude the contract;

    (b) whether or not the concluded contract will be filed by the service provider and whether it will be accessible;

    (c) the technical means for identifying and correcting input errors prior to the placing of the order; and

    (d) the languages offered for the conclusion of the contract.

(2) Unless parties who are not consumers have agreed otherwise, a service provider shall indicate which relevant codes of conduct he subscribes to and give information on how those codes can be consulted electronically.

(3) Where the service provider provides terms and conditions applicable to the contract to the recipient, the service provider shall make them available to him in a way that allows him to store and reproduce them.

(4) The requirements of paragraphs (1) and (2) above shall not apply to contracts concluded exclusively by exchange of electronic mail or by equivalent individual communications.

10. Other information requirements

Regulations 6, 7, 8 and 9(1) have effect in addition to any other information requirements in legislation giving effect to [EU] law.

11. Placing of the order

(1) Unless parties who are not consumers have agreed otherwise, where the recipient of the service places his order through technological means, a service provider shall—

    (a) acknowledge receipt of the order to the recipient of the service without undue delay and by electronic means; and

    (b) make available to the recipient of the service appropriate, effective and accessible technical means allowing him to identify and correct input errors prior to the placing of the order.

  (2) For the purposes of paragraph (1)(a) above—

    (a) the order and the acknowledgement of receipt will be deemed to be received when the parties to whom they are addressed are able to access them; and

    (b) the acknowledgement of receipt may take the form of the provision of the service paid for where that service is an information society service.

  (3) The requirements of paragraph (1) above shall not apply to contracts concluded exclusively by exchange of electronic mail or by equivalent individual communications.

12. Meaning of the term 'order'

Except in relation to regulation 9(1)(c) and regulation 11(1)(b) where 'order' shall be the contractual offer, 'order' may be but need not be the contractual offer for the purposes of regulations 9 and 11.

13. Liability of the service provider

The duties imposed by regulations 6, 7, 8, 9(1) and 11(1)(a) shall be enforceable, at the suit of any recipient of a service, by an action against the service provider for damages for breach of statutory duty.

14. Compliance with Regulation 9(3)

Where on request a service provider has failed to comply with the requirement in regulation 9(3), the recipient may seek an order from any court having jurisdiction in relation to the contract requiring that service provider to comply with that requirement.

15. Right to rescind contract

Where a person—

    (a) has entered into a contract to which these Regulations apply, and

    (b) the service provider has not made available means of allowing him to identify and correct input errors in compliance with regulation 11(1)(b),

he shall be entitled to rescind the contract unless any court having jurisdiction in relation to the contract in question orders otherwise on the application of the service provider.

Damages (Variation of Periodical Payments) Order 2005

(SI 2005, No. 841)

1. Citation, commencement, interpretation and extent

  (2) In this Order—

    (a) 'the Act' means the Damages Act 1996;

    (b) 'agreement' means an agreement by parties to a claim or action for damages which settles the claim or action and which provides for periodical payments;

    (c) 'damages' means damages for future pecuniary loss in respect of personal injury;

    (d) 'defence society' means the Medical Defence Union or the Medical Protection Society;

    (e) 'variable agreement' means an agreement which contains a provision referred to in Article 9(1);

    (f) 'variable order' means an order for periodical payments which contains a provision referred to in Article 2.

  (3) In the application of this Order to Northern Ireland—

    (a) 'claimant' means plaintiff;

    (b) 'permission' means leave;

(c) 'statements of case' means, in the High Court, the writ and pleadings and, in the county court, the civil bill and any notice of intention to defend, defence, notice for particulars, replies and counterclaim.

(4) This Order extends to England and Wales and Northern Ireland.

(5) This Order applies to proceedings begun on or after the date on which it comes into force.

2.   Power to make variable orders

If there is proved or admitted to be a chance that at some definite or indefinite time in the future the claimant will—

(a) as a result of the act or omission which gave rise to the cause of action, develop some serious disease or suffer some serious deterioration, or

(b) enjoy some significant improvement in his physical or mental condition, where that condition had been adversely affected as a result of that act or omission,

the court may, on the application of a party, with the agreement of all the parties, or of its own initiative, provide in an order for periodical payments that it may be varied.

3.   Defendant's financial resources

Unless—

(a) the defendant is insured in respect of the claim,

(b) the source of payment under the order for periodical payments is a government or health service body within the meaning of section 2A(2) of the Act,

(c) the payment is guaranteed under section 6 of or the Schedule to the Act, or

[(d) the order is made by consent and the claimant is neither a child, nor a person who lacks capacity within the meaning of the Mental Capacity Act 2005 (c.9) to administer and manage his property and affairs nor a patient within the meaning of Part VII of the Mental Health (Northern Ireland) Order 1986,]

the court will take into account the defendant's likely future financial resources in considering whether to make a variable order.

4.   Award of provisional damages

The court may make a variable order in addition to an order for an award of provisional damages made by virtue of section 32A of the [Senior Courts Act 1981] or section 51 of the County Courts Act 1984 or, in relation to Northern Ireland, paragraph 10(2)(a) of Schedule 6 to the Administration of Justice Act 1982.

5.   Contents of variable order

Where the court makes a variable order—

(a) the damages must be assessed or agreed on the assumption that the disease, deterioration or improvement will not occur;

(b) the order must specify the disease or type of deterioration or improvement;

(c) the order may specify a period within which an application for it to be varied may be made;

(d) the order may specify more than one disease or type of deterioration or improvement and may, in respect of each, specify a different period within which an application for it to be varied may be made;

(e) the order must provide that a party must obtain the court's permission to apply for it to be varied, unless the court otherwise orders.

6.   Applications to extend period for applying for permission to vary

Where a period is specified under Article 5(c) or (d)—

(a) a party may make more than one application to extend the period, and such an application is not to be treated as an application to vary a variable order for the purposes of Article 7;

(b) a party may not make an application for the variable order to be varied after the end of the period specified or such period as extended by the court.

7. Limit on number of applications to vary

A party may make only one application to vary a variable order in respect of each specified disease or type of deterioration or improvement.

8. Case file

(1) Where the court makes a variable order, the case file documents must be preserved by the court until the end of the period or periods specified under Article 5(c) or (d) or of any extension of them or, if no such period was specified, until the death of the claimant.

(2) The case file documents are, unless the court otherwise orders—

(a) the judgment as entered;

(b) the statements of case;

(c) the schedule of expenses and losses;

(d) a transcript of the judge's oral judgment;

(e) all medical reports relied on;

(f) a transcript of any parts of the claimant's own evidence which the judge considers necessary;

(g) any subsequent orders.

(3) A court officer must ensure that the case file documents are provided by the parties where necessary and filed on the court file.

(4) Where a variable order has been made, the legal representatives of the parties and, if the parties are insured, their insurers, must also preserve their own case file until the end of the period or periods specified under Article 5(c) or (d) or of any extension of them or, if no such period was specified, until the death of the claimant.

9. Variable agreements

(1) If there is agreed to be a chance that at some definite or indefinite time in the future the claimant will—

(a) as a result of the act or omission which gave rise to the cause of action, develop some serious disease or suffer some serious deterioration, or

(b) enjoy some significant improvement in his physical or mental condition, where that condition had been adversely affected as a result of that act or omission,

the parties to an agreement may agree that a party to it may apply to the court subsequently for its terms to be varied.

(2) Where the parties agree to permit an application to vary the terms of an agreement, the agreement—

(a) must expressly state that a party to it may apply to the court for its terms to be varied;

(b) must specify the disease or type of deterioration or improvement;

(c) may specify a period within which an application for it to be varied may be made;

(d) may specify more than one disease or type of deterioration or improvement and may, in respect of each, specify a different period within which an application for it to be varied may be made.

(3) A party who is permitted by an agreement to apply for its terms to be varied must obtain the court's permission to apply for it to be varied.

10. Application for permission

(1) An application for permission to apply for a variable order or a variable agreement to be varied must be accompanied by evidence—

(a) that the disease, deterioration or improvement specified in the order or agreement has occurred, and

(b) that it has caused or is likely to cause an increase or decrease in the pecuniary loss suffered by the claimant.

(2) Where the applicant is the claimant and he knows that the defendant is insured in respect of the claim and the identity of the defendant's insurers, he must serve the application notice on the insurers as well as on the defendant.

(3) Where the applicant is the claimant and he knows that the defendant is a member of a defence society and the identity of the defence society, he must serve the application notice on the defence society as well as on the defendant.

(4) The respondent to the application may, within 28 days after service of the application, serve written representations on the applicant and, if he does, must file them with the court.

(5) The court will deal with the application without a hearing.

11.   Refusal of permission

(1) Where permission is refused, the applicant may, within 14 days after service of the order, request the decision to be reconsidered at a hearing.

(2) No appeal lies from an order refusing permission after reconsideration.

12.   Grant of permission

(1) Where permission is granted, the court will also give directions as to the application for the variation of the variable order or the variable agreement.

(2) Directions must include directions as to—
   (a) the date by which the application for variation must be served and filed;
   (b) the service and filing of evidence.

(3) No appeal lies from an order granting permission.

13.   Order for variation

(1) On an application for the variation of a variable order or a variable agreement, if the court is satisfied—
   (a) that the disease, deterioration or improvement specified in the order or agreement has occurred, and
   (b) that it has caused or is likely to cause an increase or decrease in the pecuniary loss suffered by the claimant,

it may order—
   (i)   the amount of annual payments to be varied, either from the date of the application for permission or from the date of the application to vary if the order did not require the permission of the court for an application to vary, or from such later date as it may specify in the order;
   (ii) how each payment is to be made during the year and at what intervals;
   (iii) a lump sum to be paid in addition to the existing periodical payments.

(2) Section 2(3) to (9) of the Act applies to orders under this Order as it applies to orders for periodical payments.

14.   Application of rules of court

In England and Wales, the Civil Procedure Rules 1998 and in Northern Ireland, rules of court apply to applications under this Order, except where this Order makes provision inconsistent with Civil Procedure Rules or rules of court.

General Product Safety Regulations 2005

(SI 2005, No. 1803)

PART 1 GENERAL

2.   Interpretation

In these Regulations:—

   'the 1987 Act' means the Consumer Protection Act 1987;

   '[EU] law' includes a law in any part of the United Kingdom which implements a Community obligation [and does not include Regulation (EC) No 765/2008 of the European Parliament and the Council setting out the requirements for accreditation and market surveillance relating to the marketing of products and repealing Regulation (EEC) No 339/93];

'contravention' includes a failure to comply and cognate expressions shall be construed accordingly;

'dangerous product' means a product other than a safe product;

'distributor' means a professional in the supply chain whose activity does not affect the safety properties of a product;

'enforcement authority' means the Secretary of State, any other Minister of the Crown in charge of a government department, any such department and any authority or council mentioned in regulation 10;

'general safety requirement' means the requirement that only safe products should be placed on the market;

'the GPS Directive' means Directive 2001/95/EC of the European Parliament and of the Council of 3 December 2001 on general product safety;

'magistrates' court' in relation to Northern Ireland, means a court of summary jurisdiction;

'Member State' means a member State, Norway, Iceland or Liechtenstein;

'notice' means a notice in writing;

'officer', in relation to an enforcement authority, means a person authorised in writing to assist the authority in carrying out its functions under or for the purposes of the enforcement of these Regulations and safety notices, except in relation to an enforcement authority which is a government department where it means an officer of that department;

'producer' means—

    (a) the manufacturer of a product, when he is established in a Member State and any other person presenting himself as the manufacturer by affixing to the product his name, trade mark or other distinctive mark, or the person who reconditions the product;

    (b) when the manufacturer is not established in a Member State—

        (i) if he has a representative established in a Member State, the representative,

        (ii) in any other case, the importer of the product from a state that is not a Member State into a Member State;

    (c) other professionals in the supply chain, insofar as their activities may affect the safety properties of a product;

'product' means a product which is intended for consumers or likely, under reasonably foreseeable conditions, to be used by consumers even if not intended for them and which is supplied or made available, whether for consideration or not, in the course of a commercial activity and whether it is new, used or reconditioned and includes a product that is supplied or made available to consumers for their own use in the context of providing a service. 'product' does not include equipment used by service providers themselves to supply a service to consumers, in particular equipment on which consumers ride or travel which is operated by a service provider;

'recall' means any measure aimed at achieving the return of a dangerous product that has already been supplied or made available to consumers;

'recall notice' means a notice under regulation 15;

'record' includes any book or document and any record in any form;

'requirement to mark' means a notice under regulation 12;

'requirement to warn' means a notice under regulation 13;

'safe product' means a product which, under normal or reasonably foreseeable conditions of use including duration and, where applicable, putting into service, installation and maintenance requirements, does not present any risk or only the minimum risks compatible with the product's use, considered to be acceptable and consistent with a high level of protection for the safety and health of persons. In determining the foregoing, the following shall be taken into account in particular—

    (a) the characteristics of the product, including its composition, packaging, instructions for assembly and, where applicable, instructions for installation and maintenance,

   (b) the effect of the product on other products, where it is reasonably foreseeable that it will be used with other products,

   (c) the presentation of the product, the labelling, any warnings and instructions for its use and disposal and any other indication or information regarding the product, and

   (d) the categories of consumers at risk when using the product, in particular children and the elderly.

The feasibility of obtaining higher levels of safety or the availability of other products presenting a lesser degree of risk shall not constitute grounds for considering a product to be a dangerous product;

   'safety notice' means a suspension notice, a requirement to mark, a requirement to warn, a withdrawal notice or a recall notice;

   'serious risk' means a serious risk, including one the effects of which are not immediate, requiring rapid intervention;

   'supply' in relation to a product includes making it available, in the context of providing a service, for use by consumers;

   'suspension notice' means a notice under regulation 11;

   'withdrawal' means any measure aimed at preventing the distribution, display or offer of a dangerous product to a consumer;

   'withdrawal notice' means a notice under regulation 14.

Application

   3.—(1) Each provision of these Regulations applies to a product in so far as there are no specific provisions with the same objective in rules of [EU] law governing the safety of the product other than the GPS Directive.

   (2) Where a product is subject to specific safety requirements imposed by rules of [EU] law other than the GPS Directive, these Regulations shall apply only to the aspects and risks or category of risks not covered by those requirements. This means that:

   (a) the definition of 'safe product' and 'dangerous product' in regulation 2 and regulations 5 and 6 shall not apply to such a product in so far as concerns the risks or category of risks covered by the specific rules, and

   (b) the remainder of these Regulations shall apply except where there are specific provisions governing the aspects covered by those regulations with the same objective.

   4. These Regulations do not apply to a second-hand product supplied as a product to be repaired or reconditioned prior to being used, provided the supplier clearly informs the person to whom he supplies the product to that effect.

PART 2 OBLIGATIONS OF PRODUCERS AND DISTRIBUTORS

5. General safety requirement

   (1) No producer shall place a product on the market unless the product is a safe product.

   (2) No producer shall offer or agree to place a product on the market or expose or possess a product for placing on the market unless the product is a safe product.

   (3) No producer shall offer or agree to supply a product or expose or possess a product for supply unless the product is a safe product.

   (4) No producer shall supply a product unless the product is a safe product.

6. Presumption of conformity

   (1) Where, in the absence of specific provisions in rules of [EU] law governing the safety of a product, the product conforms to the specific rules of the law of part of the United Kingdom laying down the health and safety requirements which the product must satisfy in order to be marketed

in the United Kingdom, the product shall be deemed safe so far as concerns the aspects covered by such rules.

(2) Where a product conforms to a voluntary national standard of the United Kingdom giving effect to a European standard the reference of which has been published in the Official Journal of the European Union in accordance with Article 4 of the GPS Directive, the product shall be presumed to be a safe product so far as concerns the risks and categories of risk covered by that national standard. The Secretary of State shall publish the reference number of such national standards in such manner as he considers appropriate.

(3) In circumstances other than those referred to in paragraphs (1) and (2), the conformity of a product to the general safety requirement shall be assessed taking into account—

    (a) any voluntary national standard of the United Kingdom giving effect to a European standard, other than one referred to in paragraph (2),

    (b) other national standards drawn up in the United Kingdom,

    (c) recommendations of the European Commission setting guidelines on product safety assessment,

    (d) product safety codes of good practice in the sector concerned,

    (e) the state of the art and technology, and

    (f) reasonable consumer expectations concerning safety.

(4) Conformity of a product with the criteria designed to ensure the general safety requirement is complied with, in particular the provisions mentioned in paragraphs (1) to (3), shall not bar an enforcement authority from exercising its powers under these Regulations in relation to that product where there is evidence that, despite such conformity, it is dangerous.

7. Other obligations of producers

(1) Within the limits of his activities, a producer shall provide consumers with the relevant information to enable them—

    (a) to assess the risks inherent in a product throughout the normal or reasonably foreseeable period of its use, where such risks are not immediately obvious without adequate warnings, and

    (b) to take precautions against those risks.

(2) The presence of warnings does not exempt any person from compliance with the other requirements of these Regulations.

(3) Within the limits of his activities, a producer shall adopt measures commensurate with the characteristics of the products which he supplies to enable him to—

    (a) be informed of the risks which the products might pose, and

    (b) take appropriate action including, where necessary to avoid such risks, withdrawal, adequately and effectively warning consumers as to the risks or, as a last resort, recall.

(4) The measures referred to in paragraph (3) include—

    (a) except where it is not reasonable to do so, an indication by means of the product or its packaging of—

        (i) the name and address of the producer, and

        (ii) the product reference or where applicable the batch of products to which it belongs; and

    (b) where and to the extent that it is reasonable to do so—

        (i) sample testing of marketed products,

        (ii) investigating and if necessary keeping a register of complaints concerning the safety of the product, and

        (iii) keeping distributors informed of the results of such monitoring where a product presents a risk or may present a risk.

8. Obligations of distributors

(1) A distributor shall act with due care in order to help ensure compliance with the applicable safety requirements and in particular he—

(a) shall not expose or possess for supply or offer or agree to supply, or supply, a product to any person which he knows or should have presumed, on the basis of the information in his possession and as a professional, is a dangerous product; and

(b) shall, within the limits of his activities, participate in monitoring the safety of a product placed on the market, in particular by—

   (i) passing on information on the risks posed by the product,

   (ii) keeping the documentation necessary for tracing the origin of the product,

   (iii) producing the documentation necessary for tracing the origin of the product, and cooperating in action taken by a producer or an enforcement authority to avoid the risks.

(2) Within the limits of his activities, a distributor shall take measures enabling him to cooperate efficiently in the action referred to in paragraph (1)(b)(iii).

9. Obligations of producers and distributors

(1) Subject to paragraph (2), where a producer or a distributor knows that a product he has placed on the market or supplied poses risks to the consumer that are incompatible with the general safety requirement, he shall forthwith notify an enforcement authority in writing of that information and—

(a) the action taken to prevent risk to the consumer; and

(b) where the product is being or has been marketed or otherwise supplied to consumers outside the United Kingdom, of the identity of each Member State in which, to the best of his knowledge, it is being or has been so marketed or supplied.

(2) Paragraph (1) shall not apply—

(a) in the case of a second-hand product supplied as an antique or as a product to be repaired or reconditioned prior to being used, provided the supplier clearly informed the person to whom he supplied the product to that effect,

(b) in conditions concerning isolated circumstances or products.

(3) In the event of a serious risk the notification under paragraph (1) shall include the following—

(a) information enabling a precise identification of the product or batch of products in question,

(b) a full description of the risks that the product presents,

(c) all available information relevant for tracing the product, and

(d) a description of the action undertaken to prevent risks to the consumer.

(4) Within the limits of his activities, a person who is a producer or a distributor shall co-operate with an enforcement authority (at the enforcement authority's request) in action taken to avoid the risks posed by a product which he supplies or has supplied. Every enforcement authority shall maintain procedures for such co-operation, including procedures for dialogue with the producers and distributors concerned on issues related to product safety.

PART 3 ENFORCEMENT

10. Enforcement

(1) It shall be the duty of every authority to which paragraph (4) applies to enforce within its area these Regulations and safety notices.

(2) An authority in England or Wales to which paragraph (4) applies shall have the power to investigate and prosecute for an alleged contravention of any provision imposed by or under these Regulations which was committed outside its area in any part of England and Wales.

(3) A district council in Northern Ireland shall have the power to investigate and prosecute for an alleged contravention of any provision imposed by or under these Regulations which was committed outside its area in any part of Northern Ireland.

(4) The authorities to which this paragraph applies are:

    (a) in England, a county council, district council, London Borough Council, the Common Council of the City of London in its capacity as a local authority and the Council of the Isles of Scilly,

    (b) in Wales, a county council or a county borough council,

    (c) in Scotland, a council constituted under section 2 of the Local Government etc. (Scotland) Act 1994,

    (d) in Northern Ireland any district council.

(5) An enforcement authority shall in enforcing these Regulations act in a manner proportionate to the seriousness of the risk and shall take due account of the precautionary principle. In this context, it shall encourage and promote voluntary action by producers and distributors. Notwithstanding the foregoing, an enforcement authority may take any action under these Regulations urgently and without first encouraging and promoting voluntary action if a product poses a serious risk.

11. Suspension notices

(1) Where an enforcement authority has reasonable grounds for suspecting that a requirement of these Regulations has been contravened in relation to a product, the authority may, for the period needed to organise appropriate safety evaluations, checks and controls, serve a notice ('a suspension notice') prohibiting the person on whom it is served from doing any of the following things without the consent of the authority, that is to say—

    (a) placing the product on the market, offering to place it on the market, agreeing to place it on the market or exposing it for placing on the market, or

    (b) supplying the product, offering to supply it, agreeing to supply it or exposing it for supply.

(2) A suspension notice served by an enforcement authority in relation to a product may require the person on whom it is served to keep the authority informed of the whereabouts of any such product in which he has an interest.

(3) A consent given by the enforcement authority for the purposes of paragraph (1) may impose such conditions on the doing of anything for which the consent is required as the authority considers appropriate.

12. Requirements to mark

(1) Where an enforcement authority has reasonable grounds for believing that a product is a dangerous product in that it could pose risks in certain conditions, the authority may serve a notice ('a requirement to mark') requiring the person on whom the notice is served at his own expense to undertake either or both of the following, as specified in the notice—

    (a) to ensure that the product is marked in accordance with requirements specified in the notice with warnings as to the risks it may present,

    (b) to make the marketing of the product subject to prior conditions as specified in the notice so as to ensure the product is a safe product.

(2) The requirements referred to in paragraph (1)(a) shall be such as to ensure that the product is marked with a warning which is suitable, clearly worded and easily comprehensible.

13. Requirements to warn

Where an enforcement authority has reasonable grounds for believing that a product is a dangerous product in that it could pose risks for certain persons, the authority may serve a notice ('a requirement to warn') requiring the person on whom the notice is served at his own expense to undertake one or more of the following, as specified in the notice—

    (a) where and to the extent it is practicable to do so, to ensure that any person who could be subject to such risks and who has been supplied with the product be given warning of the risks in good time and in a form specified in the notice,

    (b) to publish a warning of the risks in such form and manner as is likely to bring those risks to the attention of any such person,

    (c) to ensure that the product carries a warning of the risks in a form specified in the notice.

14. Withdrawal notices

(1) Where an enforcement authority has reasonable grounds for believing that a product is a dangerous product, the authority may serve a notice ('a withdrawal notice') prohibiting the person on whom it is served from doing any of the following things without the consent of the authority, that is to say—

(a) placing the product on the market, offering to place it on the market, agreeing to place it on the market or exposing it for placing on the market, or

(b) supplying the product, offering to supply it, agreeing to supply it or exposing it for supply.

(2) A withdrawal notice may require the person on whom it is served to take action to alert consumers to the risks that the product presents.

(3) In relation to a product that is already on the market, a withdrawal notice may only be served by an enforcement authority where the action being undertaken by the producer or the distributor concerned in fulfilment of his obligations under these Regulations is unsatisfactory or insufficient to prevent the risks concerned to the health and safety of persons.

(4) Paragraph (3) shall not apply in the case of a product posing a serious risk requiring, in the view of the enforcement authority, urgent action.

(5) A withdrawal notice served by an enforcement authority in relation to a product may require the person on whom it is served to keep the authority informed of the whereabouts of any such product in which he has an interest.

(6) A consent given by the enforcement authority for the purposes of paragraph (1) may impose such conditions on the doing of anything for which the consent is required as the authority considers appropriate.

15. Recall notices

(1) Subject to paragraph (4), where an enforcement authority has reasonable grounds for believing that a product is a dangerous product and that it has already been supplied or made available to consumers, the authority may serve a notice ('a recall notice') requiring the person on whom it is served to use his reasonable endeavours to organise the return of the product from consumers to that person or to such other person as is specified in the notice.

(2) A recall notice may require—

(a) the recall to be effected in accordance with a code of practice applicable to the product concerned, or

(b) the recipient of the recall notice to—

(i) contact consumers who have purchased the product in order to inform them of the recall, where and to the extent it is practicable to do so,

(ii) publish a notice in such form and such manner as is likely to bring to the attention of purchasers of the product the risk the product poses and the fact of the recall, or

(iii) make arrangements for the collection or return of the product from consumers who have purchased it or for its disposal,

and may impose such additional requirements on the recipient of the notice as are reasonable and practicable with a view to achieving the return of the product from consumers to the person specified in the notice or its disposal.

(3) In determining what requirements to include in a recall notice, the enforcement authority shall take into consideration the need to encourage distributors, users and consumers to contribute to its implementation.

(4) A recall notice may only be issued by an enforcement authority where—

(a) other action which it may require under these Regulations would not suffice to prevent the risks concerned to the health and safety of persons,

(b) the action being undertaken by the producer or the distributor concerned in fulfilment of his obligations under these Regulations is unsatisfactory or insufficient to prevent the risks concerned to the health and safety of persons, and

(c) the authority has given not less than [ten] days notice to the person on whom the recall notice is to be served of its intention to serve such a notice and where that person has before the expiry of that period by notice required the authority to seek the advice of such person as the Institute determines on the questions of—

(i)   whether the product is a dangerous product,

(ii) whether the issue of a recall notice is proportionate to the seriousness of the risk, and the authority has taken account of such advice.

(5) Paragraphs (4)(b) and (c) shall not apply in the case of a product posing a serious risk requiring, in the view of the enforcement authority, urgent action.

(6) Where a person requires an enforcement authority to seek advice as referred to in paragraph (4)(c), that person shall be responsible for the fees, costs and expenses of the Institute and of the person appointed by the Institute to advise the authority.

(7) In paragraphs 4(c) and (6) 'the Institute' means the charitable organisation with registered number 803725 and known as the Chartered Institute of Arbitrators.

(8) A recall notice served by an enforcement authority in relation to a product may require the person on whom it is served to keep the authority informed of the whereabouts of any such product to which the recall notice relates, so far as he is able to do so.

(9) Where the conditions in paragraph (1) for serving a recall notice are satisfied and either the enforcement authority has been unable to identify any person on whom to serve a recall notice, or the person on whom such a notice has been served has failed to comply with it, then the authority may itself take such action as could have been required by a recall notice.

(10) Where—

(a) an authority has complied with the requirements of paragraph (4); and

(b) the authority has exercised its powers under paragraph (9) to take action following the failure of the person on whom the recall notice has been served to comply with that notice,

then the authority may recover from the person on whom the notice was served summarily as a civil debt, any costs or expenses reasonably incurred by it in undertaking the action referred to in sub-paragraph (b).

(11) A civil debt recoverable under the preceding paragraph may be recovered—

(a) in England and Wales by way of complaint (as mentioned in section 58 of the Magistrates' Courts Act 1980,

(b) in Northern Ireland in proceedings under Article 62 of the Magistrate's Court (Northern Ireland) Order 1981.

16.   Supplementary provisions relating to safety notices

(1) Whenever feasible, prior to serving a safety notice the authority shall give an opportunity to the person on whom the notice is to be served to submit his views to the authority. Where, due to the urgency of the situation, this is not feasible the person shall be given an opportunity to submit his views to the authority after service of the notice.

(2) A safety notice served by an enforcement authority in respect of a product shall—

(a) describe the product in a manner sufficient to identify it;

(b) state the reasons on which the notice is based;

(c) indicate the rights available to the recipient of the notice under these Regulations and (where applicable) the time limits applying to their exercise; and

(d) in the case of a suspension notice, state the period of time for which it applies.

(3) A safety notice shall have effect throughout the United Kingdom.

(4) Where an enforcement authority serves a suspension notice in respect of a product, the authority shall be liable to pay compensation to a person having an interest in the product in respect of any loss or damage suffered by reason of the notice if—

(a) there has been no contravention of any requirement of these Regulations in relation to the product; and

(b) the exercise by the authority of the power to serve the suspension notice was not attributable to any neglect or default by that person.

(5) Where an enforcement authority serves a withdrawal notice in respect of a product, the authority shall be liable to pay compensation to a person having an interest in the product in respect of any loss or damage suffered by reason of the notice if—

(a) the product was not a dangerous product; and

(b) the exercise by the authority of the power to serve the withdrawal notice was not attributable to any neglect or default by that person.

(6) Where an enforcement authority serves a recall notice in respect of a product, the authority shall be liable to pay compensation to the person on whom the notice was served in respect of any loss or damage suffered by reason of the notice if—

(a) the product was not a dangerous product; and

(b) the exercise by the authority of the power to serve the recall notice was not attributable to any neglect or default by that person.

(7) An enforcement authority may vary or revoke a safety notice which it has served provided that the notice is not made more restrictive for the person on whom it is served or more onerous for that person to comply with.

(8) Wherever feasible prior to varying a safety notice the authority shall give an opportunity to the person on whom the original notice was served to submit his views to the authority.

17. Appeals against safety notices

(1) A person on whom a safety notice has been served and a person having an interest in a product in respect of which a safety notice (other than a recall notice) has been served may, before the end of the period of 21 days beginning with the day on which the notice was served, apply for an order to vary or set aside the terms of the notice.

(2) On an application under paragraph (1) the court or the sheriff, as the case may be, shall make an order setting aside the notice only if satisfied that—

(a) in the case of a suspension notice, there has been no contravention in relation to the product of any requirement of these Regulations,

(b) in the case of a requirement to mark or a requirement to warn, the product is not a dangerous product,

(c) in the case of a withdrawal notice—

　(i) the product is not a dangerous product, or

　(ii) where applicable, regulation 14(3) has not been complied with by the enforcement authority concerned,

(d) in the case of a recall notice—

　(i) the product is not a dangerous product, or

　(ii) regulation 15(4) has not been complied with,

(e) in any case, the serving of the safety notice concerned was not proportionate to the seriousness of the risk.

(3) On an application concerning the period of time specified in a suspension notice as the period for which it applies, the court or the sheriff, as the case may be, may reduce the period to such period as it considers sufficient for organising appropriate safety evaluations, checks and controls.

(4) On an application to vary the terms of a notice, the court or the sheriff, as the case may be, may vary the requirements specified in the notice as it considers appropriate.

(5) A person on whom a recall notice has been served and who proposes to make an application under paragraph (1) in relation to the notice may, before the end of the period of seven days beginning with the day on which the notice was served, apply to the court or the sheriff for an order suspending the effect of the notice and the court or the sheriff may, in any case where it considers it appropriate to do so, make an order suspending the effect of the notice.

(6) If the court or the sheriff makes an order suspending the effect of a recall notice under paragraph (5) in the absence of the enforcement authority, the enforcement authority may apply for the revocation of such order.

(7) An order under paragraph (5) shall take effect from the time it is made until—

    (a) it is revoked under paragraph (6),

    (b) where no application is made under paragraph (1) in respect of the recall notice within the time specified in that paragraph, the expiration of that time,

    (c) where such an application is made but is withdrawn or dismissed for want of prosecution, the date of dismissal or withdrawal of the application, or

    (d) where such an application is made and is not withdrawn or dismissed for want of prosecution, the determination of the application.

(8) Subject to paragraph (6), in Scotland the sheriff's decision under paragraph (5) shall be final.

(9) An application under this regulation may be made—

    (a) by way of complaint to any magistrates' court in which proceedings have been brought in England and Wales or Northern Ireland—

        (i)   in respect of a contravention in relation to the product of a requirement imposed by or under these Regulations; or

        (ii) for the forfeiture of the product under regulation 18;

    (b) where no such proceedings have been brought, by way of complaint to any magistrates' court; or

    (c) in Scotland, by summary application to the sheriff.

(10) A person aggrieved by an order made pursuant to an application under paragraph (1) by a magistrates' court in England, Wales or Northern Ireland, or by a decision of such a court not to make such an order, may appeal against that order or decision—

    (a) in England and Wales, to the Crown Court;

    (b) in Northern Ireland, to the county court.

18. Forfeiture: England and Wales and Northern Ireland

(1) An enforcement authority in England and Wales or Northern Ireland may apply for an order for the forfeiture of a product on the grounds that the product is a dangerous product.

(2) An application under paragraph (1) may be made—

    (a) where proceedings have been brought in a magistrates' court for an offence in respect of a contravention in relation to the product of a requirement imposed by or under these Regulations, to that court,

    (b) where an application with respect to the product has been made to a magistrates' court under regulation 17 (appeals against safety notices) or 25 (appeals against detention of products and records) to that court, and

    (c) otherwise, by way of complaint to a magistrates' court.

(3) An enforcement authority making an application under paragraph (1) shall serve a copy of the application on any person appearing to it to be the owner of, or otherwise to have an interest in, the product to which the application relates, together with a notice giving him the opportunity to appear at the hearing of the application to show cause why the product should not be forfeited.

(4) A person on whom notice is served under paragraph (3) and any other person claiming to be the owner of, or otherwise to have an interest in, the product to which the application relates shall be entitled to appear at the hearing of the application and show cause why the product should not be forfeited.

(5) The court shall not make an order for the forfeiture of a product—

    (a) if any person on whom notice is served under paragraph (3) does not appear, unless service of the notice on that person is proved, or

    (b) if no notice under paragraph (3) has been served, unless the court is satisfied that in the circumstances it was reasonable not to serve notice on any person.

(6) The court may make an order for the forfeiture of a product only if it is satisfied that the product is a dangerous product.

(7) Any person aggrieved by an order made by a magistrates' court for the forfeiture of a product, or by a decision of such a court not to make such an order, may appeal against that order or decision—

    (a) in England and Wales, to the Crown Court;

    (b) in Northern Ireland, to the county court.

(8) An order for the forfeiture of a product shall not take effect until the later of—

    (i) the end of the period within which an appeal under paragraph (7) may be brought or within which an application under section 111 of the Magistrates' Courts Act 1980 or article 146 of the Magistrates' Courts (Northern Ireland) Order 1981 (statement of case) may be made, or

    (ii) if an appeal or an application is so made, when the appeal or application is determined or abandoned.

(9) Subject to the following paragraph, where a product is forfeited it shall be destroyed in accordance with such directions as the court may give.

(10) On making an order for forfeiture of a product a magistrates' court may, if it considers it appropriate to do so, direct that the product shall (instead of being destroyed) be delivered up to such person as the court may specify, on condition that the person—

    (a) does not supply the product to any person otherwise than as mentioned in paragraph (11), and

    (b) on condition, if the court considers it appropriate, that he complies with any order to pay costs or expenses (including any order under regulation 28) which has been made against him in the proceedings for the order for forfeiture.

(11) The supplies which may be permitted under the preceding paragraph are—

    (a) a supply to a person who carries on a business of buying products of the same description as the product concerned and repairing or reconditioning them,

    (b) a supply to a person as scrap (that is to say, for the value of materials included in the product rather than for the value of the product itself),

    (c) a supply to any person, provided that being so supplied the product is repaired by or on behalf of the person to whom the product was delivered up by direction of the court and that following such repair it is not a dangerous product.

20. Offences

(1) A person who contravenes regulations 5 or 8(1)(a) shall be guilty of an offence and liable on conviction on indictment to imprisonment for a term not exceeding 12 months or to a fine not exceeding £20,000 or to both, or on summary conviction to imprisonment for a term not exceeding three months or to a fine not exceeding the statutory maximum or to both.

(2) A person who contravenes regulation 7(1), 7(3) (by failing to take any of the measures specified in regulation 7(4)), 8(1)(b)(i), (ii) or (iii) or 9(1) shall be guilty of an offence and liable on summary conviction to imprisonment for a term not exceeding three months or to a fine not exceeding level 5 on the standard scale or to both.

(3) A producer or distributor who does not give notice to an enforcement authority under regulation 9(1) in respect of a product he has placed on the market or supplied commits an offence where it is proved that he ought to have known that the product poses risks to consumers that are incompatible with the general safety requirement and he shall be liable on summary conviction to imprisonment for a term not exceeding three months or to a fine not exceeding level 5 on the standard scale or to both.

(4) A person who contravenes a safety notice shall be guilty of an offence and liable on conviction on indictment to imprisonment for a term not exceeding 12 months or to a fine not exceeding £20,000 or to both, or on summary conviction to imprisonment for a term not exceeding three months or to a fine not exceeding the statutory maximum or to both.

21. Test purchases

(1) An enforcement authority shall have power to organise appropriate checks on the safety properties of a product, on an adequate scale, up to the final stage of use or consumption and for

that purpose may make a purchase of a product or authorise an officer of the authority to make a purchase of a product.

(2) Where a product purchased under paragraph (1) is submitted to a test and the test leads to—

(a) the bringing of proceedings for an offence in respect of a contravention in relation to the product of any requirement imposed by or under these Regulations or for the forfeiture of the product under regulation 18 or 19, or

(b) the serving of a safety notice in respect of the product, and

(c) the authority is requested to do so and it is practicable for the authority to comply with the request,

then the authority shall allow the person from whom the product was purchased, a person who is a party to the proceedings, on whom the notice was served or who has an interest in the product to which the notice relates, to have the product tested.

22.   Powers of entry and search etc.

(1) An officer of an enforcement authority may at any reasonable hour and on production, if required, of his credentials exercise any of the powers conferred by the following provisions of this regulation.

(2) The officer may, for the purposes of ascertaining whether there has been a contravention of a requirement imposed by or under these Regulations, enter any premises other than premises occupied only as a person's residence and inspect any record or product.

(3) The officer may, for the purpose of ascertaining whether there has been a contravention of a requirement imposed by or under these Regulations, examine any procedure (including any arrangements for carrying out a test) connected with the production of a product.

(4) If the officer has reasonable grounds for suspecting that the product has not been placed on the market or supplied in the United Kingdom since it was manufactured or imported he may for the purpose of ascertaining whether there has been a contravention in relation to the product of a requirement imposed by or under these Regulations—

(a) require a person carrying on a commercial activity, or employed in connection with a commercial activity, to supply all necessary information relating to the activity, including by the production of records,

(b) require any record which is stored in an electronic form and is accessible from the premises to be produced in a form—

(i)   in which it can be taken away, and

(ii)   in which it is visible and legible.

(c) for the purpose of ascertaining (by testing or otherwise) whether there has been any such contravention, seize and detain samples of the product,

(d) take copies of, or of an entry in, any records produced by virtue of sub-paragraph (a).

(5) If the officer has reasonable grounds for suspecting that there has been a contravention in relation to a product of a requirement imposed by or under these Regulations, he may—

(a) for the purpose of ascertaining whether there has been any such contravention, require a person carrying on a commercial activity, or employed in connection with a commercial activity, to supply all necessary information relating to the activity, including by the production of records,

(b) for the purpose of ascertaining whether there has been any such contravention, require any record which is stored in an electronic form and is accessible from the premises to be produced in a form—

(i)   in which it can be taken away, and

(ii)   in which it is visible and legible,

(c) for the purpose of ascertaining (by testing or otherwise) whether there has been any such contravention, seize and detain samples of the product,

(d) take copies of, or of an entry in, any records produced by virtue of sub-paragraph (a).

(6) The officer may seize and detain any products or records which he has reasonable grounds for believing may be required as evidence in proceedings for an offence in respect of a contravention of any requirement imposed by or under these Regulations.

(7) If and to the extent that it is reasonably necessary to do so to prevent a contravention of any requirement imposed by or under these Regulations, the officer may, for the purpose of exercising his power under paragraphs (4) to (6) to seize products or records—

    (a) require any person having authority to do so to open any container or to open any vending machine; and

    (b) himself open or break open any such container or machine where a requirement made under sub-paragraph (a) in relation to the container or machine has not been complied with.

23. Provisions supplemental to regulation 22 and search warrants etc.

(1) An officer seizing any products or records shall, before he leaves the premises, provide to the person from whom they were seized a written notice—

    (a) specifying the products (including the quantity thereof) and records seized,

    (b) stating the reasons for their seizure, and

    (c) explaining the right of appeal under regulation 25.

(2) References in paragraph (1) and regulation 25 to the person from whom something has been seized, in relation to a case in which the power of seizure was exercisable by reason of the product having been found on any premises, are references to the occupier of the premises at the time of the seizure.

(3) If a justice of the peace—

    (a) is satisfied by written information on oath that there are reasonable grounds for believing either—

        (i) that any products or records which an officer has power to inspect under regulation 22 are on any premises and that their inspection is likely to disclose evidence that there has been a contravention of any requirement imposed by or under these Regulations, or

        (ii) that such a contravention has taken place, is taking place or is about to take place on any premises, and

    (b) is also satisfied by such information either—

        (i) that admission to the premises has been or is likely to be refused and that notice of the intention to apply for a warrant under this paragraph has been given to the occupier, or

        (ii) that an application for admission, or the giving of such a notice, would defeat the object of the entry or that the premises are unoccupied or that the occupier is temporarily absent and it might defeat the object of the entry to await his return.

the justice may by warrant under his hand, which shall continue in force for a period of one month, authorise any officer of an enforcement authority to enter the premises, if need be by force.

(4) An officer entering premises by virtue of regulation 22 or a warrant under paragraph (3) may take him such other persons and equipment as may appear to him necessary.

(5) On leaving any premises which a person is authorised to enter by a warrant under paragraph (3), that person shall, if the premises are unoccupied or the occupier is temporarily absent—

    (a) leave the premises as effectively secured against trespassers as he found them,

    (b) attach a notice such as is mentioned in paragraph (1) in a prominent place at the premises.

(6) Where a product seized by an officer of an enforcement authority under regulation 22 or 23 is submitted to a test, the authority shall inform the person mentioned in paragraph (1) of the result of the test and, if—

    (a) proceedings are brought for an offence in respect of a contravention in relation to the product of any requirement imposed by or under these Regulations or for the forfeiture of the product under regulation 18 or 19; or

    (b) a safety notice is served in respect of the product; and

    (c) the authority is requested to do so and it is practicable for him to comply with the request,

then the authority shall allow a person who is a party to the proceedings or, on whom the notice was served or who has an interest in the product to which the notice relates to have the product tested.

(7) If a person who is not an officer of an enforcement authority purports to act as such under regulation 22 or under this regulation he shall be guilty of an offence and liable on summary conviction to a fine not exceeding level 5 on the standard scale.

(8) In the application of this section to Scotland, the reference in paragraph (3) to a justice of the peace shall include a reference to a sheriff and the reference to written information on oath shall be construed as a reference to evidence on oath.

(9) In the application of this section to Northern Ireland, the reference in paragraph (3) to a justice of the peace shall include a reference to a lay magistrate and the references to an information on oath shall be construed as a reference to a complaint on oath.

24. Obstruction of officers

(1) A person who—

- (a) intentionally obstructs an officer of an enforcement authority who is acting in pursuance of any provision of regulations 22 or 23; or
- (b) intentionally fails to comply with a requirement made of him by an officer of an enforcement authority under any provision of those regulations; or
- (c) without reasonable cause fails to give an officer of an enforcement authority who is so acting any other assistance or information which the officer may reasonably require of him for the purposes of the exercise of the officer's functions under any provision of those regulations,

shall be guilty of an offence and liable on summary conviction to a fine not exceeding level 5 on the standard scale.

(2) A person shall be guilty of an offence if, in giving any information which is required by him by virtue of paragraph (1)(c)—

- (a) he makes a statement which he knows is false in a material particular; or
- (b) he recklessly makes a statement which is false in a material particular.

(3) A person guilty of an offence under paragraph (2) shall be liable—

- (a) on conviction on indictment, to a fine;
- (b) on summary conviction, to a fine not exceeding the statutory maximum.

25. Appeals against detention of products and records

(1) A person referred to in regulation 23(1) may apply for an order requiring any product or record which is for the time being detained under regulation 22 or 23 by an enforcement authority or by an officer of such an authority to be released to him or to another person.

(2) An application under the preceding paragraph may be made—

- (a) to any magistrates' court in which proceedings have been brought in England and Wales or Northern Ireland—
  - (i)   for an offence in respect of a contravention in relation to the product of a requirement imposed by or under these Regulation, or
  - (ii) for the forfeiture of the product under regulation 18,
- (b) where no such proceedings have been brought, by way of complaint to a magistrates' court;
- (c) in Scotland, by summary application to the sheriff.

(3) On an application under paragraph (1) to a magistrates' court or to the sheriff, the court or the sheriff may make an order requiring a product or record to be released only if the court or sheriff is satisfied—

- (a) that proceedings
  - (i)   for an offence in respect of any contravention in relation to the product or, in the case of a record, the product to which the record relates, of any requirement imposed by or under these Regulations; or
  - (ii) for the forfeiture of the product or, in the case of a record, the product to which the record relate, under regulation 18 or 19,

  have not been brought or, having been brought, have been concluded without the product being forfeited; and

(b) where no such proceedings have been brought, that more than six months have elapsed since the product or records was seized.

(4) In determining whether to make an order under this regulation requiring the release of a product or record the court or sheriff shall take all the circumstances into account including the results of any tests on the product which have been carried out by or on behalf of the enforcement authority and any statement made by the enforcement authority to the court or sheriff as to its intention to bring proceedings for an offence in respect of a contravention in relation to the product of any requirement imposed by or under these Regulations.

(5) Where—

(a) more than 12 months have elapsed since a product or records were seized and the enforcement authority has not commenced proceedings for an offence in respect of a contravention in relation to the product (or, in the case of records, the product to which the records relate) of any requirement imposed by or under these Regulations or for the forfeiture of the product under regulation 18 or 19, or

(b) an enforcement authority has brought proceedings for an offence as mentioned in sub-paragraph (a) and the proceedings were dismissed and all rights of appeal have been exercised or the time for appealing has expired,

the authority shall be under a duty to return the product or records detained under regulation 22 or 23 to the person from whom they were seized.

(6) Where the authority is satisfied that some other person has a better right to a product or record than the person from whom they were seized, the authority shall, instead of the duty in paragraph (5), be under a duty to return it to that other person or, as the case may be, to the person appearing to the authority to have the best right to the product or record in question.

(7) Where different persons claim to be entitled to the return of a product or record that is required to be returned under paragraph (5), then it may be retained for as long as it reasonably necessary for the determination in accordance with paragraph (6) of the person to whom it must be returned.

(8) A person aggrieved by an order made under this regulation by a magistrates' court in England and Wales or Northern Ireland, or by a decision of such a court not to make such an order, may appeal against that order or decision—

(a) in England and Wales, to the Crown Court;

(b) in Northern Ireland, to the county court;

and an order so made may contain such provision as appears to the court to be appropriate for delaying the coming into force of the order pending the making and determination of any appeal (including any application under section 111 of the Magistrates' Courts Act 1980 or article 146 of the Magistrates' Courts (Northern Ireland) Order 1981 (statement of case)).

26.   Compensation for seizure and detention

Where an officer of an enforcement authority exercises any power under regulation 22 or 23 to seize and detain a product, the enforcement authority shall be liable to pay compensation to any person having an interest in the product in respect of any loss or damage caused by reason of the exercise of the power if—

(a) there has been no contravention in relation to the product of any requirement imposed by or under these Regulations, and

(b) the exercise of the power is not attributable to any neglect or default by that person.

27.   Recovery of expenses of enforcement

(1) This regulation shall apply where a court—

(a) convicts a person of an offence in respect of a contravention in relation to a product of any requirement imposed by or under these Regulations, or

(b) makes an order under regulation 18 or 19 for the forfeiture of a product.

(2) The court may (in addition to any other order it may make as to costs or expenses) order the person convicted or, as the case may be, any person having an interest in the product to reimburse an enforcement authority for any expenditure which has been or may be incurred by that authority—

(a) in connection with any seizure or detention of the product by or on behalf of the author- ity, or

(b) in connection with any compliance by the authority with directions given by the court for the purposes of any order for the forfeiture of the product.

28. Power of Secretary of State to obtain information

(1) If the Secretary of State considers that, for the purposes of deciding whether to serve a safety notice, or to vary or revoke a safety notice which he has already served, he requires information or a sample of a product he may serve on a person a notice requiring him:

(a) to furnish to the Secretary of State, within a period specified in the notice, such informa- tion as is specified;

(b) to produce such records as are specified in the notice at a time and place so specified (and to produce any such records which are stored in any electronic form in a form in which they are visible and legible) and to permit a person appointed by the Secretary of State for that purpose to take copies of the records at that time and place;

(c) to produce such samples of a product as are specified in the notice at a time and place so specified.

(2) A person shall be guilty of an offence if he—

(a) fails, without reasonable cause, to comply with a notice served on him under paragraph (1); or

(b) in purporting to comply with a requirement which by virtue of paragraph (1)(a) or (b) is contained in such a notice—

(i) furnishes information or records which he knows are false in a material particular, or

(ii) recklessly furnishes information or records which are false in a material particular.

(3) A person guilty of an offence under paragraph (2) shall—

(a) in the case of an offence under sub-paragraph (a) of that paragraph, be liable on sum- mary conviction to a fine not exceeding level 5 on the standard scale; and

(b) in the case of an offence under sub-paragraph (b) of that paragraph, be liable—

(i) on conviction on indictment, to a fine;

(ii) on summary conviction, to a fine not exceeding the statutory maximum.

29. Defence of due diligence

(1) Subject to the following provisions of this regulation, in proceedings against a person for an offence under these Regulations it shall be a defence for that person to show that he took all reason- able steps and exercised all due diligence to avoid committing the offence.

(2) Where in any proceedings against any person for such an offence the defence provided by paragraph (1) involves an allegation that the commission of the offence was due—

(a) to the act or default of another, or

(b) to reliance on information given by another,

that person shall not, without the leave of the court, be entitled to rely on the defence unless, not less than seven clear days before, in England, Wales and Northern Ireland, the hearing of the proceed- ings or, in Scotland, the trial diet, he has served a notice under paragraph (3) on the person bringing the proceedings.

(3) A notice under this paragraph shall give such information identifying or assisting in the identification of the person who—

(a) committed the act or default, or

(b) gave the information,

as is in the possession of the person serving the notice at the time he serves it.

(4) A person may not rely on the defence provided by paragraph (1) by reason of his reliance on information supplied by another, unless he shows that it was reasonable in all the circumstances to have relied on the information, having regard in particular—

(a) to the steps which he took, and those which might reasonably have been taken, for the purpose of verifying the information; and

(b) to whether he had any reason to disbelieve the information.

30.   Defence in relation to antiques

. . .

31.   Liability of person other than principal offender

(1) Where the commission by a person of an offence under these Regulations is due to an act or default committed by some other person in the course of a commercial activity of his, the other person shall be guilty of the offence and may be proceeded against and punished by virtue of this paragraph whether or not proceedings are taken against the first-mentioned person.

(2) Where a body corporate is guilty of an offence under these Regulations (including where it is so guilty by virtue of paragraph (1)) in respect of any act or default which is shown to have been committed with the consent or connivance of, or to be attributable to any neglect on the part of, any director, manager, secretary or other similar officer of the body corporate or any person who was purporting to act in any such capacity he, as well as the body corporate, shall be guilty of that offence and shall be liable to be proceeded against and punished accordingly.

(3) Where the affairs of a body corporate are managed by its members, paragraph (2) shall apply in relation to the acts and defaults of a member in connection with his functions of management as if he were a director of the body corporate.

(4) Where a Scottish partnership is guilty of an offence under these Regulations (including where it is so guilty by virtue of paragraph (1)) in respect of any act or default which is shown to have been committed with the consent or connivance of, or to be attributable to any neglect on the part of, a partner in the partnership, he, as well as the partnership, shall be guilty of that offence and shall be liable to be proceeded against and punished accordingly.

PART 4 MISCELLANEOUS

36.   Market surveillance

In order to ensure a high level of consumer health and safety protection, enforcement authorities shall within the limits of their responsibility and to the extent of their ability undertake market surveillance of products employing appropriate means and procedures and co-operating with other enforcement authorities and competent authorities of other Member States which may include:

(a) establishment, periodical updating and implementation of sectoral surveillance programmes by categories of products or risks and the monitoring of surveillance activities, findings and results,

(b) follow-up and updating of scientific and technical knowledge concerning the safety of products,

(c) the periodical review and assessment of the functioning of the control activities and their effectiveness and, if necessary revision of the surveillance approach and organisation put in place.

42.   Civil proceedings

These Regulations shall not be construed as conferring any right of action in civil proceedings in respect of any loss or damage suffered in consequence of a contravention of these Regulations.

Regulatory Reform (Unsolicited Goods and Services Act 1971) (Directory Entries and Demands for Payment) Order 2005

(SI 2005, No. 55)

1. Citation, commencement, extent and interpretation

(3) Expressions used in this Order which are also used in the Unsolicited Goods and Services Act 1971 have the same meaning as in that Act.

5. The Electronic Commerce (EC Directive) Regulations 2002

The Electronic Commerce (EC Directive) Regulations 2002 apply to—

- (a) this Order; and
- (b) any subordinate provisions order (within the meaning of section 4(4) of the Regulatory Reform Act 2001) made in respect of the Schedule to this Order.

Article 3 **SCHEDULE**

PART 1 PARTICULARS OF DIRECTORY OR PROPOSED DIRECTORY WHICH MUST BE GIVEN IN A NOTE

The particulars referred to in section 3(3) of the Unsolicited Goods and Services Act 1971 are:

- (a) the amount of the charge;
- (b) the name of the directory or proposed directory;
- (c) the name of the person producing the directory;
- (d) the geographic address at which that person is established;
- (e) if the directory is to be available in printed form, the proposed date of publication of the directory or of the issue in which the entry is to be included;
- (f) if the directory or the issue in which the entry is to be included is to be put on sale, the price at which it is to be offered for sale and the minimum number of copies which are to be available for sale;
- (g) if the directory or the issue of the directory in which the entry is to be included is to be distributed free of charge (whether or not it is also to be put on sale), the minimum numbers of copies which are to be so distributed; and
- (h) if the directory is or is to be made available in a form other than printed form, adequate details of how it may be accessed.

PART 2 CONDITIONS APPLYING TO INVOICE OR SIMILAR DOCUMENT WHICH DOES NOT ASSERT RIGHT TO PAYMENT

The conditions referred to in section 6(2) of the Unsolicited Goods and Services Act 1971 are that the invoice or similar document must:

- (a) be clear, legible and comprehensible; and
- (b) contain the following statement, displayed in uppercase lettering and in a manner that makes that statement readily apparent to a reasonable person reading that invoice or similar document—

'THIS IS NOT A DEMAND FOR PAYMENT
THERE IS NO OBLIGATION TO PAY
THIS IS NOT A BILL'

PART 3 INFORMATION REQUIRED IN WRITTEN NOTICE

The notice referred to in section 3B(1)(h)(i) of the Unsolicited Goods and Services Act 1971 must specify the following information:

    (a) the fact that the earlier contract is to be renewed or extended;

    (b) the commencement date of the new contract;

    (c) the cost to the purchaser of the new contract; and

    (d) the fact that the purchaser may, within 21 days, write to the person by whom the notice is given withdrawing his consent to the renewal or extension of the contract.

PART 4 INFORMATION TO BE GIVEN TO A PURCHASER

The following information must be given to the purchaser pursuant to section 3B(1)(i)(ii) of the Unsolicited Goods and Services Act 1971:

    (a) the name of the relevant publisher; and

    (b) the fact that, if the purchaser enters into the new contract:

        (i)   the other party to the new contract will be the relevant publisher; and

        (ii)   the parties to the earlier contract and the new contract will be different.

Transfer of Undertakings (Protection of Employment) Regulations 2006

(SI 2006, No. 246)

3.   A relevant transfer

    (1) These Regulations apply to—

    (a) a transfer of an undertaking, business or part of an undertaking or business situated immediately before the transfer in the United Kingdom to another person where there is a transfer of an economic entity which retains its identity;

    . . .

and in which the conditions set out in paragraph (3) are satisfied.

    (2) In this regulation 'economic entity' means an organised grouping of resources which has the objective of pursuing an economic activity, whether or not that activity is central or ancillary.

[4.   Effect of relevant transfer on contracts of employment

    (1) Except where objection is made under paragraph (7), a relevant transfer shall not operate so as to terminate the contract of employment of any person employed by the transferor and assigned to the organised grouping of resources or employees that is subject to the relevant transfer, which would otherwise be terminated by the transfer, but any such contract shall have effect after the transfer as if originally made between the person so employed and the transferee.

    (2) Without prejudice to paragraph (1), but subject to paragraph (6), and regulations 8 and 15(9), on the completion of a relevant transfer—

    (a) all the transferor's rights, powers, duties and liabilities under or in connection with any such contract shall be transferred by virtue of this regulation to the transferee; and

    (b) any act or omission before the transfer is completed, of or in relation to the transferor in respect of that contract or a person assigned to that organised grouping of resources or employees, shall be deemed to have been an act or omission of or in relation to the transferee.

    (3) Any reference in paragraph (1) to a person employed by the transferor and assigned to the organised grouping of resources or employees that is subject to a relevant transfer, is a reference to a person so employed immediately before the transfer, or who would have been so employed if he had not been dismissed in the circumstances described in regulation 7(1), including, where the transfer

is effected by a series of two or more transactions, a person so employed and assigned or who would have been so employed and assigned immediately before any of those transactions.

[(4) Subject to regulation 9, any purported variation of a contract of employment that is, or will be, transferred by paragraph (1), is void if the sole or principal reason for the variation is the transfer.

(5) Paragraph (4) does not prevent a variation of the contract of employment if—

    (a) the sole or principal reason for the variation is an economic, technical, or organisational reason entailing changes in the workforce, provided that the employer and employee agree that variation; or

    (b) the terms of that contract permit the employer to make such a variation.

(5A) In paragraph (5), the expression "changes in the workforce" includes a change to the place where employees are employed by the employer to carry on the business of the employer or to carry out work of a particular kind for the employer (and the reference to such a place has the same meaning as in section 139 of the 1996 Act).

(5B) Paragraph (4) does not apply in respect of a variation of the contract of employment in so far as it varies a term or condition incorporated from a collective agreement, provided that—

    (a) the variation of the contract takes effect on a date more than one year after the date of the transfer; and

    (b) following that variation, the rights and obligations in the employee's contract, when considered together, are no less favourable to the employee than those which applied immediately before the variation.

(5C) Paragraphs (5) and (5B) do not affect any rule of law as to whether a contract of employment is effectively varied.]

(7) Paragraphs (1) and (2) shall not operate to transfer the contract of employment and the rights, powers, duties and liabilities under or in connection with it of an employee who informs the transferor or the transferee that he objects to becoming employed by the transferee.

(8) Subject to paragraphs (9) and (11), where an employee so objects, the relevant transfer shall operate so as to terminate his contract of employment with the transferor but he shall not be treated, for any purpose, as having been dismissed by the transferor.

(9) Subject to regulation 9, where a relevant transfer involves or would involve a substantial change in working conditions to the material detriment of a person whose contract of employment is or would be transferred under paragraph (1), such an employee may treat the contract of employment as having been terminated, and the employee shall be treated for any purpose as having been dismissed by the employer.

(10) No damages shall be payable by an employer as a result of a dismissal falling within paragraph (9) in respect of any failure by the employer to pay wages to an employee in respect of a notice period which the employee has failed to work.

(11) Paragraphs (1), (7), (8) and (9) are without prejudice to any right of an employee arising apart from these Regulations to terminate his contract of employment without notice in acceptance of a repudiatory breach of contract by his employer.]

Business Protection from Misleading Marketing Regulations 2008

(SI 2008, No. 1276)

[Implementing Directive 2006/114/EC of the European Parliament and of the Council concerning misleading and comparative advertising [2006] OJ L376/21.]

3. Prohibition of advertising which misleads traders

    (1) Advertising which is misleading is prohibited.

(2) Advertising is misleading which—

    (a) in any way, including its presentation, deceives or is likely to deceive the traders to whom it is addressed or whom it reaches; and by reason of its deceptive nature, is likely to affect their economic behaviour; or

    (b) for those reasons, injures or is likely to injure a competitor.

(3) In determining whether advertising is misleading, account shall be taken of all its features, and in particular of any information it contains concerning—

    (a) the characteristics of the product (as defined in paragraph (4));

    (b) the price or manner in which the price is calculated;

    (c) the conditions on which the product is supplied or provided; and

    (d) the nature, attributes and rights of the advertiser (as defined in paragraph (5)).

(4) In paragraph (3)(a) the 'characteristics of the product' include—

    (a) availability of the product;

    (b) nature of the product;

    (c) execution of the product;

    (d) composition of the product;

    (e) method and date of manufacture of the product;

    (f) method and date of provision of the product;

    (g) fitness for purpose of the product;

    (h) uses of the product;

    (i) quantity of the product;

    (j) specification of the product;

    (k) geographical or commercial origin of the product;

    (l) results to be expected from use of the product; or

    (m) results and material features of tests or checks carried out on the product.

(5) In paragraph (3)(d) the 'nature, attributes and rights' of the advertiser include the advertiser's—

    (a) identity;

    (b) assets;

    (c) qualifications;

    (d) ownership of industrial, commercial or intellectual property rights; or

    (e) awards and distinctions.

6. Misleading advertising

A trader is guilty of an offence if he engages in advertising which is misleading under regulation 3.

29. Validity of agreements

An agreement shall not be void or unenforceable by reason only of a breach of these Regulations.

Consumer Protection from Unfair Trading Regulations 2008

(SI 2008, No. 1277)

PART 1 GENERAL

2. Interpretation

(1) In these Regulations—

...

'commercial practice' means any act, omission, course of conduct, representation or commercial communication (including advertising and marketing) by a trader, which is directly connected with the promotion, sale or supply of a product to or from consumers, whether occurring before, during or after a commercial transaction (if any) in relation to a product;

. . .

'invitation to purchase' means a commercial communication which indicates characteristics of the product and the price in a way appropriate to the means of that commercial communication and thereby enables the consumer to make a purchase;

'materially distort the economic behaviour' means in relation to an average consumer, appreciably to impair the average consumer's ability to make an informed decision thereby causing him to take a transactional decision that he would not have taken otherwise;

. . .

'professional diligence' means the standard of special skill and care which a trader may reasonably be expected to exercise towards consumers which is commensurate with either—

    (a) honest market practice in the trader's field of activity, or

    (b) the general principle of good faith in the trader's field of activity;

. . .

'transactional decision' means any decision taken by a consumer, whether it is to act or to refrain from acting, concerning—

    (a) whether, how and on what terms to purchase, make payment in whole or in part for, retain or dispose of a product; or

    (b) whether, how and on what terms to exercise a contractual right in relation to a product [(but the application of this definition to regulations 5 and 7 as they apply for the purposes of Part 4A is subject to regulation 27B(2))].

(6) Paragraph (5) is without prejudice to the common and legitimate advertising practice of making exaggerated statements which are not meant to be taken literally.

3.   Prohibition of unfair commercial practices

    (1) Unfair commercial practices are prohibited.

    (2) Paragraphs (3) and (4) set out the circumstances when a commercial practice is unfair.

    (3) A commercial practice is unfair if—

        (a) it contravenes the requirements of professional diligence; and

        (b) it materially distorts or is likely to materially distort the economic behaviour of the average consumer with regard to the product.

    (4) A commercial practice is unfair if—

        (a) it is a misleading action under the provisions of regulation 5;

        (b) it is a misleading omission under the provisions of regulation 6;

        (c) it is aggressive under the provisions of regulation 7; or

        (d) it is listed in Schedule 1.

5.   Misleading actions

    (1) A commercial practice is a misleading action if it satisfies the conditions in either paragraph (2) or paragraph (3).

    (2) A commercial practice satisfies the conditions of this paragraph—

        (a) if it contains false information and is therefore untruthful in relation to any of the matters in paragraph (4) or if it or its overall presentation in any way deceives or is likely to deceive the average consumer in relation to any of the matters in that paragraph, even if the information is factually correct; and

        (b) it causes or is likely to cause the average consumer to take a transactional decision he would not have taken otherwise.

    (3) A commercial practice satisfies the conditions of this paragraph if—

        (a) it concerns any marketing of a product (including comparative advertising) which creates confusion with any products, trade marks, trade names or other distinguishing marks of a competitor; or

    (b) it concerns any failure by a trader to comply with a commitment contained in a code of conduct which the trader has undertaken to comply with, if—

        (i)   the trader indicates in a commercial practice that he is bound by that code of conduct, and

        (ii) the commitment is firm and capable of being verified and is not aspirational,

and it causes or is likely to cause the average consumer to take a transactional decision he would not have taken otherwise, taking account of its factual context and of all its features and circumstances.

    (4) The matters referred to in paragraph (2)(a) are—

        (a) the existence or nature of the product;

        (b) the main characteristics of the product (as defined in paragraph 5);

        (c) the extent of the trader's commitments;

        (d) the motives for the commercial practice;

        (e) the nature of the sales process;

        (f) any statement or symbol relating to direct or indirect sponsorship or approval of the trader or the product;

        (g) the price or the manner in which the price is calculated;

        (h) the existence of a specific price advantage;

        (i) the need for a service, part, replacement or repair;

        (j) the nature, attributes and rights of the trader (as defined in paragraph 6);

        (k) the consumer's rights or the risks he may face.

    (5) In paragraph (4)(b), the 'main characteristics of the product' include—

        (a) availability of the product;

        (b) benefits of the product;

        (c) risks of the product;

        (d) execution of the product;

        (e) composition of the product;

        (f) accessories of the product;

        (g) after-sale customer assistance concerning the product;

        (h) the handling of complaints about the product;

        (i) the method and date of manufacture of the product;

        (j) the method and date of provision of the product;

        (k) delivery of the product;

        (l) fitness for purpose of the product;

        (m) usage of the product;

        (n) quantity of the product;

        (o) specification of the product;

        (p) geographical or commercial origin of the product;

        (q) results to be expected from use of the product; and

        (r) results and material features of tests or checks carried out on the product.

    (6) In paragraph (4)(j), the 'nature, attributes and rights' as far as concern the trader include the trader's—

        (a) identity;

        (b) assets;

        (c) qualifications;

        (d) status;

        (e) approval;

        (f) affiliations or connections;

        (g) ownership of industrial, commercial or intellectual property rights; and

        (h) wards and distinctions.

(7) In paragraph (4)(k) 'consumer's rights' include rights the consumer may have under Part 5A of the Sale of Goods Act 1979 or Part 1B of the Supply of Goods and Services Act 1982.

6.   Misleading omissions

(1) A commercial practice is a misleading omission if, in its factual context, taking account of the matters in paragraph (2)—

(a) the commercial practice omits material information,

(b) the commercial practice hides material information,

(c) the commercial practice provides material information in a manner which is unclear, unintelligible, ambiguous or untimely, or

(d) the commercial practice fails to identify its commercial intent, unless this is already apparent from the context,

and as a result it causes or is likely to cause the average consumer to take a transactional decision he would not have taken otherwise.

(2) The matters referred to in paragraph (1) are—

(a) all the features and circumstances of the commercial practice;

(b) the limitations of the medium used to communicate the commercial practice (including limitations of space or time); and

(c) where the medium used to communicate the commercial practice imposes limitations of space or time, any measures taken by the trader to make the information available to consumers by other means.

(3) In paragraph (1) 'material information' means—

(a) the information which the average consumer needs, according to the context, to take an informed transactional decision; and

(b) any information requirement which applies in relation to a commercial communication as a result of a Community obligation.

(4) Where a commercial practice is an invitation to purchase, the following information will be material if not already apparent from the context in addition to any other information which is material information under paragraph (3)—

(a) the main characteristics of the product, to the extent appropriate to the medium by which the invitation to purchase is communicated and the product;

(b) the identity of the trader, such as his trading name, and the identity of any other trader on whose behalf the trader is acting;

(c) the geographical address of the trader and the geographical address of any other trader on whose behalf the trader is acting;

(d) either—

(i)   the price, including any taxes; or

(ii)   where the nature of the product is such that the price cannot reasonably be calculated in advance, the manner in which the price is calculated;

(e) where appropriate, either—

(i)   all additional freight, delivery or postal charges; or

(ii)   where such charges cannot reasonably be calculated in advance, the fact that such charges may be payable;

(f) the following matters where they depart from the requirements of professional diligence—

(i)   arrangements for payment,

(ii)   arrangements for delivery,

(iii) arrangements for performance,

(iv)   complaint handling policy;

(g) for products and transactions involving a right of withdrawal or cancellation, the existence of such a right.

7. Aggressive commercial practices

(1) A commercial practice is aggressive if, in its factual context, taking account of all of its features and circumstances—

> (a) it significantly impairs or is likely significantly to impair the average consumer's freedom of choice or conduct in relation to the product concerned through the use of harassment, coercion or undue influence; and
>
> (b) it thereby causes or is likely to cause him to take a transactional decision he would not have taken otherwise.

(2) In determining whether a commercial practice uses harassment, coercion or undue influence account shall be taken of—

> (a) its timing, location, nature or persistence;
>
> (b) the use of threatening or abusive language or behaviour;
>
> (c) the exploitation by the trader of any specific misfortune or circumstance of such gravity as to impair the consumer's judgment, of which the trader is aware, to influence the consumer's decision with regard to the product;
>
> (d) any onerous or disproportionate non-contractual barrier imposed by the trader where a consumer wishes to exercise rights under the contract, including rights to terminate a contract or to switch to another product or another trader; and
>
> (e) any threat to take any action which cannot legally be taken.

(3) In this regulation—

> (a) 'coercion' includes the use of physical force; and
>
> (b) 'undue influence' means exploiting a position of power in relation to the consumer so as to apply pressure, even without using or threatening to use physical force, in a way which significantly limits the consumer's ability to make an informed decision.

29. Validity of agreements

[Except as provided by Part 4A {*consumers' rights to redress*},] An agreement shall not be void or unenforceable by reason only of a breach of these Regulations.

Regulation 3(4)(d)

SCHEDULE 1
COMMERCIAL PRACTICES WHICH ARE IN ALL CIRCUMSTANCES CONSIDERED UNFAIR

. . .

Part IV

EU Materials*

Treaty Establishing the European Economic Community

(Treaty of Rome, 25 March 1957, revised)

Article 81 (ex Art. 85)

1. The following shall be prohibited as incompatible with the common market: all agreements between undertakings, decisions by associations of undertakings and concerted practices which may affect trade between Member States and which have as their object or effect the prevention, restriction or distortion of competition within the common market, and in particular those which:
   (a) directly or indirectly fix purchase or selling prices or any other trading conditions;
   (b) limit or control production, markets, technical development, or investment;
   (c) share markets or sources of supply;
   (d) apply dissimilar conditions to equivalent transactions with other trading parties, thereby placing them at a competitive disadvantage;
   (e) make the conclusion of contracts subject to acceptance by the other parties of supplementary obligations which, by their nature or according to commercial usage, have no connection with the subject of such contracts.
2. Any agreements or decisions prohibited pursuant to this Article shall be automatically void.
3. The provisions of paragraph 1 may, however, be declared inapplicable in the case of:
   – any agreement or category of agreements between undertakings;
   – any decision or category of decisions by associations of undertakings;
   – any concerted practice or category of concerted practices;
which contributes to improving the production or distribution of goods or to promoting technical or economic progress, while allowing consumers a fair share of the resulting benefit, and which does not:
   (a) impose on the undertakings concerned restrictions which are not indispensable to the attainment of these objectives;
   (b) afford such undertakings the possibility of eliminating competition in respect of a substantial part of the products in question.

Article 82 (ex Art. 86)

Any abuse by one or more undertakings of a dominant position within the common market or in a substantial part of it shall be prohibited as incompatible with the common market in so far as it may affect trade between Member States. Such abuse may, in particular, consist in:
   (a) directly or indirectly imposing unfair purchase or selling prices or other unfair trading conditions;
   (b) limiting production, markets or technical development to the prejudice of consumers;

   (c) applying dissimilar conditions to equivalent transactions with other trading parties, thereby placing them at a competitive disadvantage;

   (d) making the conclusion of contracts subject to acceptance by the other parties of supplementary obligations which, by their nature or according to commercial usage, have no connection with the subject of such contracts.

Regulation (EC) No 864/2007 of the European Parliament and of the Council of 11 July 2007 on the law applicable to non-contractual obligations (Rome II)

[2007] OJ L199/40

Article 2   Non-contractual obligations

1. For the purpose of this Regulation, damage shall cover any consequence arising out of tort/delict, unjust enrichment, *negotiorum gestio* or *culpa in contrahendo*.

Regulation (EC) No 593/2008 of the European Parliament and of the Council of 17 June 2008 on the law applicable to contractual obligations (Rome I)

Article 1   Material scope

1. This Regulation shall apply, in situations involving a conflict of laws, to contractual obligations in civil and commercial matters.

Article 3   Freedom of choice

1. A contract shall be governed by the law chosen by the parties. The choice shall be made expressly or clearly demonstrated by the terms of the contract or the circumstances of the case. By their choice the parties can select the law applicable to the whole or to part only of the contract.

Article 9   Overriding mandatory provisions

3. Effect may be given to the overriding mandatory provisions of the law of the country where the obligations arising out of the contract have to be or have been performed, in so far as those overriding mandatory provisions render the performance of the contract unlawful.

Article 10   Consent and material validity

1. The existence and validity of a contract, or of any term of a contract, shall be determined by the law which would govern it under this Regulation if the contract or term were valid.

Proposal for a regulation of the European Parliament and of the Council on a common European sales law

(2011/0284 (COD))

Article 2   Definitions

For the purpose of this Regulation, the following definitions shall apply:

   (a) 'contract' means an agreement intended to give rise to obligations or other legal effects;

   (b) 'good faith and fair dealing' means a standard of conduct characterised by honesty, openness and consideration for the interests of the other party to the transaction or relationship in question;

(c) 'loss' means economic loss and non-economic loss in the form of pain and suffering, excluding other forms of non-economic loss such as impairment of the quality of life and loss of enjoyment;

(d) 'standard contract terms' means contract terms which have been drafted in advance for several transactions involving different parties, and which have not been individually negotiated by the parties within the meaning of Article 7 of the Common European Sales Law;

(e) 'damages' means a sum of money to which a person may be entitled as compensation for loss, injury or damage;

(f) 'obligation' means a duty to perform which one party to a legal relationship owes to another party.

Article 5   Contracts for which the Common European Sales Law can be used

The Common European Sales Law may be used for:

(a) sales contracts;

(b) contracts for the supply of digital content whether or not supplied on a tangible medium which can be stored, processed or accessed, and re-used by the user, irrespective of whether the digital content is supplied in exchange for the payment of a price.

(c) related service contracts, irrespective of whether a separate price was agreed for the related service.

Article 7   Parties to the contract

1. The Common European Sales Law may be used only if the seller of goods or the supplier of digital content is a trader. Where all the parties to a contract are traders, the Common European Sales Law may be used if at least one of those parties is a small or medium-sized enterprise ('SME').

Article 8   Agreement on the use of the Common European Sales Law

1. The use of the Common European Sales Law requires an agreement of the parties to that effect....

2. In relations between a trader and a consumer the agreement on the use of the Common European Sales Law shall be valid only if the consumer's consent is given by an explicit statement which is separate from the statement indicating the agreement to conclude a contract. The trader shall provide the consumer with a confirmation of that agreement on a durable medium.

ANNEX I COMMON EUROPEAN SALES LAW

Article 1   Freedom of contract

1. Parties are free to conclude a contract and to determine its contents, subject to any applicable mandatory rules.

2. Parties may exclude the application of any of the provisions of the Common European Sales Law, or derogate from or vary their effects, unless otherwise stated in those provisions.

Article 2   Good faith and fair dealing

1. Each party has a duty to act in accordance with good faith and fair dealing.

2. Breach of this duty may preclude the party in breach from exercising or relying on a right, remedy or defence which that party would otherwise have, or may make the party liable for any loss thereby caused to the other party.

3. The parties may not exclude the application of this Article or derogate from or vary its effects.

Article 3   Co-operation

The parties are obliged to co-operate with each other to the extent that this can be expected for the performance of their contractual obligations.

Article 5   Reasonableness

1. Reasonableness is to be objectively ascertained, having regard to the nature and purpose of the contract, to the circumstances of the case and to the usages and practices of the trades or professions involved.

2. Any reference to what can be expected of or by a person, or in a particular situation, is a reference to what can reasonably be expected.

Article 6   No form required

Unless otherwise stated in the Common European Sales Law, a contract, statement or any other act which is governed by it need not be made in or evidenced by a particular form.

Article 8   Termination of a contract

1. To 'terminate a contract' means to bring to an end the rights and obligations of the parties under the contract with the exception of those arising under any contract term providing for the settlement of disputes or any other contract term which is to operate even after termination.

2. Payments due and damages for any non-performance before the time of termination remain payable. Where the termination is for non-performance or for anticipated non-performance, the terminating party is also entitled to damages in lieu of the other party's future performance.

3. The effects of termination on the repayment of the price and the return of the goods or the digital content, and other restitutionary effects, are governed by the rules on restitution set out in Chapter 17.

Article 23   Duty to disclose information about goods and related services

1. Before the conclusion of a contract for the sale of goods, supply of digital content or provision of related services by a trader to another trader, the supplier has a duty to disclose by any appropriate means to the other trader any information concerning the main characteristics of the goods, digital content or related services to be supplied which the supplier has or can be expected to have and which it would be contrary to good faith and fair dealing not to disclose to the other party.

Article 24   Additional duties to provide information in distance contracts concluded by electronic means

5. The trader must acknowledge by electronic means and without undue delay the receipt of an offer or an acceptance sent by the other party.

Article 28   Duty to ensure that information supplied is correct

1. A party who supplies information before or at the time a contract is concluded, whether in order to comply with the duties imposed by this Chapter or otherwise, has a duty to take reasonable care to ensure that the information supplied is correct and is not misleading.

2. A party to whom incorrect or misleading information has been supplied in breach of the duty referred to in paragraph 1, and who reasonably relies on that information in concluding a contract with the party who supplied it, has the remedies set out in Article 29.

3. In relations between a trader and a consumer the parties may not, to the detriment of the consumer, exclude the application of this Article or derogate from or vary its effects.

Article 29   Remedies for breach of information duties

1. A party which has failed to comply with any duty imposed by this Chapter is liable for any loss caused to the other party by such failure.

3. The remedies provided under this Article are without prejudice to any remedy which may be available under Article 42 (2), Article 48 or Article 49.

4. In relations between a trader and a consumer the parties may not, to the detriment of the consumer, exclude the application of this Article or derogate from or vary its effects.

Article 30   Requirements for the conclusion of a contract

1. A contract is concluded if:
   (a) the parties reach an agreement;

(b) they intend the agreement to have legal effect; and

(c) the agreement, supplemented if necessary by rules of the Common European Sales Law, has sufficient content and certainty to be given legal effect.

2. Agreement is reached by acceptance of an offer. Acceptance may be made explicitly or by other statements or conduct.

3. Whether the parties intend the agreement to have legal effect is to be determined from their statements and conduct.

4. Where one of the parties makes agreement on some specific matter a requirement for the conclusion of a contract, there is no contract unless agreement on that matter has been reached.

Article 31   Offer

1. A proposal is an offer if:

(a) it is intended to result in a contract if it is accepted; and

(b) it has sufficient content and certainty for there to be a contract.

2. An offer may be made to one or more specific persons.

3. A proposal made to the public is not an offer, unless the circumstances indicate otherwise.

Article 32   Revocation of offer

1. An offer may be revoked if the revocation reaches the offeree before the offeree has sent an acceptance or, in cases of acceptance by conduct, before the contract has been concluded.

2. Where a proposal made to the public is an offer, it can be revoked by the same means as were used to make the offer.

3. A revocation of an offer is ineffective if:

(a) the offer indicates that it is irrevocable;

(b) the offer states a fixed time period for its acceptance; or

(c) it was otherwise reasonable for the offeree to rely on the offer as being irrevocable and the offeree has acted in reliance on the offer.

Article 33   Rejection of offer

When a rejection of an offer reaches the offeror, the offer lapses.

Article 34   Acceptance

1. Any form of statement or conduct by the offeree is an acceptance if it indicates assent to the offer.

2. Silence or inactivity does not in itself constitute acceptance.

Article 35   Time of conclusion of the contract

1. Where an acceptance is sent by the offeree the contract is concluded when the acceptance reaches the offeror.

2. Where an offer is accepted by conduct, the contract is concluded when notice of the conduct reaches the offeror.

3. Notwithstanding paragraph 2, where by virtue of the offer, of practices which the parties have established between themselves, or of a usage, the offeree may accept the offer by conduct without notice to the offeror, the contract is concluded when the offeree begins to act.

Article 36   Time limit for acceptance

1. An acceptance of an offer is effective only if it reaches the offeror within any time limit stipulated in the offer by the offeror.

2. Where no time limit has been fixed by the offeror the acceptance is effective only if it reaches the offeror within a reasonable time after the offer was made.

3. Where an offer may be accepted by doing an act without notice to the offeror, the acceptance is effective only if the act is done within the time for acceptance fixed by the offeror or, if no such time is fixed, within a reasonable time.

Article 37   Late acceptance

1. A late acceptance is effective as an acceptance if without undue delay the offeror informs the offeree that the offeror is treating it as an effective acceptance.

2. Where a letter or other communication containing a late acceptance shows that it has been sent in such circumstances that if its transmission had been normal it would have reached the offeror in due time, the late acceptance is effective as an acceptance unless, without undue delay, the offeror informs the offeree that the offer has lapsed.

Article 38   Modified acceptance

1. A reply by the offeree which states or implies additional or different contract terms which materially alter the terms of the offer is a rejection and a new offer.

2. Additional or different contract terms relating, among other things, to the price payment, quality and quantity of the goods, place and time of delivery, extent of one party's liability to the other or the settlement of disputes are presumed to alter the terms of the offer materially.

3. A reply which gives a definite assent to an offer is an acceptance even if it states or implies additional or different contract terms, provided that these do not materially alter the terms of the offer. The additional or different terms then become part of the contract.

4. A reply which states or implies additional or different contract terms is always rejection of the offer if:

    (a) the offer expressly limits acceptance to the terms of the offer;

    (b) the offeror objects to the additional or different terms without undue delay; or

    (c) the offeree makes the acceptance conditional upon the offeror's assent to the additional or different terms, and the assent does not reach the offeree within a reasonable time.

Article 39   Conflicting standard contract terms

1. Where the parties have reached agreement except that the offer and acceptance refer to conflicting standard contract terms, a contract is nonetheless concluded. The standard contract terms are part of the contract to the extent that they are common in substance.

2. Notwithstanding paragraph 1, no contract is concluded if one party:

    (a) has indicated in advance, explicitly, and not by way of standard contract terms, an intention not to be bound by a contract on the basis of paragraph 1; or

    (b) without undue delay, informs the other party of such an intention.

Article 48   Mistake

1. A party may avoid a contract for mistake of fact or law existing when the contract was concluded if:

    (a) the party, but for the mistake, would not have concluded the contract or would have done so only on fundamentally different contract terms and the other party knew or could be expected to have known this; and

    (b) the other party:

        (i)   caused the mistake;

        (ii)   caused the contract to be concluded in mistake by failing to comply with any pre-contractual information duty under Chapter 2, Sections 1 to 4 [*Arts 13–28*];

        (iii) knew or could be expected to have known of the mistake and caused the contract to be concluded in mistake by not pointing out the relevant information, provided that good faith and fair dealing would have required a party aware of the mistake to point it out; or

        (iv)   made the same mistake.

2. A party may not avoid a contract for mistake if the risk of the mistake was assumed, or in the circumstances should be borne, by that party.

3. An inaccuracy in the expression or transmission of a statement is treated as a mistake of the person who made or sent the statement.

Article 49   Fraud

1. A party may avoid a contract if the other party has induced the conclusion of the contract by fraudulent misrepresentation, whether by words or conduct, or fraudulent non-disclosure of any information which good faith and fair dealing, or any precontractual information duty, required that party to disclose.

2. Misrepresentation is fraudulent if it is made with knowledge or belief that the representation is false, or recklessly as to whether it is true or false, and is intended to induce the recipient to make a mistake. Non-disclosure is fraudulent if it is intended to induce the person from whom the information is withheld to make a mistake.

3. In determining whether good faith and fair dealing require a party to disclose particular information, regard should be had to all the circumstances, including:
    (a) whether the party had special expertise;
    (b) the cost to the party of acquiring the relevant information;
    (c) the ease with which the other party could have acquired the information by other means;
    (d) the nature of the information;
    (e) the apparent importance of the information to the other party; and
    (f) in contracts between traders good commercial practice in the situation concerned.

Article 50   Threats

A party may avoid a contract if the other party has induced the conclusion of the contract by the threat of wrongful, imminent and serious harm, or of a wrongful act.

Article 51   Unfair exploitation

A party may avoid a contract if, at the time of the conclusion of the contract:
    (a) that party was dependent on, or had a relationship of trust with, the other party, was in economic distress or had urgent needs, was improvident, ignorant, or inexperienced; and
    (b) the other party knew or could be expected to have known this and, in the light of the circumstances and purpose of the contract, exploited the first party's situation by taking an excessive benefit or unfair advantage.

Article 52   Notice of avoidance

1. Avoidance is effected by notice to the other party.

2. A notice of avoidance is effective only if it is given within the following period after the avoiding party becomes aware of the relevant circumstances or becomes capable of acting freely:
    (a) six months in case of mistake; and
    (b) one year in case of fraud, threats and unfair exploitation.

Article 53   Confirmation

Where the party who has the right to avoid a contract under this Chapter confirms it, expressly or impliedly, after becoming aware of the relevant circumstances, or becoming capable of acting freely, that party may no longer avoid the contract.

Article 54   Effects of avoidance

1. A contract which may be avoided is valid until avoided but, once avoided, is retrospectively invalid from the beginning.

2. Where a ground of avoidance affects only certain contract terms, the effect of avoidance is limited to those terms unless it is unreasonable to uphold the remainder of the contract.

3. The question whether either party has a right to the return of whatever has been transferred or supplied under a contract which has been avoided, or to a monetary equivalent, is regulated by the rules on restitution in Chapter 17.

Article 55   Damages for loss

A party who has the right to avoid a contract under this Chapter or who had such a right before it was lost by the effect of time limits or confirmation is entitled, whether or not the contract is avoided, to damages from the other party for loss suffered as a result of the mistake, fraud, threats or unfair exploitation, provided that the other party knew or could be expected to have known of the relevant circumstances.

Article 56   Exclusion or restriction of remedies

1. Remedies for fraud, threats and unfair exploitation cannot be directly or indirectly excluded or restricted.

2. In relations between a trader and a consumer the parties may not, to the detriment of the consumer, directly or indirectly exclude or restrict remedies for mistake.

Article 57   Choice of remedy

A party who is entitled to a remedy under this Chapter in circumstances which afford that party a remedy for non-performance may pursue either of those remedies.

Article 58   General rules on interpretation of contracts

1. A contract is to be interpreted according to the common intention of the parties even if this differs from the normal meaning of the expressions used in it.

2. Where one party intended an expression used in the contract to have a particular meaning, and at the time of the conclusion of the contract the other party was aware, or could be expected to have been aware, of that intention, the expression is to be interpreted in the way intended by the first party.

3. Unless otherwise provided in paragraphs 1 and 2, the contract is to be interpreted according to the meaning which a reasonable person would give to it.

Article 59   Relevant matters

In interpreting a contract, regard may be had, in particular, to:

   (a) the circumstances in which it was concluded, including the preliminary negotiations;
   (b) the conduct of the parties, even subsequent to the conclusion of the contract;
   (c) the interpretation which has already been given by the parties to expressions which are identical to or similar to those used in the contract;
   (d) usages which would be considered generally applicable by parties in the same situation;
   (e) practices which the parties have established between themselves;
   (f) the meaning commonly given to expressions in the branch of activity concerned;
   (g) the nature and purpose of the contract; and
   (h) good faith and fair dealing.

Article 60   Reference to contract as a whole

Expressions used in a contract are to be interpreted in the light of the contract as a whole.

Article 62   Preference for individually negotiated contract terms

To the extent that there is an inconsistency, contract terms which have been individually negotiated prevail over those which have not been individually negotiated within the meaning of Article 7.

Article 63   Preference for interpretation which gives contract terms effect

An interpretation which renders the contract terms effective prevails over one which does not.

Article 64   Interpretation in favour of consumers

1. Where there is doubt about the meaning of a contract term in a contract between a trader and a consumer, the interpretation most favourable to the consumer shall prevail unless the term was supplied by the consumer.

2. The parties may not, to the detriment of the consumer, exclude the application of this Article or derogate from or vary its effects.

Article 65   Interpretation against supplier of a contract term

Where, in a contract which does not fall under Article 64, there is doubt about the meaning of a contract term which has not been individually negotiated within the meaning of Article 7, an interpretation of the term against the party who supplied it shall prevail.

Article 66   Contract terms

The terms of the contract are derived from:

    (a) the agreement of the parties, subject to any mandatory rules of the Common European Sales Law;

    (b) any usage or practice by which parties are bound by virtue of Article 67;

    (c) any rule of the Common European Sales Law which applies in the absence of an agreement of the parties to the contrary; and

    (d) any contract term implied by virtue of Article 68.

Article 67   Usages and practices in contracts between traders

1. In a contract between traders, the parties are bound by any usage which they have agreed should be applicable and by any practice they have established between themselves.

2. The parties are bound by a usage which would be considered generally applicable by traders in the same situation as the parties.

3. Usages and practices do not bind the parties to the extent to which they conflict with contract terms which have been individually negotiated or any mandatory rules of the Common European Sales Law.

Article 68   Contract terms which may be implied

1. Where it is necessary to provide for a matter which is not explicitly regulated by the agreement of the parties, any usage or practice or any rule of the Common European Sales Law, an additional contract term may be implied, having regard in particular to:

    (a) the nature and purpose of the contract;

    (b) the circumstances in which the contract was concluded; and

    (c) good faith and fair dealing.

2. Any contract term implied under paragraph 1 is, as far as possible, to be such as to give effect to what the parties would probably have agreed, had they provided for the matter.

3. Paragraph 1 does not apply if the parties have deliberately left a matter unregulated, accepting that one or other party would bear the risk.

Article 69   Contract terms derived from certain pre-contractual statements

1. Where the trader makes a statement before the contract is concluded, either to the other party or publicly, about the characteristics of what is to be supplied by that trader under the contract, the statement is incorporated as a term of the contract unless:

    (a) the other party was aware, or could be expected to have been aware when the contract was concluded that the statement was incorrect or could not otherwise be relied on as such a term; or

    (b) the other party's decision to conclude the contract could not have been influenced by the statement.

Article 70   Duty to raise awareness of not individually negotiated contract terms

1. Contract terms supplied by one party and not individually negotiated within the meaning of Article 7 may be invoked against the other party only if the other party was aware of them, or if the party supplying them took reasonable steps to draw the other party's attention to them, before or when the contract was concluded.

2. For the purposes of this Article, in relations between a trader and a consumer contract terms are not sufficiently brought to the consumer's attention by a mere reference to them in a contract document, even if the consumer signs the document.

3. The parties may not exclude the application of this Article or derogate from or vary its effects.

Article 78   Contract terms in favour of third parties

1. The contracting parties may, by the contract, confer a right on a third party. The third party need not be in existence or identified at the time the contract is concluded but needs to be identifiable.

2. The nature and content of the third party's right are determined by the contract. The right may take the form of an exclusion or limitation of the third party's liability to one of the contracting parties.

3. When one of the contracting parties is bound to render a performance to the third party under the contract, then:

(a) the third party has the same rights to performance and remedies for non-performance as if the contracting party was bound to render the performance under a contract with the third party; and

(b) the contracting party who is bound may assert against the third party all defences which the contracting party could assert against the other party to the contract.

4. The third party may reject a right conferred upon them by notice to either of the contracting parties, if that is done before it has been expressly or impliedly accepted. On such rejection, the right is treated as never having accrued to the third party.

5. The contracting parties may remove or modify the contract term conferring the right if this is done before either of them has given the third party notice that the right has been conferred.

Article 79   Effects of unfair contract terms

1. A contract term which is supplied by one party and which is unfair under Sections 2 and 3 of this Chapter [*Arts 82–86*] is not binding on the other party.

2. Where the contract can be maintained without the unfair contract term, the other contract terms remain binding.

Article 80   Exclusions from unfairness test

1. Sections 2 and 3 [*Arts 82–86*] do not apply to contract terms which reflect rules of the Common European Sales Law which would apply if the terms did not regulate the matter.

2. Section 2 [*Arts 82–85*] does not apply to the definition of the main subject matter of the contract, or to the appropriateness of the price to be paid in so far as the trader has complied with the duty of transparency set out in Article 82.

3. Section 3 [*Art 86*] does not apply to the definition of the main subject matter of the contract or to the appropriateness of the price to be paid.

Article 81   Mandatory nature

The parties may not exclude the application of this Chapter or derogate from or vary its effects.

Article 82   Duty of transparency in contract terms not individually negotiated

Where a trader supplies contract terms which have not been individually negotiated with the consumer within the meaning of Article 7, it has a duty to ensure that they are drafted and communicated in plain, intelligible language.

Article 83   Meaning of 'unfair' in contracts between a trader and a consumer

1. In a contract between a trader and a consumer, a contract term supplied by the trader which has not been individually negotiated within the meaning of Article 7 is unfair for the purposes of this Section [*Arts 82–85*] if it causes a significant imbalance in the parties' rights and obligations arising under the contract, to the detriment of the consumer, contrary to good faith and fair dealing.

2. When assessing the unfairness of a contract term for the purposes of this Section [*Arts 82–85*], regard is to be had to:

(a) whether the trader complied with the duty of transparency set out in Article 82;

(b) the nature of what is to be provided under the contract;

(c) the circumstances prevailing during the conclusion of the contract;

(d) to the other contract terms; and

(e) to the terms of any other contract on which the contract depends.

Article 84   Contract terms which are always unfair

A contract term is always unfair for the purposes of this Section [*Arts 82–85*] if its object or effect is to:

(a) exclude or limit the liability of the trader for death or personal injury caused to the consumer through an act or omission of the trader or of someone acting on behalf of the trader;

(b) exclude or limit the liability of the trader for any loss or damage to the consumer caused deliberately or as a result of gross negligence;

(c) limit the trader's obligation to be bound by commitments undertaken by its authorised agents or make its commitments subject to compliance with a particular condition the fulfilment of which depends exclusively on the trader;

(d) exclude or hinder the consumer's right to take legal action or exercise any other legal remedy, particularly by requiring the consumer to take disputes exclusively to an arbitration system not foreseen generally in legal provisions that apply to contracts between a trader and a consumer;

(e) confer exclusive jurisdiction for all disputes arising under the contract to a court for the place where the trader is domiciled unless the chosen court is also the court for the place where the consumer is domiciled;

(f) give the trader the exclusive right to determine whether the goods, digital content or related services supplied are in conformity with the contract or gives the trader the exclusive right to interpret any contract term;

(g) provide that the consumer is bound by the contract when the trader is not;

(h) require the consumer to use a more formal method for terminating the contract within the meaning of Article 8 than was used for conclusion of the contract;

(i) grant the trader a shorter notice period to terminate the contract than the one required of the consumer;

(j) oblige the consumer to pay for goods, digital content or related services not actually delivered, supplied or rendered;

(k) determine that non-individually negotiated contract terms within the meaning of Article 7 prevail or have preference over contract terms which have been individually negotiated.

Article 85   Contract terms which are presumed to be unfair

A contract term is presumed to be unfair for the purposes of this Section if its object or effect is to:

(a) restrict the evidence available to the consumer or impose on the consumer a burden of proof which should legally lie with the trader;

(b) inappropriately exclude or limit the remedies available to the consumer against the trader or a third party for non-performance by the trader of obligations under the contract;

(c) inappropriately exclude or limit the right to set-off claims that the consumer may have against the trader against what the consumer may owe to the trader;

(d) permit a trader to keep money paid by the consumer if the latter decides not to conclude the contract, or perform obligations under it, without providing for the consumer to receive compensation of an equivalent amount from the trader in the reverse situation;

(e) require a consumer who fails to perform obligations under the contract to pay a disproportionately high amount by way of damages or a stipulated payment for non-performance;

(f) entitle a trader to withdraw from or terminate the contract within the meaning of Article 8 on a discretionary basis without giving the same right to the consumer, or entitle a trader to keep money paid for related services not yet supplied in the case where the trader withdraws from or terminates the contract;

(g) enable a trader to terminate a contract of indeterminate duration without reasonable notice, except where there are serious grounds for doing so;

(h) automatically extend a contract of fixed duration unless the consumer indicates otherwise, in cases where contract terms provide for an unreasonably early deadline for giving notice;

(i) enable a trader to alter contract terms unilaterally without a valid reason which is specified in the contract; this does not affect contract terms under which a trader reserves the right to alter unilaterally the terms of a contract of indeterminate duration, provided that the trader is required to inform the consumer with reasonable notice, and that the consumer is free to terminate the contract at no cost to the consumer;

(j) enable a trader to alter unilaterally without a valid reason any characteristics of the goods, digital content or related services to be provided or any other features of performance;

(k) provide that the price of goods, digital content or related services is to be determined at the time of delivery or supply, or allow a trader to increase the price without giving the consumer the right to withdraw if the increased price is too high in relation to the price agreed at the conclusion of the contract; this does not affect price indexation clauses, where lawful, provided that the method by which prices vary is explicitly described;

(l) oblige a consumer to perform all their obligations under the contract where the trader fails to perform its own;

(m) allow a trader to transfer its rights and obligations under the contract without the consumer's consent, unless it is to a subsidiary controlled by the trader, or as a result of a merger or a similar lawful company transaction, and such transfer is not likely to negatively affect any right of the consumer;

(n) allow a trader, where what has been ordered is unavailable, to supply an equivalent without having expressly informed the consumer of this possibility and of the fact that the trader must bear the cost of returning what the consumer has received under the contract if the consumer exercises a right to reject performance;

(o) allow a trader to reserve an unreasonably long or inadequately specified period to accept or refuse an offer;

(p) allow a trader to reserve an unreasonably long or inadequately specified period to perform the obligations under the contract;

(q) inappropriately exclude or limit the remedies available to the consumer against the trader or the defences available to the consumer against claims by the trader;

(r) subject performance of obligations under the contract by the trader, or subject other beneficial effects of the contract for the consumer, to particular formalities that are not legally required and are unreasonable;

(s) require from the consumer excessive advance payments or excessive guarantees of performance of obligations;

(t) unjustifiably prevent the consumer from obtaining supplies or repairs from third party sources;

(u) unjustifiably bundle the contract with another one with the trader, a subsidiary of the trader, or a third party, in a way that cannot be expected by the consumer;

(v) impose an excessive burden on the consumer in order to terminate a contract of indeterminate duration;

(w) make the initial contract period, or any renewal period, of a contract for the protracted provision of goods, digital content or related services longer than one year, unless the consumer may terminate the contract at any time with a termination period of no more than 30 days.

Article 86 Meaning of 'unfair' in contracts between traders

1. In a contract between traders, a contract term is unfair for the purposes of this Section only if:

(a) it forms part of not individually negotiated terms within the meaning of Article 7; and

(b) it is of such a nature that its use grossly deviates from good commercial practice, contrary to good faith and fair dealing.

2. When assessing the unfairness of a contract term for the purposes of this Section, regard is to be had to:

(a) the nature of what is to be provided under the contract;

(b) the circumstances prevailing during the conclusion of the contract;

(c) the other contract terms; and

(d) the terms of any other contract on which the contract depends.

Article 87   Non-performance and fundamental non-performance

1. Non-performance of an obligation is any failure to perform that obligation, whether or not the failure is excused, and includes:

(a) non-delivery or delayed delivery of the goods;

(b) non-supply or delayed supply of the digital content;

(c) delivery of goods which are not in conformity with the contract;

(d) supply of digital content which is not in conformity with the contract;

(e) non-payment or late payment of the price; and

(f) any other purported performance which is not in conformity with the contract.

2. Non-performance of an obligation by one party is fundamental if:

(a) it substantially deprives the other party of what that party was entitled to expect under the contract, unless at the time of conclusion of the contract the non-performing party did not foresee and could not be expected to have foreseen that result; or

(b) it is of such a nature as to make it clear that the non-performing party's future performance cannot be relied on.

Article 88   Excused non-performance

1. A party's non-performance of an obligation is excused if it is due to an impediment beyond that party's control and if that party could not be expected to have taken the impediment into account at the time of the conclusion of the contract, or to have avoided or overcome the impediment or its consequences.

2. Where the impediment is only temporary the non-performance is excused for the period during which the impediment exists. However, if the delay amounts to a fundamental non-performance, the other party may treat it as such.

3. The party who is unable to perform has a duty to ensure that notice of the impediment and of its effect on the ability to perform reaches the other party without undue delay after the first party becomes, or could be expected to have become, aware of these circumstances. The other party is entitled to damages for any loss resulting from the breach of this duty.

Article 89   Change of circumstances

1. A party must perform its obligations even if performance has become more onerous, whether because the cost of performance has increased or because the value of what is to be received in return has diminished. Where performance becomes excessively onerous because of an exceptional change of circumstances, the parties have a duty to enter into negotiations with a view to adapting or terminating the contract.

2. If the parties fail to reach an agreement within a reasonable time, then, upon request by either party a court may:

(a) adapt the contract in order to bring it into accordance with what the parties would reasonably have agreed at the time of contracting if they had taken the change of circumstances into account; or

(b) terminate the contract within the meaning of Article 8 at a date and on terms to be determined by the court.

3. Paragraphs 1 and 2 apply only if:

(a) the change of circumstances occurred after the time when the contract was concluded;

(b) the party relying on the change of circumstances did not at that time take into account, and could not be expected to have taken into account, the possibility or scale of that change of circumstances; and

(c) the aggrieved party did not assume, and cannot reasonably be regarded as having assumed, the risk of that change of circumstances.

Article 106   Overview of buyer's remedies

1. In the case of non-performance of an obligation by the seller, the buyer may do any of the following:

(a) require performance, which includes specific performance, repair or replacement of the goods or digital content, under Section 3 of this Chapter [*Arts 110–112*];

(b) withhold the buyer's own performance under Section 4 of this Chapter [*Art 113*];

(c) terminate the contract under Section 5 of this Chapter [*Arts 114–119*] and claim the return of any price already paid, under Chapter 17 [*Arts 172–177*];

(d) reduce the price under Section 6 of this Chapter [*Art 120*]; and

(e) claim damages under Chapter 16 [*Arts 159–171*].

2. If the buyer is a trader:

(a) the buyer's rights to exercise any remedy except withholding of performance are subject to cure by the seller as set out in Section 2 of this Chapter [*Art 109*]; and

(b) the buyer's rights to rely on lack of conformity are subject to the requirements of examination and notification set out in Section 7 of this Chapter [*Art 121*].

3. If the buyer is a consumer:

(a) the buyer's rights are not subject to cure by the seller; and

(b) the requirements of examination and notification set out in Section 7 of this Chapter [*Art 121*] do not apply.

4. If the seller's non-performance is excused, the buyer may resort to any of the remedies referred to in paragraph 1 except requiring performance and damages.

5. The buyer may not resort to any of the remedies referred to in paragraph 1 to the extent that the buyer caused the seller's non-performance.

6. Remedies which are not incompatible may be cumulated.

Article 108   Mandatory nature

In a contract between a trader and a consumer, the parties may not, to the detriment of the consumer, exclude the application of this Chapter, or derogate from or vary its effect before the lack of conformity is brought to the trader's attention by the consumer.

Article 116   Termination for anticipated non-performance

A buyer may terminate the contract before performance is due if the seller has declared, or it is otherwise clear, that there will be a non-performance, and if the non-performance would be such as to justify termination.

Article 159   Right to damages

1. A creditor is entitled to damages for loss caused by the non-performance of an obligation by the debtor, unless the non-performance is excused.

2. The loss for which damages are recoverable includes future loss which the debtor could expect to occur.

Article 160   General measure of damages

The general measure of damages for loss caused by non-performance of an obligation is such sum as will put the creditor into the position in which the creditor would have been if the obligation had been duly performed, or, where that is not possible, as nearly as possible into that position. Such damages cover loss which the creditor has suffered and gain of which the creditor has been deprived.

Article 161   Foreseeability of loss
The debtor is liable only for loss which the debtor foresaw or could be expected to have foreseen at the time when the contract was concluded as a result of the non-performance.

Article 162   Loss attributable to creditor
The debtor is not liable for loss suffered by the creditor to the extent that the creditor contributed to the non-performance or its effects.

Article 163   Reduction of loss
1. The debtor is not liable for loss suffered by the creditor to the extent that the creditor could have reduced the loss by taking reasonable steps.

2. The creditor is entitled to recover any expenses reasonably incurred in attempting to reduce the loss.

Article 164   Substitute transaction
A creditor who has terminated a contract in whole or in part and has made a substitute transaction within a reasonable time and in a reasonable manner may, in so far as it is entitled to damages, recover the difference between the value of what would have been payable under the terminated contract and the value of what is payable under the substitute transaction, as well as damages for any further loss.

Article 165   Current price
Where the creditor has terminated the contract and has not made a substitute transaction but there is a current price for the performance, the creditor may, in so far as entitled to damages, recover the difference between the contract price and the price current at the time of termination as well as damages for any further loss.

Article 172   Restitution on avoidance or termination
1. Where a contract is avoided or terminated by either party, each party is obliged to return what that party ('the recipient') has received from the other party.

2. The obligation to return what was received includes any natural and legal fruits derived from what was received.

3. On the termination of a contract for performance in instalments or parts, the return of what was received is not required in relation to any instalment or part where the obligations on both sides have been fully performed, or where the price for what has been done remains payable under Article 8(2), unless the nature of the contract is such that part performance is of no value to one of the parties.

Article 173   Payment for monetary value
1. Where what was received, including fruits where relevant, cannot be returned, or, in a case of digital content whether or not it was supplied on a tangible medium, the recipient must pay its monetary value. Where the return is possible but would cause unreasonable effort or expense, the recipient may choose to pay the monetary value, provided that this would not harm the other party's proprietary interests.

2. The monetary value of goods is the value that they would have had at the date when payment of the monetary value is to be made if they had been kept by the recipient without destruction or damage until that date.

3. Where a related service contract is avoided or terminated by the customer after the related service has been performed or partly performed, the monetary value of what was received is the amount the customer saved by receiving the related service.

4. In a case of digital content the monetary value of what was received is the amount the consumer saved by making use of the digital content.

5. Where the recipient has obtained a substitute in money or in kind in exchange for goods or digital content when the recipient knew or could be expected to have known of the ground for avoidance or termination, the other party may choose to claim the substitute or the monetary value of the substitute. A recipient who has obtained a substitute in money or kind in exchange for goods

or digital content when the recipient did not know and could not be expected to have known of the ground for avoidance or termination may choose to return the monetary value of the substitute or the substitute.

6. In the case of digital content which is not supplied in exchange for the payment of a price, no restitution will be made.

Article 174   Payment for use and interest on money received

1. A recipient who has made use of goods must pay the other party the monetary value of that use for any period where:

(a) the recipient caused the ground for avoidance or termination;

(b) the recipient, prior to the start of that period, was aware of the ground for avoidance or termination; or

(c) having regard to the nature of the goods, the nature and amount of the use and the availability of remedies other than termination, it would be inequitable to allow the recipient the free use of the goods for that period.

2. A recipient who is obliged to return money must pay interest, at the rate stipulated in Article 166, where:

(a) the other party is obliged to pay for use; or

(b) the recipient gave cause for the contract to be avoided because of fraud, threats and unfair exploitation.

3. For the purposes of this Chapter [Arts 172–177], a recipient is not obliged to pay for use of goods received or interest on money received in any circumstances other than those set out in paragraphs 1 and 2.

Article 175   Compensation for expenditure

1. Where a recipient has incurred expenditure on goods or digital content, the recipient is entitled to compensation to the extent that the expenditure benefited the other party provided that the expenditure was made when the recipient did not know and could not be expected to know of the ground for avoidance or termination.

2. A recipient who knew or could be expected to know of the ground for avoidance or termination is entitled to compensation only for expenditure that was necessary to protect the goods or the digital content from being lost or diminished in value, provided that the recipient had no opportunity to ask the other party for advice.

Article 176   Equitable modification

Any obligation to return or to pay under this Chapter [Arts 172–177] may be modified to the extent that its performance would be grossly inequitable, taking into account in particular whether the party did not cause, or lacked knowledge of, the ground for avoidance or termination.

Article 177   Mandatory nature

In relations between a trader and a consumer the parties may not, to the detriment of the consumer, exclude the application of this Chapter [Arts 172–177] or derogate from or vary its effects.

Part V

Codes

DRAFT COMMON FRAME OF REFERENCE (DCFR)

Principles, Definitions and Model Rules of European Private Law[*]

BOOK I GENERAL PROVISIONS

I. – 1:101: Intended field of application

(1) These rules are intended to be used primarily in relation to contracts and other juridical acts, contractual and non-contractual rights and obligations and related property matters.

I. – 1:102: Interpretation and development

(1) These rules are to be interpreted and developed autonomously and in accordance with their objectives and the principles underlying them.

(2) They are to be read in the light of any applicable instruments guaranteeing human rights and fundamental freedoms and any applicable constitutional laws.

(3) In their interpretation and development regard should be had to the need to promote:

(a) uniformity of application;

(b) good faith and fair dealing; and

(c) legal certainty.

(4) Issues within the scope of the rules but not expressly settled by them are so far as possible to be settled in accordance with the principles underlying them.

(5) Where there is a general rule and a special rule applying to a particular situation within the scope of the general rule, the special rule prevails in any case of conflict.

I. – 1:103: Good faith and fair dealing

(1) The expression "good faith and fair dealing" refers to a standard of conduct characterised by honesty, openness and consideration for the interests of the other party to the transaction or relationship in question.

(2) It is, in particular, contrary to good faith and fair dealing for a party to act inconsistently with that party's prior statements or conduct when the other party has reasonably relied on them to that other party's detriment.

I. – 1:104: Reasonableness

Reasonableness is to be objectively ascertained, having regard to the nature and purpose of what is being done, to the circumstances of the case and to any relevant usages and practices.

I. – 1:105: "Consumer" and "business"

(1) A "consumer" means any natural person who is acting primarily for purposes which are not related to his or her trade, business or profession.

(2) A "business" means any natural or legal person, irrespective of whether publicly or privately owned, who is acting for purposes relating to the person's self-employed trade, work or profession, even if the person does not intend to make a profit in the course of the activity.

(3) A person who is within both of the preceding paragraphs is regarded as falling exclusively within paragraph (1) in relation to a rule which would provide protection for that person if that person were a consumer, and otherwise as falling exclusively within paragraph (2).

I. – 1:106: "In writing" and similar expressions

(1) For the purposes of these rules, a statement is "in writing" if it is in textual form and in characters which are directly legible from paper or another tangible durable medium.

I. – 1:107: "Signature" and similar expressions

(1) A reference to a person's signature includes a reference to that person's handwritten signature, electronic signature or advanced electronic signature, and references to anything being signed by a person are to be construed accordingly.

I. – 1:108: Definitions in Annex

(1) The definitions in the Annex apply for all the purposes of these rules unless the context otherwise requires.

(2) Where a word is defined, other grammatical forms of the word have a corresponding meaning.

I. – 1:109: Notice

(1) This Article applies in relation to the giving of notice for any purpose under these rules. "Notice" includes the communication of information or of a juridical act.

(2) The notice may be given by any means appropriate to the circumstances.

(3) The notice becomes effective when it reaches the addressee, unless it provides for a delayed effect.

(4) The notice reaches the addressee:
    (a) when it is delivered to the addressee;
    (b) when it is delivered to the addressee's place of business or, where there is no such place of business or the notice does not relate to a business matter, to the addressee's habitual residence;
    (c) in the case of a notice transmitted by electronic means, when it can be accessed by the addressee; or
    (d) when it is otherwise made available to the addressee at such a place and in such a way that the addressee could reasonably be expected to obtain access to it without undue delay.

(5) The notice has no effect if a revocation of it reaches the addressee before or at the same time as the notice.

(6) Any reference in these rules to a notice given by or to a person includes a notice given by or to an agent of that person who has authority to give or receive it.

(7) In relations between a business and a consumer the parties may not, to the detriment of the consumer, exclude the rule in paragraph (4)(c) or derogate from or vary its effects.

I. – 1:110: Computation of time

. . .

BOOK II CONTRACTS AND OTHER JURIDICAL ACTS

Chapter 1: General provisions

II. – 1:101: Meaning of "contract" and "juridical act"

(1) A contract is an agreement which is intended to give rise to a binding legal relationship or to have some other legal effect. It is a bilateral or multilateral juridical act.

(2) A juridical act is any statement or agreement, whether express or implied from conduct, which is intended to have legal effect as such. It may be unilateral, bilateral or multilateral.

II. – 1:102:   Party autonomy

(1) Parties are free to make a contract or other juridical act and to determine its contents, subject to any applicable mandatory rules.

(2) Parties may exclude the application of any of the following rules relating to contracts or other juridical acts, or the rights and obligations arising from them, or derogate from or vary their effects, except as otherwise provided.

(3) A provision to the effect that parties may not exclude the application of a rule or derogate from or vary its effects does not prevent a party from waiving a right which has already arisen and of which that party is aware.

II. – 1:103:   Binding effect

(1) A valid contract is binding on the parties.

(2) A valid unilateral undertaking is binding on the person giving it if it is intended to be legally binding without acceptance.

(3) This Article does not prevent modification or termination of any resulting right or obligation by agreement between the debtor and creditor or as provided by law.

II. – 1:104:   Usages and practices

(1) The parties to a contract are bound by any usage to which they have agreed and by any practice they have established between themselves.

(2) The parties are bound by a usage which would be considered generally applicable by persons in the same situation as the parties, except where the application of such usage would be unreasonable.

(3) This Article applies to other juridical acts with any necessary adaptations.

II. – 1:105:   Imputed knowledge etc.

If a person who with a party's assent was involved in making a contract or other juridical act or in exercising a right or performing an obligation under it:

    (a) knew or foresaw a fact, or is treated as having knowledge or foresight of a fact; or

    (b) acted intentionally or with any other relevant state of mind this knowledge, foresight or state of mind is imputed to the party.

II. – 1:106:   Form

(1) A contract or other juridical act need not be concluded, made or evidenced in writing nor is it subject to any other requirement as to form.

(2) Where a contract or other juridical act is invalid only by reason of noncompliance with a particular requirement as to form, one party (the first party) is liable for any loss suffered by the other (the second party) by acting in the mistaken, but reasonable, belief that it was valid if the first party:

    (a) knew it was invalid;

    (b) knew or could reasonably be expected to know that the second party was acting to that party's potential prejudice in the mistaken belief that it was valid; and

    (c) contrary to good faith and fair dealing, allowed the second party to continue so acting.

II. – 1:107:   Mixed contracts

(1) For the purposes of this Article a mixed contract is a contract which contains:

    (a) parts falling within two or more of the categories of contracts regulated specifically in these rules; or

    (b) a part falling within one such category and another part falling within the category of contracts governed only by the rules applicable to contracts generally.

(2) Where a contract is a mixed contract then, unless this is contrary to the nature and purpose of the contract, the rules applicable to each relevant category apply, with any appropriate adaptations, to the corresponding part of the contract and the rights and obligations arising from it.

(3) Paragraph (2) does not apply where:
   (a) a rule provides that a mixed contract is to be regarded as falling primarily within one category; or
   (b) in a case not covered by the preceding sub-paragraph, one part of a mixed contract is in fact so predominant that it would be unreasonable not to regard the contract as falling primarily within one category.

(4) In cases covered by paragraph (3) the rules applicable to the category into which the contract primarily falls (the primary category) apply to the contract and the rights and obligations arising from it. However, rules applicable to any elements of the contract falling within another category apply with any appropriate adaptations so far as is necessary to regulate those elements and provided that they do not conflict with the rules applicable to the primary category.

(5) Nothing in this Article prevents the application of any mandatory rules.

II. – 1:108: Partial invalidity or ineffectiveness

Where only part of a contract or other juridical act is invalid or ineffective, the remaining part continues in effect if it can reasonably be maintained without the invalid or ineffective part.

II. – 1:109: Standard terms

A "standard term" is a term which has been formulated in advance for several transactions involving different parties and which has not been individually negotiated by the parties.

II. – 1:110: Terms "not individually negotiated"

(1) A term supplied by one party is not individually negotiated if the other party has not been able to influence its content, in particular because it has been drafted in advance, whether or not as part of standard terms.

(2) If one party supplies a selection of terms to the other party, a term will not be regarded as individually negotiated merely because the other party chooses that term from that selection.

(3) If it is disputed whether a term supplied by one party as part of standard terms has since been individually negotiated, that party bears the burden of proving that it has been.

(4) In a contract between a business and a consumer, the business bears the burden of proving that a term supplied by the business has been individually negotiated.

(5) In contracts between a business and a consumer, terms drafted by a third person are considered to have been supplied by the business, unless the consumer introduced them to the contract.

Chapter 2: Non-discrimination

II. – 2:101: Right not to be discriminated against

A person has a right not to be discriminated against on the grounds of sex or ethnic or racial origin in relation to a contract or other juridical act the object of which is to provide access to, or supply, goods, other assets or services which are available to the public.

II. – 2:102: Meaning of discrimination

(1) "Discrimination" means any conduct whereby, or situation where, on grounds such as those mentioned in the preceding Article:
   (a) one person is treated less favourably than another person is, has been or would be treated in a comparable situation; or
   (b) an apparently neutral provision, criterion or practice would place one group of persons at a particular disadvantage when compared to a different group of persons.

(2) Discrimination also includes harassment on grounds such as those mentioned in the preceding Article. "Harassment" means unwanted conduct (including conduct of a sexual nature) which violates a person's dignity, particularly when such conduct creates an intimidating, hostile, degrading, humiliating or offensive environment, or which aims to do so.

(3) Any instruction to discriminate also amounts to discrimination.

II. – 2:103: Exception

Unequal treatment which is justified by a legitimate aim does not amount to discrimination if the means used to achieve that aim are appropriate and necessary.

II. – 2:104: Remedies

(1) If a person is discriminated against contrary to II. – 2:101 (Right not to be discriminated against) then, without prejudice to any remedy which may be available under Book VI (Non-contractual liability for damage caused to another), the remedies for non-performance of an obligation under Book III, Chapter 3 (including damages for economic and non-economic loss) are available.

(2) Any remedy granted should be proportionate to the injury or anticipated injury; the dissuasive effect of remedies may be taken into account.

II. – 2:105: Burden of proof

(1) If a person who considers himself or herself discriminated against on one of the grounds mentioned in II. – 2:101 (Right not to be discriminated against) establishes, before a court or another competent authority, facts from which it may be presumed that there has been such discrimination, it falls on the other party to prove that there has been no such discrimination.

(2) Paragraph (1) does not apply to proceedings in which it is for the court or another competent authority to investigate the facts of the case.

Chapter 3: Marketing and pre-contractual duties

Section 1: Information duties

II. – 3:101: Duty to disclose information about goods, other assets and services

(1) Before the conclusion of a contract for the supply of goods, other assets or services by a business to another person, the business has a duty to disclose to the other person such information concerning the goods, other assets or services to be supplied as the other person can reasonably expect, taking into account the standards of quality and performance which would be normal under the circumstances.

(2) In assessing what information the other person can reasonably expect to be disclosed, the test to be applied, if the other person is also a business, is whether the failure to provide the information would deviate from good commercial practice.

II. – 3:102: Specific duties for businesses marketing to consumers

(1) Where a business is marketing goods, other assets or services to a consumer, the business has a duty not to give misleading information. Information is misleading if it misrepresents or omits material facts which the average consumer could expect to be given for an informed decision on whether to take steps towards the conclusion of a contract. In assessing what an average consumer could expect to be given, account is to be taken of all the circumstances and of the limitations of the communication medium employed.

(2) Where a business uses a commercial communication which gives the impression to consumers that it contains all the relevant information necessary to make a decision about concluding a contract, the business has a duty to ensure that the communication in fact contains all the relevant information. Where it is not already apparent from the context of the commercial communication, the information to be provided comprises:

(a) the main characteristics of the goods, other assets or services, the identity and address, if relevant, of the business, the price, and any available right of withdrawal;

(b) peculiarities related to payment, delivery, performance and complaint handling, if they depart from the requirements of professional diligence; and

(c) the language to be used for communications between the parties after the conclusion of the contract, if this differs from the language of the commercial communication.

(3) A duty to provide information under this Article is not fulfilled unless all the information to be provided is provided in the same language.

II. – 3:103:   Duty to provide information when concluding contract with a consumer who is at a particular disadvantage

(1) In the case of transactions that place the consumer at a significant informational disadvantage because of the technical medium used for contracting, the physical distance between business and consumer, or the nature of the transaction, the business has a duty, as appropriate in the circumstances, to provide clear information about the main characteristics of any goods, other assets or services to be supplied, the price, the address and identity of the business with which the consumer is transacting, the terms of the contract, the rights and obligations of both contracting parties, and any available right of withdrawal or redress procedures. This information must be provided a reasonable time before the conclusion of the contract. The information on the right of withdrawal must, as appropriate in the circumstances, also be adequate in the sense of II. – 5:104 (Adequate information on the right to withdraw).

(2) Where more specific information duties are provided for specific situations, these take precedence over the general information duty under paragraph (1).

(3) The business bears the burden of proof that it has provided the information required by this Article.

II. – 3:104:   Information duties in real time distance communication

(1) When initiating real time distance communication with a consumer, a business has a duty to provide at the outset explicit information on its name and the commercial purpose of the contact.

(2) Real time distance communication means direct and immediate distance communication of such a type that one party can interrupt the other in the course of the communication. It includes telephone and electronic means such as voice over internet protocol and internet related chat, but does not include communication by electronic mail.

(3) The business bears the burden of proof that the consumer has received the information required under paragraph (1).

(4) If a business has failed to comply with the duty under paragraph (1) and a contract has been concluded as a result of the communication, the other party has a right to withdraw from the contract by giving notice to the business within the period specified in II. – 5:103 (Withdrawal period).

(5) A business is liable to the consumer for any loss caused by a breach of the duty under paragraph (1).

II. – 3:105:   Formation by electronic means

(1) If a contract is to be concluded by electronic means and without individual communication, a business has a duty to provide information about the following matters before the other party makes or accepts an offer:
(a) the technical steps to be taken in order to conclude the contract;
(b) whether or not a contract document will be filed by the business and whether it will be accessible;
(c) the technical means for identifying and correcting input errors before the other party makes or accepts an offer;
(d) the languages offered for the conclusion of the contract;
(e) any contract terms used.

(2) The business has a duty to ensure that the contract terms referred to in paragraph (1)(e) are available in textual form.

(3) If a business has failed to comply with the duty under paragraph (1) and a contract has been concluded in the circumstances there stated, the other party has a right to withdraw from the contract by giving notice to the business within the period specified in II. – 5:103 (Withdrawal period).

(4) A business is liable to the consumer for any loss caused by a breach of the duty under paragraph (1).

II. – 3:106:   Clarity and form of information

(1) A duty to provide information imposed on a business under this Chapter is not fulfilled unless the requirements of this Article are satisfied.

(2) The information must be clear and precise, and expressed in plain and intelligible language.

(3) Where rules for specific contracts require information to be provided on a durable medium or in another particular form it must be provided in that way.

(4) In the case of contracts between a business and a consumer concluded at a distance, information about the main characteristics of any goods, other assets or services to be supplied, the price, the address and identity of the business with which the consumer is transacting, the terms of the contract, the rights and obligations of both contracting parties, and any available redress procedures, as may be appropriate in the particular case, must be confirmed in textual form on a durable medium at the time of conclusion of the contract. The information on the right of withdrawal must also be adequate in the sense of II. – 5:104 (Adequate information on the right to withdraw).

II. – 3:107:   Information about price and additional charges
...

II. – 3:108:   Information about address and identity of business
...

II. – 3:109:   Remedies for breach of information duties

(1) If a business has a duty under II. – 3:103 (Duty to provide information when concluding contract with a consumer who is at a particular disadvantage) to provide information to a consumer before the conclusion of a contract from which the consumer has the right to withdraw, the withdrawal period does not commence until all this information has been provided. Regardless of this, the right of withdrawal lapses after one year from the time of the conclusion of the contract.

(2) If a business has failed to comply with any duty imposed by the preceding Articles of this Section and a contract has been concluded, the business has such obligations under the contract as the other party has reasonably expected as a consequence of the absence or incorrectness of the information. Remedies provided under Book III, Chapter 3 apply to non-performance of these obligations.

(3) Whether or not a contract is concluded, a business which has failed to comply with any duty imposed by the preceding Articles of this Section is liable for any loss caused to the other party to the transaction by such failure. This paragraph does not apply to the extent that a remedy is available for non-performance of a contractual obligation under the preceding paragraph.

(4) The remedies provided under this Article are without prejudice to any remedy which may be available under II. – 7:201 (Mistake).

(5) In relations between a business and a consumer the parties may not, to the detriment of the consumer, exclude the application of this Article or derogate from or vary its effects.

Section 2: Duty to prevent input errors and acknowledge receipt

II. – 3:201:   Correction of input errors

(1) A business which intends to conclude a contract by making available electronic means without individual communication for concluding it has a duty to make available to the other party appropriate, effective and accessible technical means for identifying and correcting input errors before the other party makes or accepts an offer.

(2) Where a person concludes a contract in error because of a failure by a business to comply with the duty under paragraph (1) the business is liable for any loss caused to that person by such failure. This is without prejudice to any remedy which may be available under II.–7:201 (Mistake).

(3) In relations between a business and a consumer the parties may not, to the detriment of the consumer, exclude the application of this Article or derogate from or vary its effects.

II. – 3:202:   Acknowledgement of receipt

(1) A business which offers the facility to conclude a contract by electronic means and without individual communication has a duty to acknowledge by electronic means the receipt of an offer or an acceptance by the other party.

(2) If the other party does not receive the acknowledgement without undue delay, that other party may revoke the offer or withdraw from the contract.

(3) The business is liable for any loss caused to the other party by a breach of the duty under paragraph (1).

(4) In relations between a business and a consumer the parties may not, to the detriment of the consumer, exclude the application of this Article or derogate from or vary its effects.

Section 3: Negotiation and confidentiality duties

II. – 3:301:   Negotiations contrary to good faith and fair dealing

(1) A person is free to negotiate and is not liable for failure to reach an agreement.

(2) A person who is engaged in negotiations has a duty to negotiate in accordance with good faith and fair dealing and not to break off negotiations contrary to good faith and fair dealing. This duty may not be excluded or limited by contract.

(3) A person who is in breach of the duty is liable for any loss caused to the other party by the breach.

(4) It is contrary to good faith and fair dealing, in particular, for a person to enter into or continue negotiations with no real intention of reaching an agreement with the other party.

II. – 3:302:   Breach of confidentiality

(1) If confidential information is given by one party in the course of negotiations, the other party is under a duty not to disclose that information or use it for that party's own purposes whether or not a contract is subsequently concluded.

(2) In this Article, "confidential information" means information which, either from its nature or the circumstances in which it was obtained, the party receiving the information knows or could reasonably be expected to know is confidential to the other party.

(3) A party who reasonably anticipates a breach of the duty may obtain a court order prohibiting it.

(4) A party who is in breach of the duty is liable for any loss caused to the other party by the breach and may be ordered to pay over to the other party any benefit obtained by the breach.

Section 4: Unsolicited goods or services

II. – 3:401:   No obligation arising from failure to respond

(1) If a business delivers unsolicited goods to, or performs unsolicited services for, a consumer:
   (a) no contract arises from the consumer's failure to respond or from any other action or inaction by the consumer in relation to the goods and services; and
   (b) no non-contractual obligation arises from the consumer's acquisition, retention, rejection or use of the goods or receipt of benefit from the services.

(2) Sub-paragraph (b) of the preceding paragraph does not apply if the goods or services were supplied:
   (a) by way of benevolent intervention in another's affairs; or
   (b) in error or in such other circumstances that there is a right to reversal of an unjustified enrichment.

(3) This Article is subject to the rules on delivery of excess quantity under a contract for the sale of goods.

(4) For the purposes of paragraph (1) delivery occurs when the consumer obtains physical control over the goods.

Section 5: Damages for breach of duty under this Chapter

II. – 3:501:   Liability for damages

(1) Where any rule in this Chapter makes a person liable for loss caused to another person by a breach of a duty, the other person has a right to damages for that loss.

(2) The rules on III.–3:704 (Loss attributable to creditor) and III.–3:705 (Reduction of loss) apply with the adaptation that the reference to non-performance of the obligation is to be taken as a reference to breach of the duty.

Chapter 4: Formation

Section 1: General provisions

II. – 4:101:   Requirements for the conclusion of a contract

A contract is concluded, without any further requirement, if the parties:

    (a) intend to enter into a binding legal relationship or bring about some other legal effect; and

    (b) reach a sufficient agreement.

II. – 4:102:   How intention is determined

The intention of a party to enter into a binding legal relationship or bring about some other legal effect is to be determined from the party's statements or conduct as they were reasonably understood by the other party.

II. – 4:103:   Sufficient agreement

(1) Agreement is sufficient if:

    (a) the terms of the contract have been sufficiently defined by the parties for the contract to be given effect; or

    (b) the terms of the contract, or the rights and obligations of the parties under it, can be otherwise sufficiently determined for the contract to be given effect.

(2) If one of the parties refuses to conclude a contract unless the parties have agreed on some specific matter, there is no contract unless agreement on that matter has been reached.

II. – 4:104:   Merger clause

(1) If a contract document contains an individually negotiated term stating that the document embodies all the terms of the contract (a merger clause), any prior statements, undertakings or agreements which are not embodied in the document do not form part of the contract.

(2) If the merger clause is not individually negotiated it establishes only a presumption that the parties intended that their prior statements, undertakings or agreements were not to form part of the contract. This rule may not be excluded or restricted.

(3) The parties' prior statements may be used to interpret the contract. This rule may not be excluded or restricted except by an individually negotiated term.

(4) A party may by statements or conduct be precluded from asserting a merger clause to the extent that the other party has reasonably relied on such statements or conduct.

II. – 4:105:   Modification in certain form only

(1) A term in a contract requiring any agreement to modify its terms, or to terminate the relationship resulting from it, to be in a certain form establishes only a presumption that any such agreement is not intended to be legally binding unless it is in that form.

(2) A party may by statements or conduct be precluded from asserting such a term to the extent that the other party has reasonably relied on such statements or conduct.

Section 2: Offer and acceptance

II. – 4:201:   Offer

(1) A proposal amounts to an offer if:

    (a) it is intended to result in a contract if the other party accepts it; and

    (b) it contains sufficiently definite terms to form a contract.

(2) An offer may be made to one or more specific persons or to the public.

(3) A proposal to supply goods from stock, or a service, at a stated price made by a business in a public advertisement or a catalogue, or by a display of goods, is treated, unless the circumstances

indicate otherwise, as an offer to supply at that price until the stock of goods, or the business's capacity to supply the service, is exhausted.

II. – 4:202:   Revocation of offer

(1) An offer may be revoked if the revocation reaches the offeree before the offeree has dispatched an acceptance or, in cases of acceptance by conduct, before the contract has been concluded.

(2) An offer made to the public can be revoked by the same means as were used to make the offer.

(3) However, a revocation of an offer is ineffective if:
  (a) the offer indicates that it is irrevocable;
  (b) the offer states a fixed time for its acceptance; or
  (c) it was reasonable for the offeree to rely on the offer as being irrevocable and the offeree has acted in reliance on the offer.

(4) Paragraph (3) does not apply to an offer if the offeror would have a right under any rule in Books II to IV to withdraw from a contract resulting from its acceptance. The parties may not, to the detriment of the offeror, exclude the application of this rule or derogate from or vary its effects.

II. – 4:203:   Rejection of offer

When a rejection of an offer reaches the offeror, the offer lapses.

II. – 4:204:   Acceptance

(1) Any form of statement or conduct by the offeree is an acceptance if it indicates assent to the offer.

(2) Silence or inactivity does not in itself amount to acceptance.

II. – 4:205:   Time of conclusion of the contract

(1) If an acceptance has been dispatched by the offeree the contract is concluded when the acceptance reaches the offeror.

(2) In the case of acceptance by conduct, the contract is concluded when notice of the conduct reaches the offeror.

(3) If by virtue of the offer, of practices which the parties have established between themselves, or of a usage, the offeree may accept the offer by doing an act without notice to the offeror, the contract is concluded when the offeree begins to do the act.

II. – 4:206:   Time limit for acceptance

(1) An acceptance of an offer is effective only if it reaches the offeror within the time fixed by the offeror.

(2) If no time has been fixed by the offeror the acceptance is effective only if it reaches the offeror within a reasonable time.

(3) Where an offer may be accepted by performing an act without notice to the offeror, the acceptance is effective only if the act is performed within the time for acceptance fixed by the offeror or, if no such time is fixed, within a reasonable time.

II. – 4:207:   Late acceptance

(1) A late acceptance is nonetheless effective as an acceptance if without undue delay the offeror informs the offeree that it is treated as an effective acceptance.

(2) If a letter or other communication containing a late acceptance shows that it has been dispatched in such circumstances that if its transmission had been normal it would have reached the offeror in due time, the late acceptance is effective as an acceptance unless, without undue delay, the offeror informs the offeree that the offer is considered to have lapsed.

II. – 4:208:   Modified acceptance

(1) A reply by the offeree which states or implies additional or different terms which materially alter the terms of the offer is a rejection and a new offer.

(2) A reply which gives a definite assent to an offer operates as an acceptance even if it states or implies additional or different terms, provided these do not materially alter the terms of the offer. The additional or different terms then become part of the contract.

(3) However, such a reply is treated as a rejection of the offer if:

    (a) the offer expressly limits acceptance to the terms of the offer;

    (b) the offeror objects to the additional or different terms without undue delay; or

    (c) the offeree makes the acceptance conditional upon the offeror's assent to the additional or different terms, and the assent does not reach the offeree within a reasonable time.

II. – 4:209:   Conflicting standard terms

(1) If the parties have reached agreement except that the offer and acceptance refer to conflicting standard terms, a contract is nonetheless formed. The standard terms form part of the contract to the extent that they are common in substance.

(2) However, no contract is formed if one party:

    (a) has indicated in advance, explicitly, and not by way of standard terms, an intention not to be bound by a contract on the basis of paragraph (1); or

    (b) without undue delay, informs the other party of such an intention.

II. – 4:210:   Formal confirmation of contract between businesses

If businesses have concluded a contract but have not embodied it in a final document, and one without undue delay sends the other a notice in textual form on a durable medium which purports to be a confirmation of the contract but which contains additional or different terms, such terms become part of the contract unless:

    (a) the terms materially alter the terms of the contract; or

    (b) the addressee objects to them without undue delay.

II. – 4:211:   Contracts not concluded through offer and acceptance

The rules in this Section apply with appropriate adaptations even though the process of conclusion of a contract cannot be analysed into offer and acceptance.

Section 3: Other juridical acts

II. – 4:301:   Requirements for a unilateral juridical act

The requirements for a unilateral juridical act are:

    (a) that the party doing the act intends to be legally bound or to achieve the relevant legal effect;

    (b) that the act is sufficiently certain; and

    (c) that notice of the act reaches the person to whom it is addressed or, if the act is addressed to the public, the act is made public by advertisement, public notice or otherwise.

II. – 4:302:   How intention is determined

The intention of a party to be legally bound or to achieve the relevant legal effect is to be determined from the party's statements or conduct as they were reasonably understood by the person to whom the act is addressed.

II. – 4:303:   Right or benefit may be rejected

Where a unilateral juridical act confers a right or benefit on the person to whom it is addressed, that person may reject it by notice to the maker of the act, provided that is done without undue delay and before the right or benefit has been expressly or impliedly accepted. On such rejection, the right or benefit is treated as never having accrued.

Chapter 5: Right of withdrawal

Section 1: Exercise and effect

II. – 5:101:   Scope and mandatory nature

(1) The provisions in this Section apply where under any rule in Books II to IV a party has a right to withdraw from a contract within a certain period.

(2) The parties may not, to the detriment of the entitled party, exclude the application of the rules in this Chapter or derogate from or vary their effects.

II. – 5:102:   Exercise of right to withdraw

(1) A right to withdraw is exercised by notice to the other party. No reasons need to be given.

(2) Returning the subject matter of the contract is considered a notice of withdrawal unless the circumstances indicate otherwise.

II. – 5:103:   Withdrawal period

(1) A right to withdraw may be exercised at any time after the conclusion of the contract and before the end of the withdrawal period.

(2) The withdrawal period ends fourteen days after the latest of the following times;
  (a) the time of conclusion of the contract;
  (b) the time when the entitled party receives from the other party adequate information on the right to withdraw; or
  (c) if the subject matter of the contract is the delivery of goods, the time when the goods are received.

(3) The withdrawal period ends no later than one year after the time of conclusion of the contract.

(4) A notice of withdrawal is timely if dispatched before the end of the withdrawal period.

II. – 5:104:   Adequate information on the right to withdraw

Adequate information on the right to withdraw requires that the right is appropriately brought to the entitled party's attention, and that the information provides, in textual form on a durable medium and in clear and comprehensible language, information about how the right may be exercised, the withdrawal period, and the name and address of the person to whom the withdrawal is to be communicated.

II. – 5:105:   Effects of withdrawal

(1) Withdrawal terminates the contractual relationship and the obligations of both parties under the contract.

(2) The restitutionary effects of such termination are governed by the rules in Book III, Chapter 3, Section 5, Sub-section 4 (Restitution) as modified by this Article, unless the contract provides otherwise in favour of the withdrawing party.

(3) Where the withdrawing party has made a payment under the contract, the business has an obligation to return the payment without undue delay, and in any case not later than thirty days after the withdrawal becomes effective.

(4) The withdrawing party is not liable to pay:
  (a) for any diminution in the value of anything received under the contract caused by inspection and testing;
  (b) for any destruction or loss of, or damage to, anything received under the contract, provided the withdrawing party used reasonable care to prevent such destruction, loss or damage.

(5) The withdrawing party is liable for any diminution in value caused by normal use, unless that party had not received adequate notice of the right of withdrawal.

(6) Except as provided in this Article, the withdrawing party does not incur any liability through the exercise of the right of withdrawal.

(7) If a consumer exercises a right to withdraw from a contract after a business has made use of a contractual right to supply something of equivalent quality and price in case what was ordered is unavailable, the business must bear the cost of returning what the consumer has received under the contract.

II. – 5:106:   Linked contracts

(1) If a consumer exercises a right of withdrawal from a contract for the supply of goods, other assets or services by a business, the effects of withdrawal extend to any linked contract.

(2) Where a contract is partially or exclusively financed by a credit contract, they form linked contracts, in particular:

(a) if the business supplying goods, other assets or services finances the consumer's performance;

(b) if a third party which finances the consumer's performance uses the services of the business for preparing or concluding the credit contract;

(c) if the credit contract refers to specific goods, assets or services to be financed with this credit, and if this link between both contracts was suggested by the supplier of the goods, other assets or services, or by the supplier of credit; or

(d) if there is a similar economic link.

(3) The provisions of II.–5:105 (Effects of withdrawal) apply accordingly to the linked contract.

(4) Paragraph (1) does not apply to credit contracts financing the contracts mentioned in paragraph (2)(f) of the following Article.

Section 2: Particular rights of withdrawal

II. – 5:201:   Contracts negotiated away from business premises

(1) A consumer is entitled to withdraw from a contract under which a business supplies goods, other assets or services, including financial services, to the consumer, or is granted a personal security by the consumer, if the consumer's offer or acceptance was expressed away from the business premises.

(2) Paragraph (1) does not apply to:

(a) a contract concluded by means of an automatic vending machine or automated commercial premises;

(b) a contract concluded with telecommunications operators through the use of public payphones;

(c) a contract for the construction and sale of immovable property or relating to other immovable property rights, except for rental;

(d) a contract for the supply of foodstuffs, beverages or other goods intended for everyday consumption supplied to the home, residence or workplace of the consumer by regular roundsmen;

(e) a contract concluded by means of distance communication, but outside of an organised distance sales or service-provision scheme run by the supplier;

(f) a contract for the supply of goods, other assets or services whose price depends on fluctuations in the financial market outside the supplier's control, which may occur during the withdrawal period;

(g) a contract concluded at an auction;

(h) travel and baggage insurance policies or similar short-term insurance policies of less than one month's duration.

(3) If the business has exclusively used means of distance communication for concluding the contract, paragraph (1) also does not apply if the contract is for:

(a) the supply of accommodation, transport, catering or leisure services, where the business undertakes, when the contract is concluded, to supply these services on a specific date or within a specific period;

(b) the supply of services other than financial services if performance has begun, at the consumer's express and informed request, before the end of the withdrawal period referred to in II.–5:103 (Withdrawal period) paragraph (1);

(c) the supply of goods made to the consumer's specifications or clearly personalised or which, by reason of their nature, cannot be returned or are liable to deteriorate or expire rapidly;

(d) the supply of audio or video recordings or computer software

(i)   which were unsealed by the consumer, or

(ii) which can be downloaded or reproduced for permanent use, in case of supply by electronic means;

(e) the supply of newspapers, periodicals and magazines;

(f) gaming and lottery services.

(4) With regard to financial services, paragraph (1) also does not apply to contracts that have been fully performed by both parties, at the consumer's express request, before the consumer exercises his or her right of withdrawal.

II. – 5:202: Timeshare contracts

...

Chapter 6: Representation

...

Chapter 7: Grounds of invalidity

Section 1: General provisions

II. – 7:101: Scope

(1) This Chapter deals with the effects of:

(a) mistake, fraud, threats, or unfair exploitation; and

(b) infringement of fundamental principles or mandatory rules.

(2) It does not deal with lack of capacity.

(3) It applies in relation to contracts and, with any necessary adaptations, other juridical acts.

II. – 7:102: Initial impossibility or lack of right or authority to dispose

A contract is not invalid, in whole or in part, merely because at the time it is concluded performance of any obligation assumed is impossible, or because a party has no right or authority to dispose of any assets to which the contract relates.

Section 2: Vitiated consent or intention

II. – 7:201: Mistake

(1) A party may avoid a contract for mistake of fact or law existing when the contract was concluded if:

(a) the party, but for the mistake, would not have concluded the contract or would have done so only on fundamentally different terms and the other party knew or could reasonably be expected to have known this; and

(b) the other party;

(i) caused the mistake;

(ii) caused the contract to be concluded in mistake by leaving the mistaken party in error, contrary to good faith and fair dealing, when the other party knew or could reasonably be expected to have known of the mistake;

(iii) caused the contract to be concluded in mistake by failing to comply with a pre-contractual information duty or a duty to make available a means of correcting input errors; or

(iv) made the same mistake.

(2) However a party may not avoid the contract for mistake if:

(a) the mistake was inexcusable in the circumstances; or

(b) the risk of the mistake was assumed, or in the circumstances should be borne, by that party.

II. – 7:202: Inaccuracy in communication may be treated as mistake

An inaccuracy in the expression or transmission of a statement is treated as a mistake of the person who made or sent the statement.

II. – 7:203:   Adaptation of contract in case of mistake

(1) If a party is entitled to avoid the contract for mistake but the other party performs, or indicates a willingness to perform, the obligations under the contract as it was understood by the party entitled to avoid it, the contract is treated as having been concluded as that party understood it. This applies only if the other party performs, or indicates a willingness to perform, without undue delay after being informed of the manner in which the party entitled to avoid it understood the contract and before that party acts in reliance on any notice of avoidance.

(2) After such performance or indication the right to avoid is lost and any earlier notice of avoidance is ineffective.

(3) Where both parties have made the same mistake, the court may at the request of either party bring the contract into accordance with what might reasonably have been agreed had the mistake not occurred.

II. – 7:204:   Liability for loss caused by reliance on incorrect information

(1) A party who has concluded a contract in reasonable reliance on incorrect information given by the other party in the course of negotiations has a right to damages for loss suffered as a result if the provider of the information:

    (a) believed the information to be incorrect or had no reasonable grounds for believing it to be correct; and

    (b) knew or could reasonably be expected to have known that the recipient would rely on the information in deciding whether or not to conclude the contract on the agreed terms.

(2) This Article applies even if there is no right to avoid the contract.

II. – 7:205:   Fraud

(1) A party may avoid a contract when the other party has induced the conclusion of the contract by fraudulent misrepresentation, whether by words or conduct, or fraudulent non-disclosure of any information which good faith and fair dealing, or any pre-contractual information duty, required that party to disclose.

(2) A misrepresentation is fraudulent if it is made with knowledge or belief that the representation is false and is intended to induce the recipient to make a mistake. A non-disclosure is fraudulent if it is intended to induce the person from whom the information is withheld to make a mistake.

(3) In determining whether good faith and fair dealing required a party to disclose particular information, regard should be had to all the circumstances, including:

    (a) whether the party had special expertise;

    (b) the cost to the party of acquiring the relevant information;

    (c) whether the other party could reasonably acquire the information by other means; and

    (d) the apparent importance of the information to the other party.

II. – 7:206:   Coercion or threats

(1) A party may avoid a contract when the other party has induced the conclusion of the contract by coercion or by the threat of an imminent and serious harm which it is wrongful to inflict, or wrongful to use as a means to obtain the conclusion of the contract.

(2) A threat is not regarded as inducing the contract if in the circumstances the threatened party had a reasonable alternative.

II. – 7:207:   Unfair exploitation

(1) A party may avoid a contract if, at the time of the conclusion of the contract:

    (a) the party was dependent on or had a relationship of trust with the other party, was in economic distress or had urgent needs, was improvident, ignorant, inexperienced or lacking in bargaining skill; and

    (b) the other party knew or could reasonably be expected to have known this and, given the circumstances and purpose of the contract, exploited the first party's situation by taking an excessive benefit or grossly unfair advantage.

(2) Upon the request of the party entitled to avoidance, a court may if it is appropriate adapt the contract in order to bring it into accordance with what might have been agreed had the requirements of good faith and fair dealing been observed.

(3) A court may similarly adapt the contract upon the request of a party receiving notice of avoidance for unfair exploitation, provided that this party informs the party who gave the notice without undue delay after receiving it and before that party has acted in reliance on it.

II. – 7:208:   Third persons

(1) Where a third person for whose acts a party is responsible or who with a party's assent is involved in the making of a contract:

 (a) causes a mistake, or knows of or could reasonably be expected to know of a mistake; or

 (b) is guilty of fraud, coercion, threats or unfair exploitation, remedies under this Section
 are available as if the behaviour or knowledge had been that of the party.

(2) Where a third person for whose acts a party is not responsible and who does not have the party's assent to be involved in the making of a contract is guilty of fraud, coercion, threats or unfair exploitation, remedies under this Section are available if the party knew or could reasonably be expected to have known of the relevant facts, or at the time of avoidance has not acted in reliance on the contract.

II. – 7:209:   Notice of avoidance

Avoidance under this Section is effected by notice to the other party.

II. – 7:210:   Time

A notice of avoidance under this Section is ineffective unless given within a reasonable time, with due regard to the circumstances, after the avoiding party knew or could reasonably be expected to have known of the relevant facts or became capable of acting freely.

II. – 7:211:   Confirmation

If a party who is entitled to avoid a contract under this Section confirms it, expressly or impliedly, after the period of time for giving notice of avoidance has begun to run, avoidance is excluded.

II. – 7:212:   Effects of avoidance

(1) A contract which may be avoided under this Section is valid until avoided but, once avoided, is retrospectively invalid from the beginning.

(2) The question whether either party has a right to the return of whatever has been transferred or supplied under a contract which has been avoided under this Section, or a monetary equivalent, is regulated by the rules on unjustified enrichment.

(3) The effect of avoidance under this Section on the ownership of property which has been transferred under the avoided contract is governed by the rules on the transfer of property.

II. – 7:213:   Partial avoidance

If a ground of avoidance under this Section affects only particular terms of a contract, the effect of an avoidance is limited to those terms unless, giving due consideration to all the circumstances of the case, it is unreasonable to uphold the remaining contract.

II. – 7:214:   Damages for loss

(1) A party who has the right to avoid a contract under this Section (or who had such a right before it was lost by the effect of time limits or confirmation) is entitled, whether or not the contract is avoided, to damages from the other party for any loss suffered as a result of the mistake, fraud, coercion, threats or unfair exploitation, provided that the other party knew or could reasonably be expected to have known of the ground for avoidance.

(2) The damages recoverable are such as to place the aggrieved party as nearly as possible in the position in which that party would have been if the contract had not been concluded, with the further limitation that, if the party does not avoid the contract, the damages are not to exceed the loss caused by the mistake, fraud, coercion, threats or unfair exploitation.

(3) In other respects the rules on damages for non-performance of a contractual obligation apply with any appropriate adaptation.

II. – 7:215:   Exclusion or restriction of remedies

(1) Remedies for fraud, coercion, threats and unfair exploitation cannot be excluded or restricted.

(2) Remedies for mistake may be excluded or restricted unless the exclusion or restriction is contrary to good faith and fair dealing.

II. – 7:216:   Overlapping remedies

A party who is entitled to a remedy under this Section in circumstances which afford that party a remedy for non-performance may pursue either remedy.

Section 3: Infringement of fundamental principles or mandatory rules

II. – 7:301:   Contracts infringing fundamental principles

A contract is void to the extent that:
- (a) it infringes a principle recognised as fundamental in the laws of the Member States of the European Union; and
- (b) nullity is required to give effect to that principle.

II. – 7:302:   Contracts infringing mandatory rules

(1) Where a contract is not void under the preceding Article but infringes a mandatory rule of law, the effects of that infringement on the validity of the contract are the effects, if any, expressly prescribed by that mandatory rule.

(2) Where the mandatory rule does not expressly prescribe the effects of an infringement on the validity of a contract, a court may:
- (a) declare the contract to be valid;
- (b) avoid the contract, with retrospective effect, in whole or in part; or
- (c) modify the contract or its effects.

(3) A decision reached under paragraph (2) should be an appropriate and proportional response to the infringement, having regard to all relevant circumstances, including:
- (a) the purpose of the rule which has been infringed;
- (b) the category of persons for whose protection the rule exists;
- (c) any sanction that may be imposed under the rule infringed;
- (d) the seriousness of the infringement;
- (e) whether the infringement was intentional; and
- (f) the closeness of the relationship between the infringement and the contract.

II. – 7:303:   Effects of nullity or avoidance

(1) The question whether either party has a right to the return of whatever has been transferred or supplied under a contract, or part of a contract, which is void or has been avoided under this Section, or a monetary equivalent, is regulated by the rules on unjustified enrichment.

(2) The effect of nullity or avoidance under this Section on the ownership of property which has been transferred under the void or avoided contract, or part of a contract, is governed by the rules on the transfer of property.

(3) This Article is subject to the powers of the court to modify the contract or its effects.

II. – 7:304:   Damages for loss

(1) A party to a contract which is void or avoided, in whole or in part, under this Section is entitled to damages from the other party for any loss suffered as a result of the invalidity, provided that the first party did not know and could not reasonably be expected to have known, and the other party knew or could reasonably be expected to have known, of the infringement.

(2) The damages recoverable are such as to place the aggrieved party as nearly as possible in the position in which that party would have been if the contract had not been concluded or the infringing term had not been included.

Chapter 8: Interpretation

Section 1: Interpretation of contracts

II. – 8:101:   General rules

(1) A contract is to be interpreted according to the common intention of the parties even if this differs from the literal meaning of the words.

(2) If one party intended the contract, or a term or expression used in it, to have a particular meaning, and at the time of the conclusion of the contract the other party was aware, or could reasonably be expected to have been aware, of the first party's intention, the contract is to be interpreted in the way intended by the first party.

(3) The contract is, however, to be interpreted according to the meaning which a reasonable person would give to it:

    (a) if an intention cannot be established under the preceding paragraphs; or

    (b) if the question arises with a person, not being a party to the contract or a person who by law has no better rights than such a party, who has reasonably and in good faith relied on the contract's apparent meaning.

II. – 8:102:   Relevant matters

(1) In interpreting the contract, regard may be had, in particular, to:

    (a) the circumstances in which it was concluded, including the preliminary negotiations;

    (b) the conduct of the parties, even subsequent to the conclusion of the contract;

    (c) the interpretation which has already been given by the parties to terms or expressions which are the same as, or similar to, those used in the contract and the practices they have established between themselves;

    (d) the meaning commonly given to such terms or expressions in the branch of activity concerned and the interpretation such terms or expressions may already have received;

    (e) the nature and purpose of the contract;

    (f) usages; and

    (g) good faith and fair dealing.

(2) In a question with a person, not being a party to the contract or a person such as an assignee who by law has no better rights than such a party, who has reasonably and in good faith relied on the contract's apparent meaning, regard may be had to the circumstances mentioned in sub-paragraphs (a) to (c) above only to the extent that those circumstances were known to, or could reasonably be expected to have been known to, that person.

II. – 8:103:   Interpretation against supplier of term or dominant party

(1) Where there is doubt about the meaning of a term not individually negotiated, an interpretation of the term against the party who supplied it is to be preferred.

(2) Where there is doubt about the meaning of any other term, and that term has been established under the dominant influence of one party, an interpretation of the term against that party is to be preferred.

II. – 8:104:   Preference for negotiated terms

Terms which have been individually negotiated take preference over those which have not.

II. – 8:105:   Reference to contract as a whole

Terms and expressions are to be interpreted in the light of the whole contract in which they appear.

II. – 8:106:   Preference for interpretation which gives terms effect

An interpretation which renders the terms of the contract lawful, or effective, is to be preferred to one which would not.

II. – 8:107:   Linguistic discrepancies

Where a contract document is in two or more language versions none of which is stated to be author-
itative, there is, in case of discrepancy between the versions, a preference for the interpretation
according to the version in which the contract was originally drawn up.

Section 2: Interpretation of other juridical acts

II. – 8:201:   General rules

(1) A unilateral juridical act is to be interpreted in the way in which it could reasonably be
expected to be understood by the person to whom it is addressed.

(2) If the person making the juridical act intended the act, or a term or expression used in it,
to have a particular meaning, and at the time of the act the person to whom it was addressed was
aware, or could reasonably be expected to have been aware, of the first person's intention, the act is
to be interpreted in the way intended by the first person.

(3) The act is, however, to be interpreted according to the meaning which a reasonable person
would give to it:

    (a) if neither paragraph (1) nor paragraph (2) applies; or

    (b) if the question arises with a person, not being the addressee or a person who by law has
        no better rights than the addressee, who has reasonably and in good faith relied on the
        contract's apparent meaning.

II. – 8:202:   Application of other rules by analogy

The provisions of Section 1, apart from its first Article, apply with appropriate adaptations to the
interpretation of a juridical act other than a contract.

Chapter 9: Contents and effects of contracts

Section 1: Contents

II. – 9:101:   Terms of a contract

(1) The terms of a contract may be derived from the express or tacit agreement of the parties,
from rules of law or from practices established between the parties or usages.

(2) Where it is necessary to provide for a matter which the parties have not foreseen or provided
for, a court may imply an additional term, having regard in particular to:

    (a) the nature and purpose of the contract;

    (b) the circumstances in which the contract was concluded; and

    (c) the requirements of good faith and fair dealing.

(3) Any term implied under paragraph (2) should, where possible, be such as to give effect to
what the parties, had they provided for the matter, would probably have agreed.

(4) Paragraph (2) does not apply if the parties have deliberately left a matter unprovided for,
accepting the consequences of so doing.

II. – 9:102:   Certain pre-contractual statements regarded as contract terms

(1) A statement made by one party before a contract is concluded is regarded as a term of the
contract if the other party reasonably understood it as being made on the basis that it would form
part of the contract terms if a contract were concluded. In assessing whether the other party was
reasonable in understanding the statement in that way account may be taken of:

    (a) the apparent importance of the statement to the other party;

    (b) whether the party was making the statement in the course of business; and

    (c) the relative expertise of the parties.

(2) If one of the parties to a contract is a business and before the contract is concluded makes
a statement, either to the other party or publicly, about the specific characteristics of what is to be
supplied by that business under the contract, the statement is regarded as a term of the contract
unless:

(a) the other party was aware when the contract was concluded, or could reasonably be expected to have been so aware, that the statement was incorrect or could not otherwise be relied on as such a term; or

(b) the other party's decision to conclude the contract was not influenced by the statement.

(3) For the purposes of paragraph (2), a statement made by a person engaged in advertising or marketing on behalf of the business is treated as being made by the business.

(4) Where the other party is a consumer then, for the purposes of paragraph (2), a public statement made by or on behalf of a producer or other person in earlier links of the business chain between the producer and the consumer is treated as being made by the business unless the business, at the time of conclusion of the contract, did not know and could not reasonably be expected to have known of it.

(5) In the circumstances covered by paragraph (4) a business which at the time of conclusion of the contract did not know and could not reasonably be expected to have known that the statement was incorrect has a right to be indemnified by the person making the statement for any liability incurred as a result of that paragraph.

(6) In relations between a business and a consumer the parties may not, to the detriment of the consumer, exclude the application of this Article or derogate from or vary its effects.

II. – 9:103:   Terms not individually negotiated

(1) Terms supplied by one party and not individually negotiated may be invoked against the other party only if the other party was aware of them, or if the party supplying the terms took reasonable steps to draw the other party's attention to them, before or when the contract was concluded.

(2) If a contract is to be concluded by electronic means, the party supplying any terms which have not been individually negotiated may invoke them against the other party only if they are made available to the other party in textual form.

(3) For the purposes of this Article

(a) "not individually negotiated" has the meaning given by II.–1:110 (Terms "not individually negotiated"); and

(b) terms are not sufficiently brought to the other party's attention by a mere reference to them in a contract document, even if that party signs the document.

II. – 9:104:   Determination of price

Where the amount of the price payable under a contract cannot be determined from the terms agreed by the parties, from any other applicable rule of law or from usages or practices, the price payable is the price normally charged in comparable circumstances at the time of the conclusion of the contract or, if no such price is available, a reasonable price.

II. – 9:105:   Unilateral determination by a party

Where the price or any other contractual term is to be determined by one party and that party's determination is grossly unreasonable then, notwithstanding any provision in the contract to the contrary, a reasonable price or other term is substituted.

II. – 9:106:   Determination by a third person

(1) Where a third person is to determine the price or any other contractual term and cannot or will not do so, a court may, unless this is inconsistent with the terms of the contract, appoint another person to determine it.

(2) If a price or other term determined by a third person is grossly unreasonable, a reasonable price or term is substituted.

II. – 9:107:   Reference to a non-existent factor

Where the price or any other contractual term is to be determined by reference to a factor which does not exist or has ceased to exist or to be accessible, the nearest equivalent factor is substituted unless this would be unreasonable in the circumstances, in which case a reasonable price or other term is substituted.

II. – 9:108:   Quality

Where the quality of anything to be supplied or provided under the contract cannot be determined from the terms agreed by the parties, from any other applicable rule of law or from usages or practices, the quality required is the quality which the recipient could reasonably expect in the circumstances.

II. – 9:109:   Language

Where the language to be used for communications relating to the contract or the rights or obligations arising from it cannot be determined from the terms agreed by the parties, from any other applicable rule of law or from usages or practices, the language to be used is that used for the conclusion of the contract.

Section 2: Simulation

II. – 9:201:   Effect of simulation

(1) When the parties have concluded a contract or an apparent contract and have deliberately done so in such a way that it has an apparent effect different from the effect which the parties intend it to have, the parties' true intention prevails.

(2) However, the apparent effect prevails in relation to a person, not being a party to the contract or apparent contract or a person who by law has no better rights than such a party, who has reasonably and in good faith relied on the apparent effect.

Section 3: Effect of stipulation in favour of a third party

II. – 9:301:   Basic rules

(1) The parties to a contract may, by the contract, confer a right or other benefit on a third party. The third party need not be in existence or identified at the time the contract is concluded.

(2) The nature and content of the third party's right or benefit are determined by the contract and are subject to any conditions or other limitations under the contract.

(3) The benefit conferred may take the form of an exclusion or limitation of the third party's liability to one of the contracting parties.

II. – 9:302:   Rights, remedies and defences

Where one of the contracting parties is bound to render a performance to the third party under the contract, then, in the absence of provision to the contrary in the contract:

    (a) the third party has the same rights to performance and remedies for non-performance as if the contracting party was bound to render the performance under a binding unilateral undertaking in favour of the third party; and

    (b) the contracting party may assert against the third party all defences which the contracting party could assert against the other party to the contract.

II. – 9:303:   Rejection or revocation of benefit

(1) The third party may reject the right or benefit by notice to either of the contracting parties, if that is done without undue delay after being notified of the right or benefit and before it has been expressly or impliedly accepted. On such rejection, the right or benefit is treated as never having accrued to the third party.

(2) The contracting parties may remove or modify the contractual term conferring the right or benefit if this is done before either of them has given the third party notice that the right or benefit has been conferred. The contract determines whether and by whom and in what circumstances the right or benefit can be revoked or modified after that time.

(3) Even if the right or benefit conferred is by virtue of the contract revocable or subject to modification, the right to revoke or modify is lost if the parties have, or the party having the right to revoke or modify has, led the third party to believe that it is not revocable or subject to modification and if the third party has reasonably acted in reliance on it.

Section 4: Unfair terms

II. – 9:401:   Mandatory nature of following provisions
The parties may not exclude the application of the provisions in this Section or derogate from or vary their effects.

II. – 9:402:   Duty of transparency in terms not individually negotiated
(1) A person who supplies terms which have not been individually negotiated has a duty to ensure that they are drafted and communicated in plain, intelligible language.

(2) In a contract between a business and a consumer a term which has been supplied by the business in breach of the duty of transparency imposed by paragraph (1) may on that ground alone be considered unfair.

II. – 9:403:   Meaning of "unfair" in contracts between a business and a consumer
In a contract between a business and a consumer, a term [which has not been individually negotiated] is unfair for the purposes of this Section if it is supplied by the business and if it significantly disadvantages the consumer, contrary to good faith and fair dealing.

II. – 9:404:   Meaning of "unfair" in contracts between non-business parties
In a contract between parties neither of whom is a business, a term is unfair for the purposes of this Section only if it is a term forming part of standard terms supplied by one party and significantly disadvantages the other party, contrary to good faith and fair dealing.

II. – 9:405:   Meaning of "unfair" in contracts between businesses
A term in a contract between businesses is unfair for the purposes of this Section only if it is a term forming part of standard terms supplied by one party and of such a nature that its use grossly deviates from good commercial practice, contrary to good faith and fair dealing.

II. – 9:406:   Exclusions from unfairness test
(1) Contract terms are not subjected to an unfairness test under this Section if they are based on:
   (a) provisions of the applicable law;
   (b) international conventions to which the Member States are parties, or to which the European Union is a party; or
   (c) these rules.

(2) For contract terms which are drafted in plain and intelligible language, the unfairness test extends neither to the definition of the main subject matter of the contract, nor to the adequacy of the price to be paid.

II. – 9:407:   Factors to be taken into account in assessing unfairness
(1) When assessing the unfairness of a contractual term for the purposes of this Section, regard is to be had to the duty of transparency under II.–9:402 (Duty of transparency in terms not individually negotiated), to the nature of what is to be provided under the contract, to the circumstances prevailing during the conclusion of the contract, to the other terms of the contract and to the terms of any other contract on which the contract depends.

(2) For the purposes of II.–9:403 (Meaning of "unfair" in contracts between a business and a consumer) the circumstances prevailing during the conclusion of the contract include the extent to which the consumer was given a real opportunity to become acquainted with the term before the conclusion of the contract.

II. – 9:408:   Effects of unfair terms
(1) A term which is unfair under this Section is not binding on the party who did not supply it.

(2) If the contract can reasonably be maintained without the unfair term, the other terms remain binding on the parties.

II. – 9:409:   Exclusive jurisdiction clauses

(1) A term in a contract between a business and a consumer is unfair for the purposes of this Section if it is supplied by the business and if it confers exclusive jurisdiction for all disputes arising under the contract on the court for the place where the business is domiciled.

(2) Paragraph (1) does not apply if the chosen court is also the court for the place where the consumer is domiciled.

II. – 9:410:   Terms which are presumed to be unfair in contracts between a business and a consumer

(1) A term in a contract between a business and a consumer is presumed to be unfair for the purposes of this Section if it is supplied by the business and if it:

(a) excludes or limits the liability of a business for death or personal injury caused to a consumer through an act or omission of that business;

(b) inappropriately excludes or limits the remedies, including any right to set-off, available to the consumer against the business or a third party for non-performance by the business of obligations under the contract;

(c) makes binding on a consumer an obligation which is subject to a condition the fulfilment of which depends solely on the intention of the business;

(d) permits a business to keep money paid by a consumer if the latter decides not to conclude the contract, or perform obligations under it, without providing for the consumer to receive compensation of an equivalent amount from the business in the reverse situation;

(e) requires a consumer who fails to perform his or her obligations to pay a disproportionately high amount of damages;

(f) entitles a business to withdraw from or terminate the contractual relationship on a discretionary basis without giving the same right to the consumer, or entitles a business to keep money paid for services not yet supplied in the case where the business withdraws from or terminates the contractual relationship;

(g) enables a business to terminate a contractual relationship of indeterminate duration without reasonable notice, except where there are serious grounds for doing so; this does not affect terms in financial services contracts where there is a valid reason, provided that the supplier is required to inform the other contracting party thereof immediately;

(h) automatically extends a contract of fixed duration unless the consumer indicates otherwise, in cases where such terms provide for an unreasonably early deadline;

(i) enables a business to alter the terms of the contract unilaterally without a valid reason which is specified in the contract; this does not affect terms under which a supplier of financial services reserves the right to change the rate of interest to be paid by, or to, the consumer, or the amount of other charges for financial services without notice where there is a valid reason, provided that the supplier is required to inform the consumer at the earliest opportunity and that the consumer is free to terminate the contractual relationship with immediate effect; neither does it affect terms under which a business reserves the right to alter unilaterally the conditions of a contract of indeterminate duration, provided that the business is required to inform the consumer with reasonable notice, and that the consumer is free to terminate the contractual relationship;

(j) enables a business to alter unilaterally without a valid reason any characteristics of the goods, other assets or services to be provided;

(k) provides that the price of goods or other assets is to be determined at the time of delivery or supply, or allows a business to increase the price without giving the consumer the right to withdraw if the increased price is too high in relation to the price agreed at the conclusion of the contract; this does not affect price-indexation clauses, where lawful, provided that the method by which prices vary is explicitly described;

(l) gives a business the right to determine whether the goods, other assets or services supplied are in conformity with the contract, or gives the business the exclusive right to interpret any term of the contract;

(m) limits the obligation of a business to respect commitments undertaken by its agents, or makes its commitments subject to compliance with a particular formality;

(n) obliges a consumer to fulfil all his or her obligations where the business fails to fulfil its own;

(o) allows a business to transfer its rights and obligations under the contract without the consumer's consent, if this could reduce the guarantees available to the consumer;

(p) excludes or restricts a consumer's right to take legal action or to exercise any other remedy, in particular by referring the consumer to arbitration proceedings which are not covered by legal provisions, by unduly restricting the evidence available to the consumer, or by shifting a burden of proof on to the consumer;

(q) allows a business, where what has been ordered is unavailable, to supply an equivalent without having expressly informed the consumer of this possibility and of the fact that the business must bear the cost of returning what the consumer has received under the contract if the consumer exercises a right to withdraw.

(2) Subparagraphs (g), (i) and (k) do not apply to:

(a) transactions in transferable securities, financial instruments and other products or services where the price is linked to fluctuations in a stock exchange quotation or index or a financial market rate beyond the control of the business;

(b) contracts for the purchase or sale of foreign currency, traveller's cheques or international money orders denominated in foreign currency.

BOOK III: OBLIGATIONS AND CORRESPONDING RIGHTS

Chapter 1: General

III. – 1:101: Scope of Book

This Book applies, except as otherwise provided, to all obligations within the scope of these rules, whether they are contractual or not, and to corresponding rights to performance.

III. – 1:102: Definitions

(1) An obligation is a duty to perform which one party to a legal relationship, the debtor, owes to another party, the creditor.

(2) Performance of an obligation is the doing by the debtor of what is to be done under the obligation or the not doing by the debtor of what is not to be done.

(3) Non-performance of an obligation is any failure to perform the obligation, whether or not excused, and includes delayed performance and any other performance which is not in accordance with the terms regulating the obligation.

(4) An obligation is reciprocal in relation to another obligation if:

(a) performance of the obligation is due in exchange for performance of the other obligation;

(b) it is an obligation to facilitate or accept performance of the other obligation; or

(c) it is so clearly connected to the other obligation or its subject matter that performance of the one can reasonably be regarded as dependent on performance of the other.

(5) The terms regulating an obligation may be derived from a contract or other juridical act, the law or a legally binding usage or practice, or a court order; and similarly for the terms regulating a right.

III. – 1:103: Good faith and fair dealing

(1) A person has a duty to act in accordance with good faith and fair dealing in performing an obligation, in exercising a right to performance, in pursuing or defending a remedy for non-performance, or in exercising a right to terminate an obligation or contractual relationship.

(2) The duty may not be excluded or limited by contract or other juridical act.

(3) Breach of the duty does not give rise directly to the remedies for non-performance of an obligation but may preclude the person in breach from exercising or relying on a right, remedy or defence which that person would otherwise have.

III. – 1:104: Co-operation

The debtor and creditor are obliged to co-operate with each other when and to the extent that this can reasonably be expected for the performance of the debtor's obligation.

III. – 1:105: Non-discrimination

Chapter 2 (Non-discrimination) of Book II applies with appropriate adaptations to:

  (a) the performance of any obligation to provide access to, or supply, goods, other assets or services which are available to members of the public;

  (b) the exercise of a right to performance of any such obligation or the pursuing or defending of any remedy for non-performance of any such obligation; and

  (c) the exercise of a right to terminate any such obligation.

III. – 1:106: Conditional rights and obligations

(1) The terms regulating a right, obligation or contractual relationship may provide that it is conditional upon the occurrence of an uncertain future event, so that it takes effect only if the event occurs (suspensive condition) or comes to an end if the event occurs (resolutive condition).

(2) Upon fulfilment of a suspensive condition, the relevant right, obligation or relationship takes effect.

(3) Upon fulfilment of a resolutive condition, the relevant right, obligation or relationship comes to an end.

(4) When a party, contrary to the duty of good faith and fair dealing or the obligation to co-operate, interferes with events so as to bring about the fulfilment or non-fulfilment of a condition to that party's advantage, the other party may treat the condition as not having been fulfilled or as having been fulfilled as the case may be.

(5) When a contractual obligation or relationship comes to an end on the fulfilment of a resolutive condition any restitutionary effects are regulated by the rules in Chapter 3, Section 5, Sub-section 4 (Restitution) with appropriate adaptations.

III. – 1:107: Time-limited rights and obligations

(1) The terms regulating a right, obligation or contractual relationship may provide that it is to take effect from or end at a specified time, after a specified period of time or on the occurrence of an event which is certain to occur.

(2) It will take effect or come to an end at the time or on the event without further steps having to be taken.

(3) When a contractual obligation or relationship comes to an end under this Article any restitutionary effects are regulated by the rules in Chapter 3, Section 5, Sub-section 4 (Restitution) with appropriate adaptations.

III. – 1:108: Variation or termination by agreement

(1) A right, obligation or contractual relationship may be varied or terminated by agreement at any time.

(2) Where the parties do not regulate the effects of termination, then:

  (a) it has prospective effect only and does not affect any right to damages, or a stipulated payment, for non-performance of any obligation performance of which was due before termination;

  (b) it does not affect any provision for the settlement of disputes or any other provision which is to operate even after termination; and

  (c) in the case of a contractual obligation or relationship any restitutionary effects are regulated by the rules in Chapter 3, Section 5, Sub-section 4 (Restitution) with appropriate adaptations.

III. – 1:109:   Variation or termination by notice

(1) A right, obligation or contractual relationship may be varied or terminated by notice by either party where this is provided for by the terms regulating it.

(2) Where, in a case involving continuous or periodic performance of a contractual obligation, the terms of the contract do not say when the contractual relationship is to end or say that it will never end, it may be terminated by either party by giving a reasonable period of notice. In assessing whether a period of notice is reasonable, regard may be had to the interval between performances or counter-performances.

(3) Where the parties do not regulate the effects of termination, then:

 (a) it has prospective effect only and does not affect any right to damages, or a stipulated payment, for non-performance of any obligation performance of which was due before termination;

 (b) it does not affect any provision for the settlement of disputes or any other provision which is to operate even after termination; and

 (c) in the case of a contractual obligation or relationship any restitutionary effects are regulated by the rules in Chapter 3, Section 5, Sub-section 4 (Restitution) with appropriate adaptations.

III. – 1:110:   Variation or termination by court on a change of circumstances

(1) An obligation must be performed even if performance has become more onerous, whether because the cost of performance has increased or because the value of what is to be received in return has diminished.

(2) If, however, performance of a contractual obligation or of an obligation arising from a unilateral juridical act becomes so onerous because of an exceptional change of circumstances that it would be manifestly unjust to hold the debtor to the obligation a court may:

 (a) vary the obligation in order to make it reasonable and equitable in the new circumstances; or

 (b) terminate the obligation at a date and on terms to be determined by the court.

(3) Paragraph (2) applies only if:

 (a) the change of circumstances occurred after the time when the obligation was incurred;

 (b) the debtor did not at that time take into account, and could not reasonably be expected to have taken into account, the possibility or scale of that change of circumstances;

 (c) the debtor did not assume, and cannot reasonably be regarded as having assumed, the risk of that change of circumstances; and

 (d) the debtor has attempted, reasonably and in good faith, to achieve by negotiation a reasonable and equitable adjustment of the terms regulating the obligation.

III. – 1:111:   Tacit prolongation

Where a contract provides for continuous or repeated performance of obligations for a definite period and the obligations continue to be performed by both parties after that period has expired, the contract becomes a contract for an indefinite period, unless the circumstances are inconsistent with the tacit consent of the parties to such prolongation.

Chapter 2: Performance

III. – 2:101:   Place of performance

(1) If the place of performance of an obligation cannot be otherwise determined from the terms regulating the obligation it is:

 (a) in the case of a monetary obligation, the creditor's place of business;

 (b) in the case of any other obligation, the debtor's place of business.

(2) For the purposes of the preceding paragraph:

 (a) if a party has more than one place of business, the place of business is that which has the closest relationship to the obligation; and

(b) if a party does not have a place of business, or the obligation does not relate to a business matter, the habitual residence is substituted.

(3) If, in a case to which paragraph (1) applies, a party causes any increase in the expenses incidental to performance by a change in place of business or habitual residence subsequent to the time when the obligation was incurred, that party is obliged to bear the increase.

III. – 2:102:   Time of performance

(1) If the time at which, or a period of time within which, an obligation is to be performed cannot otherwise be determined from the terms regulating the obligation it must be performed within a reasonable time after it arises.

(2) If a period of time within which the obligation is to be performed can be determined from the terms regulating the obligation, the obligation may be performed at any time within that period chosen by the debtor unless the circumstances of the case indicate that the creditor is to choose the time.

(3) Unless the parties have agreed otherwise, a business must perform the obligations incurred under a contract concluded at a distance for the supply of goods, other assets or services to a consumer no later than 30 days after the contract was concluded.

(4) If a business has an obligation to reimburse money received from a consumer for goods, other assets or services supplied, the reimbursement must be made as soon as possible and in any case no later than 30 days after the obligation arose.

III. – 2:103:   Early performance

(1) A creditor may reject an offer to perform before performance is due unless the early performance would not cause the creditor unreasonable prejudice.

(2) A creditor's acceptance of early performance does not affect the time fixed for the performance by the creditor of any reciprocal obligation.

III. – 2:104:   Order of performance

If the order of performance of reciprocal obligations cannot be otherwise determined from the terms regulating the obligations then, to the extent that the obligations can be performed simultaneously, the parties are bound to perform simultaneously unless the circumstances indicate otherwise.

III. – 2:105:   Alternative obligations or methods of performance

(1) Where a debtor is bound to perform one of two or more obligations, or to perform an obligation in one of two or more ways, the choice belongs to the debtor, unless the terms regulating the obligations or obligation provide otherwise.

(2) If the party who is to make the choice fails to choose by the time when performance is due, then:

(a) if the delay amounts to a fundamental non-performance, the right to choose passes to the other party;

(b) if the delay does not amount to a fundamental non-performance, the other party may give a notice fixing an additional period of reasonable length within which the party to choose is required to do so. If the latter still fails to do so, the right to choose passes to the other party.

III. – 2:106:   Performance entrusted to another

A debtor who entrusts performance of an obligation to another person remains responsible for performance.

III. – 2:107:   Performance by a third person

(1) Where personal performance by the debtor is not required by the terms regulating the obligation, the creditor cannot refuse performance by a third person if:

(a) the third person acts with the assent of the debtor; or

(b) the third person has a legitimate interest in performing and the debtor has failed to perform or it is clear that the debtor will not perform at the time performance is due.

(2) Performance by a third person in accordance with paragraph (1) discharges the debtor except to the extent that the third person takes over the creditor's right by assignment or subrogation.

(3) Where personal performance by the debtor is not required and the creditor accepts performance of the debtor's obligation by a third party in circumstances not covered by paragraph (1) the debtor is discharged but the creditor is liable to the debtor for any loss caused by that acceptance.

III. – 2:108:   Method of payment

(1) Payment of money due may be made by any method used in the ordinary course of business.

(2) A creditor who accepts a cheque or other order to pay or a promise to pay is presumed to do so only on condition that it will be honoured. The creditor may not enforce the original obligation to pay unless the order or promise is not honoured.

III. – 2:109:   Currency of payment

(1) The debtor and the creditor may agree that payment is to be made only in a specified currency.

(2) In the absence of such agreement, a sum of money expressed in a currency other than that of the place where payment is due may be paid in the currency of that place according to the rate of exchange prevailing there at the time when payment is due.

(3) If, in a case falling within the preceding paragraph, the debtor has not paid at the time when payment is due, the creditor may require payment in the currency of the place where payment is due according to the rate of exchange prevailing there either at the time when payment is due or at the time of actual payment.

(4) Where a monetary obligation is not expressed in a particular currency, payment must be made in the currency of the place where payment is to be made.

III. – 2:110:   Imputation of performance

(1) Where a debtor has to perform several obligations of the same nature and makes a performance which does not suffice to extinguish all of the obligations, then subject to paragraph (5), the debtor may at the time of performance notify the creditor of the obligation to which the performance is to be imputed.

(2) If the debtor does not make such a notification the creditor may, within a reasonable time and by notifying the debtor, impute the performance to one of the obligations.

(3) An imputation under paragraph (2) is not effective if it is to an obligation which is not yet due, or is illegal, or is disputed.

(4) In the absence of an effective imputation by either party, and subject to the following paragraph, the performance is imputed to that obligation which satisfies one of the following criteria in the sequence indicated:

    (a) the obligation which is due or is the first to fall due;

    (b) the obligation for which the creditor has the least security;

    (c) the obligation which is the most burdensome for the debtor;

    (d) the obligation which has arisen first.

If none of the preceding criteria applies, the performance is imputed proportionately to all the obligations.

(5) In the case of a monetary obligation, a payment by the debtor is to be imputed, first, to expenses, secondly, to interest, and thirdly, to principal, unless the creditor makes a different imputation.

III. – 2:111:   Property not accepted

(1) A person who has an obligation to deliver or return corporeal property other than money and who is left in possession of the property because of the creditor's failure to accept or retake the property, has an ancillary obligation to take reasonable steps to protect and preserve it.

(2) The debtor may obtain discharge from the obligation to deliver or return and from the ancillary obligation mentioned in the preceding paragraph:

    (a) by depositing the property on reasonable terms with a third person to be held to the order of the creditor, and notifying the creditor of this; or

   (b) by selling the property on reasonable terms after notice to the creditor, and paying the net proceeds to the creditor.

   (3) Where, however, the property is liable to rapid deterioration or its preservation is unreasonably expensive, the debtor has an obligation to take reasonable steps to dispose of it. The debtor may obtain discharge from the obligation to deliver or return by paying the net proceeds to the creditor.

   (4) The debtor left in possession is entitled to be reimbursed or to retain out of the proceeds of sale any costs reasonably incurred.

III. – 2:112: Money not accepted

   (1) Where a creditor fails to accept money properly tendered by the debtor, the debtor may after notice to the creditor obtain discharge from the obligation to pay by depositing the money to the order of the creditor in accordance with the law of the place where payment is due.

   (2) Paragraph (1) applies, with appropriate adaptations, to money properly tendered by a third party in circumstances where the creditor is not entitled to refuse such performance.

III. – 2:113: Costs and formalities of performance

   (1) The costs of performing an obligation are borne by the debtor.

   (2) In the case of a monetary obligation the debtor's obligation to pay includes taking such steps and complying with such formalities as may be necessary to enable payment to be made.

III. – 2:114: Extinctive effect of performance

Full performance extinguishes the obligation if it is:

   (a) in accordance with the terms regulating the obligation; or

   (b) of such a type as by law to afford the debtor a good discharge.

Chapter 3: Remedies for non-performance

Section 1: General

III. – 3:101: Remedies available

   (1) If an obligation is not performed by the debtor and the non-performance is not excused, the creditor may resort to any of the remedies set out in this Chapter.

   (2) If the debtor's non-performance is excused, the creditor may resort to any of those remedies except enforcing specific performance and damages.

   (3) The creditor may not resort to any of those remedies to the extent that the creditor caused the debtor's non-performance

III. – 3:102: Cumulation of remedies

Remedies which are not incompatible may be cumulated. In particular, a creditor is not deprived of the right to damages by resorting to any other remedy.

III. – 3:103: Notice fixing additional period for performance

   (1) In any case of non-performance of an obligation the creditor may by notice to the debtor allow an additional period of time for performance.

   (2) During the additional period the creditor may withhold performance of the creditor's reciprocal obligations and may claim damages, but may not resort to any other remedy.

   (3) If the creditor receives notice from the debtor that the debtor will not perform within that period, or if upon expiry of that period due performance has not been made, the creditor may resort to any available remedy.

III. – 3:104: Excuse due to an impediment

   (1) A debtor's non-performance of an obligation is excused if it is due to an impediment beyond the debtor's control and if the debtor could not reasonably be expected to have avoided or overcome the impediment or its consequences.

(2) Where the obligation arose out of a contract or other juridical act, non-performance is not excused if the debtor could reasonably be expected to have taken the impediment into account at the time when the obligation was incurred.

(3) Where the excusing impediment is only temporary the excuse has effect for the period during which the impediment exists. However, if the delay amounts to a fundamental non-performance, the creditor may treat it as such.

(4) Where the excusing impediment is permanent the obligation is extinguished. Any reciprocal obligation is also extinguished. In the case of contractual obligations any restitutionary effects of extinction are regulated by the rules in Chapter 3, Section 5, Sub-section 4 (Restitution) with appropriate adaptations.

(5) The debtor has a duty to ensure that notice of the impediment and of its effect on the ability to perform reaches the creditor within a reasonable time after the debtor knew or could reasonably be expected to have known of these circumstances. The creditor is entitled to damages for any loss resulting from the non-receipt of such notice.

III. – 3:105:   Term excluding or restricting remedies

(1) A term of a contract or other juridical act which purports to exclude or restrict liability to pay damages for personal injury (including fatal injury) caused intentionally or by gross negligence is void.

(2) A term excluding or restricting a remedy for non-performance of an obligation, even if valid and otherwise effective, having regard in particular to the rules on unfair contract terms in Book II, Chapter 9, Section 4, may nevertheless not be invoked if it would be contrary to good faith and fair dealing to do so.

III. – 3:106:   Notices relating to non-performance

(1) If the creditor gives notice to the debtor because of the debtor's non-performance of an obligation or because such non-performance is anticipated, and the notice is properly dispatched or given, a delay or inaccuracy in the transmission of the notice or its failure to arrive does not prevent it from having effect.

(2) The notice has effect from the time at which it would have arrived in normal circumstances.

III. – 3:107:   Failure to notify non-conformity

(1) If, in the case of an obligation to supply goods, other assets or services, the debtor supplies goods, other assets or services which are not in conformity with the terms regulating the obligation, the creditor may not rely on the lack of conformity unless the creditor gives notice to the debtor within a reasonable time specifying the nature of the lack of conformity.

(2) The reasonable time runs from the time when the goods or other assets are supplied or the service is completed or from the time, if it is later, when the creditor discovered or could reasonably be expected to have discovered the non-conformity.

(3) The debtor is not entitled to rely on paragraph (1) if the failure relates to facts which the debtor knew or could reasonably be expected to have known and which the debtor did not disclose to the creditor.

(4) This Article does not apply where the creditor is a consumer.

III. – 3:108:   Business unable to fulfil consumer's order by distance communication

(1) Where a business is unable to perform its obligations under a contract concluded with a consumer by means of distance communication, it is obliged to inform the consumer immediately and refund any sums paid by the consumer without undue delay and in any case within 30 days. The consumer's remedies for non-performance remain unaffected.

(2) The parties may not, to the detriment of the consumer, exclude the application of this Article or derogate from or vary its effects.

Section 2: Cure by debtor of non-conforming performance

III. – 3:201: Scope
This Section applies where a debtor's performance does not conform to the terms regulating the obligation.

III. – 3:202: Cure by debtor: general rules
(1) The debtor may make a new and conforming tender if that can be done within the time allowed for performance.

(2) If the debtor cannot make a new and conforming tender within the time allowed for performance but, promptly after being notified of the lack of conformity, offers to cure it within a reasonable time and at the debtor's own expense, the creditor may not pursue any remedy for non-performance, other than withholding performance, before allowing the debtor a reasonable period in which to attempt to cure the non-conformity.

(3) Paragraph (2) is subject to the provisions of the following Article.

III. – 3:203: When creditor need not allow debtor an opportunity to cure
The creditor need not, under paragraph (2) of the preceding Article, allow the debtor a period in which to attempt cure if:
- (a) failure to perform a contractual obligation within the time allowed for performance amounts to a fundamental non-performance;
- (b) the creditor has reason to believe that the debtor's performance was made with knowledge of the non-conformity and was not in accordance with good faith and fair dealing;
- (c) the creditor has reason to believe that the debtor will be unable to effect the cure within a reasonable time and without significant inconvenience to the creditor or other prejudice to the creditor's legitimate interests; or
- (d) cure would be inappropriate in the circumstances.

III. – 3:204: Consequences of allowing debtor opportunity to cure
(1) During the period allowed for cure the creditor may withhold performance of the creditor's reciprocal obligations, but may not resort to any other remedy.

(2) If the debtor fails to effect cure within the time allowed, the creditor may resort to any available remedy.

(3) Notwithstanding cure, the creditor retains the right to damages for any loss caused by the debtor's initial or subsequent non-performance or by the process of effecting cure.

III. – 3:205: Return of replaced item
(1) Where the debtor has, whether voluntarily or in compliance with an order under III. – 3:302 (Enforcement of non-monetary obligations), remedied a non-conforming performance by replacement, the debtor has a right and an obligation to take back the replaced item at the debtor's expense.

(2) The creditor is not liable to pay for any use made of the replaced item in the period prior to the replacement.

Section 3: Right to enforce performance

III. – 3:301: Enforcement of monetary obligations
(1) The creditor is entitled to recover money payment of which is due.

(2) Where the creditor has not yet performed the reciprocal obligation for which payment will be due and it is clear that the debtor in the monetary obligation will be unwilling to receive performance, the creditor may nonetheless proceed with performance and may recover payment unless:
- (a) the creditor could have made a reasonable substitute transaction without significant effort or expense; or
- (b) performance would be unreasonable in the circumstances.

III. – 3:302: Enforcement of non-monetary obligations

(1) The creditor is entitled to enforce specific performance of an obligation other than one to pay money.

(2) Specific performance includes the remedying free of charge of a performance which is not in conformity with the terms regulating the obligation.

(3) Specific performance cannot, however, be enforced where:

    (a) performance would be unlawful or impossible;

    (b) performance would be unreasonably burdensome or expensive; or

    (c) performance would be of such a personal character that it would be unreasonable to enforce it.

(4) The creditor loses the right to enforce specific performance if performance is not requested within a reasonable time after the creditor has become, or could reasonably be expected to have become, aware of the non-performance.

(5) The creditor cannot recover damages for loss or a stipulated payment for non-performance to the extent that the creditor has increased the loss or the amount of the payment by insisting unreasonably on specific performance in circumstances where the creditor could have made a reasonable substitute transaction without significant effort or expense.

III. – 3:303: Damages not precluded

The fact that a right to enforce specific performance is excluded under the preceding Article does not preclude a claim for damages.

Section 4: Withholding performance

III. – 3:401: Right to withhold performance of reciprocal obligation

(1) A creditor who is to perform a reciprocal obligation at the same time as, or after, the debtor performs has a right to withhold performance of the reciprocal obligation until the debtor has tendered performance or has performed.

(2) A creditor who is to perform a reciprocal obligation before the debtor performs and who reasonably believes that there will be non-performance by the debtor when the debtor's performance becomes due may withhold performance of the reciprocal obligation for as long as the reasonable belief continues. However, the right to withhold performance is lost if the debtor gives an adequate assurance of due performance.

(3) A creditor who withholds performance in the situation mentioned in paragraph (2) has a duty to give notice of that fact to the debtor as soon as is reasonably practicable and is liable for any loss caused to the debtor by a breach of that duty.

(4) The performance which may be withheld under this Article is the whole or part of the performance as may be reasonable in the circumstances.

Section 5: Termination

III. – 3:501: Scope and definition

(1) This Section applies only to contractual obligations and contractual relationships.

(2) In this Section "termination" means the termination of the contractual relationship in whole or in part and "terminate" has a corresponding meaning.

Sub-section 1: Grounds for termination

III. – 3:502: Termination for fundamental non-performance

(1) A creditor may terminate if the debtor's non-performance of a contractual obligation is fundamental.

(2) A non-performance of a contractual obligation is fundamental if:

    (a) it substantially deprives the creditor of what the creditor was entitled to expect under the contract, as applied to the whole or relevant part of the performance, unless at the time of conclusion of the contract the debtor did not foresee and could not reasonably be expected to have foreseen that result; or

    (b) it is intentional or reckless and gives the creditor reason to believe that the debtor's future performance cannot be relied on.

III. – 3:503: Termination after notice fixing additional time for performance

(1) A creditor may terminate in a case of delay in performance of a contractual obligation which is not in itself fundamental if the creditor gives a notice fixing an additional period of time of reasonable length for performance and the debtor does not perform within that period.

(2) If the period fixed is unreasonably short, the creditor may terminate only after a reasonable period from the time of the notice.

III. – 3:504: Termination for anticipated non-performance

A creditor may terminate before performance of a contractual obligation is due if the debtor has declared that there will be a non-performance of the obligation, or it is otherwise clear that there will be such a non-performance, and if the non-performance would have been fundamental.

III. – 3:505: Termination for inadequate assurance of performance

A creditor who reasonably believes that there will be a fundamental non-performance of a contractual obligation by the debtor may terminate if the creditor demands an adequate assurance of due performance and no such assurance is provided within a reasonable time.

Sub-section 2: Scope, exercise and loss of right to terminate

III. – 3:506: Scope of right to terminate

(1) Where the debtor's obligations under the contract are not divisible the creditor may only terminate the contractual relationship as a whole.

(2) Where the debtor's obligations under the contract are to be performed in separate parts or are otherwise divisible, then:

    (a) if there is a ground for termination under this Section of a part to which a counter-performance can be apportioned, the creditor may terminate the contractual relationship so far as it relates to that part;

    (b) the creditor may terminate the contractual relationship as a whole only if the creditor cannot reasonably be expected to accept performance of the other parts or there is a ground for termination in relation to the contractual relationship as a whole.

III. – 3:507: Notice of termination

(1) A right to terminate under this Section is exercised by notice to the debtor.

(2) Where a notice under III.–3:503 (Termination after notice fixing additional time for performance) provides for automatic termination if the debtor does not perform within the period fixed by the notice, termination takes effect after that period or a reasonable length of time from the giving of notice (whichever is longer) without further notice.

III. – 3:508: Loss of right to terminate

(1) If performance has been tendered late or a tendered performance otherwise does not conform to the contract the creditor loses the right to terminate under this Section unless notice of termination is given within a reasonable time.

(2) Where the creditor has given the debtor a period of time to cure the non-performance under III.–3:202 (Cure by debtor: general rules) the time mentioned in paragraph (1) begins to run from the expiry of that period. In other cases that time begins to run from the time when the creditor has become, or could reasonably be expected to have become, aware of the tender or the non-conformity.

(3) A creditor loses a right to terminate by notice under III.–3:503 (Termination after notice fixing additional time for performance), III.–3:504 (Termination for anticipated non-performance) or III. – 3:505 (Termination for inadequate assurance of performance) unless the creditor gives notice of termination within a reasonable time after the right has arisen.

Sub-section 3: Effects of termination

III. – 3:509:   Effect on obligations under the contract

(1) On termination under this Section, the outstanding obligations or relevant part of the outstanding obligations of the parties under the contract come to an end.

(2) Termination does not, however, affect any provision of the contract for the settlement of disputes or other provision which is to operate even after termination.

(3) A creditor who terminates under this Section retains existing rights to damages or a stipulated payment for non-performance and in addition has the same right to damages or a stipulated payment for non-performance as the creditor would have had if there had been non-performance of the now extinguished obligations of the debtor. In relation to such extinguished obligations the creditor is not regarded as having caused or contributed to the loss merely by exercising the right to terminate.

Sub-section 4: Restitution

III. – 3:510:   Restitution of benefits received by performance

(1) On termination under this Section a party (the recipient) who has received any benefit by the other's performance of obligations under the terminated contractual relationship or terminated part of the contractual relationship is obliged to return it. Where both parties have obligations to return, the obligations are reciprocal.

(2) If the performance was a payment of money, the amount received is to be repaid.

(3) To the extent that the benefit (not being money) is transferable, it is to be returned by transferring it. However, if a transfer would cause unreasonable effort or expense, the benefit may be returned by paying its value.

(4) To the extent that the benefit is not transferable it is to be returned by paying its value in accordance with III.–3:512 (Payment of value of benefit).

(5) The obligation to return a benefit extends to any natural or legal fruits received from the benefit.

III. – 3:511:   When restitution not required

(1) There is no obligation to make restitution under this Sub-section to the extent that conforming performance by one party has been met by conforming performance by the other.

(2) The terminating party may elect to treat performance as non-conforming if what was received by that party is of no, or fundamentally reduced, value to that party because of the other party's non-performance.

(3) Restitution under this Sub-section is not required where the contract was gratuitous.

III. – 3:512:   Payment of value of benefit

(1) The recipient is obliged to:

    (a) pay the value (at the time of performance) of a benefit which is not transferable or which ceases to be transferable before the time when it is to be returned; and

    (b) pay recompense for any reduction in the value of a returnable benefit as a result of a change in the condition of the benefit between the time of receipt and the time when it is to be returned.

(2) Where there was an agreed price the value of the benefit is that proportion of the price which the value of the actual performance bears to the value of the promised performance. Where no price was agreed the value of the benefit is the sum of money which a willing and capable provider and a willing and capable recipient, knowing of any non-conformity, would lawfully have agreed.

(3) The recipient's liability to pay the value of a benefit is reduced to the extent that as a result of a non-performance of an obligation owed by the other party to the recipient:

    (a) the benefit cannot be returned in essentially the same condition as when it was received; or

    (b) the recipient is compelled without compensation either to dispose of it or to sustain a disadvantage in order to preserve it.

(4) The recipient's liability to pay the value of a benefit is likewise reduced to the extent that it cannot be returned in the same condition as when it was received as a result of conduct of the recipient in the reasonable, but mistaken, belief that there was no non-conformity.

III. – 3:513: Use and improvements

(1) The recipient is obliged to pay a reasonable amount for any use which the recipient makes of the benefit except in so far as the recipient is liable under III.–3:512 (Payment of value of benefit) paragraph (1) in respect of that use.

(2) A recipient who has improved a benefit which the recipient is obliged under this Section to return has a right to payment of the value of improvements if the other party can readily obtain that value by dealing with the benefit unless:

> (a) the improvement was a non-performance of an obligation owed by the recipient to the other party; or
>
> (b) the recipient made the improvement when the recipient knew or could reasonably be expected to know that the benefit would have to be returned.

III. – 3:514: Liabilities arising after time when return due

(1) The recipient is obliged to:

> (a) pay the value (at the time of performance) of a benefit which ceases to be transferable after the time when its return was due; and
>
> (b) pay recompense for any reduction in the value of a returnable benefit as a result of a change in the condition of the benefit after the time when its return was due.

(2) If the benefit is disposed of after the time when return was due, the value to be paid is the value of any proceeds, if this is greater.

(3) Other liabilities arising from non-performance of an obligation to return a benefit are unaffected.

Section 6: Price reduction

III. – 3:601: Right to reduce price

(1) A creditor who accepts a performance not conforming to the terms regulating the obligation may reduce the price. The reduction is to be proportionate to the decrease in the value of what was received by virtue of the performance at the time it was made compared to the value of what would have been received by virtue of a conforming performance.

(2) A creditor who is entitled to reduce the price under the preceding paragraph and who has already paid a sum exceeding the reduced price may recover the excess from the debtor.

(3) A creditor who reduces the price cannot also recover damages for the loss thereby compensated but remains entitled to damages for any further loss suffered.

(4) This Article applies with appropriate adaptations to a reciprocal obligation of the creditor other than an obligation to pay a price.

Section 7: Damages and interest

III. – 3:701: Right to damages

(1) The creditor is entitled to damages for loss caused by the debtor's non-performance of an obligation, unless the non-performance is excused.

(2) The loss for which damages are recoverable includes future loss which is reasonably likely to occur.

(3) "Loss" includes economic and non-economic loss. "Economic loss" includes loss of income or profit, burdens incurred and a reduction in the value of property. "Non-economic loss" includes pain and suffering and impairment of the quality of life.

III. – 3:702: General measure of damages

The general measure of damages for loss caused by non-performance of an obligation is such sum as will put the creditor as nearly as possible into the position in which the creditor would have been if the obligation had been duly performed. Such damages cover loss which the creditor has suffered and gain of which the creditor has been deprived.

III. – 3:703: Foreseeability

The debtor in an obligation which arises from a contract or other juridical act is liable only for loss which the debtor foresaw or could reasonably be expected to have foreseen at the time when the obligation was incurred as a likely result of the non-performance, unless the non-performance was intentional, reckless or grossly negligent.

III. – 3:704: Loss attributable to creditor

The debtor is not liable for loss suffered by the creditor to the extent that the creditor contributed to the non-performance or its effects.

III. – 3:705: Reduction of loss

(1) The debtor is not liable for loss suffered by the creditor to the extent that the creditor could have reduced the loss by taking reasonable steps.

(2) The creditor is entitled to recover any expenses reasonably incurred in attempting to reduce the loss.

III. – 3:706: Substitute transaction

A creditor who has terminated a contractual relationship in whole or in part under Section 5 and has made a substitute transaction within a reasonable time and in a reasonable manner may, in so far as entitled to damages, recover the difference between the value of what would have been payable under the terminated relationship and the value of what is payable under the substitute transaction, as well as damages for any further loss.

III. – 3:707: Current price

Where the creditor has terminated a contractual relationship in whole or in part under Section 5 and has not made a substitute transaction but there is a current price for the performance, the creditor may, in so far as entitled to damages, recover the difference between the contract price and the price current at the time of termination as well as damages for any further loss.

III. – 3:708: Interest on late payments

(1) If payment of a sum of money is delayed, whether or not the non-performance is excused, the creditor is entitled to interest on that sum from the time when payment is due to the time of payment at the average commercial bank short-term lending rate to prime borrowers prevailing for the currency of payment at the place where payment is due.

(2) The creditor may in addition recover damages for any further loss.

III. – 3:709: When interest to be added to capital

(1) Interest payable according to the preceding Article is added to the outstanding capital every 12 months.

(2) Paragraph (1) of this Article does not apply if the parties have provided for interest upon delay in payment.

III. – 3:710: Interest in commercial contracts

(1) If a business delays the payment of a price due under a contract for the supply of goods, other assets or services without being excused under III.–3:104 (Excuse due to an impediment), interest is due at the rate specified in paragraph (4), unless a higher interest rate is applicable.

(2) Interest at the rate specified in paragraph (4) starts to run on the day which follows the date or the end of the period for payment provided in the contract. If there is no such date or period, interest at that rate starts to run:

    (a) 30 days after the date when the debtor receives the invoice or an equivalent request for payment; or

    (b) 30 days after the date of receipt of the goods or services, if the date under (a) is earlier or uncertain, or if it is uncertain whether the debtor has received an invoice or equivalent request for payment.

(3) If conformity of goods or services to the contract is to be ascertained by way of acceptance or verification, the 30 day period under paragraph (2)(b) starts to run on the date of acceptance or verification.

(4) The interest rate for delayed payment is the interest rate applied by the European Central Bank to its most recent main refinancing operation carried out before the first calendar day of the half-year in question ("the reference rate"), plus seven percentage points. For the currency of a Member State which is not participating in the third stage of economic and monetary union, the reference rate is the equivalent rate set by its national central bank.

(5) The creditor may in addition recover damages for any further loss.

III. – 3:711:   Unfair terms relating to interest

(1) A term whereby a business pays interest from a date later than that specified in the preceding Article paragraph (2) (a) and (b) and paragraph (3), or at a rate lower than that specified in paragraph (4), is not binding to the extent that this would be unfair.

(2) A term whereby a debtor is allowed to pay the price for goods, other assets or services later than the time when interest starts to run under the preceding Article paragraph (2)(a) and (b) and paragraph (3) does not deprive the creditor of interest to the extent that this would be unfair.

(3) Something is unfair for the purposes of this Article if it grossly deviates from good commercial practice, contrary to good faith and fair dealing.

III. – 3:712:   Stipulated payment for non-performance

(1) Where the terms regulating an obligation provide that a debtor who fails to perform the obligation is to pay a specified sum to the creditor for such non-performance, the creditor is entitled to that sum irrespective of the actual loss.

(2) However, despite any provision to the contrary, the sum so specified in a contract or other juridical act may be reduced to a reasonable amount where it is grossly excessive in relation to the loss resulting from the non-performance and the other circumstances.

III. – 3:713:   Currency by which damages to be measured

Damages are to be measured by the currency which most appropriately reflects the creditor's loss.

[Chapters 4 (Plurality of debtors and creditors), 5 (Change of parties), 6 (Set-off and merger) and 7 (Prescription) are omitted.]

BOOK V BENEVOLENT INTERVENTION IN ANOTHER'S AFFAIRS

Chapter 1: Scope

V. – 1:101:   Intervention to benefit another

(1) This Book applies where a person, the intervener, acts with the predominant intention of benefiting another, the principal, and:
- (a) the intervener has a reasonable ground for acting; or
- (b) the principal approves the act without such undue delay as would adversely affect the intervener.

(2) The intervener does not have a reasonable ground for acting if the intervener:
- (a) has a reasonable opportunity to discover the principal's wishes but does not do so; or
- (b) knows or can reasonably be expected to know that the intervention is against the principal's wishes.

V. – 1:102:   Intervention to perform another's duty

Where an intervener acts to perform another person's duty, the performance of which is due and urgently required as a matter of overriding public interest, and the intervener acts with the predominant intention of benefiting the recipient of the performance, the person whose duty the intervener acts to perform is a principal to whom this Book applies.

V. – 1:103:   Exclusions

This Book does not apply where the intervener:

(a) is authorised to act under a contractual or other obligation to the principal;

(b) is authorised, other than under this Book, to act independently of the principal's consent; or

(c) is under an obligation to a third party to act.

Chapter 2: Duties of intervener

V. – 2:101:   Duties during intervention

(1) During the intervention, the intervener must:

(a) act with reasonable care;

(b) except in relation to a principal within V.–1 :102 (Intervention to perform another's duty), act in a manner which the intervener knows or can reasonably be expected to assume accords with the principal's wishes; and

(c) so far as possible and reasonable, inform the principal about the intervention and seek the principal's consent to further acts.

(2) The intervention may not be discontinued without good reason.

V. – 2:102:   Reparation for damage caused by breach of duty

(1) The intervener is liable to make reparation to the principal for damage caused by breach of a duty set out in this Chapter if the damage resulted from a risk which the intervener created, increased or intentionally perpetuated.

(2) The intervener's liability is reduced or excluded in so far as this is fair and reasonable, having regard to, among other things, the intervener's reasons for acting.

(3) An intervener who at the time of intervening lacks full legal capacity is liable to make reparation only in so far as that intervener is also liable to make reparation under Book VI (Non-contractual liability arising out of damage caused to another).

V. – 2:103:   Obligations after intervention

(1) After intervening the intervener must without undue delay report and account to the principal and hand over anything obtained as a result of the intervention.

(2) If at the time of intervening the intervener lacks full legal capacity, the obligation to hand over is subject to the defence which would be available under VII.–6:101 (Disenrichment).

(3) The remedies for non-performance in Book III, Chapter 3 apply but with the modification that any liability to pay damages or interest is subject to the qualifications in paragraphs (2) and (3) of the preceding Article.

Chapter 3: Rights and authority of intervener

V. – 3:101:   Right to indemnification or reimbursement

The intervener has a right against the principal for indemnification or, as the case may be, reimbursement in respect of an obligation or expenditure (whether of money or other assets) in so far as reasonably incurred for the purposes of the intervention.

V. – 3:102:   Right to remuneration

(1) The intervener has a right to remuneration in so far as the intervention is reasonable and undertaken in the course of the intervener's profession or trade.

(2) The remuneration due is the amount, so far as reasonable, which is ordinarily paid at the time and place of intervention in order to obtain a performance of the kind undertaken. If there is no such amount a reasonable remuneration is due.

V. – 3:103:   Right to reparation

An intervener who acts to protect the principal, or the principal's property or interests, against danger has a right against the principal for reparation for loss caused as a result of personal injury or property damage suffered in acting, if:

> (a) the intervention created or significantly increased the risk of such injury or damage; and
>
> (b) that risk, so far as foreseeable, was in reasonable proportion to the risk to the principal.

V. – 3:104:   Reduction or exclusion of intervener's rights

(1) The intervener's rights are reduced or excluded in so far as the intervener at the time of acting did not want to demand indemnification, reimbursement, remuneration or reparation, as the case may be.

(2) These rights are also reduced or excluded in so far as this is fair and reasonable, having regard among other things to whether the intervener acted to protect the principal in a situation of joint danger, whether the liability of the principal would be excessive and whether the intervener could reasonably be expected to obtain appropriate redress from another.

V. – 3:105:   Obligation of third person to indemnify or reimburse the principal

If the intervener acts to protect the principal from damage, a person who would be accountable under Book VI (Non-contractual liability arising out of damage caused to another) for the causation of such damage to the principal is obliged to indemnify or, as the case may be, reimburse the principal's liability to the intervener.

V. – 3:106:   Authority of intervener to act as representative of the principal

(1) The intervener may conclude legal transactions or perform other juridical acts as a representative of the principal in so far as this may reasonably be expected to benefit the principal.

(2) However, a unilateral juridical act by the intervener as a representative of the principal has no effect if the person to whom it is addressed rejects the act without undue delay.

BOOK VI NON-CONTRACTUAL LIABILITY ARISING OUT OF DAMAGE CAUSED TO ANOTHER

Chapter 1: Fundamental provisions

VI. – 1:101:   Basic rule

(1) A person who suffers legally relevant damage has a right to reparation from a person who caused the damage intentionally or negligently or is otherwise accountable for the causation of the damage.

(2) Where a person has not caused legally relevant damage intentionally or negligently that person is accountable for the causation of legally relevant damage only if Chapter 3 so provides.

VI. – 1:102:   Prevention

Where legally relevant damage is impending, this Book confers on a person who would suffer the damage a right to prevent it. This right is against a person who would be accountable for the causation of the damage if it occurred.

VI. – 1:103:   Scope of application

VI.–1:101 (Basic rule) and VI.–1:102 (Prevention):

> (a) apply only in accordance with the following provisions of this Book;
>
> (b) apply to both legal and natural persons, unless otherwise stated;
>
> (c) do not apply in so far as their application would contradict the purpose of other private law rules; and
>
> (d) do not affect remedies available on other legal grounds.

Chapter 2: Legally relevant damage

Section 1: General

VI. – 2:101:   Meaning of legally relevant damage

(1) Loss, whether economic or non-economic, or injury is legally relevant damage if:

   (a) one of the following rules of this Chapter so provides;

   (b) the loss or injury results from a violation of a right otherwise conferred by the law; or

   (c) the loss or injury results from a violation of an interest worthy of legal protection.

(2) In any case covered only by sub-paragraphs (b) or (c) of paragraph (1) loss or injury constitutes legally relevant damage only if it would be fair and reasonable for there to be a right to reparation or prevention, as the case may be, under VI.–1:101 (Basic rule) or VI.–1:102 (Prevention).

(3) In considering whether it would be fair and reasonable for there to be a right to reparation or prevention regard is to be had to the ground of accountability, to the nature and proximity of the damage or impending damage, to the reasonable expectations of the person who suffers or would suffer the damage, and to considerations of public policy.

(4) In this Book:

   (a) economic loss includes loss of income or profit, burdens incurred and a reduction in the value of property;

   (b) non-economic loss includes pain and suffering and impairment of the quality of life.

Section 2: Particular instances of legally relevant damage

VI. – 2:201:   Personal injury and consequential loss

(1) Loss caused to a natural person as a result of injury to his or her body or health and the injury as such are legally relevant damage.

(2) In this Book:

   (a) such loss includes the costs of health care including expenses reasonably incurred for the care of the injured person by those close to him or her; and

   (b) personal injury includes injury to mental health only if it amounts to a medical condition.

VI. – 2:202:   Loss suffered by third persons as a result of another's personal injury or death

(1) Non-economic loss caused to a natural person as a result of another's personal injury or death is legally relevant damage if at the time of injury that person is in a particularly close personal relationship to the injured person.

(2) Where a person has been fatally injured:

   (a) legally relevant damage caused to the deceased on account of the injury to the time of death becomes legally relevant damage to the deceased's successors;

   (b) reasonable funeral expenses are legally relevant damage to the person incurring them; and

   (c) loss of maintenance is legally relevant damage to a natural person whom the deceased maintained or, had death not occurred, would have maintained under statutory provisions or to whom the deceased provided care and financial support.

VI. – 2:203:   Infringement of dignity, liberty and privacy

(1) Loss caused to a natural person as a result of infringement of his or her right to respect for his or her dignity, such as the rights to liberty and privacy, and the injury as such are legally relevant damage.

(2) Loss caused to a person as a result of injury to that person's reputation and the injury as such are also legally relevant damage if national law so provides.

VI. – 2:204:   Loss upon communication of incorrect information about another

Loss caused to a person as a result of the communication of information about that person which the person communicating the information knows or could reasonably be expected to know is incorrect is legally relevant damage.

VI. – 2:205:   Loss upon breach of confidence
Loss caused to a person as a result of the communication of information which, either from its nature or the circumstances in which it was obtained, the person communicating the information knows or could reasonably be expected to know is confidential to the person suffering the loss is legally relevant damage.

VI. – 2:206:   Loss upon infringement of property or lawful possession
(1) Loss caused to a person as a result of an infringement of that person's property right or lawful possession of a movable or immovable thing is legally relevant damage.
(2) In this Article:
   (a) loss includes being deprived of the use of property;
   (b) infringement of a property right includes destruction of or physical damage to the subject-matter of the right (property damage), disposition of the right, interference with its use and other disturbance of the exercise of the right.

VI. – 2:207:   Loss upon reliance on incorrect advice or information
Loss caused to a person as a result of making a decision in reasonable reliance on incorrect advice or information is legally relevant damage if:
   (a) the advice or information is provided by a person in pursuit of a profession or in the course of trade; and
   (b) the provider knew or could reasonably be expected to have known that the recipient would rely on the advice or information in making a decision of the kind made.

VI. – 2:208:   Loss upon unlawful impairment of business
(1) Loss caused to a person as a result of an unlawful impairment of that person's exercise of a profession or conduct of a trade is legally relevant damage.
(2) Loss caused to a consumer as a result of unfair competition is also legally relevant damage if Community or national law so provides.

VI. – 2:209:   Burdens incurred by the state upon environmental impairment
Burdens incurred by the State or designated competent authorities in restoring substantially impaired natural elements constituting the environment, such as air, water, soil, flora and fauna, are legally relevant damage to the State or the authorities concerned.

VI. – 2:210:   Loss upon fraudulent misrepresentation
(1) Without prejudice to the other provisions of this Section loss caused to a person as a result of another's fraudulent misrepresentation, whether by words or conduct, is legally relevant damage.
(2) A misrepresentation is fraudulent if it is made with knowledge or belief that the representation is false and it is intended to induce the recipient to make a mistake.

VI. – 2:211:   Loss upon inducement of non-performance of obligation
Without prejudice to the other provisions of this Section, loss caused to a person as a result of another's inducement of the non-performance of an obligation by a third person is legally relevant damage only if:
   (a) the obligation was owed to the person sustaining the loss; and
   (b) the person inducing the non-performance:
      (i)   intended the third person to fail to perform the obligation, and
      (ii) did not act in legitimate protection of the inducing person's own interest.

Chapter 3: Accountability

Section 1: Intention and negligence

VI. – 3:101:   Intention
A person causes legally relevant damage intentionally when that person causes such damage either:
   (a) meaning to cause damage of the type caused; or
   (b) by conduct which that person means to do, knowing that such damage, or damage of that type, will or will almost certainly be caused.

VI. – 3:102:   Negligence

A person causes legally relevant damage negligently when that person causes the damage by conduct which either:

    (a) does not meet the particular standard of care provided by a statutory provision whose purpose is the protection of the person suffering the damage from that damage; or

    (b) does not otherwise amount to such care as could be expected from a reasonably careful person in the circumstances of the case.

VI. – 3:103:   Persons under eighteen

(1) A person under eighteen years of age is accountable for causing legally relevant damage according to VI.–3:102 (Negligence) sub-paragraph (b) only in so far as that person does not exercise such care as could be expected from a reasonably careful person of the same age in the circumstances of the case.

(2) A person under seven years of age is not accountable for causing damage intentionally or negligently.

(3) However, paragraphs (1) and (2) do not apply to the extent that:

    (a) the person suffering the damage cannot obtain reparation under this Book from another; and

    (b) liability to make reparation would be equitable having regard to the financial means of the parties and all other circumstances of the case.

VI. – 3:104:   Accountability for damage caused by children or supervised persons

(1) Parents or other persons obliged by law to provide parental care for a person under fourteen years of age are accountable for the causation of legally relevant damage where that person under age caused the damage by conduct that would constitute intentional or negligent conduct if it were the conduct of an adult.

(2) An institution or other body obliged to supervise a person is accountable for the causation of legally relevant damage suffered by a third party when:

    (a) the damage is personal injury, loss within VI.–2:202 (Loss suffered by third persons as a result of another's personal injury or death) or property damage;

    (b) the person whom the institution or other body is obliged to supervise caused that damage intentionally or negligently or, in the case of a person under eighteen, by conduct that would constitute intention or negligence if it were the conduct of an adult; and

    (c) the person whom the institution or other body is obliged to supervise is a person likely to cause damage of that type.

(3) However, a person is not accountable under this Article for the causation of damage if that person shows that there was no defective supervision of the person causing the damage.

Section 2: Accountability without intention or negligence

VI. – 3:201:   Accountability for damage caused by employees and representatives

(1) A person who employs or similarly engages another is accountable for the causation of legally relevant damage suffered by a third person when the person employed or engaged:

    (a) caused the damage in the course of the employment or engagement; and

    (b) caused the damage intentionally or negligently, or is otherwise accountable for the causation of the damage.

(2) Paragraph (1) applies correspondingly to a legal person in relation to a representative causing damage in the course of their engagement. A representative is a person who is authorised to effect juridical acts on behalf of the legal person by its constitution.

VI. – 3:202: Accountability for damage caused by the unsafe state of an immovable

(1) A person who independently exercises control over an immovable is accountable for the causation of personal injury and consequential loss, loss within VI.–2:202 (Loss suffered by third persons as a result of another's personal injury or death), and loss resulting from property damage (other than to the immovable itself) by a state of the immovable which does not ensure such safety as a person in or near the immovable is entitled to expect having regard to the circumstances including:

    (a) the nature of the immovable;

    (b) the access to the immovable; and

    (c) the cost of avoiding the immovable being in that state.

(2) A person exercises independent control over an immovable if that person exercises such control that it is reasonable to impose a duty on that person to prevent legally relevant damage within the scope of this Article.

(3) The owner of the immovable is to be regarded as independently exercising control, unless the owner shows that another independently exercises control.

VI. – 3:203: Accountability for damage caused by animals

A keeper of an animal is accountable for the causation by the animal of personal injury and consequential loss, loss within VI.–2:202 (Loss suffered by third persons as a result of another's personal injury or death), and loss resulting from property damage.

VI. – 3:204: Accountability for damage caused by defective products

(1) The producer of a product is accountable for the causation of personal injury and consequential loss, loss within VI.–2:202 (Loss suffered by third persons as a result of another's personal injury or death), and, in relation to consumers, loss resulting from property damage (other than to the product itself) by a defect in the product.

(2) A person who imported the product into the European Economic Area for sale, hire, leasing or distribution in the course of that person's business is accountable correspondingly.

(3) A supplier of the product is accountable correspondingly if:

    (a) the producer cannot be identified; or

    (b) in the case of an imported product, the product does not indicate the identity of the importer (whether or not the producer's name is indicated), unless the supplier informs the person suffering the damage, within a reasonable time, of the identity of the producer or the person who supplied that supplier with the product.

(4) A person is not accountable under this Article for the causation of damage if that person shows that:

    (a) that person did not put the product into circulation;

    (b) it is probable that the defect which caused the damage did not exist at the time when that person put the product into circulation;

    (c) that person neither manufactured the product for sale or distribution for economic purpose nor manufactured or distributed it in the course of business;

    (d) the defect is due to the product's compliance with mandatory regulations issued by public authorities;

    (e) the state of scientific and technical knowledge at the time that person put the product into circulation did not enable the existence of the defect to be discovered; or

    (f) in the case of a manufacturer of a component, the defect is attributable to:

        (i) the design of the product into which the component has been fitted; or

        (ii) instructions given by the manufacturer of the product.

(5) "Producer" means:

    (a) in the case of a finished product or a component, the manufacturer;

    (b) in the case of raw material, the person who abstracts or wins it; and

    (c) any person who, by putting a name, trade mark or other distinguishing feature on the product, gives the impression of being its producer.

(6) "Product" means a movable, even if incorporated into another movable or an immovable, or electricity.

(7) A product is defective if it does not provide the safety which a person is entitled to expect, having regard to the circumstances including:

    (a) the presentation of the product;

    (b) the use to which it could reasonably be expected that the product would be put; and

    (c) the time when the product was put into circulation,

but a product is not defective merely because a better product is subsequently put into circulation.

VI. – 3:205:   Accountability for damage caused by motor vehicles

(1) A keeper of a motor vehicle is accountable for the causation of personal injury and consequential loss, loss within VI.–2:202 (Loss suffered by third persons as a result of another's personal injury or death), and loss resulting from property damage (other than to the vehicle and its freight) in a traffic accident which results from the use of the vehicle.

(2) "Motor vehicle" means any vehicle intended for travel on land and propelled by mechanical power, but not running on rails, and any trailer, whether or not coupled.

VI. – 3:206:   Accountability for damage caused by dangerous substances or emissions

(1) A keeper of a substance or an operator of an installation is accountable for the causation by that substance or by emissions from that installation of personal injury and consequential loss, loss within VI.–2:202 (Loss suffered by third persons as a result of another's personal injury or death), loss resulting from property damage, and burdens within VI.–2:209 (Burdens incurred by the State upon environmental impairment), if:

    (a) having regard to their quantity and attributes, at the time of the emission, or, failing an emission, at the time of contact with the substance it is very likely that the substance or emission will cause such damage unless adequately controlled; and

    (b) the damage results from the realisation of that danger.

(2) "Substance" includes chemicals (whether solid, liquid or gaseous). Microorganisms are to be treated like substances.

(3) "Emission" includes:

    (a) the release or escape of substances;

    (b) the conduction of electricity;

    (c) heat, light and other radiation;

    (d) noise and other vibrations; and

    (e) other incorporeal impact on the environment.

(4) "Installation" includes a mobile installation and an installation under construction or not in use.

(5) However, a person is not accountable for the causation of damage under this Article if that person:

    (a) does not keep the substance or operate the installation for purposes related to that person's trade, business or profession; or

    (b) shows that there was no failure to comply with statutory standards of control of the substance or management of the installation.

VI. – 3:207:   Other accountability for the causation of legally relevant damage

A person is also accountable for the causation of legally relevant damage if national law so provides where it:

    (a) relates to a source of danger which is not within VI.–3:104 (Accountability for damage caused by children or supervised persons) to VI.–3:205 (Accountability for damage caused by motor vehicles);

    (b) relates to substances or emissions; or

    (c) disapplies VI.–3:204 (Accountability for damage caused by defective products) paragraph (4)(e).

VI. – 3:208:   Abandonment

For the purposes of this section, a person remains accountable for an immovable, vehicle, substance or installation which that person abandons until another exercises independent control over it or becomes its keeper or operator. This applies correspondingly, so far as reasonable, in respect of a keeper of an animal.

Chapter 4: Causation

VI. – 4:101:   General rule

(1) A person causes legally relevant damage to another if the damage is to be regarded as a consequence of that person's conduct or the source of danger for which that person is responsible.

(2) In cases of personal injury or death the injured person's predisposition with respect to the type or extent of the injury sustained is to be disregarded.

VI. – 4:102:   Collaboration

A person who participates with, instigates or materially assists another in causing legally relevant damage is to be regarded as causing that damage.

VI. – 4:103:   Alternative causes

Where legally relevant damage may have been caused by any one or more of a number of occurrences for which different persons are accountable and it is established that the damage was caused by one of these occurrences but not which one, each person who is accountable for any of the occurrences is rebuttably presumed to have caused that damage.

Chapter 5: Defences

Section 1: Consent or conduct of the person suffering the damage

VI. – 5:101:   Consent and acting at own risk

(1) A person has a defence if the person suffering the damage validly consents to the legally relevant damage and is aware or could reasonably be expected to be aware of the consequences of that consent.

(2) The same applies if the person suffering the damage, knowing the risk of damage of the type caused, voluntarily takes that risk and is to be regarded as accepting it.

VI. – 5:102:   Contributory fault and accountability

(1) Where the fault of the person suffering the damage contributes to the occurrence or extent of legally relevant damage, reparation is to be reduced according to the degree of such fault.

(2) However, no regard is to be had to:

  (a) an insubstantial fault of the person suffering the damage;
  (b) fault or accountability whose contribution to the causation of the damage is insubstantial;
  (c) the injured person's want of care contributing to that person's personal injury caused by a motor vehicle in a traffic accident, unless that want of care constitutes profound failure to take such care as is manifestly required in the circumstances.

(3) Paragraphs (1) and (2) apply correspondingly where the fault of a person for whom the person suffering the damage is responsible within the scope of VI.–3:201 (Accountability for damage caused by employees and representatives) contributes to the occurrence or extent of the damage.

(4) Compensation is to be reduced likewise if and in so far as any other source of danger for which the person suffering the damage is responsible under Chapter 3 (Accountability) contributes to the occurrence or extent of the damage.

VI. – 5:103:   Damage caused by a criminal to a collaborator

Legally relevant damage caused unintentionally in the course of committing a criminal offence to another person participating or otherwise collaborating in the offence does not give rise to a right to reparation if this would be contrary to public policy.

Section 2: Interests of accountable persons or third parties

VI. – 5:201:   Authority conferred by law

A person has a defence if legally relevant damage is caused with authority conferred by law.

VI. – 5:202:   Self-defence, benevolent intervention and necessity

(1) A person has a defence if that person causes legally relevant damage in reasonable protection of a right or of an interest worthy of legal protection of that person or a third person if the person suffering the legally relevant damage is accountable for endangering the right or interest protected. For the purposes of this paragraph VI.–3:103 (Persons under eighteen) is to be disregarded.

(2) The same applies to legally relevant damage caused by a benevolent intervener to a principal without breach of the intervener's duties.

(3) Where a person causes legally relevant damage to the patrimony of another in a situation of imminent danger to life, body, health or liberty in order to save the person causing the damage or a third person from that danger and the danger could not be eliminated without causing the damage, the person causing the damage is not liable to make reparation beyond providing reasonable recompense.

VI. – 5:203:   Protection of public interest

A person has a defence if legally relevant damage is caused in necessary protection of values fundamental to a democratic society, in particular where damage is caused by dissemination of information in the media.

Section 3: Inability to control

VI. – 5:301:   Mental incompetence

(1) A person who is mentally incompetent at the time of conduct causing legally relevant damage is liable only if this is equitable, having regard to the mentally incompetent person's financial means and all the other circumstances of the case. Liability is limited to reasonable recompense.

(2) A person is to be regarded as mentally incompetent if that person lacks sufficient insight into the nature of his or her conduct, unless the lack of sufficient insight is the temporary result of his or her own misconduct.

VI. – 5:302:   Event beyond control

A person has a defence if legally relevant damage is caused by an abnormal event which cannot be averted by any reasonable measure and which is not to be regarded as that person's risk.

Section 4: Contractual exclusion and restriction of liability

VI. – 5:401:   Contractual exclusion and restriction of liability

(1) Liability for causing legally relevant damage intentionally cannot be excluded or restricted.

(2) Liability for causing legally relevant damage as a result of a profound failure to take such care as is manifestly required in the circumstances cannot be excluded or restricted:

(a) in respect of personal injury (including fatal injury); or

(b) if the exclusion or restriction is otherwise illegal or contrary to good faith and fair dealing.

(3) Liability for damage for the causation of which a person is accountable under VI.–3:204 (Accountability for damage caused by defective products) cannot be restricted or excluded.

(4) Other liability under this Book can be excluded or restricted unless statute provides otherwise.

Section 5: Loss within VI.–2:202
(Loss suffered by third persons as a result of another's personal injury or death)

VI. – 5:501:   Extension of defences against the injured person to third persons

A defence which may be asserted against a person's right of reparation in respect of that person's personal injury or, if death had not occurred, could have been asserted, may also be asserted against a person suffering loss within VI.–2:202 (Loss suffered by third persons as a result of another's personal injury or death).

Chapter 6: Remedies

Section 1: Reparation in general

VI. – 6:101: Aim and forms of reparation

(1) Reparation is to reinstate the person suffering the legally relevant damage in the position that person would have been in had the legally relevant damage not occurred.

(2) Reparation may be in money (compensation) or otherwise, as is most appropriate, having regard to the kind and extent of damage suffered and all the other circumstances of the case.

(3) Where a tangible object is damaged, compensation equal to its depreciation of value is to be awarded instead of the cost of its repair if the cost of repair unreasonably exceeds the depreciation of value. This rule applies to animals only if appropriate, having regard to the purpose for which the animal was kept.

(4) As an alternative to reinstatement under paragraph (1), but only where this is reasonable, reparation may take the form of recovery from the person accountable for the causation of the legally relevant damage of any advantage obtained by the latter in connection with causing the damage.

VI. – 6:102: De minimis rule

Trivial damage is to be disregarded.

VI. – 6:103: Equalisation of benefits

(1) Benefits arising to the person suffering legally relevant damage as a result of the damaging event are to be disregarded unless it would be fair and reasonable to take them into account.

(2) In deciding whether it would be fair and reasonable to take the benefits into account, regard shall be had to the kind of damage sustained, the nature of the accountability of the person causing the damage and, where the benefits are conferred by a third person, the purpose of conferring those benefits.

VI. – 6:104: Multiple persons suffering damage

Where multiple persons suffer legally relevant damage and reparation to one person will also make reparation to another, Book III, Chapter 4, Section 2 (Plurality of creditors) applies with appropriate adaptation to their rights to reparation.

VI. – 6:105: Solidary liability

Where several persons are liable for the same legally relevant damage, they are liable solidarily.

VI. – 6:106: Assignment of right to reparation

The person suffering the damage may assign a right to reparation, including a right to reparation for non-economic loss.

Section 2: Compensation

VI. – 6:201: Right of election

The person suffering the damage may choose whether or not to spend compensation on the reinstatement of the damaged interest.

VI. – 6:202: Reduction of liability

Where it is fair and reasonable to do so, a person may be relieved of liability to compensate, either wholly or in part, if, where the damage is not caused intentionally, liability in full would be disproportionate to the accountability of the person causing the damage or the extent of the damage or the means to prevent it.

VI. – 6:203: Capitalisation and quantification

(1) Compensation is to be awarded as a lump sum unless a good reason requires periodical payment.

(2) National law determines how compensation for personal injury and non-economic loss is to be quantified.

VI. – 6:204:   Compensation for injury as such
Injury as such is to be compensated independent of compensation for economic or non-economic loss.

Section 3: Prevention

VI. – 6:301:   Right to prevention
(1) The right to prevention exists only in so far as:
    (a) reparation would not be an adequate alternative remedy; and
    (b) it is reasonable for the person who would be accountable for the causation of the damage to prevent it from occurring.
(2) Where the source of danger is an object or an animal and it is not reasonably possible for the endangered person to avoid the danger the right to prevention includes a right to have the source of danger removed.

VI. – 6:302:   Liability for loss in preventing damage
A person who has reasonably incurred expenditure or sustained other loss in order to prevent that person from suffering an impending damage, or in order to limit the extent or severity of damage suffered, has a right to compensation from the person who would have been accountable for the causation of the damage.

Chapter 7: Ancillary rules

VI. – 7:101:   National constitutional laws
The provisions of this Book are to be interpreted and applied in a manner compatible with the constitutional law of the court.

VI. – 7:102:   Statutory provisions
National law determines what legal provisions are statutory provisions.

VI. – 7:103:   Public law functions and court proceedings
This Book does not govern the liability of a person or body arising from the exercise or omission to exercise public law functions or from performing duties during court proceedings.

VI. – 7:104:   Liability of employees, employers, trade unions and employers' associations
This Book does not govern the liability of:
    (a) employees (whether to co-employees, employers or third parties) arising in the course of employment;
    (b) employers to employees arising in the course of employment; and
    (c) trade unions and employers' associations arising in the course of an industrial dispute.

VI. – 7:105:   Reduction or exclusion of liability to indemnified persons
If a person is entitled from another source to reparation, whether in full or in part, for that person's damage, in particular from an insurer, fund or other body, national law determines whether or not by virtue of that entitlement liability under this Book is limited or excluded.

BOOK VII UNJUSTIFIED ENRICHMENT

Chapter 1: General

VII. – 1:101:   Basic rule
(1) A person who obtains an unjustified enrichment which is attributable to another's disadvantage is obliged to that other to reverse the enrichment.
(2) This rule applies only in accordance with the following provisions of this Book.

Chapter 2: When enrichment unjustified

VII. – 2:101: Circumstances in which an enrichment is unjustified

    (1) An enrichment is unjustified unless:

        (a) the enriched person is entitled as against the disadvantaged person to the enrichment by virtue of a contract or other juridical act, a court order or a rule of law; or

        (b) the disadvantaged person consented freely and without error to the disadvantage.

    (2) If the contract or other juridical act, court order or rule of law referred to in paragraph (1)(a) is void or avoided or otherwise rendered ineffective retrospectively, the enriched person is not entitled to the enrichment on that basis.

    (3) However, the enriched person is to be regarded as entitled to an enrichment by virtue of a rule of law only if the policy of that rule is that the enriched person is to retain the value of the enrichment.

    (4) An enrichment is also unjustified if:

        (a) the disadvantaged person conferred it:

            (i)   for a purpose which is not achieved; or

            (ii) with an expectation which is not realised;

        (b) the enriched person knew of, or could reasonably be expected to know of, the purpose or expectation; and

        (c) the enriched person accepted or could reasonably be assumed to have accepted that the enrichment must be reversed in such circumstances.

VII. – 2:102: Performance of obligation to third person

Where the enriched person obtains the enrichment as a result of the disadvantaged person performing an obligation or a supposed obligation owed by the disadvantaged person to a third person, the enrichment is justified if:

        (a) the disadvantaged person performed freely; or

        (b) the enrichment was merely the incidental result of performance of the obligation.

VII. – 2:103: Consenting or performing freely

    (1) If the disadvantaged person's consent is affected by incapacity, fraud, coercion, threats or unfair exploitation, the disadvantaged person does not consent freely.

    (2) If the obligation which is performed is ineffective because of incapacity, fraud, coercion threats or unfair exploitation, the disadvantaged person does not perform freely.

Chapter 3: Enrichment and disadvantage

VII. – 3:101: Enrichment

    (1) A person is enriched by:

        (a) an increase in assets or a decrease in liabilities;

        (b) receiving a service or having work done; or

        (c) use of another's assets.

    (2) In determining whether and to what extent a person obtains an enrichment, no regard is to be had to any disadvantage which that person sustains in exchange for or after the enrichment.

VII. – 3:102: Disadvantage

    (1) A person is disadvantaged by:

        (a) a decrease in assets or an increase in liabilities;

        (b) rendering a service or doing work; or

        (c) another's use of that person's assets.

    (2) In determining whether and to what extent a person sustains a disadvantage, no regard is to be had to any enrichment which that person obtains in exchange for or after the disadvantage.

Chapter 4: Attribution

VII. – 4:101: Instances of attribution

An enrichment is attributable to another's disadvantage in particular where:

    (a) an asset of that other is transferred to the enriched person by that other;
    (b) a service is rendered to or work is done for the enriched person by that other;
    (c) the enriched person uses that other's asset, especially where the enriched person infringes the disadvantaged person's rights or legally protected interests;
    (d) an asset of the enriched person is improved by that other; or
    (e) the enriched person is discharged from a liability by that other.

VII. – 4:102: Intermediaries

Where one party to a juridical act is an authorised intermediary indirectly representing a principal, any enrichment or disadvantage of the principal which results from the juridical act, or from a performance of obligations under it, is to be regarded as an enrichment or disadvantage of the intermediary.

VII. – 4:103: Debtor's performance to a non-creditor; onward transfer in good faith

(1) An enrichment is also attributable to another's disadvantage where a debtor confers the enrichment on the enriched person and as a result the disadvantaged person loses a right against the debtor to the same or a like enrichment.

(2) Paragraph (1) applies in particular where a person who is obliged to the disadvantaged person to reverse an unjustified enrichment transfers it to a third person in circumstances in which the debtor has a defence under VII.–6:101 (Disenrichment).

VII. – 4:104: Ratification of debtor's performance to a non-creditor

(1) Where a debtor purports to discharge a debt by paying a third person, the creditor may ratify that act.

(2) Ratification extinguishes the creditor's right against the debtor to the extent of the payment with the effect that the third person's enrichment is attributable to the creditor's loss of the claim against the debtor.

(3) As between the creditor and the third person, ratification does not amount to consent to the loss of the creditor's right against the debtor.

(4) This Article applies correspondingly to performances of non-monetary obligations.

(5) Other rules may exclude the application of this Article if an insolvency or equivalent proceeding has been opened against the debtor before the creditor ratifies.

VII. – 4:105: Attribution resulting from an act of an intervener

(1) An enrichment is also attributable to another's disadvantage where a third person uses an asset of the disadvantaged person without authority so that the disadvantaged person is deprived of the asset and it accrues to the enriched person.

(2) Paragraph (1) applies in particular where, as a result of an intervener's interference with or disposition of goods, the disadvantaged person ceases to be owner of the goods and the enriched person becomes owner, whether by juridical act or rule of law.

VII. – 4:106: Ratification of intervener's acts

(1) A person entitled to an asset may ratify the act of an intervener who purports to dispose of or otherwise uses that asset in a juridical act with a third person.

(2) The ratified act has the same effect as a juridical act by an authorised intermediary. As between the person ratifying and the intervener, ratification does not amount to consent to the intervener's use of the asset.

VII. – 4:107:   Where type or value not identical

An enrichment may be attributable to another's disadvantage even though the enrichment and disadvantage are not of the same type or value.

Chapter 5: Reversal of enrichment

VII. – 5:101:   Transferable enrichment

(1) Where the enrichment consists of a transferable asset, the enriched person reverses the enrichment by transferring the asset to the disadvantaged person.

(2) Instead of transferring the asset, the enriched person may choose to reverse the enrichment by paying its monetary value to the disadvantaged person if a transfer would cause the enriched person unreasonable effort or expense.

(3) If the enriched person is no longer able to transfer the asset, the enriched person reverses the enrichment by paying its monetary value to the disadvantaged person.

(4) However, to the extent that the enriched person has obtained a substitute in exchange, the substitute is the enrichment to be reversed if:

    (a) the enriched person is in good faith at the time of disposal or loss and the enriched person so chooses; or

    (b) the enriched person is not in good faith at the time of disposal or loss, the disadvantaged person so chooses and the choice is not inequitable.

(5) The enriched person is in good faith if that person neither knew nor could reasonably be expected to know that the enrichment was or was likely to become unjustified.

VII. – 5:102:   Non-transferable enrichment

(1) Where the enrichment does not consist of a transferable asset, the enriched person reverses the enrichment by paying its monetary value to the disadvantaged person.

(2) The enriched person is not liable to pay more than any saving if the enriched person:

    (a) did not consent to the enrichment; or

    (b) was in good faith.

(3) However, where the enrichment was obtained under an agreement which fixed a price or value for the enrichment, the enriched person is at least liable to pay that sum if the agreement was void or voidable for reasons which were not material to the fixing of the price.

(4) Paragraph (3) does not apply so as to increase liability beyond the monetary value of the enrichment.

VII. – 5:103:   Monetary value of an enrichment; saving

(1) The monetary value of an enrichment is the sum of money which a provider and a recipient with a real intention of reaching an agreement would lawfully have agreed as its price. Expenditure of a service provider which the agreement would require the recipient to reimburse is to be regarded as part of the price.

(2) A saving is the decrease in assets or increase in liabilities which the enriched person would have sustained if the enrichment had not been obtained.

VII. – 5:104:   Fruits and use of an enrichment

(1) Reversal of the enrichment extends to the fruits and use of the enrichment or, if less, any saving resulting from the fruits or use.

(2) However, if the enriched person obtains the fruits or use in bad faith, reversal of the enrichment extends to the fruits and use even if the saving is less than the value of the fruits or use.

Chapter 6: Defences

VII. – 6:101:   Disenrichment

(1) The enriched person is not liable to reverse the enrichment to the extent that the enriched person has sustained a disadvantage by disposing of the enrichment or otherwise (disenrichment),

unless the enriched person would have been disenriched even if the enrichment had not been obtained.

(2) However, a disenrichment is to be disregarded to the extent that:

    (a) the enriched person has obtained a substitute;

    (b) the enriched person was not in good faith at the time of disenrichment, unless:

        (i) the disadvantaged person would also have been disenriched even if the enrichment had been reversed; or

        (ii) the enriched person was in good faith at the time of enrichment, the disenrichment was sustained before performance of the obligation to reverse the enrichment was due and the disenrichment resulted from the realisation of a risk for which the enriched person is not to be regarded as responsible; or

    (c) paragraph (3) of VII.–5:102 (Non-transferable enrichment) applies.

(3) Where the enriched person has a defence under this Article as against the disadvantaged person as a result of a disposal to a third person, any right of the disadvantaged person against that third person is unaffected.

VII. – 6:102: Juridical acts in good faith with third parties

The enriched person is also not liable to reverse the enrichment if:

    (a) in exchange for that enrichment the enriched person confers another enrichment on a third person; and

    (b) the enriched person is still in good faith at that time.

VII. – 6:103: Illegality

Where a contract or other juridical act under which an enrichment is obtained is void or avoided because of an infringement of a fundamental principle (II. – 7:301 (Contracts infringing fundamental principles)) or mandatory rule of law, the enriched person is not liable to reverse the enrichment to the extent that the reversal would contravene the policy underlying the principle or rule.

Chapter 7: Relation to other legal rules

VII. – 7:101: Other private law rights to recover

(1) The legal consequences of an enrichment which is obtained by virtue of a contract or other juridical act are governed by other rules if those rules grant or exclude a right to reversal of an enrichment, whether on withdrawal, termination, price reduction or otherwise.

(2) This Book does not address the proprietary effect of a right to reversal of an enrichment.

(3) This Book does not affect any other right to recover arising under contractual or other rules of private law.

VII. – 7:102: Concurrent obligations

(1) Where the disadvantaged person has both:

    (a) a claim under this Book for reversal of an unjustified enrichment; and

    (b) (i) a claim for reparation for the disadvantage (whether against the enriched person or a third party); or

        (ii) a right to recover under other rules of private law as a result of the unjustified enrichment,

the satisfaction of one of the claims reduces the other claim by the same amount.

(2) The same applies where a person uses an asset of the disadvantaged person so that it accrues to another and under this Book:

    (a) the user is liable to the disadvantaged person in respect of the use of the asset; and

    (b) the recipient is liable to the disadvantaged person in respect of the increase in assets.

VII. – 7:103: Public law claims

This Book does not determine whether it applies to enrichments which a person or body obtains or confers in the exercise of public law functions.

ANNEX DEFINITIONS

Advanced electronic signature An "advanced electronic signature" is an electronic signature which is (a) uniquely linked to the signatory (b) capable of identifying the signatory (c) created using means which can be maintained under the signatory's sole control; and (d) linked to the data to which it relates in such a manner that any subsequent change of the data is detectable. (I.–1:108(4))

Agent An "agent" is a person who is authorised to act for another.

Assets "Assets" means anything of economic value, including property; rights having a monetary value; and goodwill.

Assignment "Assignment", in relation to a right, means the transfer of the right by one person, the "assignor", to another, "the assignee". (III.–5:102(1))

Avoidance "Avoidance" of a juridical act or legal relationship is the process whereby a party or, as the case may be, a court invokes a ground of invalidity so as to make the act or relationship, which has been valid until that point, retrospectively ineffective from the beginning.

Barter, contract for A contract for the "barter" of goods is a contract under which each party undertakes to transfer the ownership of goods, either immediately on conclusion of the contract or at some future time, in return for the transfer of ownership of other goods. (IV. A.–1:203)

Benevolent intervention in another's affairs "Benevolent intervention in another's affairs" is the process whereby a person, the intervener, acts with the predominant intention of benefiting another, the principal, but without being authorised or bound to do so. (V.–1:101)

Business "Business" means any natural or legal person, irrespective of whether publicly or privately owned, who is acting for purposes relating to the person's self-employed trade, work or profession, even if the person does not intend to make a profit in the course of the activity. (I.–1:106(2))

Claim A "claim" is a demand for something based on the assertion of a right.

Claimant A "claimant" is a person who makes, or who has grounds for making, a claim.

Commercial agency A "commercial agency" is the legal relationship arising from a contract under which one party, the commercial agent, agrees to act on a continuing basis as a self-employed intermediary to negotiate or to conclude contracts on behalf of another party, the principal, and the principal agrees to remunerate the agent for those activities. (IV. E.–3:101)

Compensation "Compensation" means reparation in money. (VI.–6:101(2))

Complete substitution of debtor There is complete substitution of a debtor when a third person is substituted as debtor with the effect that the original debtor is discharged. (III.–5:203)

Condition A "condition" is a provision which makes a legal relationship or effect depend on the occurrence or non-occurrence of an uncertain future event. A condition may be suspensive or resolutive. (III.–1:106)

Conduct "Conduct" means voluntary behaviour of any kind, verbal or nonverbal: it includes a single act or a number of acts, behaviour of a negative or passive nature (such as accepting something without protest or not doing something) and behaviour of a continuing or intermittent nature (such as exercising control over something).

Confidential information "Confidential information" means information which, either from its nature or the circumstances in which it was obtained, the party receiving the information knows or could reasonably be expected to know is confidential to the other party. (II.–2:302(2))

Consumer A "consumer" means any natural person who is acting primarily for purposes which are not related to his or her trade, business or profession. (I.–1:106(1))

Consumer contract for sale A "consumer contract for sale" is a contract for sale in which the seller is a business and the buyer is a consumer. (IV. A.–1:204)

Contract A "contract" is an agreement which is intended to give rise to a binding legal relationship or to have some other legal effect. It is a bilateral or multilateral juridical act. (II.–1:101(1))

Contractual obligation A "contractual obligation" is an obligation which arises from a contract, whether from an express term or an implied term or by operation of a rule of law imposing an obligation on a contracting party as such.

Contractual relationship   A "contractual relationship" is a legal relationship resulting from a contract.

Co-ownership   "Co-ownership", when created under Book VIII, means that two or more co-owners own undivided shares in the whole and each co-owner can dispose of that co-owner's share by acting alone, unless otherwise provided by the parties. (Cf. VIII.–1:203)

Corporeal   "Corporeal", in relation to property, means having a physical existence in solid, liquid or gaseous form.

Costs   "Costs" includes expenses.

Counter-performance   A "counter-performance" is a performance which is due in exchange for another performance.

Court   "Court" includes an arbitral tribunal.

Creditor   A "creditor" is a person who has a right to performance of an obligation, whether monetary or non-monetary, by another person, the debtor.

Damage   "Damage" means any type of detrimental effect.

Damages   "Damages" means a sum of money to which a person may be entitled, or which a person may be awarded by a court, as compensation for some specified type of damage.

Debtor   A "debtor" is a person who has an obligation, whether monetary or non-monetary, to another person, the creditor.

Default   "Default", in relation to proprietary security, means any non-performance by the debtor of the obligation covered by the security; and any other event or set of circumstances agreed by the secured creditor and the security provider as entitling the secured creditor to have recourse to the security. (IX.–1:201(5))

Defence   A "defence" to a claim is a legal objection or a factual argument, other than a mere denial of an element which the claimant has to prove which, if well-founded, defeats the claim in whole or in part.

Delivery   "Delivery" to a person, for the purposes of any obligation to deliver goods, means transferring possession of the goods to that person or taking such steps to transfer possession as are required by the terms regulating the obligation. . . . .

Direct physical control   Direct physical control is physical control which is exercised by the possessor personally or through a possession-agent exercising such control on behalf of the possessor (direct possession). (VIII.–1:205)

Discrimination   "Discrimination" means any conduct whereby, or situation where, on grounds such as sex or ethnic or racial origin, (a) one person is treated less favourably than another person is, has been or would be treated in a comparable situation; or (b) an apparently neutral provision, criterion or practice would place one group of persons at a particular disadvantage when compared to a different group of persons. (II.–2:102(1))

Divided obligation   An obligation owed by two or more debtors is a "divided obligation" when each debtor is bound to render only part of the performance and the creditor may require from each debtor only that debtor's part. (III.–4:102(2))

Divided right   A right to performance held by two or more creditors is a "divided right" when the debtor owes each creditor only that creditor's share and each creditor may require performance only of that creditor's share. (III.–4:202(2))

Durable medium   A "durable medium" means any material on which information is stored so that it is accessible for future reference for a period of time adequate to the purposes of the information, and which allows the unchanged reproduction of this information. (I.–1:107(3))

Duty   A person has a "duty" to do something if the person is bound to do it or expected to do it according to an applicable normative standard of conduct. A duty may or may not be owed to a specific creditor. A duty is not necessarily an aspect of a legal relationship. There is not necessarily a sanction for breach of a duty. All obligations are duties, but not all duties are obligations.

Economic loss   See "Loss".

Electronic   "Electronic" means relating to technology with electrical, digital, magnetic, wireless, optical, electromagnetic, or similar capabilities.

Electronic signature   An "electronic signature" means data in electronic form which are attached to, or logically associated with, other data and which serve as a method of authentication. (I.–1:108(3))

Fraudulent   A misrepresentation is fraudulent if it is made with knowledge or belief that it is false and is intended to induce the recipient to make a mistake to the recipient's prejudice. A non-disclosure is fraudulent if it is intended to induce the person from whom the information is withheld to make a mistake to that person's prejudice. (II.–7:205(2))

Fundamental non-performance   A non-performance of a contractual obligation is fundamental if (a) it substantially deprives the creditor of what the creditor was entitled to expect under the contract, as applied to the whole or relevant part of the performance, unless at the time of conclusion of the contract the debtor did not foresee and could not reasonably be expected to have foreseen that result or (b) it is intentional or reckless and gives the creditor reason to believe that the debtor's future performance cannot be relied on. (III.–3:502(2))

Good faith   "Good faith" is a mental attitude characterised by honesty and an absence of knowledge that an apparent situation is not the true situation.

Good faith and fair dealing   "Good faith and fair dealing" is a standard of conduct characterised by honesty, openness and consideration for the interests of the other party to the transaction or relationship in question. (I.–1:103)

Goods   "Goods" means corporeal movables. It includes ships, vessels, hovercraft or aircraft, space objects, animals, liquids and gases. See also "movables".

Gross negligence   There is "gross negligence" if a person is guilty of a profound failure to take such care as is self-evidently required in the circumstances.

Harassment   "Harassment" means unwanted conduct (including conduct of a sexual nature) which violates a person's dignity, particularly when such conduct creates an intimidating, hostile, degrading, humiliating or offensive environment, or which aims to do so. (II.–2:102(2))

Immovable property   "Immovable property" means land and anything so attached to land as not to be subject to change of place by usual human action.

Incomplete substitution of debtor   There is incomplete substitution of a debtor when a third person is substituted as debtor with the effect that the original debtor is retained as a debtor in case the original debtor does not perform properly.

Incorporeal   "Incorporeal", in relation to property, means not having a physical existence in solid, liquid or gaseous form.

Indemnify   To "indemnify" means to make such payment to a person as will ensure that that person suffers no loss.

Individually negotiated   See "not individually negotiated" and II.–1:110.

Ineffective   "Ineffective" in relation to a contract or other juridical act means having no effect, whether that state of affairs is temporary or permanent, general or restricted.

Insolvency proceeding   An "insolvency proceeding" means a collective judicial or administrative proceeding, including an interim proceeding, in which the assets and affairs of a person who is, or who is believed to be, insolvent are subject to control or supervision by a court or other competent authority for the purpose of reorganisation or liquidation.

Interest   "Interest" means simple interest without any assumption that it will be capitalised from time to time.

Invalid   "Invalid" in relation to a juridical act or legal relationship means that the act or relationship is void or has been avoided.

Joint obligation   An obligation owed by two or more debtors is a "joint obligation" when all the debtors are bound to render the performance together and the creditor may require it only from all of them. (III.–4:102(3))

Joint right   A right to performance held by two or more creditors is a "joint right" when the debtor must perform to all the creditors and any creditor may require performance only for the benefit of all. (III.–4:202(3))

Juridical act   A "juridical act" is any statement or agreement, whether express or implied from conduct, which is intended to have legal effect as such. It may be unilateral, bilateral or multilateral. (II.–1:101(2))

Keeper   A keeper, in relation to an animal, vehicle or substance, is the person who has the beneficial use or physical control of it for that person's own benefit and who exercises the right to control it or its use.

Lease   A "lease" is the legal relationship arising from a contract under which one party, the lessor, undertakes to provide the other party, the lessee, with a temporary right of use in exchange for rent. (IV. B.–1:101)

Loan contract   A loan contract is a contract by which one party, the lender, is obliged to provide the other party, the borrower, with credit of any amount for a definite or indefinite period (the loan period), in the form of a monetary loan or of an overdraft facility and by which the borrower is obliged to repay the money obtained under the credit, whether or not the borrower is obliged to pay interest or any other kind of remuneration the parties have agreed upon. (IV. F.–1:101(2))

Loss   "Loss" includes economic and non-economic loss. "Economic loss" includes loss of income or profit, burdens incurred and a reduction in the value of property. "Non-economic loss" includes pain and suffering and impairment of the quality of life. (III.–3:701(3) and VI.–2:101(4))

Merger of debts   A "merger of debts" means that the attributes of debtor and creditor are united in the same person in the same capacity. (III.–6:201)

Merger clause   A "merger clause" is a term in a contract document stating that the document embodies all the terms of the contract. (II.–4:104)

Monetary loan   A monetary loan is a fixed sum of money which is lent to the borrower and which the borrower agrees to repay either by fixed instalments or by paying the whole sum at the end of the loan period. (IV. F.–1:101(3))

Movables   "Movables" means corporeal and incorporeal property other than immovable property.

Negligence   There is "negligence" if a person does not meet the standard of care which could reasonably be expected in the circumstances.

Non-economic loss   See "Loss".

Non-performance   "Non-performance", in relation to an obligation, means any failure to perform the obligation, whether or not excused. It includes delayed performance and defective performance. (III.–1:101(3))

Notice   "Notice" includes the communication of information or of a juridical act. (I.–1:105)

Not individually negotiated   A term supplied by one party is not individually negotiated if the other party has not been able to influence its content, in particular because it has been drafted in advance, whether or not as part of standard terms. (II.–1:110)

Obligation   An obligation is a duty to perform which one party to a legal relationship, the debtor, owes to another party, the creditor. (III.–1:101(1))

Ownership   "Ownership" is the most comprehensive right a person, the owner, can have over property, including the exclusive right, so far as consistent with applicable laws or rights granted by the owner, to use, enjoy, modify, destroy, dispose of and recover the property. (VIII.–1:202)

Performance   "Performance", in relation to an obligation, is the doing by the debtor of what is to be done under the obligation or the not doing by the debtor of what is not to be done. (III.–1:101(2))

Person   "Person" means a natural or legal person.

Physical control   "Physical control", in relation to goods, means direct physical control or indirect physical control. (Cf. VIII.–1:205)

Possession   Possession, in relation to goods, means having physical control over the goods. (VIII.–1:205)

Prescription   "Prescription", in relation to the right to performance of an obligation, is the legal effect whereby the lapse of a prescribed period of time entitles the debtor to refuse performance.

Presumption   A "presumption" means that the existence of a known fact or state of affairs allows the deduction that something else should be held true, until the contrary is demonstrated.

Price   The "price" is what is due by the debtor under a monetary obligation, in exchange for something supplied or provided, expressed in a currency which the law recognises as such.

Proceeds   "Proceeds", in relation to proprietary security, is every value derived from an encumbered asset, such as value realised by sale, collection or other disposition; damages or insurance payments in respect of defects, damage or loss; civil and natural fruits, including distributions; and proceeds of proceeds. (IX.–1:201(11))

Producer   "Producer" includes, in the case of something made, the maker or manufacturer; in the case of raw material, the person who abstracts or wins it; and in the case of something grown, bred or raised, the grower, breeder or raiser. A special definition applies for the purposes of VI.–3:204.

Property   "Property" means anything which can be owned: it may be movable or immovable, corporeal or incorporeal.

Ratify   "Ratify" means confirm with legal effect.

Reasonable   What is "reasonable" is to be objectively ascertained, having regard to the nature and purpose of what is being done, to the circumstances of the case and to any relevant usages and practices. (I.–1:104)

Reciprocal   An obligation is reciprocal in relation to another obligation if (a) performance of the obligation is due in exchange for performance of the other obligation; (b) it is an obligation to facilitate or accept performance of the other obligation; or (c) it is so clearly connected to the other obligation or its subject matter that performance of the one can reasonably be regarded as dependent on performance of the other. (III.–1:101(4))

Recklessness   A person is "reckless" if the person knows of an obvious and serious risk of proceeding in a certain way but nonetheless voluntarily proceeds without caring whether or not the risk materialises.

Rent   "Rent" is the money or other value which is due in exchange for a temporary right of use. (IV. B.–1:101)

Reparation   "Reparation" means compensation or another appropriate measure to reinstate the person suffering damage in the position that person would have been in had the damage not occurred. (VI.–6:101)

Representative   A "representative" is a person who has authority to affect the legal position of another person, the principal, in relation to a third party by acting in the name of the principal or otherwise in such a way as to indicate an intention to affect the principal's legal position directly. (II.–6:102(1))

Requirement   A "requirement" is something which is needed before a particular result follows or a particular right can be exercised.

Resolutive   A condition is "resolutive" if it causes a legal relationship or effect to come to an end when the condition is satisfied. (III.–1:106)

Retention of ownership device   There is a retention of ownership device when ownership is retained by the owner of supplied assets in order to secure a right to performance of an obligation. (IX.–1:103)

Revocation   "Revocation", means (a) in relation to a juridical act, its recall by a person or persons having the power to recall it, so that it no longer has effect and (b) in relation to something conferred or transferred, its recall, by a person or persons having power to recall it, so that it comes back or must be returned to the person who conferred it or transferred it.

Right   "Right", depending on the context, may mean (a) the correlative of an obligation or liability (as in "a significant imbalance in the parties' rights and obligations arising under the contract"); (b) a proprietary right (such as the right of ownership); (c) a personality right (as in a right to respect for dignity, or a right to liberty and privacy); (d) a legally conferred power to bring about a particular result (as in "the right to avoid" a contract); (e) an entitlement to a particular remedy (as in a right to have performance of a contractual obligation judicially ordered) or (f) an entitlement to do or not to do something affecting another person's legal position without exposure to adverse consequences (as in a "right to withhold performance of the reciprocal obligation").

Sale, contract for A contract for the "sale" of goods or other assets is a contract under which one party, the seller, undertakes to another party, the buyer, to transfer the ownership of the goods or other assets to the buyer, or to a third person, either immediately on conclusion of the contract or at some future time, and the buyer undertakes to pay the price. (IV.A.–1:202)

Set-off "Set-off" is the process by which a person may use a right to performance held against another person to extinguish in whole or in part an obligation owed to that person. (III.–6:101)

Signature "Signature" includes a handwritten signature, an electronic signature or an advanced electronic signature. (I.–1:108(2))

Solidary obligation An obligation owed by two or more debtors is a "solidary obligation" when all the debtors are bound to render one and the same performance and the creditor may require it from any one of them until there has been full performance. (III.–4:102(1))

Solidary right A right to performance held by two or more creditors is a "solidary right" when any of the creditors may require full performance from the debtor and the debtor may render performance to any of the creditors. (III.–4:202(1))

Standard terms "Standard terms" are terms which have been formulated in advance for several transactions involving different parties, and which have not been individually negotiated by the parties. (II.–1:109)

Subrogation "Subrogation", in relation to rights, is the process by which a person who has made a payment or other performance to another person acquires by operation of law that person's rights against a third person.

Substitution of debtor "Substitution" of a debtor is the process whereby, with the agreement of the creditor, a third party is substituted completely or incompletely for the debtor, the contract remaining in force. (III.–5:202) See also "complete substitution of debtor" and "incomplete substitution of debtor".

Supply To "supply" goods or other assets means to make them available to another person, whether by sale, gift, barter, lease or other means: to "supply" services means to provide them to another person, whether or not for a price. Unless otherwise stated, "supply" covers the supply of goods, other assets and services.

Suspensive A condition is "suspensive" if it prevents a legal relationship or effect from coming into existence until the condition is satisfied. (III.–1:106)

Tacit prolongation "Tacit prolongation" is the process whereby, when a contract provides for continuous or repeated performance of obligations for a definite period and the obligations continue to be performed by both parties after that period has expired, the contract becomes a contract for an indefinite period, unless the circumstances are inconsistent with the tacit consent of the parties to such prolongation. (III.–1:111)

Term "Term" means any provision, express or implied, of a contract or other juridical act, of a law, of a court order or of a legally binding usage or practice: it includes a condition.

Termination "Termination", in relation to an existing right, obligation or legal relationship, means bringing it to an end with prospective effect except in so far as otherwise provided.

Textual form In "textual form", in relation to a statement, means expressed in alphabetical or other intelligible characters by means of any support which permits reading, recording of the information contained in the statement and its reproduction in tangible form. (I.–1:107(2))

Transfer of contractual position "Transfer of contractual position" is the process whereby, with the agreement of all three parties, a new party replaces an existing party to a contract, taking over the rights, obligations and entire contractual position of that party. (III.–5:302)

Treatment, contract for A contract for treatment is a contract under which one party, the treatment provider, undertakes to provide medical treatment for another party, the patient, or to provide any other service in order to change the physical or mental condition of a person. (IV. C.–8:101)

Trust   A "trust" is a legal relationship in which a trustee is obliged to administer or dispose of one or more assets (the trust fund) in accordance with the terms governing the relationship (trust terms) to benefit a beneficiary or advance public benefit purposes. (X.–1:201)

Trustee   A "trustee" is a person in whom a trust fund becomes or remains vested when the trust is created or subsequently on or after appointment and who has the obligation set out in the definition of "trust" above. (X.–1:203(2))

Unjustified enrichment   An "unjustified enrichment" is an enrichment which is not legally justified.

Valid   "Valid", in relation to a juridical act or legal relationship, means that the act or relationship is not void and has not been avoided.

Void   "Void", in relation to a juridical act or legal relationship, means that the act or relationship is automatically of no effect from the beginning.

Voidable   "Voidable", in relation to a juridical act or legal relationship, means that the act or relationship is subject to a defect which renders it liable to be avoided and hence rendered retrospectively of no effect.

Withdraw   A right to "withdraw" from a contract or other juridical act is a right, exercisable only within a limited period, to terminate the legal relationship arising from the contract or other juridical act, without having to give any reason for so doing and without incurring any liability for non-performance of the obligations arising from that contract or juridical act. (II.–5:101 to II.–5:105)

Withholding performance   "Withholding performance", as a remedy for non-performance of a contractual obligation, means that one party to a contract may decline to render due counter-performance until the other party has tendered performance or has performed. (III.–3:401)

Writing   In "writing" means in textual form, on paper or another durable medium and in directly legible characters. (I.–1:107(1))

Index